Date Due

1983
The Supreme Court Review

1983

The

"Judges as persons, or courts as institutions, are entitled to
no greater immunity from criticism than other persons
or institutions . . .[J]udges must be kept mindful of their limitations and
of their ultimate public responsibility by a vigorous
stream of criticism expressed with candor however blunt."
–*Felix Frankfurter*

". . . while it is proper that people should find fault when
their judges fail, it is only reasonable that they should recognize the
difficulties. . . . Let them be severely brought to book,
when they go wrong, but by those who will take the trouble
to understand them."
–*Learned Hand*

THE LAW SCHOOL

THE UNIVERSITY OF CHICAGO

Supreme Court Review

EDITED BY

PHILIP B. KURLAND

GERHARD CASPER

AND DENNIS J. HUTCHINSON

 THE UNIVERSITY OF CHICAGO PRESS

CHICAGO AND LONDON

INTERNATIONAL STANDARD BOOK NUMBER: 0-226-46436-9

LIBRARY OF CONGRESS CATALOG CARD NUMBER: 60-14353

THE UNIVERSITY OF CHICAGO PRESS, CHICAGO 60637

THE UNIVERSITY OF CHICAGO PRESS, LTD., LONDON

© 1984 BY THE UNIVERSITY OF CHICAGO. ALL RIGHTS RESERVED. PUBLISHED 1984

PRINTED IN THE UNITED STATES OF AMERICA

CONTENTS

RACE, RELIGION, AND PUBLIC POLICY:
BOB JONES UNIVERSITY V. UNITED STATES
Mayer G. Freed and Daniel D. Polsby   1

BOB JONES UNIVERSITY V. UNITED STATES:
PUBLIC POLICY IN SEARCH OF TAX POLICY
Paul B. Stephan III   33

THE SPECIAL PLACE OF RELIGION IN THE
CONSTITUTION
Michael E. Smith   83

INS V. CHADHA: THE ADMINISTRATIVE
CONSTITUTION, THE CONSTITUTION, AND
THE LEGISLATIVE VETO
E. Donald Elliott   125

DEREGULATION AND THE HARD-LOOK DOCTRINE
Cass R. Sunstein   177

CONGRESSIONAL REGULATION OF THE "STATES
QUA STATES": FROM NATIONAL LEAGUE OF
CITIES TO EEOC V. WYOMING
Dean Alfange, Jr.   215

THE EXCLUSIONARY RULE: AN ESSENTIAL
INGREDIENT OF THE FOURTH AMENDMENT
Sam J. Ervin, Jr.   283

DEREGULATING DEATH
Robert Weisberg   305

"INTENT" AND EQUAL PROTECTION: A
RECONSIDERATION
Gayle Binion   397

CLASS ACTIONS: JOINDER OR REPRESENTATIONAL
DEVICE?
Diane Wood Hutchinson   459

COPYRIGHT, MISAPPROPRIATION, AND PREEMPTION:
CONSTITUTIONAL AND STATUTORY LIMITS OF
STATE LAW PROTECTION
Howard B. Abrams   509

BROWN V. SOCIALIST WORKERS: INEQUALITY
AS A COMMAND OF THE FIRST AMENDMENT
Geoffrey R. Stone and William P. Marshall   583

TABLE OF CASES AT BACK OF BOOK.

MAYER G. FREED
DANIEL D. POLSBY

RACE, RELIGION, AND PUBLIC POLICY: BOB JONES UNIVERSITY V. UNITED STATES

I. INTRODUCTION

By the time the Supreme Court handed down its decision in *Bob Jones University v. United States*,[1] the case was long a focus of public controversy. After the grant of certiorari, but before argument, the Reagan Administration announced its intention to abandon the position the Government had successfully urged in the courts below—that the Internal Revenue Code precluded tax-exempt status for private schools practicing racial discrimination in admissions.

The Government's new position was that to condition tax-exempt status on compliance with a "public policy" of racial nondiscrimination went beyond what Congress intended when it enacted 26 U.S.C. §501(c) (3). If such a requirement were to be imposed on institutions otherwise qualifying under §501(c) (3), Congress would have to direct its imposition and not leave it to inference.

The outcry that followed the Administration's change of position was different from the usual political hubbub over policy. It was suggested that the Reagan White House acted illegally in reinterpreting the revenue code and that reasonable people could not possibly differ about the illegality of this action. This was the position, for example, of the *New York Times*,[2] the *Washington Post*,[3] and their

Mayer G. Freed and Daniel D. Polsby are Professors of Law, Northwestern University.

AUTHORS' NOTE: We are grateful to Professors Leonard Rubinowitz and Marshall Shapo, and to the participants of faculty workshops at the Northwestern University Law School and the Center for Urban Affairs, for their comments on earlier versions of this article.

[1] 103 S. Ct. 2017 (1983).

[2] NEW YORK TIMES, Jan. 12, 1982, p. A-14; Jan. 19, 1982, p. A-26; Feb. 5, 1982, p. A-38.

[3] WASHINGTON POST, Jan. 12, 1982, p. A-16.

award-winning columnists Anthony Lewis,[4] Tom Wicker,[5] and William Raspberry.[6] After styling the Administration's position "Tax Exempt Hate," the *Times* editorialized for the better part of a month on the subject. The Administration was "picking the pocket of every American taxpayer to subsidize racism in education."[7] The Administration's position was "[c]ontrary to tax law" and "against the grain of every civil rights achievement in a generation."[8] Contrary to the President's position that previous government policy had no legal basis, "the only lawlessness here is that demonstrated by his Administration."[9]

With due respect to these authorities, however, it is a mistake to think *Bob Jones* an easy case. To suppose that the *Bob Jones* case has an obvious solution is the only indefensible position on the matter. Yet this is the position taken by Chief Justice Burger's opinion for the Court, which at least one knowledgeable journalist considers to have "demolished the legal arguments made by the Reagan lawyers,"[10] but which, in fact, fails to measure up to the Court's obligation to engage in reasoned decisionmaking.

The Court's "magisterial"[11] tone and the tenor of its argument are calculated to convey the impression of a landmark decision. But if the Court was busy speaking to the press, and to posterity, it neglected to offer a cogent basis upon which its decision might rest. Perhaps the Supreme Court's conclusion in *Bob Jones* was right, but its reasons were wrong and mischievous. Those with a special interest in and sympathy for racial equality should have a particular concern that the judicial protection of equality have a minimally lawlike aspect. The Court's argument is likely to shake even their confidence. What follows, then, is an autopsy of a good job gone bad.

II. BACKGROUND

In 1970, the Internal Revenue Service announced a change in its long-standing practice of granting tax exemptions under §501(c) (3)

---

[4] Lewis, *The Court Says No*, NEW YORK TIMES, May 26, 1983, p. 23.

[5] Wicker, *Subsidizing Racism*, NEW YORK TIMES, Jan. 12, 1982, p. A-15.

[6] Raspberry, *A Bow to Racism*, WASHINGTON POST, Jan. 15, 1982, p. A-15.

[7] NEW YORK TIMES, Jan. 12, 1982, p. A-14.

[8] NEW YORK TIMES, Jan. 19, 1982, p. A-26.

[9] NEW YORK TIMES, Feb. 5, 1982, p. A-38.

[10] Lewis, note 4 *supra*.

[11] The adjective is borrowed from Mr. Lewis. *Ibid.*

of the Internal Revenue Code to private educational institutions that practice racial discrimination. In 1971, this policy change was formalized in Revenue Ruling 71-447.[12] The question addressed by the Revenue Ruling was whether "a private school that otherwise meets the requirements of Section 501(c) (3) of the Internal Revenue Code of 1954 will qualify for exemption from federal income tax if it does not have a racially non-discriminatory policy as to students." In the course of analyzing this question, the ruling announced that "the statutory requirement [of §501(c) (3)] of being 'organized and operated exclusively for religious, charitable, *** ... or educational purposes' was intended to express the basic common law concept. This common law concept is that all charitable trusts, educational or otherwise, are subject to the requirement that the purpose of the trust may not be illegal or contrary to public policy." Having interpreted the statutes to require that tax-exempt status be granted only to institutions satisfying the foregoing common-law definition, the revenue ruling went on to indicate that a private school that does not have a racially nondiscriminatory admissions policy cannot meet the common-law test.

The IRS ruling recognized that racial discrimination in the operation of private schools was not prohibited by federal law. But the Service said that the "policy of the United States is to discourage discrimination in such schools." In support of this conclusion, the ruling noted the settled federal policy against discrimination in other fields, such as housing and employment. Further support for the IRS position was found in its own regulations stating that "promotion of social welfare" includes activities "to eliminate prejudice and discrimination."

Goldsboro Christian Schools, Inc. is a nonprofit corporation established "to conduct an institution of learning ... , giving special emphasis to the Christian religion and the ethics revealed in the Holy scriptures."[13] Goldsboro offers classes to students from kindergarten through high school and is accredited by the State of North Carolina. Since its founding in 1963, Goldsboro has excluded black applicants from admission to the school, because, in the opinion of the people who run the school, the cultural or biological mixing of people of different races is contrary to biblical law.

---

[12] Rev. Rul. 71-447, 1971-2 Cum. Bull. 230.
[13] Articles of Incorp., para. 3(a), quoted at 103 S. Ct. 2024.

Bob Jones University is an educational institutional offering classes from kindergarten through college and graduate school. Both students and teachers are required to be "Christians"—a term defined by the University—and are under strict discipline as to their religious beliefs and the consistency of their behavior with those beliefs. The tenets of the official religion of the University are that interracial dating and marriage are forbidden by the Bible, and they are accordingly forbidden by the school. At earlier times the University had other policies designed to prevent this conduct. The University was founded in 1927. Until 1971, it excluded blacks from the student body. In 1971, the school began to admit married black applicants with black spouses. In 1975, the United States Court of Appeals for the Fourth Circuit held that racial discrimination in private education violated the federal Civil Rights Act of 1866.[14] After that decision, the University adopted a new policy, pursuant to which all black students, married or unmarried, were eligible for admission on the same formal terms that white students were eligible. In conjunction with this new policy, however, the University prohibited all of its students from interracial dating or marriage—or espousal or encouragement of interracial dating or marriage—on pain of expulsion.

Pursuant to the policy announced in Revenue Ruling 71-447, the IRS informed both Goldsboro Christian and Bob Jones University that they were no longer eligible for §501(c) (3) status. Proceedings were begun by the government to collect taxes back to the time when the new IRS policy became effective. Both schools resisted the claims for back taxes, claiming that the revenue ruling was contrary to the statute that it purported to be interpreting and that even if it were consistent with the statute it would nonetheless be unconstitutional under the First Amendment as applied against religious institutions like these two schools. The Fourth Circuit Court of Appeals rejected these arguments and upheld the government's claims for back taxes, and the Supreme Court affirmed.[15]

---

[14] McCrary v. Runyon, 515 F.2d 1082 (4th Cir. 1975), aff'd, 427 U.S. 160 (1976).
[15] 639 F.2d 147 (4th Cir. 1980); 644 F.2d 879 (4th Cir. 1981), aff'd.

III. THE STATUTORY ISSUES

A. ESTABLISHING THE "LAW OR PUBLIC POLICY" CONDITION

There was a way for the Court to decide the *Bob Jones* problem cleanly. The Court did not choose to do so. Federal courts are entitled to interpret the language of federal statutes and to supply implications where the legislative will is not manifest. There is a textual basis on which the Court could have concluded that tax-exempt status under §501(c) (3) is only available to otherwise eligible institutions if they are "charitable."[16] The Internal Revenue Code does not spell out what is charitable, and it follows that deciding whether any particular institution is or is not charitable will require something like "statutory construction," for which courts are the ultimate authorities.

While there is a textual basis in the statute for reaching such a conclusion, however, it is by no means compulsory.[17] Reasonable minds might differ. Faced with a problem of this kind, courts are obviously entitled, indeed required, to make a decision. The judge's task requires an acknowledgment of uncertainty about what outcome the statute requires, because the judicial role in this context is to supply meanings that statutes do not supply by themselves. To acknowledge uncertainty and to supply the interpretation for §501(c) (3) would have been entirely appropriate in *Bob Jones*. But the Court was not content to adopt this approach. Instead it wrote an opinion that tried to make the case into the cut-and-dried matter that one encountered only on the opinion pages of newspapers, a case with an obvious outcome, dictated by clear and long-standing policy. The major elements of the Court's argument were that national public policy, as established and ascertained in various ways, is offended by private schools that practice

---

[16] Section 170 of the Internal Revenue Code provides for the deductibility of contributions to various organizations. It is reasonably viewed as a companion section to §501(c)(3), which exempts the organizations themselves from federal taxation. Although both sections accord special tax treatment to "religious," "charitable," and "educational" institutions, §170 characterizes contributions to all such entities as "charitable contributions." Relying upon this characterization, the Internal Revenue Service takes the position that all listed organizations must be "charitable," in addition to being the type of organization specified in the law. See 103 S. Ct. at 2026.

[17] The fact that §170 characterizes listed types of organizations as "charitable" does not indicate that they must meet a common-law requirement that goes beyond being the bare sort of organization listed. It is no less plausible to view the statutory list of types of organizations as the expression of Congress about what a "charitable" organization is; on this view, "charitable contribution" is merely descriptive of the conclusion that Congress reached. This is Justice Rehnquist's position on the matter. See 103 S. Ct. 2039, 2040.

racial discrimination, and that accordingly such schools are not "charitable" as that term would be understood by the common law of charitable trusts; and that being "non-charitable" in the common-law sense, an educational institution is not entitled to tax-exempt status because—according to the Court—Congress had intended that such institutions be ineligible for tax exemptions.

This sort of argument seeks to be more general and more powerful than the simpler approach that we suggested. The Court's argument pretends to speak, not to a hard and uncertain case requiring an "interstitial" exercise of interpretive power, but with the plenary voice of the Congress and the Executive in addition to its own.

1. *Deference.* In administering the provisions of the Internal Revenue Code, the IRS must have at least provisional power to decide what the language of the statute shall mean. When the Code provides that "educational" institutions are entitled to tax-exempt status, questions are bound to arise concerning what is or is not an "educational" institution within the meaning of the Code. Suppose a clatch of bowling enthusiasts decided to reconstitute itself as the Chicago School for Bowling Arts. Such a school might well be "educational," at least in the sense that it imparts knowledge and skills. The question would nevertheless remain whether it would be "educational" in the sense of the tax-exemption statute. Suppose the IRS concludes that, in order to be "educational" in the statutory sense, an institution must provide instruction "useful to the individual and beneficial to the community"[18] and that a bowling school meets neither criterion. If the bowling school contests the denial of its tax exemption, a court might uphold the IRS decision in deference to the presumed expertise of the Internal Revenue Service in administering its own statute. A decision in this mode involves a judicial recognition that a complex statute like the Internal Revenue Code will inevitably beget innumerable questions of interpretation for which no self-evident answers are available under the conventional rules of statutory construction. With respect to such issues, nothing is to be gained by a court's revisiting the agency's reading of the law. A court facing such a situation will defer unless there is a good reason for it to think that the IRS has plainly misconceived the meaning of the law. For a court to defer to the agency's interpretation here, it is not necessary to suppose that it would reach the same conclusion had it considered the matter *de novo*.

---

[18] *Cf.* 26 **CFR** §1.501(c)(3)–1(d)(3)(B).

Much of the Court's opinion is cast in this deferential mode. The Court recites the provisional authority of the IRS to interpret the Code, observing that Congress can always change interpretations that it disagrees with. It cites the history of IRS interpretations of §501(c)(3) and urges the consistency of Revenue Ruling 71-447 with that history. The holding of the case is said to be that "the IRS did not exceed its authority" when it issued the revenue ruling.

Had the Supreme Court been faced merely with Revenue Ruling 71-447 and a pattern of consistent administrative practice adhering to the position announced in that ruling, *Bob Jones* could have been a very easy case. But the government's mid stream change of position renders such a deferential position precarious. The Court's opinion makes a single passing mention of this Treasury Department flip-flop but appears to attach no significance to it at all. If, however, one is determined to defer to administrative authorities, and administrative authorities are in disagreement, deference is not a satisfactory position. The Court has to encounter the government's newly minted interpretation head-on, explaining the basis upon which to decide which of two mutually exclusive interpretations of the Code was entitled to deference.

One approach to that question might be a sort of "first in time, first in right" idea, based on the notion that administrative interpretations made closer in time to the enactment of the statute are entitled to greater weight.[19] The problem of such a rationale would be that for at least a dozen years following the enactment of §501(c)(3)—not counting the similar predecessor statute—the IRS had consistently given tax exemptions to the sort of institutions enumerated in §501(c)(3) without requiring that they meet a "law and public policy" condition as well. If the "first in time" rationale would not suffice, a different tack might be taken: administrative interpretations of statutes could be seen to have "ratchets" in them. Once an administrative interpretation has been launched and put into practice, revision of the interpretation would require more convincing reasons to be given than would be required for the initial cut.[20] The Court goes down neither of these paths. Proffering no explanation for why one IRS interpretation of the statute should be preferred to the other, the Court can hardly be adopting the deferential mode.

---

[19] *Cf.* General Electric Co. v. Gilbert, 429 U.S. 125 (1976).

[20] *Cf.* Motor Vehicle Manufacturers Association v. State Farm Mutual Automobile Ins. Co., 103 S. Ct. 2856 (1983).

2. *Subsequent legislative intent.* The Court's opinion places heavy reliance on the fact that subsequent to the issuance of Revenue Ruling 71-447, Congress failed to overturn the IRS's policy. This failure to act, said the Court, amounted to "acquiescence" in the IRS interpretation of the Revenue Code, a sort of ratification by silence:[21]

> The actions of Congress since 1970 leave no doubt that the IRS reached the correct conclusion in exercising its authority. It is, of course, not unknown for independent agencies or the Executive Branch to misconstrue the intent of a statute; Congress can and often does correct such misconceptions, if the courts have not done so. Yet for a dozen years Congress has been made aware—acutely aware—of the IRS rulings of 1970 and 1971. As we noted earlier, few issues have been the subject of more vigorous and widespread debate and discussion in and out of Congress than those related to racial segregation in education. Sincere adherents advocating contrary views have ventilated the subject for well over three decades. Failure of Congress to modify the IRS rulings of 1970 and 1971, of which Congress was, by its own studies and by public discourse, constantly reminded; and Congress' awareness of the denial of tax-exempt status for racially discriminatory schools when enacting other and related legislation make out an unusually strong case of legislative acquiescence in and ratification by implication of the 1970 and 1971 rulings.

The Court acknowledges that congressional inaction "is not often a useful guide." But its decision attaches significance to the inaction here, because numerous bills seeking to overturn the IRS policy were introduced in Congress and came to naught.[22]

The Court reasons from legislative inaction to legislative acquiescence to confirmation of the interpretation of §501(c) (3) that the Court believes it has already amply documented. Justice Powell takes a somewhat different view. Although he concedes that the "statutory terms are not self-defining," and that evidence of legislative intent is inconclusive at best, he is willing to concur in the Court's judgment

---

[21] 103 S. Ct. at 2032-33.

[22] Subsequent congressional acquiescence is divined from the enactment of §501(i) of the Code (which denies tax-exempt status to social clubs that discriminate on the basis of race, color, or religion), and from references in committee reports accompanying that bill which note that "discrimination on account of race is inconsistent with an educational institution's tax-exempt status." S. Rep. No. 1318, 94th Cong. 2d Sess., 7-8 & n.5; H.R. Rep. No. 1353, 94th Cong. 2d Sess., 8 & n.5, U.S. CODE, CONG. & ADMIN. NEWS 6058 (1976). But the legislative history is inconclusive at best. See McGlotten v. Connally, 338 F. Supp. 448 (D.D.C. 1972); Brief of Amicus Curiae, at 50-51. Green v. Connelly, 330 F. Supp. 1150 (D.D.C.), *aff'd per curiam sub nom.* Coit v. Green, 404 U.S. 997 (1971).

because he believes that Congress had ratified the IRS policy by acquiescence.[23] The Court's argument about congressional inaction as ratification is entirely unpersuasive because it does not explain why congressional inaction in the period 1971-80 should produce "law," while similar inaction in the period prior to 1971, or subsequent to 1981, should not produce "law" in the same way. Prior to 1971 and Revenue Ruling 71-447, Congress's attention was very much fixed on the subject of civil rights. The Civil Rights Act of 1964,[24] the Voting Rights Act of 1968,[25] and the Fair Housing Act[26] were all products of this heydey of the Great Society, which can fairly be described as the classical period of civil rights legislation. And yet, in all this time, the IRS followed the policy of granting tax exemptions to racially discriminatory private schools. Indeed, there was even introduced into Congress a bill that would have prohibited the IRS from granting tax exemptions to racially discriminatory schools. The bill was not enacted; it had so little support in the legislature that hearings on it were never held.[27] It could be said that congressional inaction in this period was ambiguous, but that is precisely the point. It is a point about the ambiguity of inaction itself. There is nothing special about the period before 1971 that distinguishes congressional inaction in that era from congressional inaction subsequently.

A similar point can be made for the period after the Reagan Administration announced its change of policy on the question of tax exemptions for racially discriminatory schools. There is no evidence that absent *Bob Jones*, Congress would have overturned this latest administrative interpretation of the IRS's authority under §501(c) (3). As the *New York Times* reported: "Many congressional leaders said they believed that legislation was unlikely to be enacted in the face of expected opposition from both liberal groups that feel it unnecessary and from those who say the schools have a right to choose their students however they wish."[28] On the Supreme Court's theory about ratification by legislative inaction, this 1982 interpretation of the

---

[23] 103 S. Ct. at 2037-38. The Chief Justice appears to assert that Congress's silence has ratified the entire "law and public policy" test of the revenue ruling as well as its application to discriminatory private schools. Justice Powell, however, regards the inaction of Congress only as ratification of the rule against tax exemptions for discriminatory private schools.

[24] U.S.C. §2000d *et seq.*

[25] U.S.C. §1971 *et seq.*

[26] U.S.C. §3601 *et seq.*

[27] See 111 CONG. REC. 5140, 89th Cong., 1st Sess. (1965), H.R. 6342, p.5140 (Mr. Resnick).

[28] NEW YORK TIMES, Feb. 4, 1982, p. A-1.

Internal Revenue Code would have become law if the Congress, for one reason or another, had not acted to contradict it. Granted some legislators opposed such legislation because they thought it superfluous, thus making the inaction ambiguous. Ambiguity is precisely what makes legislative inaction unacceptable as a source of law. The history of IRS treatment of tax-exempt status for discriminatory private schools and the consistent legislative inaction through all phases of that history highlight the problem of using "inaction" as a premise for inferring "action." Once again, to peek behind the curtain of talk is to learn that there is nothing there.

B. HOW "PUBLIC POLICY" IS DISCERNED

The weakness of the claim that §501(c) (3) requires tax-exempt organizations to satisfy the "law or public policy" rule is typical of other deep problems with the opinion. How is the "law or public policy" rule supposed to be implemented? The problems that can be anticipated under this head are formidable and defy any public agency—judicial or otherwise—to carry out the rule without appearing arbitrary. *Bob Jones* illustrates the difficulties that arise when "public policy" that is not law forms the basis of a legal rule. Consider some of the sources cited by the Court in support of the asserted public policy implemented in the *Bob Jones* decision:

1. The Constitution prohibits racial segregation in public education—but it does not prohibit segregation in private education.

2. Title IV of the 1964 Civil Rights Act prohibits racial discrimination in public education—but not in private education.

3. Federal law prohibits racial discrimination in various settings such as voting rights, housing, public accommodations, and private employment. But none of these statutes, and no executive order or other source of positive law relied on by the Court[29] in *Bob Jones*, directly prohibits racially discriminatory policies in private schools.

The opinion of the Court is internally inconsistent concerning the conclusions that may be drawn from inaction. In its analysis of congressional inaction in the face of the 1971 revenue ruling, the Court takes Congress's failure to act as a decision to acquiesce in—that is, to permit—the IRS's denial of tax exemptions to racially discriminatory schools. Yet in concluding that federal public policy is offended by the

---

[29] See text *infra* at notes 45–48.

practices of such schools—and that therefore governmental support (in the form of tax-exempt status) should be denied to them—the Court ignores much similar governmental inaction. Why should congressional silence toward the IRS imply acquiescence in its behavior, while congressional silence toward the practices of discriminatory private schools imply precisely the opposite attitude toward their behavior? By the logic of the *Bob Jones* approach to legislative inaction, this tissue of prohibitions and the silences that surround it could just as easily be construed, not as declarations of a public policy against discrimination in private education, but as decisions to tolerate such discrimination.

The possibility remains that a more circumscribed public policy could be made to serve as the basis for the result in *Bob Jones*. Interspersed with citations, noted above, to sources bearing on the legality of racial discrimination are sources that might give grounds for a more limited version of the public policy argument—a public policy against federal financial support for schools that practice racial discrimination.

The Court mentions Title VI of the 1964 Civil Rights Act, which prohibits racial discrimination by institutions "receiving federal financial assistance." But Title VI does not prohibit discrimination by institutions that do not receive federal financial assistance. It would be possible, of course, to construe the term "federal financial assistance" to include tax-exempt status.[30] If this statute did indeed forbid racially discriminatory institutions from receiving tax exemptions, obviously *Bob Jones* would present little difficulty, because granting a tax exemption to a racially discriminatory private school would violate positive law and there would be no need to invoke the concept of public policy. But the Court says no such thing about Title VI. It uses that statute, not as a source of positive obligation, but as a source of public policy. In so doing it would seem implicitly to reject the proposition that Congress, in forbidding recipients of federal financial assistance from discriminating, meant to count tax exemptions as such assistance. In this posture, Title VI is no better a source of public policy than those discussed above, for the same reason. Congressional inaction with respect to financial assistance taking the form of tax

---

[30] *Cf.* McGlotten v. Connally, 338 F. Supp. 448 (D.D.C. 1972).

exemptions could as easily be understood as a decision to allow such exemptions to be granted as a decision to establish a "public policy," if not a law, forbidding them.[31]

"Public policy" that is not law is completely ambivalent; it suggests equally and simultaneously that certain conduct should and should not be allowed. "Public policy" in this context is an empty idea. A rule that forbids the granting of tax exemptions to organizations that violate public policy is not a rule at all.

If, then, the Court's result in *Bob Jones* is to be sustained, it must be on the constitutional law question that the Court said it did not have to consider. Does it violate the equal protection component of the Fifth Amendment for the government to grant tax-exempt status to private schools that practice racial discrimination? If the answer is yes, it must be that government acts unconstitutionally when it renders financial assistance (in the form of tax exemptions) to activities that it could not itself engage in without violating the Constitution. But this argument surely proves too much.

Consider, for example, Wigmore Academy, a private preparatory school. Wigmore's Board of Directors has heard a rumor that some teachers have been selling drugs to students. It has ordered a surreptitious search of the desks and lockers of all faculty members. If the police were to conduct this sort of fishing expedition on the basis of unsubstantiated rumors, the Fourth Amendment would be violated. Or, suppose the Save-the-Whale Foundation decided to fire one of its staff members for having participated in a "Second Amendment Day" rally in favor of the right to bear arms. If a public employer did the same, the First Amendment would be offended. Or, suppose the Family Integrity Society offered membership to everyone except persons born out of wedlock. No office of the government could thus discriminate without acting unconstitutionally. If the tax-exempt status of the organizations in these examples were called into question, the result under the theory that tax exemptions may not be granted to entities engaged in conduct that would be unconstitutional if done by the government seems fairly clear. Yet such results do not have much cogency, either as tax law or as constitutional law.

If the tax-exempt status of private organizations is conditioned upon compliance with the limits placed upon governmental action by the

---

[31] The Court also cites Norwood v. Harrison, 413 U.S. 455 (1973), in its discussion of public policy; but for the same reason that the Title VI argument fails, the *Norwood* argument also fails.

Constitution, then the line between private conduct and state action—upon which the Court has so often been careful to insist[32]—begins to vanish. In some sense, granting tax exemptions—to anyone—is a species of state action. But to hold state action unconstitutional because of its connection with private conduct effectively saddles the government with responsibility—in both the causal and the moral sense—for that behavior. If one were seriously to pursue the notion that "state action," in the constitutional sense, ought to reach conduct that is in any way touched or facilitated by the tax laws, one would lose the capacity for a pluralistic society made possible by observing the distinction between public and private institutions. As Judge Friendly once put it:[33]

> It is the very possibility of doing something different than government can do, of creating an institution free to make choices government cannot—even seemingly arbitrary ones—without having to provide a justification that will be examined in a court of law, which stimulates much private giving and interest. If the private agency must be a replica of the public one, why should private citizens give it their money and their time?

The notion that no private activity may be "subsidized" by government if the government could not engage in that activity itself would, as suggested, raise questions about much of what government does. This is a drawback, not an advantage, of the theory. And there would appear to be only two means of escape. One could make a distinction between subsidies that are invalid because they support activities that government could not engage in and subsidies that are valid and constitutional even though they subsidize activities that government cannot engage in. In other words, we would need a theory to explain why government cannot "subsidize" racial discrimination but can "subsidize" unreasonable searches or abridgments of free speech or discriminations against persons born out of wedlock. The Court would have to develop a hierarchy of constitutional values ranging from the sacred through the sacrosanct to the inviolable in order to accommodate this sort of theory. Various analytical models of this sort are already in existence: the "tiers" of the Equal Protection Clause, "fundamental rights" theory, the "preferred place" of certain

---

[32] *E.g.*, Flagg Bros., Inc. v. Brooks, 436 U.S. 149 (1978); Jackson v. Metropolitan Edison Co., 419 U.S. 345 (1974); Moose Lodge v. Irvis, 407 U.S. 163 (1972).

[33] FRIENDLY, THE DARTMOUTH COLLEGE CASES AND THE PUBLIC-PRIVATE PENUMBRA 30 (1968).

rights as distinct from other rights in the constitutional scheme, all partake of this methodology. But the Supreme Court's opinions supporting such hierarchical approaches fall somewhere between the ad hoc and the downright hokey. The methodology is no more likely to satisfy here. The hierarchical decisions that are necessary to the definition of individual rights as against the state are ad hoc enough; a rule that requires a further ad hoc sorting of the rights already established in this process, so as to determine when such rights are infringed by government expenditures and when they are not, is excessive. It is one thing to concede the inevitability of some extemporaneity in constitutional adjudication. This is no more than a concession that there is no very well elaborated or widely accepted general theory of constitutional right. But theoretical poverty is no proud boast in a constitutional system, and there is no good reason gratuitously to call attention to it. In other connections the Court has responded to this consideration. It is precisely the difficulty in subjecting governmental expenditure or fiscal decisions to constitutional review that has led the Court to take an exceedingly deferential stance toward such decisions.[34]

The alternative to hierarchical distinctions as a limiting principle is to identify some factor in addition to the bare expenditure of money as the means of distinguishing permissible from impermissible expenditures. Although there may be other candidates for this role, "governmental purpose" would appear to be the most likely one. To impose responsibility on government for the behavior of the entities to which it grants tax exemption is to focus upon the impact of such assistance. But at least where challenged government action is facially neutral (as the tax-exemption statute is with respect to race, or with respect to the constitutional law issues contained in the illustrations heretofore suggested), the Court has usually required that an unconstitutional purpose be found in the government's behavior before it is struck down. In *Washington v. Davis*,[35] the Supreme Court rejected the argument that a civil service exam for police officers was unconstitutional simply because blacks failed it disproportionately to whites. Because the test was facially neutral, the Court held that its use by the city could be successfully attacked only by a showing that the

[34] Harris v. McRae, 448 U.S. 297 (1980); Maher v. Roe, 432 U.S. 464 (1977); Dandridge v. Williams, 397 U.S. 471 (1970); see generally, Freed, Polsby, & Spitzer, *Unions, Fairness, and the Conundrums of Collective Choice*, 56 S. CALIF. L. REV. 461, 500-03 (1983).
[35] 426 U.S. 229 (1976).

test was adopted for a racially discriminatory purpose. Similarly, in *Personnel Administrator v. Feeney*,[36] the Court held that the State's policy of preferring veterans of the armed services for state employment was not unconstitutional, even though female applicants, few of whom were veterans, were obviously burdened by this policy. As the *Feeney* Court put it, the issue was whether the veterans' preference was adopted "because of" rather than "in spite of" its effect on female applicants. The requirement of a proscribed purpose does not make what a policy's consequences turn out to be irrelevant. Consequences remain important because in conjunction with other data they may raise inferences about purposes, especially when direct information on the issue is lacking, as it often will be.

There is an inconsistency between the proposition that the government may not constitutionally grant tax exemptions to educational institutions that practice racial discrimination and the proposition that government action, in order to be unconstitutional, must have an unconstitutional purpose and not merely a discriminatory impact or effect. Although the "purpose" proposition has greater support in the Court's cases, the *Bob Jones* opinion relies on the most important case in which the government's purpose was not counted as important: *Norwood v. Harrison*.[37]

Norwood was a challenge to Mississippi's program of textbook loans to public and private schools. Mississippi had a central book depository, from which it made available to local schools, both public and private, textbooks for use in various subjects. At the time the action was brought, Mississippi's schools were under various court orders to desegregate, and it was said that the loan of textbooks to private schools, many of which practiced racial discrimination in admissions, was an unconstitutional subsidy to such schools. The textbook loan program had been adopted in Mississippi in 1940, at a time when the public schools were segregated by law and constitutionally mandated desegregation of the public schools was certainly not in the offing. The District Court in *Norwood* found, and the Supreme Court accepted the finding, that the textbook loan program at its inception did not have a racially discriminatory purpose. But the Court rejected the argument that the innocence of the statute's purpose should be dispositive: "We need not assume that the State's textbook aid to private schools has been motivated by other than a sincere interest in the educational

---

[36] 442 U.S. 256 (1979).
[37] 413 U.S. 455 (1972).

welfare of all Mississippi children. But good intentions as to one valid objective do not serve to negate the State's involvement in violation of a constitutional duty."[38]

Norwood appears to embarrass the proposition that a claim of unconstitutional racial discrimination can only be established if a racially discriminatory purpose is shown. But the issue of "purpose" is somewhat more complex in the area of school desegregation than in other areas of constitutional law. The Court has held that in a *de jure* segregated school system more is required than simply discontinuing enforced segregation. There is an affirmative duty to undo such racial isolation in the schools as is found to be the product of the previous enforcement of *de jure* segregation. This notion of an affirmative duty to undo the effects of segregated school systems may result in the invalidation of actions which are concededly not, in and of themselves, a product of segregative purpose.

The enforcement of this affirmative duty is not inconsistent with the constitutional requirement of a racially discriminatory purpose. As the Court has explained, the affirmative duty attaches only to a current condition of segregation resulting from intentional state action. "The differentiating factor between *de jure* segregation and so-called *de facto* segregation . . . is *purpose* or *intent* to segregate."[39] And there is language in *Norwood* that would justify characterizing the decision as based on the notion of an affirmative duty to desegregate schools that had heretofore been *de jure* segregated: "A state's constitutional obligation requires it to steer clear, not only of operating the old dual school system of racially segregated schools, but also of giving significant aid to institutions that practice racial or other invidious discrimination."[40] But the broad language of *Norwood* suggests[41] that the holding is not limited to situations involving prior *de jure* segregation. In this respect, it is difficult to square *Norwood* with more recent cases that say that discriminatory purpose must be shown, and this difficulty is at least as pronounced in *Bob Jones*, if that case is thought to rest on a similar constitutional basis.

---

[38] *Id.* at 466.

[39] Keyes v. School Dist. No. 1, 413 U.S. 189, 208 (1973). See also Pasadena Bd. of Ed. v. Spangler, 427 U.S. 424 (1976).

[40] 413 U.S. at 467.

[41] "An inescapable educational cost for students in both public and private schools is the expense of providing all necessary learning materials. When, as here, the necessary expense is borne by the State, the economic consequence is to give aid to the enterprise; if the school engages in discriminatory practices the State by tangible aid in the form of textbooks thereby gives support to such discrimination." *Id.* at 464-65.

The point here is not simply that *Norwood* is inconsistent with the *Washington v. Davis* line of cases. What is more important is that a purpose requirement of the *Washington v. Davis* sort seems to be the only practical limit to the otherwise unbounded notion that government may not subsidize activities that it could not engage in directly. If the "purpose" limitation is not adopted, some other boundary will necessarily have to be established instead. Given the logic of *Norwood*, for example, one would have to ask whether a Mississippi-style textbook loan program could distribute books to private schools that engaged in political censorship of student newspapers. If textbook loans to such a school would not violate the Constitution, it must be because of some constitutionally relevant difference between the *Norwood* schools and our hypothetical school. Any distinction that relies on some difference in the *gravitas* of equal protection versus First Amendment values will seem arbitrary. The tack actually adopted by the Court in *Norwood* is equally unpromising. The argument is that an educational institution that discriminates on the basis of race is pervasively "tainted" by that discrimination, and therefore grants of financial assistance to such a school can serve no valid governmental purpose. The Court in *Norwood* asserted that where racially discriminatory private schools are concerned "the legitimate educational function cannot be isolated from discriminatory practices." Such a policy[42]

> exerts a pervasive influence on the entire educational process. The private school that closes its doors to defined groups of students on the basis of constitutionally suspect criteria manifests, by its own actions, that its educational processes are based on private beliefs that segregation is desirable in education. There is no reason to discriminate against students for reasons wholly unrelated to individual merit unless the artificial barriers are considered an essential part of the educational message to be communicated to the students who are admitted.

This distinction will not suffice. Unless one is persuaded by the Court's bare *ipse dixit*, there is no basis for concluding that racial discrimination exerts a more "pervasive influence" on the educational process than, say, religious discrimination, political censorship, or detours around the due process of law. Such a bald pronouncement, then, amounts simply to a hierarchical statement in another guise.

---

[42] *Id.* at 469.

Various arguments can be adduced to support the proposition that racial discrimination in education violates "public policy," or that granting tax exemptions to private schools that so discriminate violates "public policy." All of these arguments to one degree or another need to ignore or override concrete or positive law on the way to their conclusions. Laws that prohibit X but not Y are supposed to create a public policy against Y as well as X; constitutional prohibitions on certain behavior by the state are said to create a public policy against similar behavior when indulged in by entirely private actors.

It is remarkable to compare the informality of this proposed form of quasi-law creation with Chief Justice Burger's opinion, issued less than a month later, in *Immigration and Naturalization Service v. Chadha*,[43] which held that the reservation or exercise of a legislative veto of executive administrative action is unconstitutional. In *Chadha* the Court took rather a formalistic approach to the question of what "law" is and how it is to be made under the scheme of the Constitution. Lawmaking power is vested in the Congress, subject to the checks and balances of the Constitution. In order to be "law," congressional action must satisfy certain basic requirements. There must be an affirmative vote by a majority of at least a quorum in each house of Congress. Under the scheme of Article I, such a vote may effectively create law depending on whether the President does or does not assent to the enactment. But there must be a formal enactment, and this must then be exposed to the President's constitutional power to veto the enactment. The very idea of "public policy" as contrasted with "law" would seem to be fundamentally at odds with the constitutional scheme, as characterized in *Chadha*, as the legitimating process through which formally binding public acts are made. To conclude, as the Court did in *Bob Jones*, that "public policy" is violated when a private school engages in racially discriminatory behavior even though neither the federal Constitution nor any provision of federal statutory law so provides is to erase the line between sentiments that are not law, and acts that are law, that was so important to the Court in *Chadha*.[44]

---

[43] 103 S. Ct. 2764 (1983).

[44] A similar inconsistency arises from the emphasis which the Court gives legislative inaction in the *Bob Jones* opinion. As Justice White observed in dissent in *Chadha*: "If Congress may be said to have ratified the Internal Revenue Service's interpretation without passing new legislation, Congress may also be said to approve a suspension of deportation by the Attorney General when it fails to exercise its veto authority." *Id.* at 2808. A court that treats such a legislative veto as failing to satisfy the requirements of Article I of the Constitution—even though provision for the legislative veto was itself legislated in the constitutionally standard way—ought to be embarrassed to find law in congressional inaction, as it did in *Bob Jones*.

There can be little question that the *Bob Jones* Court takes a definite position about "law"—what it is and how it is made. This position can be described as somewhat loose-jointed and informal. There could be little objection to this point of view if it were, indeed, the law of "law." But it is not: it is occasional law, mined, smelted, and struck for the particular case. Of course it is inconsistent with *Chadha;* but apart from *Chadha,* whose formalism may perhaps be criticized for running to the other extreme, the *Bob Jones* idea of how law is made is simply untenable on its own footing. It implies, in brief, a social world that is a manifold chock-full of law, either the law that was made by the actions of lawmakers or the law that was made by the lawmakers' nonaction. If there is any room at all in such a picture for private whim or liberty, it is not apparent where.

C. THE DOG THAT DIDN'T BARK

The result in *Bob Jones* cannot be convincing if it rests on the proposition that tax exemptions should not be granted to organizations that violate a public policy that is not law. In any event, the Court has no methodology for inferring the existence of such public policy from positive law sources. Equally clear are the inadequacies of an alternative theory—that tax exemptions must not be granted to institutions that behave in a way that would violate the Constitution if engaged in by government itself.

Given the difficulties that belong to these approaches, it is noteworthy that the Court fails to introduce into the analysis an argument that would have substantially reduced these difficulties. The Court's opinion, like the revenue ruling it upholds, evaluates the conduct of BJU and Goldsboro Christian from the standpoint of public policy that is not law. The Court's opinion leaves the impression that what the two schools were doing was perfectly legal although in violation of some well-established public policy. What the schools were doing is, however, apparently a violation of positive federal law. In *Runyon v. McCrary,*[45] the Supreme Court held that private schools that engage in racial discrimination violate the Civil Rights Act of 1866.

Once it is appreciated that the conduct of the schools was illegal, it is apparent that the Court's opinion might have rested on narrower and firmer ground. The Court could have decided that §501(c) (3)

---

[45] 427 U.S. 160 (1976).

prohibits tax-exempt status from being accorded to institutions whose activities violate federal law, without embracing the public policy prong of the revenue ruling, with all its attendant difficulties.[46] The Court's treatment of *Runyon*, then, is like the curious incident of the dog in the night-time that Sherlock Holmes observed in "The Silver Blaze."[47] " 'The dog did nothing in the night-time,' [said Inspector Gregory.] 'That was the curious incident,' remarked Sherlock Holmes." The Court's treatment of *Runyon*—a single mention in a string citation—requires explanation.[48]

One plausible explanation is simply that resting its decision on the wider rather than the narrower ground is the way for the Court to define its authority in the broadest possible way. In this opinion, it stakes out a broad authority indeed: it may define at will public policy that is not law. Another plausible explanation is that to a Court intent on speaking chiefly to the newspapers and the history books, a pronouncement that racial discrimination violates the "public policy" of the United States carries a certain majesty that transcends mere legal analysis. To its natural constituency, the *Bob Jones* opinion may indeed speak eloquently.

IV. FREE EXERCISE OF RELIGION

In *Bob Jones*, both petitioners were religious institutions, whose claim was that the denial of a tax exemption to them on account of their religiously motivated practices unconstitutionally interfered with the free exercise of their religion. Until recently this sort of claim to religious exemption from an otherwise concededly valid law could not have been made with much confidence in its being accepted. On the

---

[46] The ways in which a private institution can violate federal law—and administrative regulations with the force of law—are practically endless. Unless all such violations—no matter how blatant or indirect, and no matter what the law—were equal in the eyes of the Revenue Service, formidable line-drawing problems would remain. For example, now that the City University of New York has been found to have engaged in sex discrimination in hiring and compensation in violation of Title VII of the Civil Rights Act (see Melani v. Board of Higher Education, 31 FEP Cases 648 (S.D.N.Y. 1983)), must it be deprived of its tax-exempt status? What of the charitable foundation that commits an unfair labor practice in its attempts to avoid unionization?

[47] DOYLE, THE MEMOIRS OF SHERLOCK HOLMES 1, 24 (1892).

[48] One possibility is that the Court was unwilling to confront in *Bob Jones* the question it had reserved in *Runyon*—whether private schools claiming religious reasons for practicing racial discrimination might stand differently under §1981 than nonsectarian private schools. This hardly seems a probable explanation. A court that is not willing to entertain a free exercise privilege in connection with some amorphous public policy seems unlikely to defer to religious scruples when these come into conflict with the substantive lawmaking powers of the Congress.

rare occasions when the Court heard such arguments, it rejected them decisively.[49] But in 1963 the Court stood its previous free exercise law on its head, changing what could fairly be called a strong presumption against free exercise claims of exemption from valid laws to an articulated rule precisely the opposite. In *Sherbert v. Verner*,[50] the Court announced that, thereafter, statutory burdens on the practice of religion could be justified only by proof of a "compelling state interest." In *Sherbert* the Court held that South Carolina had failed to meet this burden when it found a Seventh-Day Adventist ineligible for unemployment compensation benefits on the ground that her religiously motivated refusal to work on Saturday constituted a refusal of "suitable employment" under the unemployment statute.

Following *Sherbert*, the Court upheld two other free exercise claims for exemption from otherwise applicable provisions of state law. *Wisconsin v. Yoder*[51] held that the State's compulsory education law could not constitutionally be enforced against children in the Amish community. *Thomas v. Review Board*[52] was a case something like *Sherbert*.

The Court has become quite receptive to free exercise claims. Accordingly, in a jurisprudence that makes room for a free exercise privilege even to violate the criminal law—and noting that the Court stipulates the sincerity of BJU's and Goldsboro Christian's religious sentiments—should there be no valid free exercise claim here? All the Court says in addressing the problem is that the IRS imposition on religion was justified by a "compelling governmental interest."

Sherbert establishes a presumption that free exercise claims are valid and that in order to overcome free exercise claims by individuals, a compelling governmental interest must be made out. But this standard

---

[49] Reynolds v. United States, 98 U.S. 145 (1878); Jacobson v. Massachusetts, 197 U.S. 11 (1905); Hamilton v. Regents, 293 U.S. 245 (1934); Braunfeld v. Brown, 366 U.S. 599 (1961). The few cases in which free exercise claims did succeed—*e.g.*, Cantwell v. Connecticut, 310 U.S. 296 (1940), and West Virginia State Board of Education v. Barnette 319 U.S. 624 (1943)—are not generally understood to stand on a free exercise footing at all, but involve complaints that would be good irrespective of the religious motivations of the objectors. These are obviously not cases that involve "concededly valid laws."

[50] 374 U.S. 398 (1963).

[51] 406 U.S. 205 (1972).

[52] 450 U.S. 707 (1981). Mr. Thomas, a Jehovah's Witness, worked for a foundry, initially in a department that fabricated steel sheet for various industrial uses. When that department closed, he was transferred to a department that made tank turrets. Manufacturing armaments violates the tenets of Jehovah's Witnesses, and, when it became evident that there were no other jobs available that did not also involve materials of war, he resigned. In an opinion heavily dependent on *Sherbert*, the Court held that denial of unemployment benefits to Thomas, who like Sherbert had refused work out of religious motivation, was unconstitutional.

does not help unless one can tell how the interest asserted by the government in a particular case will be characterized, and how one is supposed to know whether a particular interest, or a particular way of getting at an interest, is "compelling" or not. In the *Yoder* case, for example, there seems to be no good reason why the State's interest in assuring a universal education of its citizenry should not be thought "compelling." The Court's technique for avoiding a collision with the State's asserted interest was, simply, to jawbone it into nonexistence. Why should the State desire universal education, reasoned the Court, if not to make people able to function in society? And did not the Amish function very well within their own little enclaves? From which it follows that even if the government's purpose—making sure that everyone was educated properly—was compelling, the purpose was as well or even better satisfied by nonschooling ("learning by doing") as by schooling, and thus no "compelling interest" could be found to overcome the free exercise claim.

There is an arbitrariness about this argument that runs deeper than mere cosmetics. It is tantamount to saying that the distinction between the *Sherbert* cases and *Bob Jones* is that in the *Sherbert* cases the government loses, but in *Bob Jones* it wins. No one will deny that the governmental interest in eradicating racial discrimination in education, as elsewhere in life, is "compelling": but that does not tell us why it takes precedence over every other constitutional and social value. It is not obvious that a jurisprudence that makes room for *Sherbert*, *Thomas*, and *Yoder* does not also give (assumedly sincere) religionists the privilege to follow the dictates of their religion without being subject to reprisals by the federal government.

There is a more fruitful way to think about the free exercise problem, which has occasionally surfaced in the Court's free exercise decisions, though more frequently in dissenting opinions. Granting religious exemptions from generally applicable legal rules frequently invites strategic behavior—that is, lying about one's religious convictions in order to gain the advantage of the religious immunity. The danger that people may engage in insincere or strategic behavior, in turn, makes it necessary for government to develop a mechanism for inquiring into the *bona fides* of an assertion that one's religion requires one to deviate from a law that applies to others, for if this were not done, the integrity of the underlying governmental policy would swiftly be unraveled. The likelihood of such strategic behavior, and the accompanying need to adjudicate the sincerity of religious beliefs, were among the factors relied upon by the Court in *Braunfeld v. Brown*,[53] which upheld a state Sunday closing law as applied to Orthodox Jews whose religion requires them to refrain from doing business on Saturday. In cases subsequent to *Braunfeld*, the Court has usually discussed this problem of strategic behavior only to dismiss it, while the issue has been raised in dissent in a number of cases in which free exercise claims have been recognized by the Court.

"Strategic behavior" is the right way to think about free exercise problems and "compelling governmental interest" is the wrong way, because strategic behavior analysis asks what a free exercise claim will cost if it is granted, while the "compelling governmental interest" approach simply labels a conclusion according to whether it should be granted without illuminating the factors that might bear on that conclusion. The question that is ultimately called to judgment in free exercise cases is simply how costly, in one way or another, recognizing a religious exemption will be. Two sorts of costs count in this connection: those attributable to the undermining of the state's policy by granting exemptions to concededly sincere claimants, and the costs entailed by efforts to insure that only sincere claimants actually do get the exemption. Some free exercise claims will involve mostly costs of the first sort, because the likelihood of strategic behavior is minimal. In other cases, where something of value can be obtained at the price of telling a hard-to-detect lie, both sorts of costs need to be evaluated.

An example of the first sort of case is *Menora v. Illinois High School Ass'n*,[54] where Orthodox Jewish high school boys sought exemption from the rule against wearing headgear in interscholastic basketball competition because of religious custom of wearing a head covering at all times. The State pointed out that in the course of a basketball game, a *yarmulke* might fall to the gymnasium floor and become a slip-and-fall hazard for the players. If there are any likely costs associated with granting the sought-after exemption, they stem from the risk of injury which the State feared. It seems doubtful that there would be any incentive for basketball players to feign a religious injunction in order to be able to wear a head covering while playing competitive basketball. *Yoder*—although it is often reckoned to be the high water mark of the free exercise tide—is a similar sort of case

---

[53] 366 U.S. 599 (1961).
[54] 683 F.2d 1030 (7th Cir. 1982).

because it is difficult to envision many parents engaging in deceptive behavior in order to have the "privilege" of procuring less (free) education for their children than the State requires.[55]

But *Braunfeld v. Brown* involves both sorts of costs, and the Court so analyzed the case. First, the Court described the reasons for a state's having one compulsory day of rest. If believers in the biblical sabbath were afforded an exemption from Sunday closing laws, this "might well undermine the State's goal of providing a day that, as best possible, eliminates the atmosphere of commercial noise and activity. Although not dispositive of the issue, enforcement problems would be more difficult since there would be two or more days to police rather than one and it would be more difficult to observe whether violations were occurring."[56] The Court also recognized that a religiously based privilege to violate the Sunday closing law would be commercially valuable and that therefore a strong incentive would exist for people to manufacture religious convictions so as to obtain the economic benefit.

Similarly, *United States v. Lee*[57] involved both sorts of costs. Lee was an Amish carpenter who brought an action to establish his exemption from the requirement that he, as the employer of two Amish workmen, withhold social security taxes from their paychecks and pay

---

[55] It might well be said, of course, that the Amish have the same incentive that nineteenth-century families did to keep their children away from school and working at home—namely, that children can be valuable to the family economic unit as laborers. While that concern may have been legitimate enough to move the original enactment of compulsory education laws generally, it does seem that it is a bit far-fetched, in the case of the Amish, to suppose that the essential motive behind their behavior could possibly be to increase the wealth of the family economy: if this were indeed their motive, they would send their children to school and buy combines and other mechanical contrivances to help them out with their work. The fact that their religious practice leads them to reject the use of such efficient tools in their work gives a certain assurance that their representations are not spurious. Nevertheless, *Yoder* remains a troubling case: it is obviously not possible for Wisconsin to satisfy its desire for the children of the State to acquire a minimum degree of literacy and numeracy and simultaneously to indulge the Amish with their desire that their children not be required to undergo such education. The Court attempted to avoid this problem by defining the State's interests so generally that the household practicum offered by the Amish in lieu of education is characterized as satisfying the educational interests of the state. But so viewed it seems obvious that compulsory education laws would raise substantial due process problems when sought to be applied to any household in which the parents preferred to educate the children themselves, according to a curriculum of their own choosing, rather than subjecting them to the regime declared by the State. That the Supreme Court was willing to subordinate the State's obvious (and uncontroversial) interests in the *Yoder* case lends credence to the observation that the Free Exercise Clause is, under current case law, a potent qualification on the police power of the State and that the result in *Bob Jones* requires explanation.

[56] 366 U.S. 599, 608 (1961).

[57] 455 U.S. 252 (1982).

the employer social security portion himself. His theory was that in the Amish community, care for the elderly is a matter of religious duty, and that it is sinful both to receive benefits from and to contribute to the national social security system. The Supreme Court unanimously rejected this claim, recognizing the danger that would be posed to the social security system if conscientious exemptions from it were allowed. The solvency of such systems depends upon their universality. Moreover, there is no conceptual difference between a social security tax and a general tax such as the income tax.[58] Opening up the principle of conscientious objection to social security taxes would carry implications for income taxation as well. A tax system that allowed such conscientious objection "could not function," said the Court,[59] by which it meant that a largely self-assessed and self-policed tax system—whose functioning depends on its reputation for fairness—could not possibly survive such an exception. If a person could deduct from his tax liability some amount of money corresponding to an activity of government to which he had sincere religious objections, no doubt the country would swiftly become more religious, abuses would be widespread, and the apparent fairness of the system—not to mention its actual fairness—would suffer so greatly that honest taxpayers would appear to be fools and would therefore reduce their voluntary compliance with the system. Unless the government were content simply to surrender its tax base, then, it would have to establish some sort of administrative process to evaluate religious exemption claims on a case-by-case basis, as the Selective Service System used to do for those claiming conscientious objection to the draft. But of course, the tax objection board of inquiry would have a far harder job than Selective Service did. It would have not only to decide whether the objector's claim was a *bona fide* religious one. It would have to calculate how those religious scruples translated into a reduced tax liability. Not only would the religious scruples of the taxpayer be involved here—and these could of course change from year to year—but so also would the activities of the government, which change over time as well.

The concurring opinion of Justice Stevens more explicitly recognizes the economic incentive to acquire religious scruples that would flow from an open-ended availability of religious objections to

---

[58] *Id.* at 260.
[59] *Ibid.*

particular governmental expenditures. His opinion also emphasizes the necessity of extensive inquiry into individual religious beliefs in order to contain the damage to the tax system. Justice Stevens makes this latter point more generally by explaining that the principal objection to an expansive interpretation of the Free Exercise Clause is "the overriding interest in keeping the government—whether it be the legislature or the courts—out of the business of evaluating the relative merits of differing religious claims."[60]

On the strength of this analysis of the free exercise problem, schools that refuse to admit blacks would not be entitled to a religious exemption from the concededly valid denial of tax-exempt status to racially discriminating private schools. In a world in which many people wish to engage in racial discrimination in private school admissions, granting a religious exemption from the otherwise applicable denial of tax-exempt status will provide a significant incentive to strategic claims of religious scruples. The government is then put to the uncomfortable choice either of allowing itself to be lied to or of setting up a process to assay the sincerity of religious claims.

This argument ought to be sufficient to dispose of the free exercise claim of Goldsboro Christian. BJU's claim, however, would be more difficult to resolve. The BJU parietal rules are not so obviously racial discrimination as are race-based exclusions from eligibility for admission.[61] The parietal rule applies to all students, black and white.[62]

---

[60] Id. at 263 n.2. In this regard, Justice Stevens's emphasis is more on damage to fundamental constitutional values than it is on the expense of the administrative apparatus that would be necessary to pursue this task. The constitutional value that is said to be endangered by such inquiries is "that governmental approval of some and disapproval of others will be perceived as favoring one religion over another," a risk that the Establishment Clause is often said to have been intended to head off. This difference in emphasis is important, because it has implications for the question whether legislative decisions to grant religious exemptions are constitutional under the First Amendment Establishment Clause. If the Free Exercise Clause does not compel government to grant religious exemptions because it would be too expensive to do so, such reasoning presumably leaves discretion in the government to decide to incur such expenses. On the other hand, if the reason for denying the free exercise claim is the danger of "excessive entanglement in religion" presented by the need for government to evaluate the authenticity of religious beliefs, there is a serious question whether decisions to grant such exemptions are constitutional. See Justice Harlan's dissenting opinion in Sherbert v. Verner, 374 U.S. 418, 422 (1963).

[61] The Bob Jones University rules at issue in the case were as follows: "*There is to be no interracial dating* 1. Students who are partners in an interracial marriage will be expelled. 2. Students who are members of or affiliated with any group or organization which holds as one of its goals or advocates interracial marriage will be expelled. 3. Students who date outside their own race will be expelled. 4. Students who espouse, promote, or encourage others to violate the University's dating rules and regulations will be expelled." 103 S. Ct. at 2023.

[62] BJU argued that this ban on interracial dating did not constitute a racially discriminatory

Moreover, even conceding that the BJU parietal rule is racially discriminatory, it still is different in important respects from the Goldsboro Christian practice. BJU's rule is of a piece with its educational mission. As the Supreme Court noted, the University "is dedicated to the teaching and propagation of its fundamentalist Christian religious beliefs. It is both a religious and educational institution. Its teachers are required to be devout Christians, and all courses at the University are taught according to the Bible. Entering students are screened as to their religious beliefs, and their public and private conduct is strictly regulated by standards promulgated by University authorities."[63] In view of the concession that BJU's interracial dating ban stems from genuine religious scruples, this rule must be seen as one component in the overall policy of the University that as a condition of admission and continued good standing, all of its students subscribe to the BJU official religious dogma and conduct themselves accordingly. In a sense, then, conditioning a tax exemption on abandonment of this rule comes close to depriving the University of its conceded right to limit admissions to co-religionists.

Nevertheless, parietal rules of the BJU kind ought to be lumped together with admissions exclusions for free exercise purposes. Suppose Goldsboro Christian and similar schools were not allowed to discriminate in admissions any more than any secular segregation academy, and secular schools could not have BJU-type parietal rules either. If religiously motivated parietal rules were immune from the general prohibition, it is possible that a similar problem of strategic behavior could arise; that is, schools wishing to exclude blacks could feign religious grounds for enacting such parietal rules. If a ban on interracial dating would have a differential effect or impact on applications from black and white students, such a rule might serve as a rough-and-ready substitute for exclusion of black students.

---

practice within the meaning of the IRS Revenue Ruling, since it applied symmetrically to both black and white students. The Supreme Court summarily rejected this argument, noting that "decisions of this Court firmly establish that discrimination on the basis of racial affiliation and association is a form of racial discrimination." 103 S. Ct. at 2036, citing Loving v. Virginia, 388 U.S. 1 (1967); McLaughlin v. Florida, 379 U.S. 184 (1964); Tillman v. Wheaton-Haven Rec. Ass'n, 410 U.S. 431 (1973). That the parietal rule can reasonably be considered racially discriminatory is most easily seen in a situation where the rule is to be applied to an applicant who has an interracial relationship at the time of application. If Jane Doe, a black applicant for admission, is married to a white man, she is ineligible for admission. If she were white and otherwise similarly situated, she would be eligible under the Bob Jones policy.

[63] 103 S. Ct. at 2022.

Yet application of the "public policy" rule to the BJU parietal rule remains troubling, probably because denial of a tax exemption in the BJU situation, where the parietal rule seeks to insure that all students are co-religionists, seems about as close to a regulation of belief as it does to a regulation of action. Viewed in this way, the case would be difficult even if the parietal rules were not religiously motivated. Free exercise claims ask for exemption from generally applicable laws of presupposed constitutionality. But some cases that arise in the context of religious objections to particular laws turn out to be cases in which the religious nature of the objection is beside the point. A good example is *West Virginia v. Barnette*,[64] in which the Supreme Court held that compelling public school students to salute the flag violated the Constitution. Although the schoolchildren and their parents objected to the requirement of saluting the flag on religious grounds,[65] the Court decided the case in such a way as to make it clear that nonreligious objectors must also be exempted from the school's requirement: "[If] there is any fixed star in our constitutional constellation, it is that no official high or petty, can prescribe what shall be orthodox in politics, nationalism, religion, or other matters of opinion or force citizens to confess by word or act their faith therein."[66] Similarly, the Court's recognition in *Wooley v. Maynard*[67] of the petitioner's right to obliterate the motto, "Live Free or Die," from his automobile license plate did not depend, it appears, upon the fact that petitioner's objections were religiously motivated. Rather than whether the Free Exercise Clause is violated by denial of tax-exempt status to BJU, the question is whether it is constitutional to base denial of a tax exemption on this conduct at all, whether religiously motivated or not. In other words, is it constitutional for government to punish an educational institution for prescribing rules of conduct for its students where the underlying conduct itself is perfectly legal? Imagine that a state, pursuing its policy of eliminating invidious differentiation between the sexes, enacted a law that required residential schools to maintain sexually integrated dormitories. No doubt a religious institution with traditional values in this regard would object, but it is questionable whether its objections would stand on any higher constitutional ground than those of a nonreligious institution with

[64] 319 U.S. 624 (1943).

[65] The flag salute was considered by them to violate the prohibition on worshiping graven images.

[66] 319 U.S. at 642.

[67] 430 U.S. 705 (1977).

similar values of altogether secular origin. Of course, if one were to address the religious objections as such, the analysis of strategic behavior would lead to a likely rejection of the free exercise claim. If the traditional views were widely shared, granting a free exercise religious exemption from the otherwise applicable rule would provide an incentive for manufacturing religious objections. But in this sort of case, that observation does not lead to the conclusion that the rule can constitutionally be applied to all institutions, secular or religious. It may suggest that the rule is unconstitutional as applied to either. For many purposes, residential schools stand *in loco parentis*—no one would suggest that parents would not be allowed to prescribe similar rules of behavior.

On a similar analysis, BJU's religiously motivated ban on interracial dating may stand on no higher constitutional ground than a similar ban by a nondenominational college. And if the view that interracial dating and marriage are undesirable were widely shared, granting BJU an exemption because of its religious scruples would probably occasion strategic claims of religious scruples by competing institutions. On this view, the free exercise claim is easy to dispose of, but the constitutionality of regulating the University's rule remains a problem.[68]

It is evident that Goldsboro Christian and BJU do not present cases in which the governmental interest is more "compelling" than is usually the case. They are rather cases in which granting religious exemption from an otherwise binding rule would be very costly. Our "bottom line" on the free exercise claim, then, is the same as the Court's: no free exercise claim ought to be allowed. The Court's conclusion, however, ought to be embarrassed by the existence of its earlier decisions in *Sherbert* and *Thomas*. If those cases are right, as the Court apparently continues to think, then the free exercise claim in *Bob Jones* cannot be simply dismissed. Notwithstanding the Court's

---

[68] Nothing here suggests that it would be unconstitutional to regulate the Bob Jones practice on the ground that it was a device adopted with the unlawful purpose of excluding blacks from admission to the institution. Since regulating racially discriminatory admissions policies is constitutional, it will always be open to a court to find that a particular policy or practice was instituted as a "pretext" for invidious discrimination. For all we know, this was the situation in *Bob Jones*, where the University originally did not admit blacks at all and only later developed the policy discussed.

assertion to the contrary, *Sherbert-Thomas* and *Bob Jones* are not easily distinguishable.[69]

Although Justice Stevens disagrees,[70] *Sherbert* and *Thomas* present formidable invitations to strategic behavior. Justice Stevens says that such behavior is quite unlikely, because the claimants would be asserting that religious scruples had led them to quit their jobs and that religious scruples that required so substantial a sacrifice would not likely be counterfeit. But there are any number of people, with any number of idiosyncratic or personal reasons, who want to quit their jobs. If they do quit, they will not be eligible for unemployment compensation benefits. On the other hand, if they feign religious objection to the work that they are doing and quit, pretending it is because of that objection, then they are entitled to unemployment benefits under the doctrine of *Sherbert* and *Thomas*—unless their dissembling were uncovered. Accordingly, such people certainly do have an incentive to manipulate the system once cases like *Sherbert* and *Thomas* make such manipulation possible, if not indeed easy.

Taken together, the run of free exercise cases indicate that, notwithstanding more recent pronouncements to the contrary, the strategic behavior problem remains of central concern to the Court. Viewed in this way, the results in *Sherbert* and *Thomas* must be considered anomalous and *Bob Jones* within the mainstream of free exercise analysis.

On the free exercise issue, then, as on the statutory question, the Court's result can be defended but its opinion cannot be. The result can be reached by following the well-worn path of strategic behavior analysis; but if the Court continues to cling to the *Sherbert* line of cases, it is not at all clear why *Bob Jones* was rightly decided.

---

[69] The Court in *Sherbert* said that "there is no proof whatever" to support the State's expressed fears that a flood of fraudulent religious exemption claims would result if Sherbert's position were upheld. But how could anyone possibly prove what would happen if the State had not required unemployment insurance beneficiaries with religious objections to accept Saturday work? In the usual case the impact of a religious exemption will have to be a matter of argument. The possibility of strategic behavior was every bit as speculative in *Braunfeld* as it was in *Sherbert*. Similarly, the parade of horribles that animated the Court's conclusion in *Lee* is simply a protracted conjecture. Why was the Government's argument in the *Lee* case plausible and the argument of the State in *Sherbert* (and *Thomas*) implausible, when both arguments proceed on the basis of the theory that people are likely to engage in strategic behavior in order to get valuable benefits from the government, especially when it will be hard to uncover their lies.

[70] 455 U.S. at 263–64 n.3.

V. CONCLUSION

When the whiff of brimstone is in the air and respectable public opinion is mobilized and shrilling at a high pitch, courts have an opportunity for the only sort of heroism that usually falls in the way of lawyers. *Bob Jones* furnished that kind of opportunity, which the Supreme Court happily passed up in exchange for much favorable ink in establishment newspapers. But never mind what those newspapers said, *Bob Jones* was a difficult and uncertain case, which earned its celebrity by becoming the focus of a political feud concerning the distribution of power between Congress and the Executive. Justice required, not a different result from that reached by the Court, but only an acknowledgment of the difficulty. The klieg lights were burning, the whole world was watching, and such an acknowledgment proved to be too much to ask from the Burger Court. It would surely go too far to decry the outcome as a miscarriage of justice, for there were satisfactory reasons for allowing the Bob Jones University tax exemption to be withdrawn. But these were not the Supreme Court's reasons. It had others that will not withstand scrutiny and that will haunt and discomfit future cases.

PAUL B. STEPHAN III

BOB JONES UNIVERSITY v. UNITED STATES: PUBLIC POLICY IN SEARCH OF TAX POLICY

At first glance, the Supreme Court's decision in *Bob Jones University v. United States*[1] may seem a sport. The opinion appears to be rooted in technical minutiae and announces a rule that may ultimately govern one set of facts and no other. Relying on a melange of arguments about the structure and history of the Code, the extent of agency discretion, and the effect of congressional acquiescence in a notorious Internal Revenue Service (IRS) policy, the Court upheld the denial of federal tax exemption to schools practicing racial discrimination toward students. It determined that the Code, which exempts separately charitable, educational, and religious organizations, contains an implicit public policy standard covering all these entities. To obtain the benefits of tax exemption, *Bob Jones* declares, an organization "must demonstrably serve and be in harmony with the public interest."[2] Disclaimers in the opinion left open the questions whether the IRS could or must extend disqualification to any organizations besides schools, and could or must rely on any public policy violations other than racial discrimination.

Despite the seeming narrowness of its scope, the decision is important. Its significance lies in the Court's apparent revival of the

Paul B. Stephan III is Associate Professor, University of Virginia School of Law.

AUTHOR'S NOTE: I am grateful for valuable suggestions by Lillian R. BeVier, Richard J. Bonnie, Michael P. Dooley, Frank H. Easterbrook, Charles J. Goetz, Harry L. Gutman, Edmund W. Kitch, Douglas L. Leslie, Peter W. Low, Glen O. Robinson, George A. Rutherglen, and Robert E. Scott.

[1] 103 S. Ct. 2017 (1983).
[2] 103 S. Ct. at 2029.

public policy doctrine as a means of construing the Internal Revenue Code. This raises important questions about the proper relative roles of the IRS, the courts, and Congress in the formation of "policy" for our society.

Cases where the particular language of federal tax statutes seems to collide with more general tax policies of consistency and integrity have bedeviled the Court since the early days of the income tax. The proud if empty rhetoric of *Gregory v. Helvering*[3] that in tax cases the Court will not "elevate artifice above reality" has produced reams of elaboration in both the United States Reports and scholarly literature.[4] The public policy doctrine presents a different problem, because the question of its application arises only when an internally coherent feature of the tax system has applications that seem to conflict with the norms of a different body of public law. The doctrine, as articulated by the Court, required the denial of any deduction, exclusion, or exemption otherwise permitted by tax law if allowance would frustrate sharply defined national or state policies. Under this formula, the doctrine exists to compromise a rule of taxation, not to reconcile it with the general features of the federal tax system.

Although in some fundamental sense all legal rules implicate normative judgments, the distinction between tax and nontax policy is important. At a minimum it affects the kinds of justifications the tax bureaucracy and reviewing courts can use for particular decisions. The significance of the public policy doctrine lies in its expansion of the arsenal of arguments the taxing authorities can use to defend their actions. This expansion in turn raises questions of legitimacy—Are tax agencies or the courts the appropriate bodies for making these policy judgments?—and feasibility—Do these bodies have the necessary means to implement their policy judgments?[5]

---

[3] 293 U.S. 465, 470 (1935).

[4] See, *e.g.*, Commissioner v. Tufts, 103 S. Ct. 1826 (1983); Hillsboro Nat'l Bk. v. Commissioner, 103 S. Ct. 1134 (1983); Knetsch v. United States, 364 U.S. 361 (1960); Commissioner v. Court Holding Co., 324 U.S. 331 (1945); 1 BITTKER, FEDERAL TAXATION OF INCOME, ESTATES AND GIFTS 4-29 to -52 (1981); Blum, Knetsch v. United States: *A Pronouncement on Tax Avoidance*, 1961 SUPREME COURT REVIEW 135; Chirelstein, *Learned Hand's Contribution to the Law of Tax Avoidance*, 77 YALE L. J. 440 (1968); Isenbergh, *Musing on Form and Substance in Taxation*, 49 U. CHI. L. REV. 859 (1982).

[5] In insisting on the importance of the distinction between tax and nontax policy I am making common cause with the advocates of tax expenditure analysis. See generally SURREY, PATHWAYS TO TAX REFORM (1973); Surrey & McDaniel, *The Tax Expenditure Concept and the Budget Reform Act of 1974*, 17 B.C. IND. & COM. L. REV. 679 (1976). Tax expenditure theorists and their critics focus primarily on congressional decisions to depart from tax rules for nontax reasons; the public policy doctrine entails administrative and judicial alterations of legislative enactments.

In its heyday, the public policy doctrine gave courts and the Treasury broad discretion to disapprove tax advantages such as deductions or exemptions when the taxpayer qualified for them through conduct that violated some nontax norm of behavior. Congress in 1969 appeared to retire this canon of construction when it enacted a purportedly comprehensive codification of public policy disallowances. This legislation governed only business deductions, but it seemed to reflect a more general repudiation of administrative and judicial revisions of the Code based on nontax policy. *Bob Jones* marks the first time the Court has disregarded the implicit message of this legislation.

To see *Bob Jones* as a revival of the public policy doctrine, one first must conclude that none of the other rationales the Court advanced for the result is persuasive. In endorsing the public interest standard for charitable, educational, and religious exemptions, the Court purported both to interpret signals from Congress about this requirement and to accept arguments that insertion of the standard would best serve overriding social and moral ends. If taken seriously, the interpretive arguments would imply that *Bob Jones* is a unique case affecting nothing but racially discriminatory private schools. A review of the supporting evidence, however, suggests that the Court strained the limits of credible interpretation. In this light, one must parse the decision for alternative explanations. The other reasons the Court advanced for adding the "public interest" gloss to the statutory exemption requirements reflect the influence of the public policy doctrine, although the Court referred to it only in footnotes.

I. PUBLIC POLICY DOCTRINE AND THE SUPREME COURT

A. GENERAL CONSIDERATIONS: SELECTIVITY, PROXIMITY, AND PROPORTIONALITY

Any time a rulemaker seeks to modify a rule of taxation to serve other ends, it must confront three problems. First, it must select which public policy to serve. In a complex, highly regulated society with a hierarchy of constitutional, legislative, and common-law norms, many

---

Thus the doctrine implicates the particular problems associated with the modification of existing rules through administration and adjudication, as opposed to the initial choice of tax rules through the political process. For a fuller discussion of this distinction, see Kronman, *Contract Law and Distributive Justice*, 89 YALE L. J. 472, 503-05 (1980).

of which are in conflict, the question involves a choice among public policies rather than the discovery of a monolithic public good. The selectivity problem may seem obvious, but in the administrative actions and court decisions that developed the public policy doctrine one finds little or no acknowledgment that it exists. In general, experts in tax law, particularly those in the Treasury and the Internal Revenue Service charged with administration of these laws, claim no special competence in making the selectivity choices. *Bob Jones* nodded at the problem but provided no guidance to how it should be resolved.[6]

The rulemaker also must decide what tax rules bear so close a relationship to the public policy at issue as to require modification. The proximity issue involves judgments about tax structure, as distinguished from decisions about morality or legality implicit in the selection of public policies. Under an income tax, a range of proximity choices exists. One might deny a deduction for one or more of the following expenses: the immediate out-of-pocket costs of undertaking a disapproved activity; the capital investment associated with these costs; the sanctions incurred as punishment for the activity; or all the costs of sustaining an enterprise engaged in disapproved conduct. One also might apply different rate schedules to misbehaving taxpayers, although both the tax agencies and the courts seem to concede the exclusive power of Congress to set rates of taxation.

Like the selectivity issue, proximity questions have received almost no explicit administrative or judicial exegesis. Unlike the selectivity problem, proximity issues require for their resolution some enhanced understanding of tax law. Unless one anticipates the repercussions elsewhere in the system of a modification of tax law, one cannot begin to judge the change's impact. Treasury and IRS lawyers, familiar with both the technical aspects of tax rules and the practical side of implementation, possess this expertise in special measure, although concern about institutional bias may cloud their claim to deference.

In *Bob Jones*, the Court passed judgment only on eligibility for deductible contributions and exemption from payroll taxes, thus postponing a confrontation with the trickier technical ramifications of the case. It did not suggest how existing net-income-measuring rules

---

[6] The Court limited its holding to cases where the public policy at issue is "fundamental" and there is "no doubt" that an institution is acting contrary to it. 103 S. Ct. at 2029. It also hinted that some public policy violations may not lead to loss of exemption. *Id.* at 2031 n.21. But the opinion offers no guidance as to what constitutes a fundamental public policy or how to distinguish between acceptable and intolerable violations.

might apply to a nonprofit organization, nor did it indicate whether scholarships, fellowships, and student-dependent exemptions also would fall in the wake of a school's disqualification.[7]

Finally the rulemaker must confront the problem of proportionality.[8] Whether one regards modification of a tax rule as a form of condemnation or as an incentive to avoid misconduct, it is desirable to maintain some kind of proportion between the consequences of the modification and the public policy violation one wishes to condemn or deter. If one is expressing condemnation, whether independently derived or based on some sign of the legislative will, then a disproportionate penalty may raise new moral concerns of potentially greater moment than the judgment being expressed. If one is deterring misconduct, then one must try not to underreact or overreact. An inconsequential deterrent already in effect might discourage lawmakers from introducing more effective penalties, while too much deterrence may discourage innocent and presumably desirable behavior that might be mistaken for the proscribed conduct.[9]

When it first considered the public policy doctrine, the Court did not note the peculiar proportionality problems created by a progressive income tax, where the cost to a taxpayer of lost tax advantages turns not only on the extent of the advantage but also on the level of his taxable income. Over time, it became aware of the issue. *Bob Jones*, however, ignored the problem, even though loss of the charitable exemption creates proportionality problems that may be greater than those associated with denial of business deductions.

B. THE CASES

1. *Origin of the doctrine:* Haberle *and* Textile Mills. The Supreme Court's first attempt to reconcile income tax policy and a competing claim of public law came in *Clarke v. Haberle Crystal Springs Brewing Co.*,[10] a 1930 case involving the scope of the depreciation deduction for

---

[7] See notes 127-31 *infra* and accompanying text.

[8] I am using the term "proportionality" in its moral sense—the principle that punishment should fit the crime—and not in its technical tax sense—the principle that rates should remain constant. For elaboration of the moral principle, see, *e.g.*, BENTHAM, *Principles of Penal Law*, in 1 THE WORKS OF JEREMY BENTHAM 399-402 (Bowring ed. 1843).

[9] My use of the proportionality principle is derived from and equivalent to the economic concept of optimal sanctions. See Becker, *Crime and Punishment: An Economic Approach*, 76 J. POL. ECON. 169 (1968).

[10] 280 U.S. 384 (1934).

corporations. The taxpayer, a brewery, sought to write off against its income the adjusted basis of goodwill lost because of Prohibition. The Government objected. In retrospect the case may seem to rest on a false conflict, because the nonrecovery of basis in goodwill under any circumstances short of a sale of the business seems an entrenched feature of the income tax.[11] But at the time of the decision this rule had not taken firm shape, and the Court avoided any general remarks about the recovery of goodwill costs. Instead the majority, through a characteristically terse opinion by Justice Holmes, asserted it "plain" that Congress could not have intended a "partial compensation" for the extinction of a business "as noxious under the Constitution," because the constitutional obligation to compensate for a taking did not apply in these circumstances.[12]

What *Haberle* left unsaid was crucial. The opinion did not explain why the Court characterized the allowance of a presumptively normal deduction as compensation. Nor did *Haberle* explain why the Court selected Prohibition as a policy that might override general rules of income taxation. Grounded as it was on a constitutional amendment, Prohibition might demand special accommodation in the interpretation of inferior legislation. Public policy resting on lesser authority might not require the same kind of adjustments of the federal tax statutes. The opinion did not exclude, however, the possibility that even the most mundane administrative regulation or local ordinance might prompt a judicial reformation of the tax laws.

Another opportunity to clarify the contours of the public policy doctrine did not come to the Court for a decade. When the day arrived, a dramatic change in the Court's personnel and philosophy had occurred. *Textile Mills Securities Corp. v. Commissioner*[13] was decided in 1941, at the peak of the Court's support for New Deal administrative justice generally and the power of the taxing authorities in particular. The need for administrative agencies to have a free hand to implement their governing statutes and the value of administrative expertise in defining the legislative mandate never seemed clearer to the Court, and

---

[11] See Treas. Reg. 1.167(a)-3 (1956); Welch v. Helvering, 290 U.S. 111 (1933); 1 BITTKER, note 4 *supra*, at 20-86 to -87, 23-34 to -36. Characterization of *Haberle* as resting on tax rather than public policy principles is bolstered by a later decision holding that breweries could take a deduction for the adjusted basis of tangible property made obsolescent by prohibition. V. Loewers Gambrinus Brewery Co. v. Anderson, 282 U.S. 638 (1931).

[12] 280 U.S. at 386. In a companion case, the Court held that the personal income tax similarly did not allow a deduction. Renziehausen v. Lucas, 280 U.S. 387 (1930).

[13] 314 U.S. 326 (1941).

federal tax collectors reaped the harvest of litigative victories. *Textile Mills* exemplifies this pattern.[14]

The case concerned the validity of a Treasury regulation excluding from the definition of an "ordinary and necessary" business expense "money expended for lobbying purposes, the promotion or defeat of legislation, the exploitation of propaganda, . . . and contributions for campaign expenses."[15] The taxpayer served as the agent of German textile manufacturers who had lost property during World War I under the Trading with the Enemy Act. It launched a successful campaign for enactment of compensatory legislation and sought to deduct the costs of these efforts against the fees paid by the Germans. The income tax levied by the Revenue Act of 1928, like all of its predecessors, allowed a deduction for business expenses without reference to political activity. The Government accepted the taxpayer's assertion that the outlays had all the characteristics of a normal business expense, but relied on the regulation to deny a deduction. The Court agreed with the Government.

Although it affirmed the public policy doctrine, *Textile Mills* departed from *Haberle* in both tone and analysis. The earlier decision had rested on the Court's own judgment about the intent of Congress in the face of competing constitutional and tax policy considerations. *Textile Mills*, by contrast, emphasized the importance of administrative discretion and implied a narrower role for judicial review. The words "ordinary and necessary," asserted the Court, lack sufficient clarity to preclude administrative interpretation. The gloss imposed by the Treasury regulation simply expanded on a particular concern—the spread of "insidious influences through legislative halls"—to draw a reasonable if broad line around all expenses that run the risk of political corruption. The possibility that the Treasury might know less about the intricacies of political influence than about income measurement seemed beside the point. The issue, the Court insisted, was not what statutory construction might most appeal to its sensibility, but rather the limits of the Treasury's rulemaking authority in the absence of clearly contrary signals from Congress. Whatever the boundaries of

---

[14] See Surrey, *The Supreme Court and the Federal Income Tax: Some Implications of the Recent Decisions*, 35 ILL. L. REV. 779 (1941); Wolfman, Silver, & Silver, *The Behavior of Justice Douglas in Federal Tax Cases*, 122 U. PA. L. REV. 235, 239-52 (1973).

[15] Treas. Reg. 74, art. 262 (1928). This language originated in a 1915 Treasury Decision and first was incorporated into a regulation in 1918. T.D. 2137, 17 Treas. Dec., Int. Rev. 48, 57-58 (1915); Treas. Reg. 33, art. 143 (1918).

this authority might be, the Court believed the regulation lay comfortably within them.[16]

2. *Second thoughts about the doctrine:* Heininger *and* Lilly. Within three years of *Textile Mills* the Court made clear that it had not given the taxing authorities quite as blank a check as that case might have suggested. The issue in *Commissioner v. Heininger*[17] was the deductibility of legal expenses incurred by a taxpayer in an unsuccessful attempt to overturn a postal fraud order. No Treasury regulation applied to these facts, but the Service relied on its general authority to construe the tax laws in light of its informed judgment. Here it regarded the legal expenses as an extension of the underlying fraud and hence not "ordinary and necessary," even though they clearly arose out of the taxpayer's business. The Court disagreed.

Because the Commissioner of Internal Revenue conceded that he would have allowed the deduction if the taxpayer had prevailed in the litigation, the only issue was the taxpayer's liability under the fraud order as a reason for denying an otherwise proper business expense. "It has never been thought," asserted the Court, "that the mere fact that an expenditure bears a remote relation to an illegal act makes it nondeductible."[18] Furthermore, the taxpayer had not been convicted of mail fraud, but rather had been subject to sanctions in an administrative proceeding designed only to protect consumers, not to impose punishment. "[T]o deny the deduction would attach a serious punitive consequence to the Postmaster General's finding [of fraud] which Congress has not expressly or impliedly indicated should result from such a finding."[19]

One can analyze *Heininger* as resolving either a proximity or a selectivity issue against the Government. The decision might indicate that legal defense expenses are too distant from the initial wrongdoing to merit application of the public policy doctrine. Alternatively, the Court might have believed that the kind of misbehavior that results in administrative sanctions, as opposed to the kind for which the Government might impose criminal punishment, did not constitute the sort of public policy violation to which the doctrine should respond.

---

[16] 314 U.S. at 338-39.
[17] 320 U.S. 467 (1943).
[18] *Id.* at 474.
[19] *Id.* at 474-75.

The next case came in 1952, on the eve of the Warren Court era, and further undercut the discretion seemingly accorded the Treasury in *Textile Mills*. The narrow question for decision in *Lilly v. Commissioner*[20] was the deductibility of kickbacks paid by an optician to doctors for patient referrals. Although customary, these payments had come under increasing criticism and, after the years at issue in the tax dispute, became illegal in the taxpayer's home state. Some question existed as to whether the practice violated the Sherman Act, but no adjudication of this issue had occurred. It appeared, then, that when the taxpayer had made the kickbacks, he had exceeded no limits imposed by positive law.

In the face of the Government's claim that the kickbacks nonetheless violated public policy, the Court upheld the optician's claim to a deduction. It observed that nothing in the Internal Revenue Code or any Treasury regulation prohibited business expense deductions on general public policy grounds. Although it would assume for purposes of argument that some expenses might shed their deductibility when they " 'frustrate sharply defined national or state policies proscribing particular types of conduct,' "[21] it declared that in no case could the taxing authorities go further than Congress or the states in determining the positive content of public policy. The doctrine, if it had any validity, applied only to "national or state policies evidenced by some governmental declaration of them."[22]

The specific point decided in *Lilly*—that the range of choices of public policies for the taxing authorities to enforce did not exceed the positive enactments of some other public body—seems in retrospect far less important than the Court's hints that the entire public policy doctrine rested on shaky assumptions and lacked solid precedential support. *Lilly* confined *Textile Mills* by characterizing the decision as based on congressional acquiescence in a longstanding regulation.[23] *Haberle* received no mention at all.

---

[20] 343 U.S. 90 (1952).

[21] *Id.* at 96-97 (quoting Commissioner v. Heininger, 320 U.S. 467, 473 (1943)).

[22] *Id.* at 97.

[23] *Id.* at 95. The distinction between Treasury Regulations, on the one hand, and rulings and litigation positions, on the other, has both formal and substantive significance. Congress expressly has authorized promulgation of interpretive regulations by the Secretary of the Treasury. I.R.C. §7805(a). The notice, discussion, and approval process is elaborate and public. As a result, courts give considerable deference to the regulations. Revenue rulings, private rulings, and litigation positions are issued by the Commissioner of Internal Revenue pursuant to authority delegated by the Treasury. They are intended only to announce the application of general principles to particular facts and reflect only the judgment of IRS personnel, not that of superior officials in

3. *Contradictions and paradox: The Warren Court decisions.* In 1953, with a new occupant in the White House and an imminent turnover of personnel on the Court, the prospect of change seemed clear. At one extreme, the new Attorney General held out the possibility of denying deductions of any sort to "illegitimate" businesses.[24] At the other end, Randolph Paul, a leader of the tax bar (and counsel for the taxpayer in *Lilly*), argued against any commingling of the federal income tax and other public policies absent explicit direction from Congress.[25] The pronouncements from the Court seemed to admit of either possibility as well as a range of choices between them.

The first portent from the Warren Court was clouded by the failure of either party to argue that the public policy doctrine applied in the novel context in which it arose. In *Commissioner v. Glenshaw Glass Co.*,[26] the Court rejected a twenty-year-old line of lower court decisions and upheld the Government's claim that the punitive component of an antitrust treble-damage award constituted taxable income. Although the Government never had invoked the doctrine against the interest of the federal fisc, its logic at least superficially applied to the inclusion of rewards given taxpayers in promotion of public policy. If allowing a deduction for the cost of misbehavior blunts the force of a prohibition, then taxing a subsidy correspondingly undercuts whatever policy the incentive is designed to promote.

The punitive component of antitrust damages, intended primarily to encourage enforcement of the antitrust laws by private attorneys general, seems a plausible example. Taxation lessens the incentive and diminishes the reward, thereby undermining the goals treble damages were designed to further. Whether from dissatisfaction with the public policy doctrine generally, from unwillingness to extend it to subsidies, or from reluctance to rely on an argument not raised by either party, *Glenshaw Glass* applied a broad rule of taxing realized income absent

---

the Treasury. Pursuant to the terms of the delegation, the Secretary does not oversee or approve these rulings, although informal consultations take place. The public usually has no opportunity to discuss rulings before the Service issues them. See generally SURREY, WARREN, MCDANIEL, & AULT, FEDERAL INCOME TAXATION CASES AND MATERIALS 58-63 (1972).

[24] See Paul, *The Use of Public Policy by the Commissioner in Disallowing Deductions*, 6 U.S.C. TAX INST. 715, 715-16 (1954).

[25] *Id.*

[26] 348 U.S. 426 (1955).

an explicit congressional decision to exclude and sustained the Government's claim.[27]

The lingering dispute over the validity and scope of the public policy doctrine came to a head in a trio of decisions during the 1957 Term. Two cases involved the deductibility of state fines paid for the violation of truck weight limits; the third concerned a bookmaker's office rent and employee salaries in light of a state statute imposing criminal liability for the making of such payments as well as prohibiting the underlying business. The Court unanimously adopted the IRS's formulation of the doctrine, which denied a deduction if allowance would "frustrate sharply defined national or state policies proscribing particular types of conduct, evidenced by some governmental declaration thereof." In applying this standard, however, the Court gave the IRS only a partial victory. In *Tank Truck Rentals, Inc. v. Commissioner*,[28] it agreed that the truckers could not take a deduction for their fines. But in *Commissioner v. Sullivan*,[29] it ruled that the bookmaker could deduct the illegal payments to his landlord and employees.

Rarely has the Court unanimously produced such apparently inconsistent opinions on the same day. As indicia for the proper resolution of selectivity problems, the decisions are hopelessly in conflict. The Pennsylvania truck weight limits at issue in *Tank Truck* seem inconsequential. Violations were not only customary but essential for economic survival; the State did not impose other sanctions such as unloading, but rather levied fines that seemed indistinguishable from a road repair excise tax; and the state's own regulatory agency required the trucking companies to carry the fines on their books as business expenses.[30] By contrast, the Illinois statute involved in *Sullivan* specified a serious criminal offense for which

---

[27] One scholar relied on this point in arguing for exclusion of treble damages. See Wright, *A Tax Formula to Restore the Historical Effects of the Antitrust Treble Damage Provisions*, 65 MICH. L. REV. 245 (1966). In the related area of direct subsidies, neither the courts nor the tax agencies have recognized a "positive public policy" ground for exclusion. Some incentives, however, have been wrestled into other categories to achieve exclusion. See Rev. Rul. 72-605, 1972-2 C.B. 35; Brown Shoe Co. v. Commissioner, 339 U.S. 583 (1950); Edwards v. Cuba R.R. Co., 268 U.S. 628 (1925); McDermott v. Commissioner, 150 F.2d 585 (D.C. Cir. 1945); see generally Note, *Taxation of Nonshareholder Contributions to Corporate Capital*, 82 HARV. L. REV. 619 (1969).

[28] 356 U.S. 30 (1958). In the companion case, Hoover Motor Express Co. v. United States, 356 U.S. 38 (1958), the Court held that fines imposed for inadvertent violations of the same statute also were nondeductible.

[29] 356 U.S. 27 (1958).

[30] See Record at 116a-20a, 129a-30a, *Tank Truck*, note 28 *supra*.

nonmonetary penalties were a real possibility. Why the weight laws required adjustment of tax rules, but the antigambling statute did not, seems an unanswerable question.[31]

Nor were the decisions any more helpful in describing the contours of the proximity issue. Using "the severity and immediacy of the frustration" of state policy as the test for nondeductability, the *Tank Truck* opinion asserted that the most "complete and direct" case occurs "when the expenditure for which deduction is sought is itself prohibited by statute." Penalties for violation of the prohibition are "only slightly" more remote.[32] Yet the expenditures for which the Court permitted deduction in *Sullivan* did violate a statute and thus seemed even more eligible for nondeductibility than were the weight limit fines in *Tank Truck*. Nowhere did the Court acknowledge, much less justify, this discrepancy.

Further confusion came the following Term. In *Cammarano v. United States*,[33] the Court reaffirmed its commitment to the *Textile Mills* holding. The taxpayer, a beer distributor, sought to deduct the costs of opposing an initiative referendum that, if successful, would have abolished its business. The Service objected to the deduction on the ground that the expenditures fell within the scope of the Treasury regulation prohibiting political expense deductions.

Although *Cammarano* for the most part relied on the same congressional-ratification-by-reenactment argument that the Court had used in *Textile Mills* to sustain this regulation, it also sought to reconcile the result with the intervening decisions whittling away at the Treasury's discretion to define public policy. The Court acknowledged that *Heininger* and *Sullivan* had limited the doctrine to "sharply defined national or state policies," but explained that Treasury regulations themselves could "constitute an expression of a sharply defined national policy."[34] Evidently the Treasury still could

---

[31] Justice Douglas's opinion for the *Sullivan* Court argued that the gambling business expenses were analogous to payment of the federal wager tax, deduction of which was allowed by the Treasury. 356 U.S. at 28–29. But positive law not only permitted but compelled the tax payments; rent and wage payments, by contrast, were forbidden. The Court's further reference to rent and wages deductions as "normal" begged the question of deductibility where the payments themselves, and not simply conduct of the underlying business, constituted criminal acts.

[32] 356 U.S. at 35. Although Justice Clark's opinion for the Court describes penalties as "only slightly less remote," the remainder of the paragraph makes clear that more was meant.

[33] 358 U.S. 498, 503–04 (1959).

[34] *Id.* at 508 (quoting Commissioner v. Heininger, 320 U.S. 467, 473 (1943)).

set normative standards of behavior as long as it announced them in advance through regulations.[35]

Up to this point the unarticulated rule of thumb could be stated: absent an applicable regulation, a taxpayer may deduct the cost of illegal activity arising out of his business but not the sanctions imposed for the illegality. Unfortunately, even this fragile rationale fell apart in the face of the Court's next effort to describe the relationship between public policy and income taxation. In *United States v. James*,[36] three years after *Tank Truck*, the Court declared that an embezzler could deduct the cost of restitution to his victim. Why a deduction for this penalty does not frustrate the laws against embezzlement, although a fine paid to government would, received no explanation.

The Court's last effort to impose some order on the unruly doctrine came in 1966. It was heroic but unsatisfactory. In *Commissioner v. Tellier*,[37] it rejected a forty-year-old line of administrative and lower court decisions that consistently had denied a deduction for the costs of an unsuccessful defense against business-related criminal charges. Justice Stewart, writing for a unanimous Court, began "with the proposition that the federal income tax is a tax on net income, not a sanction against wrongdoing."[38] He cited *Sullivan, Lilly*, and *Heininger* as examples of how illegal or immoral conduct could still produce deductions to define net income, if the outlays otherwise had the characteristics of business expenses. Where Congress had not ratified a longstanding regulation or otherwise indicated a desire to implement public policy through the income tax, he explained, "only in extremely limited circumstances" has the Court tolerated exceptions to the general principle of deductibility for business expenses.[39] The hiring of a lawyer in the face of criminal charges does not violate any public policy, but rather constitutes the exercise of a constitutional right.[40]

---

[35] For reasons why regulations might be regarded as different from other actions of the tax agencies, see note 23 *supra*.

[36] 366 U.S. 213 (1961). *James* overruled Commissioner v. Wilcox, 327 U.S. 404 (1946), which had treated the embezzler's proceeds as an excludible loan. Under the *Wilcox* approach, the question of a deduction for restitution never arose.

[37] 383 U.S. 687 (1966).

[38] *Id.* at 691.

[39] *Id.* at 693-94.

[40] Although one might read *Tellier* as choosing between public policies and simply giving greater weight to the constitutional policy in favor of counsel in criminal trials, the unavailability of a deduction for nonbusiness criminal defense costs undercuts this explanation. For examples since *Tellier* where courts have applied the business-personal distinction to deny a deduction for the costs of conducting a criminal defense, see, *e.g.*, Greenway v. Commissioner, 40 T.C.M. 24, 31 (1980), Hylton v. Commissioner, 32 T.C.M. 1238 (1973).

Furthermore, the denial of a deduction for these fees would impose a burden on the taxpayer "in a measure dependent not on the seriousness of the offense or the actual sentence imposed by the Court, but on the cost of the defense and the defendant's particular tax bracket."[41] The Court refused to countenance such a disproportionate penalty imposed in the name of general hostility to wrongdoing.

With its critical analysis of the underpinnings of the public policy doctrine and its willingness to disregard a settled understanding about one particular application, *Tellier* made clear that the Court's acceptance of the verbal formulation of the doctrine did not mean endorsement of the Government's understanding of it. In one sense the Court seemed to have come full circle back to *Haberle*. But while *Haberle* had relied on public policy to avoid resolution of a difficult issue concerning the general dimensions of income taxation, *Tellier* indicated a preference for principles of taxation as a sole ground of decision. In the case of legal fees, this meant asking whether the criminal charges arose out of business activity, not whether the taxpayer had violated the law.

In all other respects more confusion surrounded the doctrine than at any previous time. Selection of a public policy to trigger its application required some pronouncement of law by a governmental body, but not all pronouncements were sufficient and the Treasury possessed some power to issue such pronouncements itself. As for proximity, *Tellier*'s discussion of *Sullivan*, a case now elevated to a norm, and its approving reference to Randolph Paul's earlier article, implied that a taxpayer usually could deduct the direct costs of illegal acts as long as he acted with profit as his goal and had not made a capital expenditure. Some sanctions remained nondeductible, but the cost of resisting sanctions would reduce a taxpayer's net income if the prosecution stemmed from his business. Clearly the articulated basis of the doctrine—frustration of well-defined federal or state policies proscribing particular conduct—could not explain or justify these disparate rules, but the Court would not unravel the mystery. Nor could longstanding administrative or lower court interpretations of this formula afford help.

---

[41] 383 U.S. at 695. In an accompanying footnote the Court quoted at length from Paul's article. *Id.* at n.11.

C. AFTERMATH

Both the Treasury and Congress found this uncertainty in the law of business deductions intolerable. In 1969 a major statutory revision codified those instances where misconduct would nullify an otherwise appropriate deduction. Fines and other penalties paid to a government, bribes paid to government officials, illegal kickbacks, and the punitive component of antitrust damage awards fell within this special category. In all other cases a taxpayer could reduce his taxable income by deducting an expense in spite of its illegality.[42] These provisions cautiously ratified the specific results the doctrine had produced, but Congress made clear its rejection of the principle of judicial and legislative discretion underlying the cases. The legislative record declared the intent of Congress to reserve to itself the exclusive authority to advance nontax policies by modifying tax rules.[43]

In the fourteen years that have passed since this enactment, the principle that Congress alone should convert income-measuring rules into sanctions for misbehavior has generally prevailed. A few technical issues remain, but none seriously undermines the basic allocation of authority in this area.[44] For the most part the public policy doctrine has enjoyed a peaceful retirement.

---

[42] Tax Reform Act of 1969, Pub. L. No. 91-172, §902(b), 83 Stat. 487, 710-11 (adding I.R.C. §162(c), (f), (g)).

[43] The Joint Committee's analysis of the change states: "The provision for the denial of the deduction for payments in these situations which are deemed to violate public policy is intended to be all inclusive. Public policy, in other circumstances, generally is not sufficiently clearly defined to justify the disallowance of deductions." Staff of Joint Comm. on Int. Rev. Tax'n, 91st Cong., 1st Sess., General Explanation of the Tax Reform Act of 1969, at 234 (1970). See S. Rep. No. 91-552, 91st Cong., 1st Sess. 274 (1969); 1 BITTKER, note 4 supra, at 20-50 to -51; Taggart, *Fines, Penalties, Bribes, and Damage Payments and Recoveries*, 25 TAX. L. REV. 611, 646 (1970). In one case the new legislation asserted the power of Congress to alter existing tax law for public policy reasons: it reversed the decision of IRS to permit deductions for the punitive component of antitrust damages. See Rev. Rul. 64-224, 1964-2 C.B. 52.

[44] One unresolved area concerns the precise meaning of the 1971 amendment of this provision. See Revenue Act of 1971, Pub. L. No. 92-178, § 310(a), 85 Stat. 497, 525 (amending I.R.C. § 162(c)). In practice the government has interpreted this language inconsistently. Compare Holt v. Commissioner, 69 T.C. 75 (1977), aff'd per curiam, 611 F.2d 1160 with Rev. Rul. 82-74, 1982-1 C.B. 110. See also Private Letter Ruling No. 7816021, IRS Letter Rul. Rep. (CCH) (1978). Some uncertainty remains about the applicability of the 1969 revision to analogous deductions for business and investment losses and inventory adjustments. See Treas. Reg. §§ 1.212-1(p), 1.471-3(d), T.D. 7345, 1975-1 C.B. 51; Rev. Rul. 77-126, 1977-1 C.B. 47; Max Sobel Wholesale Liquors v. Commissioner, 630 F.2d 670 (9th Cir. 1980); Holmes Enterprises, Inc. v. Commissioner, 69 T.C. 114 (1977). In a case arising after the 1969 revision but involving a 1965 tax year, several members of the Tax Court expressed different opinions about the applicability of the revision to personal deductions such as that for casualty losses. Compare Mazzei v.

In retrospect, this outcome seems inevitable. Assigning the Treasury or the IRS a role in the creation of nontax policy seems questionable at best. These agencies, while hardly free of political oversight, are relatively insulated from the democratic process that normally informs and shapes the formation of public policy.[45] They also enjoy almost no technical expertise in areas outside of taxation. Entrusting them with substantial policymaking power beyond the public finance arena seems a misallocation of regulatory responsibility.

Judicial review of their decisions is not an adequate corrective for such shortcomings. During the typically long intervals between administrative implementation and ultimate review lies a period of costly uncertainty. Court decisions also tend to take a piecemeal approach to policies that the Treasury and the IRS can promulgate in broad-brush regulations and rulings. Moreover, courts benefit from even fewer political checks than do the taxing agencies and do not have a legitimate claim to policy formulation in all areas. Where the underlying policy violation is a matter of state law, as in *Tank Truck*, federal courts have no authority to pass on the merits and need for augmentation of those regulatory schemes. Where the policy at issue stems from federal legislation, the courts still must consider why Congress did not choose to add tax amendments to the enactment pursuing the policy.

In addition and regardless of how one feels about the propriety of policy formulation by these institutions, there remains the matter of implementation. As *Tellier* recognized, in any given case the amount of tax at issue will depend on both the size of the expense and the taxpayer's marginal rate. Of the various methods for disassociating the tax from disapproved conduct, only a rule limiting nondeductibility to sanctions has any hope of achieving some proportionality between the

---

Commissioner, 61 T.C. 497, 503-04 (1974) (Tannenwald, J., concurring), with *id.* at 505-07 (Sterrett, J., dissenting). Finally, Congress recently has expanded public policy disallowance to deny deductions and tax credits, but not inventory adjustments, to business engaged in drug trafficking. Tax Equity and Fiscal Responsibility Act of 1982, Pub. L. No. 97-248, § 351 (a), 96 Stat. 324, 640 (adding I.R.C. § 280E); see Staff of Joint Comm. on Int. Rev. Tax'n, 97th Cong., 2d Sess., General Explanation of the Tax Equity and Fiscal Responsibility Act of 1982, at 364 (1982).

[45] The Reagan Administration's handling of the segregated schools issue illustrates the extent of the tax bureaucracy's freedom from political oversight. The President and the Justice Department were able initially to force the Treasury to change its position, but the ensuing outcry forced the administration to back down. This experience suggests that political control exists but is relatively costly.

costs of disallowance and the social harm of the misconduct. No other factor that has tax relevance—direct outlays for the harm, total expenses of the harmful enterprise, or the cost of avoiding sanctions—has any clear relationship to the strength of public policy.

But in a progressive tax system, even the proportionality between additional tax, sanctions, and harm diminishes in the face of tax rates that depend on the size of taxable income. Unless it is possible either to regard taxable income as a proxy for immorality or illegality, or to impose new rates scaled only to the social harm of misconduct, changes in the tax rules to accommodate exogenous policy concerns may produce arbitrary results. Even if one believes that penalties should reflect a malefactor's wealth in order to achieve equivalent levels of deterrence, a belief many would debate, varying the size of a penalty with taxable income is unlikely to accomplish this purpose.[46] A substantially suboptimal penalty, with attendant welfare losses, is much more likely to result.[47]

Occasions may exist where the arbitrariness and suboptimality of tax-based penalties are acceptable costs for the expression of a particularly powerful policy judgment or reflect second-best means of crafting necessary disincentives. It seems unlikely, however, that most legislatively created penalty schemes require or benefit from the kind of supplementation the public policy doctrine provides. Congress has a comparative advantage in the modification of tax rules to express nontax policy. It alone has the power to make global changes in the tax system, including adjustments in the base and rate structure. In particular it has the power to single out transactions and taxpayers for surtaxes designed to reflect judgments about the social cost and

---

[46] Some believe that in order to achieve uniform levels of deterrence, larger fines must be levied on the wealthy to achieve the same amount of "sting." This assertion depends for its validity on the assumption that personal utility derived from money diminishes at some rate, so that larger money costs are necessary to achieve the same loss of utility for a wealthy miscreant. At present the diminishing-utility-of-money theory seems in almost universal disrepute. Although some decline in the utility of money as stocks increase seems plausible, fixing the rate has proven infeasible due to the dubiousness of this kind of interpersonal utility comparison. See, e.g., MUSGRAVE & MUSGRAVE, PUBLIC FINANCE IN THEORY AND PRACTICE 97–98, 250–53 (3d ed. 1980); SIMONS, PERSONAL INCOME TAXATION 5–18 (1938); Alchian, *The Meaning of Utility Measurement*, 43 AM. ECON. REV. 26 (1953); Blum & Kalven, *The Uneasy Case for Progressive Taxation*, 19 U. CHI. L. REV. 417, 455–79 (1952). Even if one embraced the diminishing-utility-of-money theory, under our present system taxable income corresponds so poorly to either wealth or real income that graduating a fine with respect to an individual's marginal rate is unlikely to achieve the desired effect.

[47] See Becker, note 9 *supra*, at 180–85.

reprehensibility of misconduct. Even when Congress has failed to express these judgments, other institutions may do better to wait on it than to attempt inadequate and potentially counterproductive penalties. One reading of the history of the public policy doctrine would impute to the Court a growing recognition of this proposition.

II. PUBLIC POLICY AND THE CHARITABLE EXEMPTION

If public policy has not served generally as a satisfactory ground for altering tax rules, why has the Court nonetheless relied on it to reform the law of charitable exemptions? *Bob Jones* made three technical interpretivist arguments for imputing to Congress a deliberate choice to condition the charitable exemption on conformance with public policy and hinted at another functional argument asserting that a public interest standard is an inherent component of a charitable exemption. These arguments are only the same public policy doctrine in different words.

A. INTERPRETING CONGRESSIONAL INTENT

1. *The Internal Revenue Code and charitable trusts.* The so-called charitable exemption involves several different federal taxes and includes organizations besides charities. Donors to these groups can deduct contributions from the income and transfer tax bases as long as the recipient provides no reciprocal benefits.[48] The donees pay no income tax except to the extent they enjoy what the Code defines as "unrelated business income."[49] They have also enjoyed exemption from federal payroll taxes, although a 1983 amendment has ended the option of most charities to elect out of the employment tax.[50] The value of these advantages will vary among charities, depending as they do on the marginal rates and itemizing status of donors, the extent a charity

---

[48] I.R.C. §§170(c) (2) (income tax); 2055(a) (2), 2106(a) (2) (ii) (estate tax); 2522(a) (2), (b) (2), (3) (gift tax); 2602(c) (3) (generation-skipping transfer tax).

[49] *Id.* §§501(c) (3), 511.

[50] *Id.* §§3121(b) (8) (B) (employment tax), repealed by Social Security Act Amendments of 1983, Pub. L. No. 98-21, §102(b) (1), 97 Stat. 65, 71 (effective Jan. 1, 1984); 3306(c) (8) (unemployment tax).

has retained earnings or other gains on which the income tax could be levied, and the degree to which a charity is labor intensive.[51]

Eligibility criteria for these several aspects of the charitable exemption are not identical, but with minor exceptions an organization that qualifies under §501(c) (3) will be eligible for the other benefits. This provision specifies three characteristics of a qualifying organization: (1) no part of its net earnings can inure to the benefit of any private person; (2) no substantial part of its activities can comprise political action; and (3) it must be "organized and operated exclusively for religious, charitable, scientific, testing for public safety, literary, or educational purposes."[52]

Before *Bob Jones*, the Court had not been called on to fill in the statutory outlines of the charitable exemption. A few opinions contained glancing references to the advantages enjoyed by exempt entities, but these statements were neither informed nor informative.[53] Because the several aspects of the exemption are as old as the taxes out of which they are carved, their legislative history contains little evidence of what Congress thought it had achieved with their enactment.[54] The few legislative pronouncements that exist seem contradictory or incomplete.[55]

---

[51] Organizations that qualify under §501(c) (3) also may obtain certain nontax advantages such as reduced mailing rates. See Goetz & Brady, *Environmental Policy Formation and the Tax Treatment of Citizen Interest Groups*, 39 LAW & CONTEMP. PROB. (Aut. 1975), at 211, 213.

[52] I.R.C. §501(c) (3).

[53] See Helvering v. Bliss, 293 U.S. 144, 147, 151 (1934); Trinidad v. Sagrada Orden, 263 U.S. 578, 581 (1924). The day before it issued *Bob Jones*, the Court brought down Regan v. Taxation With Representation, 103 S. Ct. 1997 (1983), stressing the similarities between the exemption and a subsidization system. The Court noted, however, that the analogy was incomplete. *Id.* at 2000 n.5. See note 100 *infra*.

[54] The income tax exemption originated in the nineteenth-century tax held unconstitutional in Pollock v. Farmer's Loan and Trust Co., 158 U.S. 601 (1895). See Tariff Act of 1894, ch. 349, §32, 28 Stat. 509, 556. The deduction for charitable contributions was introduced in the first income tax to employ substantial rates. War Revenue Act of 1917, ch. 63, §1201(2), 40 Stat. 300, 330. The estate tax deduction was created in 1918, two years after enactment of that tax and at the first opportunity after creation of the income tax deduction. Revenue Act of 1918, ch. 18, §403(a) (3), 40 Stat. 1057, 1098. The gift and generation-skipping transfer tax deductions were included in the original provisions of those taxes. Revenue Act of 1924, ch. 234, §321(a) (2), 43 Stat. 253, 314 (gift tax); Tax Reform Act of 1976, Pub. L. No. 94-455, 2611(a), 90 Stat. 1520, 1882. The first social security and unemployment taxes also exempted charities. Social Security Act of 1935, Pub. L. No. 74-271, §§811(b) (8), 907(c) (7), 49 Stat. 620, 639, 643.

[55] The most extensive remarks occur in a 1938 House Report explaining a new limitation on deductions for contributions to foreign charities: "The exemption from taxation of money and property devoted to charitable and other purposes is based on the theory that the Government is compensated for the loss of revenue by its relief from financial burdens which would otherwise have to be met by appropriations from other public funds, and by the benefits resulting from the

Faced with a lack of direct evidence about what Congress meant to do when it created the charitable exemption, the Court examined the earlier state and British law of charitable trusts. Several judicial pronouncements from the nineteenth century indicated that all trusts entitled to the charitable exemption from the rule against perpetuities, including those created for educational and religious institutions, had to meet a public interest requirement. Congress, the Court asserted, must have intended to adopt this facet of charitable trust law when it carved out a special tax status for organizations dedicated to "religious, charitable, or educational purposes." Even though the language Congress chose seems to distinguish charities, schools, and churches, the Court perceived an underlying amalgamation of these institutions into the general class of charities along the lines of trust law. As a result, all of these organizations "must demonstrably serve and be in harmony with the public interest."[56]

---

promotion of the general welfare. The United States derives no such benefit from gifts to foreign institutions, and the proposed limitation is consistent with the above theory. If the recipient, however, is a domestic organization the fact that some portion of its funds is used in other countries for charitable and other purposes (such as missionary and educational purposes) will not affect the deductibility of the gift." H.R. Rep. 1860, 75th Cong., 3d Sess. 19-20 (1938) (first sentence quoted in 103 S. Ct. at 2028). To similar effect was a statement by Senator Hollis made during enactment of the first charitable contribution deduction: "For every dollar that a man contributes to these public charities, educational, scientific, or otherwise, the public gets 100 percent." 55 Cong. Rec. 6728 (1917) (quoted in 103 S. Ct. at 2027).

Putting aside the question of contributions for religious activity, which does not substitute for something government does, the government compensation explanation does not account even for the 1938 amendment. This provision, which has been carried forward in all subsequent internal revenue statutes, failed to limit significantly the overseas use of tax-deductible contributions. It required substantial domestic use only for transfers by corporations to noncorporate charities. Then, as now, all individual contributions and corporate contributions to incorporated charities could be used overseas as long as the initial donee had a domestic charter. See Rev. Rul. 66-79, 1966-1 C.B. 48. Moreover, foreign charities remain exempt from the income and payroll taxes and can produce transfer tax deductions for their contributors. See Rev. Rul. 74-523, 1974-2 C.B. 304; Liles & Blum, *Development of the Federal Tax Treatment of Charities*, 39 LAW & CONTEMP. PROB., Aut. 1975, at 6; Rabin, *Charitable Trusts and Charitable Deductions*, 41 N.Y.U. L. REV. 912, 928-30 (1966).

[56] 103 S. Ct. at 2027 (citing Perin v. Carey, 24 How. 465, 501 (1861); Ould v. Washington Hospital for Foundlings, 95 U.S. 303, 311 (1878); Commissioners v. Pemsel, [1891] A.C. 531, 583). The Court added, however, that it did not mean to rely on this history to resolve any question other than the existence of a public interest gloss: "We need not consider whether Congress intended to incorporate into the Internal Revenue Code any aspects of charitable trust law other than the requirements of public benefit and a valid public purpose." 103 S. Ct. at 2026-27 n.12. The Court also attached significance to the grammatical structure of §170, which defines "charitable contributions" as transfers for, *inter alia*, religious, charitable, or educational purposes. Rather than regarding this definition as elaborating on the meaning of a technical term, the Court saw it as equating charitable and educational activities. 103 S. Ct. at 2026 & n.11.

A number of objections to the Court's reliance on the law of charitable trusts spring to mind. Why state and British laws designed to suspend the rule against perpetuities and mortmain statutes should have any relevance to tax exemption is something of a mystery.[57] More important, Congress used in the tax laws a classification system that diverged from that found in trust law. It created a category of entities—social welfare organizations—that fit under the trust law definition of a charity but to which it did not extend the more important aspects of the tax law charitable exemption.[58] The most telling point against reliance on this historical analogy, however, is the fact that Congress specifically excluded charitable trusts when it enacted the first post-Sixteenth Amendment income tax exemption in 1913 and the first charitable contribution deduction in 1917.[59] Trusts enjoyed no benefits of exemption until 1921 and could not receive deductible contributions until 1924.[60] It seems unlikely that Congress intended to model on the law of charitable trusts an exemption that did not comprise these entities or that its belated inclusion of trusts somehow altered the scope of exempt activities.

2. *The administrative history of the charitable exemption.* The *Bob Jones* opinion also emphasized the importance of the Service's position that racially discriminatory schools violated public policy and therefore could not enjoy the benefits of the charitable exemption. It

---

[57] Commissioners v. Pemsel, [1891] A.C. 531, one of the cases cited by the Court, did involve a tax exemption rather than the rule against perpetuities. In referring to the law of charitable exemptions to interpret this act of Parliament, however, the judges made clear that their decision rested on particular signs of the legislative will rather than on any general equivalence between trust and tax law. Moreover, the exemption at issue arose in a tax structure significantly different from that in the United States, and in particular did not involve a deduction for contributions.

[58] The exemption for these organizations appeared in the first post-Sixteenth Amendment income tax, see Tariff Act of 1913, ch. 16, §II.G.(a), 38 Stat. 114, 172, and currently can be found in I.R.C. §501(c) (4). Unlike charities, they neither can receive deductible contributions nor enjoy exemption from the payroll taxes.

[59] The Bureau of Internal Revenue did not regard this omission as an oversight. See A.R.M. 104, 2 C.B. 262 (1921). The Bureau did recognize an exemption for trusts benefiting public schools, but only because it believed the Constitution forbade the taxation of income belonging to state institutions. See S. 1374, 2 C.B. 96 (1920).

The nineteenth-century income tax held unconstitutional in Pollock v. Farmers' Loan and Trust Co., 158 U.S. 601 (1895), did contain an exemption for the funds of trusts dedicated to "charitable, religious, or educational purposes." Tariff Act of 1894, ch. 349, §32, 28 Stat. 509, 556. In *Bob Jones*, the Court, while noting that the earlier statute served as a model for the charitable exemptions enacted in the 1909 corporate income tax and the 1913 personal income tax, failed to observe that the latter acts departed from the model with respect to charitable trusts. See 103 S. Ct. at 2027 n.14.

[60] Revenue Act of 1921, ch. 136, §231(6), 42 Stat. 227, 253; Revenue Act of 1924, ch. 234, §214(a) (10), 43 Stat. 253, 271.

stressed this point with boilerplate references to the Service's broad authority to interpret the Code.[61] Again, however, the administrative record does not provide as much support for the public policy gloss as the Court asserted. Since the inception of the income tax, the Service and the Treasury have taken different and occasionally inconsistent stands on the scope of the charitable exemption. A review of their pronouncements suggests, if anything, stronger support for a construction of the exemption that does not contain a separate public interest prerequisite.

During the first decade of the income tax, two components of the Bureau of Internal Revenue took different approaches to the charitable exemption. The Office of the Solicitor advocated a liberal interpretation, arguing that the pursuit of any public benefit constituted a charitable purpose.[62] The Income Tax Unit employed a more technical analysis, stressing the separate enumeration of religious, educational, charitable, and social welfare purposes. To give independent meaning to each of the categories, the Unit maintained that "charitable" had to be understood "in its popular and ordinary sense" as pertaining "to the relief of the poor."[63] In 1924 the Treasury appeared to resolve the dispute in favor of the Unit and its narrower interpretation. In the first regulation defining the charitable exemption, the Treasury distinguished each type of exempt activity and declared that "charitable purposes comprise, in general, . . . the relief of the poor."[64] This more focused approach avoided any general inquiry into public benefits or harms.

Subsequent regulations carried forward this language for the next thirty-five years. Toward the end of the Eisenhower administration, however, signs of change began to appear. As late as 1956, the Service had argued that a hospital, to qualify as a charity, had to provide free services to the poor and not merely benefit the general public by

---

[61] 103 S. Ct. at 2031–32 (citing, *inter alia, Textile Mills*). The Court saw no incongruity in its reliance on the Service's expertise in the face of the Treasury's recent repudiation of the policy that this expertise produced.

[62] Sol. Op. 159, III-1 C.B. 480 (1924); S.M. 1836, III-I C.B. 273 (1924); O.D. 510, 2 C.B. 209 (1920); S. 992, 1 C.B. 145 (1919).

[63] I.T. 1800, II-2 C.b. 152 (1923).

[64] Treas. Reg. 65, art. 517 (1924). In keeping with this particularized and narrow approach to the separate categories of exempt purposes, the Treasury later issued a regulation confining "educational" activities to instruction of a student body by a faculty. Instruction of the general public would qualify as educational only "under exceptional circumstances." Treas. Reg. 86, art. 101(6)-1 (1934).

offering health care to the community.[65] But in 1958 an article by Herman Reiling, the Service's Assistant Chief Counsel, revived the arguments for broader use of the charitable exemption. He maintained that the class of organizations eligible for the exemption should be regarded as homogeneous and including all disinterested activity promoting the broad public welfare.[66] The following year the Treasury issued new regulations that embraced his position. Henceforth social-welfare-organization status would be limited primarily to entities that otherwise qualified as charities but engaged in political activity.[67]

No evidence exists as to what prompted the Treasury to shift directions in this manner, but the regulation's list of examples of charitable activity is suggestive. Exempt purposes now included efforts "(i) to lessen neighborhood tensions; (ii) to eliminate prejudice and discrimination; (iii) to defend human and civil rights secured by law; or (iv) to combat community deterioration and juvenile delinquency."[68] Although the Eisenhower Administration had not greeted the Supreme Court's desegregation mandate with unqualified delight, after the Little Rock episode and the enactment of the Civil Rights Act of 1957 it had begun to give at least lukewarm support to the growing civil rights movement. Whether the 1959 amendment was a conscious political ploy or only the product of reconsideration prompted by the movement's moral force, it clearly bore the movement's mark. The

---

[65] Rev. Rul. 56-185, 1956-1 C.B. 202. In light of the 1959 redefinition of charitable purposes, the Service later ruled that a hospital need not provide substantial services to indigents to qualify for an exemption. Rev. Rul. 69-545, 1969-2 C.B. 117. A court challenge to this later ruling ultimately failed because of the challengers' lack of standing. Simon v. Eastern Kentucky Welfare Rights Org., 426 U.S. 26 (1976).

[66] Reiling, *Federal Taxation: What Is a Charitable Organization?* 44 A.B.A. J. 525 (1958).

[67] Treas. Reg. §1.501(c) (4)-1(a) 2 (ii) (1959). By political activity, the Treasury did not mean to include participation in the campaigns of candidates for public office. *Id.* Candidate-oriented organizations remained in limbo until the enactment of I.R.C. §527 in 1974. See Schoenblum, *From De Facto to Statutory Exemption: An Analysis of the Evolution of Legislative Policy Regarding the Federal Taxation of Campaign Finance,* 65 VA. L. REV. 513 (1979).

[68] The new definition of charitable activities stated in full: "The term 'charitable' is used in section 501(c) (3) in its generally accepted legal sense and is, therefore, not to be construed as limited by the separate enumerations in section 501(c) (3) or other tax-exempt purposes which may fall within the broad outlines of 'charity' as developed by judicial decisions. Such term includes: Relief of the poor and distressed or of the underprivileged; advancement of religion; advancement of education of science; erection or maintenance of public buildings, monuments, or works; lessening of the burdens of government; and promotion of social welfare by organizations designed to accomplish any of the above purposes, or (i) to lessen neighborhood tensions; (ii) to eliminate prejudice and discrimination; (iii) to defend human and civil rights secured by law; or (iv) to combat community deterioration and juvenile delinquency." Treas. Reg. §1.501(c) (3)-1(d) (2) (1959).

earlier regulations had favored traditional institutions tending to shore up the status quo; the new interpretation indicated a willingness to accommodate efforts to bring about social change, particularly the struggle for racial equality, within the confines of charity.

While the extension of charitable status to activities in the general public interest served initially as a shield to protect the civil rights movement from the burdens of taxation, the question soon arose whether the concept could also work as a sword to require removal of the tax advantages enjoyed by the movement's targets. This step meant using the public interest standard, which had expanded the administrative interpretation of charitable activities, to narrow the scope of noncharitable exempt activities such as churches and schools. In particular the Service began to consider whether schools engaged in racial discrimination could be considered "educational" organizations.[69] In 1965 it suspended action on applications for exemption by segregated public schools until it could study the issue.

After two years of reflection, the Service announced its first response to the problem. It used a revenue ruling to explain the application of the public interest criterion to an organization created to run a segregated park. Because segregation undercut the public benefit derived from the park, the enterprise could not be considered charitable.[70] This step did not resolve the general issue of exemption and public interest, however, because parks and similar recreational facilities qualified for exemption only because of the expansion of charitable purposes outlined in the 1959 regulations.[71] In a simultaneous press release, the Service announced it would resume recognition of exemptions for segregated private schools. The cryptic announcement could be interpreted as holding either that an organization need not meet the public interest standard to qualify as an educational, as

---

[69] The 1959 amendment broadened the definition of "educational." It dropped the "under exceptional circumstances" language found in earlier regulations, see note 64 *supra*, and treated as equally educational the "instruction or training of the individual for the purpose of improving or developing his capabilities" and the "instruction of the public on subjects useful to the individual and beneficial to the community." Treas. Reg. §1.501(c) (3)-1(d) (3) (i) (1959). The regulation did not refer to its concept of charitable activity as a limiting factor on educational functions.

[70] Rev. Rul. 67-325, 1967-2 C.B. 113.

[71] Before the issuance of the 1959 regulation, the Service had opposed according exempt status to public recreational facilities. Peters v. Commissioner, 21 T.C. 55 (1953), nonacquiescence, 1955-1 C.B. 8. Simultaneously with the announcement of the new regulation, the Service published a ruling that recognized the exempt status of these facilities as long as they served a generally recognized public purpose which tends to lessen the burdens of government. Rev. Rul. 59-310, 1959-2 C.B. 147, 148.

opposed to a charitable, institution or that private segregation, not violating the Constitution or other federal law, could not be considered inimical to the public interest.[72]

The Service never had a chance to clarify its position. Following the issuance of the press release, parents of black schoolchildren in Mississippi sued the Service to halt all exemptions for segregated schools in that State. In 1970 a three-judge federal court granted a preliminary injunction in favor of the plaintiffs. Six months later the Service announced it would reverse its earlier position. It declared its belief that the public interest limitation overlay all of §501(c) (3)'s prescribed purposes and that the explicit prohibitions of positive law were not the only means of identifying the public interest. In the eyes of the Service, racial segregation in private schools violated federal public policy even if no provision of the Constitution or act of Congress forbade it, and this public policy violation mandated loss of exempt status.[73]

The final episode in the Service's public interest gloss came after the *Bob Jones* case had reached the Supreme Court. As a result of pressure from the White House and the Justice Department, the Treasury announced it had realized the error in the Service's 1970 position and intended to return to its earlier interpretation of educational activities. The ensuing public reaction and a lower court injunction produced by collateral litigation blocked implementation of this decision. The government then declared it would take no steps inconsistent with the immediately prior policy pending the Court's resolution of the *Bob Jones* case.[74]

In sum, the administrative interpretation of the charitable exemption did not contain the public interest gloss until late in the exemption's history. Even after this addition the Service limited the gloss to organizations claiming charitable, but not educational or religious, status. Upon first considering the question of discriminatory schools, the Service first ruled in favor of exemption. Only in the face of judicial hostility did the Service change its position, and when later confronted with opposition from the executive branch it flip-flopped again. One

---

[72] The news release stated that the Service would not recognize an exemption if a school's "involvement with the state or political subdivision is such as to make the operation unconstitutional or a violation of the laws of the United States." Internal Revenue Service News Release (Aug. 2, 1967).

[73] Internal Revenue Service Press Release (Jul. 10, 1970), Internal Revenue Service Press Release (Jul. 19, 1970). A year later the Service issued a ruling stating its position more elaborately. Rev. Rul. 71-447, 1971-2 C.B. 230.

[74] See Hearing, *supra* note 2, at 419-703; 103 S. Ct. at 2025 n.9.

cannot plausibly talk of deference to administrative expertise in the face of such a history, at least if one wishes to sustain the gloss rejected in both 1967 and 1982.

3. *Ratification by Congress.* When the first court to consider the matter held that racially discriminatory schools could not enjoy exempt status, it relied explicitly on the *Tank Truck* line of cases. The charitable trust analogy seemed insufficient alone to sustain the public interest gloss, and the Service's *volte-face* on the issue was too recent to inspire any reliance.[75] When the Court decided *Bob Jones* twelve years later, the passage of time had altered the context of the dispute. The Court claimed to attach great significance to the failure of Congress in the intervening years to repudiate the Service's position. Whatever the initial validity of the 1970 shift in policy, the Court argued, at some point it became the will of Congress.[76]

The Court acknowledged that ratification-by-inaction arguments, when applied to Congress, seldom carry the day.[77] This disclaimer was too modest. The Court usually discards these contentions out of hand. Although its opinions do not often discuss the functional underpinnings of its posture, presumably its hostility rests on a recognition that the Constitution's manifold deliberate impediments to the enactment of legislation make congressional inaction insignificant. To impose on Congress any general obligation affirmatively to renounce agency rulemaking would, as a practical matter, transfer substantial legislative authority from Congress to the agencies.[78] More typical of the Court's attitude toward ratification claims is *Tellier*, where a Service position of much greater continuity and antiquity than that in *Bob Jones* was discarded.[79]

---

[75] Green v. Connally, 330 F. Supp. 1150 (D.D.C.), *aff'd per curiam sub nom.* Coit v. Green, 404 U.S. 997 (1971). The Fourth Circuit, the only other lower court to consider the issue, also rested its decision on *Tank Truck*. Bob Jones University v. United States, 639 F.2d 147 (4th Cir. 1980), *aff'd*, 103 S. Ct. 2017 (1983).

[76] 103 S. Ct. at 2032–34.

[77] "Ordinarily, and quite appropriately, courts are slow to attribute significance to the failure of Congress to act on particular legislation." *Id.* at 2033.

[78] If the Court were serious about imposing a consistent burden on Congress to disavow agency action, the resulting shift in lawmaking authority would raise issues similar to those involved in the debate about the delegation doctrine. In each case, the core problem is the degree of positive and explicit authorization required from Congress before an agency can act. For a discussion of these issues, compare ELY, DEMOCRACY AND DISTRUST 131–34 (1980), and Aronson, Gellhorn, & Robinson, *A Theory of Legislative Delegation*, 68 CORNELL L. REV. 1 (1982), with Posner, *Economics, Politics, and the Reading of Statutes and the Constitution*, 49 U. CHI. L. REV. 263, 288–90 (1982).

[79] The few cases in the tax area where the Court has given any credence to the ratification-by-inaction argument involve Treasury regulations, for which both additional

Some kernels of positive legislative steps bolster the Court's ratification argument, although a fair appraisal of the actions of Congress would suggest at least as much evidence of hostility toward the Service's 1970 discriminatory schools policy.[80] If the Court truly relied on these points, *Bob Jones* would have no general significance. We would know nothing about the validity of the public interest gloss aside from its disqualification of discriminatory schools, because the Service has taken no other actions to which congressional acquiescence might apply. So ready a cabining of the case to its particular facts seems implausible, however.

B. THE FUNCTION OF THE CHARITABLE EXEMPTION

One cannot avoid the suspicion that the *Bob Jones* majority accepted the interpretivist arguments because it found the result congenial, not because the evidence of congressional intent was persuasive.[81] The Court apparently believed that an enlightened Congress would recognize the public interest gloss as appropriate, whether or not such recognition had yet occurred. From this perspective, construction of

---

statutory authority and specific rules of promulgation exist. No such regulation applied to *Bob Jones*. See notes 23, 35 *supra* and accompanying text.

[80] The most significant event suggesting congressional support for the Service's position is a 1976 amendment withdrawing income tax exemption from segregated social clubs. Act of Oct. 20, 1976, Pub. L. No. 94-568, §2(a), 90 Stat. 2697 (adding I.R.C. §501(i)). The Senate and House reports indicated that the enactment was in response to McGlotten v. Connally, 338 F. Supp. 448 (D.D.C. 1972), which had held that racially discriminatory fraternal organizations would lose their income tax exemption under § 501(c) (8), but that segregated social clubs could retain their exemption under § 501(c) (7). See 103 S. Ct. at 2033-34 n.26. While citing this event as indicative of congressional support for the 1970 segregated schools policy emplanted in § 501(c) (3), the Court did not distinguish cases in which it had rejected similar efforts to use the legislative history of one provision to amend the meaning of another. See, *e.g.*, Southeastern Community College v. Davis, 442 U.S. 397, 410-11 n.11 (1979). See generally Easterbrook, Statutes' Domains, 50 U. CHI. L. REV. 533, 538-39 (1983). Nor did it acknowledge the significant differences between the bare income tax exemption at stake in *McGlotten* and the various aspects of the charitable exemption. The Court also did not discuss the effect of the 1969 revisions of the charitable exemption on the ratification argument. These changes, which represent the most extensive overhaul of the exemption by Congress since its enactment, took place during the period in which the Service maintained that segregated schools came within the exemption. See generally Taggart, *The Charitable Deduction*, 26 TAX L. REV. 63 (1970).

[81] Justice Powell alone based his decision solely on the congressional ratification argument. While finding the evidence of congressional support for the IRS's segregated schools policy adequate to sustain the outcome of the case, he disputed the existence of a more diffuse public policy component to the charitable exemption. 103 S. Ct. at 2036-39. The majority opinion's response to his arguments is terse to a fault, but appears to say that congressional ratification is a sufficient but not a necessary ground for the decision. *Id.* at 2032 n.23.

the public interest gloss seems to complete a task Congress left unfinished, and further extensions to new public policy violations would be appropriate as long as they were consistent with the underlying purposes of the gloss.

Parts of the opinion seem to say as much. Early in its analysis of the charitable exemption, it invokes the traditional platitude that the Court, in interpreting legislation, must go beyond the plain language when the words Congress chose would "defeat the plain purpose of the statute."[82] Jumbled in with its efforts to translate legislative signals are arguments based on the perceived purpose of the exemption. These perceptions provide a likely explanation of the Court's readiness to hear the message it received.

That *Bob Jones* constitutes an act of independent judicial lawmaking, rather than a conscientious effort to interpret the legislative will, may give some critics a sufficient ground for condemning the decision. The point is valid but weak. Since enactment of the federal income tax the Court has assumed a creative role in the development of tax rules. Some form of interstitial lawmaking has been a part of this interpretive function, and the Court has acquitted this task with frequent if not uniform success.[83] Whether or not the Court should undertake such a responsibility hardly seems noteworthy at this late date.

The critical question remains whether *Bob Jones* fulfills the basic purpose of the charitable exemption. This issue turns on whether courts generally should view the exemption as an incentive for the kind of activities in which covered organizations engage, or rather as an attempt to reconcile the broad goal of taxing income with the necessity of excluding some types of economic gain. The Court apparently assumed that the former function best explains the exemption. A careful look at the federal tax structure, however, uncovers strong objections to this assumption.

1. *Charitable activity and public functions.* Perhaps because its functional analysis was dispersed among its interpretive arguments, the

---

[82] 103 S. Ct. at 2025.

[83] One prominent example from the 1982 Term is Commissioner v. Tufts, 103 S. Ct. 1826 (1983), which held that the "amount realized" in a sale of property included relief from inadequately secured nonrecourse debt. The Court supported the decision with arguments about the basic structure of the Code's treatment of financing, not with inferences about the result Congress wished to embrace. Nor did the Court concern itself, as the public policy doctrine might have indicated, with whether the initial exclusion of loan proceeds from a debtor's income constitutes a subsidy for borrowing that might be suspended if the loan proceeds were used in a way that did not benefit the public.

Court did not say much about what purposes it thought the exemption fulfilled. The opinion's discussion of the issue did not go beyond an assertion that the exemption serves "to encourage the development of private institutions that serve a useful public purpose or supplement or take the place of public institutions of the same kind."[84] Although the phrase "useful public purpose" does nothing more than restate the public interest gloss, the Court may have meant to invoke the mainstream scholarly analysis of the exemption—the public function thesis.

Beginning with Reiling, most commentators who have tried to make sense of the exemption have emphasized how much it departs from what they have depicted as a general pattern of taxing economic gain. They have assumed that whatever justification the exemption has must rest on special policies rather than on general considerations for defining the tax base. They have found such a policy in the perceived need to accommodate and encourage private expenditures that complement and compete with governmental functions.[85]

Charitable contributions lessen the burdens of government and improve the quality of government services, these commentators have contended, by promoting private production of similar goods. The tax system does not regard the private assumption of public functions as identical to the conduct of government, because it does not allow

---

[84] 103 S. Ct. at 2026.

[85] See COMM'N ON PRIVATE PHILANTHROPY AND PUBLIC NEEDS, GIVING IN AMERICA 103-05 (1975); GOODE, THE INDIVIDUAL INCOME TAX 160-68 (rev. ed. 1976); KAHN, PERSONAL DEDUCTIONS IN THE FEDERAL INCOME TAX 13 (1960); SURREY, note 5 supra, at 223-32; Cohen, Exempt Status for Segregated Schools: Does the Constitution Permit Lower Standards for Tax Benefits Than for Direct Grants? 17 TAX NOTES 259, 267-68 (1982); Feldstein, The Income Tax and Charitable Contributions: Part I—Aggregate and Distributional Effects, 28 NAT'L TAX J. 81 (1975); Goetz & Brady, note 51 supra, at 227-28; Hansmann, The Rationale for Exempting Nonprofit Organizations from Corporate Income Taxation, 91 YALE L. J. 54, 71-72 (1981); Hochman & Rodgers, The Optimal Tax Treatment of Charitable Contributions, 30 NAT'L TAX J. 1 (1977); Kelman, Personal Deductions Revisited: Why They Fit Poorly in an "Ideal" Income Tax and Why They Fit Worse in a Far from Ideal World, 31 STAN. L. REV. 831 (1979); Liles & Blum, note 55 supra; McDaniel, Federal Matching Grants for Charitable Contributions: A Substitute for the Income Tax Deduction, 27 TAX L. REV. 377 (1972); Rabin, note 55 supra; Reiling, note 66 supra; Simon, The Tax-Exempt Status of Racially Discriminatory Religious Schools, 36 TAX L. REV. 477, 483-96 (1981); Stone, Federal Tax Support of Charities and Other Exempt Organizations: The Need for a National Policy, 20 U.S.C. TAX INST. 27 (1968); Taggart, note 80 supra; Taussig, Economic Aspects of the Personal Income Tax Treatment of Charitable Contributions, 20 NAT'L TAX J. 1 (1967); White, Proper Income Tax Treatment of Deductions for Personal Expense, in 1 House Comm. on Ways and Means, 86th Cong., 1st Sess., Tax Revision Compendium 365, 369-70 (Comm. Print 1959); Wolfman, Federal Tax Policy and the Support of Science, 114 U. PA. L. REV. 171 (1965); Wolkoff, Proposal for a Radical Alternative to the Charitable Deduction, 1973 U. ILL. L. F. 279.

contributors full credit against tax liability. Instead, we seem to regard charitable activity as parallel to but separate from government services. We maintain the separation between the government and charity by excluding contributions from the kinds of consumption that go into the definition of taxable income and by exempting charitable institutions from most tax obligations.

The public function thesis rests on the assumption that charitable activity produces benefits comparable to those generated by government. It follows that extension of the exemption to a particular activity implicitly recognizes that the activity contains such benefits. This further implies a need for some kind of weighing of costs and benefits to make sure functions with net social harms do not come under the exemption. The scope of this monitoring, however, might be modest because of its cost.

2. *The exemption as a refinement of taxable income.* Not everyone has agreed that the charitable exemption constitutes a stark departure from the general pattern of taxation. Comparing the present system with the exemption to a world in which we tax all economic gain is misleading, because no one believes that a workable system could tax every form of gain. Individuals derive satisfaction from a wide range of activities outside the exchange economy, including the consumption of government services (streets, schools, national security), parental pride, aesthetic satisfaction, public praise, and freedom from work. If reasons exist to exclude these kinds of economic income from the tax base, then we may be able to find related justifications for not levying taxes on charitable activity. Such justifications imply limits different from those suggested by the public function thesis on what we should characterize as charitable for purposes of exemption.

In a series of articles published between 1967 and 1972, Professors Boris Bittker and William Andrews argued that the charitable exemption follows logically from an income tax that contains the systemic exclusion of goods received outside the normal processes of exchange.[86] They exploit the famous Haig-Simons equation of income with net savings plus consumption to establish that charitable

---

[86] See Bittker, *A "Comprehensive Tax Base" as a Goal of Income Tax Reform*, 80 HARV. L. REV. 925, 938-40, 951 (1967); Bittker, *Churches, Taxes, and the Constitution*, 78 YALE L. J. 1285 (1969); Bittker, *Accounting for Federal "Tax Subsidies" in the National Budget*, 22 NAT'L TAX J. 244, 255-57 (1969); Bittker, *Charitable Contributions: Tax Deductions or Matching Grants?* 28 TAX L. REV. 37 (1972); Andrews, *Personal Deductions in an Ideal Income Tax*, 86 HARV. L. REV. 309, 344-75 (1972). See also Bittker & Rahdert, *The Exemption of Nonprofit Organizations from Federal Income Taxation*, 85 YALE L. J. 299 (1976).

contributions, which they contend differ significantly from other forms of personal consumption, reduce income by the amount contributed.[87] Bittker points out that contributions may substitute for unpaid services rendered to charities. A deduction for money given produces a result equivalent to the exclusion from the donor's income of the value of contributed services.[88] Andrews expands on this insight by arguing that as a general matter the federal income tax makes a distinction between personal consumption that diverts real goods and services away from other consumers and consumption that entails less tangible satisfactions. Charitable contributions do not divert goods or services to the use of the contributor's household and hence fall outside the category of personal consumption that taxable income comprises.[89] The satisfactions they purchase seem more akin to the kind of intangible pleasures obtained from leisure or a low-paying but high-esteem job, benefits not embraced by our current definition of the income tax base.[90]

Some have argued that the deductions for contributions, although justifiable as an income-measuring device when the donor is viewed in isolation, becomes untenable when combined with the recipient's freedom from taxation. The case for also excluding charitable transfers from the recipient's income must be made in two stages. With respect to the initial recipient, the charitable organization, Bittker has argued persuasively that concepts used to define the gross income and permissible deductions of profit-seeking enterprises fit poorly when applied to nonprofit entities. On the income side, distinguishing included income from excluded contributions to capital or gifts seems

---

[87] "Personal income may be defined as the algebraic sum of (1) the market value of rights exercised in consumption and (2) the change in the value of the store of property rights between the beginning and end of the period in question." SIMONS, note 46 *supra*, at 50.

[88] Bittker, 28 Tax L. Rev. 37, note 86 *supra*, at 59-60.

[89] The line between tangible and intangible satisfactions is incorporated explicitly into the income tax's definition of charitable contributions through its exclusion of transfers to organizations some "part of the net earnings of which inures to the benefit of any private shareholder or individual." I.R.C. §170(c) (2) (C). This requirement has been especially useful in challenges to the *bona fides* of religions. Rather than attacking the sincerity of a bogus religion's founders or followers, the government traditionally has focused on the presence of private profit to deny charitable status. See, *e.g.*, Founding Church of Scientology v. United States, 412 F.2d 1197 (Ct. Cl. 1969), *cert. denied*, 397 U.S. 1009 (1970). The requirement that the recipient of a deductible contribution not be an individual, but rather some kind of institution, further bolsters the line between private benefits and disinterested gratification. See DeJong v. Commissioner, 309 F.2d 373 (9th Cir. 1962). See generally Kurtz, *Difficult Definitional Problems in Tax Administration: Religion and Race*, 23 CATH. LAW. 301 (1978). But see Kelman, note 85 *supra*, at 849-58.

[90] *Id* at 356.

awkward at best. Nor does existing law readily lend itself to defining appropriate deductions for charities. Direct distribution of benefits to worthy recipients does not qualify for the charitable contribution deduction, and avowedly nonprofit entities, not having a business or profit-seeking purpose, lack the prerequisites to most other deductions. Furthermore, taxation of the entity as a substitute for taxation of the ultimate recipient presents the difficulty of ascertaining the appropriate rate in light of the disparate income levels of the recipients.[91]

As for those who end up with the benefits, the taxability of receipts turns on the character of the charity. Pure redistribution of wealth—alms for the poor—presents no problem, because almost all the recipients have incomes that fall within the zero tax bracket. Religious activities undoubtedly are as diverse as the sects that engage in them, but they consist mostly of either redistribution of wealth to low-income recipients or the generation of intangible satisfactions that generally fall outside the income tax base.[92]

With respect to educational organizations, the focus of our inquiry, the answer is more complex. To the extent that contributions produce higher salaries for teachers, the benefit generally is taxed. To the extent that they lead to reduced charges for students, they merely create a benefit for which nontaxation is the norm in our system. By far the largest price reductions offered to students come from public institutions supported by taxes rather than from private schools sustained by charitable contributions. Primary and secondary public school students receive free education without incurring tax liability. At the college and graduate school levels, across-the-board tuition reduction by public institutions is still the norm and remains tax free.[93] Another feature of our system that benefits students is the nontaxability of human capital accumulation produced by education.[94] In light of these features, which stem from technical problems of income measurement rather than from any desire to reward students,

---

[91] See Bittker, 78 YALE L. J. 1285 note 86 *supra*, at 1291-1301; Bittker & Rahdert, note 86 *supra*, at 307-14; Andrews, note 86 *supra*, at 358-62. But see Hansmann, note 85 *supra*, at 58-62.

[92] Bittker & Rahdert, note 86 *supra*, at 342-45.

[93] See Aaron, *What Is a Comprehensive Tax Base Anyway?* 22 NAT'L TAX J. 543 (1969). Both public and private schools can engage in price discrimination among students through the award of rebates in the form of scholarships. As long as the student undertakes no additional reciprocal obligation, this benefit also escapes taxation. I.R.C. §117(a) (1) (A),(b) (1). See Rev. Rul. 77-263, 1977-2 C.B. 47.

[94] See CHIRELSTEIN, FEDERAL INCOME TAXATION 113-14 (3d ed. 1982); Klein, *Timing in Personal Taxation*, 6 J. LEG. STUDIES 461 (1977).

it seems only fair not to tax the reduced tuition produced by contributions to educational organizations.[95]

Just as the public function thesis implies limits on the charitable exemption—in particular that it should not embrace activities with net social costs—the arguments characterizing the exemption as a refinement on the concept of taxable income suggest some implicit boundaries to exempt functions. The Service or a court, informed by this analysis, would not automatically recognize the exempt status of an organization claiming to be religious, educational, or charitable. In asking whether a school, for example, qualified for exemption, it would use as a test something like what is found in the applicable Treasury regulation, which refers to the "instruction or training of the individual for the purpose of improving or developing his capabilities."[96] This standard captures the idea that the school should provide services comparable, from the student's perspective, to those rendered by a public educational institution. Although the decisionmaker would not further inquire into the overall social benefit of the type of instruction at issue, it would look hard for private benefits, in cash or in kind, enjoyed by those maintaining the school. Deductions for payments made by the families of students would be particularly suspect because of the likelihood of reciprocal payoffs in the form of reduced tuition.[97] In addition, the taxable income thesis would disqualify proprietary operations, such as the infamous school for pickpockets run by *Oliver Twist*'s Fagin, because of entrepreneurial profits.[98]

---

[95] An offsetting cost for students is the usual nondeductibility of out-of-pocket expenses associated with eduction. Treas. Reg. §1.162-5 (1958). Although this rule departs from a sweeping exclusion of education-related benefits, it suggests a refinement of the perceived pattern. That portion of education that a household must finance itself may produce a more certain return than those benefits attributable either to opportunity costs, which probably vary greatly among students at the same institution and thus may correspond to consumer surplus, or to nonhousehold funding. If these assumptions are valid, then one can characterize the direct costs as analogous to either personal consumption or investment in an intangible asset of indefinite useful life, neither of which is deductible under general principles of taxation. For a case that seems to rest on these assumptions, see Sharon v. Commissioner, 66 T.C. 515 (1976), aff'd, 591 F.2d 1273 (9th Cir. 1979), cert. denied, 442 U.S. 941 (1979).

[96] Treas. Reg. §1.501(c) (3)-1(d) (3) (i) (a) (1959).

[97] In recent years the Service has taken a hard look at such contributions. See Rev. Rul. 83-104, 1983 I.R.B. 30, 5. At the behest of private schools, Congress barred implementation of an earlier ruling on this issue. See Cohen, note 85 *supra*, at 265-66.

[98] The example of Fagin's school was first cited in *Green*, and the Court's opinion in *Bob Jones* made a similar argument to show the unacceptability of an exemption without the public interest gloss. 103 S. Ct. at 2028-29 n.18; Green v. Connally, 330 F. Supp. 1150, 1160 (D.D.C. 1971) (opinion of Leventhal, J.). For real cases where schools have not qualified for the exemption because of private profits, see Cleveland Chiropractic College v. Commissioner, 312 F.2d 203 (8th

3. *Comparison of the two theses.* The public function thesis is far from useless. The charitable exemption has enough of the characteristics of a subsidy to invite the kind of analysis economists generally apply to incentive systems.[99] Its resemblance to a subsidy may also be relevant to certain constitutional and nontax statutory issues.[100] Moreover, the public function thesis is no less successful than the taxable income analysis in providing an ultimate justification for the

---

Cir. 1963); Birmingham Business College, Inc. v. Commissioner, 276 F.2d 476 (5th Cir. 1960); Gemological Institute of America, Inc. v. Commissioner, 17 T.C. 1604 (1952), *aff'd per curiam,* 212 F.2d 205 (9th Cir. 1954); John Marshall Law School v. United States, 1981-2 U.S. Tax Cas. ¶9514 (Ct. Cl., Trial Div.), *aff'd per curiam,* 1981-2 U.S. Tax Cas. ¶9745 (Ct. Cl. 1981). Although the taxable income approach deals only with those features of the exemption found in the income tax, the other features are not hard to justify without resorting to the kind of special pleading that public function thesis implies. Assuming one can define a normative transfer tax base, compare Bittker, 22 NAT'L TAX J. 244, note 86 *supra,* at 260, with Gutman, *Federal Wealth Transfer Taxes after ERTA: An Assessment,* 69 VA. L. REV. 1183, 1188-97 (1983), one logically can distinguish transfers that keep wealth within a family (defined broadly to include the transferor's friends as well as blood relatives) from those that produce no tangible benefits for anyone connected with the transferor. See COMM'N ON PRIVATE PHILANTHROPY AND PUBLIC NEEDS, *supra* note 85, at 149. The employment tax exemption has been abolished, and when it did exist had as its price the inability of employees to qualify for social security. See I.R.C. §3121(k), amended by Social Security Act Amendments of 1983, Pub. L. No. 98-21, §102 (b) (1), 97 Stat. 65, 71. The unemployment tax exemption is not significant because of other features of that tax inducing states to levy comparable charges on charities that are employers. See I.R.C. §§3304 (a) (6), 3309.

[99] Whatever the purpose of Congress in creating the charitable exemption, a system without it would have different behavioral consequence than those of the status quo. For examples of the economic analysis of these differences, see Feldstein, note 85 *supra;* Goetz & Brady, note 52 *supra;* Hochman & Rodgers, note 85 *supra;* Schwartz, *Personal Philanthropic Contributions,* 78 J. POL. ECON. 1264 (1970); Taussig, *supra* note 85.

[100] For reasons that have nothing to do with tax law, the Court applies more relaxed standards of constitutional review to things termed subsidies. Compare Maher v. Roe, 432 U.S. 464 (1977), and Califano v. Jobst, 434 U.S. 47 (1977), with Zablocki v. Redhail, 434 U.S. 374 (1978), and Roe v. Wade, 410 U.S. 113 (1973). In Regan v. Taxation With Representation, 103 S. Ct. 1997 (1983), a decision one day before *Bob Jones,* a unanimous Court characterized the charitable exemption as tantamount to a subsidy for purposes of triggering more lenient judicial review. Characterization of the exemption as a subsidy or similar form of substantial entanglement also is important for determining whether it constitutes state action sufficient to trigger certain constitutional limits on the recipients. *Taxation With Representation* reserved the issue of state action with a footnote pointing out that the charitable exemption need not be considered in all respects identical to a cash subsidy. 103 S. Ct. at 2000 n.5. In *Bob Jones* the Court also declined to discuss the issue. 103 S. Ct. at 2032 n.24. Finally, Title VI of the Civil Rights Act of 1964 applies to "any program or activity receiving Federal financial assistance." 42 U.S.C. §2000d (1976). One court has held that the charitable contribution deduction constitutes such assistance, although it conceded that neither the language of Title VI nor the legislative history supported this result. McGlotten v. Connally, 338 F. Supp. 448, 460-62 (D.D.C. 1972) (opinion of Bazelon, J.). Whether this interpretation is true to the intent of Congress is a matter of Title VI law. Academic criticism of this decision has been devastating, and no other court has followed it. If Congress did choose not to include tax advantages among the kinds of assistance that would carry Title VI nondiscrimination obligations, then it is ironic that *Bob Jones,* through the medium of tax law interpretation, achieved exactly the result Congress rejected.

exemption, and both may fail in this task.[101] But as a touchstone administrators and courts can use for resolving close cases concerning the dimensions of the charitable exemption now contained in the Code, the public function thesis suffers in comparison to the taxable income approach.

Although the concept of a public function may seem concrete enough, it takes little probing to reveal its shortcomings. Unless the thesis is completely circular, the concept must mean something other than those things that government does or that government is permitted to do. It is rare but not unknown, for example, for the federal government to run a business that competes with the private sector, yet private businesses are exactly what the public function concept is meant not to cover. Furthermore, government under our laws may not engage in religious functions, yet the charitable exemption explicitly extends to this activity. Nor can the economic concept of public or social goods help much. This defines a class of goods for the benefits of which the providers are not compensated through the exchange system.[102] The public function thesis justifies denying exemption to activities with positive externalities but overall social costs.

It might be possible to characterize the public function thesis as embracing those public goods (in the economic sense) that a significant portion of our society would regard as desirable. An immediate problem with this solution, however, is its inconsistency with the charitable exemption that the thesis is supposed to explain. Under present law religious activities qualify for exemption, while substantial political involvement will disqualify an otherwise exempt organization. Granting that both religion and politics have positive externalities—in both cases the passive observer is edified and perhaps

---

[101] The income tax with the charitable exemption might have greater social costs than one without it either if the increase in welfare produced the charitable sector induced by the exemption were less valuable than that generated within the private or governmental sector due to fewer contributions would produce, or if the costs of uncertainty and disputes created by the exemption exceeded its benefits. Cf. Hochman & Rodgers, note 85 supra. On the other hand, these costs might be offset by the deadweight loss that the deduction arguably prevents by its recognition of individuals' greater inclination to sacrifice intangible satisfactions as income diminishes. See Andrews, note 85 supra, at 361-62. For a theoretical argument that the substitution effect is larger for altruistic satisfactions, see Becker, A Theory of Social Interactions, 82 J. POL. ECON. 1063, 1070-74 (1974). For distributional critiques of the exemption, see SURREY, note 5 supra; Kelman, note 85 supra; McDaniel, note 85 supra; and Rabin, note 55 supra.

[102] See ALCHIAN & ALLEN, EXCHANGE AND PRODUCTION: COMPETITION, COORDINATION AND CONTROL 122-24 (2d ed. 1977); MUSGRAVE & MUSGRAVE, PUBLIC FINANCE IN THEORY AND PRACTICE 54-87 (3d ed. 1980).

enlightened as opposing interests clash—how can one assert that religion provides greater or wider social benefits than politics? Not only is political advocacy widely regarded as the civic religion of our secular society, but we generally consider it essential to the continued existence of our free and pluralist society.[103]

Beyond this obvious conflict between the thesis and the law it purports to explain lies a broader problem of sorting out those public goods that constitute public functions from those that do not enjoy sufficiently broad societal support. If we took this process seriously, the Service should inquire widely into harmful encroachments on the public welfare by charities. Yet the taxing authorities have not attempted to incorporate into the definition of a charity either antidiscrimination rules involving factors other than race (*e.g.*, gender, alienage, physical or mental disability) or other strong federal policies such as free speech, due process, antitrust, or environmental protection.[104]

One conceivably might condition loss of exemption on the occurrence of public policy violations that cause great social harm or that the Service can detect easily. It seems unlikely, however, that either criterion justifies the singling out of segregated schools. Although racial discrimination is pernicious, it is not the only serious wrong charities can inflict. Moreover, its detection can be costly, due to the difficulty of sorting out legitimate from pretextual reasons for disfavoring particular students. At least until the Service or the courts alter their present practice, the public function thesis cannot be reconciled with the public interest standard provided by *Bob Jones.*

---

[103] A skeptic might dismiss as empty rhetoric the First Amendment tradition of assigning a high social value to political speech and insist that political action has little general utility due to the offsetting nature of opposing interests. From this point of view, government action to reduce political expenditures resolves a kind of Prisoner's Dilemma by inducing opponents to buy fewer wasteful offsets. While this theory is intriguing, it fails to explain why religious expenditures should have any higher overall value. Even though religious activity is not as overtly competitive as is politics, it seems reasonable to assume that the problem of envy is even greater. As a member of one sect, I may abhor government support for those whose dogmas I have repudiated even though I enjoy my own government handout. I am grateful to Charles J. Goetz for pointing out this problem.

[104] The Court declared that racially discriminatory schools "cannot be deemed to confer a benefit on the public" and put off the question of exemption for an institution that both causes social harm and provides public benefits. 103 S. Ct. at 2031 n.21. This explanation is merely semantic, as even segregated schools provide some social benefits, although the harm they cause easily may exceed the good they do. The Court acknowledged as much elsewhere in its opinion. 103 S. Ct. at 2035 n.29. What remains unresolved is how to tell which public policy violations vitiate the basic purpose of a beneficial institution and which do not.

If we look to the public function thesis, not for an understanding of the status quo of the charitable exemption, but rather for hints as to the shape of the exemption's future, the result is not much more satisfying. One possibility is to let the concept of public benefit merge with a notion of legality, so that an organization engaged in any illegal activity would lose its exemption. A problem with this solution is its conflict with the spirit, if not the letter, of *Tellier* and the 1969 amendment of the business deduction rules, both of which rejected the notion that illegality and nondeductibility should be coextensive. Once one looks for ways of choosing among illegal acts to determine which will lead to loss of exemption, the public function thesis provides little guidance.

The taxable income approach does a better job of explaining comprehensively the various facets of the charitable exemption and related features of the income tax. Its principal shortcoming is its apparent inconsistency with the current treatment of noncharitable gifts and political contributions, which may seem to produce equally intangible satisfactions for the transferor but which do not qualify for deduction. A plausible explanation for this discrepancy is the greater difficulty of monitoring intrafamilial transfers and political transactions for hidden payoffs. Although personal gifts may produce intangible gratification for their donors, as a class they often take place in a network of reciprocal obligations that produce tangible returns. One might think of a family gathered at Christmas to exchange presents. Even when the reciprocity is not immediate or explicit, a general pattern of mutual courtesies may serve to define family boundaries. Moreover, intrafamilial transactions are more frequent and informal than are charitable transfers, which makes a rule distinguishing reciprocal from nonreciprocal family transfers too costly to implement. As for political contributions, a politician has considerably more flexibility than do particular charities in the kind of benefits they can distribute. Moreover, politicans can deliver rewards through the medium of government, while charities generally must deliver benefits directly. As a result, we have adopted an irrebuttable presumption against nonreciprocity. With charitable transfers, by contrast, the Service has enjoyed some success in distinguishing on a case-by-case basis altruistic contributions from those that entail payoffs to the donor.[105]

---

[105] See Goetz & Scott, *Enforcing Promises: An Examination of the Basis of Contract*, 89 YALE L. J. 1261, 1306-8 & n.112 (1980). For cases where the Service has succeeded in showing that a

Another and perhaps more important strength of the taxable income approach is that by reconciling the exemption with the general pattern of federal taxation, it forces the tax agencies and the courts to focus on issues they have confronted repeatedly and successfully in a variety of contexts. The inquiry into the presence of private benefits is pervasive in tax law, existing not only to define the charitable exemption but also to distinguish nondeductible personal from deductible profit-seeking expenses.[106] The public function thesis, by contrast, enlists the Service in particular in the definition and enforcement of a host of policies that are foreign to its customary concerns.

One might regard this strength equally as a flaw, because the inquiry into an institution's eligibility for exemption would be unresponsive to compelling moral issues and legal claims. It could produce exemptions for harmful activity, of which segregated schools are a striking example, as long as no individuals received private benefits from the enterprise. It further seems to put the government in the position of rewarding behavior that Congress or some other body has sought to prohibit. For these schools, loss of exemption would come, if at all, from factors perhaps associated with, but not directly a result of, their antisocial conduct.

If Dickens's observations of human nature can be generalized, Fagin's school may typify enterprises designed to flout "fundamental public policy." In many cases, the penalties associated with transgressing legal or social norms may be so great as to compel creation of proprietary profits as a necessary inducement to those able to run the operation. This relation between misconduct and proprietary profits is not fixed, however, and the record in *Bob Jones* does not reveal the presence of the private benefits on which the taxable income approach would make the exemption turn. The public function theory avoids this problem by making the objectionable nature of an organization a ground for denying the exemption. At a minimum, the public function approach prevents the appearance of

---

transfer to a charity produced reciprocal benefits, see, *e.g.*, Ottawa Silica Co. v. United States, 699 F.2d 1124 (Fed. Cir. 1983); Winters v. Commissioner, 468 F.2d 778 (2d Cir. 1972); Summers v. Commissioner, 33 T.C.M. 695 (1974). In other cases the Service has been able to assign a value to the reciprocal benefit and has allowed a deduction for that portion of a contribution in excess of the benefit. See Rev. Rul. 67-246, 1967-2 C.B. 104.

[106] For an example of an area where the courts have turned from a public policy inquiry to a search for private consumption, see the cases concerning deductions for criminal defense costs, note 40 *supra*.

government support of conduct that, however altruistic it may be, offends fundamental moral principles or other expressions of public policy.

But the last point is simply the affirmative case for the public policy doctrine. *Bob Jones* may have meant to recognize this equivalence with its footnote reference to the *Tank Truck* line of cases.[107] However attractive may seem the idea that tax rules should contain sufficient elasticity to mirror broader social policies, experience has demonstrated severe problems. Although one cannot condemn categorically every potential application of the doctrine, this history suggests strong grounds for skepticism toward its present invocation. Nor is there any reason why the charitable exemption presents the special case where the doctrine offers a second-best solution to an otherwise intractable dilemma. An examination of selectivity, proximity, and proportionality problems both resolved and left open by *Bob Jones* suggests that the Court's exhumation of the public policy doctrine here was a mistake.

III. SEGREGATED SCHOOLS AND THE CHARITABLE EXEMPTION

Bob Jones seems clear enough in its result. Private schools that otherwise meet the requirements of §501(c) (3) will lose the advantages associated with the provision if they practice racial discrimination toward their students. Beyond this holding, however, many questions remain. These pending issues, as well as the result itself, illustrate the pitfalls of selectivity, proximity, and proportionality the Court must confront once it unleashes the public policy doctrine.

A. SELECTIVITY ISSUES: WHAT KINDS OF DISCRIMINATION AND WHY ONLY SCHOOLS?

Bob Jones University and Goldsboro Christian Schools present easy cases for denial of the exemption. Both admitted to racial discrimination. Bob Jones imposed racially based restrictions on its students and Goldsboro Christian Schools simply refused to admit blacks. Because of these factual concessions, the Court had no need to consider what

---

[107] 103 S. Ct. at 2028 n.17. See also *id.* at 2037 n.1 (Powell, J., concurring in the judgment).

devices the government could employ to disprove a school's claim of innocence. More basically, it did not explore what antidiscrimination principle the public policy doctrine required.

In practice, the procedural and substantive questions merge. Burdens of proof and safe harbors, among other devices, shape the standard of conduct to which the regulated entity must comply. In the case of antidiscrimination rules, the problem is distinguishing legitimate breakdowns in racial mixing from impermissible discrimination. The Service's enforcement experience with its segregated schools policy is illustrative. For eight years after announcement of its position, the Service generally accepted the declaration of a school that it did not discriminate on the basis of race.[108] Concerned that this practice might allow dishonest schools to evade the policy, the Carter Administration in 1978 attempted to formulate stricter evidentiary burdens for schools that had few or no minority students. Congress blocked implementation of these proposals, but a lower court has read them into the statute. The Court will have an opportunity to join in the controversy in the 1983 Term.[109]

The Carter rules, if they had gone into effect, would have identified a class of schools that would have borne significant minority recruitment obligations. As originally proposed, they would have imposed on schools whose minority-student enrollment was less than 20 percent of the percentage of minority students in the surrounding school-age population and which either came into being or substantially expanded their student body during the desegregation of local public schools an affirmative duty to obtain more minority students and faculty. Failure to execute this duty would have lead to loss of exemption.[110]

One might compare this standard to the series of presumptions the Court has mandated or approved to cope with the problem of public school desegregation. Although the Court has barred finding a constitutional violation in the absence of purposeful discrimination by school officials, it has allowed a finding of a system's earlier segregation coupled with a high present incidence of one-race schools

---

[108] The Service's guidelines required a school to make these declarations not only in its application for recognition as an exempt organization but also as part of its publicity in recruiting students. See Rev. Proc. 75-50, 1975-2 C.B. 587; Rev. Proc. 72-54, 1972-2 C.B. 834.

[109] See Wright v. Regan, 656 F.2d 820 (D.C. Cir. 1981), *cert. granted*, 103 S. Ct. 3109 (1983).

[110] See Prop. Rev. Proc. §3.03, 43 Fed. Reg. 37,296, 37,297 (1978). See also Prop. Rev. Proc. §3.03, 44 Fed. Reg. 9451, 9452-53 (1979).

to sustain a presumption of ongoing purposeful discrimination.[111] The presumption permits a court to order redistribution of students to obtain a more even racial mix. Although some have criticized this device because it permits judicial intervention without serious inquiry into the causes of racial distributions in the affected system, the Carter rules would go even further.[112] They would impose affirmative duties without any proof of historical discrimination, much less present segregation.

I do not mean to suggest that these methods of implementing antidiscrimination principles are immoral or unwise. A gap necessarily must exist between any principle and the technical rules designed to implement it. One should recognize, however, that the business of crafting these rules requires a sense of both the historical background and the immediate environment in which breakdowns in racial mixing take place, and some awareness of the behavioral effects of particular legal rules. Failure to take account of these factors will lead to rules bearing only the faintest trace of the principles that inspired them.

For whatever reason, Congress, the federal courts, and the Civil Rights Division of the Justice Department traditionally have been the source of the racial discrimination policies for our society. Absent a transformation of the training and experience of its personnel, the Internal Revenue Service cannot claim similar expertise and may operate at cross-purposes with these other rulemakers.[113] It is true that courts will have a chance to review the Service's choices, at least if exempt organizations dislike them. But judicial review takes time, as evidenced by the thirteen-year interval between the Service's announcement of its antisegregation policy and the Court's en-dorsement of it. These lags make the costs of Service errors substantial.

---

[111] See Dayton Bd. of Educ. v. Brinkman, 443 U.S. 526 (1979); Columbus Bd. of Educ. v. Penick, 443 U.S. 449 (1979).

[112] For the critics' view, see Kitch, *The Return of Color-Conciousness to the Constitution: Weber, Dayton, and Columbus,* 1979 SUPREME COURT REVIEW 1.

[113] Even if the expertise problem could be conquered through a transformation of the Service, there are reasons for apprehension about merging such disparate functions as tax collection and civil rights enforcement in a single agency. The history of private firms reveals substantial costs associated with the conglomeration of unrelated activities in a single enterprise. See Coase, *The Nature of the Firm,* 4 ECONOMICA 386 (1937); Panzar & Willig, *Economies of Scope,* 71 AM. ECON. REV. PAPERS AND PROC. 268 (1981). Firms have tended to lower these costs by developing forms of management that segregated the firm's different operations. Comparable costs from failure to achieve what Professor Williamson calls optimal hierarchical decomposition might exist if the Service took on major civil rights responsibilities. See Williamson, *The Modern Corporation: Origins, Evolution, Attributes,* 19 J. ECON. LIT. 1537 (1981).

Furthermore, judicial review tends to be piecemeal, as all of the unanswered questions left by *Bob Jones* illustrate. The Service and Treasury, by contrast, can issue broad pronouncements in legislative form. These differences give the taxing authorities residual power to implement their decisions even when the courts demonstrate their hostility.[114] On balance, the prospect of finding ultimate wisdom in the courts seems an insufficient corrective for an initial misallocation of regulatory authority.

Other selectivity problems further illustrate the dubious wisdom of giving the Service substantial power to set civil rights policy. The issue whether racial discrimination used to rectify breakdowns in racial mixing is either unconstitutional or immoral has divided both the country and the Court in the past decade. To cite two recent decisions by a badly splintered Court, *Bakke*[115] indicates that some kinds of reverse discrimination in the selection of public school students may violate federal law, while *Weber*[116] suggests a more benevolent stance toward reverse discrimination in the private labor market. In light of these cases, no one can say with complete confidence whether private schools violate federal law when they engage in particular kinds of affirmative action programs, or if so what distinguishes permissible from improper reverse discrimination. What seems to follow from *Bob Jones* is an obligation on the part of the Internal Revenue Service to deal with the issue.[117] Any answer it may give—that reverse racial discrimination either is or is not equivalent to the kind of discrimination condemned in *Bob Jones*—will profoundly dismay many.

---

[114] One recent example concerns sales and leasebacks. The Service developed strict standards for determining when such a transaction constituted a disguised financing arrangement with less favorable tax consequences for the putative buyer/lessor. Rev. Rul. 72-543, 1972-2 C.B. 87. Although the Court expressed a more liberal attitude toward these transactions in Frank Lyon Co. v. United States, 435 U.S. 561 (1978), cautious investors remained constrained by the narrow but precise Service guidelines because of the absence of definite rules from the Court.

[115] Regents v. Bakke, 438 U.S. 265 (1978).

[116] United Steelworkers v. Weber, 443 U.S. 193 (1979). See also Fullilove v. Klutznick, 448 U.S. 448 (1980).

[117] See 4 BITTKER, note 4 *supra*, at 100-06. The Service's rulings to date concerning the scope of its policy are suggestive only. In a public ruling it held that a school's discrimination in favor of American Indians does not produce a loss of exemption. Rev. Rul. 77-272, 1977-2 C.B. 191. This result is consistent with Morton v. Mancari, 417 U.S. 535 (1974), which upheld a federal hiring preference for Indians. In a private letter ruling the Service has maintained that §501(i)'s explicit prohibition of racial discrimination by social clubs does not apply to discrimination on the basis of ethnic background or national origin. Private Letter Ruling 8317004, IRS Letter Rul. Rep. (CCH) (1983).

The merits of the issue aside, one might argue that this decision ought to be made by officials directly accountable to the public through the political process. Alternatively, one might believe that the moral claims at stake are such as to require determination by an institution, such as the courts, that has the responsibility for defining individual rights and is insulated from the short-term frenzies of the political process.[118] It is inconceivable that civil service bureaucrats, isolated from public accountability and trained, at least for the present, in matters wholly unrelated to individual rights, should have the initial responsibility for shaping our nation's policy on affirmative action in education.

Another selectivity problem that the Service has not confronted, but that seems a logical extension of the *Bob Jones* policy, involves racial discrimination by public schools. A glance at the Supreme Court's docket indicates that a number of public school systems appear to remain in violation of the Court's desegregation mandate as well as of various federal antidiscrimination statutes.[119] Schools run by state and local governments receive a number of tax advantages comparable to the charitable exemption and enjoy the further benefit of tax-favored financing.[120] If *Bob Jones* applies to anything other than its own facts, these advantages must be forfeit where evidence of discrimination exists. One might object that an elaborate regulatory structure, including supervision by federal courts and the Justice Department, already governs public schools, and that any additional benefits from the Service's regulation would be offset by its costs. If redundancy is

[118] For a sample of views on the structural question of decisionmaking authority as it relates to the affirmative action-reverse discrimination dilemma, see DWORKIN, TAKING RIGHTS SERIOUSLY 223-39 (1977); GOLDMAN, JUSTICE AND REVERSE DISCRIMINATION (1979); Ely, *The Constitutionality of Reverse Racial Discrimination*, 41 U. CHI. L. REV. 723 (1974); Posner, *The De Funis Case and the Constitutionality of Preferential Treatment of Racial Minorities*, 1974 SUPREME COURT REVIEW 1.

[119] See, *e.g.*, Washington v. Seattle School Dist. No. 1, 458 U.S. 457 (1982); Mississippi University for Women v. Hogan, 458 U.S. 718 (1982); Plyler v. Doe, 457 U.S. 202 (1982); North Haven Bd. of Educ. v. Bell, 456 U.S. 512 (1982); New York City Bd. of Educ. v. Harris, 444 U.S. 130 (1979); Dayton Bd. of Educ. v. Brinkman, 443 U.S. 526 (1979); Columbus Bd. of Educ. v. Penick, 443 U.S. 449 (1979).

[120] I.R.C. §§103 (income tax exclusion for interest from certain state and local governmental indebtedness); 164 (income tax deduction for certain general levies); 170 (c) (1) (income tax deduction for contributions dedicated to "exclusively public purpose"); 2055 (a) (1) (estate tax deduction for same); 2106 (a) (2) (A) (i) (same); 2522 (a) (1), (b) (1) (gift tax deduction for same); 2602 (c) (2) (generation-skipping transfer tax deduction for same); 3121 (b) (7) (employment tax exemption); 3306 (c) (7) (unemployment tax exemption).

a valid objection, however, one must ask what justifies the Service's policing of private schools.[121]

Besides the problem of identifying when the absence of racial mixing should constitute a violation of public policy, there exists a matter that the Court did address in *Bob Jones*. In a society where religious practice as well as belief enjoys certain legally enforced privileges, does religiously inspired discrimination stand on a different footing than secular education? While admitting to discrimination, both Bob Jones University and Goldsboro Christian Schools maintained their actions had a religious basis and claimed constitutional protection for them. In light of the Court's past free exercise decisions, the assertion of a First Amendment privilege to discriminate was not frivolous.[122] I am not concerned here with the merits of the Court's ultimate rejection of the free exercise claim. What does seem disturbing is the Service's contention, made in 1975, that it had initial responsibility for balancing these interests, both of which are alien to the normal concerns of a tax collector.[123]

The Service's nonchalance toward these difficult choices is ominous when one considers that *Bob Jones*'s public interest gloss logically should apply to all religious activities, not just to sectarian schools. Section 501(c) (3) lumps together charitable, educational, and religious activities, and at first blush segregation in religious organizations seems no more charitable than segregation in schools.[124] Some large denominations, such as the Church of Jesus Christ of the Latter-Day Saints, impose racial restrictions even when they permit nominal membership on the part of minorities. Do these rules, analogous to the ban on interracial dating imposed by Bob Jones University, constitute breaches of public policy sufficient to require a loss of exemption?

It seems certain that the Service now must confront this issue. Those attempting to distinguish congregations from schools will insist on both free exercise and associational rights. Those opposing them will give greater weight to antidiscrimination principles. As with the affirmative action-reverse discrimination problem, advocates on each side will argue about the proper forum for resolution of the dispute.

---

[121] See notes 133-35 *infra* and accompanying text.

[122] For one argument in support of the free exercise claim, see Laycock, *Tax Exemptions for Racially Discriminatory Religious Schools*, 60 TEX. L. REV. 259 (1982).

[123] Rev. Rul. 75-231, 1975-1 C.B. 158.

[124] A footnote in *Bob Jones* hints that discrimination in schooling has a greater harmful effect on society, and therefore is a more fundamental defeat of the public interest, than is discrimination in a purely religious activity. 103 S. Ct. at 2035 n.29.

Although some will support politicians and some philosophers, no one can advance a principled basis for granting the Internal Revenue Service the initial authority to weigh the balance, or take comfort from the prospect of subsequent litigation over the Service's conclusion.

Beyond these obvious selectivity ·issues lurk a host of potential problems. *Bob Jones* concerned discrimination toward students, but what about faculty hiring? If employment discrimination disqualifies an organization from tax-exempt status, should the Service define discrimination by reference to the Constitution and §1981 or by incorporating the stricter rules of Titles VI and VII?[125] What about other federal policies, such as procedural due process, free speech, antitrust, environmental protection, or food and drug safety?[126] If we truly are concerned about the appearance of subsidizing illegal behavior, violations of any of these statutes should result in denial of the charitable exemption. But if we want to limit the public policy doctrine, on what basis can we construct a hierarchy of illegality?

B. PROXIMITY ISSUES: WHAT SUBSTITUTES FOR THE CHARITABLE EXEMPTION?

Segregated schools no longer may qualify for any tax attribute conditioned on meeting the requirements of §501(c) (3). Despite the apparent simplicity of this result, several questions remain unresolved.

Qualification under §501(c) (3) results in certain advantages, not only for the school, but also for faculty, students, and the parents of the latter. Fellowships and scholarships will constitute taxable income unless the recipient can meet the requirements of §117. For fellowships

---

[125] See Guardians Ass'n v. Civil Service Comm'n, 103 S. Ct. 3221 (1983); General Building Contractors Ass'n, Inc. v. Pennsylvania, 458 U.S. 375 (1982); North Haven Bd. of Educ. v. Bell, 456 U.S. 512 (1982). There would be some paradox in a denial of the charitable exemption based on employment discrimination, as businesses may deduct the cost of carrying out employment discrimination that violates the Civil Rights Act of 1964. See Rev. Rul. 74-323, 1974-2 C.B. 40.

[126] Up until now the advocates of the public interest gloss have not been ambitious in their proposals. The Civil Rights Commission has argued only that any Title VI or Title IX violation should lead to loss of exemption. Under this interpretation, schools engaged in employment, gender, or national origin discrimination would lose the exemption. U.S. CIVIL RIGHTS COMM'N, THE FEDERAL CIVIL RIGHTS ENFORCEMENT EFFORT—1974: Vol. 3—TO ENSURE EQUAL EDUCATIONAL OPPORTUNITY 387 (1975). See also Ginsburg, *Sex Discrimination and the IRS: Public Policy and the Charitable Deduction,* 10 TAX NOTES 27 (1980). But *cf.* Private Letter Ruling 8317004, IRS Letter Rul. Rep. (CCH) (1983).

to qualify, they must be provided by either a governmental entity or a §501(c) (3) organization.[127] Scholarships are excluded only if their recipients are degree candidates at what §170(b) (1) (A) (ii) defines as a school, and this provision in turn refers back to §501(c) (3).[128] Parents can take a dependency exemption for a child over eighteen only if he is a full-time student at a similarly defined institution, unless the child has less than $1,000 income.[129] Each of these benefits bears only the most attenuated relationship to the issues on which *Bob Jones* has made exempt status turn, yet loss of exemption now would appear to defeat all of them.

There also remains the problem Bittker has discussed at length: How does the Code define the income of a nonprofit organization? The Service has avoided confronting the issue by declining to levy an income tax on schools expelled from charitable status by their racial practices, but it has not explained or even acknowledged its policy of nontaxation.[130] Although *Bob Jones* indicated no dissatisfaction with this solution, sooner or later the Service or the courts will be called on to address the problem explicitly.[131]

Even if one distorts the existing law for measuring net income, predicated as much of it is on a profit-seeking purpose, to provide rules for inclusions and deductions of a nonprofit entity, do the public policy concerns embraced in *Bob Jones* extend to income measurement, or does the repudiation by Congress of the doctrine in the context of business deductions prevail? If public policy predominates, can any of the expenses necessary to maintain a segregated institution—faculty salaries, rent, interest, utility charges, for example—be used to offset gross receipts? What should be characterized as taxable income, and what qualifies for exclusion as contributions to capital or gifts? For organizations that are neither corporations nor trusts, what is the

---

[127] See I.R.C. §117 (b) (2). The Treasury maintains that §117 provides the only test for excludibility of fellowships and scholarships, preempting exclusion as a gift or as a prize or award. See Treas. Reg. §1.117-1(a) (1956).

[128] See I.R.C. §117(b) (1).

[129] See I.R.C. §151 (e)(4). In addition, scholarship funds not excluded from income under §117 (b) (1) count as outside support, thus making it more difficult for a parent to provide at least one-half of the child's support as required by §152 (a). See *id.* §152 (d).

[130] The Service's rulings on discriminatory schools are silent as to income tax liability, and no dispute about the income tax levied on such an organization has reached any court.

[131] The call might come from an administration more inclined to attack discriminatory schools than is the present one, or through third-party lawsuits if the Court adopts the exception to the *Eastern Kentucky Welfare Rights Organization* standing rules carved out by the District of Columbia Circuit in *Wright*. See note 109 *supra*. See also Abortion Rights Mobilization, Inc. v. Regan, 544 F. Supp. 471 (S.D.N.Y. 1982).

taxpaying entity, and do the corporate or individual rates apply?[132] If *Bob Jones* extends to public school systems, may taxpayers deduct taxes, and bondholders exclude interest, used to finance discriminatory schools?

None of these questions is unanswerable, but each takes us further away from the sweeping moral vision that produced the Service's original antisegregation policy and leads us into a welter of technical detail. Moreover, resolution of these issues probably will be achieved by reference to the general structure of taxation, not to the nature and degree of racial discrimination an organization perpetuates. This paradox will heighten the proportionality problem.

C. PROPORTIONALITY ISSUES: HOW MUCH SHOULD SEGREGATED SCHOOLS PAY?

Racial segregation is reprehensible, and discrimination in schools is especially bad because of the memories it revives and the injuries it inflicts on children. Agreement on this point, however, does not take us very far. Presumably we as a society should make segregation costly, either as a means of expressing our condemnation or to discourage this behavior. The problem then becomes one of deciding how costly segregated schools should be.

Existing laws outside the Internal Revenue Code, were they exploited, could impose significant costs on segregated schools. After *Runyon v. McCrary*,[133] the Justice Department apparently has the authority to seek criminal penalties and injunctions to close private schools outright or to obtain less drastic decrees tailored to the offense.[134] Although the Supreme Court has not addressed the issue, it appears courts can also assess punitive as well as actual damages against these schools.[135] These powers are sufficiently flexible to permit the

---

[132] The Code definition of a corporation comprises unincorporated associations. I.R.C. §7701(a)(3). Both judicial and administrative interpretations of this provision, however, insist on a business purpose as an essential characteristic of such organizations. Treas. Reg. §301.7701-2(a) (1960); Morrisey v. Commissioner, 296 U.S. 344 (1935). For the limited object of imposing the unrelated-income tax on charitable organizations, the Code classifies all entities other than trusts as corporations. I.R.C. §511 (a) (2) (A).

[133] 427 U.S. 160 (1976).

[134] See 18 U.S.C. §241 (1976); 28 U.S.C. §1343(4) (1976); *cf.* Cannon v. University of Chicago, 441 U.S. 677, 733 n.3 (1979) (Powell, J., dissenting); United States v. Republic Steel Corp., 362 U.S. 482 (1960); Pennsylvania v. Porter, 659 F.2d 306 (3d Cir. 1981) (*en banc*). But see United States v. City of Philadelphia, 644 F.2d 187 (3d Cir. 1980).

[135] See Smith v. Wade, 103 S. Ct. 1625 (1983).

government, private plaintiffs, and courts to scale sanctions to the gravity and harm of individual instances of discrimination. Alternatively, Congress might supplement existing law by providing a schedule of fines and other penalties for schools that discriminate. In either case, an opportunity exists to bring into line the nature of the wrong and its consequences to the wrongdoer.

Compared to these sanctions, loss of exempt status seems significantly deficient. The flexibility to base punishment on the severity of misconduct is entirely absent. In its place will be a cost related only randomly to the harm imposed.

The cost of nonexemption has three components: reduced contributions; the possibility of income tax liability; and liability under the unemployment tax.[136] At present it is unclear whether the Service will levy any income taxes on nonprofit schools that discriminate, and the burden of unemployment taxes is offset by the amount already paid to a State for unemployment insurance.[137] Reduced contributions, then, seem the most significant concern for schools facing loss of exemption, and this will turn on donors' elasticity of giving.

Elasticity of giving appears to depend largely on a donor's income. This stems from both the effect of progressive taxation, which makes deductions more valuable as tax rates increase, and the fact that most charitable deductions are available only if the taxpayer has excess itemized deductions (a factor closely related to level of income).[138] Because there is no reason to suspect that any relation exists between the income level of contributors and the extent of a disqualified school's misconduct, the disqualification sanction can lead to bizarre results. An aberrant but highly publicized act of wrongdoing, such as discrimination in a single department of a large university, could lead to a major drop in contributions by wealthy alumni and friends.[139] Discrimination by a subordinate body, such as a student fraternity, conceivably could cost a university its exemption and produce the same result.[140] Conversely, a school established to substitute almost

---

[136] An organization may also suffer other costs depending on its exploitation of nontax benefits conditioned on qualification for the charitable exemption. See note 52 *supra*. The discussion in the text ignores these costs as well as the effects of loss of exemption on faculty and students. See notes 127–29 *supra* and accompanying text.

[137] See I.R.C. § §3302.

[138] All but a small amount of charitable contributions are itemized deductions, and most itemizers have relatively high incomes. See I.R.C. § §63 (b) (1) (c); 170(i).

[139] See Grove City College v. Harris, 687 F.2d 684 (3d Cir. 1982), *cert. granted*, 103 S. Ct. 1181 (1983).

[140] See Iron Arrow Honor Soc'y v. Heckler, 702 F.2d 549 (5th Cir.), *dismissed as moot*, 104 S. Ct. 373 (1983).

completely for integrated public schools might suffer no losses at all if it depended exclusively on tuition or contributions from low-income supporters for its upkeep. Religiously grounded schools may prove especially resilient because of the relatively low income of their supporters and the enthusiasm that motivates contributions to them.[141]

The potential for unfairness is not a disproportionate penalty's only problem. The lack of any relationship between the harm and a sanction's burden may have negative behavioral consequences. Penalties have social costs, because of both the expense of administration and the possibility of deterring worthwhile conduct, such as the provision of private schooling, that might be mistaken for the proscribed behavior.[142] As a result, it is possible to speak of optimal and suboptimal penalties, the latter defined by their failure to minimize the sum of these costs and the social harm of the proscribed conduct. The penalty embodied in the added cost of nonexemption will be optimal only by accident if at all. It is much more likely that nonexemption will lead to insufficient deterrence of segregation or excessive discouragement of legitimate private education.

IV. CONCLUSION

Bob Jones reflects a simplistic belief that the government, when confronted with something bad (whether illegal or immoral is unimportant), must attack the offending act with every resource at its disposal. The conviction that withholding any potential means of attacking a problem demonstrates a lack of commitment to its solution suffers from two flaws. First, it ignores the possibility that some agencies of government may have comparative advantages as prosecutors of particular policy violations. Second, it ignores the fact that the failure to mold a penalty system to match the policy it enforces has both moral and welfare costs. *Bob Jones* illustrates each of these flaws.

---

[141] Clotfelter & Salamon, *The Impact of the 1981 Tax Act on Individual Charitable Giving*, 35 NAT'L TAX J. 171 (1982); Feldstein, *The Income Tax and Charitable Contributions: Part II—The Impact on Religious, Educational, and Other Organizations*, 28 NAT'L TAX J. 209 (1975). *Cf.* Clotfelter, *Tax Incentives and Disincentives for Charitable Giving*, in WORKING PAPERS FOR SPRING RESEARCH FORUM: SINCE THE FILER COMMISSION 353 (1983).

[142] See Becker, note 9 *supra*, at 179-85.

In a society where a growing public sector requires increasing taxation for its support, the influence of tax rules and the importance of controversies about them can only increase. There is nothing sacred about tax law, and no intrinsic reason why revenue collection should be the only policy taxes serve. But given the Leviathan the federal tax system has become, the likelihood that piecemeal introduction of new policies will backfire is too great to permit casual injection of public policy arguments into the creation of new tax rules and the resolution of disputes about old ones. As the arena of tax debate grows, both the temptation to take this misstep and the need to resist it will become greater.

Bob Jones displays exactly the wrong posture toward the problem. Although the invitation for the time being is only implicit, it encourages the Service and courts to develop a public policy overlay for every tax rule whose base-definition role is not immediately apparent. This is what makes the case important and the outcome regrettable.

MICHAEL E. SMITH

THE SPECIAL PLACE OF RELIGION IN THE CONSTITUTION

I. INTRODUCTION

A. REASONS FOR THE INQUIRY

Religion presently has a special place in the United States Constitution: government action concerning religion is particularly likely to be judged unconstitutional by the courts.

For example, the United States Supreme Court has interpreted the Free Exercise Clause to mean that government may not hinder the exercise of religion without a strong nonreligious reason. In *Sherbert v. Verner*,[1] the Court ruled that a Seventh-Day Adventist could not be denied unemployment compensation because of her refusal to work on Saturday, and in *Wisconsin v. Yoder*,[2] the Court barred criminal prosecution of Amish parents who refused to send their children to public school past the eighth grade.

Similarly, although over strong objections, the Supreme Court has interpreted the Establishment Clause to mean that government may not aid religion unless, among other things, the purpose and "primary effect" are secular.[3] Accordingly, the Court has invalidated released-time religion courses, prayers, and religious readings in the public schools.[4] It has also invalidated a variety of financial aids to private religious schools, such as teacher salary supplements, but it has been equivocal on tax credits for parents.[5]

Michael E. Smith is Professor of Law, University of California, Berkeley.

[1] 374 U.S. 398 (1963).

[2] 406 U.S. 205 (1972).

[3] *E.g.*, Abington School Dist. v. Schempp, 374 U.S. 203, 222 (1963); Lemon v. Kurtzman, 403 U.S. 602, 612-13 (1971). In *Lemon*, the Court added a third requirement, that the program not unduly "entangle" government and religion.

[4] *E.g.*, McCollum v. Board of Educ., 333 U.S. 203 (1948); Abington School Dist. v. Schempp, 374 U.S. 203 (1963).

[5] *E.g.*, Lemon v. Kurtzman, 403 U.S. 602 (1971); Committee for Pub. Educ. v. Nyquist, 413 U.S. 756 (1973).

A third category of government action consists of treating some religious groups more favorably or unfavorably than others. The Supreme Court has repeatedly declared that government may not do so on religious grounds.[6]

By comparison, economic activity at present has no such special place in the Constitution. Government may hinder the exercise of economic liberty for any debatable reason, including economic belief.[7] The Court would brush off objections that government is aiding economic activity for economic reasons.[8] No constitutional rule denies government the power to prefer some economic activities over others, even on economic grounds.[9]

Indeed, religion has a special constitutional place even by comparison with so high a present constitutional value as political thought and action. In *Wisconsin v. Yoder*, the Supreme Court stated that its ruling did not extend to those whose objection to public schooling was based on a nonreligious philosophy.[10] Likewise, in the Court's first ruling against school prayers, the Justices expressly distinguished the teaching of patriotic propositions in the public schools.[11] And in a major freedom of speech case, they upheld government financial aid to political candidates against a challenge based on the analogy of the Establishment Clause.[12]

At the same time, the special constitutional place of religion presents the courts with unusually difficult doctrinal questions. Chief Justice Burger, writing for the Court in *Lemon v. Kurtzman*, acknowledged in all "candor" that "we can only dimly perceive the lines of demarcation in this extraordinarily sensitive area of constitutional law," that "the line of separation . . . is a blurred, indistinct, and variable barrier."[13] The most difficult question is how to effectuate both halves of the rule that government may neither aid nor hinder religion for religious (or antireligious) reasons. For example, at issue in *Abington*

---

[6] *E.g.*, Gillette v. United States, 401 U.S. 437, 449-50 (1971); Larson v. Valente, 456 U.S. 228, 246 & n. 23 (1982).

[7] *E.g.*, Ferguson v. Skrupa, 372 U.S. 726 (1963); North Dakota Bd. of Pharm. v. Snyder's Drug Stores, Inc., 414 U.S. 156 (1973).

[8] See, *e.g.*, United States v. Gerlach Live Stock Co., 339 U.S. 725 (1950); Hughes v. Alexandria Scrap Corp., 426 U.S. 794 (1976).

[9] See, *e.g.*, Williamson v. Lee Optical Co., 348 U.S. 483 (1955) (optometrists and ophthalmologists vs. opticians); Ferguson v. Skrupa, 372 U.S. 725 (1963) (lawyers vs. debt adjustors).

[10] 406 U.S. at 215-16.

[11] Engel v. Vitale, 370 U.S. 421, 435 n.21 (1962).

[12] Buckley v. Valeo, 424 U.S. 1, 92-93 (1976).

[13] 403 U.S. 602, 612, 614 (1971).

School Dist. v. Schempp[14] was Bible reading and recitation of the Lord's Prayer in public schools. The majority of the Supreme Court invalidated these practices as a forbidden aid to religion. The dissenting Justice, however, argued that for the Court to exclude all religious activities from the public schools might constitute improper hindrance of religion.

Sherbert v. Verner, decided the same day as *Schempp*, provides a reverse example. It involved denial of unemployment compensation to a Seventh-Day Adventist who would not work on Saturday. The majority of the Court invalidated the action as a forbidden hindrance of religion. Two dissenting Justices, however, took note of the argument that for the Court to favor the religiously motivated in this way constituted improper aid to religion.

Justices on both sides in *Schempp* and *Sherbert* expressly recognized the possibility of conflict between the Establishment Clause and the Free Exercise Clause. The point has since become something of a favorite with the Supreme Court. Chief Justice Burger wrote in *Walz v. Tax Comm'n:* "The Court has struggled to find a neutral course between the two Religion Clauses, both of which are cast in absolute terms, and either of which, if expanded to a logical extreme, would tend to clash with the other."[15]

Under these circumstances, there are at least two good reasons to ask how the Supreme Court justifies the special constitutional place of religion. The answer will enhance our understanding of our present pattern of constitutional values. It may also help us to resolve the difficult doctrinal problems to which the special place of religion gives rise.

B. AN APPROACH TO THE PROBLEM

To the question, What justifies the special constitutional place of religion? perhaps the most straightforward answer is what current commentators would call "interpretivist."[16] The very language of the Constitution gives religion a special place in Article VI, section 3, and in the First Amendment. Moreover, the framers of the Constitution had urgent reasons for giving religion a special place. Some scholars stress the Enlightenment rationalism of leaders such as Thomas

---

[14] 374 U.S. 203 (1963).
[15] 397 U.S. 664, 668–69 (1970).
[16] ELY, DEMOCRACY AND DISTRUST 1 (1980).

Jefferson.[17] Others emphasize the free church Protestantism of the followers of Roger Williams.[18] Still others argue that the framers had a nonideological desire to allay potential social conflict.[19]

In reality, however, interpretivism has affected our constitutional practice only to a limited extent. Insofar as the Justices at present maintain the special constitutional place of religion, they do so mainly for present-day policy reasons. Religion had no special constitutional place until after the constitutional revolution of 1937. Before that time, the Supreme Court readily upheld government actions concerning religion that seem highly problematic by present standards. For example, in *Davis v. Beason*,[20] an 1890 case, a Mormon challenged an Idaho statute that required voters to swear that they did not belong to any group that taught or practiced polygamy. The Court rejected the challenge unanimously, saying little more than that "on this point there can be no serious discussion or difference of opinion. . . . Probably never before in the history of this country has it been seriously contended that the whole punitive power of the government for acts, recognized by the general consent of the Christian world in modern times as proper matters for prohibitory legislation, must be suspended in order that the tenets of a religious sect encouraging crime may be carried out without hindrance."[21]

During World War I the draft law exempted as conscientious objectors only members of a "well-recognized religious sect . . . whose existing creed or principles forbid its members to participate in war."[22] When the statutory classification was challenged as a violation of the Religion Clauses of the Constitution, the Court responded unanimously that "we pass [the challenge] without anything but statement . . . because we think its unsoundness is too apparent to require us to do more."[23] By contrast, economic liberty, which at present has no special constitutional place, was perhaps the Supreme Court's most cherished constitutional value between 1890 and 1937.[24]

Indeed, some Justices of the Supreme Court have begun to acknowledge openly that, in their view, the language and history of the

---

[17] *E.g.*, see dissenting opinion of Justice Rutledge in Everson v. Board of Education, 330 U.S. 1, 33-43 (1947).

[18] *E.g.*, HOWE, THE GARDEN AND THE WILDERNESS, ch. 1 (1965).

[19] *E.g.*, MURRAY, WE HOLD THESE TRUTHS, ch. 2 (1960).

[20] 133 U.S. 333 (1890).

[21] 133 U.S. at 341, 343.

[22] Selective Draft Law Cases, 245 U.S. 366, 389-90 (1918).

[23] *Id.*

[24] McCLOSKEY, THE AMERICAN SUPREME COURT 131-69 (1960).

Religion Clauses are largely beside the point as compared with present-day policy considerations. Justice White wrote in dissent in *Committee for Pub. Educ. v. Nyquist:*[25]

> No one contends that he can discern from the sparse language of the Establishment Clause that a State is forbidden to aid religion in any manner whatsoever or, if it does not mean that, what kind of or how much aid is permissible. And one cannot seriously believe that the history of the First Amendment furnishes unequivocal answers to many of the fundamental issues of church-state relations. In the end, the courts have fashioned answers to these questions as best they can, the language of the Constitution and its history having left them a wide range of choice among many alternatives. But decision has been unavoidable; and, in choosing, the courts necessarily have carved out what they deemed to be the most desirable national policy governing various aspects of church-state relationships.

Justice Powell was even blunter in his separate opinion in *Wolman v. Walter:* "At this point in the 20th century we are quite far removed from the dangers that prompted the Framers to include the Establishment Clause in the Bill of Rights. . . . The risk [of great harm from financial aid to private religious schools] is remote, and when viewed against the positive contributions of sectarian schools, any such risk seems entirely tolerable. . . ."[26]

Little has been written on the Supreme Court's present-day policy justifications for the special constitutional place of religion. The writings of Professors Kurland and Howe and Father Murray, among others, are full of important perceptions, but they do not treat the subject systematically.[27] The contrast with political speech is especially vivid. There have been many powerful essays, judicial and scholarly, on the justifications for the special constitutional place of the latter.[28]

C. DESCRIPTION OF THE INQUIRY

I shall describe the Supreme Court's articulated justifications for the special constitutional place of religion, concentrating on the views of

---

[25] 413 U.S. 756, 820 (1973).

[26] 433 U.S. 229, 263 (1977).

[27] *E.g.*, KURLAND, RELIGION AND THE LAW, ch. 1 (1962); HOWE, note 18 *supra;* MURRAY, note 19 *supra.*

[28] *E.g.*, the dissenting opinion of Justice Holmes in Abrams v. United States, 250 U.S. 616, 624 (1919); concurring opinion of Justice Brandies in Whitney v. California, 274 U.S. 357, 372 (1927); MEIKLEJOHN, FREE SPEECH AND ITS RELATION TO SELF-GOVERNMENT (1948); Emerson, *Toward a General Theory of the First Amendment*, 72 YALE L. J. 877 (1963).

the Justices since 1937. Before the constitutional revolution of 1937, religion had no special constitutional place. In 1940, however, the Court first ruled that the Free Exercise Clause is applicable against the states,[29] and during the next four years it enforced the Clause rigorously.[30] In 1947, the Court ruled that the Establishment Clause also applies against the states,[31] and it invalidated state aid to religion one year later.[32] The constitutional rules that give religion its special place are the product of these path-breaking decisions.

Between 1940 and 1952, the Supreme Court decided a fairly continuous series of religion cases, and during that period it was dominated by Justices appointed by President Roosevelt. When I refer to the first generation of Justices or cases, these are the ones I have in mind. For the next eight years, the Court decided no major cases. Since 1960, its decisions on religion have again become abundant, and during this period it has been increasingly dominated by the appointees of Republican Presidents, Eisenhower and Nixon. These I refer to as the second generation of Justices or cases.

None of the Justices has written at length on the justifications for the special constitutional place of religion. The Justices tend to be unreflective or reticent about larger issues. They have a special reason for caution with regard to religion. Since they have interpreted the Constitution to mean that government may neither aid nor hinder religion for religious reasons,[33] they may well feel that an explicit statement of the justifications for the constitutional place of religion might somehow run afoul of this rule.

To be sure, their opinions abound with observations that purport to justify the special constitutional place of religion. Most of these, however, do little more than to reformulate the inquiry. For example, the Justices may say that the Constitution expresses our commitment to freedom of religious conscience. We must still ask why freedom of religious conscience is regarded as so high a value compared with other freedoms. Likewise, the Justices may suggest that the Constitution prevents discrimination against religious minorities. Again, we must still ask why, among life's innumerable inequalities, religious discrimination is of special concern.

---

[29]Cantwell v. Connecticut, 310 U.S. 296 (1940).

[30]*E.g.*, Murdock v. Pennsylvania, 319 U.S. 105 (1943); Follett v. Town of McCormick, 321 U.S. 573 (1944).

[31]Everson v. Board of Education, 330 U.S. 1 (1947).

[32]McCollum v. Board of Education, 333 U.S. 203 (1948).

[33]See text at notes 1-5 *supra.*

Part II deals with the justifications for religion's special constitutional place that the Justices have articulated. Trying to grasp these justifications, however, I found underlying them certain views of religion itself. These underlying views may be just as pertinent to understanding the constitutional place of religion as the articulated justifications, and they are treated in Part III along with the important decisions of the last Term.

When I refer to the Justices' underlying views of religion, I mainly mean whether they regard religion favorably or unfavorably. Religion, however, can take many forms. For example, it can be embodied in a corporate institution such as the Catholic Church, with a structure of hierarchical authority and a claim to universal jurisdiction; or, at the other extreme, it can be the impulse of a lone person, one of billions, questing for God in his or her own inimitable way. Religion can be mainly concerned with the material conditions of this life, as are many religious groups today, progressive and reactionary, or mainly with the eternal and spiritual, the object of worship.

Exploring the Justices' underlying views on these matters, the evidence of the opinions may be checked against readily available nonjudicial sources. One source is biographical material on the Justices. This material is particularly helpful for four Justices now dead who played an important part in giving religion its special constitutional place—Black, Frankfurter, Douglas, and Murphy. Regrettably, the biographical material on other Justices now dead is much less helpful, and there is hardly any readily available for those still alive. Another nonjudicial source is sociological studies of American attitudes concerning religion. This material is relevant insofar as the Justices, even in their official actions, reflect popular opinion.

D. DEFINITIONS

A leading American dictionary defines religion primarily as "[t]he service and adoration of God . . . as expressed in forms of worship [and] in obedience to divine commands . . ."[34] God, in turn, is primarily defined as "[t]he Supreme Being; the eternal and infinite Spirit, Creator and Sovereign of the universe."[35] This, of course, is a traditional, theistic definition of religion. This definition adequately describes what the Justices have been writing about in their opinions. Most of

---

[34]WEBSTER'S NEW INTERNATIONAL DICTIONARY 2105 (2d ed. 1954).
[35]Id. at 1072.

the cases before the Supreme Court have involved traditional, theistic religion. The justifications articulated in their opinions, and the views of religion underlying them, have thus been tied to this definition.

Of course, the constitutional definition of religion, at least in the Free Exercise Clause, may be considerably broader than Webster's.[36] One implication of this study might be that the Religion Clauses should apply to activities beyond the accepted definition.

A distinction is drawn herein between "corporate" and "individual" religion. "Corporate religion" is used to mean group belief, worship, and morality. Typically, the group imposes a discipline on individual members by seeking to inculcate its views and to deter deviation from them. Certain corporate religions are highly expansionist. They aspire to gain converts, indeed to convert the entire world to their beliefs, worship, and morality. "Individual religion," on the other hand, is a matter of personal choice. Often its proponents disavow any desire to sway others; individuals are to be let alone to find their own way. And they evince a strong preference for religious pluralism, which assures that individuals have a wide range of choice and that they will be free of social pressures.

Thus financial aid to Catholic parochial schools exemplifies government action concerning corporate religion. The mission of these schools, at least traditionally, has been to indoctrinate children to the beliefs, worship, and morality prescribed by the Church.[37] On the other hand, drafting a conscientious objector with unique views of the moral universe exemplifies government action concerning individual religion. For example, in *United States v. Seeger*, the views of one of the objectors were based on what the Supreme Court described as "research in religious and cultural fields," including such thinkers as Plato, Aristotle, and Spinoza.[38]

The classification between "corporate" and "individual" is not always easy or evident. For example, the Jehovah's Witnesses have traditionally been a highly disciplined, proselytizing group. When they appeared before the Supreme Court in the early 1940s, however, the Justices mainly pictured them as individuals whose autonomous religious choices were at stake.[39] On the other hand, in *Wisconsin v.*

[36] See Torcaso v. Watkins, 367 U.S. 488, 495 & n.11 (1961).

[37] *E.g.*, Everson v. Board of Education, 330 U.S. 1, 22-23 (1947) (dissenting opinion).

[38] 380 U.S. 163, 166-67 (1965).

[39] *E.g.*, West Virginia Board of Education v. Barnette, 319 U.S. 624, 631 (1943) (complainants "stand on a right of self-determination in matters that touch individual opinion and personal attitude"); *id.* at 646 (social benefits insufficient "to justify the invasion of freedom and privacy

Yoder, the Court granted individual Amish parents an exemption from a burdensome governmental obligation. In doing so, however, Chief Justice Burger relied heavily on the fact that the corporate life of the Amish was jeopardized.[40]   There is also the need to distinguish between "secular" and "religious" matters. Herein, "secular" refers to the material conditions of our life in this world. The "religious," on the other hand, concerns our spiritual condition. As the dictionary definition suggests, it values worship of God and obedience to his commands for their own sake, without substantial regard to material, temporal consequences.

II. THE ARTICULATED JUSTIFICATIONS

A. PERSONAL FREEDOM

Following the constitutional revolution of 1937, the first cases to come before the Supreme Court under the Religion Clauses concerned certain inhibitions on religious behavior, especially that of the Jehovah's Witnesses. At that time, freedom of speech doctrine was already fairly fully developed, and freedom of religion was closely linked to freedom of speech in these early cases. Those challenging government hindrance of religion typically invoked both parts of the First Amendment, and when the Court granted their claims, it sometimes did so on both grounds.[41] Moreover, the Justices explicitly associated the two freedoms with each other. In *Prince v. Massachusetts*, for example, Justice Rutledge wrote for the Court: "All [the liberties of the First Amendment] are interwoven there. . . . [T]hey have unity in the charter's prime place because they have unity in their human sources and functionings. . . . [T]hese variant aspects of personality find inseparable expression in a thousand ways. They cannot be altogether parted in law more than in life."[42]

It is significant that in these cases the Justices offered justifications for the special constitutional place of religion analogous to prevalent freedom of speech justifications. In a most perceptive article on the demise of economic liberty under the Constitution, Professor

---

that is entailed or to compensate for a restraint on the freedom of the individual to be vocal or silent according to his conscience or personal inclination") (concurring opinion).

[40] 406 U.S. at 215-19.

[41] *E.g.*, Cantwell v. Connecticut, 310 U.S. 296 (1940); Murdock v. Pennsylvania, 319 U.S. 105 (1943).

[42] 321 U.S. 158, 164-65 (1944).

McCloskey summarized the justifications commonly offered for the special constitutional place of freedom of speech:

> [First] it is sometimes argued that laws limiting freedom of expression impinge on the human personality more grievously than do laws curbing mere economic liberty. . . . The individual has, *qua* individual, "the right to be let alone." . . . [Second,] another suggested rationale looks toward the community rather than the separate individuals within it. Progress, it is said, "is to a considerable extent the displacement of error which once held sway as official truth by beliefs which in turn have yielded to other beliefs."[43]

In the early cases, the Justices emphasized what Professor McCloskey called the community rationale. That is, they repeatedly espoused the view that in order to attain the truth or, if that is a quixotic objective, in order to serve social needs, a free marketplace of ideas is indispensable. Thus on the first hearing of *Jones v. Opelika*, Justice Reed wrote for the Court: "Too many settled beliefs have in time been rejected to justify this generation in refusing a hearing to its own dissentients."[44] Justice Murphy, concurring in *Martin v. Struthers*, stated: "If a religious belief has substance, it can survive criticism . . . with the aid of truth and reason alone. By the same method, those who follow false prophets are exposed."[45] In *West Virginia Bd. of Educ. v. Barnette*, Justices Black and Douglas in concurrence wrote: "If, as we think, [these beliefs] are groundless, time and reason are the proper antidotes for their errors."[46] Concurring in a case two decades later, *McGowan v. Maryland*, Justice Frankfurter stated that with freedom from government intervention, "[religious] beliefs and institutions shall continue, as the needs and longings of the people shall inspire them, to exist, to function, to grow, to wither, and to exert [influence] with whatever innate strength they may contain. . . ."[47]

This justification for the constitutional place of religion has, however, all but disappeared from Supreme Court opinions. Cases in which it might plausibly have been adduced tend to be treated as matters of speech. The major exception is *McDaniel v. Paty*, a freedom of religion case, in which Justice Brennan wrote in concurrence: "The

[43] *Economic Due Process and the Supreme Court*, 1962 SUPREME COURT REVIEW 34, 48, 49.

[44] 316 U.S. 586, 594 (1942).

[45] 319 U.S. 141, 149-50 (1943).

[46] 319 U.S. 624, 644 (1943).

[47] 366 U.S. 420, 461 (1961).

antidote which the Constitution provides against zealots who would inject sectarianism into the political process is to subject their ideas to refutation in the marketplace of ideas and their platforms to rejection at the polls."[48]

Professor McCloskey had doubts about this justification. He conceded that freedom of expression promotes social welfare, especially in a democracy, but insisted that freedom of economic activity, which has no special constitutional place, may be of comparable social value. He observed, for example:[49]

> Few historians would deny that the growth of entrepreneurial and occupational freedom helped to promote material progress in England in the eighteenth and nineteenth centuries and in America after the Civil War.... We can refuse to swallow whole the dogmas of nineteenth-century rugged individualism and can still believe that some freedom of occupation and economic choice is also instrumental to the development of [the] self-determining and sensitive citizen-governor.

In the later cases, there has been much greater emphasis on Professor McCloskey's other suggested rationale, the right to be let alone. Intrusion into parts of our psyche, especially the realm of religious belief, may be too painful and destructive of our psychological well-being. We must be spared certain trials of conscience. Thus, as early as *West Virginia Bd. of Educ. v. Barnette*, Justices Black and Douglas, concurring, deplored the "fear of spiritual condemnation" to which the youthful Jehovah's Witnesses were being subjected.[50] Two decades later, in *Braunfeld v. Brown*, Justice Stewart, in dissent, characterized the situation of the Orthodox Jews there as a "cruel choice."[51] In one of the conscientious objector cases, *Welsh v. United States*, Justice Black sided with those "whose consciences, spurred by deeply held moral, ethical, or religious beliefs, would give them no rest or peace."[52] Writing for the Court in a later conscientious objector case, *Gillette v. United States*, Justice Marshall referred repeatedly to the "hard choice," the "painful dilemma," of the defendants.[53]

Indeed, for years the Supreme Court has endorsed tests that apply this justification in cases involving hindrance of religion. The courts

---

[48] 435 U.S. 618, 642 (1978).
[49] McCloskey, note 43 *supra*, at 45–46.
[50] 319 U.S. at 644.
[51] 366 U.S. 599, 616 (1961).
[52] 398 U.S. 333, 344 (1970).
[53] 401 U.S. 437, 445, 453, 454 (1971).

ask whether the dissenter's objection is sincere, and how central it is to the dissenter's religious belief.[54] Most commentators seem to agree that these tests are appropriate if not applied too rigorously.[55]

Nevertheless, Professor McCloskey also objected to this justification. He acknowledged the "inarguable importance" to the human personality of freedom of expression generally but doubted that giving it a special constitutional place reflected the "real preferences of the commonality of mortals. . . . [M]ost men would probably feel that an economic right, such as freedom of occupation, was at least as vital to them as the right to speak their minds. Mark Twain would surely have felt constrained in the most fundamental sense, if his youthful aspiration to be a riverboat pilot had been frustrated by a State-ordained system of nepotism" such as the one upheld by the Supreme Court.[56]

B. SOCIAL HARM

In the earliest hindrance of religion cases, the Justices suggested another set of justifications for the special constitutional place of religion. The alternative justifications, however, were not fully elaborated until the Court began hearing cases concerning government aid to religion, in particular aid to religious education. The justifications offered in these cases were social harms peculiar to religion.

First. The Justices claimed that government action concerning religion is apt to degenerate into persecution. Justice Murphy, dissenting in *Prince v. Massachusetts*, put the point especially forcefully:[57]

> No chapter in human history has been so largely written in terms of persecution and intolerance as the one dealing with religious freedom. From ancient times to the present day, the ingenuity of man has known no limits in its ability to forge weapons of oppression for use against those who dare to express or practice unorthodox religious beliefs.

A majority of the Court adopted the point in *Everson v. Board of Educ.*, where Justice Black summarized the European past as follows:

---

[54] Cases discussed in TRIBE, AMERICAN CONSTITUTIONAL LAW 859-65 (1978).
[55] *Id.*
[56] McCloskey, note 43 *supra*, at 46.
[57] 321 U.S. at 175-76.

"Catholics had persecuted Protestants, Protestants had persecuted Catholics, Protestant sects had persecuted other Protestant sects, Catholics of one shade of belief had persecuted Catholics of another shade of belief, and all of these had from time to time persecuted Jews."[58] Later, in *Engel v. Vitale*, in the course of another historical essay, Justice Black took it as "historical fact that governmentally established religions and religious persecution go hand in hand."[59]

By "persecution," Justice Black and the others presumably meant something more than the mere hindrance of religion. Otherwise, in some cases they would have been saying hardly more than that hindrance of religion degenerates into itself. Presumably they meant cruelty, that is, the intentional infliction of a high degree of pain without a defensible justification. Thus, Justice Black, dissenting in *Zorach v. Clauson*, referred to "zealous sectarians entrusted with governmental power" who would "torture, maim and kill those they branded 'heretics,' 'atheists' or 'agnostics.'"[60] Concern about this degree of persecution has disappeared almost entirely from Supreme Court opinions in recent years.

Second. The Justices asserted that government action aiding or hindering religion is particularly damaging to social unity. They commonly linked this concern to the religious diversity of our people. Sometimes they contemplated outright social conflict among religious groups. For example, dissenting in *Board of Educ. v. Allen*, Justice Black claimed: "The First Amendment's prohibition against governmental establishment of religion was written on the assumption that state aid to religion and religious schools generates discord, disharmony, hatred, and strife among our people. . . ."[61] At other times they warned against the less dramatic harm of social separatism. Probably the most ardent expression of this concern was Justice Frankfurter's concurring opinion for four members of the Court in *McCollum v. Board of Educ.*[62] No one ever put the point more articulately, however, than Justice Brennan, concurring in *Abington School Dist. v. Schempp*, when he extolled "the training of American citizens in an atmosphere free of parochial, divisive, or separatist influences of any sort—an atmosphere in which children may

---

[58] 330 U.S. at 9.
[59] 370 U.S. 421, 432 (1962).
[60] 343 U.S. at 319. See KURLAND, note 27 *supra*, at 16.
[61] 392 U.S. 236, 254 (1968).
[62] 333 U.S. 203, 212 (1948).

assimilate a heritage common to all American groups and religions."[63]
At still other times, the Justices feared animosity toward government.
Thus, writing for the Court in *Engel v. Vitale*, Justice Black claimed
that "whenever government had allied itself with one particular form
of religion, the inevitable result had been that it had incurred the
hatred, disrespect and even contempt of those who held contrary
beliefs."[64]

Of the justifications for the special constitutional place of religion,
fear of social disunity has probably been the one most commonly
articulated. Nearly all of the Justices writing on the subject have
recited this fear. Some Justices, especially Frankfurter, have adduced
hardly any other justification.[65] Moreover, unlike the concern about
persecution, this justification continues to be invoked repeatedly.
Justice Harlan forcefully asserted the point when he wrote, concurring
in *Walz v. Tax Comm'n*, that undue "government involvement in
religious life . . . is apt to lead to strife and frequently strain a political
system to the breaking point."[66] Indeed, since *Lemon v. Kurtzman* and
Tilton v. Richardson, under the name "political entanglement," the
concern has been raised to an independent test of unconstitutionality
in cases involving aid to religion.[67] Justice Brennan has come to rely
heavily on this test, as in his recent opinion for the Court in *Larson v.
Valente*.[68]

On the other hand, some of its early exponents have begun to
express doubts about this test. Dissenting from invalidation of certain
aids to religious schools in *Meek v. Pittenger*, Chief Justice Burger
argued, "I see at least as much potential for divisive political debate in
opposition to the crabbed attitude the Court shows in this case."[69]
Likewise, Justice Powell asserted in a separate opinion in *Wolman v.
Walter:* "At this point in the 20th century we are quite far removed
from the dangers that prompted the Framers to include the
Establishment Clause in the Bill of Rights. . . . The risk . . . even of

---

[63] 374 U.S. 203, 242 (1963).

[64] 370 U.S. at 431.

[65] Father Murray charged Justice Frankfurter with having made a religion of secular unity.
Murray, *Law or Prepossessions?* 14 LAW & CONTEMP. PROB. 23, 37–40 (1949). Justice
Frankfurter's predilection was shared by two scholars who were close to him. Freund, *Public Aid
to Parochial Schools*, 82 HARV. L. REV. 1680, 1692 (1969); BICKEL, POLITICS AND THE WARREN
COURT , chs. 17, 18 (1965).

[66] 397 U.S. 664, 694 (1970).

[67] 403 U.S. 602, 622–23 (1971); 403 U.S. 672, 688–89 (1971).

[68] 456 U.S. at 251–53.

[69] 421 U.S. 349, 386 (1975).

deep political division along religious lines . . . is remote. . . ."[70] Even
Justice Brennan, an enthusiast for this justification, acknowledged in
McDaniel v. Paty that it is limited by other constitutional values such
as the free marketplace of religious ideas.[71]

As Dean Choper has pointed out, there are strong reasons to agree
with Chief Justice Burger and Justice Powell.[72] But even if government
aid to religion may still be a source of social strife, that alone does not
justify singling it out constitutionally. Proponents of this justification
must establish further that religion is significantly more divisive than
other sources of social discord, such as economic condition, race, sex,
and political ideology. There are strong reasons to think otherwise.

For example, in 1968, Professor Morgan argued cogently that while
the potential occasions for political conflict along religious lines were
increasing in number, the underlying sources of religious conflict in
our country were continuing to abate. He pointed to several
developments, including the waning importance of dogma, both
religious and atheistic; the willingness of Jews and conservative
Protestants to reconsider their commitment to strict separationism; the
greater acceptability of the Catholic Church following Vatican II; the
increasing social integration of people of different religions and
nonreligions; the convergence of Catholic parochial schools and other
kinds of American schooling.[73]

Even more probative is the comparison of religion with other
sources of social disunity. Our most divisive social issues since the
constitutional revolution of 1937 have included the completion of
industrial unionization in the late 1930s; McCarthyism in the early
1950s; the campaign for racial equality from the middle 1950s onward;
prolongation of the Vietnam War; and perhaps the Watergate scandal.
It is perhaps too early to tell whether abortion and other sexual issues
of the last decade should be added to this list. Even if so, they would
be the only ones inherently involving religion.

Some people may suppose that we have not had destructive religious
conflict in recent generations because of the very constitutional
restraints on aid to religion that this justification has produced. But the
most heated recent controversies over aid to religion have concerned

---

[70] 433 U.S. at 263.

[71] 435 U.S. at 640-42.

[72] *The Religion Clauses of the First Amendment: Reconciling the Conflict*, 47 U. PITT. L. REV.
673, 684-85 (1980); *cf. Defining "Religion" in the First Amendment*, 1982 U. ILL. L. REV. 579,
596.

[73] MORGAN, THE POLITICS OF RELIGIOUS CONFLICT 133-39 (1968).

religion in the public schools and financial aid to private religious schools, especially aid by the federal government. The first controversy was triggered by Supreme Court decisions forbidding aid to religion.[74] The second dispute, even though it came at a time when the constitutional restraints on financial aid were still highly uncertain, was relatively tame.[75]

Third. In the cases involving aid to religion, another justification for religion's special constitutional place eventually came to light. It had various aspects, but central to it was that corporate religion itself is apt to be bad for society and ought not to be encouraged. There were hints of this view in the early cases, but it was not until the late 1960s that two members of the first generation of Justices, Black and Douglas, expressed it clearly. On the whole, the other Justices have declined to join them.

The first charge against corporate religion was greed. Dissenting alone in *Walz v. Tax Comm'n,* Justice Douglas warned: "The religiously used real estate of the churches today constitutes a vast domain. . . . And the extent to which they are feeding from the public trough is alarming."[76] Joined by two other Justices in *Tilton v. Richardson,* Justice Douglas repeated these charges. He also quoted with approval the warning of a leading liberal Protestant that "with reasonably prudent management, the churches ought to be able to control the whole economy of the nation within the predictable future," and Justice Douglas added, "The mounting wealth of the churches makes ironic their incessant demands on the public treasury."[77]

The second charge against corporate religion was totalitarianism. That is, it tends to dominate the thinking and behavior of everyone within its reach. Thus, Justice Black, dissenting in *Board of Educ. v. Allen,* prophesied: "The same powerful sectarian religious propagandists who have succeeded in securing passage of the present law to help religious schools carry on their sectarian religious purposes can and doubtless will continue their propaganda, looking toward complete domination and supremacy of their particular brand of religion."[78] Likewise, in *Lemon v. Kurtzman,* for himself and Justice Black, Justice

---

[74] Engel v. Vitale, 370 U.S. 421; Abington School Dist. v. Schempp, 374 U.S. 203.

[75] MORGAN, note 73 *supra*, at 84–94.

[76] 397 U.S. at 714.

[77] 403 U.S. 672, 695, 696 (1971).

[78] 392 U.S. 236, 251 (1968).

Douglas quoted with approval an exposé of parochial schools: "The whole education of the child is filled with propaganda. . . . Their purpose is not so much to educate, but to indoctrinate and train, not to teach Scripture truths and Americanism, but to make loyal Roman Catholics. The children are regimented, and are told what to wear, what to do, and what to think."[79]

The third charge against corporate religion was political and scientific ignorance. Justice Douglas again was the leading spokesman for this view. In cases involving aid to religious schools, he strongly implied that teachers with corporate religious beliefs are bound to purvey unenlightened views. For example, dissenting in *Board of Educ. v. Allen*, he drew a series of harsh comparisons between nonreligious and religious schooling, including the following: "Is the slaughter of the Aztecs by Cortes and his entourage to be lamented for its destruction of a New World culture . . . or forgiven because the Spaniards 'carried the true Faith' to a barbaric people who practiced human sacrifice . . . ?"[80] Similarly, in *Lemon v. Kurtzman*, writing for himself and Justice Black, he observed: "One can imagine what a religious zealot, as contrasted to a civil libertarian, can do with the Reformation or with the Inquisition."[81]

Perhaps the clearest example of charging religion with promoting ignorance, however, was Justice Fortas's opinion for the Court in *Epperson v. Arkansas*.[82] The case involved a 1928 Arkansas statute that forbade public schools to teach that mankind evolved from a lower form of animals. Justice Fortas noted "the discomfort which the statute's quixotic prohibition necessarily engenders in the modern mind," and he also quoted with evident approval a sarcastic comment on such laws by Clarence Darrow, a defense lawyer in the famous Scopes trial, and the observation of two scholars that Charles Darwin's opponents had exhibited " 'a kind of phylogenetic snobbery [which led them] to think that Darwin had libelled the [human] race by discovering simian rather than seraphic ancestors.' "[83]

The target of many of these charges was the Catholic Church. It was nearly the only beneficiary of the statutes challenged in *Board of Educ. v. Allen* and *Lemon v. Kurtzman*, as the Court noted in the latter case,[84]

---

[79] 403 U.S. 602, 635 n.20 (1971).
[80] 392 U.S. at 261.
[81] 403 U.S. at 635-36.
[82] 393 U.S. 97 (1968).
[83] *Id.* at 102 & nn.9-10.
[84] 403 U.S. 602, 608, 610 (1971).

and it also had a very heavy stake in the outcome of *Walz v. Tax Comm'n* and *Tilton v. Richardson*. In *Board of Educ. v. Allen*, Justice Douglas directed nine pages of his dissenting opinion against the Catholic Church.[85] But the Church was not the only object of these charges. In *Epperson v. Arkansas*, this time over the objection of Justice Black, the blow fell on fundamentalist Protestants,[86] and in *Wisconsin v. Yoder*, Justice Douglas asserted that if a child "is harnessed to the Amish way of life by those in authority over him and if his education is truncated, his entire life may be stunted and deformed."[87]

C. SOCIAL BENEFIT

From almost the first of the cases, it was argued that aid to religion may be socially beneficial and, therefore, constitutional. These arguments moved to the fore in the 1960s with the coming of the second generation of Justices. It is possible that these arguments have had nothing to do with justifying the special constitutional place of religion. They may have asserted no more than that certain government interests limit the principle that government may not aid religion. Likewise, in the one hindrance of religion case cited in this section, *Wisconsin v. Yoder*, the passages quoted may have gone only to show that the government interest in limiting religion was inadequate. But these arguments are typically recited with a fervor appropriate to constitutional values. They constitute a new set of justifications for the principle that government should not hinder religion.

First. The Justices have suggested that the special constitutional place of religion is justified by historical tradition. Religion, including corporate religion, has been deeply entrenched in American social life. The way that government has treated religion has also become deeply entrenched. Traditionally, government has treated religion benignly, without unduly favoring it. Much social harm would be done if legislatures or courts were to disturb such a strong and persistent tradition.

In one of the most renowned passages in the whole line of cases, Justice Douglas, writing for the majority in *Zorach v. Clauson*, espoused this justification: "We are a religious people whose

---

[85] 392 U.S. at 258-64, 268-69.
[86] 393 U.S. 97.
[87] 406 U.S. at 245-46.

institutions presuppose a Supreme Being. . . . When the state
encourages religious instruction . . . , it follows the best of our
traditions. For it then respects the religious nature of our people and
accommodates the public service to their spiritual needs."[88] Numerous
Justices of the second generation have quoted this passage, while others
have put the point in their own words. Dissenting in one of the first
aid to religion cases, *McCollum v. Board of Educ.*, Justice Reed noted
"the many instances of close association of church and state in
American society" and added that "many of these relations are so much
a part of our tradition and culture that they are accepted without
more," and he then argued: "This Court cannot be too cautious in
upsetting practices embedded in our society by many years of
experience."[89] Dissenting in *Engel v. Vitale*, Justice Stewart asserted:
"What is relevant to the issue here is . . . the history of the religious
traditions of our people." He then defended certain aids to religion as
calculated "to recognize and to follow the deeply entrenched and
highly cherished spiritual traditions of our nation."[90] Even while
concurring in a decision invalidating certain aids to religion, *Abington
School Dist. v. Schempp*, Justices Goldberg and Harlan asserted:
"Neither government nor this Court can or should ignore the
significance of the fact that a vast portion of our people believe in and
worship God and that many of our legal, political and personal values
derive historically from religious teachings."[91] Chief Justice Burger,
writing for the Court in *Walz v. Tax Comm'n*, stated: "Few concepts
are more deeply embedded in the fabric of our national life, beginning
with pre-Revolutionary colonial times, than for the government to
exercise at the very least this kind of benevolent neutrality toward
churches and religious exercise. . . ."[92]

Two of our most profound scholars of the subject also espoused this
justification for religion's special constitutional place. In the last
section of his published lectures on religion and government in
American constitutional history, Professor Howe repeatedly invoked
as criteria for interpreting the Religion Clauses "America's way of
life," "the presuppositions of our society," "the society's history," "the
mandate of a recognized tradition," "the living practices of the

---

[88] 333 U.S. at 239, 256.
[89] 343 U.S. at 313-14.
[90] 370 U.S. at 446, 450.
[91] 374 U.S. at 306.
[92] 397 U.S. at 676-77.

American people," "the subtle gradations of past and present reality."[93]
Father Murray argued that the Religion Clauses are not theology but
only "a matter of prejudice."[94]

> [That is, their] origins are in our peculiar context and [their] validity
> has been demonstrated by the unique course of American
> history.... They are not destitute of reason, but their chief
> corroboration is from experience. They are part of the legacy of
> wisdom from the past; they express an ancestral consensus....
> [O]ther prejudices may obtain elsewhere—in England, in Sweden,
> in Spain. Their validity in their own context and against the
> background of the history that generated them does not disturb
> [our] conviction that [our] own prejudice, within [our] own context
> and against the background of [our] own history, has its own
> validity.

Dean Ely has raised troubling objections to the use of tradition as a
test for deciding constitutional cases. He doubts that we have any
traditions that are specific enough to help in deciding particular cases,
and even if we do, he doubts that judges have any special competence
to discern these traditions.[95] Ely's point is not uniformly compelling.
For example, tradition was an inconclusive guide in the cases involving
prayers and religious readings in the public schools,[96] but it seems to
have provided a firm basis for upholding tax exemptions for church
property.[97]

Second. The special constitutional place of religion is justified by its
social functions. The key opinion here is Justice Brennan's
concurrence in *Walz v. Tax Comm'n.* He contended that "religious
organizations ... uniquely contribute to the pluralism of American
society by their religious activities.... [E]ach group contributes to the
diversity of association, viewpoint, and enterprise essential to a
vigorous, pluralistic society."[98] Moreover, Justice Brennan asserted that
through their "public service activities," "religious organizations
contribute to the well-being of the community in a variety of
non-religious ways, and thereby bear burdens that would otherwise

[93] HOWE, note 18 *supra*, at 167, 168, 174, 176.

[94] MURRAY, note 19 *supra*, at 46, 47.

[95] ELY, note 16 *supra*, at 60–69.

[96] Compare Engel v. Vitale, 370 U.S. at 446–50 (Stewart, J., dissenting), with *Abington*, 374 U.S.
at 267–76 (Brennan, J., concurring).

[97] Walz v. Tax Comm'n, 397 U.S. at 676–80, 681–86.

[98] *Id.* at 689. See also *id.* at 693.

either have to be met by general taxation, or be left undone, to the detriment of the community."[99]

The latter justification was explicitly disavowed by the majority in *Walz v. Tax Comm'n*,[100] but in numerous contemporaneous and later cases involving aid to religious schools, other Justices have argued to the same effect. For example, dissenting in *Committee for Pub. Educ. v. Nyquist,* Chief Justice Burger, referred to the "debt owed by the public" to religious schools and the "wholesome diversity" that they engender.[101] Justice Rehnquist wrote sympathetically of the "service" to the public rendered by parents who send their children to private schools and of their efforts to "keep alive pluralism" in education.[102] Justice White called the private schools "an educational resource that could deliver quality education at a cost to the public substantially below the per-pupil cost of the public schools."[103]

These justifications apparently apply to freedom of association generally. As such, they are subject to the same objection that Professor McCloskey raised against the special constitutional place of freedom of expression: freedom of noneconomic association may promote social welfare, but freedom of economic association, which has no special constitutional place, may be of comparable social value.

Third. The Justices have suggested that religion, particularly corporate religion, may contribute to the development of good personal character. Hinted at in some early opinions, this view was expressed clearly in Chief Justice Burger's opinion for the Court in *Wisconsin v. Yoder.* Referring to the Amish community, he wrote, "Its members are productive and very law-abiding members of society; they reject public welfare in any of its usual modern forms," because the Amish inculcate "habits of industry and self-reliance," "qualities of reliability, self-reliance, and dedication." In short, "the Amish communities singularly parallel and reflect many of the virtues of Jefferson's ideal of the 'sturdy yeoman' who would form the basis of what he considered as the ideal of a democratic society."[104]

---

[99] *Id.* at 687. See also *id.* at 692.

[100] *Id.* at 674.

[101] 413 U.S. at 805.

[102] *Id.* at 812, 813.

[103] *Id.* at 818.

[104] 406 U.S. at 222, 224, 225–26. See also *id.* at 222–23 n.11.

D. RELIGIOUS JUSTIFICATION

In later cases before the Supreme Court, there appeared clearly for the first time a quite different justification for the special constitutional place of religion, a strictly religious justification. That is, religion's place was justified by the intrinsic value of religion. The justification rests on the foundation of traditional, theistic religion—obedience to God's will.

This justification has been hinted at by several Justices. For example, concurring in *Abington School Dist. v. Schempp,* Justice Brennan contended, for the first of many times, that the rule against aiding religion was partly meant to protect "the devout believer who fears the secularization of a creed which becomes too deeply involved with and dependent upon government."[105]

The only Justice to assert a religious justification at all explicitly, however, was Douglas. Dissenting in *McGowan v. Maryland,* he wrote: "The institutions of our society are founded on the belief that there is an authority higher than the authority of the State; that there is a moral law which the State is powerless to alter; that the individual possesses rights, conferred by the Creator, which government must respect."[106] Likewise, concurring in *Abington School Dist. v. Schempp,* he quoted the following with approval: "This pure Religious Liberty" . . . "declared [all forms of church-state relationships] and their fundamental idea to be oppressions of conscience and abridgments of that liberty which God and nature had conferred on every living soul."[107]

Justice Douglas's views may appear paradoxical. On the one hand, he was a strong advocate of the personal freedom justifications. No Justice of the Supreme Court since 1960 voted more consistently in favor of individual believers. In *Zorach v. Clauson,* he wrote the most famous judicial statement in defense of aid to corporate religion. He alone explicitly sought to justify protecting religion for its own sake. On the other hand, since 1960 his criticisms of corporate religion were by far the harshest of any Justice, and he consistently voted against it.

If his remarks in *Zorach v. Clauson* are put to one side, Justice Douglas's position is reasonably coherent. Justice Douglas was very sympathetic to religion as an individual activity. After 1960 he was

[105] 374 U.S. 203, 259 (1963).
[106] 366 U.S. at 562.
[107] 374 U.S. at 228.

very hostile to corporate religion, particularly corporate Christianity and Judaism. What happened to Douglas between *Zorach v. Clauson* and the 1960s? This essay is not concerned with judicial biography, so I shall do no more than to suggest two possibilities.[108] First, he may genuinely have changed his mind about corporate religion in the interim. Second, what he said in *Zorach v. Clauson* may have been an oddity, reflecting political ambition or some other personal impulse.

III. UNDERLYING VIEWS OF RELIGION

A. THE FIRST GENERATION

1. *Social harm.* The views of corporate religion of Justices Black and Douglas were unusually explicit. They thought that much of corporate religion is socially harmful. It is apt to be greedy, totalitarian, and politically and scientifically backward. These observations applied especially to the Catholic Church. Justice Black may have been somewhat more sympathetic to fundamentalist Protestantism.

Biographical sources confirm the evidence of the opinions. Justice Black's son wrote of his father's strong suspicion of the Catholic Church and, to a lesser extent, of public religion generally.[109] Similarly, in his autobiography, Justice Douglas expressed his contempt for conventional American religion and its chief spokesmen.[110] The sociological evidence may point in the same direction. Characteristically, foes of aid to religion outside the Supreme Court were quite hostile to the most rigorous of the large corporate religions, the Catholic Church.[111]

A similar unease about corporate religion was apt to underlie the views of other Justices, that government action concerning religion often degenerates into "persecution." Persecution is a highly pejorative term. Moreover, the blame fell on corporate religion. Of course, under some circumstances, nonreligious persons might persecute the religious. But concern about persecution was mainly expressed in cases involving aid to religion, and there the initiators of government action were the Catholic Church, mainline Protestant denominations, and branches of Judaism.

---

[108] Louisell, *The Man and the Mountain: Douglas on Religious Freedom*, 73 YALE L. J. 975, 993-96 (1964); Note, *The "Released Time" Cases Revisited*, 83 YALE L. J. 1202, 1228 nn.151-55 (1974).

[109] BLACK, MY FATHER 104, 176 (1975).

[110] GO EAST, YOUNG MAN 14-16, 109-11, 203-04 (1974).

[111] SANDERS, PROTESTANT CONCEPTS OF CHURCH AND STATE 161-65, 212-16 (1964).

It is harder to infer unease about corporate religion from the most widely espoused justification, that government action concerning religion is apt to lead to social disunity and strife. In our country, causing social conflict, at least if it is nonviolent, has not been regarded nearly as unfavorably as causing persecution. It has seemed more a concomitant of pluralism and freedom. Moreover, the responsibility for social conflict need not fall entirely on the initiators of government action. It may also be caused by undue sensitivity on the other side. Opponents of government action concerning religion may be unduly ready to fight about it.

There is wide scope for disagreement about the underlying character of religion that fosters social conflict. Many Justices refer to religion as an unusually sensitive matter. Concurring in *Abington School Dist. v. Schempp*, Justice Brennan called religious questions "highly charged."[112] Justice Powell, writing for the Court in *Committee for Pub. Educ. v. Nyquist*, described the issue of church-state relations as "deeply emotional."[113] In the majority opinion in *Committee for Pub. Educ. v. Regan*, Justice White acknowledged that cases involving government aid to religion "stir deep feelings."[114] The Justices have not tried to explain why religion happens to be so sensitive a matter.

Nevertheless, underlying this justification, too, may be an unfavorable view of corporate religion. Among the first generation of Justices, social conflict along religious lines was often linked with the propensity of corporate religion to promote persecution. Justices Black and Douglas went even further, tying religious conflict to the other faults that they found in corporate religion—greed, totalitarianism, and barbarism. Other Justices implicitly agreed, as in Justice Rutledge's famed dissent in *Everson v. Board of Educ.*, where social conflict was associated with the appetite of corporate religion for financial aid:[115]

> Public money devoted to payment of religious costs, educational or other, brings the quest for more. It brings too the struggle of sect against sect for the larger share or for any. . . . The end of such strife cannot be other than to destroy the cherished liberty. The dominating group will achieve the dominant benefit; or all will embroil the state in their dissensions.

---

[112] 374 U.S. at 241.
[113] 413 U.S. at 797.
[114] 444 U.S. 646, 662 (1980).
[115] 330 U.S. at 53, 54.

The Justices' fear of religious divisiveness was greatly dispropor-tionate both to the evidence on which they relied and to the reality. There is strong reason to doubt that recent government action concerning religion is especially apt to cause social strife. What little evidence the Justices have adduced, mainly the religious history of Europe and America before 1791, is scarcely pertinent now. An underlying distaste for corporate religion may have caused their special sensitivity to religious disputes.

If the Justices were uneasy about corporate religion, it is understandable that they would prefer to emphasize its supposed tendency to produce social conflict. The Supreme Court has held that government may not act toward religion for religious (or antireligious) purposes. "Religious purposes" presumably include value judgments about religion that relate to religion alone. Thus the other justifications for not aiding religion—its greed, totalitarianism, barbarism, and cruelty—are based on religious reasons. Their use violates the very rule against religious purposes to which they ostensibly give rise.

Justice Murphy's views on the matter appear paradoxical. He deplored the tendency of government action concerning religion to degenerate into persecution. This view was apt to reflect an unease about corporate religion and particularly about the Catholic Church. Yet Murphy was a Catholic. Nonjudicial sources suggest that although Murphy was a devoted member of the Church, he was anticlerical from childhood, a staunch Jeffersonian, and a syncretistic humanist. His main commitment was to certain Catholic moral values rather than to the institution.[116]

2. *Personal freedom.* When the Justices of the first generation turned from justifications involving social harm to those involving personal freedom, their view of religion also changed. Their main concern was no longer to prevent aid to religion but to prevent its hindrance. Accordingly, their view of religion was no longer unfavorable but indifferent or even favorable. The kind of religion of which they were thinking also changed. No longer were they concerned with corporate religion, particularly large religious groups. Instead, they had in mind the religion of individuals and of a plurality of small sects.

This may simply have reflected the facts of the cases. Hindrance of religion cases did not affect the Catholic Church or the mainline Protestant denominations. Rather, in virtually every case in the first

---

[116] HOWARD, MR. JUSTICE MURPHY 4, 444–45, 455–56 (1968).

generation, the victims of government action were Jehovah's Witnesses. The particular justifications offered by the Justices suggested that the kind of religion they thought worthy of constitutional protection was individual, pluralistic religion. First, the Justices suggested that people have a strong psychological need to be let alone in religious matters. This justification emphasized individual autonomy, the person's independence from external authority. Second, the Justices contended that social welfare requires a free marketplace of religious ideas. Here they extolled vigorous competition among a plurality of ideological alternatives.

To be sure, the Justices might have thought that the only danger lay in government hindrance of religion. They might have accepted with equanimity private ecclesiastical authority and a nonestablished universal church. Yet the justifications they offered seem to apply equally to private interference with individualism and pluralism.

The Justices repeatedly emphasized that they were protecting individual choice. Thus, concurring in *West Virginia Bd. of Educ. v. Barnette,* Justice Murphy touted "the freedom of the individual to be vocal or silent according to his conscience or personal inclination."[117] In his famed dissent in *Everson v. Board of Educ.,* Justice Rutledge stated: "The realm of religious training and belief remains, as the Amendment made it, the kingdom of the individual man and his God. It should be kept inviolately private."[118] Writing for the Court in *Engel v. Vitale,* Justice Black opposed government involvement in religious matters on the ground that "religion is too personal."[119] Justice Douglas was the most explicit. Dissenting in *McGowan v. Maryland,* he approvingly quoted Dean Pound to the effect that the Puritans who "helped shape our constitutional law" " 'put individual conscience and individual judgment in the first place.' "[120] And in his dissent in *Wisconsin v. Yoder,* he asserted, "Religion is an individual experience"; objected to allowing parents to "impose [their] notions of religious duty upon their children"; and hoped that Amish children would not be "harnessed to the Amish way of life by those in authority over [them]."[121]

---

[117] 319 U.S. at 646.

[118] 330 U.S. at 57-58. Father Murray called this passage an "echo" of "Madison's radically individualistic concept of religion." See Murray, note 65 *supra,* at 29-30 & n.29.

[119] 370 U.S. at 432.

[120] 366 U.S. at 563.

[121] 406 U.S. at 242, 243, 245-46.

To highlight the religious individualism of these passages, it is helpful to compare another opinion from the period, Justice Jackson's dissent in *Everson v. Board of Educ.* There he thoughtfully compared the Catholic policy of "early and indelible indoctrination in the faith and order of the Church" with the common Protestant assumption that "after the individual has been instructed in worldly wisdom he will be better fitted to choose his religion," and Jackson in no way suggested that the individualistic view of religion was preferable.[122]

The opinions also repeatedly stressed the pluralism of American religious life. This was sometimes treated not simply as a fact but as a value producing affirmative benefits. For example, concurring in *Martin v. Struthers*, Justice Murphy wrote: "[U]nity and strength are best accomplished, not by enforced orthodoxy of views, but by diversity of opinion through the fullest possible measure of freedom of conscience and thought."[123] Even more pointedly, Justice Douglas asserted in dissent in *Walz v. Tax Comm'n*: "[O]ne of the mandates of the First Amendment is to promote a viable pluralistic society. . . ."[124] Justice Frankfurter valued pluralism for a less affirmative reason. In his opinion for the Court in *Minersville School Dist. v. Gobitis*, he endorsed the "plurality of principles which, as a matter of history, underlies protection of religious toleration."[125] Whereas Justices Murphy and Douglas viewed pluralism as a desirable expression of personal freedom, Frankfurter valued it as a defense against the social harms of religion.[126]

Nonjudicial sources confirm the evidence provided by the opinions. Justice Black's son recorded his father's view that the only true religion is personal religion.[127] Most other Americans of Black's time also viewed religion as properly individual and pluralistic.[128]

One must not overstate the extent to which the Justices of the first generation, even those appointed by President Roosevelt, were disposed to rule against corporate religion or in favor of individual believers. For example, a majority of them voted to uphold financial aid to religion in the form of bus transportation for children attending

---

[122] 330 U.S. at 23-24.

[123] 319 U.S. at 150.

[124] 397 U.S. at 716.

[125] 310 U.S. 586, 594 (1940).

[126] Professor Kurland made the same point more emphatically in *Foreword—Church and State in the United States*, 1966 WIS. L. REV. 215, 216.

[127] BLACK, note 109 *supra*, at 176.

[128] HERBERG, PROTESTANT, CATHOLIC, JEW 85-87 (rev. paperback ed. 1960); SANDERS, note 111 *supra*, at 199-203.

parochial schools.[129] They also upheld a criminal statute that forbade young Jehovah's Witnesses to sell religious literature on the streets.[130] In both cases, the Justices found the health and safety of children, a conventional New Deal cause, to be overriding. Moreover, at least one Justice of this generation, Reed, was consistently more sympathetic to corporate than to individual religion. He joined the dissenters in a number of cases in which the majority of the Court invalidated hindrances of Jehovah's Witnesses,[131] and he alone dissented from the decision invalidating released-time religion courses in the public schools.[132]

* * *

During the first generation, many of the Justices appear to have had a coherent set of underlying views about religion. The group included four of the leaders of the Court in religion cases during the period—Black, Douglas, Rutledge, and, in a special way, Frankfurter. Their views were characteristic of social progressivism. When the Justices thought of corporate religion, it was apt to strike them as socially harmful, and the larger and more rigorously corporate the religion, the more harmful it might be. Insofar as they thought of religion sympathetically, it was apt to be individual, pluralistic religion.

On the latter point, there was some disagreement within this group. Justice Frankfurter appears to have had an unfavorable view of religion generally. He apparently thought that individual religion is also often harmful and that even at its best it is not of much positive social value. He cherished it mainly as a barrier against the threat of corporate religion. The others of this group, especially Douglas, appear to have viewed religion as a generally valuable human activity which, however, becomes corrupted in corporate form: they thought that individual religion is of positive social value and worthy of special protection.

That the Justices held these underlying views of religion can be substantiated in another way. For Justices, such as Frankfurter, who have the generally unfavorable view of religion, the appropriate cardinal rule in constitutional cases might be no aid to religion. The

---

[129] Everson v. Board of Education, 330 U.S. 1.

[130] Prince v. Massachusetts, 321 U.S. 158.

[131] E.g., Murdock v. Pennsylvania, 319 U.S. at 117; Martin v. Struthers, 319 U.S. at 154; Barnette, 319 U.S. at 642; and see Follett v. Town of McCormick, 321 U.S. 573, 578 (1944).

[132] McCollum v. Board of Education, 333 U.S. at 238.

Supreme Court should readily grant any plausible claim that government is improperly aiding religion. Moreover, the Court should be wary of granting a claim that government is hindering religion; if religious believers are given a constitutional exemption from secular burdens, as in *Sherbert v. Verner* or *Wisconsin v. Yoder*, the effect may be to aid religion. The Court should be most ready to grant claims of hindrance of religion when the effect of burdening some religions is to advantage others.

All of Justice Frankfurter's votes arguably conformed to this pattern. The only substantial claim of aid to religion that he rejected concerned the Sunday closing laws, where he was convinced that the main purpose and effect of the laws was to promote social welfare rather than religion.[133] The only claims of hindrance of religion that he supported involved aid to other religions, or freedom of expression generally.[134]

Justice Frankfurter came close to expressly asserting that the rule in constitutional cases should be no aid to religion. In his famed dissent in *West Virginia Bd. of Educ. v. Barnette*, he argued that sectarians ought not to be exempted from secular burdens by "waving the banner of religious freedom. . . . Otherwise the doctrine of separation of church and state, so cardinal in the history of this nation and for the liberty of our people, would mean not disestablishment of a state church but the establishment of all churches and of all religious groups."[135]

Justice Frankfurter is a special case. Ordinarily the leading apostle of judicial restraint, as in *West Virginia Bd. of Educ. v. Barnette*, hardly anyone in the Supreme Court's history has been more eager to invalidate government aid to religious groups. Moreover, no one on the Court was more inclined to base his position on the single justification of preventing social disunity and strife. On these points, he may have had a significant influence on certain other members of the Court, particularly his allies, Justices Jackson and Harlan.

From his own experience, Justice Frankfurter was acutely aware that in this country, Jews, even those brought up in obscurity, might rise to political and cultural eminence, and he was intensely grateful for this circumstance. He attributed it largely to the absence of religious divisions in our society, which he said depended on at least two

---

[133] McGowan v. Maryland, 366 U.S. at 459.
[134] Torcaso v. Watkins, 367 U.S. at 496; Cantwell v. Connecticut, 310 U.S. 296.
[135] 319 U.S. at 655.

conditions. First, the government must continue to seek to strengthen our social unity, especially through the public schools. Second, religious groups must suppress their inclination to resist the secular demands of the rest of society.[136]

So much may be reasonably obvious. A deeper insight into Justice Frankfurter's views of corporate religion may have been provided by his admirer, Alexander Bickel. Writing while Frankfurter was still alive and active, Bickel suggested that, because of its polarizing tendencies, corporate religion is a public nuisance. We are "bound to suffer" it because of the Constitution. But government ought to strive hard to replace religion with a unifying secular ethos, and the public schools are a key instrument in this policy.[137]

The sociological evidence suggests that we might expect Justice Frankfurter to have thought in this way. Professor Herberg noted that many American Jews believe that corporate Christianity, even when private, inevitably tends to cause discrimination against Jews. Accordingly, they favor not just the exclusion of corporate religion from government programs, but its elimination from private culture as well.[138]

On the other hand, for Justices, such as Douglas, who favor individual although not corporate religion, the appropriate policy might be strenuous protection of minorities against both aid to religion and its hindrance. The Supreme Court should readily uphold any substantial claim that government is aiding religion, since for political reasons government benefits are generally given to corporate religion. The Court also should readily uphold any substantial claim that government is hindering religion, since for the same political reasons government burdens are generally imposed on individual religion. The Court should uphold government action concerning religion only when, because of peculiar political circumstances, its effect is to hinder corporate religion or aid individual religion.

In every second-generation case in which he participated, Justice Douglas voted in accord with this prescription. For example, he was the only Justice who would have invalidated Sunday closing laws and tax exemptions for church property as forbidden aids to religion.[139] And he was the only Justice who would have invalidated, as a

---

[136] HIRSCH, THE ENIGMA OF FELIX FRANKFURTER 191-93, 195 (1981).

[137] BICKEL, note 65 *supra*, at ch. 17.

[138] HERBERG, note 128, *supra*, at 239.

[139] McGowan v. Maryland, 366 U.S. at 561; *Walz*, 397 U.S. at 700.

forbidden hindrance of religion, certain limitations on the exemption of conscientious objectors from military service.[140] In the only case involving a claim of hindrance of religion in which Douglas gave less than full support to the claim, *Wisconsin v. Yoder*, he regarded the state law as a potential protection for dissenting individual members of the religious group.[141] Other Justices whose votes, and expressions of viewpoint, approximated this pattern were Black, Rutledge, and from the second generation, Marshall.

The Justices of the first generation by no means originated these views. They can be traced back to the period in which our Constitution was framed. In the years from the start of the War of Independence to the adoption of the Constitution and the Bill of Rights, corporate religion generally, and the established churches in particular, were in sharp decline. Two of the most potent forces in American religious life were Enlightenment rationalism, typified by Thomas Jefferson, and the free church Protestants, heirs of Roger Williams. These forces concurred in hostility to established churches and a strongly individualistic view of religion.[142]

This attitude was also part of the climate of opinion among enlightened people in the decade or two immediately before the first generation of cases. During the 1920s and 1930s, the social effectiveness of the mainline Protestant denominations declined sharply. At the same time, there was a rise in rationalist skepticism, typified by the defenders of modern science at the time of the Scopes trial, Clarence Darrow and H. L. Mencken. There was also a marked increase in the popularity of the minority sects.[143]

B. THE SECOND GENERATION

1. *Social benefit.* Many Justices of the second generation have taken substantially different underlying views of religion. They have been more favorably disposed toward corporate religion. They have showed this by espousing different justifications for the special constitutional place of religion. First, they have largely avoided the justifications involving social harm that most clearly disparage corporate religion.

---

[140] *Gillette*, 401 U.S. at 463, 470.

[141] 406 U.S. at 241.

[142] AHLSTROM, A RELIGIOUS HISTORY OF THE AMERICAN PEOPLE, ch. 23 (1975); MURRAY, note 19 *supra*, at 49-53; SANDERS, note 111 *supra*, at 185-91.

[143] Handy, *The American Religious Depression, 1925-35*, 29 CHURCH HIST. 3 (1960); HERBERG, note 128 *supra*, at 46-47, 53, 259-60.

Justice Fortas's opinion for the Court in *Epperson v. Arkansas* is the only one by a latter-day Justice to emulate the open hostility of Justices Black and Douglas. Concern about persecution has also largely disappeared from opinions of the second generation of Justices. Some Justices have even begun to question the claim that corporate religion contributes to social disunity.

Second, they have offered new justifications based on the social benefits of corporate religion. These include religion's contribution to social diversity, to public welfare programs, and to the development of good moral character. These justifications are far more favorable to corporate religion even than the personal freedom justifications.

This more approving view of corporate religion is also demonstrated by the kind of cases in which the new justifications have been offered. The cases have not involved hindrance only of individuals or small sects. On the contrary, they have mainly concerned aid to the Catholic Church, mainline Protestant denominations, and branches of Judaism.

The Justices have expressed the new view of corporate religion in their opinions. Insofar as the older opinions referred to religion sympathetically, it was almost always individual, autonomous religion that the Justices had in mind. More recently, however, they have showed an appreciation for corporate aspects of religion, for external influences on a person's religious development such as church and family. The new view was probably expressed most clearly in Chief Justice Burger's opinion for the Court in *Wisconsin v. Yoder*. There, the Court explicitly undertook to defend, not individual religious belief, but "the way of life of the Amish faith community" and "parental control over the religious upbringing and education of their minor children."[144] Justice Douglas, the inveterate individualist, strongly objected to this aspect of the Court's decision.[145]

There is also evidence that some Justices of the second generation may be less sympathetic than their predecessors to individual religion. Dissenting in *Welsh v. United States*, the three Justices who have probably been most favorable to corporate religion, Burger, Stewart, and White, gave a relatively narrow definition of "religious belief" in the conscientious objector statute and defended their definition as constitutional.[146] Likewise, in *Wisconsin v. Yoder*, Chief Justice Burger

---

[144] 406 U.S. at 218, 231.

[145] *Id.* at 241–46.

[146] 398 U.S. 333, 367 (1970).

emphasized that the claim of the Amish was "[a]ided by a history of three centuries as an identifiable religious sect and a long history as a successful and self-sufficient segment of American society," and he explicitly distinguished a hypothetical group "claiming to have recently discovered some 'progressive' or more enlightened process for rearing children for modern life."[147]

One must not overstate the extent of the shift in the Justices' view of religion. Some Justices of the second generation have apparently continued to think of the religion protected by the Constitution from government hindrance as individual, pluralistic religion. For example, writing for the Court in *Gillette v. United States,* Justice Marshall somewhat sarcastically compared "conventional piety and religiosity" with "the imperatives of a personal faith,"[148] and dissenting in *Trans World Airlines, Inc. v. Hardison,* he expressed his preference for "a society that truly values religious pluralism."[149] Likewise, in *Larson v. Valente,* Justice Brennan's majority opinion echoed Justice Frankfurter's endorsement of "a multiplicity of sects" as a defense against oppressive corporate religion.[150]

Moreover, in cases involving government aid to religion, some Justices have continued to express concern about its tendency to produce social disunity and strife. In recent years, the cases evoking these expressions of concern have mainly involved aid to Catholic parochial schools. Indeed, in *Lemon v. Kurtzman,* Chief Justice Burger emphasized that the case was mainly about such schools,[151] as did Justice Powell in two successor cases.[152] It is possible that even the Justices of the second generation who view corporate religion favorably and are not hostile to the Catholic Church are still uneasy about religious institutions that are thought to be unduly disciplined and expansionist. In other words, even these Justices may share with their predecessors a limited predilection for individual autonomy and pluralism in religion.

---

[147] 406 U.S. at 235. See also the Supreme Court's denials of certiorari in cases involving eccentric religious beliefs and practices, some of which are cited in LOCKHART, KAMISAR, & CHOPER, CONSTITUTIONAL LAW 1232, 1234, 1235 (5th ed. 1980). Professor Kurland claimed that in *Yoder* the Court favored corporate religion ahead of the individual conscience. *The Supreme Court, Compulsory Education, and the First Amendment's Religion Clauses,* 75 W. VA. L. REV. 213, 237-38 (1973).

[148] 401 U.S. at 454.

[149] 432 U.S. 63, 87 (1977).

[150] 456 U.S. at 245.

[151] 403 U.S. at 608.

[152] *Nyquist,* 413 U.S. at 768; Sloan v. Lemon, 413 U.S. 825, 830 (1973).

This should come as no surprise. Sociological evidence suggests that people outside the Supreme Court who favor some government aid to religion still have felt uneasy about certain features of Catholicism, including parochial schools.[153]

Finally, the Supreme Court of the second generation has not invariably ruled in favor of corporate religion and against individual believers. On the contrary, most of the cases invalidating religion in the public schools and financial aid to religious schools were decided after 1960. The same is true of the cases that have exempted religious dissenters, even those belonging to no religious group, from nonreligious legal requirements.

2. *Religious justifications.* The social benefit justifications of the second generation of Justices are revealing in another way. The benefits attributed to corporate religion may properly be called secular benefits. Social diversity, public welfare programs, industrious character—these are apt to be regarded primarily as temporal, material goods, not as means of worshiping and obeying God. In other words, even the second generation of Justices seems to have viewed the religion worthy of being protected by the Constitution primarily as a secular activity.

This may be somewhat confirmed by at least one major opinion. Concurring in *Walz v. Tax Comm'n,* Justice Brennan, after reciting the contributions of corporate religion to social diversity and public welfare programs, sought to refute the argument that the means of attaining these benefits are essentially religious: "The means churches use . . . are the same means used by any purely secular organization— money, human time and skills, physical facilities."[154]

The same is true of the personal freedom justifications, insofar as they too imply that religion is beneficial. The advantages attributed to individual, pluralistic religion—psychological well-being and socially useful ideas—are apt to be regarded primarily as temporal, material values. Likewise, the means of achieving these benefits, psychological "space" and competitive ideological markets, are secular processes. Indeed, the very propensity to identify freedom of religion with freedom of speech implies that religion is primarily a secular activity. It assumes that thought and expression, whether in the realm of politics, science, or religion, are basically alike.[155]

---

[153] SANDERS, note 111 *supra,* at 263-65.

[154] 397 U.S. at 693.

[155] Professor Howe agreed with the last point. See HOWE, note 18 *supra,* at 109.

I do not claim that all of the Justices have viewed religion primarily as a secular activity. At least this was not true of Justice Douglas. To be sure, he was inclined to judge corporate religion by its greed and lack of social enlightenment. But toward the end of his life, he gave a religious justification for the special constitutional place of individual religion. That is, he based its place ultimately on conformity with God's will. This is confirmed in his nonjudicial writings. On the one hand, his main criticism of corporate religion was its complicity in economic inequality and abuse of the natural environment.[156] On the other hand, Justice Douglas expressed a commitment to the universe as God's creation that, although somewhat pantheistic by Jewish or Christian standards, was essentially religious.[157]

It is possible that other Justices have also viewed religion primarily as a religious activity, or at least have seriously entertained the possibility. Supposing that they did, it is understandable that they have still refrained from giving religious justifications for the special constitutional place of religion. The Supreme Court has laid down the rule that government may not act toward religion for religious purposes. Presumably, "religious purposes" include contentions about God's will and value judgments that relate to religion alone. If so, not to hinder religion because that is what God wills is to act for religious reasons. This justification violates the very rule against religious purposes to which it ostensibly gives rise. The same may be said of some Justices' view that religion, particularly corporate religion, contributes, to an unusual extent, to the development of good moral character, a major social benefit.

Nevertheless, it is doubtful that many of the Justices have shared Douglas's view of religion as a religious activity. People who believe in God and are convinced that religion is a transcendent human activity are also capable of seeing what it has in common with secular activities. They are apt to balk, however, at reciting the secular benefits of religion as if religion were primarily a means of obtaining those benefits as many Justices have done.[158]

Nonjudicial sources confirm here, too, the evidence of the opinions. Justice Black's son reported that for his father, ethical conduct was all there was to true religion.[159] Likewise, Justice Murphy, a devoted

---

[156] GO EAST, YOUNG MAN, note 110 *supra*, at 14-16, 110-11, 203-04.

[157] *Id.* at 112-14, 204-05; Louisell, note 108 *supra*, at 975-79.

[158] See C. S. LEWIS, THE SCREWTAPE LETTERS 108-09 (paperback ed. 1962), for the truly religious viewpoint.

[159] BLACK, note 109 *supra*, at 173-75.

Catholic, identified his religious belief with democratic values, the crux of both being "brotherhood and equality, human dignity and natural rights."[160] Professor Herberg described Americans of the 1950s as strongly secular in their religious attitudes.[161]

In their opinions, the Justices must often distinguish between religious and secular activities. This need not mean that they regard the two as essentially dissimilar. It need only mean that in their eyes, religion has distinctive temporal, material characteristics.

*   *   *

Like their predecessors, many Justices of the second generation appear to have a coherent set of underlying views about religion. This group has included three of the most articulate members of the Supreme Court in recent religion cases—Burger, Stewart, and White. Their views are characteristic of moderate social conservatism. They tend to regard religion as socially useful, especially corporate religion. True to the American religious tradition, they prefer corporate religion that is not highly disciplined and expansionist.

Concerning individual religion, there could be a difference of view within this group. Some Justices might have a generally favorable view of all religion. If so, they would think that individual religion is also socially useful and worthy of special protection. Other Justices might view religion as a valuable human activity which, however, becomes warped when it shrinks to individual dimensions. That is, individual religion is only irregularly worthy of special protection.

For Justices who have a generally favorable view of all religion, the appropriate cardinal rule might be no hindrance of religion. The Supreme Court should readily grant any substantial claim that government is hindering religion. Moreover, it should be wary of granting a claim that government is improperly aiding religion, for if government cannot aid religion, for example, by granting tax exemptions to religious property, the effect may be to hinder religion. The Court should be most ready to grant claims of improper aid to religion when the effect of benefiting some religions is to disadvantage others.

There have been no Justices since 1937 whose votes have consistently fit this pattern. During the 1960-62 Supreme Court Terms, however, when the Court heard an unusual number of important religion cases, Justice Stewart seems to have adopted no

---

[160] HOWARD, note 116 supra, at 455-56.
[161] HERBERG, note 128 supra, at 74-84.

hindrance as his predominant rule. He voted to uphold the Sunday closing laws and at the same time was one of only three Justices who would have exempted Orthodox Jews;[162] twice, he was the only Justice who would have upheld prayer in the public schools;[163] and he joined in exempting Seventh-Day Adventists from Saturday work-requirements.[164]

During these terms, Justice Stewart also came close to asserting expressly that the cardinal rule should be no hindrance of religion. In dissent in *Abington School Dist. v. Schempp*, he argued that the practice invalidated as an aid to religion should have been understood rather as a means of relieving religion of a hindrance:[165]

> Unlike other First Amendment guarantees, there is an inherent limitation upon the applicability of the Establishment Clause ban on state support to religion. . . . [T]he limitation [is] one which [is] itself compelled by the free exercise guarantee. . . . [T]he central value embodied in the First Amendment . . . is the safeguarding of an individual's right to free exercise of his religion. . . .

On the other hand, for Justices who favor corporate but not individual religion, the appropriate policy might be deference to majorities concerning both aid to religion and its hindrance. The Supreme Court should be wary of granting claims that government is improperly aiding religion, since government benefits are generally given to corporate religion. The Court should also be wary of granting claims that government is improperly hindering religion, since government burdens are generally imposed on individual religion. The Court might most properly invalidate government action concerning religion when, because of peculiar political circumstances, its effect is to hinder corporate religion.

There have been no Justices since 1937 whose votes have consistently fit this pattern. Chief Justice Burger, however, has come reasonably close. In the last dozen years, since *Lemon v. Kurtzman* and *Tilton v. Richardson*, he has not voted to uphold a single claim of improper aid to religion.[166] And in the most important of the cases in which he voted to uphold a claim of hindrance of religion, *Wisconsin*

---

[162] Braunfeld v. Brown, 366 U.S. at 616.

[163] Engel v. Vitale, 370 U.S. at 444; *Abington*, 374 U.S. at 308.

[164] Sherbert v. Verner, 374 U.S. at 413.

[165] 374 U.S. at 311, 312.

[166] *E.g.*, *Nyquist*, 413 U.S. at 798; Wolman v. Walter, 433 U.S. at 255; Stone v. Graham, 449 U.S. 39, 43 (1980).

v. Yoder, he regarded the religion being hindered as strongly corporate.[167] Other Justices whose votes and views approximate this pattern are White and, from the first generation, Reed.

Again, these views hardly originated with the Justices of the second generation. Although we often think of Enlightenment rationalism and free church Protestantism as the main forces in American religion at the time that the Constitution and the Bill of Rights were adopted, some of the major founders of our nation, including John Adams, defended establishment of religion on the state level.[168] They avowed, in the words of the Massachusetts Declaration of Rights, that "the happiness of a people, and the good order and preservation of civil government, essentially depend upon piety, religion and morality."[169] Indeed, the greatest founder of all, George Washington, not only shared this view of private religion but was the leading proponent of an American "civil religion." He repeatedly used his public position to preach that we owe thanks and obedience to the God who watches over our new nation.[170]

This attitude was also part of the climate of opinion in the decade immediately preceding the second generation of cases. During the 1940s and 1950s, Americans overwhelmingly approved of corporate religion. They identified it mainly with secular benefits and values. At the same time, they cherished religious individualism and pluralism. Accordingly, they remained uneasy about certain features of the Catholic Church.[171]

C. OCTOBER TERM 1982

At the end of the 1982 Term, the Supreme Court decided three important religion cases. In *Bob Jones University v. United States,*[172] the Court upheld, against a claim of hindrance of religion, the denial of exemption from federal income taxes to private religious schools that practice racial discrimination. In *Mueller v. Allen,*[173] it upheld, as a permissible aid to religion, a Minnesota income tax deduction for certain expenses of sending children to elementary and secondary

---

[167] 406 U.S. at 215-19.

[168] GAUSTAD, A RELIGIOUS HISTORY OF THE UNITED STATES 127-28 (1966).

[169] Quoted in HOWE, note 18 *supra,* at 26-27.

[170] BELLAH, BEYOND BELIEF 173-75 (1970).

[171] HERBERG, note 128 *supra,* at chs. 1, 4, 5, 9-11; SANDERS, note 111 *supra,* at 262-70.

[172] 76 L. Ed. 2d 157 (1983).

[173] 103 S. Ct. 3062 (1983).

schools, including private religious schools. In *Marsh v. Chambers*,[174] it again upheld an aid to religion—the Nebraska practice of opening each legislative session with a prayer by a paid chaplain.

The two decisions upholding aids to religion further confirm my thesis about the underlying views of religion held by the second generation of Justices. In the former case, the beneficiaries were religious elementary and secondary schools, a major component of corporate religions such as the Catholic Church. In the latter case, the practice supported mainstream corporate religion generally. The legislative chaplain for the previous sixteen years was a Presbyterian minister whose prayers were "in the Judeo-Christian tradition," with "elements of the American civil religion."[175] Moreover, at least the former decision signified an important shift in favor of upholding aid to corporate religion. Just ten years before, the Court had struck down programs that were not markedly different.[176]

It is even more important that the Court's opinions in these cases carried forward the views expressed in preceding decisions. First, in the school aid case, a majority of the Court openly disparaged the main social harm justification, that government action concerning religion is apt to cause undue social strife. After repeating a prior assertion of this justification, Justice Rehnquist quoted with approval Justice Powell's skeptical response in *Wolman v. Walter:* "At this point in the 20th century we are quite far removed from the dangers that prompted the Framers to include the Establishment Clause in the Bill of Rights. . . . The risk . . . even of deep political division along religious lines . . . is remote. . . ."[177] Later, Justice Rehnquist characterized the test based on this justification—the political entanglement test—as a "rather elusive inquiry," claimed that it had been "interpreted differently in different cases," and most important of all, attempted to confine its application to a limited class of aid cases.[178]

Second, the majority strenuously embraced the social benefit justifications. In the school aid case, Justice Rehnquist twice repeated the arguments that private religious schools perform a social service at reduced public expense and diversify the educational alternatives available to the public.[179] Indeed, he significantly elaborated on the

---

[174] 103 S. Ct. 3330 (1983).
[175] 103 S. Ct. at 3336 & n.14.
[176] *Nyquist*, 413 U.S. 756; Sloan v. Lemon, 413 U.S. 825.
[177] 103 S. Ct. at 3069.
[178] *Id.* at 3071 n.11.
[179] *Id.* at 3067, 3070.

latter justification, claiming that "private schools may serve as a benchmark for public schools, in a manner analogous to the 'TVA yardstick' for private power companies."[180] And in the legislative prayer case, Chief Justice Burger relied almost wholly on the argument from tradition. The practice, he wrote, "is deeply embedded in the history and tradition of this country" and "has become part of the fabric of our society."[181] He ended the discussion by once again repeating Justice Douglas's dictum in *Zorach v. Clauson*.[182]

Third, the Court, more clearly than before, expressed a predominantly secular view of religion. It went so far as to characterize legislative prayer as nonreligious "conduct" which only incidentally "harmonizes with religious canons."[183] The dissenters understandably responded by reciting a more conventional view: "It is prayer which distinguishes religious phenomena from all those which resemble them or lie near to them, from the moral sense, for example, or aesthetic feeling."[184]

Meanwhile, in the same dissenting opinion, Justice Brennan came closer than before to expressing an underlying view of religion characteristic of the first generation. Not only did he again stress the social harm of strife and alienation along religious lines that follows government aid to religion,[185] but he also echoed the emphasis placed by earlier Justices such as Black on the intensely individual nature of true religion.[186] Indeed, he may have taken another step toward espousing Justice Douglas's religious justification for the special constitutional place of religion.[187]

It is more difficult to show a coincidence between the recent decision rejecting the claim of hindrance of religion—the *Bob Jones* decision—and the Justices' underlying views of religion. The ruling on the constitutional issue was virtually unanimous. Indeed, Justices with ostensibly different views of religion concurred in a single opinion. Perhaps for that reason, the opinion was relatively unrevealing. Chief Justice Burger disposed of the constitutional issue in two pages, with no reference to the justifications for the special place of religion. Under

---

[180] *Id.* at 3067.
[181] 103 S. Ct. at 3332, 3336.
[182] *Id.* at 3336.
[183] *Id.* at 3335.
[184] *Id.* at 3345.
[185] *Id.* at 3342-43.
[186] *Id.* at 3342; see *id.* at 3350 n.47.
[187] *Id.* at 3342, 3345, 3349.

these circumstances, it is enough to show that the holding is not inconsistent with the views of religion attributed to the Justices.

For nearly all of the Justices, whatever their generations, religion is primarily a secular activity. That is, they are apt to view religion according to its temporal, material consequences. At the same time, Justices of both generations have been firmly committed to racial equality as a secular value. To be sure, the extent of their commitment has varied, and so may their reasons. For social progressives characteristic of the first generation, racial equality is presumably a matter of absolute morality. For moderate conservatives of the kind who have dominated the second generation, it may be valued more as a useful unifying ethos under particular conditions. In any event, both generations of Justices might be disposed to view religious groups that practice racial discrimination, especially in education, as unworthy either of government aid or of protection from government hindrance.

This predilection might be strongly reinforced by the way in which the Justices categorized the government action and the religious groups involved. Heirs of the first generation might view the case as mainly concerning the propriety of aid to corporate religion. At stake was a valuable tax exemption for groups that, in the eyes of these Justices, may have all of the failings of disciplined, expansionist religion. Foes would accuse them of being greedy for government financial benefits, totalitarian in dealing with their students,[188] and benighted in their racial attitudes. They practice the very kind of religion that, in this view, would be apt to subject our society to persecution and civil war.

On the other hand, Justices characteristic of the second generation might view the case more nearly as what it purported to be, a claim of hindrance of religion by dissenting sects. The groups involved will suffer a competitive disadvantage by losing the tax exemption, and these Justices might feel that they deserve to do so because they exemplify the harm that supposedly results from excessive religious individualism. To be sure, like the Amish, fundamentalist Protestant groups may seem to these Justices to be socially beneficial corporate religions in many ways. On the point of racial equality, however, they are heretics who disrupt social harmony by disavowing a major article of the American creed.

---

[188] 76 L. Ed. 2d at 166.

E. DONALD ELLIOTT

INS v. CHADHA: THE ADMINISTRATIVE CONSTITUTION, THE CONSTITUTION, AND THE LEGISLATIVE VETO

> The law is administered by able and experienced men, who know too much to sacrifice good sense to a syllogism. . . .
> [OLIVER WENDELL HOLMES, JR. (1881)][1]

> [T]he fact that a given law or procedure is efficient, convenient, and useful in facilitating functions of government, standing alone, will not save it if it is contrary to the Constitution.
> [CHIEF JUSTICE WARREN BURGER (1983)][2]

Holmes's view that policy, not logic, shapes the law is particularly apt for constitutional law. There are some who deplore that judges base constitutional decisions on their personal views of good policy,[3] but hardly anyone denies that judges are in fact guided by "sense" as well as "syllogism." Judicial policymaking remains controversial in many areas of constitutional law, but in some it has long since been widely accepted that judgment as well as reason should influence judicial decisions. Historically cases involving the separation of powers have been in this category.

The main line of the tradition, dominant at least since *McCulloch v. Maryland,*[4] is that practical effects, not abstract formulas alone, should

E. Donald Elliott is Associate Professor, Yale Law School.

AUTHOR'S NOTE: I would like to thank Stephen Carter, Owen Fiss, Joe Goldstein, Jerry Mashaw, Peter Schuck, Cass Sunstein, and Harry Wellington for their helpful comments on an earlier draft.

[1] HOLMES, THE COMMON LAW 32 (Howe ed. 1963).

[2] Immigration and Naturalization Service v. Chadha, 103 S. Ct. 2764, 2780-81 (1983).

[3] See, *e.g.,* Easterbrook, *Substance and Due Process,* 1982 SUPREME COURT REVIEW 85, 125; KURLAND, POLITICS, THE CONSTITUTION, AND THE WARREN COURT (1970).

[4] 4 Wheat. 316, 407 (1819). For a discussion of McCulloch v. Maryland from a separation of powers perspective, see TRIBE, AMERICAN CONSTITUTIONAL LAW, 228-29 (1978).

guide the Court in separation of powers cases. This is not to say, of course, that "syllogism" counts for naught; to go that far would be to repudiate the core of constitutionalism. Instead, an unresolved tension between sense and syllogism has sustained constitutional jurisprudence in separation of powers cases at least since Holmes.

The conflict between instrumentalism and interpretivism—between policy and text—is, of course, not limited to separation of powers cases. Tension between these competing approaches to interpreting the Constitution underlies most areas of law. But in separation of powers cases, where few deny that both sense and syllogism must have weight, the conflict often breaks out into the open. Speaking for a unanimous Supreme Court in upholding the Iranian hostage release agreements, Justice Rehnquist wrote:[5]

> [I]t is doubtless both futile and perhaps dangerous to find any epigrammatical explanation of how this country has been governed.... [W]e freely confess that we are obviously deciding only one more episode in the never-ending tension between ... a world that presents each day some new challenge ... and the Constitution ... which no one disputes embodies some sort of system of checks and balances.

In this area, the Court has sought to maintain a balance between generalizations and practical accommodations. Thus, Chief Justice Burger's formalistic opinion for the Court in *Immigration and Naturalization Service v. Chadha* [6] came as a shock. In *Chadha*, the Court held unconstitutional the legislative veto in §244(c)(2) of the Immigration and Nationality Act,[7] which authorized either House of Congress to disapprove by resolution the Attorney General's decision to suspend deportation of an alien. For years, distinguished legal scholars as well as officials of the Department of Justice have questioned the constitutionality of the legislative veto,[8] arguing that it

---

[5] Dames & Moore v. Regan, 101 S. Ct. 2972, 2976-78 (1981).

[6] 103 S. Ct. 2764 (1983).

[7] 8 U.S.C. §1254(c)(2) (1976). "Legislative veto" herein refers to a statutory provision by which Congress has reserved to itself, or to one of its houses or committees, the power to override actions by officials of the Executive branch or of independent agencies.

[8] The list of scholars who have testified in congressional hearings that the legislative veto is probably unconstitutional is a virtual Who's Who of American constitutional law, and includes Charles Black, Alexander M. Bickel, Philip B. Kurland, and Laurence Tribe. Statements by scholars and officials of the Department of Justice questioning the constitutionality of the legislative veto are collected in McGowan, *Congress, Court and Control of Delegated Power*, 77 COL. L. REV. 1119, 1136-45 (1977); BOLTON, THE LEGISLATIVE VETO: UNSEPARATING THE POWERS 9-13, 43-46 (1977).

infringes on the President's veto power, and in the case of the one-house veto, that it violates the principle of bicameralism as well. What was astonishing about *Chadha* was not the result, but the scope and inflexibility of the Court's opinion.[9]

Justice White, who alone dissented from the merits of the Court's separation of powers analysis,[10] proclaimed *Chadha* to be of "surpassing importance" because it "sounds the death knell for nearly 200 other statutory provisions in which Congress has reserved a 'legislative veto'.... Today's decision strikes down in one fell swoop provisions in more laws enacted by Congress than the Court has cumulatively invalidated in its history."[11] Justice Powell, concurring in the judgment on the "narrower ground"[12] that the legislative veto in this particular case infringed on judicial power, seconded Justice White's assessment: "The Court's decision ... apparently will invalidate every use of the legislative veto."[13]

Dissenting opinions are a notoriously inaccurate source of insight into the implications of Supreme Court decisions, but in this instance, the predictions were quickly confirmed. Only days after *Chadha*, the Court affirmed summarily two decisions declaring legislative vetoes unconstitutional in circumstances arguably distinguishable from *Chadha*.[14] Again Justice White dissented, protesting that "[w]here the

---

[9] *Cf.* Tribe, note 4 *supra*, at 162-63: "There is some appeal in the argument that any congressional veto of an executive or administrative act taken pursuant to a prior delegation must constitute either a usurpation of the judicial function of interpreting the scope of the original delegation, or a change in that delegation's initial scope. If it is the former, the legislative veto impermissibly interferes with the judicial power; if it is the latter, the legislative veto is tantamount to a new law and must therefore be passed by both Houses and submitted to the President for his approval or veto. *But the difficulty with any such syllogistic approach is that it appears to exalt rigid formulas in an area where doctrine must be responsive to basic problems of political accountability and due process rather than to any mechanistic separation of functions* [emphasis added]." See also McGowan, note 8 *supra*, at 1152: "[C]onventional legal analysis alone is unlikely to establish definitively the constitutionality vel non of the one-house veto or similar legislative control devices. In the final accounting, one's position is likely to depend much more on a subjective assessment of how our constitutional system will best function than on close textual analysis of constitutional language...."

[10] Justice Rehnquist filed a separate dissenting opinion, in which Justice White joined, questioning the Court's determination that the legislative veto was severable. 103 S. Ct. at 2816-17.

[11] *Id.* at 2792, 2810-11.

[12] 103 S. Ct. at 2789.

[13] *Id.* at 2788.

[14] Process Gas Consumers Group v. Consumer Energy Council, 103 S. Ct. 3556 (1983), *affirming* Consumer Energy Council of America v. FERC, 673 F.2d 425 (D.C. Cir. 1982); United States Senate v. FTC, 103 S. Ct. 3556 (1983), *affirming* Consumers Union of U.S., Inc. v. FTC, 691 F.2d 575 (D.C. Cir. 1982).

[legislative] veto is placed as a check upon the actions of the independent regulatory agencies, the Article I analysis relied upon in *Chadha* has a particularly hollow ring."[15] The Court, however, refused to hear argument in the cases, or even to remand them to the lower courts for reconsideration in the light of *Chadha*. It appeared, for the moment at least, that the Court had definitively disposed of the legislative veto in *Chadha*. The popular press concurred.[16]

Something even more fundamental than the ruling on the legislative veto was at issue in *Chadha*. According to the Court, the case turned on the plain wording of "[e]xplicit and unambiguous provisions of the Constitution [which] prescribe and define the respective functions of the Congress and of the Executive in the legislative process."[17] Justice White denounced the majority's approach, however, as "reflect[ing] a profoundly different conception of the Constitution than that held by the Courts which sanctioned the modern administrative state."[18] To the majority, on the other hand, Justice White seemed to be offering a mere "utilitarian argument" that the legislative veto is a "useful 'political invention',"[19] an argument which the Court dismissed as raising policy considerations not rising to the level of constitutional significance. Thus, the difference between Justice White and the majority goes deeper than disagreement over the legislative veto. It goes to the very nature of the Constitution and to how judges are to go about relating it to the rapidly evolving structure of the "modern administrative state."

I

A. THE FACTUAL BACKGROUND

Jagdish Rai Chadha came to the United States from Kenya on a British passport in 1966. After his student visa expired, the Immigration and Naturalization Service (INS) began deportation proceedings. Chadha conceded that he had overstayed his visa and applied for suspension of deportation on grounds of extreme hardship.[20]

---

[15] *Consumer Energy Council*, 103 S. Ct. at 3558.

[16] *E.g.*, Greenhouse, *Supreme Court, 7-2, Restricts Congress's Right to Overrule Actions by Executive Branch*, NEW YORK TIMES, June 24, 1983, at 1, col. 6; *An Epic Court Decision*, TIME, July 4, 1983, at 12.

[17] 103 S. Ct. at 2781.

[18] *Id.* at 2810.

[19] *Id.* at 2781.

[20] Under §244(a)(1) of the Immigration and Nationality Act, the Attorney General "may, in his discretion" suspend deportation and grant permanent resident status to an alien who has been

An INS immigration judge ruled in June 1974 that Chadha's request for a suspension of deportation should be granted, in part because he had been born of Indian parents and "it would be extremely difficult, if not impossible, for [Chadha] to return to Kenya or go to Great Britain by reason of his racial derivation."[21]

The suspension of deportation was duly reported to Congress as required by statute,[22] and on December 16, 1975, the House of Representatives, without debate or recorded vote, adopted a resolution disapproving the suspension of deportation in the cases of Chadha and five other aliens. The chairman of the House Subcommittee on Immigration, Citizenship, and International Law, who sponsored the resolution of disapproval, stated that after reviewing 340 cases in which suspension of deportation had been granted by the INS, the subcommittee had concluded that in six of them the statutory criteria had not been met, "particularly as it relates to hardship."[23] Under the terms of the Immigration and Nationality Act, if either house of Congress passes a resolution "stating in substance that it does not favor the suspension of . . . deportation, the Attorney General shall thereupon deport such alien. . . ."[24] Thus, the House resolution had the effect of overruling the INS's order suspending Chadha's deportation and reasserting the INS's statutory duty to deport him.

Chadha filed a petition for judicial review of the INS proceedings, arguing, among other things, that the legislative veto of the Attorney General's suspension of deportation was unconstitutional, and the United States Court of Appeals for the Ninth Circuit agreed. Although the INS had supported Chadha's position in the court of appeals that the legislative veto was unconstitutional, it filed an appeal to the Supreme Court, and the House and Senate both filed petitions for certiorari.

The constitutionality of the legislative veto had been challenged before, but the Supreme Court had always declined to reach the constitutional issues.[25] In *Chadha*, however, the Court brushed aside

---

in the United States for seven years, is of good moral character, and whose deportation would "in the opinion of the Attorney General, result in extreme hardship" to the alien or other persons including "a spouse." 8 U.S.C. §1254(a)(1) (1976).

[21] 634 F.2d 408, 411 (9th Cir. 1980), *affirmed*, 103 S. Ct. 2764 (1983).

[22] 8 U.S.C. §1254(c)(1) (1976).

[23] 103 S. Ct. at 2771.

[24] §244(c)(2), 8 U.S.C. §1254(c)(2) (1976).

[25] Buckley v. Valeo, 424 U.S. 1, 140 n.176 (1976); *cf. id.*, 257, 284-86 (White, J., concurring); see also Atkins v. United States, 556 F.2d 1028 (Ct. Cl. 1977); Clark v. Valeo, 559 F.2d 642 (D.C. Cir.) (*en banc*) (*per curiam*), *aff'd sub nom.* Clark v. Kimmitt, 431 U.S. 950 (1977).

several threshold issues that offered promising opportunities for avoiding the merits.[26] The Court's handling of two threshold issues was particularly curious. First, the Court held that the INS was an "aggrieved party" entitled to appeal under 28 U.S.C. §1252 (1976), although in the court of appeals the INS had supported Chadha's position that the legislative veto was unconstitutional.[27]

The Court's rejection of a second threshold argument was even more dubious. In 1980, Chadha married a United States citizen, and thus became eligible to apply for permanent resident status as an immediate relative of a United States citizen.[28] Congress suggested that the Supreme Court should decline to reach the merits of Chadha's constitutional claims since other, narrower avenues of relief were now available.[29] The Court brushed this point aside with the curt rejoinder that whether Chadha would prevail if he pursued alternative avenues of relief was "speculative."[30] But in other contexts which do not involve constitutional issues, and where the grounds for judicial restraint are therefore less weighty, the Court routinely requires the exhaustion of administrative remedies even though it is not certain that the claimant will prevail.[31] It is hard to understand why the Court should rule on a major constitutional issue if routine statutory grounds for granting relief could make the constitutional ruling unnecessary.

Chadha's marriage to a citizen also provided a second reason for declining to reach the merits, which the Court apparently overlooked. The stated explanation for the House's exercise of its veto was that there had been an insufficient showing of hardship in Chadha's case. Hardship "to a spouse" is an additional statutory ground for granting suspension of deportation. If the Court had remanded to the INS for reconsideration, it is possible, perhaps even likely, that the INS could have found additional new grounds for suspending Chadha's deportation based on the hardship to his spouse. It is doubtful that the House would have exercised its legislative veto over a new suspension of deportation based on hardship to Chadha's spouse, since this ground is far less innovative and controversial than the racial discrimination rationale originally relied on by the INS.

---

[26] 103 S. Ct. at 2772–80.

[27] 103 S. Ct. at 2777.

[28] See 8 U.S.C. §§1255(a) and 1203(a)(2) (1976).

[29] Cf. Ashwander v. TVA, 297 U.S. 288, 346 (1936) (Brandeis, J., concurring)

[30] 103 S. Ct. at 2777.

[31] See Myers v. Bethlehem Shipbuilding Corp., 303 U.S. 41 (1938).

The Court in *Chadha* was not compelled to decide the constitutional issues, but had to overcome formidable obstacles to reach them. The fact that several other cases challenging legislative vetoes were already on the Court's docket may explain why the Court chose to face the constitutional issues squarely in *Chadha*,[32] but it does not excuse the Court's action in reaching out to decide important questions of constitutional law unnecessarily. The function of the case or controversy requirement in disciplining the Court's view of the law might have been better served had the Court waited for another case.

B. THE COURT'S REASONING

The Supreme Court's analysis of the legislative veto in *Chadha* turns on relatively narrow constitutional issues. The Constitution contains three "[e]xplicit and unambiguous provisions"[33] governing lawmaking by Congress. Before a bill becomes a law, it must be "presented" to give the President an opportunity to exercise his veto.[34] This presentment requirement applies not only to "Bills," but also to "[e]very Order, Resolution, or Vote to which the Concurrence of the Senate and House of Representatives may be necessary."[35] In addition, the Constitution vests the legislative power of the United States in a bicameral legislature composed of a Senate and a House of Representatives.[36] Before a bill becomes a law, it must be passed by both houses of Congress. The central question presented in *Chadha* was whether the procedural requirements for passing laws— presentment and bicameral action—also apply to the legislative veto.[37]

---

[32] Consumer Energy Council v. FERC, 673 F.2d 425 (D.C. Cir. 1982), *app. docketed sub nom.* Process Gas Consumers Group v. Consumer Energy Council, 51 U.S.L.W. 3002 (April 29, 1982) (Nos. 81-2008 etc.), *aff'd*, 103 S. Ct. 3556 (1983); Consumers Union v. FTC, 691 F.2d 575 (D.C. Cir. 1982) (*en banc*), *app. docketed sub nom.* U.S. Senate v. FTC, 51 U.S.L.W. 3470 (Dec. 12, 1982) (Nos. 82-935 etc.), *aff'd*, 103 S. Ct. 3556 (1983); see also Martin, *The Legislative Veto and the Responsible Exercise of Congressional Power*, 68 VA. L. REV. 253, 294 n.105 (1982).

[33] 103 S. Ct. at 2781.

[34] "Every Bill which shall have passed the House of Representatives and the Senate, shall, before it become a Law, be presented to the President of the United States; . . ." Art. I, sec. 7, cl. 2.

[35] Art. I, sec. 7, cl. 3.

[36] Art. I, sec. 1.

[37] See Scalia, *The Legislative Veto: A False Remedy for System Overload*, REGULATION 19, 20 (Nov./Dec. 1979): "The validity of the legislative veto, then, turns quite simply upon whether it in reality constitutes lawmaking" which must comply with the requirements of presentment and bicameralism. It has been suggested that the legislative veto may also violate a more general

Chief Justice Burger's opinion for the Court in *Chadha,* which was joined by five other Justices, gives three reasons for concluding that the legislative veto is legislative action of the kind to which the Constitution's presentment and bicameralism requirements apply. None of the three is ultimately persuasive.

1. *Presumption.* The Court begins with the proposition that the Constitution divides the powers of the federal government into "three defined categories, legislative, executive and judicial."[38] While conceding that they are not " 'hermetically' sealed from one another,"[39] the Court contends that the powers of each branch are "functionally identifiable" and that "[w]hen any Branch acts, it is presumptively exercising the power the Constitution has delegated to it. See *Hampton & Co. v. United States,* 276 U.S. 394, 406 (1928)."[40]

The Court's reasoning is unpersuasive for several reasons. In the first place, the Court is mistaken when it asserts that the framers "defined" the categories legislative, executive, and judicial in the Constitution. Not only is the Court incorrect—the Constitution does not define these terms—but the slip is revealing. The Court's conceptualistic approach to analyzing the issues conflicts with the more pragmatic approach which the framers actually espoused. In Federalist No. 37, for instance, Madison warns that any attempt to define the categories legislative, executive, and judicial in abstract, theoretical terms is bound to fail.[41] The most that can be said is that the Constitution uses the terms "legislative," "executive," and "judicial," but that rather than attempt to define these concepts in the abstract, the framers left to subsequent history the working out of the relationships among them.

Nor is the Court's conceptualistic approach to the issues in *Chadha* supported by the case which it cites, *Hampton & Co. v. United States.* *Hampton* is a 1928 decision in which the Court upheld a statute giving

---

constitutional "separation of powers principle." Consumer Energy Council v. FERC, *supra,* 673 F.2d at 470-77 (Wilkey, J.). The Supreme Court specifically declined to rest its analysis in *Chadha* on separation of powers principles as "an abstract generalization," but focused instead on specific provisions of the Constitution. 103 S. Ct. at 2781.

[38] *Id.* at 2784.

[39] *Ibid.*

[40] *Ibid.*

[41] "Experience has instructed us that no skill in the science of government has yet been able to discriminate and define with sufficient certainty its three great provinces—the legislative, executive and judiciary; or even the privileges and provinces of the different legislative branches. Questions daily occur in the course of practice, which prove the obscurity which reigns in these subjects, and which puzzle the greatest adepts in political science." Federalist No. 37 (Madison), in THE FEDERALIST PAPERS (Fairfield ed. 1961).

the President power to modify tariffs against a claim that it constituted an impermissible delegation of legislative powers to the Executive.[42] If anything, the result in *Hampton* contradicts the Court's claim that the powers of each branch are "functionally identifiable." Nor is there any discussion of "presumptions" in *Hampton*, the proposition for which the Court ostensibly cites it. In *dictum*, Chief Justice Taft does say that it would be "a breach of the National fundamental law if Congress gives up its legislative power and transfers it to the President."[43] On a superficial, linguistic level, then, the case might be read to support the proposition that when Congress acts it must be exercising "legislative" power. It is one thing, however, to deploy a presumption of regularity to conclude that when Congress acts it is within the scope of authorized legislative powers, but quite another to rely on presumption to support the conclusion that a branch has acted in an unconstitutional manner.[44]

Even on its own terms, however, the Court's presumption sweeps in too much and proves too little. Conceding that the legislative veto is an exercise of Article I legislative power (as opposed to executive or judicial powers) does not resolve, but only poses the question before the Court. The Constitution does not require presentment to the President of all congressional actions within Article I legislative power. On the contrary, the text restricts presentment to "Bills" and to "Every Order, Resolution or Vote to which the Concurrence of the Senate and House of Representatives may be necessary. . . ." The most that can be said about the drafting history is that the Constitutional Convention wanted the presentment requirement to apply to bills and to functional equivalents of bills.[45] Not every exercise of Article I legislative power comes within these categories, as the Court concedes.[46] Congress has developed extensive powers to oversee the Executive's administration of the laws, for example, as an exercise of

---

[42] 276 U.S. at 404.

[43] *Id.* at 406.

[44] See also 103 S. Ct. at 2791 n.7 (Powell, J., concurring: "The Court's presumption provides a useful starting point, but does not conclude the inquiry.")

[45] Madison wanted to eliminate the possibility that bills could avoid the President's veto by being passed under a different label, 103 S. Ct. at 2782; *id.* at 2799-2800 (White, J., dissenting); 5 ELLIOT'S DEBATES 431 (1845) ("if the negative of the President was confined to bills, it would be evaded by acts under the form and name of resolutions, votes &c."). See Martin, note 32 *supra*, at 295.

[46] See 103 S. Ct. at 2784. But *cf. ibid.*: "It emerges clearly that the prescription for legislative action in Art. I, §§1, 7 represents the Framers' decision that the legislative power of the Federal government be exercised in accord with a single, finely wrought and exhaustively considered procedure."

Article I legislative powers,[47] but no one would suggest that these forms of legislative oversight by congressional committees require presentment to the President for his veto.

The question to be decided in *Chadha* was not whether the legislative veto is an exercise of Article I legislative power, but whether it is an exercise of Article I legislative power of the kind that requires presentment and bicameral action.[48] The Court's presumption that the legislative veto is an exercise of Article I legislative power should only frame, rather than decide, the issue.

2. *Altering legal rights.* The Court does not rely on presumption alone. It goes on to argue that the House resolution vetoing the suspension of Chadha's deportation was "essentially legislative in purpose and effect."[49] The Court's formalistic approach to the issues is disappointing, but given its source, not surprising. The Court bases its analysis on a nineteenth-century congressional report which construed the Presentment Clause as applicable to any matter which is "legislative in its character and effect."[50] The core of the Court's reasoning is conceptual and formalistic: the legislative veto is "legislative" because it has the effect of "altering legal rights."[51]

The legislative veto "alters legal rights," however, only because the Court chooses to characterize its effect that way. The Court's

[47] McGrain v. Daugherty, 273 U.S. 135, 174 (1927). See also Barenblatt v. United States, 360 U.S. 109, 111 (1959). For a general description of the panoply of oversight techniques available to Congress, see generally KIRST, GOVERNMENT WITHOUT PASSING LAWS (1969); SENATE COMM. ON GOVERNMENT OPERATIONS, STUDY OF FEDERAL REGULATION, II: CONGRESSIONAL OVERSIGHT OF REGULATORY AGENCIES (Comm. Print 1977).

[48] See Scalia, note 37 *supra*. The narrow textual issue is whether the legislative veto is a resolution "to which the concurrence of the Senate and House of Representatives may be necessary. . . ." Art. I, sec. 7, cl. 3. It is hard to question that a two-house veto comes under this language. By definition, a two-house veto is a vote to which the concurrence of both houses is required. Therefore, it is hard to escape the conclusion that a two-house veto not presented to the President is clearly unconstitutional. A one-house veto, however, like that at issue in *Chadha*, is a different matter. In the case of the one-house veto, a statute authorizes one house to act through a resolution to which the concurrence of both houses is not literally "necessary." Antonin Scalia points out that for this reason, at least on a superficial level, the one-house veto stands on a stronger constitutional footing than a legislative veto under a statute which explicitly requires the concurrence of both houses. Scalia contends, however, that this argument is "obviously wrong because it assumes that the Founding Fathers were careful to preserve the presidential veto as a check upon disguised legislative action by both houses of Congress, but were quite willing to let a single house proceed unchecked." Scalia, note 37 *supra*, at 22. In addition, Scalia also argues that a legislative veto requires bicameral action. With due respect, Scalia's analysis, like the Court's in *Chadha*, is circular. It implicitly assumes that the legislative veto, like passage of a statute, is the sort of legislative action that requires the "check" of a presidential veto and bicameral adoption.

[49] 103 S. Ct. at 2784.

[50] S. Rep. No. 1335, 54th Cong., 2d Sess. 8 (1897), quoted, 103 S. Ct. at 2784. See also Martin, note 32 *supra*, at 296 n.107.

[51] 103 S. Ct. at 2784.

manipulation of legal categories could just as easily be turned to support the opposite conclusion that the legislative veto does not alter legal rights.[52]

The Court maintains that the legislative "purpose and effect" of the legislative veto is clear because:[53]

> The House took action that had the purpose and effect of altering the legal rights, duties and relations of persons, including the Attorney General, Executive Branch officials and Chadha, all outside the legislative branch. . . . The one-House veto operated in this case to overrule the Attorney General and mandate Chadha's deportation; absent the House action, Chadha would remain in the United States.

The first thing to notice about the quoted passage is that the first and the last sentences are not equivalent. There is no question that "absent House action, Chadha would remain in the United States." But does that really prove that the House resolution had "the effect of altering . . . legal rights"? Not at all, any more than when a prosecutor drops charges for possession of marijuana the defendant thereby acquires the "legal right" to smoke the substance. Admittedly, prior to the House resolution Chadha was in the country legally as a result of the Attorney General's decision to suspend deportation as a matter of grace. But that does not necessarily support the conclusion that Chadha had a legal right to remain that could only be altered by statute.

Even if it could be said that Chadha had acquired "legal rights," how were those rights "altered" by the House resolution? After all, the statute authorizing the Attorney General to suspend deportation on grounds of hardship also provided that either house of Congress could veto the Attorney General's action. Why was the nature of Chadha's legal rights not defined by the statute creating them?[54] If Chadha's only right was what the statute gave him—the right to remain in the country unless one house exercised its legislative veto—then the House's action did not alter Chadha's rights: the possibility of a legislative veto was built into them in the first place.

These questions imply, not that the Court's analysis is incorrect, but that it is arbitrary. The legislative veto "alters legal rights" only because the Court superimposes that conceptualization on the House resolution canceling the suspension of deportation. It would be equally

---

[52] See text *infra* at notes 56-61.
[53] 103 S. Ct. at 2784-85.
[54] *Cf.* Arnett v. Kennedy, 416 U.S. 134, 152 (1974).

plausible (and equally arbitrary) to manipulate the Court's abstract legal categories to say that the legislative veto did not alter legal rights.[55]

Justice White makes precisely that argument in dissent when he describes the legislative veto as authority that Congress had "reserved"[56] in the statute. He goes on to argue from this premise that the legislative veto does not work a "change in the legal status quo,"[57] and hence that the Constitution's procedural requirements for passing statutes do not apply to the legislative veto. The only case to have squarely upheld the legislative veto, the Court of Claims decision in *Atkins v. United States*,[58] rested on a similar analysis.[59] A distinction could be drawn between the *Atkins* statute and the *Chadha* statute. The difference is between a statute which casts the legislative veto as a condition precedent (executive action only goes into effect if Congress does not veto it) as opposed to a statute which makes the legislative veto a condition subsequent (executive action is effective immediately but Congress may nullify it).[60] In a footnote, however, the Supreme

---

[55] The ease with which the "altering legal rights" test may be manipulated is illustrated by events during the Carter Administration. Attorney General Griffin Bell had given an opinion that the one-house legislative veto was constitutional in legislation authorizing the President to reorganize government departments. Letter from Griffin B. Bell to President Carter (Jan. 31, 1977), reprinted in Providing Reorganization Authority to the President: Hearings Before the Legislation and National Security Subcomm. of the House Comm. on Government Operations, 95th Cong., 1st Sess. 40 (1977). A few months later, Assistant Attorney General (now Judge) Wald attacked a different proposal for a legislative veto as unconstitutional, distinguishing it as a situation in which one House could "effect [*sic*] the implementation of a substantive statute which determines the rights of those subject to it." Letter from Patricia M. Wald to Rep. Peter W. Rodino Jr., 6 (May 5, 1977), quoted McGowan, note 8 *supra*, at 1141.

[56] 103 S. Ct. at 2804.

[57] *Id.* at 2806.

[58] 556 F.2d 1028 (Ct. Cl. 1977) (plurality opinion).

[59] In *Atkins*, the Court of Claims held that a one-house veto of a Presidential recommendation to increase judicial salaries did not alter existing legal rights but merely cancelled an expectancy. The veto is "certainly not making new law . . . but only preserves the legal status quo." 556 F.2d at 1063. The Court went on to acknowledge that the President's "recommendations" would have "become the law" if there had been no legislative veto, but maintained that it was significant that "the Act did not make them law automatically, but only gave them that effect absent objection from either House of Congress." *Ibid.*

[60] The Salary Act, upheld in *Atkins*, was construed to contemplate a "recommendation" which would only go into effect if it were not vetoed, whereas the portions of the Immigration and Nationality Act struck down in *Chadha* authorized a "suspension" of deportation which was effective until vetoed. Perhaps the legislative veto in §244 of the Immigration Act would have passed constitutional muster had it been written in terms of an Attorney General's "recommendation for a suspension of deportation" which would become effective if not vetoed by Congress. *Cf.* Lewis, *Legislative Veto Case Leaves Much Unsettled*, NEW YORK TIMES, July 3, 1983, at E5 (reporting vote by the House to require Consumer Product Safety Commission rules to be adopted by Joint Resolution of both houses and signed by the President before taking effect). Perhaps it would even be enough if Congress amended the statute to state explicitly that

Court in *Chadha* appears to reject outright the Court of Claims' analysis in *Atkins*.[61]

> Neither can we accept the suggestion that the one-House veto provision in §244(c) (2) either removes or modifies the bicameralism and presentation requirements for the enactment of future legislation affecting aliens. See *Atkins v. United States*, 556 F.2d 1028, 1063-64 (Ct. Cl. 1977). *cert. denied*, 431 U.S. 1009 (1978); Brief for the United States House of Representatives 40. The explicit prescription for legislative action contained in Article I cannot be amended by legislation.

The Court's answer in *Chadha* is, of course, no answer at all. The Court merely asserts the unimpeachable (but irrelevant) proposition that a statute cannot alter the constitutional procedure for passing legislation. But the Court's argument assumes that legislation is necessary, whereas the issue under discussion is whether there was any alteration of existing legal rights so as to make legislation necessary. The point in *Atkins* is logically prior to the question of how legislation must be passed under the Constitution; it was that legislation was not necessary since there were no "rights" to alter.

The Court's opinion in *Chadha* does not turn solely on the Court's construction of Chadha's rights, however. The opinion can also be read to hold that the legislative veto is unconstitutional if it alters legal rights of any persons "including the Attorney General, Executive Branch officials *and* Chadha, all outside the legislative branch."[62] The Court's reasoning is no less arbitrary and formalistic in discussing the "rights" of the Executive branch. The Court declares:[63]

> Disagreement with the Attorney General's decision on Chadha's deportation . . . no less than Congress' original choice to delegate to the Attorney General the authority to make that decision, involves determination of policy that Congress can implement only one way; bicameral passage followed by presentment to the President. Congress must abide by its delegation of authority until that delegation is legislatively altered or revoked.

---

it conferred no legal rights until after the time for Congress to exercise its legislative veto had passed.

[61] 103 S. Ct. at 2787, n.22.

[62] 103 S. Ct. at 2784 (emphasis added). The Attorney General of the United States has adopted the broad reading of *Chadha*, see William French Smith, *Congress: No Loss in Ruling by Court*, NEW YORK TIMES, July 12, 1983, at A21. (Any congressional action "with the purpose and effect of altering the legal rights of people outside the legislative branch" must be enacted by both houses and presented to the President.)

[63] 103 S. Ct. at 2786.

The first sentence merely restates the Court's conclusion in different words. The question was whether Congress could affect policy through the legislative veto without passing a statute. It is no answer to say that the legislative veto affects policy, and therefore a statute is required.

As for the second proposition—that Congress must "abide" its delegation of authority to the Attorney General—one can only ask "Why?" Again, the question is whether the legislative veto is a permissible technique for controlling exercises of delegated authority. Not a word of the Court's opinion is spent explaining why it would be contrary to the framers' principles of constitutional design or otherwise legally suspect for Congress to retain supervision over exercises of power that it has delegated.[64]

The absence of any other explanation suggests that the Court regards its conclusion as implicit in the very concept of delegation: once power has been delegated, it is beyond recall. But there is nothing inherently implausible about some powers being delegated while others are retained.

There may be sound reasons of constitutional significance to prohibit Congress from making partial delegations of power to the Executive, but the Court does not reach that level of analysis. Instead, the opinion rests on two legal fictions,[65] "altering legal rights" and "delegation." The Court treats these abstractions as if they had independent and immutable existences, rather than recognizing them as constructs that serve purposes which should define their reach and measure.[66] This approach to deciding cases by manipulating formal legal concepts is a throwback to what Llewellyn called the Formal Style of conceptualistic judicial reasoning prevalent late in the nineteenth century.[67]

---

[64] The Court's opinion does include a short discussion of "the purposes underlying the Presentment Clauses ... and the bicameral requirement." See 103 S. Ct. at 2781-84. After the obligatory bow to the records of the Constitutional Convention and THE FEDERALIST, however, the framers' purposes never figure in the Court's analysis of the issues, see also 103 S. Ct. at 2799 (White, J., dissenting: "I do not dispute the Court's truismatic [sic] exposition of these clauses").

[65] Cf. MAINE, ANCIENT LAW 20-41 (Firth ed. 1963). The modern connotations of the term "fictions" should not mislead us to think that the concept applies only if judges are consciously dissembling. See id. at 29.

[66] Cf. Holmes, Law in Science and Science in Law, 12 HARV. L. REV. 443, 462 (1899) ("different rights ... stand on different grounds of policy. ... [I]f you simply say all rights shall be [absolute], that is only a pontifical or imperial way of forbidding discussion ...").

[67] See LLEWELLYN, THE COMMON LAW TRADITION: DECIDING APPEALS 5-6 (1960).

3. *Expressio unius est exclusio alterius.* Decision by presumption and legal fiction would be bad enough, but the Court makes a third argument even weaker and more palpably unreasonable than the first two: "Finally, we see that when the Framers intended to authorize either House of Congress to act alone and outside of its prescribed bicameral legislative role, they narrowly and precisely defined the procedure for such action."[68]

The Court proceeds to list "four provisions in the Constitution, explicit and unambiguous, by which one House may act alone with the unreviewable force of law, not subject to the President's veto,"[69] and to concede in a footnote that in 1798 the Supreme Court created a fifth exception by holding that proposed constitutional amendments are not subject to the President's veto.[70] From the existence of these exceptions, the Court concludes:[71] "Clearly, when the Draftsmen sought to confer special powers on one House, independent of the other House, or of the President, they did so in explicit, unambiguous terms."

Here the Court is engaged in another example of the style of reasoning based on mechanical legal "rules" fashionable in the late nineteenth century. The principle of construction which the Court invokes was once in common use for construing contracts and deeds to land under the maxim *expressio unius est exclusio alterius.*[72] While the maxim is occasionally still cited in cases today to buttress interpretations of contracts and certain types of statutes,[73] it is quite a different matter juristically to rely on *expressio unius* to interpret the Constitution. The Constitution is not a mere private contract.[74] The

---

[68] 103 S. Ct. at 2786.

[69] *Ibid.* The exceptions are: the House's power to initiate impeachments, Art. I, sec. 2, cl. 6; the Senate's power to try impeachments, Art. I, sec. 3, cl. 5; the Senate's power to approve Presidential appointments, Art. II, sec. 2, cl. 2; and the Senate's power to ratify treaties, Art. II, sec. 2, cl. 2.

[70] 103 S. Ct. at 2786 n.20, citing Hollingsworth v. Virginia, 3 Dall. 378 (1798).

[71] 103 S. Ct. at 2786.

[72] ("The expression of one thing is the exclusion of the other.") See BROOM, A SELECTION OF LEGAL MAXIMS, CLASSIFIED AND ILLUSTRATED 505 (2d ed. 1848); see also Walla Walla v. Walla Walla Water Co., 172 U.S. 1, 22 (1898). It should be noted that Broom warned that "great caution [is] always requisite" in applying this maxim. BROOM at 506.

[73] See, *e.g.*, National Railroad Passenger Corp. v. National Association of Railroad Passengers, 414 U.S. 453, 458 (1974). On other occasions, however, the Supreme Court has cautioned against using this ancient maxim to construe modern statutes. SEC v. C. M. Joiner Leasing Corp., 320 U.S. 344, 350-51 (1943).

[74] "A constitution, establishing a frame of government, declaring fundamental principles, and creating national sovereignty, and intended to endure for ages and to be adapted to the various crises of human affairs, is not to be interpreted with the strictness of a private contract." The Legal Tender Cases, 110 U.S. 421, 439 (1884).

Constitution was intended to set in motion a process of government that would adapt to changing conditions over generations, and consequently linguistic aids to ascertaining the intent of "the Draftsmen" should carry relatively little weight in interpreting the Constitution.

Moreover, even in its native sphere of private law, *expressio unius* is subject to significant qualifications, one of which should preclude using it here. *Expressio unius* is actually a principle of evidence, not substantive law: If a writing lists some members of a class specifically, a permissive inference may be drawn that other members of the same class were meant to be excluded or else it would have been natural to list them also.[75] The inference is only a weak one, however, and it is negated entirely if other circumstances show that the list of specifics was not intended to be exhaustive. In particular, if there is general language in addition to the enumeration of specifics, the inference suggested by *expressio unius* does not apply since the inclusion of the general language contradicts the premise that the drafters intended to include everything in the enumeration.[76]

The Court's use of *expressio unius* in *Chadha* ignores this well-established limitation on the principle. Clearly the Constitution does not purport to specify all the ways in which Congress may exercise power, and hence the inference suggested by *expressio unius* is not applicable. Perhaps the strongest reason to conclude that the framers did not intend to include everything in the enumeration of specifics is the fact that, in John Marshall's phrase, "it is a *Constitution* we are expounding."[77] If the government established by the Constitution is to sustain itself, Congress, like the other branches, must be able to exercise not only those powers that are mentioned specifically in the text of the Constitution but also those that may be fairly implied from the overall structure that the Constitution establishes.

In the past, the Court has frequently recognized that the wording of the Constitution does not purport to enumerate Congress's powers exhaustively. Thus, even though neither power is mentioned specifically in the text of the Constitution, it has been held that Congress may approve amendments to the Constitution without

---

[75] See 3 CORBIN ON CONTRACTS: §552 at 203-06 (1960).

[76] Springer v. Philippine Islands, 277 U.S. 189, 206 (1928); Corbin, note 75 *supra*, §552 at 206.

[77] McCulloch v. Maryland, 4 Wheat. at 407 (1819).

presenting them to the President for veto, and that Congress may investigate and engage in other oversight activities without bicameral action or presentment.[78] Admittedly, neither of these recognized exceptions to the requirements of presentment and bicameral action is directly analogous to the legislative veto, but they do illustrate that there is a category of congressional powers not mentioned in the text in addition to the power to pass statutes. Hence it is clear that the text does not enumerate Congress's powers exhaustively, and that the Court's reliance on *expressio unius* is invalid.

The doctrine that powers may be implied as well as enumerated is so fundamental that it is probably inherent in the nature of any constitution, but in the case of our Constitution the doctrine of implied powers is also codified in the Necessary and Proper Clause.[79] The Necessary and Proper Clause is clear, textual evidence that the framers did not intend to enumerate every way in which Congress may exercise power, and hence its existence undermines the premise for invoking *expressio unius* for the same reasons that general language in a contract shows that a listing of specifics was not intended to be exhaustive.

The Court, however, dismisses the Necessary and Proper Clause with the statement that "what is challenged here is whether Congress has chosen a constitutionally permissible means of implementing" its authority rather than Congress's authority to regulate immigration *vel non*.[80] The Court is surely correct that Congress's power under the Necessary and Proper Clause is not limitless,[81] but the Court's analysis overlooks a crucial logical distinction. The Necessary and Proper Clause would not immunize an exercise of power by Congress that was otherwise impermissible under the Constitution, but that is not the situation before the Court. On the contrary, the point is that the existence of the Necessary and Proper Clause undermines one of the premises for the Court's conclusion that the legislative veto is unconstitutional, not that the Necessary and Proper Clause redeems a practice which is unconstitutional for independent reasons.

A more sophisticated argument could be made against using the Necessary and Proper Clause to refute the Court's *expressio unius* rationale. It could be argued that the Necessary and Proper Clause is

---

[78] McGrain v. Daugherty, note 47 *supra;* see generally KIRST, note 47 *supra.*

[79] Art. I, sec. 8, cl. 18.

[80] 103 S. Ct. at 2779.

[81] Buckley v. Valeo, 424 U.S. at 132; Casper, *Constitutional Constraints on the Conduct of Foreign and Defense Policy: A Nonjudicial Model,* 43 U. CHI. L. REV. 463, 483 (1976).

irrelevant because it only relates to the subjects on which Congress may "make laws," but it does not affect the procedures for making them.[82] But this argument is also wide of the mark. Congress did "make laws" in accordance with the constitutional requirements of bicameral action and presentment when it passed the statutes creating legislative vetoes. As long as Congress's claim to a legislative veto is grounded on a statute, duly passed following constitutional procedures, the proper question is whether such a statute is within the range of subjects on which Congress is empowered to legislate. Any confusion on this point arises from the Court's insistence on framing the issue as whether "the Framers intended to authorize either House of Congress to act" without following proper procedures for legislating,[83] when in fact Congress has legislated in accordance with constitutional procedures when it passed the legislative veto statutes. The proper question should be whether legislative veto statutes are within the range of subjects on which the Constitution authorizes Congress to legislate. The Necessary and Proper Clause is surely germane to that inquiry.

In analyzing whether the Constitution gives Congress power to enact legislative veto statutes, it must be borne in mind that Congress's power to legislate under the Necessary and Proper Clause is not restricted to effectuating Congress's own enumerated powers. In addition, Congress may also legislate in aid of "all other Powers vested by this Constitution in the Government of the United States, or in any Department or Officer thereof."[84] Consequently, the *Chadha* Court's conclusion that delegated lawmaking authority is an executive, not a legislative, function[85] actually supports Congress's authority to pass legislative veto statutes. Congress may base its legislation in an area on powers conferred by the Constitution on other branches of government. For example, Congress's power to modify maritime law is based on the grant of admiralty jurisdiction to the federal courts, not on any legislative power independently granted to Congress itself by the text of the Constitution.[86] If the authority to make "quasi-legislative" rules can be delegated to the Executive branch and

---

[82] See 634 F.2d at 433.

[83] 103 S. Ct. at 2786.

[84] Art. I, sec. 8, cl. 18. See Van Alstyne, *The Role of Congress in Determining Incidental Powers of the President and the Federal Courts: A Comment on the Horizontal Effect of the Sweeping Clause*, LAW & CONTEMP. PROB. 102 (Spring 1976).

[85] 103 S. Ct. at 2785 n.16.

[86] Art. III, sec. 2, cl. 1; Detroit Trust Co. v. The Thomas Barlum, 293 U.S. 21 (1934).

independent agencies, the Necessary and Proper Clause gives Congress a general power to "make laws" controlling the exercise of that authority.

This is not to say, of course, that the legislative veto is constitutional. Prohibitions elsewhere in the Constitution might preclude the legislative veto even though Congress has general authority to legislate to control delegated lawmaking by the Executive. But the Court never reaches that level of analysis, nor does it identify either the source or the nature of such prohibitions. Rather, the thrust of the Court's *expressio unius* analysis is that Congress lacks power to create legislative vetoes because the legislative veto is not mentioned anywhere in the Constitution. That argument is clearly invalid. At least since *McCulloch v. Maryland*, it has been clear that powers are not necessarily denied to Congress merely because they are not enumerated specifically in the text.

It is hard to imagine why the Court deviates from a principle of our constitutional law as fundamental as the doctrine of implied powers in analyzing the legislative veto, but perhaps the explanation lies in the term "legislative veto" itself.[87] The name associated with a legal device can carry subtle but powerful implications for the ways that we think about it.[88] The text of the Constitution gives a veto over legislation to the President explicitly,[89] but it makes no mention of any similar "veto" for the Congress. By calling the device at issue in *Chadha* a "legislative veto," we may unconsciously consign it to constitutionally suspect territory. The word itself creates a vague, unreasoning sense that if the framers had intended Congress to have a veto, they would have said so, just as they did for the President.

But the analogy buried inside the term legislative "veto" is an imperfect one. Unlike the President's veto, most legislative "vetoes" do not create a check on a power that the Constitution confides in another branch; instead, the legislative "veto" usually checks only powers of delegated lawmaking that are themselves conferred by statute. There is nothing anomalous about using statutory sources to create a limitation on a power which is itself statutory in origin. Yet the associations of the term "veto" imply the opposite: To be valid a "veto"

---

[87] The term "legislative veto" was used first in Millett & Rogers, *The Legislative Veto and the Reorganization Act of 1939*, 1 PUB. AD. REV. 176 (1941); see Schwartz, *The Legislative Veto and the Constitution: A Reexamination*, 46 GEO. WASH. L. REV. 351, 351 n.3 (1978).

[88] As Humpty Dumpty said (anticipating Wittgenstein), words sometimes become our masters, rather than we theirs, see CARROLL, THE ANNOTATED ALICE 269 (Gardner ed. 1960).

[89] Art. I, sec. 7.

must find its source in the Constitution, which creates the presidential "veto." One cannot know, of course, but the ultimate source for the Court's curious *expressio unius* rationale may be a misnomer buried so deep in conventional legal terminology that we are no longer attuned to its implications. Imagine that from the beginning the legal device at issue in *Chadha* had been called "the conditional delegation" rather than the legislative veto. Its constitutional pedigree might well be beyond question by now.

C. THE COURT'S DUBIOUS JURISPRUDENTIAL PREMISES

The legislative veto may well be unconstitutional. Many thoughtful people have concluded that it is, at least in some circumstances. But if the legislative veto is unconstitutional, it is not unconstitutional for the reasons stated in *Chadha*. Whatever one's view about the merits, the *Chadha* opinion is a disappointment.

The Court's analysis in *Chadha* is unpersuasive but also fails to come to grips with important issues raised by the legislative veto. Even an "apostle of strict construction" was taken aback by the literalism of the Court's opinion, writing that the Chief Justice "gave us strict construction with a vengeance."[90] Representative Elliott Levitas, a leading congressional supporter of the legislative veto, ventured a less charitable assessment: the Court's opinion was "not just simple" but "simplistic."[91]

The underlying source of the problems is jurisprudential. The Court insists that the texts of the presentment clauses and the vesting of legislative power in a bicameral Congress dispose of the legislative veto *ex proprio vigore*. But constitutional texts do not apply themselves.[92] Justice White is surely right that the Constitution is silent on the "precise question" of the legislative veto and neither "directly authorize[s]" nor "prohibit[s]" it.[93] In order to treat the texts as dispositive, the Court must tacitly assume the postulate which should be under examination: whether the legislative veto is congressional

---

[90] Kilpatrick, *Decision Not Catastrophic after All*, NEW HAVEN REGISTER, July 8, 1983, at 9.

[91] Levitas, *Letter to the Editor*, NEW YORK TIMES, July 7, 1983.

[92] See Brest, *The Fundamental Rights Controversy: The Essential Contradictions of Normative Constitutional Scholarship*, 90 YALE L. J. 1063, 1090 (1981): "Like other formalist strategies, strict intentionalism pretends to constrain constitutional decisionmaking while inviting, if not demanding, arbitrary manipulation of sources and outcomes."

[93] 103 S. Ct. at 2798.

action of the sort to which the requirements of bicameralism and presentment should apply. To answer this question necessarily requires a perspective from outside the system: "Syllogism" alone is incapable of resolving such questions.

The Court's literal approach does not really exclude policy judgments about the legislative veto, as its adherents claim;[94] it only drives them underground, where it is more difficult to scrutinize and criticize them. It would be better if the Court were open and aboveboard about its conclusions concerning the pernicious effects of the legislative veto, rather than slipping hints into footnotes,[95] while insisting that the language of the Constitution is dispositive and that the utility of the legislative veto is not in question.

The second reason that the Court's approach in *Chadha* is unsatisfactory grows out of the first. The Court's linguistic arguments and analytical approach depend on dividing government power into three stark categories—legislative, executive, and judicial—and are troublesome because they are unpersuasive on their own terms.[96] But the Court's approach is also troubling because it excludes other considerations that should be relevant. It is as if the Court were determined to avoid acknowledging what the case is really about. Representative Levitas has charged:[97]

> The framers of our Constitution would be most surprised to find that regulations that have the force and effect of law are today put into effect by unelected officials in the executive branch and in independent agencies rather than by the Congress. Those "laws" are not passed by either the House and Senate, nor are they signed by the President. As this practice developed over the years, Congress

---

[94] See 103 S. Ct. at 2780-81 ("[The] wisdom [of the legislative veto] is not the concern of the courts; . . . JUSTICE WHITE undertakes to make a case for the proposition that the one-House veto is a useful 'political invention'. . . . But policy arguments supporting even useful 'political inventions' are subject to the demands of the Constitution which defines powers and, with respect to this subject, sets out just how those powers are to be exercised").

[95] See 103 S. Ct. at 2771 n.3 (suggesting that "it is not at all clear" that the House "correctly understood the relationship between" the resolution it passed and Chadha's deportation, but may have thought that it was confirming rather than overruling the Attorney General's decision).

[96] Only a few years ago the Court declared that the proper inquiry in separation of powers cases was not to be found in the "archaic view" of "three airtight departments of government" but rather by assessing the actual "impact" a measure would have on the functioning of other branches of government. Nixon v. GSA, 433 U.S. 425, 443 (1977); *cf. id.* at 504 (Burger, C.J., dissenting).

[97] Levitas, note 91 *supra.* See also SUNDQUIST, THE DECLINE AND RESURGENCE OF CONGRESS 345 (1981) (describing increasing use of the legislative veto in the 1970s as one of the best indicators of the resurgence of Congress after decades of decline).

> attempted to redress the balance with the legislative veto. The
> Court's opinion . . . failed to mention that it was a response to this
> evolving system.

Levitas has a valid point, although he overstates it. The Court does
mention "lawmaking" by administrative agencies, but only in a
footnote and only in the distorted context of answering a rhetorical
question from one of the briefs: "Why is the Attorney General exempt
from submitting his proposed changes in the law to the full bicameral
process?"[98] The answer, the Court responds in a footnote that would
do Lewis Carroll proud, is that while administrative rulemaking may
"resemble" lawmaking,[99] and while by statute agency rules do
"prescribe law,"[100] agency rulemaking is not really "legislative" but
only "quasi-legislative" "Executive action."[101] Besides, the Court adds,
the bicameral process is "not necessary" in the case of rulemaking by
agencies because the courts are available to insure that "the will of
Congress has been obeyed."[102]

The Court makes short work of the argument by assigning
administrative rulemaking to a different pigeonhole. But the exercise in
semantics misses the point. The growth of the bureaucracy in the
Executive branch and in agencies independent of presidential control
is not of constitutional significance because it raises a nice point of
classification that can be laid to rest once the Court decides whether the
legal category "executive" or "legislative" is more appropriate.
Concern exists because of the reality that most of the federal law
affecting most of the people most of the time is not made through the
bicameral legislative process that the Court's opinion enshrines, but by
administrative decisionmakers, who are not elected and who are not,
by and large, subject to either effective presidential or judicial
control.[103]

The growth of lawmaking power in a vast administrative
bureaucracy may be seen as a threat to the essence of the constitutional
principle of separation of powers. Madison (not Hamilton, as the
Court mistakenly states)[104] summarized that fundamental constitutional
principle in Federalist No. 51 as "contriving the interior structure of

---

[98] 103 S. Ct. at 2785 n.16 (quoting from brief for the House of Representatives).

[99] 103 S. Ct. at 2785 n.16.

[100] 5 U.S.C. §551(4) (1976).

[101] 103 S. Ct. at 2785 n.16.

[102] Ibid.

[103] BREYER, REGULATION AND ITS REFORM 1-3 (1982).

[104] 103 S. Ct. at 2783.

the government as that its several constituent parts may, by their mutual relations, be the means of keeping each other in their proper places." [105] The "constant aim" of this strategy, Madison continues, "is to divide and arrange the several offices in such a manner as that each may be a check on the other."[106] It is ironic that the Court in *Chadha*, in the name of the constitutional principles of checks and balances and separation of powers, ends up striking down one of the few existing checks on lawmaking by the bureaucracy.[107]

II

It is not unusual for the Supreme Court to begin a foray into a new and unexplored area of constitutional law with a decision like *Chadha*. The Court's first opinions in a strange area often are mechanical, literal, and admit of no exceptions. In the past the Court solemnly declared, for example, that manufacturing was not interstate commerce;[108] that a state could not regulate terms of employment;[109] that the First Amendment does not prevent government discharge of an employee for her beliefs.[110] In each case, the Court propounded a flat rule based on abstract reasoning. Each decision appeared as absolute and unyielding as *Chadha* does now, and each did not last.

The Court's early decisions in an area are often rigid and mechanical because when the Court first faces new issues, it analyzes them in terms of existing legal concepts which were refined in other contexts. As the law grows, its logic is tailored to the needs of new situations as experience demonstrates inadequacies in the existing approach. The judicial process works like the "anchoring and adjusting" heuristic; a possible solution is proposed, often one which is suggested by the structure of the problem, and then adjusted to fit new circumstances.[111]

---

[105] THE FEDERALIST PAPERS, note 41 *supra*, at 355. See also Sharp, *The Classical American Doctrine of "The Separation of Powers*," 2 U. CHI. L. REV. 385 (1935).

[106] THE FEDERALIST PAPERS, note 41 *supra*, at 356.

[107] See Karl, *Letter to the Editor, Rule-Making Powers: An American Dilemma*, NEW YORK TIMES, July 6, 1983, at A18, col. 3. See also Schwartz, *The "Legislative Veto"—Now That It's Gone*, NEW YORK TIMES, June 30, 1983, at A19, col. 2; Miller & Knapp, *The Congressional Veto: Preserving the Constitutional Framework*, 52 IND. L. J. 367 (1977). But see Martin, note 32 *supra*, at 262-67 (rejecting arguments that the legislative veto "actually promotes the aims" of separation of powers doctrine).

[108] United States v. E. C. Knight Co., 156 U.S. 1, 12 (1895).

[109] Coppage v. Kansas, 236 U.S. 1, 14 (1915).

[110] Adler v. Board of Education, 342 U.S. 485, 492 (1952).

[111] See Tversky & Kahneman, *Judgment under Uncertainty: Heuristics and Biases*, in JUDGMENT UNDER UNCERTAINTY: HEURISTICS AND BIASES 3, 14-18 (Kahneman, Slovic, & Tversky eds.

Chadha is such an "anchor." It remains to be seen to what degree the legal system will "adjust" this initial result.

It is inherent in the nature of the judicial process that legal doctrines evolve through a process of what Eugene Rostow described as "back and fill, zig and zag":[112]

> [N]o court has ever achieved perfection in its reasoning in its first, or indeed in its twentieth opinion on the same subject. . . . In the nature of law as a continuing process, constantly meeting the shocks of social change, and of changes in people's ideas of justice, this characteristic of law must be true, even for our greatest and most insightful judges. They grapple with a new problem, deal with it over and over again, as its dimensions change. They settle one case, and find themselves tormented by its unanticipated progeny. They back and fill, zig and zag, groping through the mist for a line of thought which will in the end satisfy their standards of craft and their vision of the policy of the community they must try to interpret. . . . There are cases that lead nowhere, stunted branches and healthy ones. . . . Yet the felt necessities of society have their impact, and the law emerges, gnarled, asymmetrical, but very much alive. . . .

Rostow's description is surely correct for those parts of the law where we can look back and see lines of cases developing over time. When courts confront the same or similar issues over and over again, they do explore, modify, refine, and develop the law. But Rostow gives only half the picture. The judicial process does not inevitably erode a decision like *Chadha*.[113] Sometimes, perhaps most of the time, lawyers and the community at large accept the Court's initial decision as settling the law. Unfortunately, no one has come up with an entirely satisfactory explanation for why the community recognizes some Supreme Court opinions as precedents while others become stunted branches of the law.

Often it is not the Court but the community reaction which signals that a decision is unacceptable and initiates a new cycle of legal evolution.[114] It is not so much the formal checks in the Constitution

1982). See also Elliott, *Holmes and Evolution: Legal Process as Artificial Intelligence*, 13 J. LEGAL STUD. (Jan. 1984); Ackerman, *The Structure of Subchapter C: An Anthropological Comment*, 87 YALE L. J. 436, 444-45 (1977).

[112] Rostow, *American Legal Realism and the Sense of the Profession*, 34 ROCKY MT. L. REV. 123, 141-42 (1962).

[113] But see LEVI, AN INTRODUCTION TO LEGAL REASONING 9 (1949).

[114] See generally BICKEL, THE MORALITY OF CONSENT 110-11 (1975). But *cf.* Burt, *Constitutional Law and the Teaching of the Parables*, 93 YALE L. J. (forthcoming).

that select which of the Supreme Court's "anchor" decisions stand and which are "adjusted."[115] Rather, a combination of criticism and the rhythm of litigation itself acts as an invisible hand leading the Court to reexamine decisions which have not been accepted by the community.

If the principles of law declared in an opinion are recognized as dispositive, the Court's statement of the law will stand, literally unchallenged.[116] On the other hand, if people continue to litigate, and lawyers and courts continue to have doubts about how these cases should be resolved, the Supreme Court is eventually moved to reexamine its previous statement of the law. No decision, not even a unanimous decision of the Supreme Court, is a precedent on the day it is decided. It becomes a precedent if it is recognized and accepted as authoritative to resolve other controversies.[117] The process of legal evolution which Rostow describes is brought into play only when a significant number of people do not accept existing statements of the law as ending controversy in the area.[118]

The question that remains for the legislative veto is how this court which sits in judgment on the judgments of the Supreme Court will respond to *Chadha*. It is easy to get so caught up in criticizing Supreme Court opinions that we lose sight of the fact that a poor opinion is not the same thing as a bad decision. The craft of writing opinions is important, because method may sometimes lead courts to decisions wiser than the individual judges who make them and because opinions may influence the community's reaction to a decision. But courts, no less than the rest of us, sometimes reach a right—or at least an acceptable—result for the wrong reasons.

Once the Court has spoken, as it has in *Chadha*, evaluation must move to a new level. It is less important now what the Court should

---

[115] See also ELY, DEMOCRACY AND DISTRUST 46-47 (1980).

[116] See Rubin, *Why Is the Common Law Efficient?* 6 J. LEGAL STUD. 51 (1977); Priest, *The Common Law Process and the Selection of Efficient Rules*, 6 J. LEGAL STUD. 65 (1977). The Rubin-Priest thesis is couched in terms of selecting rules for relitigation and modification if they are not economically efficient. In principle, however, any values that are systematically held by the community could make themselves felt on the law through a similar mechanism, see Elliott, note 111 *supra*. Absolute unanimity is not required for a legal issue to remain settled, of course. It is usually enough to prevent an issue from being reexamined by the Supreme Court, for example, if the lower federal courts have no difficulty deciding the cases that follow based on existing legal principles.

[117] Deutsch, *Law as Metaphor: A Structural Analysis of Legal Process*, 66 GEO. L. J. 1339, 1340 (1978). See also Eisenberg, *Private Ordering through Negotiation: Dispute-Settlement and Rulemaking*, 89 HARV. L. REV. 637, 649-53 (1976).

[118] See JHERING, THE STRUGGLE FOR LAW (Lalor tr. 1879).

have done than how other parts of the total lawmaking system should respond to the Court's decision. In deciding whether to acquiesce in the Supreme Court's decision in *Chadha*, or to pursue variations of the legislative veto in the hope that the Court will eventually soften its statement of the law, the legislative veto must be viewed from a different perspective. The germane question is whether the legislative veto is too valuable a part of the evolving structure of government to be abandoned because of one Supreme Court decision, or whether we should get along without it.

A. EFFECTS OF THE LEGISLATIVE VETO

Although the literature debating the legal issues posed by the legislative veto is extensive, relatively little attention has been paid to how the veto actually works in practice.[119] Legislative vetoes are not alike. They exist in different statutory and political environments, their purposes and effects differ. How well the legislative veto works under the immigration laws has little bearing on the device's utility under the War Powers Resolution,[120] where its function is quite different.[121]

1. *An effective check on the bureaucracy?* The arguments in favor of the legislative veto were summarized by Representative Elliott Levitas when introducing a bill to create a comprehensive legislative veto over agency rules.[122] According to Levitas, the legislative veto "give[s] the public, through their elected representatives, an input into and a control over the rules which govern their lives:"[123]

> If you ask the man on the street who makes the laws in this country, he would likely tell you that Congress does. But he would be wrong, because more edicts regulating his life are promulgated by unelected bureaucrats than are passed by the elected Congress.

Expanded use of the legislative veto, according to Representative Levitas, would "help cut down on bureaucratic red tape, reduce the

[119] Bruff & Gellhorn, *Congressional Control of Administrative Regulation: A Study of Legislative Vetoes*, 90 HARV. L. REV. 1369 (1977) (case studies under five statutes providing legislative vetoes); see also CONGRESSIONAL RESEARCH SERVICE, STUDIES ON THE LEGISLATIVE VETO, 96th Cong., 2d Sess. (Comm. Print 1980) (historical studies of legislative vetoes in sixteen areas of law) (cited hereafter as STUDIES).

[120] Pub. L. No. 93-148, §5, 87 Stat. 555, 556-57 (1973), 50 U.S.C. §1544 (1976).

[121] See Fisher, *A Political Context for Legislative Vetoes*, 93 POL. SCI. Q. 241 (1978); *compare* McClure, *Legislative Veto Provisions under the Immigration Laws*, in STUDIES, note 119 *supra*, at 378, *with* Nanes, *Legislative Vetoes: The War Powers Resolution, id.* at 579.

[122] 129 CONG. REC. H931-34 (daily ed., March 8, 1983) (statement of Rep. Levitas).

[123] *Id.* at H931-32.

regulatory outpouring from Federal agencies, and make the rules that
are adopted more reasonable."[124]

Opponents of the legislative veto dispute the claim that it is an
effective check on the bureaucracy. It is certainly true that Congress
seldom actually invokes the legislative veto. Precise statistics are not
available, but it seems clear that there are many more statutes creating
legislative vetoes than there are instances in which the veto has actually
been exercised. There have been a few well-publicized cases in which
Congress used the legislative veto to reject major agency rules. In May
1982, for example, Congress used a two-house legislative veto to
override an FTC rule requiring dealers to disclose known defects in
used cars to potential customers.[125] In that instance, however, an
ordinary statute, passed by both houses and subject to presidential veto,
almost certainly would have been forthcoming to nullify the rule if the
legislative veto had not been available. Well-organized, politically
effective groups do not need the legislative veto to see to it that an
agency rule is reversed by Congress if it imposes significant costs on
them but the beneficiaries of the rule are diffuse and disorganized.[126]

If the legislative veto is worth saving, it must be because it provides
something distinctive that is not available through the ordinary,
statutory process. Antonin Scalia has argued that the legislative veto
achieves nothing of substance that could not be done at least as well
through the ordinary legislative process, except to avoid the President's
veto and the requirement of passage by the other house.[127] That is not
entirely correct, nor are these small differences. Proponents of the
legislative veto point out that the process of passing a statute to
overrule agency actions is "cumbersome and time-consuming."[128] In
contrast, a legislative veto is a resolution of disapproval which, because
it has no substantive content, cannot be amended, either on the floor
or in committee.[129] Moreover, the statutory time limits within which a
legislative veto must be exercised impose a discipline on the legislative
process which means that as a practical matter subcommittee hearings

---

[124] *Id.* at H932.
[125] 128 CONG. REC. S5402 (daily ed., May 18, 1982); 128 CONG. REC. H2883 (daily ed., May 26, 1982), *vetoing* 46 FED. REG. 41328-78 (1981).
[126] See generally Wilson, *Introduction,* in THE POLITICS OF REGULATION (Wilson ed. 1980); see also MAYHEW, CONGRESS: THE ELECTORAL CONNECTION (1974).
[127] Scalia, note 37 *supra,* at 24. See also Martin, note 32 *supra,* at 288-90.
[128] Levitas, note 122 *supra,* at H933.
[129] See Javits & Klein, *Congressional Oversight and the Legislative Veto: A Constitutional Analysis,* 52 N.Y.U. L. REV. 455, 456 (1977); Fisher, *Introduction,* in STUDIES at 1, 4; but *cf.* Consumer Energy Council v. FERC, 673 F.2d at 476 (Wilkey, J.).

are rarely held, and committee reports are almost never written to accompany legislative veto resolutions.

The legislative veto does involve a simplification of the legislative process, but what is gained in speed is lost in understanding. Stripped of hearings, reports, and committee deliberations, members of Congress have no way to reach informed, independent decisions about how to vote on legislative veto resolutions. Moreover, without subcommittee hearings and internal deliberation even members of the subcommittee directly involved become virtual prisoners of their staff. It is a mistake, therefore, to conceive of the legislative veto as action by Congress, or by a single house, in the same sense that passing a statute is action by Congress; statutes creating legislative vetoes in effect delegate power to review agency actions to the staff of a congressional subcommittee, at least in the first instance.[130] Agencies tend to enter into negotiations at an early stage to ensure that the agency's proposals will be acceptable, rather than run the risk of suffering a legislative veto later.[131] Thus, a legislative veto may affect policy even though it has not been exercised, and, as at least one lower court has correctly held, the fact that the veto has not been exercised should not immunize a statute from challenge under *Chadha*.[132]

The true significance of the legislative veto cannot be measured by the infrequency with which it has been used. The legislative veto creates the most effective kind of power, the kind that does not have to be used to be effective. It is no exaggeration to say that "the main benefit of the congressional veto is that it exists. Its very existence will sensitize the bureaucracy and make it more responsive."[133] The key question, however, is "more responsive" to what? The political calculus for a group potentially affected by agency action changes once a legislative veto enters the picture. No longer does effective political recourse involve waiting until after agency and court have ruled and then attempting to move a majority of 535 legislators to act. Instead, it becomes possible to influence policy before the agency acts by persuading a few key members of Congress and/or congressional staff members.

Many public interest lawyers oppose the legislative veto for this reason, contending that it would only increase the influence of

---

[130] See Levitas, note 122 *supra*, at H933.

[131] See Bruff & Gellhorn, note 119 *supra*, at 1409-12.

[132] "A retained one-house veto is unconstitutional even when not exercised." EEOC v. Allstate Ins. Co., 52 U.S.L.W. 2152 (Sept. 20, 1983).

[133] Levitas, note 122 *supra*, at H933; see also BOLTON, note 8 *supra*, at 22-24.

industry and other "[w]ealthy, well-organized and experienced special interests."[134] Former Representative Robert Eckhardt has been quoted as saying that "[r]ather than increasing Congressional control" legislation to expand the legislative veto "would simply provide more business for the high-priced Washington lobbyist."[135]

Which groups would actually gain in influence if the legislative veto moved debate over "administrative regulations and their ultimate decisions into the private arena of congressional offices"[136] is not self-evident. The dominance of subcommittee staff under legislative veto statutes might lead decisionmaking to be less "political" than when the ordinary statutory process is the only congressional mechanism available for overturning agency decisions. On the other hand, because the legislative veto poses a much more credible threat to the substance of agency decisions, it probably does tend to reduce agency independence and the degree to which decisions can be based on "expertise," and to increase the political component in agency decisions. As former FTC Chairman Michael Pertschuk points out, the legislative veto "invite[s] an affected industry to try its case in a political forum rather than go through the painstaking process of building a record and arguing its case on the merits."[137]

The legislative veto affects the administrative process procedurally as well as substantively by opening up a new congressional arena in which to debate issues that are before agencies. In the congressional arena, however, procedural requirements which are intended to insure fairness and equality of access in the administrative process do not apply.[138] As a consequence, the procedural due process issues raised by the legislative veto can be substantial.[139] Even if it does not violate the Constitution, it certainly is problematic that the legislative veto creates an "appeal" from administrative decisions to a forum that typically listens to representations of fact *ex parte*, does not give all sides equal opportunities to be heard, does not explain its decisions, and from which there is no appeal. But the threat to the integrity of

---

[134] Green & Zwenig, *The Legislative Veto Is Bad Law*, NATION, Oct. 28, 1978, at 434 (Director and staff attorney of Nader-affiliated Congress Watch); McGowan, note 8 *supra*, at 1149.

[135] Eckhardt is quoted in Green & Zwenig, note 134 *supra*, at 434.

[136] Hearings before the Subcommittee on Administrative Law and Government Relations of the House Comm. on the Judiciary on H.R. 3658, H.R. 8231, and Related Bills, 94th Cong., 1st Sess. 257 (1975) (statement of Professor Walter Gellhorn).

[137] See Mulock, *Legislative Vetoes in Selected Regulatory Agencies*, in STUDIES, note 119 *supra*, 560, 569.

[138] See Bruff & Gellhorn, note 119 *supra*, at 1412-14.

[139] See Martin, note 32 *supra*, at 261 n.22; see also Javits & Klein, note 129 *supra*, at 466.

administrative procedures is more subtle as well. Agencies may be encouraged to avoid public rulemaking proceedings altogether, resorting to ad hoc methods of making policy to evade the legislative veto.[140] The real difference of opinion is not over the effects of the legislative veto, but whether it is a good idea to employ a mechanism that cuts through bureaucratic red tape, subverts administrative due process, and makes unelected bureaucrats more responsive to the people yet increases the power of special interests.[141]

2. *The effect on Congress.* A second set of objections, in its simplest form, is that the legislative veto encourages Congress to make broad delegations of power to administrative decisionmakers. Without the veto, the argument runs, Congress would be forced to write better (more detailed) statutes[142] or even to return power to "the people."[143] A more sophisticated version of the thesis, put by Professor David Martin, is that the legislative veto gives Congress a means to "make a public show of addressing an important issue, while yet evading direct responsibility for the necessary affirmative choices."[144]

Both versions of the argument depend, however, on the dubious premise that it is a bad thing for Congress to "avoid" deciding issues, at least those issues worth characterizing as "of an essentially political nature."[145] Professor Martin writes:[146]

> Broad delegations are not an inevitable affliction visited on Congress by some outside force. They are inevitable only in the sense that the courts are not currently disposed to employ the nondelegation doctrine to save Congress from the consequences. But Congress itself, provided it musters the political will, can curb its delegates through more precise standards that channel the exercise of delegated power.

---

[140] See Levinson, *Legislative and Executive Veto of Rules of Administrative Agencies,* 24 WM. & MARY L. REV. 79, 91-92 (1982); see also Schuck, *When the Exception Becomes the Rule: Regulatory Equity and the Formulation of Energy Policy through an Exceptions Process,* DUKE L. J. (forthcoming).

[141] See LANDIS, THE ADMINISTRATIVE PROCESS 77-78 (1938) (praising British techniques of "laying on the table" which is similar to legislative veto as providing regular and open way for individual legislators to influence administrative policy, whereas in U.S. legislators must use "other measures" to put pressure on administrators).

[142] See BOLTON, note 8 *supra,* at 49-50; see also Martin, note 32 *supra,* at 289-93.

[143] See Scalia, note 37 *supra,* at 25.

[144] Martin, note 32 *supra,* at 273.

[145] Scalia, note 37 *supra,* at 26.

[146] Martin, note 32 *supra,* at 288.

Ironically, these arguments against the legislative veto can be traced back to an attitude common among lawyers today that romanticizes the role of statutes in the total lawmaking system.

Lawyers, aware of limits to the institutional competence of courts, are naturally attracted to the idea of "leaving" tough issues to the legislature. Most lawyers view legislatures through the eyes of judges. Under the doctrine of legislative supremacy, courts are supposed to act, with few exceptions, as if legislatures were omniscient when they have spoken within their purview. But this does not mean that legislatures are omniscient, or that they ought to decide as many issues as possible. The truth is that often the decision that Congress would have made is not as good as the one that was made by another lawmaking body to which Congress delegated power. Prevailing constitutional theory is, of course, that the legislature must make basic policy decisions to "canalize" administrative discretion "within banks that keep it from overflowing."[147] But it does not follow that the narrower the banks, the better the statute. On the contrary, there are instances in which it is clear that Congress erred by writing statutes which were too specific, and by deciding issues on political grounds that might better have been left to agency expertise.[148]

At least sometimes it is a virtue, not a defect, that the legislative veto enables Congress to feel comfortable making a delegation when it is "unable or unwilling to delimit the precise boundaries of executive action."[149] The same considerations that counsel courts to avoid deciding issues which are not "ripe" often apply to Congress as well.

There is, of course, a balance between the over general and the over specific in writing statutes, but the dream of a perfect code remains an illusion, as it always has been. Those who condemn the legislative veto because it encourages Congress to delegate power without writing detailed standards are moved by too great a thirst for certainty in the law. Ambiguity is often valuable, even necessary in affairs of state. Consider the War Powers Resolution.[150] Suppose Congress were to write detailed standards into law as conditions on the President's use of force, and suppose further that a situation arose in which the President felt it necessary to disobey them. Only two things could

---

[147] Schechter Poultry Corp. v. U.S., 295 U.S. 495, 551 (1935) (Cardozo, J., concurring).
[148] See ACKERMAN & HASSLER, CLEAN COAL/DIRTY AIR 121-28 (1981).
[149] Javits & Klein, note 129 *supra*, at 456.
[150] Note 120 supra.

happen, and neither would be desirable. It could become clear, either by judicial decision or through acquiescence, that the President alone decides to use military force, or it could be decided that Congress, not the President, has exclusive power to act in this area. The thirst for certainty would have been satisfied, but the state of the law would not necessarily have been improved. We might well have been better off to preserve the Constitution that the framers gave us, which with studied ambiguity makes the President Commander-in-Chief and gives Congress the power to declare war and raise armies.[151] One need not accept the extreme view that all separation of powers issues should be left to the ebb and flow of political forces[152] to recognize that there are situations in which it is desirable for Congress and the Executive to share power, while preserving ambiguity as to the precise authority of each.

To the extent that the legislative veto permits Congress to make delegations that it would not otherwise make, and to the extent that the legislative veto is used judiciously or not at all, it may be a useful tool in some contexts for maintaining a healthy balance between executive and legislative authority.

B. ALTERNATIVES TO THE LEGISLATIVE VETO

A variety of alternatives to the legislative veto have been suggested and their advantages and disadvantages debated.[153] Substitutes suggested for the legislative veto range from full-scale statutory action by Congress to oversight by a committee, including: (1) direct statutory repeal of agency action;[154] (2) amendments limiting an agency's jurisdiction;[155] (3) appropriations riders restricting the use of funds for specified purposes;[156] (4) rewriting statutes to require that agency rules

---

[151] A leading analysis of the historical record concludes that the original intention of the framers was to give Congress "at least a coordinate, and probably the dominant, role in initiating all but the most obviously defensive wars." Lofgren, *War-Making under the Constitution: The Original Understanding*, 81 YALE L. J. 672, 701 (1972). The suggestion in the text of this article is that Lofgren's first interpretation, "coordinate" authority, is the correct one.

[152] See CHOPER, JUDICIAL REVIEW AND THE NATIONAL POLITICAL PROCESS 260-379 (1980).

[153] Kaiser, *Congressional Action to Overturn Agency Rules: Alternatives to the "Legislative Veto,"* 32 AD. L. REV. 667 (1980); Bruff & Gellhorn, note 119 *supra*, at 1420-23; see also Levinson, note 140 *supra*, at 96-111 (reviewing state systems); CONGRESSIONAL OVERSIGHT OF REGULATORY AGENCIES, note 47 *supra*.

[154] Kaiser, note 153 *supra*, at 669-73.

[155] *Id.* at 673-87.

[156] *Id.* at 687-96. See also Martin, note 32 *supra*, at 274 n.61.

must be enacted affirmatively by Congress;[157] (5) statutory requirements for consultation among agencies;[158] (6) requirements for notification of Congress or of a committee before action is taken;[159] (7) committee reports;[160] and (8) to "stage an embarrassing oversight hearing."[161] At the statutory end of the spectrum, the alternatives are generally effective when they are actually invoked, but suffer from the disadvantage that they require overcoming the massive institutional inertia of Congress, not to mention surviving the President's veto. At the other end of the spectrum, the substitutes that rely on committee action are, like the legislative veto, easier to effect but also less effective.

The single substitute that comes closest to duplicating the legislative veto is an appropriations rider—a condition prohibiting the agency from using funds for a particular purpose which is written into the legislation to appropriate funds. While technically voted by the Congress as a whole, as a practical matter a rider often can be added in committee. Action is generally required by the appropriations committee, however, rather than by the standing committee that has substantive jurisdiction.[162] The appropriations bill to which the rider is attached is subject to the President's veto, but as a practical matter, a veto is unlikely. As it has become increasingly difficult for Congress to agree on a budget in recent years, however, it has also become more difficult to use the appropriations process as a means of controlling agency action. Even if it is possible to get a rider adopted, there is no guarantee that it will be effective. If an agency receives funding under more than one appropriation, as many do, the Executive branch retains some power to evade the effect of a rider by "re-programming" unrestricted funds and using them to pursue the policy which had incurred Congress's ire.[163] And even if the rider is effective, its effect is only temporary, since a rider only lasts as long as the appropriations authority to which it is attached, usually only a single fiscal year.

None of the alternatives is an exact substitute for the legislative veto, but from among the total array of techniques available, one or another can usually be found that is tolerably serviceable if Congress is

[157] See Lewis, note 60 *supra*.
[158] Kaiser, note 153 *supra*, at 696–701.
[159] *Id.* at 701–04.
[160] *Id.* at 704–09.
[161] Bruff & Gellhorn, note 119 *supra*, at 1423.
[162] See generally Fisher, *Congressional Budget Reform: The First Two Years*, 14 HARV. J. LEGIS. 413, 416–17 (1977).
[163] See Kaiser, note 153 *supra*, at 689.

determined to overturn agency or Executive action.[164] The real significance of the legislative veto, however, is found less in the instances in which it is invoked than in the way that its existence alters the working relationship between agency and subcommittee staff. Here too the divergence between the legislative veto and the alternatives is greatest. None of the suggested substitutes is nearly as certain or predictable as the legislative veto, and none so clearly gives the committee with substantive jurisdiction (as opposed to the appropriations committee) and its staff the primary say over an agency's proposals.[165] The threat of congressional review by means other than legislative veto is less likely to produce the advance negotiations between agencies and congressional committee staffs that are the hallmark of legislative vetoes.

This is not necessarily a great loss, however. Only the most extreme partisan of Congress could think that congressional staff are the best body imaginable to exercise essentially unreviewable power over Executive and agency decisionmaking. To be sure, some of the problems that accompany the legislative veto would also result from any other reviewing institution; for example, extra costs and delay would result from any additional level of review of agency decisions. But most of the problems which accompany the legislative veto are not inherent in the concept of creating an additional mechanism to review agency decisions. They result from using congressional staff to perform the reviewing function. If one broadens the focus, so that substitutes for the legislative veto may include mechanisms outside Congress, a number of alternatives to the legislative veto are attractive.

Most states provide a mechanism, in addition to judicial review and statutory amendment, for overriding agency rules.[166] State mechanisms for reviewing agency rules take a number of different forms, including one- and two-house legislative vetoes. In addition to those with legislative vetoes, however, nine states allow a legislative committee to suspend a rule temporarily pending final legislative action; at least

---

[164] See also Carter, *The Political Aspects of Judicial Power: Some Notes on the Presidential Immunity Decision*, 131 U. PA. L. REV. (forthcoming).

[165] For an account of authorization and appropriations committees as competing "subsystems" and an interpretation of the legislative veto as an attempt by authorization committees to increase their own authority, see DODD & SCHOTT, CONGRESS AND THE ADMINISTRATIVE STATE 222-24, 233-34 (1979).

[166] Levinson, note 140 *supra*, at 81-83; NATIONAL CONFERENCE OF STATE LEGISLATURES, RESTORING THE BALANCE: LEGISLATIVE REVIEW OF ADMINISTRATIVE REGULATIONS (1977).

fifteen states have advisory committees that systematically review administrative rules and make recommendations to the legislature concerning those that should be set aside; and in another three states, the advisory committee not only recommends which rules should be set aside, but if it finds a rule objectionable, the burden of proof shifts against the agency on judicial review. This last approach, an advisory committee recommendation that shifts the burden of proof, is also recommended in the latest revision of the Model State Administrative Procedure Act.[167]

Direct review of administrative rules by legislatures has been challenged on separation of powers grounds in several states,[168] and the challenges are likely to intensify after *Chadha*.[169] An independent commission to review administrative rules is, however, an attractive alternative to the legislative veto at the federal level. A new body could be created by Congress with authority to review and suspend exercises of delegated lawmaking authority, or even to set them aside entirely. If Congress may delegate power to make rules, presumably it may provide by statute that the rules do not become effective unless they are approved by an administrative review commission. An administrative review commission could act as a check on arbitrary or unwise uses of administrative authority at least as well as the legislative veto, thus meeting one of the primary objectives claimed by supporters of the legislative veto. On the other hand, because the administrative review commission would be outside Congress, the procedural and substantive problems raised by the legislative veto would be ameliorated. It is possible that Congress could make appointments to some forms of an administrative review commission, but the Constitution would require that appointments to others be made by the President.[170]

---

[167] NATIONAL CONFERENCE OF COMMISSIONERS ON UNIFORM STATE LAWS, MODEL STATE ADMIN. PROCEDURE ACT §3-204(d) (rev. 1981).

[168] Levinson, note 140 *supra*, at 83 nn.17-21.

[169] Peterson, *Court's Outlawing Of Congress's Veto Casts Shadows on State Legislatures*, NEW YORK TIMES, July 22, 1983, at A8, cols. 1-3.

[170] The course least vulnerable to challenge would be an independent commission insulated by statute from both Congress and the President, whose members would be nominated by the President and confirmed by the Senate. The configuration most vulnerable to challenge would be to give the power to suspend rules to a commission composed of members of Congress *ex officio*. See Art. I, sec. 6, cl. 2. Between the two, in a debatable area, lies a commission some or all of whose members would be appointed by Congress. See Buckley v. Valeo, 424 U.S. 1, 109-43 (1976). The Court did recognize exceptions to the requirement of presidential appointment, however. If the rulemaking review commission's role were limited to investigating and recommending to Congress which rules be set aside by statute—and perhaps even if the commission were given power to suspend rules temporarily, or to affect the burden of proof on judicial review—Congress might well be able to appoint its members. 424 U.S. at 141.

It may seem odd that Congress can create a commission to do what Congress cannot do itself,[171] but the parts of the Constitution relied on by the Court in *Chadha* are limitations on Congress, not on the instrumentalities that Congress may create. The Constitution does not require that the commission's action (as opposed to Congress's) must be presented to the President for his or her veto. An administrative review commission would not infringe on the judiciary's power, as long as an ultimate right of appeal to the courts is preserved,[172] nor would an administrative review commission be performing a judicial function. The commission's role would be to second-guess agencies on discretionary decisions within the ambit of their authority, a function which the courts steadfastly disclaim for themselves.[173]

C. THE LEGISLATIVE VETO IN PERSPECTIVE

Legislative veto statutes range along a spectrum. On one end is the public law, represented by the War Powers Resolution or the Congressional Budget and Impoundment Control Act of 1974. In these instances, Congress has used the legislative veto to control affirmative exercises of power by the Executive. By and large, the powers at issue have not been delegated by Congress, but are powers that the President claims as inherent, a claim that Congress generally disputes. In some instances, judicial review is not available to resolve the controversy, in others it may not be desirable to resolve the issue in the courts.[174] The need for the legislative veto here may be greatest. Substitutes for legislative vetoes of this kind are not easy to imagine. Those that exist lack one of the virtues of the legislative veto statute: Congress can call into question the President's assertion of unilateral power without actually having to do anything. Viewed from this perspective, the War Powers Resolution may be a success after all.[175]

At the other end of the spectrum, the private law end, are the legislative veto statutes in which the public law implications are much more attenuated, but the interests of individuals in fair treatment are more pronounced. Immigration cases like *Chadha* are at this end of the spectrum.

---

[171] See 103 S. Ct. at 2803 (White, J., dissenting).

[172] *Cf.* Johnson v. Robison, 415 U.S. 361 (1974).

[173] See Vermont Yankee Nuclear Power Corp. v. Natural Resources Defense Council, 435 U.S. 519, 557–58 (1978).

[174] See generally Casper, note 81 *supra;* see also Choper, note 152 *supra.*

[175] But *cf.* Nanes, *Legislative Vetoes: The War Powers Resolution,* in STUDIES, at 579, 602.

At the private law end of the spectrum, no unique need for the legislative veto is apparent. If Congress regards the Executive's practices in granting suspensions of deportation to aliens as too lenient, it has a variety of effective techniques available for sending signals to the INS. To be sure, most other techniques are prospective only, and in the meantime a number of decisions that Congress regards as erroneous may stand, but that may not be an unacceptable price. On the other hand, the problems that the legislative veto raises are most intense at the private law end of the spectrum. Even if not ultimately a violation of the Due Process Clause, the lack of equal treatment and fair and regular procedures accompanying the legislative veto are most bothersome here, as are the opportunities for special influence, be it political or financial.

Between the two poles lie a range of situations in which the public and private dimensions are intermingled in varying degrees: FTC rules defining unfair trade practices[176] and EPA rules concerning hazardous wastes[177] are two examples which lie somewhere in the middle. Here too are plenty of substitutes for the legislative veto, although none is its exact equivalent. In the middle range, a balance is called for. Generally the benefits are speculative and are not worth the costs in arbitrariness, both procedural and substantive. Congress and the President, which together may create a statutory scheme for delegated lawmaking, ought, however, to have discretion to choose that politics play a larger role in regulating unfair trade practices than in cleaning up hazardous waste disposal sites or vice versa. To pick the right mix of politics and expertise to be built into delegated lawmaking is a prototypical political question of the sort that ought to be left to Congress and the President, not put out of their reach by the Court.

Chadha, of course, would not leave such choices to the political branches, but strikes down the legislative veto all along the spectrum. *Chadha* is not a disaster, however. In most areas, passable substitutes are available for the legislative veto. It is unlikely, consequently, that community reaction will lead to major "adjustment" of the "anchor" staked out by the Court in *Chadha*. In the few areas where the legislative veto is uniquely valuable (such as the War Powers Resolution), opportunities for litigation are few and far between, and it is unlikely that the judicial process will be able to correct itself by carving out exceptions through the "ebb and flow" of cases about

[176] 15 U.S.C. §57a-1.
[177] 42 U.S.C. §9655.

which Rostow wrote.[178] Perhaps under a torrent of criticism the Court would pull back. Perhaps even a consensus among scholars that *Chadha* does not reach the public law end of the spectrum would suffice to keep the legislative veto alive under the War Powers Resolution by keeping the issue open. But neither seems likely.

Chadha has probably stated the law for some time to come.

III

From one perspective, writing a broad, all-encompassing opinion in *Chadha* may have been a wise exercise of judicial statesmanship. Sometimes the Supreme Court can unlock latent, creative forces by eliminating weak or deficient parts of the existing legal order, thereby clearing room for new growth.[179]

In statutes, as elsewhere, new concepts are slow to emerge if an existing device is available to fill a need. Occasionally accidents or circumstances do give birth to a new device such as the legislative veto. If it meets a need that no existing device satisfies, there is a strong tendency for the "mutant" to reproduce rapidly as it is copied from one statute to another. Without competitors or obvious countervailing considerations to limit its growth, such a new legal device may spread rapidly until it becomes so established that it dominates the field and squeezes out the possibility of alternatives. The geometric growth of recent statutes incorporating legislative vetoes is evidence that this phenomenon has been occurring. Congress has been writing legislative vetoes into statutes where the need for the veto is weak at best.[180] Moreover, as the legislative veto has become fashionable, Congress has not been inclined to give serious consideration to possible alternatives for controlling administrative discretion under broad delegations.

Paradoxically, then, by striking down the legislative veto, in the long run the Court may have advanced the professed goals of supporters of the legislative veto to control administrative discretion.

---

[178] See note 112 *supra*.

[179] *Cf.* CALABRESI, A COMMON LAW FOR THE AGE OF STATUTES 8-15 (1982).

[180] Examples include a legislative veto over President's extension of production period for Naval petroleum reserves, Pub. L. No. 94-258, 90 Stat. 303 §201(3), (1976); a veto over rules establishing grievance procedures for institutionalized persons, §7(b)(1), Pub. L. No. 96-247, 94 Stat. 349, 352-55 (1980); a veto over changes to the rules governing airline pension plans, §43(f)(3), Pub. L. No. 95-504, 92 Stat. 1705, 1752 (1979), or to retirement plans for employees of the District of Columbia, §164, Pub. L. No. 96-122, 93 Stat. 866, 891-92 (1979).

Deprived of the legislative veto, Congress may now be forced to consider alternative devices.

The idea that *Chadha* may advance the cause of controlling administrative discretion, however, is only speculation. There is no cause for rejoicing when the Court strikes down a legal device that it assumes is "efficient, convenient and useful in facilitating the functions of government."[181] To be sure, there may be a difference between good policy and what the Constitution requires. One of the things "unconstitutional" means is that something violates principles so fundamental that no other considerations may save it. It is, however, no virtue in a constitutional law that it lays to waste political innovations which are efficient, convenient, and useful (as the Court says it assumes the legislative veto to be).

A. TOWARD AN ALTERNATIVE APPROACH

A starting point for an alternative approach to the issues in *Chadha* can be found in Justice White's dissent. There are two distinct levels to the dissent. White answers the majority's formalistic, textual arguments with a conceptual argument of his own. The legislative veto is not the equivalent of a statute, White argues, because Congress has "reserv[ed]" a veto in the delegation and hence the veto does not make a change in the "legal status quo."[182] White supports his view that a condition built into a statute is not an independent exercise of legislative authority with two cases from the late 1930s which had upheld statutes giving "vetoes" to private groups.[183] If this were all there were to White's opinion, it would be little better than the majority's equally mechanical approach.

White's dissent, however, operates on a second level as well. He sees the legislative veto in a larger perspective of evolving constitutional structure and relationships.[184] White begins by tracing the history of the legislative veto, concluding that "it has not been a sword with which Congress has struck out to aggrandize itself at the expense of the other branches" but a "reservation of ultimate authority necessary if

---

[181] 103 S. Ct. at 2780-81.

[182] *Id.* at 2806-07.

[183] Currin v. Wallace, 306 U.S. 1 (1939); and U.S. v. Rock Royal Co-operative, 307 U.S. 533, 577 (1939), cited 103 S. Ct. at 2803 (White, J., dissenting). But *cf.* Martin, note 32 *supra*, at 297-98 (distinguishing *Currin* on ground that requirements of presentation and bicameral action apply "only to members of Congress").

[184] *Cf.* BLACK, STRUCTURE AND RELATIONSHIP IN CONSTITUTIONAL LAW (1969).

Congress is to fulfill its designated role under Article I as the nation's lawmaker."[185] White then describes the growth of the "modern administrative state" in which "legislative authority is routinely delegated to the Executive branch, to the independent regulatory agencies and to private individuals and groups."[186] Quoting Justice Jackson, White asserts that the rise of the administrative state has been "the most significant legal trend of the last century."[187] A plethora of administrative bodies with lawmaking authority has now "become a veritable fourth branch of Government, which has deranged our three-branch legal theories."[188]

White criticizes the majority for not "facing the reality of administrative lawmaking,"[189] but what significance White himself ascribes to administrative lawmaking is a bit murky. He suggests that the "wisdom and the constitutionality of these broad delegations [to administrative lawmakers] are matters that still have not been put to rest."[190] White turns around, however, and argues in a key passage that "If Congress may delegate lawmaking power to independent and executive agencies, it is most difficult to understand Article I as forbidding Congress from also reserving a check on legislative powers for itself."[191] Strictly speaking, White's point is a non sequitur: The fact that Congress may delegate legislative authority, without more, has nothing to do with whether Congress may reserve a legislative veto in the delegation. White comes back to the supposed inconsistency between the result in *Chadha* and the growth of administrative lawmaking at the conclusion of his opinion: "[The Court's holding] reflects a profoundly different conception of the Constitution than that held by the Courts which sanctioned the modern administrative state."[192] It is clear that Justice White considers the growth of the "modern administrative state" to be relevant, but just exactly how it bears on the questions before the Court he never explains.

White indicates that he would not necessarily hold all legislative vetoes constitutional.[193] Instead of the majority's approach that the texts of Article I are dispositive, White contends that the "Constitution does

---

[185] 103 S. Ct. at 2796.
[186] *Id.* at 2801.
[187] *Id.*, quoting FTC v. Ruberoid Co., 343 U.S. 470, 487 (1952) (Jackson, J., dissenting).
[188] *Ibid.*
[189] 103 S. Ct. at 2803.
[190] *Id.* at 2802.
[191] *Ibid.*
[192] *Id.* at 2810.
[193] *Ibid.*

not directly authorize or prohibit the legislative veto," and that in the face of the "silence of the Constitution on the precise question," the Court should "determine whether the legislative veto is consistent with the purposes of Art. I and the principles of Separation of Powers."[194] Justice White would analyze each legislative veto in its individual context. It turns out, however, that White's general "constitutional principle of separation of powers"[195] has very little content. Measures would violate the separation of powers principle only if they were contrary to "some express provision in the Constitution" assigning authority to another branch,[196] or if they "prevent" another branch "from accomplishing its constitutionally assigned functions."[197] Most legislative vetoes would easily survive these tests, although Justice White maintains that "a legislative check on an inherently executive function, for example that of initiating prosecutions, [would pose] an entirely different question."[198]

There is obvious appeal to White's approach as contrasted with the majority's literalism, but several important weaknesses are apparent. For one thing, the textual basis for a general separation of powers principle is unclear, a factor to which the majority alludes in explaining its own refusal to follow this line of analysis. The separation of powers principle that Justice White describes has little if any independent content beyond what is already expressed or implied by other provisions of the Constitution. White's approach would, moreover, call into question those exercises of the legislative veto at the public law end of the spectrum, where the legislative veto is arguably most valuable, while doing nothing to remedy the abuses of the legislative veto in the private law area, where it seems least fitted to its task.

The weaknesses in his approach are even deeper and more fundamental. White's opinion fails to persuade at least in part because both the concept of the "administrative state" and the jurisprudential underpinnings that make it relevant to the issue before the Court remain unclear. Nonetheless there is great intuitive appeal to Justice White's recognition that the federal government "has become an endeavor far beyond the contemplation of the Framers," and that the

---

[194] *Id.* at 2798.
[195] *Id.* at 2808.
[196] *Id.* at 2809.
[197] *Id.*, quoting Nixon v. GSA, 433 U.S. 425, 433 (1977).
[198] *Id.* at 2810.

Constitution must be interpreted "with the flexibility to respond to contemporary needs."[199]

B. THE PROBLEM OF QUASI-CONSTITUTIONAL INSTITUTIONS

Underlying the debate between White and the majority is a problem with ramifications that go far beyond the legislative veto. In a nutshell, the problem is that the text of the Constitution creates not four branches of government, but three. White and the majority differ both conceptually and jurisprudentially over the significance of the changes in the structure of the federal government which have occurred since the New Deal. White conceives of these changes as creating the "modern administrative state." The majority, on the other hand, sees them as merely a series of delegations to the Executive,[200] a phenomenon that goes back to the beginning of the Republic.

White's term, "the modern administrative state," is used with "increasing regularity" by contemporary political scientists,[201] but is only beginning to achieve currency among lawyers.[202] The concept of an "administrative state" goes well beyond the idea of delegation of lawmaking power to administrative decisionmakers. Indeed, the concept of an "administrative state" goes even further than the metaphor of a Fourth Branch. Describing administrative lawmakers as a "Fourth Branch" implies that they have achieved parity with the three original branches of government. The "administrative state," on the other hand, suggests that the growth of administrative decision-making is significant, not only in its own right, but also because administrative lawmaking has become the central lawmaking institution, and thereby that it has transformed the functions and relationships among other institutions of government. The term "the modern administrative state" implies, in short, that a qualitative change in the nature of government as a whole has resulted from the growth of administrative lawmaking.

To spell out the implications of Justice White's term is not to endorse it. Lumping a number of institutional changes together under the rubric of "the administrative state" substitutes a slogan for more precise analysis of particular institutions. In at least one crucial respect,

---

[199] *Id.* at 2798.
[200] See 103 S. Ct. at 2785 n.16.
[201] FREEMAN, CRISIS AND LEGITIMACY 3 (1978); see also DODD & SCHOTT, note 165 *supra.*
[202] See Monaghan, *Marbury and the Administrative State*, 83 COLUM. L. REV. 1 (1983).

however, White's metaphor is more perspicacious than the familiar concept of delegation which the majority employs. Delegation is a mechanistic metaphor: it implies that the thing which is delegated is the same in the hands of the recipient as it was before, and that both parties are otherwise left unchanged by the transaction. The "administrative state," on the other hand, suggests a concept of government as a holistic system. Changing one part of such a system necessarily alters the whole.

In this respect, at least, White's understanding of the significance of the rise of administrative lawmaking is superior to the majority's. The growth of a vast administrative bureaucracy with lawmaking powers is not a mere additive change to the structure of government. Inevitably it has transformed the nature and functions of existing institutions as well. The increasing importance of administrative modes of lawmaking has, for example, transformed the role of the courts in many areas of law. Rather than make common-law tort rules, for example, today federal courts are more likely to review generic rulemaking by agencies such as the National Highway Transportation Safety Administration. No longer are the courts the primary expositors of the law as they were in the nineteenth century. Instead, they review law made by others.[203] Federal courts have become part of a composite lawmaking system, in which they function in conjunction with legislatures and administrative decisionmakers so that the law is the joint product of all three.

Similarly, the rise of a vast administrative bureaucracy with lawmaking powers has transformed the role of Congress. For one thing, it has stimulated the growth of congressional staff and ancillary institutions, but even more importantly it has altered the nature of federal legislation itself. Most significant legislation passed by Congress today is not addressed to the citizenry, but to supposedly expert administrative decisionmakers, who in turn formulate the level of rules that touch the populace.

Justice White and the majority differ not only in how they conceive of the changes in the structure of government since the New Deal, but also in the jurisprudential significance that they ascribe to them. White senses that "the most significant legal trend of the last century" must somehow alter existing constitutional relationships. It is downright

---

[203] *Ibid.*

silly, White maintains, to read the language of the Constitution concerning the legislative process in isolation, without taking into account massive changes that have taken place in other lawmaking institutions. White gropes for a recognized legal doctrine that will legitimize the idea that a change in institutions of a magnitude as fundamental as the growth of the "modern administrative state" should alter the meaning and relationships among existing provisions of the Constitution. White never finds it, and perhaps no such doctrine now exists in American constitutional law. The majority dismisses White's point, characterizing it as a mere "utilitarian argument" that the legislative veto is a "useful 'political invention'."[204] According to the majority, the growth of the administrative state and the concomitant need to control it are mere "policy arguments," which do not rise to the level of constitutional significance.

Perhaps the majority's answer suffices for a case like *Chadha*, since reasonable substitutes for the legislative veto are available. The difference between White and the majority in *Chadha* is, however, symptomatic of a deeper confusion in our law over the constitutional status and significance of lawmaking by administrative bodies, a confusion that could cause great harm if it is not resolved. Because existing constitutional doctrines were made to accommodate three branches of government, not four, it is the lawyer's equivalent of child's play to raise questions about the "uneasy constitutional position of the administrative agency,"[205] or to yearn for the day when the courts will invoke the nondelegation doctrine to return us to a simpler era in which Congress made the laws, as the framers intended.[206]

Ultimately, what White is up against in *Chadha* is the problem created by the growth of "quasi-constitutional" institutions. The dimensions of the problem can be clarified by referring to an article written several years ago by Kenneth Dam describing the "American Fiscal Constitution."[207] Dam began by noting that "the notion of an American Fiscal Constitution may strike most American constitutional lawyers as odd," since the Constitution itself has comparatively little to say about financial matters.[208] Adapting the concept of "framework

---

[204] 103 S. Ct. at 2781.

[205] BREYER & STEWART, ADMINISTRATIVE LAW AND REGULATORY POLICY 37-39 (1979).

[206] See McGowan, note 8 *supra*, at 1128-30; but see Easterbrook, note 3 *supra*, at 118-19: "The nondelegation doctrine is a name without a doctrine."

[207] Dam, *The American Fiscal Constitution*, 44 U. CHI. L. REV. 271 (1977).

[208] *Id.* at 271.

statutes" proposed originally by Gerhard Casper,[209] Dam suggested that the American Fiscal Constitution could be understood as extending beyond the test of the Constitution itself:[210]

> Supplementing the rules of taxation and expenditure found in the Constitution are several statutes that are so far-reaching in their implications for year-by-year fiscal decisions that they deserve to be thought of as quasi-constitutional. . . . American constitutional law does not have a separate category to describe these "framework" statutes, though they are increasing in importance. Although such statutes can be amended under the same congressional majority rule as any other statute and must comply with the Constitution, it would be a triumph of form over substance to treat them as ordinary legislation.

In addition to the "framework statutes" defining the budgetary process, the American Fiscal Constitution includes certain customary rules including the "widespread consensus in American society about the respective roles of the federal, state and local governments."[211] Taken together "this evolving structure is at least as important as the provisions of the Constitution, and perhaps can be described as the constitution (with a lower-case 'c') underlying the process of public choice" in the fiscal area.[212] Although never quite put into these words, the central idea of a fiscal constitution is the insight that one core function of a constitution—creating the basic institutions of government and defining power relationships among them—is being performed for fiscal matters in the United States by legal structures that are not part of the Constitution.[213]

The United States has at least one other "constitution (with a lower-case 'c')," which we might call the "constitution of the administrative state." Its functions are to provide structure and control over the enormous array of federal departments, independent commissions, agencies, government corporations, banks, boards, committees, and quasi-official agencies and authorities that now

---

[209] Casper, note 81 *supra*, at 482.

[210] Dam, note 207 *supra*, at 272–73. Dam mentions the War Powers Resolution as an example of another "framework" statute. *Id.* at 271 n.6.

[211] *Id.* at 273.

[212] *Id.* at 273–74.

[213] The German Constitution (*Grundgesetz*, or Basic Law) defines fiscal relationships in much greater detail than in the United States, "giving fiscal federalism in the Federal Republic a constitutional explicitness and structure almost totally lacking in the United States." *Id.* at 294.

exercise power to make law in various forms.[214] This network of legal principles, usually thought of as part of administrative law, includes "framework" statutes such as the Administrative Procedure Act,[215] the Freedom of Information Act,[216] the Federal Advisory Committee Act,[217] the common law of judicial review of administrative action, even Executive Orders[218] and unwritten rules concerning informal interagency consultation. Together the constitution of the administrative state creates a system of law by which government instrumentalities are supposedly controlled and managed.[219]

American lawyers do not yet have terms and concepts to enable them comfortably to handle bodies of law of this sort.[220] The word "quasi-constitutional"[221] has been suggested by some to describe such law,[222] but it is awkward. Moreover, it carries the unfortunate implication that this law is not really of constitutional stature.[223] The truth is that quasi-constitutional law has some, but not all, of the characteristics of constitutional law.

Quasi-constitutional law is unlike formally amending the text of the Constitution. A lowercase constitution can be modified more easily as conditions change, or, more to the point, as experiments with different approaches for controlling administrative discretion are tried one after another until one works.[224] At the moment the law is in the midst of a major exercise in revising the constitution of the administrative state. At issue is how to extend the Constitution's system of checks and balances to the array of lawmaking institutions exercising delegated powers. Another generation of administrative lawyers, led by Louis

---

[214] Over 600 pages are required simply to catalog them, see THE UNITED STATES GOVERNMENT MANUAL 1982-83.

[215] 5 U.S.C. §551 et seq. (1976).

[216] 5 U.S.C. §552 (1976).

[217] 5 U.S.C. App. I (Supp. I, 1977).

[218] See, e.g., Executive Order No. 12291, 46 FED. REG. 13193 (Feb. 19, 1981).

[219] See BREYER & STEWART, note 205 supra, at 10-11 (1979); DAVIS, ADMINISTRATIVE LAW TEXT §1.01 at 1 (3d ed. 1972).

[220] Elsewhere I have used the term "meta-law" to describe law of this kind, Elliott, Holmes and Evolution, note 111 supra (1984); Elliott, The Disintegration of Administrative Law, 92 YALE L. J. (1983) (forthcoming).

[221] Dam, note 207 supra, at 272.

[222] See Stewart, The Development of Administrative and Quasi-Constitutional Law in Judicial Review of Environmental Decisionmaking: Lessons from the Clean Air Act, 62 IOWA L. REV. 713, 740 (1977); GUNTHER, CASES AND MATERIALS ON CONSTITUTIONAL LAW 429 (9th ed. 1975).

[223] Dam himself later abandons the term; see Dam, note 207 supra, at 278 (referring to "framework" statutes as "part of the Fiscal Constitution in its larger sense").

[224] See BREYER, note 103 supra, at 3; see also Shapiro, On Predicting the Future of Administrative Law, REGULATION 18 (May/June 1982).

Jaffe, maintained that judicial review could control and coordinate administrative actions.[225] Many now see this role as too ambitious for the courts and have begun to look elsewhere for new, or at least supplementary, techniques for controlling administrative action.[226]

Some have argued that the President should be given broad powers to supervise and control administrative lawmaking.[227] This approach to strengthening coordination and control within the Executive branch received strong reinforcement recently with the enactment of the Paperwork Reduction Act of 1980,[228] which for the first time gives the President, through OMB, veto power over virtually all new rules by administrative entities.[229]

Others, however, dispute that control over administrative lawmaking is an appropriate role for the President, arguing for enhancing legislative control instead. They applaud the resurgence of Congress, as reflected in enhanced oversight activity and the legislative veto,[230] or imagine that the nondelegation doctrine might be a way of forcing Congress to take more responsibility.[231] Another faction takes the position that the agencies should remain independent, insulated from politics as much as possible.[232] And finally, still others suggest enhancing judicial control by creating new causes of action for the beneficiaries of regulatory programs.[233] From this perspective of continuing constitutional development, *Chadha* can be understood as one episode in a struggle among the three established branches of government to redefine their roles in the evolving "constitution of the administrative state," with the Court having adopted its traditional stance of joining with the Executive against the Congress.[234]

---

[225] See JAFFE, JUDICIAL CONTROL OF ADMINISTRATIVE ACTION (1965).

[226] See BREYER, note 103 *supra*, at 3; Elliott, note 220 *supra*.

[227] Cutler & Johnson, *Regulation and the Political Process*, 84 YALE L. J. 1395 (1975); see also Executive Order No. 12291, note 218 *supra* (giving the Office of Management and Budget broad authority to review major proposed new rules).

[228] 44 U.S.C. §3501 *et seq.* (Supp. V, 1981).

[229] See 44 U.S.C. §3508 (administrative entities may not promulgate new rules requiring collection of any information from outside government unless Director of OMB concurs in the "necessity" for the rules).

[230] See SUNDQUIST, note 97 *supra*.

[231] McGowan, note 8 *supra;* see also BOLTON, note 8 *supra*, at 49 (calling on Congress to enact "more carefully structured" grants of discretion instead of the legislative veto).

[232] *Cf.* Sierra Club v. Costle, 657 F.2d 298, 404-10 (D.C. Cir. 1981) (rejecting argument by the Environmental Defense Fund that interference in EPA rulemaking by Congress and White House officials after close of record was improper); see also ACKERMAN & HASSLER, note 148 *supra*, at 116-28.

[233] See Stewart & Sunstein, *Public Programs and Private Rights*, 95 HARV. L. REV. 1193 (1982).

[234] See KURLAND, WATERGATE AND THE CONSTITUTION 83 (1978): the "combination of the

A lowercase constitution facilitates both experimentation with different approaches and adaptation to a changing environment to a greater degree than would be possible by amending the text of the Constitution. Using nonconstitutional sources of law to perform essentially constitutional functions has worked reasonably well. But the quasi-constitutional approach to institutional change depends for its success on there being no strong sources of tension between the rapidly evolving constitutional structure and the formal Constitution. Thus, Dam suggests that the quasi-constitutional approach has worked in the fiscal area, in part because the formal Constitution is open-textured on fiscal matters: "The lacunae in the written Constitution have been filled by Supreme Court interpretations and by statutes, which can be changed when conditions change."[235]

Grave difficulties can arise, however, when basic changes in institutional relationships are made without changing the text of the Constitution. It is possible to use quasi-constitutional methods to walk into the legal equivalent of a cul-de-sac: gradual, piecemeal modifications of institutional relationships may be upheld as constitutional (as broad delegations of legislative power have been), but doctrines may be lacking that permit the meaning of other, related parts of the formal constitutional structure to be altered if the new institutional developments have "mere" statutory sources. This is becoming an increasingly serious problem as the importance of administrative lawmaking continues to grow; hence "the uneasy constitutional position of the administrative agency."[236]

The problem can be illustrated by imagining that there had been a formal amendment to the Constitution establishing a Fourth Branch. Lawyers do not have much difficulty conceiving that established meanings change as a result of modifications that are embodied as changes to the text of the Constitution (or Supreme Court interpretations, which are another way of incorporating change into a text). Amendments to one part of a text may change the meaning of other provisions whose language remains the same; the new and old are read together and a new whole is created. Thus, the Fourteenth Amendment changes the meaning of the First Amendment by revising the relationship between federal and state governments.

---

executive branch and the judicial branch against the congressional branch . . . is pervasive in our constitutional history, except on rare occasions."

[235] Dam, note 207 *supra*, at 274.

[236] See note 205 *supra*.

An amendment creating a Fourth Branch of government would also have altered existing constitutional relationships. The amendment might have made it clear that neither the Congress nor the President was to have a veto over actions by administrative bodies. Indeed, if the imaginary Fourth Branch amendment had been adopted in 1946, when the Administrative Procedure Act was passed, it probably would have embodied the then prevailing (and since discredited) theory that judicial review alone would be adequate to control administrative discretion. But leave the particular content of the Fourth Branch amendment aside for the moment. The point is that inevitably an amendment would have affected other portions of the structure and relationships created by the Constitution;[237] a coherent, new whole is created each time a text is changed, either by amendment or judicial interpretation.

Therein is the crux of Justice White's problem in *Chadha:* the "most significant legal trend of the last century" was not accomplished by amending the Constitution, but by developing a constitution of the administrative state piecemeal. The problem cannot be solved now by adopting an amendment to the Constitution codifying the results, even if that were politically feasible. The process of quasi-constitutional evolution is still proceeding too rapidly to be fixed in a formal amendment to the Constitution, and it is questionable whether the need for change and experimentation in this area will ever diminish to the point at which an amendment to the Constitution would become practical. The solution must be to find a way to interpret the Constitution so that quasi-constitutional developments and the original text can be harmonized.

C. CHADHA REVISITED

Justice White's argument in *Chadha* goes astray once he concedes that the "wisdom and the constitutionality of . . . broad delegations [to administrative lawmakers] are matters that still have not been put to rest."[238] On the contrary, it is hard to imagine any proposition of constitutional law that is more firmly established de facto than that law may be made by administrative institutions acting under broad delegations. It would be fatuous to believe that the courts are actually capable of declaring unconstitutional the vast administrative apparatus

---

[237] See generally BLACK, note 184 *supra.*
[238] 103 S. Ct. at 2802.

that has developed during the fifty years since the New Deal, no matter
how suspect its foundations may be in terms of existing legal doctrines.
The administrative state exists. It is beyond the practical power of the
Supreme Court to make it go away or even to modify its essentials
significantly. Sooner or later constitutional doctrines will have to be
modified accordingly. When institutional reality refuses to accommodate itself to legal doctrine, eventually doctrine has to accommodate
itself to reality.

In principle, moreover, broad delegations of lawmaking authority to
administrative decisionmakers are not some accident or incidental
development that has come about through a combination of judicial
timidity and congressional laziness, although undoubtedly there are
particular statutes which are ill-advised or poorly drafted. The growth
of administrative lawmaking over the half-century since the New Deal
has been fueled by fundamental political and cultural currents[239] that
the law is powerless to reverse and to which it must therefore
accommodate itself.

The existence of a sprawling administrative bureaucracy with broad
powers to make law should no longer be regarded as an open
constitutional question. It is constitutional fact. It must become one of
the fundamental premises from which our reasoning about constitutional structure and relationships begins. In this sense, the rise of
administrative lawmaking, although accomplished gradually and
without benefit of a formal amendment to the Constitution, now
constitutes an amendment to the Constitution de facto. The changes in
structure and working relationships which are hinted at by the term
"the administrative state" are at least as fundamental as any of the
changes in governmental institutions that have been embodied in
constitutional amendments during the twentieth century.[240]

It is a necessary first step to acknowledge that administrative
lawmaking under broad delegations is constitutional, but it is only a
first step. Next must come a recognition that the Constitution as a
whole changes not only when the text changes, but also when its
institutional context changes. No text draws meaning from its words
alone. Meaning is also determined by a context, which includes a

---

[239] See Schuck, *The Politics of Regulation*, 90 YALE L. J. 702, 725 (1981); see also Elliott,
Anthropologizing Environmentalism, 92 YALE L. J. (1983) (forthcoming).

[240] *Cf.* Amendment XVI (income tax); Amendment XVII (direct election of Senators);
Amendment XXII (President limited to two terms). It could be argued, however, that the federal
income tax is the change in the framers' design that has made possible the growth of the federal
government described in the text.

structure of institutional relationships in which the text is embedded. Imagine, for example, a constitution with words identical to ours, but without the inferior federal courts. Although the words would be the same, inevitably meanings would have diverged because of the different institutional contexts in which the words would be set.[241]

Despite its obvious importance, institutional context did not often present major problems for constitutional interpretation until this century. The basic structure of government either was established in the Constitution itself, or fundamental changes to it were ratified through amendments or interpretations by the Supreme Court, and thereby were incorporated into the text itself. But in the twentieth century this tradition has eroded and we have come to rely more and more on quasi-constitutional sources of law to create and shape the institutional context on which the meaning of the Constitution depends.

From a lawyer's perspective, the resulting problem is how the meaning of our fundamental law, the Constitution, can be affected by "mere" statutory sources of law such as the lowercase constitution of the administrative state. One possible answer is through the Necessary and Proper Clause, which Justice White mentions in *Chadha* but does not exploit.[242] Part of the wisdom of the framers of the Constitution was their recognition that they could not anticipate more than the most rudimentary outlines of the government that would be necessary if the enterprise they launched were to succeed. The text of the Constitution does not purport to create all necessary institutions once and for all. Instead, the Constitution gives Congress power to create such institutions as shall be necessary and proper to carry into effect the powers of government.[243] The changes in the structure of government encompassed under the rubric "the administrative state" were, ultimately, created through Congress's exercise of its powers under the Necessary and Proper Clause. As such, these institutions are as much a part of the structure and relationships established by the Constitution as if they were created in the text itself.[244]

This is not to say that the legislative veto is constitutional. But it is to say that the majority in *Chadha* was wrong—dead wrong—to dismiss Justice White's arguments about the rise of the administrative

---

[241] See also SCHUCK, SUING GOVERNMENT 169-81 (1983).

[242] 103 S. Ct. at 2801 (White J., dissenting).

[243] See First National Bank v. Fellows *ex rel*. Union Trust Co., 244 U.S. 416, 419 (1917).

[244] In his Storrs Lectures, delivered after the present article was in press, Professor Bruce Ackerman develops several parallel ideas. See Ackerman, "Discovering the Constitution"

state as mere points of policy irrelevant to the constitutional question. Administrative lawmaking is now a central part of the Constitution. The task for the Court should have been to reinterpret the Constitution to create a harmonious new whole, just as that would have been the Court's task if a Fourth Branch had been created by constitutional amendment.

The legislative veto at issue in *Chadha* is unconstitutional, not because the words of Article I read in splendid, sterile isolation prohibit all legislative vetoes, but because this particular legislative veto is inconsistent with the Constitution, the administrative state included. The legislative veto at issue in *Chadha* is not unconstitutional because it is an attempt by Congress to exercise legislative power without following the proper procedures for legislation, as the Court held, but because it is an attempt by Congress to exercise powers that can no longer properly be considered legislative. Whatever role the framers may have intended for private bills in immigration cases originally, today it has become an administrative function to say whether an individual case involves "extreme hardship." Thus, the legislative veto is inconsistent with the scheme of the Immigration and Nationality Act as a whole, and with our evolving notions of what constitutes a proper legislative function. In the context of suspensions of deportation for individual aliens, the legislative veto therefore violates what John Marshall called the "spirit of the Constitution," and what today we might call due process, or the deep structure of the Constitution's evolving grammar.

The Court decided *Chadha* too broadly and on the wrong grounds. In the end, however, those are not the reasons why the case is so troubling. What is haunting about *Chadha* is the revelation that the Supreme Court has not yet developed a theory to harmonize administrative lawmaking and the Constitution. If need be, the law will survive the loss of the legislative veto. There will be real trouble, however, if the Court has forgotten that there is more to the Constitution than just words.

(Lectures delivered at the Yale Law School, November 8-10, 1983). Ackerman also portrays the New Deal as bringing about fundamental changes which are tantamount to amending the Constitution. According to Ackerman's theory, however, the legitimacy of these changes depends largely upon the "critical election" of 1936. The present article, on the other hand, conceives of a de facto amendment to the Constitution as coming about through a gradual process of related developments and community acceptance, like the common law.

CASS R. SUNSTEIN

DEREGULATION AND THE HARD-LOOK DOCTRINE

In the last fifteen years, courts have begun to command regulatory initiatives and to invalidate deregulation. These developments reflect a shift in the underlying premises of administrative law, a shift that appears to be leading, for the first time, to a public law divorced from traditional principles of private law.

It should not be surprising that this is occurring. The consequence of the New Deal and the enormous growth of regulatory activity since World War II has been the creation of a vast administrative apparatus. The existence of that apparatus represents a substantial rejection of the common-law system of private ordering—a system that afforded the original basis for judicial doctrines controlling administrative action: Public law was built on private law. But things have changed. The electoral process has proved insufficient to discipline agency decisions, and courts have rejected the notion that political supervision is an adequate safeguard against unlawful or arbitrary failure to regulate. Federal common law,[1] statutory interpretation,[2] and constitutional

Cass R. Sunstein is Assistant Professor of Law, The University of Chicago.

AUTHOR'S NOTE: I am grateful to Douglas G. Baird, Mary E. Becker, Walter J. Blum, David P. Currie, Frank H. Easterbrook, E. Donald Elliott, Richard A. Epstein, Geoffrey P. Miller, Michael J. Perry, Richard A. Posner, Deborah L. Rhode, Carol M. Rose, Geoffrey R. Stone, David A. Strauss, and James Boyd White for helpful comments on a previous draft. Carrie Huff provided valuable research assistance. I am also grateful to participants in the faculty workshop at the Northwestern University Law School. For financial support I thank the Law and Economics Program of the University of Chicago.

[1] See, e.g., Chaney v. Heckler, 718 F.2d 1174 (D.C. Cir. 1983); Bargmann v. Helms, 715 F.2d 638 (D.C. Cir. 1983); WWHT, Inc. v. FCC, 656 F.2d 807 (D.C. Cir. 1981); NRDC v. SEC, 606 F.2d 1031 (D.C. Cir. 1979); Environmental Defense Fund, Inc. v. Ruckelshaus, 439 F.2d 584 (D.C. Cir. 1971).

[2] See, e.g., Dunlop v. Bachowski, 421 U.S. 560 (1975); Environmental Defense Fund v. Gorsuch, 713 F.2d 802 (D.C. Cir. 1983).

doctrines[3] have been worked, individually and in concert, to turn regulatory protection into an entitlement enforceable by the courts.[4]

Traditional legal doctrines do not easily square with an affirmative right to regulatory protection. These doctrines were built on an understanding that the courts were to aid private citizens in fending off unauthorized regulatory initiatives, not that judicial aid could be invoked to require the government to proceed against third parties. The last two decades have seen important developments, largely judge-made, that attempt to adapt to the changing landscape of administrative law. The judicial effort is no longer primarily to protect private rights, but instead to facilitate identification and implementation of the values at stake in regulation. These developments represent an effort, still somewhat tentative, to formulate an independent public law—a body of doctrine to control agency action (and inaction) that does not derive from traditional common-law principles or statutory provisions or constitutional commands.

The new developments have been given impetus by the Supreme Court's recent decision in *Motor Vehicle Manufacturers Association v. State Farm Mutual Insurance Company*,[5] where the Court invalidated the rescission of a regulation requiring "passive restraints"—automatic seatbelts and airbags—in new automobiles. To some degree, the Court's decision ratified the lower courts' effort to grant the beneficiaries of regulation the same protection accorded to regulated classes. Equally important, it endorsed a number of aspects of the controversial "hard-look" doctrine developed by the lower courts, particularly the United States Court of Appeals for the District of Columbia Circuit. And the decision has implications for judicial review of the largely novel phenomenon of deregulation. For these reasons, the decision is one of the more important administrative law pronouncements of the past decade, and one of the more surprising. *State Farm*, in short, calls for a renewed assessment of the premises underlying the new directions in which administrative law has been moving.

---

[3] See Logan v. Zimmerman Brush Co., 455 U.S. 422 (1982).

[4] It is an entitlement, however, of very special sort, for there are severe difficulties in treating regulatory protection as a conventional common-law entitlement. See Stewart & Sunstein, *Public Programs and Private Rights*, 95 HARV. L. REV. 1193, 1271-75 (1982); see text at notes 42-48 *infra*.

[5] 103 S. Ct. 2856 (1983).

I. THE HARD-LOOK DOCTRINE AND RIGHTS OF INITIATION: THE CHANGING CONTOURS OF ADMINISTRATIVE LAW

Judicial review of deregulation—a development largely of the last five years—can be understood only in the context of a number of more general developments in administrative law. It is necessary here to outline those developments and their underlying rationale. Traditional doctrines of administrative law grew out of efforts by private entities—individuals or institutions—to limit regulatory initiatives. Judicial review was available when the private entity alleged that the government had invaded a right protected at common law. The official could defend successfully only on the ground that the legislature had authorized the invasion.

This basic framework explains much of American administrative law for its first half-century. Both the idea of standing to secure judicial review and the notion of "liberty" and "property" interests grew directly out of this framework. The existence of a common-law right was a necessary basis for the invocation of judicial relief. If no such right was at stake, judicial review was unavailable.[6] Thus, if a plaintiff complained of an action that offended a statute but invaded no common-law right—such as the right to be free from competition or a general consumer interest—he would lack standing to sue and have no liberty or property interest to protect.[7] The realm of common-law rights corresponds closely to those recognized by libertarian individualism.[8] The last twenty-five years, however, have seen a dramatic breakdown in this traditional private law basis of public law. The elements of the breakdown are familiar.

---

[6] See, *e.g.*, Alabama Power Co. v. Ickes, 302 U.S. 464 (1938). See generally Stewart, *The Reformation of American Administrative Law*, 88 HARV. L. REV. 1667, 1671-76 (1975).

[7] See, *e.g.*, Bailey v. Richardson, 182 F.2d 46 (D.C. Cir. 1950), *aff'd by equally divided court*, 341 U.S. 918 (1951). I speak here of rights of procedural due process, but substantive due process doctrines were also originally built on common-law principles. See, *e.g.*, Lochner v. New York, 198 U.S. 45 (1905). There have not (yet) been developments in the area of substantive due process parallel to those in the procedural context—notwithstanding scholarly support for such developments. See, *e.g.*, Michelman, *Foreword: On Protecting the Poor through the Fourteenth Amendment*, 83 HARV. L. REV. 7 (1969).

[8] See, *e.g.*, VINING, LEGAL IDENTITY (1978); Epstein, *A Theory of Strict Liability*, 2 J. LEGAL STUDIES 151 (1973).

A. STANDING

First, standing to secure review has been recognized not merely for those asserting common-law interests—rights against governmental invasion of the realm of private autonomy—but also for others suffering any "injury in fact" as a result of agency action or inaction.[9] The required injury in fact includes a wide range of harms that were not recognized at common law. A person will have standing if he can show an adverse effect that has resulted from a failure to comply with some statutory command. It is unnecessary to invoke a legally protected interest, and it is also irrelevant that many people may have been affected by the alleged violation.[10]

The result, produced in part by statute but mostly by the courts, has been to authorize suit in nearly every case in which an agency action or failure to act has adversely affected some identifiable public value.[11] Beneficiaries of regulation—for example, civil rights organizations— may often bring suit even though no common-law right is at stake. Standing is thus accorded not only to those who can show a governmental invasion of private autonomy as defined by traditional private law, but also to others whose interests have been affected because the government has ignored or impaired some value associated with a regulatory provision. This is a dramatic departure from the private law foundations of administrative law, because it is the existence of an interest associated with a statute, rather than a traditional private right, that serves as the basis for invoking judicial relief.

B. LIBERTY AND PROPERTY INTERESTS

Second, a broad range of interests have been understood as "liberty" or "property" entitled to protection under the Due Process Clause. Welfare benefits, government employment, and other forms of state

---

[9] See, e.g., Association of Data Processing Service Organizations v. Camp, 397 U.S. 150 (1970); Duke Power Co. v. Carolina Environmental Study Group, 438 U.S. 59 (1978). The changes discussed in the text cannot be attributed to the APA provisions on standing. See 5 U.S.C. §702. Those provisions are codifications of preexisting standards which had evolved from the exclusive reliance on common-law interests, but which were significantly changed by *Data Processing*. See Stewart, *The Reformation of American Administrative Law*, 88 HARV. L. REV. at 1723–48; Currie, *Misunderstanding Standing*, 1981 SUPREME COURT REVIEW 31.

[10] See, e.g., Duke Power Co. v. Carolina Environmental Study Group, 438 U.S. 59 (1978).

[11] See VINING, note 8 *supra; cf.* Stewart, *Standing for Solidarity*, 88 YALE L. J. 1559 (1979) (book review).

largesse have been given procedural protection.[12] In a potentially revolutionary development, the Court has held that protection against statutory violations by private parties can also be a property interest.[13] These developments, too, depart from the common-law roots of constitutional checks on administrative agencies.

C. THE HARD-LOOK DOCTRINE

Under traditional principles of administrative law, the central function of judicial review was to test whether Congress had authorized an invasion of a common-law right. There was little room for review of "discretionary" administrative action. In most contexts, however, the Administrative Procedure Act also allows courts to set aside agency action if such action is "arbitrary, capricious, an abuse of discretion, or otherwise not in accordance with law."[14] This language allowed some judicial supervision of agency discretion, but it was traditionally understood to require a highly deferential judicial approach.[15]

In a third development, the courts have used this language to force agencies to take, and later to initiate on their own, a "hard look" at the factual and policy issues involved in regulation.[16] The purpose of the hard-look doctrine is primarily to facilitate review of the reasonableness of the exercise of discretion, not to ascertain whether agency action has been authorized by the governing substantive law. The doctrine, which is largely the creation of the United States Court of Appeals for the District of Columbia Circuit, has both procedural and substantive components.

The procedural components include four central requirements. First, agencies must offer detailed explanations for their decisions.[17] The statutory anchor for this requirement is the APA's provisions for

---

[12] See Arnett v. Kennedy, 416 U.S. 134 (1974); Vitek v. Jones, 445 U.S. 480 (1980); Goldberg v. Kelly, 397 U.S. 254 (1970).

[13] See Logan v. Zimmerman Brush Co., 455 U.S. 422 (1982).

[14] 5 U.S.C. §706 (1976).

[15] See, e.g., Van Curle Broadcasting Corp. v. U.S., 236 F.2d 722 (D.C. Cir. 1956); Hoving Corp. v. FTC, 290 F.2d 803 (2d Cir. 1961).

[16] See Leventhal, *Environmental Decisionmaking and the Role of the Courts*, 122 U. PA L. REV. 509 (1974).

[17] See, e.g., Citizens to Preserve Overton Park, Inc. v. Volpe, 401 U.S. 402 (1971); Office of Communication of United Church of Christ v. FCC, 707 F.2d 1413 (D.C. Cir. 1983); NAACP v. FCC, 682 F.2d 993 (D.C. Cir. 1982).

judicial review,[18] which, it is thought, cannot be meaningfully exercised absent such explanations. The explanations must show that agencies have given "adequate consideration" to all factors made relevant by the controlling statute. They must also demonstrate that factors made irrelevant by that statute have not entered into the decision. The "concise statement of basis and purpose" required by the Administrative Procedure Act for notice-and-comment rulemaking is insufficient.[19]

Second, agencies must justify departures from past practices. Such practices are presumptively legitimate and deviations must be explained.[20] This principle holds whether the agency is increasing or decreasing the extent of regulation. This requirement is also based on the judicial review provisions of the APA.

Third, agencies must allow effective participation in the regulatory process by a broad range of affected interests.[21] Participation requirements have taken the form of liberal intervention rights and, until recently, remands for procedures that facilitate opportunities to take part in agency decisionmaking.[22]

Finally, agencies must give consideration to possible alternative measures. Failure to explain why certain, apparently reasonable, alternatives were not selected is a well-established basis for reversal or remand. The APA does not expressly require identification and consideration of alternatives, as do some statutes, but courts have held that it is nonetheless "arbitrary" within the meaning of the APA to disregard plausible alternatives.[23]

All of these developments can be understood as an effort to ensure that the agency's decision was a "reasoned" exercise of discretion and not merely a response to political pressures. The consequence has been

---

[18] See 5 U.S.C. §706 (1976). For one of the many cases to this effect, see Amoco Oil Co. v. EPA, 501 F. 2d 722 (D.C. Cir. 1974).

[19] 5 U.S.C. §553(c) (1976).

[20] *United Church of Christ*, 707 F.2d at 1425-26; Baltimore & Annapolis R. R. Co. v. WMATC, 642 F.2d 1365, 1370 (D.C. Cir. 1980); Nat'l Tour Brokers Ass'n v. ICC, 671 F.2d 528, 532 (D.C. Cir. 1982); Greater Boston Television Corp. v. FCC, 444 F.2d 841, 852 (D.C. Cir. 1970).

[21] See Environmental Defense Fund, Inc. v. Ruckelshaus, 439 F.2d 584 (D.C. Cir. 1971); National Welfare Rights Organization v. Finch, 429 F.2d 725 (D.C. Cir. 1970).

[22] For examples and discussion of such remands, see Scalia, *Vermont Yankee: The APA, The D.C. Circuit, and the Supreme Court*, 1978 SUPREME COURT REVIEW 345; BREYER & STEWART, ADMINISTRATIVE LAW AND REGULATORY POLICY 509-16 (1979). Of course, Vermont Yankee Nuclear Power Corp. v. Natural Resources Defense Council, 435 U.S. 519 (1978), severely undermined such rulings. But subsequent cases, involving remands for a more complete record, have accomplished the same basic goals. See BREYER & STEWART, 1982 SUPPLEMENT TO ADMINISTRATIVE LAW AND REGULATORY POLICY 77-88, and cases cited.

[23] See, *e.g.*, National Citizens Committee for Broadcasting v. FCC, 567 F.2d 1095, 1110-115 (D.C. Cir. 1977); Pillai v. CAB, 485 F.2d 1018, 1029 (D.C. Cir. 1973).

to assimilate administrative to judicial decisionmaking and to blur the traditionally sharp distinction between rulemaking and adjudication. Even in rulemaking, agencies must show that they responded to the arguments raised by all parties and that they exercised their discretion in a reasonable fashion.

One of the underlying purposes of these developments has been to replicate a pluralist approach to administration by ensuring representation of all affected interests. The notion is that if all private interests are given a chance to be heard, all will be protected. Representation thus serves as a means of aggregating private interests and maximizing the opportunity of all groups to gratify their private desires.[24] But another theme, conflicting but perhaps dominant, is that agency decisions should not be merely a response to private interests equipped with preexisting preferences. They should instead be an attempt to decide upon and implement the public values at stake in regulatory choices.[25] There are reasons to doubt whether and to what extent judicial remedies, including requirements of explanations, will be able to achieve such purposes. However that question may be resolved, the procedural elements of the hard-look doctrine are efforts to discipline agency decisions to facilitate this process.

The substantive component of the hard-look doctrine is a judicial willingness to overturn decisions that appear unjustified in light of the evidentiary record.[26] This aspect of the doctrine has been rarely exercised. There is a clear preference for "procedural" remands over substantive invalidation.[27]

The procedural and substantive elements of the hard-look doctrine are a controversial gloss on judicial review for arbitrariness, which is authorized by the APA. The doctrine is sometimes characterized as an exercise of federal common-law authority that the APA was intended

---

[24] See Stewart, *The Reformation of American Administrative Law*, 88 HARV. L. REV. 1667 (1975); Rhode, *Class Conflicts in Class Actions*, 34 STAN. L. REV. 1183, 1221-32 (1983). For criticism of this approach, see MANSBRIDGE, BEYOND ADVERSARY DEMOCRACY (1980); HABERMAS, LEGITIMATION CRISIS 123-24 (1977).

[25] See Stewart & Sunstein, note 4 *supra*, at 1278-82; VINING, note 8 *supra*; Unger, *The Critical Legal Studies Movement*, 96 HARV. L. REV. 561, 584-85 (1983). See generally ARENDT, ON REVOLUTION (1965); WOOD, THE CREATION OF THE AMERICAN REPUBLIC, 1776-1787 57 (1969). For discussion of an analogous conception of legislation, see Sunstein, *Public Values, Private Interests, and the Equal Protection Clause*, 1982 SUPREME COURT REVIEW 127; Michelman, *Politics and Values, or What's Really Wrong with Rationality Review*, 13 CREIGHTON L. REV. 487 (1979).

[26] See, *e.g.*, NRDC v. USNRC, 685 F.2d 459 (D.C. Cir. 1982), *reversed*, United States Nuclear Regulatory Com'n v. NRDC, 103 S. Ct. 2246 (1983).

[27] For criticism of this preference, see Sax, *The (Unhappy) Truth about NEPA*, 26 OKLA. L. REV. 239 (1973).

to displace. The *Vermont Yankee*[28] decision reasserted a conception of the APA as an ordinary statute which does not allow for the exercise of such authority.[29] But as *State Farm* demonstrates, *Vermont Yankee*'s holding that the courts may not impose procedural requirements beyond those provided in the APA did not affect other aspects of the hard-look doctrine—perhaps because those aspects are a reasonable gloss on the judicial review provisions of the APA, perhaps because the *Vermont Yankee* understanding of that statute will be unable to stand the test of time.[30]

D. RIGHTS OF PARTICIPATION AND INITIATION; REVIEWABILITY

Finally, the courts have allowed beneficiaries of regulatory statutes both to participate in agency activity[31] and to initiate agency action.[32] This is a revolutionary development, for the traditional role of the courts was to allow regulated entities to avoid governmental intrusions. If inadequate regulatory protection was forthcoming, the remedy was to come from political pressures, not the courts.[33]

The rejection of the traditional approach is attributable to two perceptions.[34] The first underlies all three of the previous developments as well: the common-law catalog of private rights is an inadequate yardstick for judicial intervention in a heavily regulated society. That catalog, based on liberal-individualist premises of the role of government, has been substantially eroded by legislative and

---

[28] Vermont Yankee Nuclear Power Corp. v. Natural Resources Defense Council, 435 U.S. 519 (1978).

[29] See Stewart, *Vermont Yankee and the Evolution of Administrative Procedure*, 91 HARV. L. REV. 1805 (1978).

[30] The *Vermont Yankee* Court itself concluded that detailed justification was required in order to allow for judicial review, see 435 U.S. at 549, a conclusion that seemed inconsistent with the Court's attempt to reassert what it viewed as the original understanding of the APA. In this sense, *Vermont Yankee* presaged the *States Farm* outcome.

[31] See cases cited note 21 *supra*.

[32] See notes 1-3 *supra*. See also Stewart & Sunstein, note 4 *supra*, at 1205-06, 1208-16; Note, *Judicial Review of Administrative Inaction*, 83 COLUM. L. REV. 627, 648-52 (1983).

[33] See, *e.g.*, Vaca v. Sipes, 386 U.S. 171, 181-83 (1967); Moog Indus. v. FTC, 355 U.S. 411, 413 (1958); Kixmiller v. SEC, 492 F.2d 641 (D.C. 1974). The provisions of the APA are inconclusive on the point. Reviewing courts are authorized to "compel agency action unlawfully withheld or unreasonably delayed," 5 U.S.C. §706(1), but courts may not review agency action "committed to agency discretion by law," 5 U.S.C. §701 (a) (2). It is unclear, from the text and history of the statute, to what extent agency failure to act is unreviewable because committed to agency discretion. Nor do governing statutes generally resolve the problem, for they fail to distinguish between action and inaction.

[34] See Stewart & Sunstein, note 4 *supra*, at 1278-79.

administrative developments before and after the New Deal. It would be odd indeed if the judiciary adhered to a highly controversial political theory repudiated by other branches of government and maintained its original posture after the common-law catalog had been supplemented through the imposition of affirmative duties on government.[35] Judicial reluctance to recognize initiation rights was founded in large part on faith in the availability of political remedies for agency inaction. But those remedies have seemed inadequate for the often unorganized beneficiaries of regulation.[36]

The second perception involves the risk of capture of regulatory power by factions seeking to redistribute wealth or opportunities in their own favor. Agencies are not directly accountable to the electorate. And there is developing recognition that the authority exercised by Congress and the President is intermittent.[37] The consequence has been an increased danger that well-organized private groups would be able to use governmental power for their own ends.[38]

Administrative agencies have thus been a severe intrusion into the original constitutional structure in the familiar sense that they displaced lawmaking authority vested in Congress. They have been an intrusion as well in the less obvious sense that they usurped authority to allocate resources that was the original province of the state and federal courts. The common law, as recent writers have reminded us, was above all a regulatory system.[39] This system helped to guard against the most obvious forms of "capture"[40] by factions seeking to redistribute wealth or opportunities in their favor. But the dis-

---

[35] The "take Care" clause, Art. II, sec. 3, cl. 4, obliges the President to ensure faithful execution of all laws, not only those of which he approves. As a general rule, judicial review should be available whenever the President has violated that responsibility—whether through action or inaction. See Nader v. Saxbe, 497 F.2d 676, 679 (D.C. Cir. 1974).

[36] See Stewart & Sunstein, note 4 *supra*, at 1284-86.

[37] See Litan & Nordhaus, *Reforming Federal Regulation* 60-81 (1983). But see Weingast & Moran, *The Myth of Runaway Bureaucracy—the Case of the FTC*, REGULATION (May-June 1982) at 33.

[38] See, for recent discussion, Aranson, Gellhorn, & Robinson, *A Theory of Legislative Delegation*, 68 CORNELL L. REV. 1 (1982).

[39] See POSNER, ECONOMIC ANALYSIS OF LAW (2d ed. 1977); HORWITZ, THE TRANSFORMATION OF AMERICAN LAW, 1780-1860 (1977); but *cf.* Epstein, *The Social Consequences of Common Law Rules*, 95 HARV. L. REV. 1717 (1982).

[40] This is not to deny that common-law rules may reflect a distinct ideology that may operate in the interest of particular groups. See Kennedy, *Form and Substance in Private Law Adjudication*, 89 HARV L. REV. 1685 (1976). In some circumstances they affect the distribution of wealth. See HORWITZ, note 39 *supra*.

placement of the common-law system by a vast administrative apparatus has created a renewed risk of capture of governmental power by narrow interest groups.

The risk can appear in the form of redirection of governmental power by regulatory beneficiaries as well as by regulated industries. Indeed, judicial review of agency action is sometimes understood as a response to the former phenomenon. But agency inaction, or lax enforcement, is often conspicuously the product of sustained organizing efforts of regulated entities. Creation of rights of participation—in the form of review of enforcement activity—might be justified as a partial response to the possibility that the values identified in regulatory statutes will be subverted in the enforcement process.[41] Such rights serve as a mechanism, admittedly highly imperfect, for the identification and implementation of those values, which will sometimes be found in governing statutes and sometimes sought by the courts through a more open-ended process. In this sense, the effort to promote participation by all those affected is intended to serve as a rough surrogate for legislative control.[42]

In short, judicial protection of private ordering—freedom to go about one's business without unauthorized regulatory intrusions—has been accompanied by a willingness to protect citizens from public law torts as well: freedom from racial discrimination, from pollution, from the wide range of torts statutorily proscribed by an affirmative state. And that protection takes the form, not of safeguarding "rights" in the ordinary sense, but of attempting to structure a process through which such public torts will be identified and remedied.[43]

All of these developments show that administrative law is shifting away from an understanding that the role of the courts is to police a realm of private autonomy by demanding legislative authorization for government intrusions. That understanding produced a public law that was distinctly private, in the sense that it owed its origin and shape to private law principles and treated government officials like any other person invading the realm protected by common-law doctrines.

---

[41] See Stewart & Sunstein, note 4 *supra*, at 1278-82.

[42] See the discussion of "responsive law" in NONET & SELZNICK, LAW AND SOCIETY IN TRANSITION: TOWARD RESPONSIVE LAW 73-113 (1977). See also HABERMAS, COMMUNICATION AND THE EVOLUTION OF SOCIETY (1967); Teubner, *Substantive and Reflexive Elements in Modern Law*, 17 LAW & SOC. REV. 239 (1983).

[43] These developments have close parallels outside of the context of administrative law. See Rhode, note 24 *supra* (class actions); Sunstein, *Judicial Relief and Public Tort Law*, 92 YALE L. J. 450 (1983) (injunctions). See also VINING, note 8 *supra*, at 179-81, for a provocative discussion of the "possible unity of public and private law."

The new developments are leading toward a public law that is to a substantial degree independent of private law principles. But because of the absence of a historical tradition, the effort to define the elements of such a public law remain tentative and ill-formed. For present purposes, it may be sufficient to begin with two suggestions. The first is that courts have disciplined administrative decisions by requiring close justification in instrumental terms. The effort is to control the exercise of discretion—a task handled uneasily by traditional administrative law—through requiring explanations that resemble those offered in the judicial process. As applied to administrative agencies, this requirement of "comprehensive rationality" borrows from contemporary policy analysis to require precise identification of goals and detailed exploration of the ways in which various alternatives might achieve those goals. Belief in the potential of such approaches tends to be associated with belief in a more or less objective public interest and with skepticism toward the notion that collective decisions are simply a matter of mediating the terms of a battle among competing social groups.[44]

The second and somewhat more general suggestion is that the function of judicial review is no longer to protect private interests from governmental intrusion, but instead to facilitate the identification and enforcement of regulatory values. Under this approach, the effort is not to implement or trade off preexisting private interests but rather to ascertain the public values that ought to control the controversy.[45] There should be nothing mysterious in this process. Sometimes the relevant values can be found in the governing statute. On occasion, the statute is obscure, and the courts' role becomes more open ended. In such cases, the judicial task requires procedural and substantive rules designed to ensure public scrutiny and review in the regulatory process and to guard against the possibility that government power will be taken over by a particular faction. Public values are what emerge from the process of discussion of statutorily relevant factors and are thus defined in procedural rather than in substantive terms.

---

[44] See Diver, *Policymaking Paradigms in Administrative Law*, 95 HARV L. REV. 393 (1981); LINDBLOM, THE INTELLIGENCE OF DEMOCRACY (1965); Bruff & Gellhorn, *Congressional Control of Administrative Regulation: A Study of Legislative Vetoes*, 90 HARV. L. REV. 1369, 1375-77 (1977).

[45] Such an approach must be understood as an effort to return to the Constitution's roots in civil republicanism. See WOOD, note 25 *supra*; SULLIVAN, RECONSTRUCTING PUBLIC PHILOSOPHY (1982). *Cf.* Unger, *The Critical Legal Studies Movement*, 96 HARV. L. REV. 561, 584-85, 592-93 (1983); Tribe, *Technology Assessment and the Fourth Discontinuity: The Limits of Instrumental Rationality*, 46 U.S.C. L. REV. 617 (1973).

The hard-look doctrine may, in short, be understood as an effort to develop rules to govern this process.

There is, moreover, a relationship between the requirements of technocratic rationality and the attempt to select public values. The former device—careful reasoning in many ways reminiscent of the judicial process—is designed to filter out or expose the "political" factors that often underlie agency decisions. Often, of course, consideration of such factors is unobjectionable, and it would be naive to suggest that courts can or should attempt to remove them.[46] One of the central dilemmas of administrative law grows out of recognition that "politics" sometimes should and often does play a major role in agency decisions, and by fear that such considerations are sometimes made irrelevant by statute and in any event threaten to mask capture of the regulatory process by factions. The goal of the requirement of technocratic rationality is to ensure that the relevant considerations are opened up to public scrutiny and review and not shielded behind discussion of the factual data alone. In this respect, judicial examination of means-ends connections under the hard-look doctrine serves functions similar to those of means-ends scrutiny under the Equal Protection Clause.

It is important to be realistic about the limitations of judicial remedies, and one may find it highly implausible to think that such remedies will by themselves be able to transform the regulatory process into a forum for collective self-determination. That process, with or without judicial intervention, tends to be dominated by private groups pressing their private interests. The notion that, under current conditions, rights of participation and initiation can produce a kind of Habermasian "ideal speech situation"[47] is wildly romantic. There is, moreover, the familiar risks that judicial remedies will be based on a skewed understanding of a complex regulatory scheme or serve the preferences of the judges rather than promote genuine public interests. But to recognize the limits of judicial remedies is not to deny that those remedies may redress persistent biases in the administrative process, or that the reformulated doctrine points in the direction of a normative framework altogether different from that which formed the original basis for public law doctrines.

---

[46] See Bazelon, *Coping with Technology through the Legal Process*, 62 CORNELL L. REV. 817 (1977).

[47] See Habermas, note 42 *supra*. See also ACKERMAN, SOCIAL JUSTICE AND THE LIBERAL STATE (1980).

All four of the developments I have outlined can be understood as responses to one or both of the primary themes. And the *State Farm* case directly tested the developments and the themes in the important context of deregulation.

II. STATE FARM: THE REGULATORY BACKGROUND

We are in the midst of considerable controversy over the functions served by regulation,[48] a controversy that has dramatically affected contemporary debate over governmental efforts to promote automobile safety.[49] The federal government's decision to regulate automobile safety might be justified on a number of grounds. Under an economic approach, for example, the government might believe that the decision to allow an unregulated market produces significant externalities,[50] that people have inadequate information about the benefits of safety precautions,[51] or that consumers react irrationally to dangerous situations where the probability of the danger is low.[52] Alternatively, the government might conclude that paternalism is justified in this context because even if armed with perfect information, consumers will make decisions that they will or should regret.[53] Justifications of this sort compete with a more cynical theory that regulation is often sought and obtained by narrow interest groups intent on redistributing wealth or opportunities in their favor.[54]

---

[48] See, *e.g.*, BREYER, REGULATION AND ITS REFORM (1982); NOLL & OWEN, THE POLITICAL ECONOMY OF DEREGULATION (1983); Kennedy, *Distributive and Paternalist Motives in Contract and Tort Law, with special reference to compulsory terms and unequal bargaining power*, 41 MD. L. REV. 563 (1982).

[49] See, *e.g.*, BREYER, note 48 *supra*. On the effectiveness of automobile regulation, *compare* Peltzman, *The Effects of Automobile Safety Regulations*, 83 J. POL. ECON. 677 (1975), *with* Nelson, *Comments on Peltzman's Paper on Automobile Safety Regulation*, in MANNE & MILLER, eds. AUTO SAFETY REGULATION 63 (1976); and MacAvoy, *The Regulations of Accidents, id.* at 83.

[50] See Dahlman, *The Problem of Externality*, 22 J. L. & ECON. 141 (1979); Kennedy, *Cost-Benefit Analysis of Entitlement Problems: A Critique*, 33 STAN. L. REV. 387 (1981).

[51] *Cf.* Posner, *Strict Liability: A Comment*, 2 J. LEGAL STUDIES 205, 211 (1973).

[52] See Tversky & Kahneman, *Availability: A Heuristic for Judging Frequency and Probability*, 5 COGNITIVE PSYCHOL. 207 (1973); Kunreuther, *Limited Knowledge and Insurance Protection*, 24 PUB. POL. 227 (1976); Arnould & Brabowski, *Auto Safety Regulation: An Analysis of Market Failure*, 12 BELL J. ECON. 27 (1981).

[53] See Kennedy, note 48 *supra*; Kelman, *Choice and Utility*, 1979 WIS. L. REV. 769. An argument based on distributional consequences would seem implausible here. See Markovits, *The Distributive Impact, Allocative Efficiency, and Overall Desirability of Ideal Housing Codes: Some Theoretical Clarifications*, 89 HARV. L. REV. 1815 (1976); Ackerman, *Regulating Slum Housing Markets on Behalf of the Poor: Of Housing Codes, Housing Subsidies and Income Redistribution Policy*, 80 YALE L. J. 1093 (1971).

[54] See Stigler, *The Theory of Economic Regulation*, 2 BELL J. ECON. 3 (1971); Peltzman, *Toward a More General Theory of Regulation*, 19 J. L. & ECON. 211 (1976); Jordan, *Producer Protection*,

Deregulation is the object of considerable enthusiasm nowadays.[55] The enthusiasm may be attributed to two different perceptions. The first is that regulation itself imposes significant costs on government, on those regulated, and (sometimes) even on the purported beneficiaries of regulation. The second is that the effect of regulation is often not to promote economic (or any other) welfare, but instead to redistribute resources to groups that have no special claim to public assistance. For example, the federal food and drug laws might protect existing sellers at the expense of new entrants and the public at large.[56] Whether such perceptions are accurate in a particular context requires examination of the force of the various rationales for government intervention. Both of the perceptions are reflected in recent executive orders drawing attention to the costs and benefits of regulation[57] and in deregulation of a number of substantive areas.[58]

Deregulation has, moreover, been subject to judicial challenge with increasing frequency.[59] The usual basis for attack is that the decision to allow an unregulated market is inconsistent with the governing statute or that it is otherwise arbitrary. An example of the first claim is deregulation on the basis of a conclusion that regulation does not promote economic "efficiency"[60] although the statute is not concerned with efficiency at all.[61] An example of the second is deregulation when the evidence shows that the advantages of regulation substantially outweigh the disadvantages.[62] Both claims assert something like a right to regulation, or at least to consideration of a particular range of factors and a particular sort of procedure in deciding whether and how much regulation is appropriate. Challenges of this kind have had varying

---

Prior Market Structure and the Effects of Government Regulation, 15 J. L. & ECON. 151 (1972).

[55] See NOLL & OWEN, note 48 *supra;* BREYER, note 48 *supra;* Presidential Task Force on Regulatory Relief, Reagan Administration Regulatory Achievements (1983); TOLCHIN & TOLCHIN, DISMANTLING AMERICA: THE RUSH TO DEREGULATE (1983).

[56] See Peltzman, *An Evaluation of Consumer Protection Legislation: The 1962 Drug Amendments,* 81 J. POL. ECON. 1049 (1973).

[57] See Executive Order No. 12,291, 46 Fed. Reg. 13,193 (1981); see also Presidential Task Force Report, note 55 *supra.*

[58] Including, most prominently, communications, airlines, and trucking.

[59] See, *e.g.,* United Church of Christ v. FCC, note 17 *supra;* Action on Smoking and Health v. CAB, 699 F.2d 1209 (D.C. Cir. 1983); NAACP v. FCC, 682 F.2d 993 (D.C. Cir. 1982); CCIA v. FCC, 693 F.2d 198 (D.C. Cir. 1982); Building & Construction Trade Dept. v. Donovan, 553 F. Supp. 352 (D.D.C. 1982).

[60] See *Symposium: Cost-Benefit Analysis and Agency Decision-Making: An Analysis of Executive Order No. 12,291,* 23 ARIZ L. REV. 1195 (1981).

[61] See, *e.g.,* American Textile Mfrs. Inst. v. Donovan, 452 U.S. 490 (1981).

[62] The *State Farm* case is itself an example.

degrees of success.[63] The difficulty has been to apply the principles of judicial review developed in the past twenty-five years to this novel phenomenon.

A. PASSIVE RESTRAINTS IN NHTSA AND THE LOWER COURTS

The *State Farm* decision involved the National Traffic and Motor Vehicle Safety Act of 1966,[64] a statute typical of modern safety legislation. The Act requires the Secretary of Transportation to issue motor vehicle safety standards that "shall be practicable, shall meet the need for motor vehicle safety, and shall be stated in objective terms."[65] The Secretary must consider "relevant available motor vehicle safety data,"[66] whether the standard in question is "reasonable, practicable, and appropriate" for the relevant motor vehicle,[67] and the extent to which the standard "will contribute to carrying out the purposes" of the Act.[68] Judicial review is provided for all "orders establishing, amending, or revoking a Federal motor vehicle safety standard."[69] It is pursuant to this Act that the federal government elected to require passive restraints in automobiles.

The interest in passive restraints originated because manual belts have had relatively low usage rates—about 11 percent. Such belts are termed "active" because passengers must take action to connect them. Inertia results in nonuse. With passive restraints, the protection is automatic. Inertia results in use. Significant gains in safety could result. According to one NHTSA (National Highway Traffic Safety Administration) estimate, 7,000 lives would be saved annually by passive restraints and 130,000 injuries would be prevented.

Three kinds of passive restraints are pertinent here. The first is the detachable belt, which operates like an ordinary seatbelt except that it is automatically connected when a rider enters the automobile. It can, however, be detached permanently. The second kind of passive restraint is the continuous or nondetachable belt, which is identical to the detachable belt except that it is much harder to disconnect. The third kind of passive restraint is the airbag. Airbags, which are installed

---

[61] See cases cited in note 59 *supra*.
[64] 15 U.S.C. § § 1381 *et seq.* (1976 and Supp. IV. 1980).
[65] *Id.* at § 1392(a).
[66] *Id.* at § 1392 (f).
[67] *Id.* at § 1392 (f) (3).
[68] *Id.* at § 1392 (f) (4).
[69] *Id.* at § 1392(b).

in the dashboard of the car, are invisible and are activated only in a crash.

The Transportation Department's lengthy involvement with passive restraints began in 1969 with a notice of proposed rulemaking. After three years of administrative proceedings, the Department issued its final rule, requiring installation of passive restraints in all vehicles manufactured after late 1975. In the period of transition—1973 to 1975—manufacturers could comply with the rule by installing either passive restraints or manual belts combined with ignition interlocks. Shortly after its promulgation, the regulation was challenged in court, where it was upheld,[70] and in Congress, which promptly amended the Safety Act so as to prohibit ignition interlocks or continuous buzzers designed to indicate that safety belts are not in use.[71] Congress did not otherwise enact any provision dealing with passive restraints.

In 1977,[72] the Transportation Department, under Secretary Brock Adams, again proposed passive restraints. The relevant regulation would have required their installation in new automobiles. It would, however, have given manufacturers a choice among detachable belts, nondetachable belts, and airbags. A judicial challenge was again unsuccessful,[73] and this time efforts to obtain congressional action failed. In its final form, the regulation required adoption of passive restraints in large cars in model year 1982 and in all cars by 1984.

In 1981, the Reagan Administration—one month after assuming office—proposed to postpone implementation of the passive restraints rule by one year, citing the economic problems of the automobile industry. Two months later, the new administrator proposed rescission of the existing rules, and on October 29, 1981, he rescinded the rule.[74]

The administrator agreed that if usage rates increased by 13 percent—from the current rate of 11.4 percent to 24.4 percent—the benefits of the passive restraint standard would justify the costs. But he concluded that no such increase would be likely to occur. The administrator relied heavily on the fact that the "overwhelming majority of new cars would be equipped with automatic belts that are

[70] Chrysler Corp. v. Department of Transportation, 472 F.2d 659 (6th Cir. 1972).

[71] 15 U.S.C. § 1410(b) (1) (1976).

[72] In 1976, Secretary Coleman had initiated rulemaking on the same problem, but eventually proposed a demonstration project to ensure public support and ascertain the benefits. See 42 FED. REG. 5071 (1977).

[73] Pacific Legal Foundation v. Department of Transportation, 593 F.2d 1338 (D.C. Cir.).

[74] 46 FED. REG. 53,419 (Oct. 29, 1981).

detachable."[75] Several of the automobile manufacturers that had participated in the proceedings indicated their plan to use detachable belts. Detachable belts, however, would suffer from some of the same defects as the manual belts: they can be permanently detached.

The administrator concluded that he could not "reliably predict even a five percentage point increase as the minimum level of expected usage increase."[76] There was thus substantial uncertainty that the rule would do much good. At the same time, the rule would be quite costly. Imposition of a passive restraint requirement would have an annual cost of about $1 billion resulting from an increase of about $89 per car. It could also produce a "poisoning of popular sentiment toward efforts to improve occupant systems in the future," and might lead dissatisfied consumers to cut "automatic belts out of their cars, thus depriving subsequent owners of the cars of the protection of any occupant restraint system."[77]

This analysis would not bar other sorts of passive restraints, including continuous, or nondetachable, belts and airbags. With respect to the former, the administrator invoked considerations of cost, equity, public reception, and safety. Ignition interlocks had produced a hostile public reaction culminating in a statute prohibiting the proposed regulatory action. This history suggested that Congress might respond unfavorably to nondetachable belts as well. Moreover, such belts could be counterproductive in view of reaction by potential users, who would fear being trapped. NHTSA did not, however, discuss the possibility of requiring airbags, saying that the issue was not before it.[78]

In a lengthy decision, the court of appeals reversed.[79] It began by meeting the argument that judicial review of deregulation should be identical to review of a failure to act. According to the court, the fact that NHTSA had changed directions so sharply and so suddenly created "danger signals" justifying relatively intensive scrutiny.[80] This conclusion, according to the court, was especially powerful in light of Congress's repeated failure to overturn passive restraint standards proposed by previous administrations. The court referred in particular

---

[75] *Id.* at 53,421.
[76] *Id.* at 53,423.
[77] *Id.* at 53,424.
[78] See 103 S. Ct. at 2869.
[79] 680 F.2d 206 (D.C. Cir. 1982).
[80] *Id.* at 228–230.

to the failure to outlaw passive restraints when Congress invalidated the ignition interlock rule, the failure to apply the legislative veto in 1977, and certain floor action on a 1980 authorization bill, in which Congress failed to ban passive restraints.

Under this heightened scope of review, the court held that the decision could not stand. It relied on two lines of argument. First, NHTSA failed to show that seatbelt usage would not increase in the way originally anticipated. To be sure, most manufacturers planned to use detachable passive belts. But there was considerable record evidence showing that even with detachable belts, a substantial increase in usage would result. NHTSA, according to the court, faced some burden to explain why "a regulation once considered to prevent deaths and injuries efficiently can no longer be expected to do so."[81]

Second, the court held that the agency erred in failing to give adequate consideration to alternatives.[82] There was insufficient discussion of the possibility of requiring nondetachable belts and no discussion at all of the installation of airbags. In this respect, the court's decision reflected the traditional use of the hard-look doctrine to require consideration of reasonable alternatives.

B. THE SUPREME COURT'S DECISION

The Supreme Court accepted major portions of the lower court's reasoning.[83] Two aspects of the Court's opinion are of primary importance. The first relates to the scope of review of deregulation. The second involves the Court's approach to the merits, which reflects a willingness to scrutinize agency decisions with considerable care.

1. *Scope of review.* Three major claims had been made by various petitioners with respect to scope of review. The court of appeals, echoed rather unenthusiastically by respondents, had added a fourth. Acceptance of any one of them would have had dramatic implications for administrative law. But the Supreme Court, unanimous on these points, rejected all four claims.

The first claim began with the premise that review of a refusal to promulgate a rule in the first instance is extraordinarily deferential. According to petitioners, review of deregulation should also be

---

[81] *Id.* at 231.

[82] *Id.* at 233. Judge Edwards did not join this part of the opinion. See *id.* at 242.

[83] The Court did not, however, affirm, but vacated the judgment of the court of appeals and remanded for further administrative proceedings. See note 92 *infra.*

deferential, because it is functionally identical to review of inaction. Without commenting on the premise, the Court found the claim unpersuasive on two grounds. First, the governing statute applies its review provisions "to all orders establishing, amending, or revoking" a standard. In the Court's view, the attempted distinction between establishment and revocation of a rule would therefore be inconsistent with congressional intent. Second, the Court noted that revocation, unlike a mere failure to act, amounts to "a reversal of the agency's former view as to the proper course."[84] Any departure from a prior course obligates an agency to "supply a reasoned analysis for the change beyond that which may be required when an agency does not act in the first instance."[85] The Court rejected the notion that courts should intervene primarily to protect private ordering, for "the forces of change do not always or necessarily point in the direction of deregulation," and "the direction in which an agency chooses to move does not alter the standard of judicial review established by law."[86]

The second claim relating to scope of review was that the test for arbitrariness under the APA is identical to the rationality requirements of the Due Process Clause. Drawing on the history of the APA and some early cases,[87] the Department of Transportation had argued that the constitutional and statutory tests were identical. The Court rejected the claim flatly, without explanation.

The third contention was that under the arbitrary and capricious test, administrative agencies are under no obligation to consider alternatives. But in the Court's view, "an agency rule would be arbitrary and capricious if the agency has relied on factors which Congress has not intended it to consider, entirely failed to consider an important aspect of the problem, offered an explanation for its decision that runs counter to the evidence before the agency, or is so implausible that it could not be ascribed to a difference in view or [be] the product of agency expertise."[88]

Finally, the Court rejected the court of appeals' view that the inaction of Congress justified heightening the standard of review. According to the Court, the failure to apply the legislative veto, and other related events relied on by the lower court, provided no reason

---

[84] *Id.* at 2866.
[85] *Id.*
[86] *Id.*
[87] See note 103 *infra.*
[88] 103 S. Ct. at 2867.

to believe that Congress approved of the passive restraints requirements.

In short, the Court endorsed the basic elements of the hard-look doctrine as formulated by the United States Court of Appeals for the District of Columbia Circuit—an endorsement that, as discussed below, is responsive to that court's effort to generate public law doctrines that do not grow out of private law. At the same time, the Court rejected the notion that deregulation is subject to any special standard. There is no one-way ratchet in favor of regulation, as some language in the lower court's opinion could be read to suggest, nor is special deference to be granted to deregulation.

2. *The merits.* The Court made two major rulings on the merits. The first, on which the Court was unanimous, involved the failure to consider the alternative of requiring airbags. The second, on which the Court divided five to four, involved the legality of the agency's decisions with respect to both detachable and nondetachable belts.

The Court first concluded that the rescission was arbitrary, because the agency did not explain why it failed to modify the standard to require airbags. The rescission rested on an understanding that manufacturers would use detachable belts, which would not substantially increase usage. But the fact that manufacturers had chosen an ineffective means of compliance, the Court said, was insufficient to justify rescission. The agency could have responded simply by disallowing detachable belts and by requiring airbags. "At the very least this alternative way of achieving the objectives of the Act should have been addressed and adequate reasons given for its abandonment."[89]

Second, the Court agreed with the court of appeals that the rescission of the detachable and nondetachable belts requirements was arbitrary. The Court acknowledged that substantial uncertainty that an existing standard was beneficial would be a proper basis for rescission. But such a conclusion must be supported by reasons, and those reasons must include an explanation "for rescinding the regulation before engaging in a search for further evidence."[90] Here, the Court found the agency's reasons insufficient. There were uncertainties in the evidence showing that usage rates would increase substantially with detachable belts. But the agency failed to consider that with passive belts, whether or not detachable, inertia "works in favor of, not against, use of the

---

[89] *Id.* at 2869.
[90] *Id.* at 2871.

protective device."[91] This factor was sufficiently important to require reconsideration of the agency's conclusion that there would be no significant gain in expected usage from passive belts.

Finally, the agency failed to explain why it did not require nondetachable belts. Because such belts would not be detachable, they would, by hypothesis, increase usage rates. The agency had previously concluded that this belt design would allow easy extricability. And the mere reference to irrational fear on the part of the public was insufficient.

At the same time, the Court rejected the court of appeals' conclusion that the passive restraints rule promulgated by the Carter Administration should be ordered into effect. The effect of the Court's ruling was only to require reconsideration of the entire question. There was sufficient basis for **NHTSA** to suspend the effective date of the rule pending that consideration.[92]

In a separate opinion dissenting in part, Justice Rehnquist, joined by the Chief Justice and Justices Powell and O'Connor, agreed with the ruling on airbags, but he rejected the holding with respect to detachable belts. According to Justice Rehnquist, it was sufficient for the administrator to say that there would be some increase in usage whose costs would outweigh its benefits. In Justice Rehnquist's view, the changed view of costs and benefits was attributable "to the election of a new President of a different political party."[93] A new administration "may consider public resistance and uncertainties to be more important than do their counterparts in a previous administration," and there was nothing wrong with that.[94] In a footnote, however, he added: "Of course, a new administration may not choose not to enforce laws of which it does not approve, or to ignore statutory standards in carrying out its regulatory functions."[95]

III. THE HARD-LOOK DOCTRINE AND DEREGULATION

A. SCOPE OF REVIEW

The Court's conclusions in *State Farm* were both important and correct on all four issues with respect to scope of review.

---

[91] *Id.* at 2872.

[92] In the Court's view, "the agency had sufficient justification to suspend, although not to rescind, Standard 208, pending the further consideration. . . ." *Id.* at 2874 n.21. There is presumably some time limit affixed to the permission to suspend, so as to prevent evasion of the Court's decision.

[93] *Id.* at 2875.

[94] *Id.*

[95] *Id.* at 2875 n.*.

1. Congress's failure to apply the legislative veto can hardly be taken as evidence of legislative approval of passive restraints. Here, as elsewhere, inaction may be attributable to a number of factors other than approval: belief that the courts would invalidate the measure, indifference, lack of time, and so forth. In some contexts, to be sure, subsequent congressional approval of administrative practice may be relevant in ascertaining the original legislative intent, even if the approval has not manifested itself in positive law but merely in repeated informal expressions of awareness and agreement.[96] But there was nothing of that sort in the *State Farm* case. The Court was thus correct to hold that congressional inaction was, at least in this context, entitled to no weight in considering the legality of the rescission.

2. For two related reasons, the Court was also correct in rejecting the notion that agency action is to be assessed under the standards of due process rationality. First, administrative agencies exercising broad discretionary power do not have a strong constitutional pedigree.[97] As an historical matter, a judicial check—ensuring that agencies stay within the bounds set by Congress and guarding against arbitrariness— has been an important, if imperfect, means of fulfilling some of the purposes underlying the original constitutional structure. Such a judicial role has worked to promote predictability on the part of regulated actors and regulatory beneficiaries, to ensure that agencies adhere to the will of the politically accountable branches of government, and to reduce the risk that governmental power will be used by powerful factions to redistribute wealth or opportunities in their favor.[98] No such argument is applicable when the decisionmaker is Congress.

Second, Congress recognized the need for a relatively aggressive judicial role in the Administrative Procedure Act. The APA grew out of competing forces with different motivations, but two central points are clear. The first is that the statute was largely a product of dissatisfaction with the legitimacy of the administrative agency in American government. The second is that at least one response was to increase the authority of the federal courts over agency decisions. The increased risk that administrative agencies might be captured by factional interests; the connection of that risk to the breach of the twin

---

[96] See United States v. Midwest Oil, 236 U.S. 459, 472–73 (1914); Zemel v. Rusk, 381 U.S. 1, 11–12 (1965); Haig v. Agee, 453 U.S. 280, 297–301 (1981); Bob Jones University v. United States, 103 S. Ct. 2017, 2032–34 (1983).

[97] See Stewart & Sunstein, note 4 *supra*, at 1232–33.

[98] See generally Stewart & Sunstein, note 4 *supra*.

safeguards of electoral accountability and separation of powers; and the potential virtues of a check by an independent, decentralized judiciary—all of these were prominent themes behind the enactment of the APA.[99]

The original APA framework for judicial review was, of course, designed for two polar cases. The first involved adjudication, which was to be reviewed for "substantial evidence."[100] As the Court made clear in *Universal Camera*,[101] such review both reflected and expressed a "mood" to the effect "that courts must now assume more responsibility for the reasonableness and fairness" of agency decisions.[102] The second category of cases involved notice-and-comment rulemaking, sometimes called "informal" rulemaking, which was to be reviewed pursuant to the "arbitrary and capricious" standard generally applicable to administrative decisions. The nature of this standard received little independent discussion in the legislative history of the APA.[103]

For two reasons,[104] it should not be surprising that most of the legislators' interest focused on judicial review of adjudicatory decisions and that little attention was paid to rulemaking. Only recently has

[99] See, *e.g.*, Legislative History, Administrative Procedure Act, S. Doc. No. 248, 79th Cong., 2d Sess. 48 (concern that agencies threaten "to develop a 'fourth branch' of the Government for which there is no sanction in the Constitution"); *id.* at 305 ("I desire to emphasize ... the provisions for judicial review, because it is something in which the American public has been and is much concerned, harkening back, if we may, to the Constitution of the United States, which sets up the judicial branch of the Government for the redress of human wrongs"); *id.* at 217 ("the enforcement of the bill, by the independent judicial interpretation and application of its terms, is a function which is clearly conferred upon the courts ... Judicial review is of utmost importance ... It is indispensable since its mere existence generally precludes the arbitrary exercise of powers not granted"); *id.* at 311; *id.* at 312; *id.* at 382-85. For contemporaneous commentary to the same effect, see, *e.g.*, Sherwood, *The Federal Administrative Procedure Act*, 41 AM. POL. SCI. REV. 271 (1947), and sources cited; Dickinson, *Administrative Procedure Act: Scope and Grounds of Broadened Judicial Review*, 33 A.B.A.J. 434 (1947); McCarran, *Improving "Administrative Justice": Hearings and Evidence; Scope of Judicial Review*, 32 A.B.A.J. 827 (1946).

[100] 5 U.S.C. § 706 (1976).

[101] Universal Camera Corp. v. NLRB, 340 U.S. 474 (1951).

[102] *Id.* at 490.

[103] There was a suggestion that the provision in general would "restate the several categories of questions of law subject to judicial review ... The several categories, constantly repeated by courts in the course of judicial decisions or opinions, were first established by the Supreme Court as the minimum requisite under the Constitution and have also been carried into State practice, in part at least, as the result of the identical due process clause of the Fourteenth Amendment, applicable to the States, and the Fifth Amendment, applicable to the Federal Government." Senate Judiciary Committee Print (1945), as reproduced in Legislative History, Administrative Procedure Act, S. Doc. No. 248, 79th Cong., 2d Sess. 39 (1946) (citations omitted). But it would be a mistake to read such language to suggest a highly deferential judicial role, since the cases cited for due process standards were decided during the heyday of substantive due process.

[104] The points are discussed in Scalia, *Vermont Yankee: The APA, the D.C. Circuit, and the Supreme Court*, 1979 SUPREME COURT REVIEW 345; Stewart, *Vermont Yankee and the Evolution of Administrative Procedure*, 91 HARV. L. REV. 1805 (1978).

notice-and-comment rulemaking become a dominant method of agency decisionmaking. And it also has been only recently that judicial review has come in the form of pre-enforcement challenges to regulations, usually in the courts of appeals. This was a critical development. Most important, it made it impossible to comply with what some regard as the APA drafters' original desire to ensure that the validity of rules would be decided in a *de novo* proceeding in the district court.[105] The administrative record became the sole basis for upholding or invalidating the agency's decision. There was no opportunity to develop additional facts in court.

Paradoxically, the consequence of these two developments was to make strict adherence to the original APA framework quite incongruous, especially from the standpoint of the original intention of the APA drafters. If the "arbitrary and capricious" approach is taken to be highly deferential, one of the dominant purposes of the APA—to increase judicial supervisory power—would be frustrated by a shift to rulemaking and the rise of pre-enforcement review. Judicial review would become a simple exercise of assessing whether there was a rational justification for the regulation, with the statement of basis and purpose serving as the only articulated grounds for the agency's decision—hardly what was foreseen by the APA drafters as the method of review in the great range of cases. To be sure, the intention to increase judicial supervision was in many quarters accompanied by an understanding that such supervision would help to fend off, rather than require, regulatory impositions. But the judicial review provisions of the APA do not include any such one-way ratchet.

Some of these considerations should be familiar, for they surfaced in recent discussion of the propriety of judicial imposition of procedural requirements in notice-and-comment rulemaking.[106] The same considerations apply, and with more force, in evaluating the "mood" set by the APA for scope of review of rulemaking. To argue, under present circumstances, that such review is equivalent to current constitutional tests of "rationality" seems inconsistent with the underlying purposes of the APA.

3. The third contention, involving the attempted equation of review of inaction and review of deregulation, is the most difficult to assess.

---

[105] See Nathanson, *Probing the Mind of the Administrator: Hearing Variations and Standards of Judicial Review under the Administrative Procedure Act and Other Federal Statutes*, 75 COLUM. L. REV. 721 (1975); Nathanson, *The Vermont Yankee Nuclear Power Opinion: A Masterpiece of Statutory Misinterpretation*, 16 SAN DIEGO L. REV. 183 (1979).

[106] See note 104 *supra*.

In rejecting the claim, the Court relied on the statutory provision for review of "revocation" as well as for promulgation of regulations. But the provision for review does not resolve the problem of scope of review, and it does not preclude a conclusion that special deference is due in the context of revocation. To understand the problem, it will be useful to examine why review of inaction is said to require an especially deferential judicial role.[107] The question is more difficult than it might at first appear. The APA does not provide much guidance on the question, and it hardly provides a deferential standard for review of inaction.[108] Moreover, governing substantive statutes rarely distinguish action from inaction. Instead the distinction is largely a creation of courts exercising common-law powers.

As an historical matter, principles of prosecutorial discretion help to account for the traditional deference. Those principles rest at least in part on the availability of alternative forms of private relief, including tort remedies. But in addition, they rest on a fear that judicial oversight of an agency's exercise of its enforcement powers often requires assessment of a complex variety of factors that are not well suited to judicial review. An agency's decision not to act depends in part on the legality of the private conduct in question, but also on the wide variety of considerations that must be brought to bear whenever an agency is allocating its limited resources. Thus, for example, a decision not to bring enforcement proceedings against an alleged violator of the securities laws may depend on the likelihood of receiving a favorable precedent, the existence of other cases having broader implications, the consequences of enforcement proceedings on appropriations, and so forth. Moreover, a decision not to act may be made informally, without a record for judicial review. At the agency level at least, there is little or nothing at which a court can look to assess the legality of the agency's decision.

It is for these reasons that some courts still refuse to recognize private rights of initiation and that the courts that recognize such rights tend to emphasize that judicial review should be unusually deferential.[109] Many cases involving review of inaction tend to have features in common with the conventional case in which there is "no law to apply"—the classic context for a conclusion that an agency's decision

---

[107] For more detailed discussion, see Stewart & Sunstein, note 4 *supra* at 1210-11, 1267-71.
[108] See note 33 *supra*.
[109] See NRDC v. SEC, 606 F.2d 1031 (D.C. Cir. 1979); WWHT, Inc. v. FCC, 656 F.2d 807 (D.C. Cir. 1981); Pendleton v. Trans Union Sys. Corp. 430 F. Supp. 95 (E.D. Pa. 1977).

is unreviewable because it is "committed to agency discretion by law."[110] If the plaintiff claims a complete default in the enforcement process, or identifies statutorily irrelevant factors as the basis for the decision, there will of course be law to apply. And in such cases, review of inaction is not substantially different from review of action.[111] But if the plaintiff has simply alleged that the agency acted "arbitrarily"—as, for example, by refusing to initiate rulemaking proceedings on a particular matter—there are no readily ascertainable standards for assessing the claim.

Deregulation is different from inaction: no one denies that deregulation is, as a general rule, subject to judicial review. The APA itself defines rulemaking, which is generally reviewable, as "agency process for formulating, amending, or repealing a rule."[112] But there are three common features to inaction and deregulatory measures that might be thought to justify a deferential judicial role.

First, a decision to deregulate may be, at least in part, based on a belief that the agency's limited resources should not be devoted to the problem at hand. To be effective, regulation requires enforcement, and enforcement requires resources. A decision to deregulate may be based on a conclusion that enforcement resources are best allocated to different problems.

Second, regulation imposes costs on the admittedly limited resources of the regulated class. To impose a particular set of regulatory requirements will require regulated entities to expend their resources on one problem rather than another. An agency may decide that even if a particular regulation does some good, the money would be better spent on another matter altogether. Deregulation and inaction are, on this score, identical.

Third, to the extent that the distinct role of the courts is thought to be the promotion of private ordering,[113] deregulation and inaction are indistinguishable. Both serve to immunize private actors from regulation. The fact that deregulation disturbs the *status quo*—by

[110] 5 U.S.C. § 706. The "no law to apply" interpretation comes from Citizens to Preserve Overton Park v. Volpe, 401 U.S. 402 (1971).

[111] In part, refusal to review inaction may depend on a concern that courts lack authority to order the executive to enforce the law. See *e.g.*, Note, *Dunlop v. Bachowski and the Limits of Judicial Review under Title IV of the LMRDA: A Proposal for Administrative Reform*, 86 YALE L. J. 885, 901-02 & nn.61-62 (1977). But there is no separation of powers concern if a court orders an agency to obey the will of Congress as expressed in the governing statute or the APA—even if conformity requires the agency to act. See note 35 *supra*; Sunstein, *Cost-Benefit Analysis and the Separation of Powers*, 23 ARIZ. L. REV. 1267 (1981).

[112] 5 U.S.C. § 551 (5).

[113] See text at notes 6-10 *supra*.

removing a preexisting burden—is, from this standpoint, irrelevant. What is critical is that both deregulation and inaction do not interfere with private conduct.

At the same time, however, there are major differences between review of inaction and review of deregulation. First, review of deregulation involves an inquiry into a well-defined, actual decision, one that is ordinarily based on a record. Review of inaction, by contrast, may involve an inquiry into no decision at all, or instead into a decision having only an informal basis. A "hard look" is thus much more easily made of a deregulatory measure. By hypothesis, an agency has allocated its resources to consideration of the measure in question, and usually in a well-documented fashion.

Judicial reluctance to interfere with an agency's failure to act is based in part on fear of interfering with administrative decisions on how best to allocate limited enforcement resources. To require an agency to investigate the matter of passive restraints when it has not yet looked into the matter at all, for example, is to deflect resources from other ways of promoting automobile safety. There are no easily administrable standards for deciding whether an agency has been arbitrary in allocating its resources to one problem rather than another. Much of this constraint disappears in the context of deregulation. In such a case, an agency has already expended resources on the problem. A judicial decree that deregulation not take place does not divert agency resources in the same way as an order that an agency initiate rulemaking in the first instance.

As the history of administrative law over the past two decades reflects, it is no longer feasible to understand the exclusive, or even the primary, judicial role as the promotion of private ordering. The role is instead to ensure that administrative agencies develop and implement the relevant public values—often authoritatively reflected in the will of Congress, to the extent that it is discernible—and to guard against arbitrariness, which often takes the form of undue solicitude for a narrow interest group. Deregulation cannot be distinguished from regulation on this score.

In *State Farm*, the Court relied on the additional fact that deregulation, unlike inaction, is a departure from established practices. As the Court understood it, such a departure demands justification—a principle that generates a presumption in favor of the *status quo* whether or not the *status quo* involves regulation. But the source of the presumption is not obvious. Certainly Congress has said nothing to require such a presumption. And the presumption might be questioned on the ground that regulatory policy often requires flexibility in meeting new conditions and in responding to changing social views of the advantages and disadvantages of regulation.

Perhaps the Court's view is best understood as an effort to protect expectations and reliance. When an agency undertakes to regulate a particular field, an entire system of private ordering develops on the basis of the regulation. Indeed, the resulting system of expectations resembles statutory entitlements treated as "property" in recent Supreme Court decisions for purposes of procedural due process.[114] A departure from the *status quo*, even in the form of deregulation, may disrupt the expectations that regulation has built up and impede planning on the part of regulatory beneficiaries.

Alternatively, the presumption may be an application of the more general principle that agency interpretations of statutory requirements are entitled to deference.[115] When an agency has for some period of time adhered to a particular interpretation of its statutory duty, it is under an obligation to explain departures. Perhaps, too, the presumption may reflect concern for the possibility that a hasty shift from the *status quo* will reflect only political preferences rather than the reasoned decisionmaking deemed critical in *State Farm*. Similar notions underlie traditional judicial doctrines of *stare decisis* in the courts. Efforts to apply those doctrines in the administrative context fit well with the general effort to diminish the risk of factional takeover by dressing agency actions with many of the trappings of adjudication.

These considerations make it inappropriate to accord special deference to deregulatory decisions, even if special deference is due in the context of inaction. An agency may deregulate on the ground that its own enforcement budget, or the available compliance resources of regulated industries, should be devoted to other problems. But those factors may be taken into account in assessing the reasonableness of the decision to deregulate and do not justify an unusually deferential scope of review. The *State Farm* decision should not, however, be understood to create a presumption against changes in regulatory policy, whether those changes increase or decrease regulation. It should instead stand for the basic proposition that administrative action, including deregulation, must be reviewed to ensure that it

---

[114] See, *e.g.*, cases cited in note 12 *supra*.
[115] See, *e.g.*, Whirlpool Corp. v. Marshall, 445 U.S. 1, 11 (1980).

conforms to the governing statute and that it is not arbitrary in light of the record.

There are of course permissible and impermissible bases for decisions to deregulate. The ordinary way to tell the difference is to look at the governing substantive statute. Some general guidelines may be helpful. Deregulatory decisions may lawfully be based on a conclusion that regulation does not help regulatory beneficiaries. Regulation, as the *State Farm* Court recognized, imposes costs, and costs should not be imposed without benefits. Under some statutes, deregulation may be based on a cost-benefit calculus:[116] Under others, cost is relevant, but a cost-benefit approach is proscribed.[117] Moreover, a conclusion that regulation has unanticipated adverse consequences—for example, decreasing incentives for research and development—is a relevant factor supporting deregulation. New knowledge[118] or changed circumstances[119] showing that the existing scheme is ineffective or unnecessary are also legitimate bases for repeal.

Harder questions are raised by deregulation based on more diffuse considerations—a preference for private autonomy, a fear that regulation may breed resentment among particular segments of society or the public at large, a heightened concern with costs growing out of a renewed interest in promoting economic well-being. What makes such considerations at least superficially troublesome is that they may be irrelevant or unimportant under regulatory statutes, some of which express a legislative judgment that the interest in private autonomy has in the circumstances been overcome. If taken sufficiently far, generalized interests of these sorts would justify complete default under many statutes—not what Congress anticipated. As a general rule, however, federal agencies do have discretion at least to take into account such admittedly diffuse considerations. Few statutes make them irrelevant. This is not to suggest that they can be made dispositive where regulation does produce substantial benefits. It will always be necessary to examine carefully the weighing process used by the agency for conformity to the governing statute and the more general APA prohibition on arbitrariness.

---

[116] See, *e.g.*, 15 U.S.C. § 2058 (f) (3) (a) (1976) (Consumer Product Safety Act); *id.* at § 1261(s) (Child Protection and Toy Act), both of which refer to "unreasonable risks," a term that might plausibly be read to allow for some form of cost-benefit test.

[117] See, *e.g.*, the National Traffic and Motor Vehicle Safety Act at issue in *State Farm* itself.

[118] See NAACP v. FCC, 682 F.2d 993 (D.C. Cir. 1982).

[119] See, *e.g.*, *United Church of Christ*, note 17 *supra*. *Cf.* ASH v. FCC, 699 F.2d 1209, 1217 (D.C. Cir. 1983).

In any event, an agency's decision to deregulate must have the normal supporting basis required for any agency action. This is not to suggest that an agency is prohibited from revoking a regulation unless it can affirmatively show that the regulation will not do some good. It is hardly arbitrary or capricious to decide that a regulation—which presumably imposes costs—should not remain on the books when there is substantial uncertainty whether it will produce any benefits at all. But if an agency revokes a rule on the ground that it will not help the purported beneficiaries, a mere assertion will not suffice. Here, as elsewhere, an agency must give some reasoned explanation for its decision. It must also consider reasonable alternatives to deregulation—including a reduction, rather than elimination, of regulation, and different sorts of regulatory strategies. And here as elsewhere the normal *Chenery* principle applies: a court may not uphold agency action on any basis other than that offered by the agency.[120]

4. Finally, there is no reason to question the Court's conclusion that an agency must consider alternatives. It is certainly arbitrary to disregard measures that would fulfill regulatory goals without imposing significant costs. The difficult questions are what sorts of alternatives must be considered and what kind of consideration must be given to them. With respect to these questions, it is necessary to turn to the merits.

B. THE MERITS: THE HARD LOOK IN PRACTICE

1. *Airbags and the problem of alternatives.* At one level, it is hard to object to the Court's conclusion that the failure to examine the airbags option was arbitrary. The agency rescinded the entire regulation simply because regulated industries indicated that they would opt for the least effective means of fulfilling the rule's requirements. Particularly when implementing a statute passed because of dissatisfaction with industry's response to safety concerns, an agency should not be permitted to default on its statutory obligations whenever industry chooses an ineffective means of compliance. In this respect, *State Farm* strikes a familiar chord in the decisions invalidating failure to act. The fear is that in the implementation process, the regulated industries will be permitted to obtain a victory in the administrative process that could not be won in the legislative process.

---

[120] SEC v. Chenery Corp., 318 U.S. 80 (1943).

As a result, the values that the statute was supposed to reflect become perverted or ignored.[121] Judicial review thus becomes a means of ensuring that the statutory standard is not defeated during the implementation process.

Investigation of alternatives, however, can be costly. Airbags raise a host of questions different from those involved in the decision whether to require detachable belts. To resolve these questions, a substantial investment of resources may be required. Why should it not be sufficient for the agency to note that fact, to point to the various demands on its budget, to rescind the (by hypothesis) defective existing rule, and to say that it would be preferable to take up the question of airbags at some later date? The Court did not explain.

The question itself suggests that the problem of judicial review of inaction cannot be neatly separated from the requirement of investigation of alternatives. In both cases, the court is interfering with the agency's allocation of its resources among various enforcement strategies. And in both cases, there is no obvious reason why the courts should be dissatisfied with an explanation that invokes the limited size of the agency budget and that explains why other competing problems have a comparatively stronger claim on that budget.

In both cases, however, the mere fact that resources are limited and must be allocated should not be sufficient to immunize the decision from review. The agency's allocation may still be arbitrary within the meaning of the APA. Whether an alternative must be investigated depends on (1) the amount of work already done on the proposed alternative, (2) the proximity between the matter under review and the alternative, (3) the costs of investigating the advantages and disadvantages of the alternative, and (4) the strength, in light of existing information, of the claim that the alternative is a good one. Where work has been done on the alternative; where it is closely related to the proposal at issue; where additional costs seem low; and where there is a colorable basis for believing the alternative to be effective and desirable, a decision to rescind the proposal rather than to undertake additional work seems arbitrary. If the factors are reversed, the case approaches that of a pure, nonarbitrary failure to act on the ground that resources are best allocated to other problems.

---

[121] See, *e.g.*, Carpet, Linoleum & Resilient Tile Layers, Local Union No. 419 v. Brown, 656 F.2d 564 (10th Cir. 1981); Adams v. Richardson, 480 F.2d 1159, 1163-64 (D.C. Cir. 1973); Environmental Defense Fund, Inc. v. Ruckelshaus, 439 F.2d 584 (D.C. Cir. 1971).

Under the proposed test, the Court's decision with respect to airbags seems correct. The agency had already done considerable work on the problem. That problem in turn was closely related to the question of nondetachable belts, with overlapping issues of fact and policy. The costs of completing the investigation of airbags seemed comparatively low. Finally, there was reason, on the existing record, to believe that the airbags option would be desirable. For these reasons, the Court correctly concluded that the rescission was arbitrary.

2. *Detachable and nondetachable belts.* Here the Court's position is more aggressive and more difficult to sustain. The key question was whether the Secretary of Transportation had supported his conclusion that there was serious uncertainty about whether the detachable belt would produce substantial safety benefits. That question in turn depended on whether there would be a significant increase in usage. The Court relied on the fact that, in the case of detachable belts, the "burden of inertia" is on the side of usage. That fact, according to the Court, constituted "grounds to believe that seatbelt use . . . will be substantially increased."[122]

Whether and to what extent the reversal of the burden of inertia will increase seatbelt usage is an enormously difficult question. It calls for an assessment of inconclusive factual data and for predictive judgments on questions on which the existing data shed little light. That is precisely the sort of matter on which, the Court has suggested, administrative agencies are entitled to particular deference.[123] But the Court was apparently persuaded, on the basis of its own reading of the record, that it was highly unlikely that there would not be a significant increase in seatbelt usage if the burden of inertia were shifted.

It is in this respect that the Court's ruling on the problem of detachable belts goes considerably further than the ruling on airbags. The latter ruling reflected the principle that agencies must give adequate consideration to reasonable alternatives—one of the less controversial aspects of the hard-look doctrine. The detachable belts ruling, by contrast, has a decidedly substantive flavor, for it rests on straightforward disagreement with the agency's assessment of the facts.

The Court's conclusion with respect to nondetachable belts is in the same vein. The agency had not considered that option in much detail.

---

[122] 103 S. Ct. at 2872.

[123] See, *e.g.*, United States Nuclear Regulatory Com'n v. NRDC, 103 S. Ct. 2246 (1983); FCC v. National Citizens Committee for Broadcasting, 436 U.S. 775 (1978).

That there would be significant gains from continuous belts was undisputed. The agency thought that those gains were outweighed, first, because it speculated that people would fear being trapped—a fear that was unjustified in light of the emergency release mechanisms—and second, because of the adverse public reaction to interlocks. Interlocks, of course, require affirmative action on the part of drivers and passengers, a feature that makes them different from continuous belts. Here too, the Court's reversal appears to depend on a straightforward conclusion that the agency's weighing of advantages and disadvantages was unsatisfactory.

Both of these rulings reflect the requirement of technocratic rationality that typifies the hard-look doctrine. The approach taken by the Court can be best understood as an effort to promote decisionmaking based on careful application of statutorily relevant factors to the existing data. But the decision cannot be easily squared with earlier suggestions to the effect that in the realm of predictive judgments on which reasonable people may differ, agencies are to be given considerable deference.[124] Those decisions may be understood to reflect a perception that administration is a battle among competing interest groups and thus skepticism about the usefulness of detailed explanations in generating better regulatory decisions. By contrast, *State Farm*, with its emphasis on the need for careful justifications, can be associated with belief in a more objective public interest and in the value of written justifications in filtering out irrelevant or illegitimate factors.[125]

IV. General Implications: From Private to Public Administrative Law?

In the view of some,[126] *Vermont Yankee* and other Supreme Court decisions[127] had threatened to overturn many lower court decisions adopting an aggressive approach to notice-and-comment rulemaking and informal decisionmaking, especially in the context of attempts to require agencies to implement agency directives. *State Farm*, by contrast, reads like a number of decisions by the United States Court of Appeals for the District of Columbia Circuit in the

---

[124] See *id.*
[125] *Cf.* Diver, note 44 *supra.*
[126] See, *e.g.*, DAVIS, 1 ADMINISTRATIVE LAW TREATISE 6:35–6:37 (2d ed. 1978).
[127] See cases cited in note 123 *supra.*

1970s—decisions that attempted to create the fabled "partnership" between administrative agencies and the federal courts. At the most general level, the decision may be read as part of an effort to generate a unitary body of public law doctrine that is substantially independent of private law principles. There are two primary elements to that doctrine. The first is a requirement of technocratic rationality. The second is the decision to develop surrogate safeguards for electoral control by abandoning any preference for private autonomy in favor of a general effort to identify and implement regulatory values.

The *State Farm* decision expressly endorses the primary elements, both substantive and procedural, of the hard-look doctrine. It requires detailed consideration of statutorily relevant factors, persuasive justifications for departures from past practices, and consideration of reasonable alternatives. It also reflects willingness to overturn decisions based on an unjustifiable balance of advantages and disadvantages.

The APA provides no clear authorization for the hard-look doctrine, which might therefore be regarded as a creation of federal common law. Nonetheless, it would be a mistake to conclude that the doctrine is for that reason illegitimate. The APA was born in a period of dissatisfaction with agency performance, and the prohibition on arbitrariness is sufficiently flexible to accommodate the Court's approach in *State Farm*. All of the elements of that approach—the prohibition on consideration of statutorily irrelevant factors, the requirement that alternatives be considered, and the judicial look at the merits—are reasonable glosses on the statutory standard.

The hard-look doctrine, moreover, is designed to require decision-making that is highly structured, that identifies goals in a way that conforms to the governing statute, and that selects methods of achieving those goals in a logical manner. One may doubt whether judicial review is well suited to accomplishing that task,[128] and it seems clear that alternative mechanisms of control would at least in some respects be far more fruitful.[129] Decisions such as *State Farm* may generate boilerplate discussion designed to placate the courts but having little substantive effect on agency decisionmaking.[130] Because

---

[128] See MASHAW, BUREAUCRATIC JUSTICE (1983); ACKERMAN, ROSE-ACKERMAN, SAWYER, & HENDERSON, THE UNCERTAIN SEARCH FOR ENVIRONMENTAL QUALITY 147-61 (1974).

[129] For example, President Reagan has recently attempted to ensure that decisionmakers within the executive branch undertake a cost-benefit analysis of major rules. See Exec. Order 12291, 46 Fed. Reg. 13,193 (1981).

[130] See Sax, note 27 *supra*.

State Farm—unlike the decision of the court of appeals—requires only reconsideration by the agency and does not order the passive restraints rule into effect, it is peculiarly vulnerable to the conventional challenge that it will serve only to produce needless formality. But these criticisms are often overstated. Remands, and requirements of explanations, have had real effects on agency outcomes. Recent developments suggest that the issue of passive restraints may itself be an illustration.[131] Judicial control of that sort can fulfill an important, if imperfect, means of promoting agency fidelity to statutory norms.

The technocratic rationality required by *State Farm* and similar decisions should be understood as a device, admittedly highly imperfect, for reducing the risk that agency decisions will result from "political" considerations that are sometimes illegitimate and that at any rate ought not to be concealed. In this respect, the emphasis of the hard-look doctrine on careful identification of goals and detailed explanation of how various alternatives might achieve those goals is in tension with a conception of the administrative process not as a search for the public interest but as a struggle among competing interest groups for economic welfare. Justice Rehnquist's reference to the political orientation of the new Administration highlights the point.

It is of course true that a new political administration may value certain factors, such as cost and private autonomy, more highly than its predecessors. Technocratic rationality can get one only part of the way in regulatory decisionmaking. It is a commonplace that expertise cannot serve to generate some objective public interest.[132] But if a new valuation of statutorily relevant factors is the basis for deregulation, the agency's justification should at least be articulated. The premise of the *State Farm* approach is that judicial examination of an agency's decisionmaking can expose changes in underlying values so as to ensure conformity with the governing statute as well as public scrutiny of those changes. It is in this light that *State Farm* is best understood. The concern is that in the absence of a relatively firm judicial hand, the statutory standard may be subverted by an agency responding to interests that had been largely defeated in Congress. In the Court's view, the primary defect in the agency's action was its deference to industry's methods for achieving safety, methods whose inadequacy was the very basis for the Act. This fear of subversion of statutory

---

[131] See 48 FED. REG. 48622 (1983). See Stewart & Sunstein, note 4 *supra*, at 1283 and n. 379, for other examples.

[132] See Bazelon, note 46 *supra*.

programs by factional interests is a primary theme of the recent cases. Such subversion may result from deregulation and inaction as much as from regulation itself.

Under a public law divorced from private law principles, deregulation, like regulation itself, must conform to the governing statute and the APA. A decision to deregulate may lawfully be based on a number of factors. It may, for example, rest on changed circumstances or on new information with respect to the subject at hand, or on a finding that regulation has unanticipated consequences, or on a conclusion that regulation has not in fact helped those it was designed to benefit. Under many statutes, moreover, overtly political considerations—like a greater preference for private autonomy or a heightened concern about cost—may be taken into account. At the same time such considerations will sometimes be made irrelevant by statute. Even if they are relevant, however, they must be balanced against the benefits of regulation. In any event alternatives must be considered.

The final point relates to the separation of powers. With the apparent demise of the legislative veto,[133] it has become all the more important to ensure that in executing the laws, administrative agencies adhere to the will of Congress. In cases involving inaction and deregulation, the primary goals of Congress may be undermined in the enforcement process, as the agency acts on the basis of concerns that are irrelevant or at best secondary in the governing statute. In these circumstances an active judicial posture does not intrude on congressional prerogatives but promotes them. For this reason, it may not be too much to expect the *State Farm* decision eventually to stand for the proposition that the beneficiaries of regulation ought to be granted the same protection accorded to regulated industries—even to the extent of a right to initiate regulatory action when an agency has simply failed to act. And whether the case involves regulation, inaction, or deregulation, judicial protection will take the form, not of a conventional common-law right, but of a right to a process of decision designed to ensure that the relevant public values will be properly identified and implemented. Such a development, which seems inevitable, will be a critical signal in the shift from private to public administrative law.

---

[133] See INS v. Chadha, 103 S. Ct. 2764 (1983).

CONCLUSION

State Farm at once ratifies the major elements of the hard-look doctrine and rejects the notion that the judicial role should embody a presumption in favor of private ordering. Both of these conclusions fit well with the changing nature of administrative law, as courts adapt traditional doctrines, first meant exclusively to check regulation, in order to facilitate the definition and implementation of regulatory values.

It is not difficult to identify what administrative law is moving away from. Because the occasions for judicial intervention were derived from common-law principles, American public law was built directly on private law. In administrative law, there has never been a public law with distinct principles of its own. And because of the absence of a background tradition, there are formidable difficulties in the effort to formulate such principles, especially when that effort is undertaken primarily or exclusively by the courts.[134] But the past twenty-five years, culminating in decisions such as *State Farm*, have begun to set out the elements of an independent public law.

Such an approach would contain no presumption in favor of private ordering and would not be primarily designed to protect private interests from government intrusion. It would instead be intended, above all, to facilitate the emergence and implementation of the public values at stake in regulation,[135] and in the process to minimize the risk that regulatory policy will be responsive to private factions. In time, the *State Farm* decision may be seen as an important step in the transition.

---

[134] See generally MASHAW, note 128 *supra;* MELNICK, REGULATION AND THE COURTS: THE CASE OF THE CLEAN AIR ACT (1983).

[135] It is of course a premise of this whole enterprise that such values at least potentially exist and that the regulatory process may serve to define them. That premise may be questioned by those who believe that, at least under current conditions, the result will be not dialogue but domination. See, *e.g.,* Hand, *Is There a Common Will?* (1929), in THE SPIRIT OF LIBERTY (Phoenix ed. 1977); Freeman, *Truth and Mystification in Legal Scholarship,* 90 YALE L. J. 1229 (1981); Unger, *The Critical Legal Studies Movement,* 95 HARV. L. REV. 561 (1982); Brest, *Interpretation and Interest,* 34 STAN. L. REV. 765 (1982). Compare ACKERMAN, RECONSTRUCTING AMERICAN LAW 96-101, 110 (1984).

DEAN ALFANGE, JR.

CONGRESSIONAL REGULATION OF THE "STATES QUA STATES": FROM NATIONAL LEAGUE OF CITIES TO EEOC V. WYOMING

In *EEOC v. Wyoming*,[1] the Supreme Court upheld, by a vote of five to four, the constitutionality of the 1974 amendment[2] to the Age Discrimination in Employment Act (ADEA) of 1967[3] extending the Act to employees of "a State or political subdivision of a State."[4] It thereby sustained the claim of the Equal Employment Opportunity Commission that, under the amended law, Wyoming was prohibited from conditioning the employment of its game and fish wardens after the age of fifty-five upon "the approval of the employer."[5] Commenting on this decision on the following day in the *New York Times*, Linda Greenhouse wrote that the Court had "effectively overruled, albeit not in so many words,"[6] its 1976 decision in *National League of Cities v. Usery*.[7] In that case, the Court had invalidated the 1974 amendment[8] to the Fair Labor Standards Act of 1938[9] (ironically enacted together with the ADEA amendment upheld in the *Wyoming* case), extending the wage and hour provisions of the Act to employees

Dean Alfange, Jr., is Professor of Political Science at the University of Massachusetts—Amherst.

[1] 103 S. Ct. 1054 (1983).
[2] 88 Stat. 74.
[3] 81 Stat. 602; 29 U.S.C. §§621-34.
[4] 29 U.S.C. §630(b).
[5] Wyo. Stat. Ann. §31-3-107(c) (1977).
[6] NEW YORK TIMES, March 3, 1983, A20.
[7] 426 U.S. 833 (1976).
[8] 88 Stat. 55, 59.
[9] 52 Stat. 1060; 29 U.S.C. §§201-19.

of "a State, or a political subdivision of a State,"[10] on the ground that that "exercise of congressional authority [did] not comport with the federal system of government embodied in the Constitution."[11] Although it is clear that faithful adherence to the reasoning of Justice Rehnquist's majority opinion in *National League of Cities* would have led to the invalidation of the ADEA amendment (only one of the eight Justices who participated in the decision of both cases—Justice Blackmun—appeared to believe that the two cases should have been decided differently),[12] and although *National League of Cities* has had no progeny among Supreme Court decisions, it cannot be said to have been overruled by *Wyoming*. The dissenters in *National League of Cities* (who were four-fifths of the new majority) applied in *Wyoming*—and thereby legitimated—the approach to the issue of constitutionality set forth by Justice Rehnquist in the earlier case. The differences that were seen to require a different result were merely differences of fact. Thus, a minor reassessment of the factual situation in a subsequent case is all that is required to restore the vitality of the earlier decision. In Justice Jackson's phrase, *National League of Cities* still "lies about like a loaded weapon"[13] ready for use by a Court that is prepared to circumscribe congressional authority to satisfy its own conception of proper public policy.

I. NATIONAL LEAGUE OF CITIES

The reasoning of *National League of Cities v. Usery* has been subjected to severe scholarly criticism,[14] and justifiably so.[15] Not the

---

[10] 29 U.S.C. §203(x).

[11] 426 U.S. at 852.

[12] Justice Blackmun, who joined the Court's opinion in *National League of Cities* and added a brief concurrence (*id.* at 856), subscribed without comment to the majority opinion in *Wyoming*. It is not clear whether he saw the cases as distinguishable or whether he had simply changed his mind in the intervening seven years. Although the suggestion that he had changed his mind is not implausible in the light of what has been aptly described as his "changing social vision" (see Note, *The Changing Social Vision of Justice Blackmun*, 96 HARV. L. REV. 717 (1983)), the fact that the majority opinion in *Wyoming* sought ostensibly to employ the approach suggested in his *National League of Cities* concurrence strongly suggests that he was not yet ready fully to recant his earlier position.

[13] Korematsu v. United States, 323 U.S. 214, 246 (1944) (dissenting opinion).

[14] See, *e.g.*, Barber, *National League of Cities v. Usery: New Meaning for the Tenth Amendment?* 1976 SUPREME COURT REVIEW 161, 176-81; Tribe, *Unraveling National League of Cities: The New Federalism and Affirmative Rights to Essential Government Services*, 90 HARV. L. REV. 1065, 1069-75 (1977); Matsumoto, *National League of Cities—From Footnote to Holding—State Immunity from Commerce Clause Regulation*, 1977 ARIZ. ST. L. J. 35, 62-76; Cox, *Federalism and Individual Rights under the Burger Court*, 73 NW. U. L. REV. 1, 22-25 (1978); Kaden, *Politics,*

least of the bases for its critical reception was its startling break with established precedent. Since the end, in 1937, of the era in which the Court had employed restrictive definitions of the commerce clause and the doctrine of substantive due process to protect American business from state and federal regulation,[16] the Court had not employed state autonomy to invalidate an act of Congress based on the commerce power.[17] In *United States v. California*[18] in 1936, the Court had unanimously rejected the contention that Congress could not, under that power, require a railroad owned and operated by a state to comply with the provisions of the Federal Safety Appliance Act.[19] The Court distinguished precedents holding that state instrumentalities were immune from federal taxation, declaring that "there is no such limitation upon the plenary power to regulate commerce. The state can no more deny the power if its exercise has been authorized by Congress than can an individual."[20] This view remained good law for forty years,[21] and the reasoning had been extended in 1946 to cover congressional regulation of state activity under the war power.[22]

In 1966, Congress for the first time extended the coverage of the Fair Labor Standards Act to include certain employees of state and local governments—those employed in hospitals, institutions, and schools.[23] The constitutionality of this extension was upheld in *Mary-*

Money, and State Sovereignty: The Judicial Role, 79 COLUM. L. REV. 847, 886-88 (1979); Tushnet, *Constitutional and Statutory Analyses in the Law of Federal Jurisdiction,* 25 U.C.L.A. L. REV. 1301, 1337-43 (1978); La Pierre, *The Political Safeguards of Federalism Redux: Intergovernmental Immunity and the States as Agents of the Nation,* 60 WASH. U. L. Q. 779, 807-14 (1982); Note, *Municipal Bankruptcy, the Tenth Amendment and the New Federalism,* 89 HARV. L. REV. 1871, 1881-84 (1976). See also Shapiro, *Mr. Justice Rehnquist: A Preliminary View,* 90 HARV. L. REV. 293, 306-07 (1976); Powell, *The Compleat Jeffersonian: Justice Rehnquist and Federalism,* 91 YALE L. J. 1317, 1325-26, 1348 (1982). But *cf.* Nagel, *Federalism as a Fundamental Value: National League of Cities in Perspective,* 1981 SUPREME COURT REVIEW 81. Professor Nagel describes the decision as "understandable and admirable." *Id.* at 97.

[15] Mark Tushnet has commented that "the opinion [is] characterized by what might be called the argument from strident assertion." Tushnet, note 14 *supra,* at 1322-23.

[16] See generally JACKSON, THE STRUGGLE FOR JUDICIAL SUPREMACY 39-175 (1941).

[17] See the discussion in Matsumoto, note 14 *supra,* at 43-56.

[18] 297 U.S. 175 (1936).

[19] 27 Stat. 531 (1893), as amended 29 Stat. 85 (1896).

[20] 297 U.S. at 185. See also Sanitary District of Chicago v. United States, 266 U.S. 405 (1925).

[21] See, *e.g.,* California v. United States, 320 U.S. 577 (1944), upholding the application of the Shipping Act of 1916, 39 Stat. 734, as amended 49 Stat. 1518, 1987, to port facilities operated by the state of California and the city of Oakland; California v. Taylor, 353 U.S. 553 (1957), upholding the application of the Railway Labor Act of 1926, 44 Stat. 577, to the same state-owned railroad involved in United States v. California, note 18 *supra.*

[22] Case v. Bowles, 327 U.S. 92 (1946).

[23] 80 Stat. 831 (1966).

land v. Wirtz[24] in 1968. In an opinion by Justice Harlan, the Court stated that the controlling principle was that laid down in *United States v. California*: there could be no denial of the reach of "the commerce power to protect enterprises indistinguishable in their effect on commerce from private businesses, simply because those enterprises happen to be run by the States for the benefit of their citizens."[25] Justice Douglas, joined by Justice Stewart, dissented, arguing that if Congress were as free to regulate the activities of states under the commerce power as it is to regulate individuals, "then the National Government could devour the essentials of state sovereignty."[26]

As late as 1975, in *Fry v. United States*,[27] with only Justice Rehnquist in dissent, the Court relied on both *Maryland v. Wirtz* and *United States v. California* to uphold the application of the salary increase restrictions that had been authorized by the Economic Stabilization Act of 1970[28] to prevent the State of Ohio from awarding wage and salary increases to its employees larger than those that were permissible under the administrative regulations that had been promulgated to implement the provisions of the Act. The Court devoted scarcely any discussion to the constitutional question beyond noting that the State's position was "foreclosed" by *Wirtz*.[29] Yet, only thirteen months later, four members of the majority in that case joined with Justice Rehnquist in *National League of Cities* to explain away the significance of *Fry*,[30] to declare the language of *United States v. California*, on which the subsequent line of cases had been based,[31] to be "simply wrong,"[32] and to overrule *Maryland v. Wirtz*.[33]

To accommodate its ruling with precedents it was not prepared to overrule and with federal law it was not prepared to invalidate, the Court in *National League of Cities* attempted to draw four distinctions,

---

[24] 392 U.S. 183 (1968), overruled in National League of Cities v. Usery, note 7 *supra*.

[25] 392 U.S. at 198-99.

[26] *Id.* at 205 (dissenting opinion).

[27] 421 U.S. 542 (1975).

[28] 84 Stat. 799 (1970).

[29] 421 U.S. at 548. It was an augury of things to come that the majority opinion in *Fry* included an enigmatic footnote that stated that the Tenth Amendment "is not without significance," and that its meaning was "that Congress may not exercise power in a fashion that impairs the States' integrity or their ability to function effectively in a federal system." *Id.* at 547 n.7. It was quickly noted, however, that the Court was "convinced that the wage restriction regulations constituted no such drastic invasion of state sovereignty." *Id.* at 547-48 n.7.

[30] 426 U.S. at 852-53.

[31] See text at note 20 *supra*.

[32] 426 U.S. at 854-55.

[33] *Id.* at 855.

none of which proved to be tenable. It sought to distinguish (1) between the scope of Congress's authority over the states under the commerce power and under other delegated powers; (2) between congressional regulation of private activities within a state and regulation of the activities of the State itself; (3) between traditional and nontraditional functions of state and local governments; and (4) between necessary, desirable, insubstantial, or benign effects on state autonomy and effects which are unnecessary, undesirable, significant, or harsh.

A. THE COMMERCE POWER AND OTHER DELEGATED POWERS

One of the principal difficulties with Justice Rehnquist's opinion is that he changes his argument in the midst of making it. He begins by conceding that the regulation of the wages and hours of state and local employees is "undoubtedly within the scope of the Commerce Clause,"[34] but notes that, even so, "there are attributes of sovereignty attaching to every state government which may not be impaired by Congress, not because Congress may lack an affirmative grant of legislative authority to reach the matter, but because the Constitution prohibits it from exercising the authority in that manner."[35] To protect these "attributes of sovereignty"—the existence of which is reflected in the Tenth Amendment—Congress is forbidden to "exercise power in a fashion that impairs the States' integrity or their ability to function effectively in a federal system."[36] It may not directly regulate the "States *qua* States,"[37] by displacing their "freedom to structure integral operations in areas of traditional governmental functions."[38]

The Tenth Amendment cannot, of course, by its terms place a limit on the exercise of a delegated power. It merely provides that "powers not delegated to the United States . . . are reserved to the States," and, therefore, any aspect of a power which *is* delegated to the United States is not, by definition, reserved to the states.[39] But that is not the heart of

---

[34] *Id.* at 841. That this was not a grudging concession may be seen from Justice Rehnquist's dissenting opinion in Fry v. United States, 421 U.S. at 551, where he spoke of "the anachronistic and doctrinally unsound constructions of the Commerce Clause which had [prior to 1937] been used to deny both to the States and to Congress authority to regulate economic affairs."

[35] 426 U.S. at 845.

[36] *Id.* at 843, quoting from Fry v. United States, 421 U.S. at 547 n.7. See note 29 *supra.*

[37] 426 U.S. at 847.

[38] *Id.* at 852.

[39] It was on this basis that Justice Stone made his often quoted remark that the Tenth Amendment "states but a truism that all is retained which has not been surrendered." United States v. Darby, 312 U.S. 100, 124 (1941).

the problem here. Constitutional prohibitions may be implicit as well as expressly stated.[40] The principal problem is that Justice Rehnquist ultimately does not rest his argument on the existence of a constitutional prohibition at all, whether drawn from the Tenth Amendment or from any other source. He concludes—in direct contradiction to his initial concession—that the statutory amendment was invalid, not because it violated a prohibition, but because it was "not within the authority granted Congress by [the Commerce Clause]."[41]

The logical dilemma Justice Rehnquist faced was that, as he constructed his argument, the invalidity of the law both had to be and could not be based on a constitutional prohibition. It had to be based on a prohibition, because—given his concession that the law was within the scope of the commerce power—it could not be unconstitutional unless it violated a prohibition. It could not be based on a prohibition, because the Court was not prepared to hold that Congress could not interfere with the states' "freedom to structure integral operations" through the use of delegated powers other than the commerce power. (In a footnote, the Court expressly reserved judgment on that question.)[42] But constitutional prohibitions cannot merely limit one power; they must apply equally to all. If Congress is in fact forbidden to interfere with "the States' freedom to structure integral operations," then it cannot do so under any of its powers. Conversely, if it can validly do so under one of its powers, then it cannot be constitutionally prohibited from doing so.

Only four days after *National League of Cities* was issued, the Court confirmed the implications of its footnote in another opinion by Justice Rehnquist,[43] when, without dissent, it accepted as beyond question that Congress was empowered under section 5 of the Fourteenth Amendment to extend the prohibitions against employment discrimination contained in §703(a) of Title VII of the Civil Rights Act of 1964[44] to states (or local governments) as employers[45]—despite the fact

---

[40] See, *e.g.*, McCulloch v. Maryland, 4 Wheat. 316, 426 (1819), where Chief Justice Marshall found a prohibition against state taxation of federal instrumentalities in "a principle which so entirely pervades the constitution, is so intermixed with the materials which compose it, so interwoven with its web, so blended with its texture, as to be incapable of being separated from it, without rending it into shreds."

[41] 426 U.S. at 852.

[42] *Id.* at 852 n.17.

[43] Fitzpatrick v. Bitzer, 427 U.S. 445 (1976).

[44] 78 Stat. 255; 42 U.S.C. §2000e-2(a).

[45] The extension was enacted as part of the Equal Employment Opportunity Act of 1972, 86 Stat. 103; 42 U.S.C. §2000e(a).

that this prohibition operated upon the "States *qua* States" and "displace[d] the States' freedom to structure integral operations" every bit as much as did the provisions of the Fair Labor Standards Act that had been invalidated for doing so a few days earlier. "There can be no doubt," Justice Rehnquist declared, that "Congress, acting under the Civil War Amendments, [may intrude] into the judicial, executive, and legislative spheres of autonomy previously reserved to the States."[46] It can do so, he explained, because the authority granted by the enforcement clauses of those amendments is delegated expressly for the purpose of ensuring compliance with the prohibitory provisions, "which themselves embody significant limitations on state authority."[47] Thus it can hardly be impermissible for Congress to restrict state autonomy in areas where that autonomy is already limited by the Constitution.

Such a distinction might be valid if Congress's power under the Civil War Amendments were limited to providing sanctions or remedies to deal with acts of states that were, in themselves, prohibited by the Constitution.[48] But Congress's power is not so limited, and, in fact, Justice Rehnquist relied on *South Carolina v. Katzenbach*,[49] which upheld provisions of the Voting Rights Act of 1965,[50] whose encroachments on state sovereignty were about as sweeping as could be imagined. While the Voting Rights Act was a congressional response to the widespread practice of racial discrimination in voting,[51] its principal provisions (which included disallowing literacy tests as a means of determining voter eligibility in states covered by the Act,[52] authorizing the appointment of federal examiners to supplant state and local officials in carrying out the traditional state functions of determining voting qualifications and registering voters,[53] and

---

[46] 427 U.S. at 455, citing and quoting at length from *Ex parte* Virginia, 100 U.S. 339, 345-48 (1880), which had upheld a federal indictment against a state judge for excluding persons from service on state court juries "on account of race, color, or previous condition of servitude" in violation of §4 of the Civil Rights Act of 1875, 18 Stat., Pt. 3, 336. The Court rejected the argument that interference with the performance of official duties by a state judge was an unconstitutional invasion of state sovereignty. *Id.* at 346.

[47] 427 U.S. at 456.

[48] It was the thesis of the Civil Rights Cases, 109 U.S. 3 (1883), that Congress's power under the Civil War Amendments was so limited.

[49] 383 U.S. 301 (1966).

[50] 79 Stat. 437; 42 U.S.C. §1973a-p.

[51] See the discussion in 383 U.S. at 308-15.

[52] 79 Stat. 438; 42 U.S.C. §1973b. See also Katzenbach v. Morgan, 384 U.S. 641 (1966); Gaston County v. United States, 395 U.S. 285 (1969); Oregon v. Mitchell, 400 U.S. 112 (1970). For a discussion of the breadth of congressional power in this area, see Cohen, *Congressional Power to Interpret Due Process and Equal Protection,* 27 STAN. L. REV. 603 (1975).

[53] 79 Stat. 439; 42 U.S.C. §1973d.

requiring states and localities to obtain prior federal approval before putting into effect what might be perfectly valid new laws relating to voting[54] were affirmed without the need to show actual unconstitutional behavior on the part of the states. And in 1980, in *City of Rome v. United States*[55] and *Fullilove v. Klutznick*,[56] the Court reaffirmed both that the reach of Congress's power under the Civil War Amendments extended to the regulation of state actions that were in themselves perfectly constitutional and that this enforcement power was not subject to the restrictions imposed on the commerce power in *National League of Cities.*

But as long as the state policies being displaced by congressional action are ones that the Constitution leaves the states free to adopt, it can make no difference to the integrity or autonomy of the states whether Congress displaces those policies through the use of the commerce power or any other power. In either case, it is Congress, not the Constitution, that takes authority away from the states. It is of no relevance that the Civil War Amendments were intended to "embody significant limitations on state authority."[57] For it is certainly no less true that the Commerce Clause was also intended to limit state authority.[58] The constitutional grant to Congress of authority over

---

[54] 79 Stat. 439; 42 U.S.C. §1973c. South Carolina v. Katzenbach was unanimous except that Justice Black alone dissented on this single aspect of the case, insisting that the constitutional guarantees of federalism must "mean at least that the States have power to pass laws and amend their constitutions without first sending their officials hundreds of miles away to beg federal authorities to approve them." 383 U.S. at 359 (concurring and dissenting opinion).

[55] 446 U.S. 156, 173-80 (1980). For a vigorous criticism of the Court's holding in *Rome* on the breadth of congressional power to enforce the Civil War Amendments and on the inapplicability of the restrictions of *National League of Cities* to these enforcement powers, see Note, *Toward Limits on Congressional Enforcement Power under the Civil War Amendments*, 34 STAN. L. REV. 453, 473-79 (1982).

[56] 448 U.S. 448, 476-78 (1980) (plurality opinion). See Bohrer, *Bakke, Weber, and Fullilove: Benign Discrimination and Congressional Power to Enforce the Fourteenth Amendment*, 56 IND. L. J. 473, 507-10 (1981).

[57] Fitzpatrick v. Bitzer, 427 U.S. at 456. See text at note 47 *supra*.

[58] See, *e.g.*, CORWIN, THE COMMERCE POWER VERSUS STATES RIGHTS (1936). Professor Corwin observed that one of the "immediate objectives back of the commerce clause" was "to bring to an end either directly or through Congressional action, all State power in relation to both foreign and interstate commerce." *Id.* at 23. While there may be reason to doubt that the commerce clause itself took away all state power over interstate or foreign commerce, see Currie, *The Constitution in the Supreme Court: State and Congressional Powers, 1801-1835*, 49 U. CHI. L. REV. 887, 942-47 (1982), a view which has been rejected by the Supreme Court—see, *e.g.*, Cooley v. Board of Wardens, 12 How. 299 (1851)—surely at the very least it invested Congress with full authority to remove from the states whatever power over interstate or foreign commerce they had previously possessed that Congress deemed incompatible with the national interest. Thus, if Professor Corwin meant that the commerce clause provided the potential, "either directly or through Congressional action," to end all state power over interstate and foreign commerce, he was unquestionably correct. For a review of the meager history of the adoption of the commerce

commerce is, at bottom, simply a power to displace state choices."[59]

The only other power mentioned by Justice Rehnquist, in his *National League of Cities* footnote,[60] by which Congress might possibly be able to "affect integral operations of state governments" in ways it could not validly accomplish under the Commerce Clause was the spending power—which, since 1937, has consistently been interpreted as empowering Congress to tell the states how to carry out particular governmental responsibilities, even in areas where it lacks direct regulatory authority.[61] Since the basic provisions of the Social Security Act of 1935[62] were upheld by the Supreme Court in *Steward Machine Co. v. Davis*[63] and *Helvering v. Davis*,[64] the ability of Congress to use the power to tax and spend to induce the states to maintain particular programs has become a prominent and broadly accepted feature of the federal system.[65] The very purpose of imposing these conditions frequently is to require the states to make choices regarding their "integral operations" that they might otherwise be disinclined to make.[66] But only in the quickly repudiated decision in *United States v.*

---

clause, see Stern, *That Commerce Which Concerns More States than One*, 47 HARV. L. REV. 1335, 1337-48 (1934).

[59] In his dissent in EEOC v. Wyoming, 103 S. Ct. at 1072-73, Chief Justice Burger suggested another reason for distinguishing the extent of the limits imposed by the principles of state autonomy embodied in the Tenth Amendment on the commerce power of Congress from the limits on its power to enforce the Fourteenth Amendment: the Tenth Amendment was adopted after the commerce clause and thus limits it; it was adopted before the Civil War Amendments and thus is limited by them. See text at notes 311-14 *infra*.

[60] See text at note 42 *supra*.

[61] See, *e.g.*, Oklahoma v. Civil Service Commission, 330 U.S. 127 (1947), upholding an order of the United States Civil Service Commission for the removal from office of a state highway commissioner who was also chairman of the Democratic State Central Committee, on pain of loss of a specified amount of federal highway funds.

[62] 49 Stat. 620, 42 U.S.C. §301 *et. seq.*

[63] 301 U.S. 548 (1937).

[64] 301 U.S. 619 (1937).

[65] See generally [UNITED STATES] ADVISORY COMMISSION ON INTERGOVERNMENTAL RELATIONS, THE INTERGOVERNMENTAL GRANT SYSTEM: AN ASSESSMENT AND PROPOSED POLICIES (1975-78). An extremely informative summary may be found in Kaden, note 14 *supra*, at 871-81.

[66] In recent years, scholarly commentators have expressed concern over the potential reach of Congress's power to require the states to do its bidding by the imposition of conditions on federal grants. A thorough and balanced analysis of the constitutional issues is in Stewart, *Pyramids of Sacrifice? Problems of Federalism in Mandating State Implementation of National Environmental Policy*, 86 YALE L. J. 1196, 1250-62 (1977). See also Kaden, note 14 *supra*, at 889-97; Kolker, *National League of Cities, the Tenth Amendment and the Conditional Spending Power*, 21 URBAN L. ANN. 217, 225-36 (1981); Note, *Taking Federalism Seriously: Limiting State Acceptance of National Grants*, 90 YALE L. J. 1694 (1981); Note, *Federal Grants and the Tenth Amendment: "Things As They Are" and Fiscal Federalism*, 50 FORDHAM L. REV. 130 (1981). But there is virtually unanimous agreement among commentators that, without more, there is no constitutional prohibition against constitutional grants merely because they displace state choices regarding the conduct of state business. See, *e.g.*, Stewart, *supra*, at 1255.

Butler[67] in 1936 has the Supreme Court held that state sovereignty limits the spending power. In rejecting *Butler*'s conclusion that such use of the spending power was void because of its "coercive purpose and intent,"[68] the new majority of the following year (which included Justice Roberts, the author of *Butler*) held that the provisions of the Social Security Act were not, in fact, "weapons of coercion, destroying or impairing the autonomy of the states."[69] "[T]emptation," the Court intimated, is not "equivalent to coercion."[70]

It is on this basis that courts have traditionally dismissed constitutional complaints that conditional grants impair state autonomy.[71] Insofar as the assumption is correct, Congress does not displace, through the spending power, the states' freedom to act as they see fit. It merely encourages them successfully to exercise that freedom in different ways. An advantage of this assumption, of course, is that it avoids the problem of differentiating between Congress's capacity to interfere with state autonomy through the spending power and the commerce power. If the spending power does not interfere with state autonomy, then there is no need to explain why Congress has broader authority to interfere with the states here than under the commerce power.

But the assumption is a transparent fiction. In the first place, as Richard Stewart has noted: "Debating whether conditions on federal grants . . . 'coerce' the states is an unhelpful anthropomorphism. The structure of the federal system under current social and economic conditions makes it inevitable that states will become subject to the federal spending power, just as it makes it inevitable that they will become subject to the federal commerce power."[72] Second, it is analytically not very useful to assert that Congress interferes with state autonomy when it achieves a modification of state policies through the commerce power, but that it does not interfere with state autonomy when it achieves the identical modification through the spending power.

At the close of his dissent in *National League of Cities*, Justice Brennan pointed out that Congress could restore the wage and hour

---

[67] 297 U.S. 1 (1936).

[68] *Id.* at 71.

[69] Steward Machine Co. v. Davis, note 63 *supra*, at 586.

[70] *Id.* at 590.

[71] See the cases collected in Kaden, note 14 *supra*, at 875-81. See also Schwartz, *National League of Cities v. Usery—The Commerce Power and State Sovereignty Redivivus*, 46 FORDHAM L. REV. 1115, 1129-32 (1978).

[72] Stewart, note 66 *supra*, at 1254.

requirements invalidated by the majority "by conditioning grants of federal funds upon compliance with federal minimum wage and overtime standards,"[73] and there is no reason to believe that the Court would not uphold congressional power if exercised in that manner. But surely the interference with state autonomy, or the degree of displacement of state choices, would be no greater in the one case than in the other. If, as the Court has consistently held, Congress may effectively control integral operations of state governments through the spending power, it can only be because no constitutional prohibition is involved.

There would be no particular utility to canvassing each of the other delegated powers to demonstrate that, with the possible exception of the taxing power—which will be discussed later[74]—there is no basis for drawing a constitutional distinction between the degree to which Congress may interfere with state autonomy through them and through the power to regulate interstate commerce. Suffice it to say that although Justice Rehnquist only made express reference to the spending power and to section 5 of the Fourteenth Amendment in suggesting, in his *National League of Cities* footnote, that there may be greater room for Congress to displace state choices under other powers than under the commerce power, the Court has made quite clear in other cases—including some contemporaneous with or subsequent to *National League of Cities*—that Congress is not limited by considerations of state autonomy when exercising a wide range of different powers. The doctrine of *National League of Cities* appears specific to the power to regulate interstate commerce.[75]

[73] 426 U.S. at 880 (dissenting opinion). Recognizing the apparent validity of Justice Brennan's observation, Bernard Schwartz was prompted to comment: "If that is the case, was there any real point to the *National League of Cities* decision? Was it truly necessary for the Court to march the king's men up the hill in a commerce clause case only to offer to march them down ignominiously if the spending power were instead invoked?" Schwartz, note 71 *supra*, at 1132. See also Kolker, note 66 *supra*, at 225.

[74] See text at notes 125-27 *infra*.

[75] With regard to the power to regulate foreign commerce, as opposed to interstate commerce, the Court has specifically declared the doctrine of *National League of Cities* to be inapplicable because, while "Congress' power to regulate interstate commerce may be restricted by considerations of federalism and state sovereignty[, i]t has never been suggested that Congress' power to regulate foreign commerce could be so limited." Japan Line, Ltd. v. County of Los Angeles, 441 U.S. 434, 448-49 n.13 (1979). With regard to the treaty power, see Missouri v. Holland, 252 U.S. 416 (1920), specifically rejecting the proposition that Congress "had no power to displace" state choices on matters within the scope of their reserved powers through a valid treaty with a foreign nation. *Id.* at 432-35. With regard to the war power, it was held not to be limited by considerations of state autonomy in Case v. Bowles, note 22 *supra*, upholding the application of the Emergency Price Control Act of 1942, 56 Stat. 23, to timber on public lands sold by the state of Washington. The Court there held that price control was a valid exercise of the war power, and that "the Tenth Amendment 'does not operate as a limitation upon the

B. THE REGULATION OF THE "STATES *QUA* STATES"

The authority of Congress under the Commerce Clause to displace state policies regulating private activity has, since 1937, been held to be virtually without limit as long as there is "a rational basis for finding a chosen regulatory scheme necessary to the protection of commerce."[76] On this basis, the power of Congress to control the wages and hours of those who work for private employers is as settled as any proposition of constitutional law can be.[77] Justice Rehnquist made no effort whatever to deny Congress's plenary authority in this regard,[78] but declared that it was an entirely different matter "to uphold a similar exercise of congressional authority directed, not to private citizens, but to the States as States."[79] The perceived difference was that, apparently unlike congressional regulation of private activity, the control of what state and local governments pay to their employees—or at least those of their employees engaged in "traditional governmental functions"—

---

powers, express or implied, delegated to the national government.' " 327 U.S. at 102, quoting from Fernandez v. Wiener, 326 U.S. 340, 362 (1945). With regard to the power under Art. IV, sec. 3, to make rules respecting federal property, the Court has held that the exercise by Congress of its "power over the public land . . . is without limitations" and may constitutionally be employed to displace the choices of a state and a municipal government as to how water and electrical energy obtained from public lands "shall be disposed of in San Francisco"—that is, whether it should be made available to consumers through public or private agencies. United States v. San Francisco, 310 U.S. 16, 28, 29 (1940). See also Kleppe v. New Mexico, 426 U.S. 529 (1976), and the cases cited therein, *id.* at 539.

[76] Katzenbach v. McClung, 379 U.S. 294, 304 (1964).

[77] As originally enacted, the Fair Labor Standards Act of 1938, note 9 *supra*, controlled only the wages and hours of employees "engaged in commerce or in the production of goods for commerce." 52 Stat. 1062. A unanimous Court upheld this law in United States v. Darby, note 39 *supra*, in part on the ground that it was rationally related to the regulation of interstate commerce. But since the test of the scope of this power is that Congress may act when it has "a rational basis for finding a chosen regulatory scheme necessary to the protection of commerce," see text at note 76 *supra*, Congress had authority under the commerce power to regulate the wages and hours of a much broader category of employees. In 1961, Congress extended coverage of the Act to all employees of an "enterprise engaged in commerce or in the production of goods for commerce," whether or not they themselves were engaged in these activities. 75 Stat. 66; 29 U.S.C. §203(s). Since there was a reasonable basis for believing that the total labor costs of such an enterprise would affect interstate commerce, the extension was upheld. Maryland v. Wirtz, note 24 *supra*, at 188–93. But even as thus extended, the Act covered a much narrower category of employees than was constitutionally required. Congress may reach the wages and hours of all employees, no matter how local or far removed from commerce their employment may be. That was the net effect of the 1966 and 1974 amendments, which extended the coverage of the Act to employees of enterprises in which persons are engaged in "handling, selling, or otherwise working on goods or materials that have been moved in or produced for commerce by any person." 80 Stat. 831, 88 Stat. 59. Since there is scarcely any employee who does not work in an organization in which someone handles "materials that have been moved in or produced for commerce by any person," and since the working conditions of such persons are rationally related to interstate commerce in those materials, Congress is constitutionally empowered to control the wage and hour levels of all of these employees.

[78] See text at note 34 *supra*.

[79] 426 U.S. at 845.

involves impermissible interference with the states' "attributes of sovereignty."[80] Justice Rehnquist drew an analogy to *Coyle v. Smith*,[81] in which it was held that Congress could not use its power under Article IV, section 3, to admit new states to deny a state authority to relocate its capital, because such decisions are within what are "essentially and peculiarly state powers."[82]

It would be difficult to deny that there are some "attributes of sovereignty" belonging to the states that have constitutional protection against impairment by Congress, but very few have absolute protection. Some of these "attributes of sovereignty" find express protection in the Constitution: for example, Article IV, section 3, guarantees each state sovereignty over its territorial integrity by providing that no new state shall be created by carving territory from an existing state or group of states without the consent of the states concerned; Article V provides that the Constitution shall not be amended to eliminate the guarantee that a state may not be deprived of equal representation in the Senate without its consent; the Eleventh Amendment protects states from being sued in federal court by citizens of other states or citizens of foreign countries.[83] Other sovereign attributes may exist even though not expressly mentioned in the Constitution.[84] The power to tax, the power to legislate with regard to activities not subject to federal regulation, and the power to determine both the form and structure of the state government and the terms of office of state officials would be in this category.[85] The states' very existence has absolute constitutional protection: Congress "could not abolish the states on the grounds that they adversely affect interstate commerce."[86] Other attributes of sovereignty may have absolute protection at a general, but not at a particular, level against

---

[80] *Ibid.* See text at note 35 *supra.*

[81] 221 U.S. 559 (1911), discussed in National League of Cities *sub nom.* Coyle v. Oklahoma at 845.

[82] *Id.* at 565.

[83] For a discussion of the extent to which the Eleventh Amendment actually does protect state sovereignty, see Tribe, *Intergovernmental Immunities in Litigation, Taxation, and Regulation: Separation of Powers Issues in Controversies about Federalism,* 89 HARV. L. REV. 682, 683-99 (1976).

[84] These protections may be said to be derived from the Tenth Amendment, although, in the light of the language of that Amendment, such a proposition would be difficult to maintain. They are more properly derivable from the nature of federalism inherent in the constitutional system, of which the Tenth Amendment is merely another reflection. See BLACK, PERSPECTIVES IN CONSTITUTIONAL LAW 29-30 (1963).

[85] Similar lists may be found in Tribe, note 14 *supra,* at 1070, and Stewart, note 66 *supra,* at 1231-32.

[86] Note, *Is Federalism Dead? A Constitutional Analysis of the Federal No-Fault Automobile Insurance Bill: S. 354,* 12 HARV. J. LEGIS. 668, 681 (1975).

congressional impairment. Certainly Congress may not forbid a state to lay and collect taxes. It may, however, through its delegated powers, including the commerce power, prohibit many possible exertions of a state's taxing power.[87]

Some attributes may appear to be absolute, such as the power to decide on the location of the state capital or on the terms of office of state officials, but the appearance of absoluteness probably rests more on the difficulty of imagining a legitimate reason for congressional interference than with the existence of an unyielding constitutional prohibition against interference if a legitimate reason were to be found. Justice Brennan was undoubtedly correct in his *National League of Cities* dissent when he declared that the Court's power to protect state sovereignty from destruction by Congress is to be found in its ability to invalidate laws that are not legitimately within the scope of the delegated powers.[88] When Congress has been found to have a legitimate reason within the scope of its delegated powers to act, it may intrude even so far into the attributes of state sovereignty as to require a state or local government to obtain federal authorization prior to amending its election laws.[89]

The power to determine the wages and hours of its employees may be an attribute of state sovereignty, but there appears to be little reason for treating it as more immune from congressional control than a state's tax structure or its election machinery. More to the point, there is little reason for treating it as more immune from congressional control than a state's power to make policy judgments regarding the conditions of employment of private employees within its jurisdiction and to embody those judgments in legislation. As Justice Brennan stated, "the paradigm of sovereign action—action *qua* State—is in the enactment and enforcement of state laws. . . . [T]he ouster of state laws obviously curtails or prohibits the States' prerogatives to make policy choices respecting subjects clearly of greater significance to the 'State *qua* State' than the minimum wage paid to state employees."[90] Yet, under the

---

[87] See, *e.g.*, Maryland v. Louisiana, 451 U.S. 725, 746-52 (1981).

[88] 426 U.S. at 860, 861-62 n.4 (dissenting opinion). For a discussion in which this proposition is supported, see Ely, *The Irrepressible Myth of Erie*, 87 HARV. L. REV. 693, 700-06 (1974).

[89] South Carolina v. Katzenbach, note 49 *supra*, at 334, where, in discussing this requirement, the Court stated: "This may have been an uncommon exercise of congressional power . . . but the Court has recognized that exceptional conditions can justify legislative measures not otherwise appropriate." See text at notes 49-56 *supra*.

[90] 426 U.S. at 875 (dissenting opinion). The Court has since declared that the power to make policy "is perhaps the quintessential attribute of sovereignty. . . . Indeed, having the power to make decisions and to set policy is what gives the State its sovereign nature." FERC v. Mississippi, 456 U.S. 742, 761 (1982).

curious doctrine of *National League of Cities*, Congress is entirely free, without regard to considerations of state sovereignty, to override state policy relating to the wages and working conditions of virtually every private employee within the state's borders, but is not free to regulate the wages and working conditions of employees of state and local governments because that would "impair[ ] the States' integrity or their ability to function effectively in a federal system."[91] From a moral perspective, Frank Michelman has arrestingly observed, this distinction is[92]

> just precisely wrong: congressional action in areas of disputable federal competence would be most vulnerable insofar as it displaced the state from its role of universal legislator and law-enforcer, and least vulnerable insofar as it curbed the state in its guise of active agent having particular interests opposed to other particular interests such as those of its employees.

The majority opinion in *National League of Cities* makes little effort to explain why the power to set the wages of its own employees is more essential to a state's sovereignty than its power to control the wages paid by private employers. It merely asserts that, without such authority, "there would be little left of the States' ' "separate and independent existence." ' "[93] But such an assertion could be at least as easily made with respect to the authority of the state to regulate its internal economy, and no analysis supporting a coherent distinction is provided. The Court does discuss the financial strains that might be placed on the budgets of state and local governments by the

---

[91] Fry v. United States, 421 U.S. at 547 n.7. quoted in *National League of Cities*, 426 U.S. at 843. As Justice Brennan commented in 1977: "One may rightfully feel unease that the Court is in the process of developing a concept of state sovereignty that is marked neither by consistency nor intuitive appeal." United States Trust Co. v. New Jersey, 431 U.S. 1, 51 n.15 (1977) (dissenting opinion).

[92] Michelman, *States' Rights and States' Roles: Permutations of "Sovereignty" in National League of Cities v. Usery*, 86 YALE L. J. 1165, 1168 (1977). See also *id.* at 1168-69; Tribe, note 14 *supra*, at 1074-75. For an interesting development in another area of constitutional law in which the Court has distinguished "the state in its guise of active agent having particular interests opposed to other particular interests"—in this case the state as market participant rather than as market regulator with regard to transactions in interstate commerce—and has granted the state greater freedom in its role as "active agent" rather than as lawmaker, see White v. Massachusetts Council of Construction Employees, 103 S. Ct. 1042 (1983); Reeves, Inc. v. Stake, 447 U.S. 429 (1980); Hughes v. Alexandria Scrap Corp., 426 U.S. 794 (1976).

[93] 426 U.S. at 851, citing Coyle v. Smith, note 81 *supra*, at 580, which in turn quotes from the eloquent dictum in Lane County v. Oregon, 7 Wall. 71, 76 (1869): "[T]he people of each State compose a State, having its own government, and endowed with all the functions essential to separate and independent existence."

requirement that they meet the federal minimum-wage and maximum-hour standards, and the possibility that these governments might be forced to cut essential services, such as police or fire protection, to remain solvent.[94] But the state's inability to control the wages and hours of employees in the private sector makes it impossible for the state to compete for private business by lowering standards, and thus it may lose tax revenues and the quality or quantity of governmental services it can provide may be correspondingly circumscribed.

Ultimately, the Court did not in fact assess the financial impact on the states of the federal wage and hour requirements, because it held that that question was immaterial. Regardless of the amount of strain involved, the federal standards "will nonetheless significantly alter or displace the States' abilities to structure employer-employee relationships" with regard to the provision of traditional governmental services[95] — that is, they will reduce or eliminate altogether the freedom of a state to provide these services through such means as the use of volunteer assistance, specially designed hours for special areas such as the police or fire departments,[96] the summertime use of teenage help, or the employment of persons "who for some . . . reason do not possess minimum employment requirements, and [who thus may be paid] less than the federally prescribed minimum wage."[97]

Obviously, these requirements would affect state and local governments and could easily require them to restructure their delivery of essential services, but to say that they would leave the states without a "separate and independent existence" or that they would "impair[ ] the States' integrity or their ability to function effectively in a federal system" is unwarranted hyperbole. They may create significant financial problems,[98] but they hardly threaten the states' independent existence. If, in fact, a state chooses to curtail its level of performance of "traditional governmental functions,"[99] it is only

---

[94] It was the Court's emphasis on the impact of the federal wage and hour standards on the states' ability to provide essential governmental services that led Professors Michelman and Tribe to find in its opinion the beginnings of a doctrine that states have an affirmative constitutional obligation to provide such services to those who require them. See Michelman, note 92 *supra*, at 1178-80; Tribe, note 14 *supra*, at 1072-78.

[95] 426 U.S. at 851.

[96] *Id.* at 850.

[97] *Id.* at 848.

[98] It is, of course, well established that the Constitution is not violated by the mere fact that the federal government imposes financial obligations directly on the states. See, *e.g.*, Fitzpatrick v. Bitzer, note 43 *supra;* see also Hutto v. Finney, 437 U.S. 678, 693-700 (1978).

[99] 426 U.S. at 852.

because it exercises its sovereign prerogative not to raise the additional revenue or not to impose equivalent cutbacks in "nontraditional" services.[100]

This is not to argue that the federal courts do not have "power to prevent . . . 'the utter destruction of the State as a sovereign political entity.' "[101] But to suggest that such destruction is a risk of enforcement of the federal standards with regard to state and local employees is wholly unreasonable.[102] *National League of Cities* was not a case in which a state was being required to relocate its capital or to change the term of office of its governor. It was not even a case in which a state was being required to provide a service or to discontinue a service or to increase or decrease the level of service it chose to provide. Moreover, since the Court treats the actual financial impact on the states as immaterial, its rule would apparently apply even where that impact was minimal and necessitated no diminution of governmental services whatever.[103]

Wage and hour standards do not implicate the issue that has, within the past decade, aroused considerable concern among constitutional scholars—whether the federal government has constitutional authority to "commandeer" agencies of state government to implement and enforce federal policies of which the states may not approve.[104] This

---

[100] See Cox, note 14 *supra*, at 23.

[101] Maryland v. Wirtz, 392 U.S. at 196, quoted in *National League of Cities*, 426 U.S. at 842.

[102] See Tribe, note 14 *supra*, at 1072.

[103] In his dissenting opinion in Maryland v. Wirtz, Justice Douglas distinguished the obligations imposed on the states by the Act from those imposed by earlier acts of Congress, such as the Federal Safety Appliance Act, note 19 *supra*, whose application to a state-owned railroad was upheld in United States v. California, note 18 *supra*. Unlike the extension of the Fair Labor Standards Act, he asserted, the earlier obligations did not "overwhelm state fiscal policy" by requiring the states "either to spend several million more dollars on hospitals and schools or substantially reduce services in these areas." 392 U.S. at 203 (dissenting opinion). But there is no reason to believe that the magnitude of the financial impact on the states of the 1966 extension of the Fair Labor Standards Act was as great as Justice Douglas suggested. In his *National League of Cities* dissent, Justice Brennan declared that the Court's unwillingness to rest its decision on an assessment of the actual impact on the states of the 1974 extension of the Act was "advisable" in the light of evidence showing that this impact was likely to be insubstantial. 426 U.S. at 874 n.12 (dissenting opinion).

[104] See, *e.g.*, Kaden, note 14 *supra*, at 869-70, 890-92; Stewart, note 66 *supra*, at 1243-50; Dorsen, *The National No-Fault Motor Vehicle Insurance Act: A Problem in Federalism*, 49 N.Y.U. L. REV. 45, 58-62 (1974); Salmon, *The Federalist Principle: The Interaction of the Commerce Clause and the Tenth Amendment in the Clean Air Act*, 2 COLUM. J. ENVT'L L. 290, 324-41 (1976). See also the testimony of then Attorney General Edward Levi before the Senate Committee on Commerce, relative to the constitutional questions pertaining to federalism raised by the proposed (but not enacted) legislation to establish national standards for no-fault automobile insurance, to be implemented by the states. National Standards No-Fault Motor Vehicle Insurance Act: Hearings Before the Committee on Commerce, United States Senate, 94th Cong., 1st Sess., 496-516 (1975). See also the dissenting opinion of Justice O'Connor in FERC v. Mississippi, 456 U.S. 742, 776-96 (1982).

issue is substantial and is entitled to the serious consideration it has received. Perhaps a constitutional prohibition against "commandeering" could be fashioned that would have general application and would not simply provide an ad hoc basis for invalidating a congressional policy disliked by the courts.[105] However, the wage and hour requirements merely call upon the states to comply with federal law; they do not call upon them to develop, promulgate, or implement a regulatory program mandated by the federal government to be enforced through state governmental machinery, or to create a state agency to carry out such functions. Lewis Kaden, who strongly believes that the "commandeering" by Congress of state governmental machinery is unconstitutional, nevertheless sees the issue in *National League of Cities* as fundamentally different: "Neither the fiscal nor the governmental impact of fair labor standards . . . significantly alters a state's political process."[106] Inasmuch as such standards do not involve federal control of "the performance of a uniquely sovereign power: the

---

[105] Any such rule would have to take into account the fact that some congressional "commandeering" of state governmental agencies has already been upheld. See Testa v. Katt, 330 U.S. 386 (1947). Those who would treat Testa v. Katt as not dispositive of the "commandeering" question argue that state courts, by the express provision of Art. VI, sec. 2, have the constitutional obligation to consider themselves bound by federal law, an obligation which is not imposed on state administrative agencies or other branches of state government, and that, in any event, the state courts, under *Testa*, were not required to assume jurisdiction that was not granted them under state law, but were merely required to enforce the terms of federal law when that was invoked in a case in which the state courts had jurisdiction under state law. See *id.* at 394. For statements of this argument, see, *e.g.*, La Pierre, note 14 *supra*, at 944-45; Stewart, note 66 *supra*, at 1246-47; Dorsen, note 104 *supra*, at 53-55; and the dissenting opinions of Justices Powell and O'Connor in FERC v. Mississippi, 456 U.S. at 773-74 n.4, 784-85. The fact remains that Testa v. Katt stands for the proposition that at least one state agency—the state courts—may, when properly vested with jurisdiction, be required by Congress to enforce provisions of federal law of which the state may not approve. See the discussion in FERC v. Mississippi, *id.* at 758-63. As for the requirement that the state authorities specifically consider the adoption of certain conservation measures, the Court resolved this issue without "mak[ing] a definitive choice between competing views of federal power to compel state regulatory activity." *Id.* at 764. While the Court found that Testa v. Katt, as well as Fry v. United States, note 27 *supra*, and Washington v. Washington State Commercial Passenger Fishing Vessel Ass'n, 443 U.S. 658 (1979), demonstrated that "the Federal Government has some power to enlist a branch of state government . . . to further federal ends," 456 U.S. at 762, it did not believe that the issue had to be squarely addressed, because whatever may be the scope of the power of Congress to compel state administrative agencies to enforce federal law or to compel "the States to enact a legislative program," *id.* at 765, in an area where Congress "could have pre-empted the field" by direct regulation under the commerce power, its actions "should not be invalid simply because, out of deference to state authority, Congress adopted a less intrusive scheme and allowed the States to continue regulating in the area on the condition that they *consider* the suggested federal standards." *Ibid.* The Court specifically repudiated the "rigid and isolated statement" in Kentucky v. Dennison, 24 How. 66, 107 (1861), that Congress "has no power to impose on a State officer, as such, any duty whatever, and compel him to perform it." But see 456 U.S. at 779-91 (O'Connor, J., dissenting). See also EPA v. Brown, 431 U.S. 99 (1977). *Cf.* Pennsylvania v. EPA, 500 F.2d 246 (3d Cir. 1974).

[106] Kaden, note 14 *supra*, at 890.

authority to enact laws for the regulation of conduct by public or private interests," he believes that they should properly be upheld.[107] If, as Justice Rehnquist maintains, the constitutional problem arises when congressional action affects the "States *qua* States," the case against constitutionality should be at its weakest when only a state's salary schedule, and not its capacity to govern, is at stake.

C. TRADITIONAL AND NONTRADITIONAL GOVERNMENTAL FUNCTIONS

Perhaps the most widely criticized of the artificial distinctions in Justice Rehnquist's opinion was the line he drew between the "traditional governmental functions" of states and municipalities and their other functions.[108] To begin with, by conceding that the federal government has plenary power under the Commerce Clause "over areas of private endeavor, even when its exercise may pre-empt express state-law determinations contrary to the result which has commended itself to the collective wisdom of Congress,"[109] the Court has not only allowed congressional regulation that "displaces state policies"[110] in the area most central to the core interests of the "States *qua* States," but it has also authorized sweeping interference with the most traditional governmental function of all: governing. Probably the most severe of the anomalies of *National League of Cities* is its persistent equation of state sovereignty not with the ability to govern but with the ability to provide services.[111]

But even if one dismisses that anomaly and focuses on the notion of "traditional governmental functions" exclusively in terms of the provision of services, it is difficult to understand how a distinction drawn by a federal court between what could be described as nontraditional services (subject to federal control) and traditional services (not subject to federal control) would not itself make severe inroads into a state's "sovereign prerogative of choice."[112] For, as Frank

[107] *Id.* at 891. See also Dorsen, note 104 *supra*, at 57 n.79.

[108] See, *e.g.*, Tribe, note 14 *supra*, at 1072-74; Matsumoto, note 14 *supra*, at 72-76; Kaden, note 14 *supra*, at 886-87; Tushnet, note 14 *supra*, at 1339-40; La Pierre, note 14 *supra*, at 806-12; Stewart, note 66 *supra*, at 1234 n.144, 1267-69; Michelman, note 92 *supra*, at 1171-72. For a thorough discussion of the various uses in constitutional law of the distinction between "governmental functions" and "proprietary functions," see Wells & Hellerstein, *The Governmental-Proprietary Distinction in Constitutional Law*, 66 VA. L. REV. 1073 (1980).

[109] 426 U.S. at 840.

[110] *Id.* at 847.

[111] See Tribe, note 14 *supra*, at 1074; Stewart, note 66 *supra*, at 1267-69.

[112] The phrase, of course, belongs to Oliver Wendell Holmes. HOLMES, COLLECTED LEGAL PAPERS 239 (1920).

Michelman has observed, "a state's (or locality's) political choice to extend the range of its public involvements into some nontypical or nontraditional area would apparently be a quintessential instance of that very political vitality that the Constitution supposedly meant to nurture and protect."[113] Not only is the distinction between traditional and nontraditional functions extremely difficult to define and to apply in concrete instances,[114] but any attempt to define it by reference to past practice would tend to freeze constitutional law into a static, historically determined pattern,[115] and, as Felix Frankfurter put it: "Such a static concept of government denies its essential nature."[116] On the other hand, if "traditional" is redefined to mean "important" or "essential,"[117] the concept becomes boundless. Surely there is no better standard for measuring what is an important or essential service than observing what the legislature, within the limited scope of its resources, has decided to provide.

One of the routine justifications for respecting state autonomy is the classic argument of Justice Brandeis in *New State Ice Co. v. Liebmann*[118] (dissenting from a decision that state regulation of the ice industry was novel and not sufficiently important to the public interest to be constitutionally justified): "It is one of the happy incidents of the federal system that a single courageous state may, if its citizens choose, serve as a laboratory; and try novel social and economic experiments without risk to the rest of the country."[119] If by traditional governmental functions the Court meant what it said, then it both affirmed the virtues of state sovereignty and—by limiting the states' freedom from federal control in the provision of services to those services that are time-tested and nonexperimental—curtailed one of the principal reasons for recognizing that sovereignty: the preservation of the states' ability to experiment that Justice Brandeis extolled.[120]

---

[113] Michelman, note 92 *supra*, at 1172.

[114] Justice Brennan caustically dismissed the Court's attempt to rely on this distinction in *National League of Cities* by adding parenthetically: "whatever that may mean." 426 U.S. at 875 (dissenting opinion).

[115] See, *e.g.*, Matsumoto, note 14 *supra*, at 73-74.

[116] New York v. United States, 326 U.S. 572, 579 (1946) (opinion announcing the judgment of the Court).

[117] Throughout its opinion, the Court uses the term "traditional" interchangeably with the terms "essential," "integral," "typical," "important," or "require[d]." The imprecision is no help in providing a definition. See the analysis of the Court's use of these terms in *National League of Cities* in Michelman, note 92 *supra*, at 1171-72 and n.26.

[118] 285 U.S. 262 (1932).

[119] *Id.* at 311 (dissenting opinion).

[120] See Tushnet, note 14 *supra*, at 1339-40.

Apparently the Court did mean what it said. In the course of invalidating the wage and hour standards for state and local employees performing "traditional governmental functions," it specifically reaffirmed the result, if not the reasoning, of *United States v. California*,[121] in which congressional regulation of a state-owned railroad had been upheld. And, six years later, it reiterated this position by defining "traditional" purely in static, historical terms to uphold federal regulation of a state-owned commuter railroad on the ground that running a railroad is a nontraditional governmental activity,[122] thus entirely ignoring the importance of providing commuter transportation in urban areas.

Such precedential basis as the Court had for its distinction between traditional and nontraditional governmental functions was derived from the area of intergovernmental tax immunity—not one of the most admired doctrines of American constitutional history. Tax immunity was granted the states as an indirect means of ensuring that state governments could not be "crippled, much less defeated" by the federal taxing power.[123] But, in *South Carolina v. United States*[124] in 1905, the Court refused to grant a state immunity from federal liquor license taxes when it took over from private dealers the business of selling liquor. Business enterprises of the state were not to be accorded the same degree of constitutional protection as the states' traditional functions, and states were not given the ability to immunize activities within the legitimate scope of the federal taxing power from the reach of that power by the expedient of taking them over.[125] But neither the justification for granting the states immunity from federal taxation nor the justification for distinguishing in this area between traditional and nontraditional functions of states has any application to areas in which Congress is exercising regulatory authority.

The taxing power of Congress is more difficult to cabin than its

---

[121] 297 U.S. 175 (1936). See text at notes 18-21 *supra*.

[122] United Transportation Union v. Long Island Rail Road Co., 455 U.S. 678 (1982). See text at notes 214-33 *infra*.

[123] Collector v. Day, 11 Wall. 113, 125 (1871).

[124] 199 U.S. 437 (1905). The distinction between traditional and nontraditional functions of government for the purpose of determining the scope of state immunity from federal taxation was continued—see Ohio v. Helvering, 292 U.S. 360 (1934) (liquor sales); Helvering v. Powers, 293 U.S. 214 (1934) (municipal transit system); Allen v. Regents, 304 U.S. 439 (1938) (state university athletic events); but *cf.* New York v. United States, 326 U.S. 572 (1946) (sale of mineral waters)—but was ultimately described by the Court as "unworkable," Case v. Bowles, 327 U.S. 92, 101 (1946), and has now apparently been discarded. See Massachusetts v. United States, 435 U.S. 444, 457-58 (1978) (plurality opinion).

[125] 199 U.S. at 454-58.

regulatory powers. Justice Brennan noted in his *National League of Cities* dissent that the Court could effectively protect the states from destruction through the commerce power by limiting congressional exercise of that power to enactments that have a legitimate relation to commerce.[126] But the taxing power is not susceptible to that kind of control.[127] Congress is free to choose the subjects it wishes to tax virtually without direct constitutional limitation. The immunity doctrine thus serves as an artificial means of ensuring that Congress will no more be able to destroy the states through taxation than through regulation. Although the relevant constitutional prohibition on the taxing power of Congress is no different from that which applies to all the delegated powers—that is, Congress may not, under any of its powers, strip the states of the ability to carry out any function essential to their continued existence—the special guarantee of tax immunity was provided to preclude any possibility of the circumvention of that prohibition through the instrument of taxation.

Since the distinction between the traditional and nontraditional functions of government was established in the tax immunity area to avoid the adverse effects on federal power of granting unnecessarily broad immunity to the states, there is no reason to invoke it in an area where immunity does not exist to begin with. Moreover, inasmuch as it was created, not for the purpose of imposing a limitation on the power of Congress, but to lessen the restrictiveness of a limitation already established, its importation into *National League of Cities* to impose a limitation on the commerce power is particularly inappropriate. When Congress restricts the freedom of the states through a regulatory power, the constitutional questions to be asked are whether Congress can reasonably be said to have acted within the scope of the power invoked and whether the particular exercise of that power genuinely threatens the "separate and independent" existence of the states. These inquiries require no distinction to be made between traditional and nontraditional governmental functions.

---

[126] 426 U.S. at 860 (dissenting opinion). See text at note 88 *supra*.

[127] As Justice Brennan has described it, the granting of intergovernmental tax immunity "reflected the view that the awesomeness of the taxing power required a flat and absolute prohibition against a tax implicating an essential state function because the ability of the federal courts to determine whether particular revenue measures would or would not destroy such an essential function was to be doubted." Massachusetts v. United States, note 125 *supra*, at 456 (plurality opinion).

D. PROTECTING STATE AUTONOMY THROUGH JUDICIAL POLICYMAKING

1. The legacy of Fry. In his brief but elegant dissent in *National League of Cities*,[128] Justice Stevens declared that he personally disagreed with the policy underlying the federal minimum-wage requirement but that his disagreement "merely reflects my views on a policy issue which has been firmly resolved by the branches of government having power to decide such questions."[129] He concluded: "Since I am unable to identify a limitation on ... federal power that would not also invalidate federal regulation of state activities that I consider unquestionably permissible, I am persuaded that this statute is valid."[130] His assessment that the decision reflected no principle of constitutional law of general applicability, but merely the majority's dissatisfaction with the wisdom of the policy embodied in the statute, is widely shared.[131] Archibald Cox, for example, described the decision as one which "illustrates with unusual clarity the Burger Court's affinity for pragmatic and particularistic policymaking."[132]

The problem is, as Justice Stevens pointed out, that the Court articulated no rule in support of its decision that could not be shown to have been transgressed by similar exercises of congressional power affecting the states. If the argument is that Congress cannot impose regulations on the "States *qua* States," it is plain that Congress frequently does so in ways that are not seriously challenged and that affect the "States *qua* States" at least as centrally as the requirement that they pay a minimum wage to their employees.[133] Nor does the fact that the rule of *National League of Cities* applies only to "traditional" or "essential" governmental functions provide a principle capable of general application.[134] Ignoring the difficulty of providing workable definitions of "traditional" or "essential," a difficulty that the Court

---

[128] 426 U.S. at 880-81 (dissenting opinion).

[129] 426 U.S. at 881.

[130] *Ibid.* See also Justice Brennan's observation that the majority's reasoning "can only be regarded as a transparent cover for invalidating a congressional judgment with which they disagree." *Id.* at 867 (dissenting opinion). See also *id.* at 872.

[131] See, *e.g.*, Barber, note 14 *supra*, at 176-81; Cox, note 14 *supra*, at 22-25; Kaden, note 14 *supra*, at 848-49, 886-88; La Pierre, note 14 *supra*, at 784, 804, and *passim;* Tushnet, *The Dilemmas of Liberal Constitutionalism*, 42 OHIO ST. L. J. 411, 420 (1981).

[132] Cox, note 14 *supra*, at 22.

[133] See, *e.g.*, text at notes 43-56 *supra*.

[134] See Wechsler, *Toward Neutral Principles of Constitutional Law*, 73 HARV. L. REV. 1 (1959), reprinted in WECHSLER, PRINCIPLES, POLITICS, AND FUNDAMENTAL LAW 3-48 (1961); Greenawalt, *The Enduring Significance of Neutral Principles*, 78 COLUM. L. REV. 982 (1978).

made no effort to overcome, and ignoring the fact that the very attempt to define for a state what is essential to its needs is itself a serious incursion into state autonomy, it remains that functions of state and local governments every bit as traditional or essential as the provision of basic services may be interfered with by Congress if its action is reasonably related to the discharge of its responsibilities under the delegated powers.[135] Even if one accepts the unacceptable distinction between Congress's capacity to interfere with state choices relating to the performance of traditional functions under the commerce power and under its power to enforce the Civil War Amendments[136] or other delegated powers,[137] the fact is that Congress has been recognized as having power to interfere with such state choices under the Commerce Clause as well. In *Fry v. United States*,[138] only one year prior to *National League of Cities*, the Court upheld Congress's use of the commerce power to impose limitations on the authority of state and local governments to offer salary increases to their employees.

The absence of any general principle of decision in *National League of Cities* is most clearly apparent in the Court's attempt to distinguish rather than to overrule *Fry*. It identified four reasons for regarding the congressional imposition of salary increase limitations on the employees of state and local governments as valid under the commerce power while regarding the imposition of wage and hour limitations on these same employees as invalid. The reasons were that the anti-inflation salary freeze that had been upheld in *Fry* (1) dealt with "an extremely serious problem . . . which only collective action by the National Government might forestall"; (2) was to be in effect for only "a very limited, specific period of time"; (3) "displaced no state choices as to how governmental operations should be structured"; and (4) "operated to reduce the pressures upon state budgets rather than increase them."[139] Justice Rehnquist declared: "The limits imposed upon the commerce power when Congress seeks to apply it to the States are not so inflexible as to preclude temporary enactments tailored to combat a national emergency."[140] In the light of this, it is not

---

[135] See, *e.g.*, *Ex parte* Virginia, note 46 *supra;* South Carolina v. Katzenbach, note 49 *supra;* Rome v. United States, note 55 *supra;* Fullilove v. Klutznick, note 56 *supra;* Helvering v. Davis, note 64 supra; and the cases cited in notes 52 & 75 *supra.*

[136] See *National League of Cities*, 426 U.S. at 852 n.17; EEOC v. Wyoming, 103 S. Ct. at 1072–75 (Burger, C.J., dissenting).

[137] See note 75 *supra.*

[138] 421 U.S. 542 (1975). See text at notes 27–29 *supra.*

[139] 426 U.S. at 853.

[140] *Ibid.*

correct to say, as the Court did, that congressional displacement of "the States' freedom to structure integral operations in areas of traditional governmental functions" is outside the scope of the commerce power.[141] The statement must be rewritten: Congress may not displace the states' freedom in this area under the commerce power unless it really needs to do so and promises to cease doing so when the need is over. Moreover, it has greater power to do so when it seeks to prevent the states from amending their previous decisions (as opposed to making new decisions for them) and when it seeks to prevent them from being overly munificent as opposed to overly parsimonious.[142]

Each of the four asserted grounds for distinguishing *Fry* is manifestly untenable. The questions how badly legislation is needed and whether it is important that it be applied to the states are preeminently legislative. If Congress perceives a need and acts on that perception, the Court would not be performing a judicial function in substituting its judgment for that of Congress.[143] And if Congress can determine the existence of the need, it must also be able to determine how long the need continues. Although Congress authorized the imposition of the wage freeze upheld in *Fry* for a period of limited duration,[144] that fact cannot seriously be taken to have a bearing on the constitutionality of its action. Surely, the Court could not have been suggesting that a congressional effort to renew the restriction beyond the time of its expiration would have been of dubious constitutionality. And suppose Congress were to have decided that the continuing threat of inflation was so serious that a permanent system of wage controls needed to be instituted. Whatever might be said of the merits of such a conclusion, it could scarcely be argued that Congress's constitutional authority to maintain such controls would lapse after a period of six months or a year—perhaps to be revived once more after a passage of time.

The contention that the salary increase limitations upheld in *Fry*

---

[141] *Id.* at 852.

[142] See Barber, note 14 *supra*, at 180–81, for a similar attempt to derive a constitutional rule from the National League of Cities opinion. As Professor Barber convincingly demonstrates, such a rule would have to be extraordinarily convoluted—one which "[n]o one ... could knowingly intend." *Id.* at 181.

[143] The classic statement of Chief Justice Marshall is directly in point: "But where the law is not prohibited, and is really calculated to effect any of the objects entrusted to the government, to undertake here to inquire into the degree of its necessity, would be to pass the line which circumscribes the judicial department, and to tread on legislative ground." McCulloch v. Maryland, note 40 *supra*, at 423.

[144] See Fry v. United States, 421 U.S. at 543 n.1.

"displaced no state choices" but "merely required that the wage scales
... which the States themselves had chosen be maintained" is, of
course, specious. If a state believes that a choice that it had previously
made has become obsolete and needs to be modified, denying it the
capacity to make that modification is no less a displacement of the
state's power of choice than the imposition on it of a federally
determined salary scale.[145] As Justice Brennan forcefully pointed out:
"It is absurd to suggest that there is a constitutionally significant
distinction between curbs against increasing wages and curbs against
paying wages lower than the federal minimum."[146] In any event, it is
particularly difficult to see how, if the Court could claim to see a
distinction of constitutional dimension between acts of Congress that
reduce the strain on state budgets and those that increase them, it could
have arrived at its decision in *National League of Cities* without
resolving the question whether the wage and hour restrictions there
actually increased significantly the strains on the budgets of the
governments involved.[147]

   In short, the only visible basis for a distinction between *National
League of Cities* and *Fry* is that in the former case the Court did not
believe that the need for federally mandated labor standards was
sufficiently great, as a matter of policy, to justify imposing them on
state and local governments. That the Court was, in reality, employing
a "balancing of interests"—or, more accurately, a "balancing of policy
considerations"—approach was made even clearer by the express
recognition of that fact in Justice Blackmun's one-paragraph
concurring opinion. Justice Blackmun joined the opinion of the Court,
thus making it a majority rather than a plurality opinion,[148] but stated
that he did not believe that the balancing approach that he saw the
Court as adopting would "outlaw federal power in areas such as
environmental protection, where the federal interest is demonstrably
greater and where state facility compliance with imposed federal
standards would be essential."[149] Apparently because he saw the federal

---

[145] As Justice Brennan argued, the Court's distinction here was "sophistry." 426 U.S. at 872 (dissenting opinion).

[146] *Ibid.*

[147] *Id.* at 851. See text at note 95 *supra*.

[148] Because Justice Blackmun's position in his concurrence is inconsistent with the Court's opinion, which claims to be setting forth a flat rule free of balancing of interests considerations, some commentators speak of the Court's opinion in *National League of Cities* as a plurality opinion. See, *e.g.*, La Pierre, note 14 *supra*, at 804-14.

[149] 426 U.S. at 856 (concurring opinion). But, as Mark Tushnet has noted, Justice Blackmun "did not demonstrate why" the federal interest in environmental protection is greater than the

interest in imposing wage and hour requirements on the states as less great, he was prepared to deny Congress authority to require the states to meet these standards even though it would have power under the Commerce Clause, in other areas, to displace state choices with regard to the structuring of "integral operations" of their affairs. That surely is also the Court's position—no other explanation makes sense—but the Court would have greatly added to the coherency of its opinion if it had openly followed a balancing approach rather than to pretend to state a general constitutional rule and to hide its use of balancing by avoiding discussion of the factors that would have to have been balanced.[150]

What is the justification for balancing interests in this area—that is, for making the judgment of constitutionality turn on the Court's assessment of the wisdom, desirability, or necessity of the policy embodied in the challenged law? Since no question of individual rights is at stake here,[151] this would appear to be a proper case for the judicial self-restraint endorsed by the Court since 1937 in the area of economic regulation.[152] This is not to quarrel with Charles Black's observation that, "as a matter of constitutional law, one must conclude that some limits on federal power arise by mere implication from the fact of there being states, with general authority over their own local concerns."[153] Rather, if the "limits on federal power [that] arise . . . from the fact of there being states" are to be judicially enforced, it should be through the articulation of rules or principles of general applicability—designed to ensure the continued existence of the states and to protect their powers to maintain a government, to legislate, to lay and collect taxes, to decide on their own "internal processes of decision making"[154] and perhaps also their right not to have their governmental agencies

---

federal interest in maintaining adequate labor standards, nor did he explain what "such a demonstration would look like." Tushnet, note 14 *supra*, at 1341.

[150] For one thing, if the Court had conceded that it was employing a balancing approach, it would have had to enter into an examination of one point to which no attention was paid in its opinion: the actual importance to the attainment of essential national goals of the application to state and local governments of federally designated labor standards. The significance of denying to Congress any power to control the wages of a sizable number of state and local employees, who, in total, constitute some 12 percent of the national civilian work force (13,103,000 out of a total civilian work force in 1981 of 108,670,000, STATISTICAL ABSTRACT OF THE UNITED STATES, 1982-83, at 303, 379), is probably not trivial, but the Court's opinion gives no consideration whatever to that side of the balance.

[151] Notwithstanding the ingenious arguments of Professors Michelman and Tribe. See note 92 *supra*.

[152] See generally JACKSON, note 16 *supra*.

[153] BLACK, note 84 *supra*, at 29.

[154] Tushnet, note 14 *supra*, at 1323.

commandeered for service under federal direction.[155] It should not be through a process of balancing that allows judges free rein to approve one act of Congress as constitutional, even though it restricts the autonomy of the states, and to disapprove another, whose impact on the states is no different from that of the first, because they do not happen to agree with Congress's judgment that the law is needed. To paraphrase Justice Stevens, if the Court cannot "identify a limitation on . . . federal power that would not also invalidate federal regulation of state activities that [is] unquestionably permissible,"[156] it should allow the congressional judgment to stand.

2. *Political safeguards for the states.* The classic statement of the proposition that the states are protected by political safeguards in the national political process was made by Herbert Wechsler.[157] Substantial changes in the structure and realities of that process— together with the vast expansion of federal programs in areas once left entirely to state control—have occurred in the thirty years since he wrote and have rendered much of his argument obsolete.[158] Its ultimate conclusion, however, that the degree of permissible "[f]ederal intervention as against the states is . . . primarily a matter for congressional determination in our system as it stands,"[159] still is sound.[160] While it may no longer be possible to argue that state interests dominate the national political process, the critical point is not whether they are dominant but whether they can be assured a respectful and sympathetic hearing.[161] And, indeed, there is also no small degree of

---

[155] See note 105 *supra* and the discussion there in text. Another way to approach the problem of judicial enforcement of the constitutional "limits on federal power [that] arise . . . from the fact of there being states" would be to inquire whether adequate political safeguards exist that would render Congress politically accountable for its actions and check possible irresponsible exertions of its authority. See La Pierre, note 14 *supra*, at 977–1052; Note, *Redefining the National League of Cities State Sovereignty Doctrine*, 129 U. PA. L. REV. 1460 (1981). See text at notes 157–67 *infra*.

[156] See text at note 130 *supra*.

[157] Wechsler, *The Political Safeguards of Federalism: The Role of the States in the Composition and Selection of the National Government*, 54 COLUM. L. REV. 543 (1954), reprinted in WECHSLER, note 134 *supra*, at 49–82. See also James Madison's discussion of the political safeguards of federalism in Federalist Nos. 45 and 46. THE FEDERALIST 311–13, 317–20 (Cooke ed. 1961).

[158] See Kaden, note 14 *supra*, at 857–68.

[159] Wechsler, note 157 *supra*, at 559.

[160] See the recent argument of Jesse Choper, which presents an effective restatement of the Wechsler thesis with up-to-date data. CHOPER, JUDICIAL REVIEW AND THE NATIONAL POLITICAL PROCESS 176–81 (1980). See also Tushnet, note 14 *supra*, at 1328–37, and the plurality opinion of Justice Brennan in Massachusetts v. United States, 435 U.S. at 456, 456–57 n.13.

[161] See, *e.g.*, Justice Brennan's discussion in *National League of Cities* regarding the amount of federal assistance that is given annually to the states as a measure of what he describes as "the

irony in the observation that since the political reforms of the past thirty years (such as the elimination of malapportionment in state delegations to the House of Representatives and the removal of many discriminatory barriers to voting) have eroded the states' capacity to influence the national political process, Congress should no longer be considered to be adequately solicitous of state interests.[162] Can it really be true that a malapportioned Congress chosen by an electorate from which many persons have been discriminatorily excluded is entitled to greater deference from the courts on questions of federalism than one chosen by a process from which these evils have been eradicated?

In a footnote to his opinion in *National League of Cities*,[163] Justice Rehnquist attempted to counter the argument that the courts should defer to Congress on such issues because, as Justice Brennan argued, "the States are fully able to protect their own interests in the premises."[164] If, Justice Rehnquist maintained, judicial protection should not be accorded to active participants in the governing process because their role provides them with adequate ability to protect themselves, then the Court should not have protected the President against invasions by Congress of his constitutional authority because Presidents have the capacity to protect their interests in the legislative process through the use of the veto.[165] This misses the point. The Court may provide protection for the constitutional authority of the President, just as it may provide protection for whatever degree of state autonomy is constitutionally guaranteed, but not by an ad hoc balancing of interests process through which it might conclude that the policy Congress sought to advance was not sufficiently important or desirable to justify an invasion of presidential (or state) authority that might be acceptable under other circumstances. To protect presidential or state authority, the Court should be prepared to rely on constitutional standards of general applicability. If such a standard can be articulated and defended, it may be applied in concrete cases without regard to the existence of the presidential veto power or the influence possessed by the states in the national political process. But where, as

---

enormous impact of the States' political power." 426 U.S. at 878 (dissenting opinion). See also his discussion of the compromises reached in the course of enacting the challenged amendments to the Fair Labor Standards Act. *Id.* at 877 n.13.

[162] See Kaden, note 14 *supra*, at 860-62.

[163] 426 U.S. at 841-42 n.12.

[164] *Id.* at 876 (dissenting opinion).

[165] *Id.* at 841-42 n.12, citing, as examples of cases in which the Court has protected the President's constitutional authority against congressional invasion, Myers v. United States, 272 U.S. 52 (1926) (removal power); Buckley v. Valeo, 424 U.S. 1 (1976) (appointing power).

in *National League of Cities*, there was no such reliance on a general rule,[166] but merely a judicial assertion of the need to protect state autonomy, the degree of influence possessed by the states in the political process becomes extremely relevant. For if the states can command a serious hearing for their concerns, it is not a proper judicial function to reassess the outcome of the legislative process to see whether it is desirable. It is not the Court's function to protect losers in the legislative process when the process has been fairly conducted. As long as the question is one of policy, the fact that the losers may be states ought not to change this.[167]

A stronger argument in defense of judicial power to protect the constitutional essentials of state sovereignty was implicit in Justice Rehnquist's dissent in *Fry*. If, he suggested, Congress may impose on the states whatever restrictions it deems proper that are rationally related to its delegated powers, and if the Court may intervene only when the restrictions are so serious as actually to threaten "the continued existence of the state,"[168] then it is possible that the degree of sovereignty to which the states are constitutionally entitled may be withdrawn, not by one dramatic act of the federal government, but by a succession of smaller actions each of which may seem innocuous enough on its face.[169] As Robert Nagel has phrased it: "Discrete governmental restrictions do threaten these larger values cumulatively and in the long run."[170]

This concern is not without merit, but it would appear to apply equally to discrete instances of congressional action preempting state power to regulate private activity. It is no longer challenged that courts should defer to Congress in this regard, despite the fact that these actions cumulatively pose at least as great a threat to the preservation

---

[166] Whatever rule the Court may have thought it found was declared to be "not so inflexible as to preclude temporary enactments tailored to combat a national emergency." 426 U.S. at 853. A rule that is "not so inflexible" that it cannot be ignored whenever the Court chooses to ignore it is, needless to say, not a rule of general applicability.

[167] Mark Tushnet provides an alternative basis for rejecting the argument in Justice Rehnquist's footnote. See Tushnet, note 14 *supra*, at 1342.

[168] The term is from Helvering v. Gerhardt, 304 U.S. 405, 421 (1938).

[169] 421 U.S. at 550 (dissenting opinion). Justice Rehnquist cited United States v. California, note 18 *supra*, Maryland v. Wirtz, note 24 *supra*, and Fry v. United States, the case before him, and declared that "the danger to our federal system which is emphasized by these three cases taken together, as it is not by any one taken separately, seems to me quite manifest." *Ibid.* He also cited Justice Douglas's dissent in Maryland v. Wirtz, referring to a hypothetical succession of actions which "could devour the essentials of state sovereignty though that sovereignty is attested by the Tenth Amendment." *Ibid.*, quoting from 392 U.S. at 205 (dissenting opinion).

[170] Nagel, note 14 *supra*, at 96. See also TRIBE, AMERICAN CONSTITUTIONAL LAW 302 (1978).

of an effective role for the states in the federal system as do congressional decisions to regulate the activities of the states themselves. This very concern was consistently expressed by the Court in the pre-1937 period,[171] but was emphatically rejected afterward. Yet, despite the enormous increase in federal regulation of private activity that has taken place since the New Deal, and despite the dire predictions that the states would be destroyed if that were allowed to occur, the states remain effective actors in the American constitutional system.

There is little reason to believe that the similar fear of the possible consequences of allowing Congress freedom from judicial supervision in the direct regulation of state activity is not equally exaggerated. On the basis of this fear, restrictions well within the scope of the delegated powers may be struck down, not because they appear to pose an immediate threat to the effective functioning of the states, but because if Congress may impose an innocuous regulation, it might subsequently do other things which—individually or cumulatively—would pose such a threat. Robert Bork, arguing the federal government's case in *National League of Cities* as Solicitor General, was asked what the courts should do if Congress were to try to bankrupt the states by imposing on them a minimum wage of $50 an hour. His answer on reargument was correct: Congress would not do it.[172] As Justice Stone stated in his classic dissent in *United States v. Butler*, the occurrence of such a hypothetical example "would be possible only by action of a legislature lost to all sense of public responsibility."[173] As long as the states retain the degree of influence on the legislative process in Congress that they possess—that is, the ability to command a fair hearing on the effects that proposed legislation would have on them—they should not be any less able to convince Congress of the destructive impact of an accumulation of regulations than of the destructive impact of a single law. This is particularly true because, in arguing the case of cumulative impact, states would be presenting not merely conjecture about possible future results, but concrete evidence of what a succession of pieces of previous congressional legislation had already specifically done.

---

[171] See, *e.g.*, United States v. E. C. Knight Co., 156 U.S. 1, 13 (1895); Carter v. Carter Coal Co., 298 U.S. 238, 295-96 (1936).

[172] LANDMARK BRIEFS AND ARGUMENTS OF THE SUPREME COURT OF THE UNITED STATES 860-61, 903-04 (Kurland & Casper eds. 1977), cited in La Pierre, note 14 *supra*, at 1001 n.877.

[173] 297 U.S. 1, 87 (1936) (dissenting opinion). See also ELY, DEMOCRACY AND DISTRUST 181-83 (1980).

Federalism is an integral feature of the American governmental system. It is a constitutional imperative that the states continue to exist as independent, functioning units. But to recognize this fact is not to say anything about what the boundaries between federal and state authority are or how or by whom the boundary lines are to be determined. The Constitution offers little guidance in this regard, and the Tenth Amendment offers no guidance at all, because it merely reserves to the states that which is on their side of the boundary without explaining how the boundary line is to be drawn.[174] The dominant view at the time of the adoption of the Constitution, as reflected in the debates in the Constitutional Convention and the ratifying conventions,[175] the Federalist Papers,[176] the language of the Supremacy Clause and the "Necessary and Proper" Clause, and the early opinions of the Supreme Court,[177] was that the critical factor in determining the scope of national power should be national need, not conceptions of state sovereignty, and that the existence of national need should be determined by Congress, on whom the principal checks were to be the political safeguards of the constitutional system.[178] Certainly this was the view that the Marshall Court embedded in the basic principles of American constitutional law—too deeply to be easily removed—in cases such as *McCulloch v. Maryland*[179] and *Gibbons v. Ogden*.[180] The Supreme Court's assertion in *National League of Cities* of authority to impose restrictions on congressional power through an ill-disguised process of balancing interests, by which it necessarily claims for itself greater wisdom than Congress about the importance of particular policies for the enhancement of the national welfare, has no justification in history or precedent (except the

---

[174] As Walter Berns has stated, the Tenth Amendment is merely "an accessory to interpretation of the Constitution; it is not and cannot provide a rule of law of the Constitution." Berns, *The Meaning of the Tenth Amendment*, in A NATION OF STATES 132 (Goldwin ed. 1963).

[175] William Murphy, in his thorough study of the expressed views on the subjects of federalism and state sovereignty during the framing and ratification of the Constitution, concludes: "While there was no intention to create a national government of unlimited power, it is clear that the limitations were not to be imposed by considerations of state sovereignty." MURPHY, THE TRIUMPH OF NATIONALISM 410 (1967).

[176] Federalist No. 45 (Madison), THE FEDERALIST, note 157 *supra*, at 309.

[177] See, *e.g.*, Justice Wilson's statement in Chisholm v. Georgia, 2 Dall. 419, 457 (1793): "As to the purposes of the union . . . Georgia is not a sovereign state." While the decision in this case led to the adoption of the Eleventh Amendment to restore state sovereignty to the extent of not making states subject to suit in federal courts by foreign citizens or citizens of other states, Justice Wilson's point retains its validity.

[178] See, *e.g.*, Federalist No. 44, THE FEDERALIST, note 157 *supra*, at 305.

[179] 4 Wheat. 316 (1819).

[180] 9 Wheat. 1 (1824). See *id*. at 197.

discredited precedents of the pre-1937 era) or in defensible theories of the role of courts in a democratic society.[181]

II. NATIONAL LEAGUE OF CITIES AS PRECEDENT

As a commentator recently noted: "In the six [now seven] years since *NLC* was decided, the Supreme Court has not addressed, much less resolved, the basic theoretical deficiencies of that decision."[182] At the same time, however, it has not again employed the doctrine to invalidate an act of Congress.[183] Between 1976 and 1980, the Court on three occasions confirmed the suggestion in its *National League of Cities* footnote[184] that the limitations it found on the power of Congress "to affect integral operations of state government" did not apply when Congress was exercising power under section 5 of the Fourteenth Amendment or section 2 of the Fifteenth Amendment.[185] Within a week following *National League of Cities*, the Court, in *Fitzpatrick v. Bitzer*,[186] expressly recognized, without dissent, that when Congress acts under the Civil War Amendments, it may intrude into all areas of state autonomy, specifically including the structuring of the state's relations with its employees even in areas relating to the delivery of traditional governmental services.[187] In *City of Rome v. United States*,[188] the Court, citing *Fitzpatrick v. Bitzer*, held that "[t]he decision in *National League of Cities* was based solely on an assessment of congressional power under the Commerce Clause,"[189] and that "principles of federalism that might otherwise be an obstacle to congressional authority are necessarily overridden by the power to enforce the Civil War Amendments . . . [because t]hose Amendments were specifically designed as an expansion of federal power and an

---

[181] It certainly has no justification in the theory of the role of the courts in a democratic society that is espoused by Justice Rehnquist. See Rehnquist, *The Notion of a Living Constitution*, 54 TEXAS L. REV. 693, 699 (1976): "However socially desirable the goals sought to be advanced . . . , advancing them through a freewheeling, nonelected judiciary is quite unacceptable in a democratic society."

[182] La Pierre, note 14 *supra*, at 814.

[183] For an exhaustive survey of the history of *National League of Cities* as a precedent in federal and state courts to 1982, see *id.* at 814-955.

[184] 426 U.S. at 852 n.17.

[185] See text at notes 43-56 *supra*.

[186] 427 U.S. 445 (1976).

[187] 427 U.S. at 455. See note 43 *supra*.

[188] 446 U.S. 156 (1980). See note 55 *supra*.

[189] 446 U.S. at 178.

intrusion on state sovereignty."[190] And in *Fullilove v. Klutznick*,[191] Chief Justice Burger, in a plurality opinion, wrote that "complications" that might arise when Congress uses "the Commerce Power to regulate the actions of state and local governments" may be avoided when it relies on "section 5 of the Fourteenth Amendment for the power to regulate the procurement practices of state and local grantees of federal funds."[192]

Also in 1980, the Court held that the sanctity of a state's legislative process is not immune to invasion by federal criminal law. In *United States v. Gillock*,[193] it held that evidence relating to the performance of official legislative activities could be introduced in the federal trial of a state legislator under an indictment charging various bribery and racketeering offenses. The Court held that the federal prosecution was a regulation of an individual, not of the state, and noted that it had been "recognized in *National League of Cities* that the regulation by Congress under the Commerce Clause of individuals is quite different from legislation which directly regulates the internal functions of States."[194] The Court conceded that the prosecution of a legislator on the basis of his performance of official duties "might conceivably influence his conduct while in the legislature," but it said that this was "not in any sense analogous to the direct regulation imposed by the federal wage-fixing legislation in *National League of Cities*."[195] Why it was not analogous was not explained.

It is true that federal bribery and racketeering statutes do not directly control the legislative process of the state, but it is also true that the official acts of a state legislator are hardly an example of the "wholly private activity" that Congress had been conceded plenary power to regulate under the Commerce Clause, in contradistinction to its power to regulate state activity.[196] If Congress regulates the official actions of state officials directly engaged in the conduct of a function no less traditional or integral than the operation of the state legislature, it is

---

[190] *Id.* at 179.

[191] 448 U.S. 448 (1980). See note 56 *supra*.

[192] 448 U.S. at 476 (plurality opinion). Although the Chief Justice's opinion was written for a plurality rather than a majority (it was joined by Justices White and Powell), there is little doubt that this was the expression of a majority view, for the concurring Justices—Brennan, Marshall, and Blackmun—could have no less broad a view than Chief Justice Burger as to the power of Congress to interfere with the "States *qua* States."

[193] 445 U.S. 360 (1980).

[194] *Id.* at 371.

[195] *Ibid.*

[196] 426 U.S. at 840.

necessarily regulating the activity of the "States *qua* States," for the states can act only through the official actions of their officials, and the official actions of legislatures, in particular, are the sum of the actions of individual legislators.[197] Surely it is understandable that the Court would be unwilling to employ the doctrine of *National League of Cities* to place limits on the commerce power in the context of a bribery case, just as it is understandable that it would be unwilling to employ it in cases involving congressional efforts to eradicate discrimination under its power to enforce the Civil War Amendments. The very fact that the Court may be unwilling to extend a doctrine to analogous cases is itself evidence that the doctrine is of questionable validity.

In 1981, in *Hodel v. Virginia Surface Mining & Reclamation Assn.*,[198] presumably in response to the difficulties some lower courts experienced with the inherent contradictions in the *National League of Cities* reasoning,[199] the Court sought to codify what had been held there by creating a three-part test emphasizing its narrow applicability. "[I]n order to succeed," the Court declared, "a claim that congressional commerce power legislation is invalid under the reasoning of *National League of Cities* must satisfy each of the three requirements":[200]

> First, there must be a showing that the challenged statute regulates the "States as States." . . . Second, the federal regulation must address matters that are indusputably "attribute[s] of state sovereignty." . . . And third, it must be apparent that the States' compliance with the federal law would directly impair their ability "to structure integral operations in areas of traditional governmental functions."

---

[197] Thus, Justice Frankfurter, whose view of the unrestricted breadth of congressional power to regulate state activity has not been exceeded by any member of the Court—see, *e.g.*, his statement in Bethlehem Steel Co. v. New York State Labor Relations Board, 330 U.S. 767, 780 (1947) (separate opinion): "Congress can, if it chooses, entirely displace the States to the full extent of the far-reaching Commerce Clause"—has declared that to assume "that Congress has constitutional power to limit the freedom of State legislators acting within their traditional sphere" "would be a big assumption." Tenney v. Brandhove, 341 U.S. 367, 376 (1951). In that case, Justice Frankfurter quoted from the statement in Coffin v. Coffin, 4 Mass. 1, 27 (1808), that the protection accorded to legislators against inquiry into their official actions is not granted to them as individuals "for their own benefit, but to support the rights of the people, by enabling their representatives to execute the functions of their office without fear of prosecutions, civil or criminal." Quoted in 341 U.S. at 373-74. None of this, of course, demonstrates that the result in United States v. Gillock, note 193 *supra*, was incorrect, but it certainly casts doubt on the Court's suggestion that the prosecution of a legislator for the manner in which official legislative acts were performed is merely an example of "the regulation . . . of individuals," *id.* at 371.

[198] 452 U.S. 264 (1981).

[199] See, *e.g.*, the cases collected in La Pierre, note 14 *supra*, at 899-900 n.464. The "lower court decisions illustrate the problems inherent in the tests of state immunity derived from *NLC.*" *Id.* at 816.

[200] 452 U.S. at 287-88 (1981).

In a footnote, the Court then added a fourth consideration, which further narrowed the scope of the limitations imposed on congressional power:[201]

> Demonstrating that these three requirements are met does not, however, guarantee that a Tenth Amendment challenge to congressional commerce power action will succeed. There are situations in which the nature of the federal interest advanced may be such that it justifies state submission.

This codification had the unanimous support of the Court.[202] It resolved some of the ambiguities in *National League of Cities* by confirming the suggestions in the opinion about its narrowness. It confirmed that it was only a limitation on the commerce power, that it had no application to congressional regulation of private activity, and that, even with regard to direct regulation of state activity, it could be overridden if the federal interest involved were great enough. But the codification did little to explain or justify the mystifying distinctions of *National League of Cities;* it merely restated them.[203] It offered no elucidation of what "attribute[s] of state sovereignty" were protected against impairment by an exercise of the commerce power, and it failed to resolve the tension between what were now the first and second parts of the new test by explaining how it could provide a coherent definition of constitutionally protected attributes of state sovereignty that included only the activities of "States as States" and excluded the ability of the states to make the rules to govern private behavior. Nor did it make any effort to deal with the uncertainties created by such terms as "traditional governmental functions" or "integral operations."

The *Virginia Surface Mining* case and its companion, *Hodel v.*

---

[201] *Id.* at 288 n.29. Citation of Justice Blackmun's concurring opinion in *National League of Cities*, 426 U.S. at 856, would seem to confirm that the balancing test put forward here was an acceptance of his argument of the need for balancing in this type of case. See text at notes 148-50 *supra.*

[202] All Justices joined the Court's opinion except Justice Rehnquist, who concurred in the judgment but refrained from joining the majority solely because he wished to stress that the proper test for determining the scope of Congress's power over interstate commerce was whether the "regulated activity has a *substantial effect* on that commerce," not that it "merely 'affects' " it. 452 U.S. at 312 (concurring opinion). By expressly noting that he would otherwise have been prepared to join the majority, *id.* at 313, he left no doubt that he, too, was in agreement as to the Court's test.

[203] Professor La Pierre's observation is sound: "Notwithstanding the superficial allure of an enumerated test, the *Hodel* three-prong test is an intellectual sham because it does not resolve the basic issues left unanswered in *NLC.*" La Pierre, note 14 *supra,* at 895.

Indiana,[204] dealt with various challenges to the Surface Mining Control and Reclamation Act of 1977,[205] which put into effect a national system for regulating surface coal mining and reclaiming the land after the mining activity ceases.[206] As well as finding various provisions of the law constitutionally deficient on other grounds, federal district courts in Virginia[207] and Indiana[208] had found it to contravene *National League of Cities,* because, although the regulatory provisions of the Act controlled the activities of coal mine operators, not states, they impaired the states' ability to make essential decisions regarding land use, which is one of the most important of their "traditional governmental functions."[209] The Supreme Court unanimously rejected this argument because the law was not directed at the governmental operations of the "States as States," but at private activity, an area in which the states are subject to the total preemption of their laws with regard to any matter affecting interstate commerce.[210] The Court declared: "[a]lthough such congressional enactments obviously curtail or prohibit the States' prerogatives to make legislative choices respecting subjects the States may consider important, the Supremacy Clause permits no other result."[211] Nor did the Court find merit in the argument that the Act was invalid because it had a coercive effect upon the states, in that it allowed them to take over the regulation of surface mining and reclamation from the federal government—but only if they adopted a regulatory program that met standards spelled out in the act.[212] Because the states were not required to adopt a plan meeting federal standards, but were given the choice either to do so or to allow direct federal regulation of mining and reclamation activities, the Court felt that "there can be no suggestion that the Act commandeers the legislative processes of the States by directly compelling them to enact and enforce a federal regulatory program."[213]

In 1982, the Court rejected two additional challenges to congression-

---

[204] 452 U.S. 314 (1981).

[205] 91 Stat. 445; 30 U.S.C. §§1201-1328.

[206] See, *e.g.,* Harvey, *Paradise Regained? Surface Mining Control and Reclamation Act of 1977,* 15 HOUS. L. REV. 1147 (1978); Brion, *Federal Regulation of Surface Mining in Virginia,* 67 VA. L. REV. 329 (1981).

[207] Virginia Surface Mining and Reclamation Assn. v. Andrus, 483 F. Supp. 425 (W.D. Va. 1980).

[208] Indiana v. Andrus, 501 F. Supp. 452 (S.D. Ind. 1980).

[209] See 483 F. Supp. at 431-35; 501 F. Supp. at 461-68.

[210] Hodel v. Virginia Surface Mining & Reclamation Ass'n, 452 U.S. at 290-91.

[211] *Id.* at 290.

[212] 30 U.S.C. §§1251-79. See 483 F. Supp. at 432-35; 501 F. Supp. at 464-65.

[213] 452 U.S. at 288. The Court's position on the "commandeering" question appears sound. Some

al enactments based on *National League of Cities*. In *United Transportation Union v. Long Island Rail Road Co.*,[214] the Court unanimously and tersely reversed a Court of Appeals decision[215] that had held that, under *National League of Cities*, the provisions of the Railway Labor Act of 1926[216] could not constitutionally supersede state labor relations law as applied to a state-owned commuter railroad. The lower court said that the provision of commuter transportation in a metropolitan area was "a very important public service," and thus an "integral governmental function,"[217] and, on balance, the state's interest in the operation of its commuter railroad was greater than any countervailing federal interest under the Commerce Clause.[218] The Supreme Court did not agree with these conclusions, both because it did not accept the contention that the operation of a railroad was a "traditional governmental function"—with the result that the third part of the *Hodel* test was not satisfied[219]—and because it did not see the federal interest involved as inferior to that of the state.[220]

On the question whether the operation of a commuter railroad was a traditional or integral governmental function, the Court fell back, to a large extent, on its gratuitous assertion in *National League of Cities* that the result in *United States v. California*[221] (which had upheld federal regulation of a state-owned railroad) had been correct because the operation of a railroad was not an essential aspect of government activity.[222] The Court concluded that since the operation of a railroad is not "among the functions *traditionally* performed by state and local governments,"[223] its regulation by Congress "simply does not impair a

commentators who have expressed concern over the power of the federal government to require state governments to enforce federal law have distinguished between that situation and the situation presented by the Surface Mining Act, which gives the states the option either to implement and enforce federally mandated standards or to accept direct federal regulation, federally enforced. 30 U.S.C. §1254(a). See Harvey, note 206 *supra*, at 1155-56. See also Hearings, note 104 *supra*, at 496-516. Dorsen, note 104 *supra*, at 57. But see La Pierre, note 14 *supra*, at 927-32.

[214] 455 U.S. 678 (1982). Ironically, Lewis Kaden, who had tellingly criticized the reasoning and the result in *National League of Cities*—Kaden, note 14 *supra*, at 886-88; see text at notes 106-07 *supra*—argued the case for the state before the Supreme Court urging that the reasoning of that case be extended to prohibit federal regulation of labor relations in a state-owned commuter railroad.

[215] United Transportation Union v. Long Island Rail Road Co., 634 F.2d 19 (2d Cir. 1980).

[216] 44 Stat. 577, as amended; 45 U.S.C. §§151-63.

[217] 634 F.2d at 26, 27.

[218] *Id.* at 29-30.

[219] 455 U.S. at 684-87.

[220] *Id.* at 687-90.

[221] 297 U.S. 175 (1936). See text at notes 18-20 *supra*.

[222] 426 U.S. at 854 n.18.

[223] 455 U.S. at 686.

state's ability to function as a state."[224] Although the latter proposition
is undoubtedly true, the Court did not explain, as it had not explained
in *National League of Cities*, why federal regulation of employee
relations in more traditional areas would be more likely to endanger a
state's ability to function as a state.

Although the Court insisted that its emphasis on tradition "was not
meant to impose a static historical view of state functions,"[225] it offered
no response to the Court of Appeal's apparently unexceptionable
observation that "there is now no reasoned basis for finding that the
operation of an intrastate passenger service which transports tens of
thousands to and from their jobs every day is any less a governmental
function than are sanitation or public parks and recreation,"[226]
particularly where, as the Court of Appeals noted in this case,
economic realities dictate that the service will be provided by the
government or not provided at all.[227] Aside from mere reliance on
history, the only reasons adduced by the Supreme Court to support its
conclusion were those that it had employed in *South Carolina v. United
States*[228] when it introduced the distinction between governmental and
proprietary functions into the law of intergovernmental tax
immunity:[229] that a state should not be granted any encouragement to engage in business ventures[230] and that it should not be
allowed to remove activities from the reach of federal power simply by
taking them over.[231] Strikingly, the Court totally ignored the
unchallenged conclusion of the Court of Appeals that, in the light of
the unprofitability of the line, the government here had no choice but
to take it over. Thus, not only was this an essential governmental
service, it was a service that could only be provided by the
government.[232]

Unless the Court, contrary to its assertion, was merely imposing
"a static historical view," it is difficult to see what its distinction
between traditional (or essential) and other governmental functions

---

[224] *Ibid.*
[225] 455 U.S. at 686.
[226] 634 F.2d at 27.
[227] *Id.* at 26–27.
[228] 199 U.S. 437 (1905).
[229] See text at notes 124–25 *supra.*
[230] 455 U.S. at 685 n.11, citing City of Lafayette v. Louisiana Power & Light Co., 435 U.S. 389,
424 (1978) (Burger, C.J., concurring): "[T]he running of a business enterprise is not an integral
operation in the area of traditional governmental functions." Cf. South Carolina v. United States,
199 U.S. at 457–58.
[231] 455 U.S. at 687. *Cf.* 199 U.S. at 454–55.
[232] 634 F.2d at 26–27.

can possibly mean. The Court's opinion in this case therefore serves to reduce this distinction, which is part of the very core of the *National League of Cities* approach, to utter vacuity. And its dispute with the Court of Appeals over whether the state interest in maintaining effective commuter service outweighs the federal interest in preserving an efficient national rail system demonstrates both the futility and the undesirability of resolving such issues by balancing interests in the courts.[233]

The second 1982 case, *FERC v. Mississippi*,[234] involved a challenge to particular provisions of the Public Utility Regulatory Policies Act of 1978,[235] in which Congress had sought to steer a middle course between national preemption of all state and local public utility regulation, in order to conserve energy resources, and the more constitutionally dubious approach of "commandeering" state and local agencies to implement and enforce federal conservation policies. What it did was spell out certain apparently desirable techniques for the conservation of energy and require state and local regulatory agencies to give full and formal consideration to adopting them.[236] The Court noted that there was "a significant difference" between the issue in this case and that in *National League of Cities*, because the latter relates to "the extent to which state sovereignty shields the States from generally applicable federal regulations," while the former relates to "attempts to use state regulatory machinery to advance federal goals."[237] Perhaps because it saw the issue as one "of first impression,"[238] it did not invoke the *Hodel* test as a measure of the constitutionality of the Act. However, Justice O'Connor, who was joined by Chief Justice Burger and Justice Rehnquist in dissent on this aspect of the case, had no doubt either that the *Hodel* test was the proper standard or that all three parts of the test had been met.[239] Affirmance of the Act, she declared,

---

[233] That this issue may be better left to congressional resolution is shown by Congress's amendment of the Railway Labor Act, while this case was pending before the Court, to provide special procedures for dealing with labor disputes involving publicly owned commuter railroads. 95 Stat. 681; 45 U.S.C. §159a. See 455 U.S. at 689 n.21.

[234] 456 U.S. 742 (1982). See notes 104 & 105 *supra*.

[235] 92 Stat. 3117; 15 U.S.C. §§3201-11; 16 U.S.C. §§2601-45.

[236] For a more detailed explanation of the intricate statutory plan, see 456 U.S. at 746-50. One provision of the Act (Title II, §210; 92 Stat. 3144; 16 U.S.C. §824a-3) does require state regulatory agencies to implement federal policy with regard to encouraging use of nontraditional energy sources. See 456 U.S. at 750-51. The Court found the question of the constitutional validity of this requirement "more troublesome," *id.* at 759, but it upheld it on the reasoning of Testa v. Katt, 330 U.S. 386 (1947). See the discussion in note 105 *supra*.

[237] 456 U.S. at 758, 759.

[238] *Id.* at 759.

[239] *Id.* at 778-81 and n.7 (dissenting opinion). Justice O'Connor noted that *Hodel* had stipulated

"permits Congress to kidnap state utility commissions into the national regulatory family."[240]

The "commandeering" issue in *Mississippi* was distinct from that in *Hodel*,[241] because in *Hodel* the states were given the option either to adopt an acceptable plan for the regulation of surface mining or to accept full federal preemption of their regulatory authority. In *Mississippi*, there was to be no federal preemption, and the states' choice was either to consider adoption of the measures that Congress required them to consider or to withdraw altogether from the field of public utility regulation. Although Justice O'Connor was obviously justified in declaring that the assumption that the states were left with any real choice was an "absurdity,"[242] the Court relied both on the existence of an apparent choice and on the fact that the states were not being required to adopt regulations, but only to consider their adoption, to avoid "mak[ing] a definitive choice between competing views of federal power to compel state regulatory activity."[243] It left for another day the question of the constitutionality of a congressional act that would require the states to adopt and enforce federally prescribed regulations and allow them no option except compliance. The decisive factors for the Court in this case were that Congress, under the Commerce Clause, had full authority to preempt the entire field of utility regulation, and that it was not actually compelling the states to adopt specific regulations. Because the challenged provisions of the act "simply condition continued state involvement in a pre-emptible area on the consideration of federal proposals, they do not threaten the States' 'separate and independent existence,' . . . and do not impair the ability of the States 'to function effectively in a federal system.' "[244]

---

that even if all three of the requirements of the test were satisfied, congressional authority might still be upheld if "the nature of the federal interest . . . justifies state submission." 452 U.S. at 288 n.29. Although this would appear to have been an appropriate case for the invocation of this criterion in the light of the magnitude of the federal interest in energy conservation, Justice O'Connor sidestepped the issue, stating merely that "the Court has not yet explored the circumstances that might justify such an exception." 456 U.S. at 778 n.4.

[240] *Id.* at 790.

[241] See text at notes 212-13 *supra.*

[242] 456 U.S. at 781. See also, for a vigorous argument to the same effect, La Pierre, note 14 *supra*, at 945-47.

[243] 456 U.S. at 764. The Court noted that there were precedents upholding federal authority to compel state officials and state governmental institutions to implement and enforce federal law. See note 105 *supra.*

[244] *Id.* at 765-66. The argument that because Congress has unquestioned authority completely to preempt state regulation of private activity it may validly stop short of such preemption and simply require the states to enforce prescribed regulations has generally been found wanting. See Stewart, note 66 *supra*, at 1222-24; Dorsen, note 104 *supra*, at 46-49; and see Hearings, note 104 *supra*, at 497, 503, and *passim.*

The cases following *National League of Cities* demonstrate rather starkly the central difficulty with that decision: the irrelevance of its categories and the emptiness of its reasoning make it impossible to derive from it any constitutional rules that can be applied coherently and evenhandedly in subsequent cases. If it is not overruled, it is likely to remain simply a sport in the law, as it is today, or, even worse, a precedent that may be employed from time to time without conceptual consistency but merely as a convenient device to allow judges to invalidate occasional acts of Congress with which they disagree.

The interest putatively to be advanced by the *National League of Cities* doctrine is the preservation of the "States' integrity or their ability to function effectively in a federal system."[245] However, in the light of the breadth and importance of congressional responsibilities relating to interstate commerce and the supremacy of Congress in the constitutional scheme, the integrity of state authority is inescapably compromised, and *National League of Cities* can, at best, provide only random and marginal protection. As summarized in *Hodel*, the doctrine has five limiting aspects, each of which helps to make it both incoherent and incapable of preserving the interests of the states:

1. It applies only to acts of Congress under the commerce power. However, there appears to be no understandable basis for such a limitation, and as *Fitzpatrick*, *Rome*, and *Fullilove* demonstrate, the most sweeping impairments of state autonomy can be accomplished by Congress through the enforcement powers granted it in the Civil War Amendments, as well as through enactments under such grants of authority as the spending power, the war power, or even the power to regulate foreign commerce,[246] and *National League of Cities* does not affect these at all.

2. It applies only to congressional regulation of the "States *qua* States," but, as defined by the Court, this excludes both the states' power to govern and, as *United States v. Gillock* demonstrates, the performance of official duties by those officials on whom the "States *qua* States" must depend for their ability to carry out their most vital functions.

3. It applies only where the law affects a state's indisputable "attributes of sovereignty," but the attributes of sovereignty that are protected do not include the ability to make and enforce the laws and policies needed to govern individual and corporate behavior within the

---

[245] Fry v. United States, 421 U.S. at 547 n.7.

[246] See note 75 *supra*.

state. Thus, the state can be stripped, as it was in *Hodel*, of complete authority to govern even with respect to a matter as central to legitimate local concern as land use, and, as in *FERC v. Mississippi*, its administrative officials may be denied authority to set their own agendas for carrying out their governmental responsibilities.

4. It applies only to protect the states in the performance of traditional or essential governmental functions, yet, apparently to preserve the bounds of this category, the states are denied the sovereign prerogative of determining what functions are essential for the welfare of their residents. This determination is to be made for them by the federal courts—apparently, if the approach taken in *Long Island Rail Road* is maintained, by reference to narrow historical considerations that exclude from the category of essential services the provision of public transportation in a metropolitan area.

5. Even if all the previous conditions are satisfied, congressional abridgment of state autonomy may still be upheld if the federal interest to be advanced is sufficiently great to warrant it. This judgment calls for a balancing process that will necessarily involve the courts, as in *Long Island Rail Road*, in the task—emphatically inappropriate to them—of assessing the magnitude of the federal interest in such matters as keeping national transportation systems free from obstructions caused by labor disputes, and comparing it with the state interest affected.

These limitations are salutary in that they reduce the danger that considerations of state sovereignty may cripple the ability of the federal government to protect the national welfare. But, given the potentially massive restrictions on state sovereignty that they allow, and given the fact that state and local governments have substantial political resources to protect their interests in the legislative process in Congress, it seems both needless and quixotic for the Court to distort the Constitution, and devise a doctrine that defies rational analysis, merely to insure that Congress is denied power to impose on states and municipalities regulations pertaining to the employment of those responsible for carrying out their traditional governmental functions. Surely the "States' integrity or their ability to function effectively in a federal system" is not jeopardized more by such regulations than by the myriad other requirements that can be imposed on them by Congress and that are unquestionably constitutional.

III. EEOC v. Wyoming

A. THE MAIN PLOT

In *EEOC v. Wyoming*,[247] as in each of the other successors to *National League of Cities*, the Court made no effort to come to grips with the problems inherent in that case. With total ingenuousness, the four dissenters in *National League of Cities*, now joined by Justice Blackmun to compose a new majority,[248] simply stated that the challenge to the 1974 amendment to the Age Discrimination in Employment Act (ADEA) of 1967,[249] which extended the protection of the Act to employees of state and local governments, did not satisfy the third part of the *Hodel* test[250] and dismissed it on that ground.[251] The soundness of the entire constitutional exercise was not examined.

Justice Brennan, writing for the majority, discussed at some length the legislative history of the ADEA to demonstrate that Congress and the executive had united, at the time of the initial passage of the Act, in the view that[252]

> arbitrary age discrimination was profoundly harmful in at least two ways. First, it deprived the national economy of the productive labor of millions of individuals and imposed on the governmental treasury substantially increased costs in unemployment insurance and federal Social Security benefits. Second, it inflicted on individual workers the economic and psychological injury accompanying the loss of the opportunity to engage in productive and satisfying occupations.

Although the Act initially applied only to private employers, it was extended to apply to the federal, state, and local governments in 1974[253]

---

[247] 103 S. Ct. 1054 (1983).

[248] See note 12 *supra*.

[249] See notes 2 & 3 *supra*.

[250] See text at note 200 *supra*.

[251] 103 S. Ct. at 1062.

[252] 103 S. Ct. at 1058.

[253] 29 U.S.C. §633a (federal government); 29 U.S.C. §630(b) (state and local governments). As Chief Justice Burger pointedly noted in his dissenting opinion, Congress has seen fit to provide exceptions to the requirements of the act for various categories of federal employees: "early retirement is still required of federal air traffic controllers, 5 U.S.C. §8335(a), federal law enforcement officers, §8335(b), federal firefighters, *id.*, employees of the Panama Canal Commission and the Alaska Railroad, §8335(c), members of the Foreign Service, 22 U.S.C. §4052, and members of the Armed Services, 10 U.S.C. §1251." 103 S. Ct. at 1074-75 (dissenting opinion).

after Congress "found this gap in coverage to be serious."[254] There was no question that the provisions of the Act were within the scope of the commerce power. The sole question raised was whether, "at least with respect to state game wardens, application of the ADEA to the States is precluded by virtue of external constraints imposed on Congress's commerce powers by the Tenth Amendment."[255]

The fact situation in *Wyoming* was more closely analogous to that in *National League of Cities* than that of any of the other cases that had come to the Court in the interim since 1976.[256] The ADEA applied to the state as employer, rather than as legislator, administrator, or adjudicator, and the challenge thus fit that single, narrow category where state sovereignty appears to have constitutional significance under the *National League of Cities* doctrine. As the Court recognized, "[t]he management of state parks is clearly a traditional state function,"[257] so the pitfall that led to the dismissal of the constitutional challenge in *Long Island Rail Road* was avoided. One potential distinction, however, was that arguably the prohibition against age discrimination was an exercise of power under section 5 of the Fourteenth Amendment to enforce the Equal Protection Clause,[258] to which it had been clearly established that *National League of Cities* did not apply. However, the majority was content to set the Fourteenth Amendment aside and to treat the law as an exercise of the commerce power.[259] The dissenters rejected the contention that it was sustainable as an exercise of power under the Fourteenth Amendment.[260] With that concern removed, the case was on all fours with *National League of Cities*. By interfering with the states' ability to determine the terms and

---

[254] *Id.* at 1059.

[255] *Id.* at 1060.

[256] Nevertheless, the vast majority of the lower federal courts that had dealt with the issue presented in this case had sustained the ADEA amendments against constitutional challenge. Justice Brennan lists eighteen cases in which the Act had been upheld in the lower courts. *Id.* at 1059 n.6. On the other hand, it had been held invalid in only three lower court cases—the decision of the District Court in this case, EEOC v. Wyoming, 514 F. Supp. 595 (D. Wyo. 1981); Taylor v. Dept. of Fish and Game, 523 F. Supp. 514 (D. Mont. 1981); Campbell v. Connelie, 542 F. Supp. 275 (N.D.N.Y. 1982).

[257] 103 S. Ct. at 1062.

[258] See La Pierre, note 14 *supra*, at 876-77 n.373, where the lower court cases relying on sec. 5 of the Fourteenth Amendment to uphold the application of the ADEA to the states are collected. But *cf.* the opinion of the District Court, which found that "[t]here is not a word or even a smidgen in the 1974 amendments to the ADEA or the legislative history of the amendments supporting the contention that Congress was exercising its powers under the Fourteenth Amendment." EEOC v. Wyoming, 514 F. Supp. at 599.

[259] 103 S. Ct. at 1064.

[260] *Id.* at 1072-75 (dissenting opinion).

conditions of employment of their employees, the ADEA had "displace[d] state policies regarding the manner in which they will structure delivery of those governmental services which their citizens require."[261]

Justice Brennan readily conceded that the first part of the *Hodel* test was met—the ADEA regulates the "States as States" by denying them authority to require the retirement of certain of their employees at age fifty-five.[262] He bypassed the second, and most inscrutable, part of the test—whether the law addresses "matters that are indisputably 'attribute[s] of state sovereignty' "—simply by noting that it was unnecessary to resolve it,[263] although he very accurately observed in a footnote that "[p]recisely what [is] meant by an 'undoubted attribute of state sovereignty' is somewhat unclear."[264] On this point, the Court had offered little explanation in *National League of Cities*: it merely cited the prohibition recognized in *Coyle v. Smith*[265] against the use of the power to admit new states to prevent a state from relocating its capital as an example of the protection of such an attribute, and it asserted that the power to determine the wages and hours of "those whom they employ in order to carry out their governmental functions" was "undoubted[ly]" another such attribute.[266] It determined whether a particular aspect of state autonomy was protected by asking whether it was among the "functions essential to separate and independent existence,"[267] which, of course, is not a definition but merely the substitution of one phrase for another.

In that same footnote, Justice Brennan did retreat significantly from his argument in *National League of Cities* that the only safeguard against federal impairment of state sovereignty that could be derived from the Tenth Amendment was the requirement that Congress not exercise power that was not delegated to it.[268] He stated, however, that "some employment decisions are so clearly connected to the execution of underlying sovereign choices that they must be assimilated into them for purposes of the Tenth Amendment,"[269] which plainly implies that some congressional actions squarely within the scope of the

[261] 426 U.S. at 847.
[262] 103 S. Ct. at 1061.
[263] *Ibid.*
[264] *Id.* at 1061 n.11. See text at notes 80–92 *supra.*
[265] 221 U.S. 559 (1911). See notes 81–82 *supra.*
[266] 426 U.S. at 845.
[267] *Ibid.* The quoted phrase is from Lane County v. Oregon, note 93 *supra*, at 76.
[268] 426 U.S. at 862 n.4 (dissenting opinion).
[269] 103 S. Ct. at 1061 n.11.

commerce power may nevertheless be held unconstitutional because of Tenth Amendment considerations. Among these protected employment decisions, he suggested, are those related to the "unimpeded exercise of State's role as provider of emergency services" and essential to the performance of its " 'dual functions of administering the public law and furnishing public services.' "[270] But, he added, "not . . . every state employment decision aimed simply at advancing a generalized interest in efficient management—even the efficient management of traditional state functions—should be considered to be an exercise of an 'undoubted attribute of state sovereignty,' "[271] thus leaving the issue every bit as murky as before.

In his dissenting opinion (in which he was joined by Justices Powell, Rehnquist, and O'Connor), Chief Justice Burger expressed no doubt that the 1974 amendment to the ADEA interfered with a constitutionally protected attribute of state sovereignty. Given that the maintenance of state parks and the provision of recreation services are clearly traditional state functions, a state may "assure the physical preparedness" of those who are employed to assist in carrying out these functions.[272] The Chief Justice suggested a quantitative test as a "persuasive" but not "conclusive" measure for determining whether a particular state action was entitled to constitutional protection as an attribute of sovereignty: one should look to see "whether other government entities have attempted to enact similar legislation."[273] Since he found that most states have mandatory retirement laws that contravene the ADEA,[274] and since Congress has excluded certain categories of federal employees (most notably, law enforcement personnel) from the coverage of the Act,[275] he concluded that the requirements of this test were fully satisfied. But his judgment that the establishment of mandatory retirement laws was a protected attribute of sovereignty was more fundamentally based on the principle that "it

---

[270] *Ibid,* quoting from *National League of Cities,* 426 U.S. at 851. Although the Michelman and Tribe articles are not cited, it is difficult to escape the thought, in the light of the Court's particular emphasis here on the constitutional dimension of the states' ability to provide basic public services in an "unimpeded" fashion, that it had been influenced by their arguments that the Constitution should be read as denying Congress authority unduly to interfere with the states' ability to meet their residents' constitutional rights to the provision of such services. See note 94 *supra.*

[271] 103 S. Ct. at 1061 n.11.

[272] *Id.* at 1069 (dissenting opinion).

[273] *Ibid.*

[274] See *id.* at 1069–70 n.2.

[275] See note 253 *supra.*

is the essence of state power to choose—subject only to *constitutional* limits—who is to be part of the state government."[276]

That is surely a clear and comprehensible standard, which would, if capable of general application, provide a concrete example of what is meant by a protected attribute. The problem is that it is not capable of general application. At best it applies only to those parts of the state government engaged in performance of traditional governmental functions, for it is not the Constitution but the Railway Labor Act that, by denying an employer the right to discharge an employee for labor union activity,[277] limits the state's capacity to determine who is to be part of that agency of government responsible for commuter rail transit services, a limitation upheld in *Long Island Rail Road* by a unanimous Court in an opinion by Chief Justice Burger.[278] It is also inconsistent with the opinion of the Chief Justice in *Fullilove v. Klutznick*,[279] which affirmed the requirement of the Public Works Employment Act of 1977 that at least 10 percent of federal grant funds awarded to states and local governments for public works projects be used to purchase goods and services from minority business enterprises. Surely it should be no less an attribute of state sovereignty to determine who shall be awarded a state contract than to determine who is to be given state employment, and clearly the Constitution does not require observance of the 10 percent set-aside requirement, but the Chief Justice saw no objection to Congress's displacement of the states' choices in this regard.[280] To be sure, the 10 percent requirement was sustained in part as an exercise of congressional power under section 5 of the Fourteenth Amendment rather than the Commerce Clause. But that makes it no less clear that no rule of constitutional law prohibits Congress from interfering with a state's "power to choose—subject only to *constitutional* limits—who is to be part of the state government."[281]

---

[276] 103 S. Ct. at 1069.

[277] 45 U.S.C. §152.

[278] See text at notes 214-33 *supra*. In *Long Island Rail Road*, Chief Justice Burger wrote that that exercise of congressional authority (which, of course, includes the power to control "who is to be part of the state government") "simply does not impair a state's ability to function as a state." 455 U.S. at 686.

[279] 448 U.S. 448 (1980).

[280] *Id.* at 472-80 (plurality opinion).

[281] In Oklahoma v. Civil Service Commission, 330 U.S. 127 (1947), the Court upheld the power of Congress to condition grants to states on the requirement that persons employed to carry out the functions financed by grant funds not be active in political organizations or political campaigns. This, of course, interfered with the state's power to determine "who is to be part of the state government" even though the state's choice was in no way limited by the Constitution. See note 61 *supra*.

It was the third part of the *Hodel* test—whether "the States' compliance with the federal law would directly impair their ability 'to structure integral operations in areas of traditional governmental functions' "—that the Court used as its basis for rejecting the challenge to the constitutionality of the ADEA. Although the majority in *National League of Cities* had examined at some length the claims of states and local governments regarding the damaging financial impact of the Fair Labor Standards Act, it did not rely on those claims in concluding that the Act was unconstitutional because of its interference with structuring integral operations of those governments.[282] The mere displacement of state choices in this area was enough. Nevertheless, Justice Brennan based his opinion with regard to this part of the *Hodel* test squarely on an assessment of the actual impact the ADEA would be likely to have on the states,[283] and on the conclusion that the impact would be "sufficiently less serious than it was in *National League of Cities*" to justify a different result.[284]

The conclusion that the likely impact of the ADEA on the states was insufficient "to turn the color of legal litmus paper"[285] was based not on "particularized assessments"[286] but on a general discussion of what the nature of the impact could be expected to be on any state whose mandatory retirement laws were overridden. Justice Brennan offered three reasons for the Court's judgment. (1) If the state's concern is with the physical preparedness of its game wardens, the Act does not preclude it from attaining that goal both because it permits the state to require wardens to undergo periodic physical examinations (and to retire those who are not sufficiently fit) and because it allows exceptions to its provisions where it can be shown that age is a "bona fide occupational qualification" for a particular job.[287] (2) The financial pressures on state budgets resulting from observance of the ADEA

---

[282] 426 U.S. at 852. See *id.* at 846: "[R]esolution of the factual disputes as to the effect of the amendments is not critical to our disposition of the case." See also *id.* at 851.

[283] 103 S. Ct. at 1062-64.

[284] *Id.* at 1062. Justice Brennan's assertion that the decision in *National League of Cities* was also dependent upon "considerations of degree," *ibid.*, is simply untrue, at least as far as it relates to the majority opinion. Justice Blackmun, who provided the fifth vote necessary to make Justice Rehnquist's opinion in *National League of Cities* a majority opinion, clearly had "considerations of degree" in mind, as his concurring opinion—426 U.S. at 856—shows, but the majority specifically disclaimed reliance on any assessment of the degree of impact on the states. See note 282 *supra*.

[285] The phrase is from Abrams v. United States, 250 U.S. 616, 629 (Holmes, J., dissenting).

[286] 103 S. Ct. at 1063, quoting from *National League of Cities*, 426 U.S. at 851.

[287] 103 S. Ct. at 1062.

should be insubstantial. Whatever strain may be imposed on a state's pension system by allowing workers to accrue more seniority (and thus earn larger benefits) and on its salary budget by requiring the retention of more senior (and thus more highly paid) employees, should be offset, at least in large part, by the fact that as long as the senior employees remain on the payroll they will not be drawing any pension benefits at all; when they do retire, they will be drawing from the pension fund for a smaller number of years.[288] The increase in costs for health insurance or similar benefits that would result from the requirement that older employees be retained need not be great, because the Act allows adjustments in the benefit packages for these employees that could preclude a major increase.[289] (3) Unlike the wage and hour requirements, which might prevent a state from accomplishing certain broader social purposes (the Court cited as its example the possibility mentioned in *National League of Cities* of providing jobs to untrained persons),[290] the prohibition against mandatory retirement does not appear to pose a barrier to the attainment of any broader social goals.[291]

Chief Justice Burger viewed the likely impact on the states quite differently. He saw the strains on the state pension systems and salary budgets brought about by the elimination of mandatory early retirements to be significant,[292] and the "[n]on-economic hardships . . . equally severe."[293] Because older game wardens must be retained in service, the state is "prevented from hiring those physically best able to do the job,"[294] and the state is prevented from attaining important broader social goals such as providing incentives to the young and meeting affirmative action goals.[295] He found that the exceptions to the ADEA in other federal statutes for various categories of federal employees[296] demonstrated Congress's awareness of the desirability of requiring early retirement in certain areas of government employment and illustrated the absence of a valid purpose in "forcing the states to

---

[288] *Id.* at 1063.
[289] *Ibid.*
[290] *Id.* at 1064, citing 426 U.S. at 848.
[291] 103 S. Ct. at 1064.
[292] *Id.* at 1070 (dissenting opinion).
[293] *Id.* at 1071.
[294] *Ibid.*
[295] *Ibid.*
[296] *Id.* at 1074–75. See note 253 *supra.*

comply with rigid standards."[297] Nor did he believe that it was realistic
to expect that the states could escape the economic difficulties imposed
on them by adjusting the health insurance or benefit packages for older
employees in occupations covered by mandatory early retirement laws,
for "these employees . . . are, for the most part, in the most physically
hazardous occupations, and thus most need protection."[298] In any event,
he argued, adjusting the insurance plans would require new laws and
regulations, and "[d]rafting and enacting these new laws is a burden
Congress has no power to impose on the states."[299] Finally, he declared
that the burden of proof that age is a "bona fide occupational
qualification" for a particular job is likely to be so great that no escape
from the rigidity of the federal requirement will be available through
this avenue.[300]

The majority and the dissenters were equally far apart in their
judgments relative to the additional, "balancing of interests," segment
of the *Hodel* test. Justice Brennan felt it unnecessary to address the

---

[297] 103 S. Ct. at 1071 (dissenting opinion). The Court refused to treat the exceptions to the
ADEA provided by law for certain categories of federal employees as undermining the validity
of the federal interest asserted. It declared that these exceptions reflect "the ebbs and flows of
political decisionmaking," and need not lead to the conclusion that "Congress was insincere."
The "sufficiency of the federal interest [must be evaluated] as a matter of law rather than of
psychological analysis." *Id.* at 1064 n.17. That is, of course, unless it is possible that Congress is
seeking to achieve an illegitimate ulterior purpose, which is hardly the case here. See Alfange, *Free
Speech and Symbolic Conduct: The Draft-Card Burning Case*, 1968 SUPREME COURT REVIEW 1,
27-38.

[298] 103 S. Ct. at 1071 (dissenting opinion).

[299] *Ibid.* It is, of course, hardly fair to say that Congress is requiring the states to draft and enact
new laws. The situation presented here is one in which the states may decide that it is wise to
enact new laws in the light of a valid enactment by Congress under one of its delegated powers
that renders previous state legislation obsolete or inappropriate. One would imagine that this is
a common occurrence.

[300] *Id.* at 1071-72, citing, as a likely example of the standard of proof that might be required to
demonstrate that age is a "bona fide occupational qualification" for a job, the standard employed
by the Fourth Circuit in Arritt v. Grisell, 567 F.2d 1267, 1271 (4th Cir. 1977), that there be "a
factual basis for believing that all or substantially all persons within the class . . . would be unable
to perform safely and efficiently the duties involved, or that it is impossible or impractical to deal
with persons over the age limit on an individualized basis." This language is a paraphrase of that
of the Fifth Circuit in Usery v. Tamiami Trail Tours, 531 F.2d 224, 236 (1976), involving the
application of the ADEA to a private employer, which in turn, paraphrased the language of
Weeks v. Southern Bell Telephone & Telegraph Co., 408 F.2d 228, 235, 235 n.5 (1969), involving
Title VII of the Civil Rights Act of 1964, 42 U.S.C. §2000e-2. The suggestion that it would
essentially be impossible to meet this standard in an age discrimination case appears to be wrong.
Some federal courts have sustained claims that age is a "bona fide occupational qualification." See,
e.g., Hodgson v. Greyhound Lines, 499 F.2d 859 (7th Cir. 1974), *cert. denied sub nom.* Brennan
v. Greyhound Lines, 419 U.S. 1122 (1975) (initial hiring of bus drivers); Usery v. Tamiami Trail
Tours, *supra* (initial hiring of bus drivers); Murnane v. American Airlines, 667 F.2d 98 (D.C. Cir.
1981), *cert. denied*, 456 U.S. 915 (1982) (initial hiring of flight officers). In any event, if the courts
are using too rigid a standard for determining what constitutes a "bona fide occupational
qualification," the proper response of the Court would seem to be to loosen the standard, not to
declare an act of Congress unconstitutional.

issue, because the Court had found that the challenge failed to meet the third part of the test. He paused to note that even if it could have been held that that part of the test had been satisfied, it might still have been necessary to conclude that the federal interest underlying the statute was sufficiently great to justify its intrusion into state autonomy.[301] Chief Justice Burger, on the other hand, believed that the federal interest was "largely theoretical" and did not outweigh the strong state interest in insuring the physical preparedness of law enforcement and fire prevention personnel.[302]

Little would be served by an effort to choose between the arguments in the majority opinion and in the dissent about the degree of impact that the federal prohibition against mandatory early retirement laws would be likely to have on the states. It is equally fruitless to debate whether the federal interest in preventing the exclusion of able individuals from productive labor in the national economy outweighs the state interest in insuring the physical preparedness of game wardens or other law enforcement or fire prevention personnel. It is difficult to escape the conclusion that the resolution of the constitutional issue in this case did not turn, either for the majority or the dissenters, on an objective assessment of the impact on the states or of the comparative strengths of the federal and state interests involved, but rather that the process worked in reverse: the individual Justices decided first how they thought the constitutional question should be answered and then magnified or disparaged the federal or state concerns accordingly.

The incoherence of a concept such as structuring the integral operations of state or local governments is, of course, an open invitation to engage in a process of conclusion first, reasoning second. If the purpose of prohibiting the federal government from interfering with integral state operations—whatever that means—is to preserve the "separate and independent existence" of the states (which is what the Court suggested in *National League of Cities*)[303] then only by engaging in the grossest exaggeration can it be said that requiring the states to observe the requirements of the ADEA would have that effect. If, as is more probable, the intended purpose of the prohibition is to allow the Court to find interference with integral operations whenever it concludes that Congress is imposing unnecessary or unjustified

---

[301] 103 S. Ct. at 1064 n.17.

[302] *Id.* at 1072 (dissenting opinion).

[303] 426 U.S. at 851. For the history of the quoted phrase, see note 93 *supra.*

requirements on the states, then it is nothing but a vehicle by which the Court, in the guise of constitutional law, can replace policy determinations of Congress concerning interstate commerce with its own.

There are no valid reasons for shifting policymaking responsibility to the courts in this area. Not only are the "political safeguards of federalism" fully applicable,[304] but the additional political safeguards created by the fact that the law also covers those working for private employers[305] — including employees responsible for the safety and security of individuals or of the public[306] — are present. This means that, if the requirements of the law are indeed unreasonable, the Members of Congress responsible for its passage can surely be expected to be exposed to the political repercussions of imposing such requirements generally on the society as a whole. Since it is conceded that Congress has constitutional authority to prohibit age discrimination against airline pilots,[307] there is hardly greater justification, in terms of public safety, for denying it constitutional authority to prohibit the same form of discrimination against state game wardens.

The very fact that Congress has allowed exceptions to the ADEA for various categories of federal employees demonstrates that it is willing to grant exceptions in cases where it can be persuaded that there are cogent reasons for doing so. Since there is no reason to assume congressional hostility toward the states, it should be expected that Congress would be prepared to grant them similar exceptions for those of their employees performing physically strenuous jobs if it can be shown to its satisfaction that these exceptions are warranted. There is thus no basis for arguing that when Congress makes the policy determination that an exception is not warranted, the issue may be reopened in the courts. Because the Court's reasoning in *Wyoming* necessarily calls for a judicial reexamination of what is a purely policy question, it marks the triumph, not the demise, of the *National League of Cities* approach. That approach has now been given the stamp of approval by its opponents, and courts will thus continue to resolve

---

[304] See text at notes 157-67 *supra*.

[305] See La Pierre, note 14 *supra*, at 1000-04.

[306] See, *e.g.*, Hodgson v. Greyhound Lines, note 300 *supra* (bus driver); Usery v. Tamiami Trail Tours, note 300 *supra* (bus driver); Houghton v. McDonnell Douglas, 553 F.2d 561 (8th Cir. 1977), *cert. denied*, 434 U.S. 966 (1977) (test pilot); Smallwood v. United Air Lines, 661 F.2d 303 (4th Cir. 1981), *cert. denied*, 456 U.S. 1007 (1982) (airline pilot); Murnane v. American Airlines, note 300 *supra* (airline flight officer); Tuohy v. Ford Motor Co., 675 F.2d 842 (6th Cir. 1982) (company pilot).

[307] See Smallwood v. United Air Lines, note 306 *supra*.

issues of state autonomy by evaluating the merits of congressional policy. One can certainly understand the new majority's apparent concern for the principle of *stare decisis*, but what is involved here is not merely an erroneous interpretation of a statute, or even an erroneous interpretation of the Constitution—where the case for *stare decisis* is weaker[308]—but an erroneous assertion of judicial authority to decide on the merits or wisdom of a policy chosen by Congress. In the latter context, *stare decisis* need play no part at all.[309]

B. THE SOLILOQUY

There was an additional issue in *Wyoming:* whether Congress had authority to extend the ADEA to the states on the basis of its power under section 5 of the Fourteenth Amendment. Because the majority upheld the application of the Act to the states under the commerce power, it had no need to discuss whether it could also have been sustained as an exercise of Fourteenth Amendment and did not do so, except to reiterate that the *National League of Cities* doctrine was inapplicable to congressional enactments grounded in that authority.[310] However, the dissenters' conclusion that the law could not be upheld as an exercise of the commerce power required them to examine the issue.

Chief Justice Burger began his discussion of this question with the startling assertion that the Tenth Amendment does not impose the same limitations on Congress's power under section 5 of the Fourteenth Amendment as it does on Congress's commerce power, because, unlike the Commerce Clause, the Fourteenth Amendment was adopted after the Tenth Amendment.[311] The implications of this line of reasoning—that the chronological order of the adoption of individual provisions of the Constitution has a bearing on how they are to be interpreted relative to one another—are quite remarkable. Congress would have more authority to abridge freedom of speech when acting under a power granted to it subsequent to the adoption of

---

[308] See Burnet v. Coronado Oil & Gas Co., 285 U.S. 393, 405-11 (1932) (Brandeis, J., dissenting).

[309] Because *National League of Cities* called for judicial reevaluation of the policy decisions of Congress relative to interstate commerce, Justice Stevens declared, in his concurring opinion in *Wyoming*, that *National League of Cities* was "inconsistent with the central purpose of the Constitution itself, . . . [and] not entitled to the deference that the doctrine of *stare decisis* ordinarily commands for this Court's precedents." 103 S. Ct. at 1067 (concurring opinion).

[310] *Id.* at 1064 n.18.

[311] *Id.* at 1072 (dissenting opinion).

the First Amendment than when acting under powers granted in Article I, section 8. Perhaps the states might be able to disregard the requirements of due process or equal protection in legislating on the subject of intoxicants under the Twenty-first Amendment.[312] Surely this argument—which was apparently still another vain effort to explain how federalism can place limits on Congress's commerce power but not its power to enforce the Fourteenth Amendment—collapses quickly of its own weight. Even if it could be accepted, it would offer no justification for interpreting the Tenth Amendment to limit the commerce power. It is obviously true that the Tenth Amendment was added to the Constitution after the Commerce Clause; it is settled that it did not change the Constitution in any way but was "merely declaratory of the distribution of powers made in the original Constitution."[313] Thus, even if it could be read as a prohibition—which it emphatically cannot—it places no limitations on the commerce power that were not inherent in the Commerce Clause itself.[314]

On the merits of the Fourteenth Amendment question, the Chief Justice's argument was that Congress lacked power to override state mandatory retirement laws as a means of enforcing the Equal Protection Clause, because such laws have never been held to violate that Clause.[315] He conceded that Congress's power under the Fourteenth Amendment may enable it "to enact legislation that prohibits conduct not in itself unconstitutional" but only where "the prohibition [is] necessary to guard against enroachment of guaranteed rights or to rectify past discrimination."[316] Congress may thus prohibit state action not itself in violation of the Constitution as a rational means of precluding discrimination on the basis of race but not on the basis of age, because the Equal Protection Clause has never been held to forbid discrimination on the basis of age; and in the absence of such a

---

[312] That is perhaps the basis of the Court's reasoning that states have greater authority to interfere with conduct arguably protected by the First Amendment when they are exercising authority under the Twenty-first Amendment. See New York State Liquor Authority v. Bellanca, 452 U.S. 714 (1981); California v. La Rue, 409 U.S. 109 (1972).

[313] Berns, note 174 *supra*, at 145.

[314] Justice Powell, who joined Chief Justice Burger's dissent, stressed the purely declaratory nature of the Tenth Amendment in his own dissenting opinion. 103 S. Ct. at 1078 n.6.

[315] *Id.* at 1073. The Chief Justice cited two cases in which mandatory retirement laws had been upheld by the Court against Fourteenth Amendment challenges. A state law imposing mandatory retirement requirements on state police was upheld in Massachusetts Board of Retirement v. Murgia, 427 U.S. 307 (1976); the federal requirement of mandatory retirement for Foreign Service Officers was upheld in Vance v. Bradley, 440 U.S. 93 (1979).

[316] 103 S. Ct. at 1073.

determination—presumably by the Court—Congress may not prohibit the states from engaging in such discrimination.[317]

This is an extreme statement from one side in a constitutional debate that has continued unresolved since the Supreme Court held precisely the contrary in 1966 in *Katzenbach v. Morgan*[318] and a hopelessly fragmented Court, four years later in *Oregon v. Mitchell*,[319] failed to reaffirm that decision. But some discrimination on the basis of age would be difficult to defend as constitutional—for example, establishing a maximum age for attendance at a state university or the right to vote in a state election. Since age is not a suspect classification, courts will uphold classifications based on age unless they cannot be said to be rationally related to the achievement of a legitimate public purpose.[320] This extremely relaxed standard is maintained so that courts will not substitute their own views of proper public policy for those of the states.[321] But because of the liberality of this test some arguably unconstitutional acts of age discrimination may be upheld by the courts. Unlike the courts, however, Congress has policymaking responsibility, which it should be free to exercise. It may, therefore, legitimately substitute its views on policy for those of the states with regard to Fourteenth Amendment questions and need not be limited by the rationality standard that limits the courts. Its constitutional responsibility to enforce the Equal Protection Clause should carry with it the authority to require state laws establishing discriminatory classifications to meet a stricter standard of public necessity.[322]

C. THE SUBPLOT

In both the opinion of the Court in *Wyoming* and the Chief Justice's

---

[317] *Id.* at 1073–74.

[318] 384 U.S. 641, 652–56 (1966), upholding the constitutionality of §4(e) of the Voting Rights Act of 1965, 79 Stat. 439; 42 U.S.C. §1973b(e), prohibiting the denial of the right to vote by a state for lack of English literacy to one who has completed the sixth grade in an American-flag school in which the predominant classroom language was other than English.

[319] 400 U.S. 112 (1970), striking down a provision of the Voting Rights Act Amendments of 1970, 84 Stat. 318, prohibiting the denial by a state of the right to vote on account of age in state elections to anyone who had reached the age of 18. This decision was, of course, subsequently rendered moot by the Twenty-sixth Amendment.

[320] See Massachusetts Board of Retirement v. Murgia, 427 U.S. at 313–14; Vance v. Bradley, 440 U.S. at 96–97.

[321] See, *e.g.*, San Antonio Independent School District v. Rodriguez, 411 U.S. 1, 40–44 (1973).

[322] This was the argument of the federal government in *Wyoming* which Chief Justice Burger would reject. See 103 S. Ct. at 1073–74 n.7 (dissenting opinion). See also Alfange, *Congressional Power and Constitutional Limitations*, 18 J. PUB. L. 103, 126–27 (1969); Cohen, note 52 *supra*, at 619.

dissent, it was assumed that the constitutional issue turned on whether the challenge to the ADEA satisfied the *Hodel* test; the soundness of the *Hodel/National League of Cities* approach was not questioned. There were two other opinions in the case. Justice Stevens, who joined the opinion of the Court (thereby making it an opinion for the Court), wrote a separate concurrence directly challenging the assumptions on which the majority's reasoning rested. Justice Powell, who was joined by Justice O'Connor, added a separate dissent for the sole purpose of responding to Justice Stevens.

Justice Stevens found the focus on whether constitutional limitations drawn from the Tenth Amendment or from principles of federalism inherent in the Constitution were transgressed in this case to be fundamentally misconceived. The question, as he saw it, had nothing to do with constitutional limitations, because none was "even arguably applicable."[323] The question was "purely one of constitutional power."[324] *National League of Cities*, he argued, was "pure judicial fiat"[325] and, therefore, like the cases prior to 1937 that gave an artificially narrow construction to the Commerce Clause and "whose . . . rejection is now universally regarded as proper," it should be given a "prompt rejection" as "inconsistent with the central purpose of the Constitution itself."[326] The "central purpose" was, for him, embodied in the Commerce Clause, because it was the perceived need for effective national authority to regulate interstate commerce that was the primary reason for the drafting of the Constitution.[327] The execution of that responsibility is the national government's "central mission."[328]

The ADEA, like the Fair Labor Standards Act, thus reflects a congressional policy judgment about the legislation that is needed to carry out an aspect of that "central mission"—regulation of the "American labor market."[329] Although Justice Stevens indicated his personal disagreement with the policy of prohibiting mandatory early retirement—as, in his *National League of Cities* dissent, he had

---

[323] 103 S. Ct. at 1067 (concurring opinion).

[324] *Id.* at 1068.

[325] *Id.* at 1067.

[326] *Ibid.*

[327] *Id.* at 1065. Justice Stevens here quotes at length from a lecture by Justice Rutledge, in which he declared that the existence of barriers to trade among the states was "the particular problem causative of" the establishment of the Constitution. RUTLEDGE, A DECLARATION OF LEGAL FAITH 26 (1947). Other sources relied on by Justice Stevens in support of his contention are cited in 103 S. Ct. at 1065 n.1.

[328] *Id.* at 1066.

[329] *Ibid.*

indicated his disagreement with the policy underlying the minimum-wage requirement[330]—he insisted again that his views on the policy issue were "totally irrelevant."[331] The only question to be decided was whether Congress, in carrying out its "central mission" through regulation of the labor market, may "regulate both the public sector and the private sector of that market, or must . . . confine its regulation to the private sector."[332] "Because of the interdependence of the segments of the economy and the importance and magnitude of government employment,"[333] he concluded, "that question can have only one answer."[334]

Justice Powell took sharp issue with these conclusions. Unfortunately, his opinion is largely a succession of non sequiturs. He begins by challenging Justice Stevens's contention that the concern that led to the adoption of the Commerce Clause was the *"central problem* that gave rise to the Constitution itself."[335] Although he conceded that this "was *one* of the Constitution's purposes,"[336] he insisted that "one can be reasonably sure that few of the Founding Fathers thought that trade barriers among the States were 'the central problem,' or that their elimination was the 'central mission' of the Constitutional Convention."[337] The true central mission, in Justice Powell's view, was "[c]reating a national government within a federal system,"[338] a proposition which he supported by noting that the focus of the 1787 convention was heavily on issues of the structure of the national government and its relationship to the states, that the regulation of commerce was not listed among the purposes for the adoption of the Constitution set forth in the Preamble, and that the commerce power was not even listed first among the powers delegated to Congress in Article I, section 8.[339]

Justice Powell's point confuses the purpose in establishing the Constitution with the problems of detail that had to be faced once the decision to establish it was reached. Whatever the time devoted to

---

[330] 426 U.S. at 881 (dissenting opinion). See text at note 129 *supra*.
[331] 103 S. Ct. at 1068 (concurring opinion). *Cf.* 426 U.S. at 881 (dissenting opinion).
[332] 103 S. Ct. at 1068.
[333] *Id.* at 1066-67.
[334] *Id.* at 1068.
[335] *Id.* at 1075 (dissenting opinion), quoting *id.* at 1065.
[336] *Id.* at 1076.
[337] *Ibid.*
[338] *Ibid.*
[339] *Id.* at 1076-77.

structural issues at the convention, the Constitution was certainly not established for the purpose of assuring that there be two houses of Congress, with the representatives in one to be chosen by the people and apportioned among the states according to their population, and the representatives in the other to be chosen by the state legislature, each state having equal representation, and so on. The fact that the grant of power to Congress to regulate commerce was so little debated and occupied so little of the attention of the convention[340] is itself testimony that the imperative need for this grant was universally understood and accepted by the delegates, and suggests in context that they may have recognized it as a prime purpose of their endeavors. Nor can much be made of the absence of any specific mention of commerce among the purposes for the adoption of the Constitution set forth in the Preamble. Justice Powell recognized that the protection of commerce could be subsumed within the end of "promot[ing] the general welfare," even though he expressed some doubt about whether it really was, since the term "general welfare" had not encompassed interstate commerce when it was employed in the Articles of Confederation.[341] But in any event, the protection of interstate commerce surely falls squarely within the very first of the purposes mentioned in the Preamble—"to form a more perfect Union." The absence of any central authority to control interstate commerce was a principal imperfection in the Union under the Articles of Confederation.[342]

It is difficult to take seriously an argument that denigrates the significance of the commerce power because it was not listed first in Article I, section 8. To be sure, it was not. It is preceded by the power "to lay and collect Taxes," which power is given for the purpose of enabling Congress to appropriate money "to pay the Debts and provide for the common Defence and general Welfare," and by the power to

---

[340] See *e.g.*, MURPHY, note 175 *supra*, at 182-83: "Commercial reform was, of course, the stated reason for the convening of the Annapolis convention, which led to the calling of the Philadelphia convention. In light of this background, it is not surprising that the draft reported to the convention by the Committee of Detail contained the broad and unqualified grant of power to Congress 'to regulate commerce with foreign nations and among the several states.' Nor is it surprising that when this clause came up for consideration on August 16, it was approved by the convention without discussion and without dissent. So easily and readily was a huge and vitally important area of legislative power transferred from the states to the nation." See also the statement of James Madison in Federalist No. 45 that the grant to Congress of the commerce power was one "which few oppose." THE FEDERALIST, note 157 *supra*, at 314.

[341] 103 S. Ct. at 1077. See Articles of Confederation, Art. III.

[342] See, *e.g.*, Stern, note 58 *supra*, at 1337.

"borrow money on the credit of the United States." Justice Powell seems to conclude from this that "[i]t is evident that the authority to tax and to 'provide for the common Defence' loomed larger among the concerns of the Founders than other powers granted Congress."[343] If his point is merely that the framers were also profoundly concerned with the need to grant Congress an effective power of taxation and the means to defend the nation, it is unobjectionable. But this in no way contradicts Justice Stevens's contention that commercial concerns provided the direct motivation for calling the convention. Moreover, the "rank order" argument for establishing priority of importance among the powers delegated in Article I, section 8, that Justice Powell appears to be espousing is itself problematic, to say the least. It would not explain, for example, why the power to borrow money appears so high on the list, and, since the powers relating to defense are not actually granted in the first clause, it would not explain why one would have to wait until Clauses 11-13 (after the power to grant patents and copyrights) until the war power and the power to raise and support an army and navy are reached.

The main difficulty with Justice Stevens's opinion, in Justice Powell's view, was that it ignored the fact that the system of government embodied in the Constitution recognized the existence of "state governments that retained a significant measure of sovereign authority."[344] But Justice Stevens did not dispute this. He merely assumed—as would appear inescapably necessary in the light of the Supremacy Clause—that a fundamental principle of the constitutional system is that the sovereignty of the states must yield to an exercise by Congress of one of its delegated powers.[345] Given the Supremacy Clause, the only question, for Justice Stevens, was whether complete regulation of the American labor market, including the public sector, was within the reach of the commerce power, a question he saw as having "only one answer."[346]

Justice Powell makes no real effort to challenge the proposition that regulation of the labor market is a valid exercise of the commerce power, but he suggests that that power must be limited by considerations of state sovereignty and declares that it was not the

---

[343] 103 S. Ct. at 1077.
[344] *Ibid.*
[345] See text at notes 174-80 *supra.*
[346] 103 S. Ct. at 1068. See text at notes 332-34 *supra.*

intention of the framers, in drafting the Commerce Clause, to "empower the Federal Government to intrude expansively upon the sovereign powers reserved to the States."[347] In support of that rather extraordinary contention, he cites the provisions of the Constitution that recognize the existence of the states as a fundamental component of the governmental system; the understanding of the framers, as described by Madison in Federalist No. 45, that the delegated powers of the national government "are few and defined," while the reserved powers of the states "are numerous and indefinite;"[348] and, incredibly, the various arguments for the doctrine of interposition that were asserted from the time of the Kentucky and Virginia Resolutions of 1798 and 1799[349] to the assertion by John Calhoun[350] of state power of nullification of acts of Congress.[351]

Recognition of the existence of the states as an integral aspect of the American system tells nothing in itself about where the boundary line between federal and state authority is to be located or who is to determine its location.[352] William Murphy, in his study of the influence of the concept of state sovereignty on the framing and ratification of the Constitution, concluded that, whatever the limitations on the powers of Congress may be, "it is clear that [they] were not to be imposed by considerations of state sovereignty."[353] Unless the Marshall Court is to be accused of overriding completely the intent of the framers, that is the only conclusion compatible with its decisions establishing the bedrock principles of the federal-state relationship in cases such as *Martin v. Hunter's Lessee,*[354] *McCulloch v. Maryland,*[355] and *Gibbons v. Ogden.*[356]

Justice Powell dismisses *Gibbons v. Ogden* as "essentially irrelevant" to the *Wyoming* case, because it dealt with the power to grant a monopoly of the use of the state's waterways, which he said, "clearly

---

[347] 103 S. Ct. at 1079 n.8.

[348] THE FEDERALIST, note 157 *supra*, at 313.

[349] See 4 DEBATES ON THE FEDERAL CONSTITUTION 528-29 (Elliot ed. 1836) (Virginia Resolution of 1798); *id.* at 540-44 (Kentucky Resolution of 1798); *id.* at 544-45 (Kentucky Resolution of 1799); *id.* at 546-80 (Madison's Report on the Virginia Resolutions).

[350] See, *e.g.,* Letter to Governor James Hamilton, Jr., in 11 THE PAPERS OF JOHN C. CALHOUN 613-24 (Wilson ed. 1978).

[351] 103 S. Ct. at 1078-80.

[352] See text at note 174 *supra.*

[353] MURPHY, note 175 *supra*, at 410.

[354] 1 Wheat. 304 (1816).

[355] 4 Wheat. 316 (1819).

[356] 9 Wheat. 1 (1824).

is not one of a State's traditional sovereign powers," while *Wyoming* "concerns the power to determine the terms and conditions of employment for the officers and employees who constitute a State's government ... [which] is as sovereign a power as any that a State possesses."[357] But that assertion once again begs the question left unaddressed in *National League of Cities*, to which no answer has yet been provided by the Court: Why is controlling the use of a state's waterways any less an exercise of sovereign authority than setting the terms of employment of state employees so that considerations of state sovereignty (which have no limiting effect whatsoever on federal authority to override state policy with regard to the former) suddenly become a constitutional obstacle to a congressional decision to override state policy with regard to the latter?[358] Justice Powell confidently claims that the Constitution would not "have been recommended by the Convention, much less ratified, if it had been understood that the Commerce Clause ... [had given Congress power to regulate] the personnel practices of state and local governments,"[359] an observation which is entirely ahistorical. Even if it were true, it could also be claimed, with equal confidence, that the Constitution would never have been ratified if it had been understood that Congress would have power under the Commerce Clause to control the terms and conditions of employment of the employees of local business enterprises within the states. Today the power of Congress to regulate private employment contracts is beyond challenge, but that proposition would have been no less shocking in 1787 (as the congressional authority to do so is no less destructive of the concept of state sovereignty) than the proposition that once the power to regulate the national labor market is conceded, that power, to be effective, must extend to public as well as private employment.

It is true that, as noted by Madison in Federalist No. 45, the powers of Congress "are few and defined" while those of the states "are numerous and indefinite." But it is also true that the deliberate refusal of the First Congress to amend the proposal that was to become the Tenth Amendment to reserve to the states those powers not "expressly" delegated to Congress—a refusal that Madison played a central role in ensuring[360]—meant that the ultimate definition of the

---

[357] 103 S. Ct. at 1077 n.5.

[358] See text at notes 90-100 *supra*.

[359] 103 S. Ct. at 1077.

[360] See Berns, note 174 *supra*, at 138.

breadth of those "few" powers was to be provided by the federal government's conception of national need.[361] It strains credibility that Justice Powell would seek to counter the evidence of this proposition by reliance, as an indication of the framers' intent, on the assertions of the doctrines of interposition and nullification that were made from time to time in the early years of the nation's history and which were later resurrected by the South to protest the Supreme Court's school desegregation decisions of 1954.[362] The idea of interposition or nullification—that it was within the power of a state to determine when the federal government had exceeded its constitutional authority, and that it could declare such actions to be "unauthoritative, void, and of no force"[363]—could in no sense be reflective of the framers' intent. If accepted, it would defeat the purpose of the Constitution to ensure that the federal government had the authority necessary to carry out its responsibilities without dependence upon the cooperation or agreement of individual states. It would mean that the federal government would have no constitutional authority that the states themselves were not prepared to accept, which would, in turn, necessarily mean that there would be as many versions of the Constitution and of federal law as there were states. As Justice Story observed in a related context: "The public mischiefs that would attend such a state of things would be truly deplorable; and it cannot be believed that they could have escaped the enlightened convention which formed the constitution."[364]

To be sure, Justice Powell disavowed any "suggest[ion] that either the doctrine of interposition or that of nullification was constitutionally sound."[365] But he nevertheless implied that they had a serious claim

---

[361] It should be recalled that, in the same paper quoted by Justice Powell, Madison also declared that the fundamental needs of the nation were not to be sacrificed so that "individual States . . . might enjoy a certain extent of power, and be arrayed with certain dignities and attributes of sovereignty." Federalist No. 45, in THE FEDERALIST note 157 *supra*, at 325. See note 176 *supra*.

[362] Brown v. Board of Education, 247 U.S. 483 (1954); Bolling v. Sharpe, 347 U.S. 497 (1954). See, for a statement of interposition theory written in this period, KILPATRICK, THE SOVEREIGN STATES (1957). The definitive appraisal of this theory was given by a three-judge District Court in Louisiana in 1960, which declared that "interposition is not a *constitutional* doctrine. If taken seriously, it is illegal defiance of constitutional authority." Bush v. Orleans Parish School Board, 188 F. Supp. 916, 926 (1960), *summarily affirmed*, 364 U.S. 500 (1960). See also Cooper v. Aaron, 358 U.S. 1, 17-20 (1958).

[363] Kentucky Resolution of 1798, 4 DEBATES, note 349 *supra*, at 540, quoted by Justice Powell, 103 S. Ct. at 1078-79 n.7.

[364] Martin v. Hunter's Lessee, note 354 *supra*, at 348.

[365] 103 S. Ct. at 1079 n.8.

to legitimacy until "they were laid to rest" by the Civil War,[366] and that they constitute valid evidence relative to the extent to which it was the intent of the framers to allow Congress to override state sovereignty through the commerce power.[367] But these doctrines are so fundamentally at odds with the notion of a Union that they cannot be evidence of the actual intent of the framers unless one assumes that the framers had no concern for the maintenance of the Union. Their only serious claim to legitimacy is that their initial formal statement—made in response to the notorious Alien and Sedition Acts of 1798[368]—came in the Kentucky and Virginia Resolutions, drafted by Thomas Jefferson and James Madison, respectively. But these were not accurate expressions of either man's understanding of the meaning of the Constitution, but declarations of protest against an instance of tyrannical behavior. Jefferson's statements were tailored for the specific occasion. As Dumas Malone has observed, in Jefferson's writings in the period 1798-99, he "went further in his emphasis on the rights and powers of the states vis-à-vis the general government than he had ever done before or was ever to do again."[369] For Madison, the doctrine of interposition was antithetical to his views as expressed at the Constitutional Convention, in *The Federalist*, and in Congress. Not surprisingly, he later expressed vigorous opposition to it. He noted correctly that, at bottom, it was only coherent as a theory of secession. In his "Notes on Nullification," written in the final year of his life, he provided a fitting description of the theory that Justice Powell claims to constitute evidence of the intention of the framers of the Constitution on the question of state sovereignty:[370]

> But it follows, from no view of the subject, that a nullification of a law of the U.S. can as is now contended, belong rightfully to a single State, as one of the parties to the Constitution; the State not ceasing to avow its adherence to the Constitution. A plainer contradiction in terms, or a more fatal inlet to anarchy, cannot be imagined.

Justice Powell's conclusion that "[t]he Founding Fathers . . .

---

[366] *Ibid.*

[367] *Ibid.*

[368] 1 Stat. 566, 570, 577, 596.

[369] MALONE, JEFFERSON AND THE ORDEAL OF LIBERTY 395 (1962).

[370] 9 THE WRITINGS OF JAMES MADISON 575 (Hunt ed. 1910).

understood the States' reserved powers to be a limitation on Congress's power"[371] is patently false, as is his contention that "the Court has recognized and accepted this fact for almost 200 years."[372] As for his view of the framers' understanding, it is contradicted by the language of the Tenth Amendment, which reserves to the states only that which has not been delegated to the United States, and by the language of the Supremacy Clause. A more accurate statement of the framers' understanding of the relationship of the reserved powers of the states to the delegated powers of Congress was offered by James Madison, in the First Congress, speaking in opposition to the establishment of the Bank of the United States. Madison believed that establishing the bank would be unconstitutional because the power to do so was not within the scope of the powers delegated to Congress by the Constitution. If it were within the scope of a delegated power, however, state sovereignty would not, in his view, have been relevant to the question of its constitutionality. He declared that:[373]

> Interference with the power of the States was no constitutional criterion of the power of Congress. If the power was not given, Congress could not exercise it; if given, they might exercise it, although it should interfere with the laws, or even the Constitution of the States.

Justice Powell's view that the Supreme Court has recognized and accepted for almost two hundred years that the delegated powers of Congress were limited by the reserved powers of the states is directly contrary to the position taken by the Court in the most famous decisions of the Marshall era, which established the basic principles of American constitutional jurisprudence.[374] Far more accurate was Justice Brennan's observation in *National League of Cities* that "our decisions over the last century and a half have explicitly rejected the existence of any such restraint on the commerce power."[375] As Justice Holmes stated in 1918: "I should have thought that the most conspicuous decisions of this Court had made it clear that the power to regulate commerce and other constitutional powers could not be cut

---

[371] 103 S. Ct. at 1080-81.

[372] *Id.* at 1081.

[373] 2 ANNALS OF CONGRESS (1st Cong., 3d sess.), quoted in CORWIN, note 58 *supra*, at 121.

[374] See cases cited at notes 354-56 *supra*.

[375] 426 U.S. at 858 (dissenting opinion).

down or qualified by the fact that it might interfere with the carrying out of the domestic policy of any State."[376]

Justice Stevens, alone among the Justices on the Court, expressed concern in *Wyoming* over the propriety of the judicially conceived and imposed limitations on the commerce power of Congress, in which the other Justices in the majority were now apparently prepared silently to acquiesce. Justice Brennan, joined by Justices White and Marshall, had made a similar point in dissent in *National League of Cities*,[377] but did not press it in this case, perhaps out of respect for *stare decisis* or perhaps out of a desire to bring Justice Blackmun into the majority.[378] But in the face of the Court's inability or unwillingness to provide a reasoned basis for the *National League of Cities* approach, its continued use of the doctrine of that case as a potential vehicle for invalidating acts of Congress under the commerce power is accurately described by Justice Stevens as "pure judicial fiat."[379] Arbitrary judicial interference with congressional ability to control the public sector of the economy at the state and local level can have a potentially serious impact, as Justice Stevens has noted, in light of the significant proportion of the overall work force that is made up of state and local employees.[380]

IV. CONCLUSION

The Court's decision in *EEOC v. Wyoming* is likely to satisfy no one. Those who would defend the Court's decision in *National League of Cities* can only be chagrined at the Court's failure once again to duplicate the result of that case and to strike down an act of Congress on its authority. In the light of the near identity of the facts in the two cases, they may well see in *Wyoming* an ominous portent that *National League of Cities* will never have progeny—that, while it may not be immediately overruled, it will be distinguished away in every case and thus limited to its precise facts.

On the other hand, those who view *National League of Cities* as an unfortunate and unjustified exercise in judicial review, in which an act of Congress was struck down on the basis of what Justice Brennan described as an "abstraction without substance, founded neither in the

---

[376] Hammer v. Dagenhart, 247 U.S. 251, 278 (1918) (dissenting opinion).
[377] 426 U.S. at 858–68 (dissenting opinion).
[378] See note 12 *supra*.
[379] 103 S. Ct. at 1067 (concurring opinion).
[380] *Id.* at 1066–67. See note 150 *supra*.

words of the Constitution nor on precedent,"[181] and by Justice Stevens as "pure judicial fiat," will be dissatisfied by the majority's failure even to question, let alone to repudiate, that decision, and by its allowing the decision on the constitutional question presented to turn on a test that is directly based on its definitionless standards.

The problems in the reasoning of *National League of Cities* are substantial. The Court's failure in *Wyoming*—as in every other case since 1976 in which the opportunity to do so has been presented—to attempt to confront and resolve these problems is regrettable. If, as seems likely, the problems are too intractable to be resolved adequately, it would be better for the Court frankly to acknowledge that *National League of Cities* was in error and to abandon it than to continue the practice that *Wyoming* seems to exemplify—of distinguishing it either on the basis of minor differences in the facts or by magnifying the importance of the federal interest to be protected, or of downplaying the impact of the challenged law on the states. Until then, the threat will always be present that the *National League of Cities* doctrine will be revived and a critical aspect of Congress's power over commerce subjected to limitations that are derived, not from any constitutional principles of general applicability, but solely from the Justices' conception of desirable public policy.

---

[181] 426 U.S. at 860 (dissenting opinion).

SAM J. ERVIN, JR.

THE EXCLUSIONARY RULE: AN ESSENTIAL INGREDIENT OF THE FOURTH AMENDMENT

The Fourth Amendment to the Constitution declares "the right of the people to be secure in their persons, houses, papers, and effects, against unreasonable searches and seizures, shall not be violated, and no warrants shall issue, but upon probable cause, supported by oath or affirmation, and particularly describing the place to be searched, and the person or things to be seized."

I. THE ORIGIN OF THE AMENDMENT

This constitutional guaranty against unreasonable searches and seizures has its roots deeply implanted in the human heart, the common law of England, and tyrannies perpetrated by government on the people of England and the colonies.

The oldest and deepest hunger of the human heart is for a place where one may dwell in peace and security and keep inviolate from public scrutiny one's innermost aspirations and thoughts, one's most intimate associations and communications, and one's most private activities. This truth was documented by Micah, the prophet, 2,700 years ago when he described the Mountain of the Lord as a place where "they shall sit every man under his own vine and fig tree and none shall make them afraid" (MICAH 4:4).

The common law of England originated in the instincts, the habits, and the customs of the people. Hence, it is not surprising that on

Sam J. Ervin, Jr., practices law in Morganton, North Carolina, and is former Justice of the North Carolina Supreme Court and former United States Senator from North Carolina. This paper is based on remarks delivered to the Escambia-Santa Rosa Bar Association at Pensacola, Florida, April 29, 1983.

emerging from the mists of unrecorded history, the English common law embraced as a fundamental principle that every man's home is his castle and the correlative rule that every man may resist to the utmost unidentified persons who seek to enter his home against his will. Moreover, the common law supplemented the protection of privacy, personal security, and private property inherent in this principle by the crimes of burglary and eavesdropping and the law of trespass.

The principle of the common law that every man's home is his castle was recognized and applied by the English judiciary in *Semayne's Case,* which was decided in 1603 and held: "The house of everyone is to him as his castle and fortress, as well as for his defense against injury and violence as for his repose."[1] This principle of law was not absolute in the sense that it prevailed at all times and in all circumstances. It yielded on rare occasions if overriding public purpose demanded that government make an entry into a home. But even on those occasions, government was permitted to enter only if it used means that ensured that its power to enter would not be abused.

In recognition of this, the English court further declared in *Semayne's Case:* "In all cases where the King is party, the Sheriff (if the doors be not open) may break the party's house, either to arrest him, or do other execution of the King's process, if otherwise he cannot enter. But before he breaks it he ought to signify the cause of his coming, and to make request to open doors."[2] The common-law courts of England, such as the Court of King's Bench, which had jurisdiction of most criminal charges, and the Court of Common Pleas, which had jurisdiction of most civil cases, recognized that a salutary principle of substantive law is destitute of practical value unless it is enforceable by suitable rules of procedure. They authorized searches and seizures only by special warrants, which were based on oaths disclosing the reasons for their issuance and describing the places to be searched and the persons or things to be seized.

The courts of England that were independent of the common law, such as the Court of Star Chamber, which was concerned primarily with the prerogatives of the king, and the Court of High Commission, which was concerned solely with the prerogatives of the established church, did not respect the principle of the common law that every man's home is his castle.

---

[1] 5 Co. Rep. 91a, 91b; 77 Eng. Rep. 194, 195.
[2] *Ibid.*

They authorized searches and seizures by general warrants, which were based on mere suspicion and commanded searches and seizures for the enforcement of particular laws without specifying the places to be searched or the persons or things to be seized. In so doing, the general warrants delegated to the persons executing them the autocratic power to decide according to their own notions what places should be searched, what persons should be arrested, and what things should be seized. Their excessive use of general warrants, incriminatory practices, and other tyrannies inspired hatred for the Court of Star Chamber and the Court of High Commission throughout England; and the Long Parliament, which met in 1640, abolished these tribunals.

Parliamentary resentment of general warrants proved to be short-lived. For more than one hundred years after the abolition of the Court of Star Chamber and the Court of High Commission, Parliament either expressly or tacitly permitted the Secretary of State to issue general warrants on mere suspicion to enforce the Licensing Act, which forbade the publication of any book or pamphlet in England without the prior license of the king, and the laws creating the crimes of seditious and blasphemous libel. After the Licensing Act expired in 1695, the Secretary of State, acting without any parliamentary authority, continued to issue general warrants of search and seizure on suspicion to enforce libel laws. Parliament also conferred on the Court of Exchequer jurisdiction to issue general warrants of search and seizure to enforce the revenue laws.

These uses of general warrants engendered intense hatred of such warrants among Englishmen everywhere. One of the revenue laws, which was enacted by Parliament in 1763, laid an excise tax on cider and gave the officers of excise virtually unlimited power to invade and search private dwellings for its enforcement. The actions of officers of excise under it aroused resistance in the apple-growing areas of England and resentment among lovers of liberty in other parts of the realm.

In an unsuccessful effort to persuade the House of Commons to reject the proposals embodied in this law, William Pitt the Elder, the most eloquent parliamentary orator of the age, extolled the principle that every man's home is his castle in these unforgettable words: "The poorest man may in his cottage bid defiance to all the forces of the Crown. It may be frail; its roof may shake; the wind may blow through it; the storm may enter; the rain may enter; but the King of England can not enter; all his force dares not cross the threshold of the ruined tenement!"[3] As the commerce of the English colonies in America increased, customs officers were given blanket authority to make general searches for goods imported into the colonies in violation of the laws of England.

They were given this blanket authority by a form of general warrant known as a writ of assistance, which derived its name from the legal circumstances that all civil officers and subjects of the Crown were required by it to assist the officer of the customs to whom it was issued in its execution. Instead of describing the place to be searched and the things to be seized, the writ of assistance gave the officer of customs to whom it was issued by the court the absolute power to enter and search at his own pleasure any building, ship, or other place where he suspected smuggled goods to be and to seize and remove any goods he discovered which he believed to be of that character.

The tyranny sanctioned by the writ of assistance aroused resentment in all the colonies and particularly in Massachusetts, where the writ was most widely employed. Historians agree that this resentment was one of the causes of the American Revolution.

A spectacular event occurred in 1761 when Oxenbridge Thatcher and James Otis, attorneys for more than threescore Boston merchants, appeared before Chief Justice Hutchinson and his colleagues on the Superior Court bench in a crowded and tense courtroom in Boston and eloquently but unsuccessfully challenged the jurisdiction of the Superior Court to issue writs of assistance.[4] As a young bystander, John Adams, afterward second President of the United States, was present in the Boston courtroom and heard Otis speak.[5] He later declared that "Otis was a flame of fire"[6] and that his "oration against the writs of assistance breathed into this nation the breath of life."[7]

II. THE EXCLUSIONARY RULE

The exclusionary rule is as follows: When challenged by an appropriate and timely motion to suppress or objection, evidence obtained by government by a violation of the Fourth Amendment must be excluded in a criminal prosecution of the person whose Fourth

[3] Quoted in Miller v. U.S., 357 U.S. 301, 307 (1958).

[4] See generally SMITH, THE WRITS OF ASSISTANCE CASE (1978).

[5] See 2 WROTH & ZOBEL (eds.), LEGAL PAPERS OF JOHN ADAMS 107 ff. (1965).

[6] Letter to William Tudor, March 29, 1817.

[7] Letter to Hezekiah Niles, Jan. 14, 1818.

Amendment right has been violated.[8] Despite honest beliefs of sincere persons to the contrary, the exclusionary rule is an essential ingredient of the Fourth Amendment. Apart from it, the Amendment's guaranty against unreasonable searches and seizures is worse than solemn mockery, and the Amendment might well be expunged from the Constitution as a meaningless expression of a merely pious hope. The Supreme Court rightly and unanimously so declared and adjudged in *Weeks v. United States*,[9] the leading case on the subject. In that case, the Court said:[10]

> If letters and private documents can be thus seized and held and used in evidence against a citizen accused of an offense, the protection of the Fourth Amendment declaring his right to be secure against such searches and seizures is of no value, and, so far as those thus placed are concerned, might as well be stricken from the Constitution. The efforts of the courts and their officials to bring the guilty to punishment, praiseworthy as they are, are not to be aided by the sacrifice of those great principles established by years of endeavor and suffering which have resulted in their embodiment in the fundamental law of the land.

The indispensable nature of the exclusionary rule was revealed in cases past numbering in state courts before the landmark decision in *Mapp v. Ohio*,[11] where the Supreme Court held that the Fourth Amendment is made binding on the states by the Due Process Clause of the Fourteenth Amendment. Prior to *Mapp*, the courts of many states admitted in criminal prosecutions evidence obtained by the states in violation of their constitutions outlawing general warrants and prohibiting unreasonable searches and seizures, and thus converted solemn constitutional guaranties into dead letters. The exclusionary rule is, in reality, the only breakwater against conviction-prone courts and overzealous law enforcement officers. Those who maintain the contrary are like the comforters of Job: they multiply words without knowledge.

After the colonies revolted against England and converted themselves into self-governing states, they adopted state constitutions. The constitutions of the states of Delaware, Maryland, North

---

[8] Weeks v. U.S., 232 U.S. 383 (1914); Gouled v. U.S., 255 U.S. 298 (1921); Jones v. U.S., 362 U.S. 257 (1960); Mapp v. Ohio, 367 U.S. 643 (1961); Wong Sun v. U.S., 371 U.S. 471 (1962). See also Rule 41(f), Fed. R. Cr. P.

[9] 232 U.S. 383 (1914).

[10] *Id.* at 393.

[11] See note 8 *supra*.

Carolina, Pennsylvania, and Virginia, which were adopted in 1776, and that of Vermont, which was adopted in 1777, contained prototypes of the Fourth Amendment.[12] The prototype whose phraseology is very similar to that of the Fourth Amendment was drafted by John Adams and was incorporated into the constitution of Massachusetts, which was adopted in 1780, and that of New Hampshire, which was adopted in 1783.[13]

> Every subject has a right to be secure from all unreasonable searches, and seizures of his person, his houses, his papers, and all his possessions. All warrants, therefore, are contrary to this right, if the cause or foundation of them be not previously supported by oath or affirmation, and if the order in the warrant to a civil officer, to make search in suspected place, or to arrest one or more suspected persons, or to seize their property, be not accompanied with a special designation of the persons or objects of search, arrest, or seizure: and no warrant ought to be issued but in cases, and with the formalities, prescribed by the laws.

A. DISLIKE FOR THE EXCLUSIONARY RULE

Some judges, prosecutors, law enforcement officers, politicians, and others dislike the exclusionary rule and demand that it be abolished or substantially modified. The reasons for their dislike and demand are stated most ably by the most famous of them, Chief Justice Warren Burger, in his dissenting opinion in *Bivens v. Six Unknown Federal Narcotics Agents*,[14] and his concurring opinion in *Stone v. Powell*.[15] Let us analyze these reasons and ascertain their validity.

For their convenient consideration, I state the arguments of the opponents of the exclusionary rule in Chief Justice Burger's words and in this numerical fashion:

1. The rule is a judge-made rule without support in the Constitution. The function of the rule is to exclude "truth from the factfinding process" in criminal prosecutions.[16] Unlike the Fifth Amendment's ban of self-incrimination, the rule excludes reliable rather than dubious evidence. "The direct beneficiaries of the rule can be none but persons

---

[12] Schwartz, The Bill of Rights: A Documentary History 278, 282, 287, 265, 235, 323 (1971).

[13] *Id.* at 342, 377–78.

[14] 403 U.S. 388, 411 (1971).

[15] 428 U.S. 465, 496 (1976).

[16] *Id.* at 496.

guilty of crimes,"[17] and the rule results in a "bizarre miscarriage of justice"[18] because it prevents the conviction of the guilty.

2. The rule was devised "for the protection of private papers against governmental intrusion,"[19] and not to prevent "the search for and seizure of stolen or forfeited goods, or goods liable to duties and concealed to avoid"[20] their payment. The rule has been perverted in large measure from its original purpose and "is now used almost exclusively to exclude from the evidence articles which are unlawful to be possessed or tools and instruments of crimes."[21]

3. The rule "rests upon its purported tendency to deter police"[22] violation of the Fourth Amendment. The rule does "nothing to punish the wrong-doing official," frees "the wrong-doing defendant," "deprives society of its remedy against one lawbreaker because he is pursued by another,"[23] and "offers no relief whatever to victims of overzealous police work who never appear in court."[24] "Despite its avowed deterrent objective, proof is lacking that the exclusionary rule . . . serves the purpose of deterrence. Notwithstanding Herculean efforts, no empirical study has been able to demonstrate that the rule does in fact have any deterrent effect. . . . To vindicate the continued existence of this . . . rule, it is incumbent on those who seek its retention . . . to demonstrate that it serves its declared deterrent purpose and to show that the results outweigh the rule's heavy costs to rational enforcement of the criminal law."[25]

4. "The rule has long been applied to wholly good-faith mistakes and to purely technical deficiencies in warrants."[26] The English and Canadian legal systems, which are highly regarded, have not adopted the rule.

B. COMMENTS ON THE ARGUMENTS AGAINST THE RULE

The assertion that the courts of England and Canada have not adopted the exclusionary rule is wholly irrelevant. Unlike the United

---

[17] *Id.* at 501.
[18] *Id.* at 496.
[19] *Id.* at 497.
[20] *Ibid.*, quoting from Boyd v. U.S., 116 U.S. 616, 623 (1886).
[21] Note 15 *supra*, at 498.
[22] *Ibid.*
[23] *Bivens*, note 14 *supra*, at 368, quoting from Irvine v. California, 347 U.S. 128, 136 (1954).
[24] Stone v. Powell, note 15 *supra*, at 501.
[25] *Id.* at 499–500.
[26] *Id.* at 499.

States, neither of them has a written constitution containing a Fourth Amendment and constituting its supreme law. The arguments of the opponents of the rule otherwise lack validity and indicate that they do not understand the rule or its origin or objective. The Chief Justice argues in his concurring opinion in the *Stone* case that the exclusionary rule is "a judge-made rule" without support in the Constitution, "a Draconian discredited device," and "a judicially contrived doctrine."[27]

The response to these arguments necessitates a slight repetition. Some spurious color of support for them and similar arguments may be found in meaningless *obiter dicta* in some of the many cases on the subject, and in this wholly irrelevant and virtually incomprehensible statement of Justice Stewart in his opinion in *Elkins v. United States:* "What is here invoked is the Court's supervisory power over the administration of criminal justice in the federal courts, under which the Court has 'from the very beginning of its history formulated rules of evidence to be applied in federal criminal prosecutions.' *McNabb v. United States*, 318 U.S. 332, 341."[28]

Despite these considerations, there are two absolute and incontrovertible answers to these and all other arguments offered in support of the proposition that the Supreme Court ought to divorce the exclusionary rule from the Fourth Amendment. Such arguments are totally repugnant to the Constitution in general and to the Fourth Amendment in particular. The Supreme Court is obligated to support the Constitution in its entirety and is destitute of power to alter the meaning of a single syllable of it.

The exclusionary rule is implicit and inherent in the Fourth Amendment itself. When they are interpreted aright, the words of the Amendment incorporate the exclusionary rule as a permanent and inseparable element, and by so doing make the Fourth Amendment a living constitutional guaranty that the right of the people to be secure in their persons, houses, papers, and effects against unreasonable searches and seizures shall not be violated by government. What the Fourth Amendment joins together Supreme Court Justices cannot put asunder. This conclusion is in full accord with the applicable Supreme Court decisions.[29]

---

[27] *Id.* at 501.

[28] 364 U.S. 206, 216 (1960).

[29] Weeks v. U.S., note 8 *supra;* Silverthorne Lumber Co. v. U.S., 251 U.S. 385 (1920); Gouled v. U.S., note 8 *supra;* Amos v. U.S., 255 U.S. 313 (1921); Agnello v. U.S., 269 U.S. 20 (1925);

The function of the rule is not to exclude truth from the fact-finding process in criminal prosecutions. On the contrary, its objective is most laudatory. The recognition and enforcement of the rule is necessary to make the Fourth Amendment's guaranty against unreasonable searches and seizures effective and thus enable Americans to enjoy personal privacy, personal security, and private property free from arbitrary and Gestapo-like governmental invasions.

What has just been said is made indisputable by the sound decision in *Gouled v. United States*, where the Supreme Court enforced the Fourth Amendment and the self-incrimination clause of the Fifth Amendment and made these emphatic declarations concerning them:[30]

> It would not be possible to add to the emphasis with which the framers of our Constitution and this court [citing authorities] have declared the importance to political liberty and the welfare of our country of the due observance of the rights guaranteed under the Constitution by these two Amendments. The effect of the decisions cited is: that such rights are declared to be indispensable to the "full enjoyment of personal security, personal liberty, and private property"; that they are to be regarded as of the very essence of constitutional liberty; and that the guaranty of them is as important and as imperative as are the guaranties of the other fundamental rights of the individual citizen,—the right to trial by jury, to the writ of *habeas corpus* and to due process of law. It has been repeatedly decided that these Amendments should receive a liberal construction, so as to prevent stealthy encroachment upon or "gradual depreciation" of the rights secured by them, by imperceptible practice of the courts, or by well-intentional but mistakenly over-zealous executive officers.

Inasmuch as the Fourth Amendment is indispensable to the enjoyment of personal privacy, personal security, and private property, there is no merit in the argument that no persons are its direct beneficiaries except those guilty of criminal offenses. All human beings within the borders of our land are its direct beneficiaries because it enables them to enjoy their persons, their houses, their papers, and

---

Harris v. U.S., 331 U.S. 145 (1947); Jones v. U.S., 362 U.S. 257 (1960); Mapp v. Ohio, note 8 *supra;* Wong Sun v. U.S., note 8 *supra.* In addition to these cases so ruling in virtually express terms, there are numerous other cases so adjudging by necessary implication. While legal literature is replete with statements that the Supreme Court first recognized and applied the exclusionary rule in *Weeks*, note 8 *supra*, in 1914, I submit that it did so for all practical purposes in *Boyd*, note 20 *supra*, in 1886.

[30] Note 8 *supra* at 303-04.

effects free from arbitrary and Gestapo-like searches and seizures by government.

Opponents of the exclusionary rule cannot resist the temptation to quote Judge Benjamin N. Cardozo's catchy aphorism: "The criminal is to go free because the constable has blundered."[31] Unfortunately, Judge Cardozo's aphorism does not display his customary illuminating power, and many opponents of the exclusionary rule accept it as a substitute for thought on the subject. Judge Cardozo ought to have said, "The accused goes free because government, acting through a blundering constable, denied him his constitutional right to be exempt from an unreasonable search or seizure." The arguments which harp on the circumstance that judicial enforcement of the exclusionary rule sometimes permits guilty persons to escape conviction and punishment shed no light on the questions of the constitutionality or objective of the rule.

These questions are answered with unmistakable clarity by the emphatic declaration of the Fourth Amendment that "the right of the people to be secure in their persons, houses, papers, and effects, against unreasonable searches and seizures, shall not be violated." By these words, the Fourth Amendment emulates the impartiality of the rains of heaven, which fall on the just and unjust alike, and clearly extends to all men the protection of its guaranty against unreasonable searches and seizures irrespective of whether they be innocent or guilty. As the inevitable consequence, the Fourth Amendment condemns every search or seizure that is unreasonable and protects those suspected or known to be offenders as well as the innocent.[32] Under the Amendment, a search is constitutional or unconstitutional at its inception, and does not change its character by what it brings to light.[33]

The argument that the rule was devised solely "for the protection of private papers against governmental intrusion," and is now used almost exclusively "to exclude from evidence articles" which it is unlawful for

---

[31] People v. Defore, 242 N.Y. 13, 21; 150 N.E. 585, 587 (1926).

[32] Go-Bart Importing Co. v. U.S., 282 U.S. 344 (1931); McDonald v. U.S., 335 U.S. 451 (1948); Ker v. California, 374 U.S. 23 (1963). As stated in *McDonald*: "This guarantee of protection against unreasonable searches and seizures extends to the innocent and guilty alike. It marks the right of privacy as one of the unique values of our civilization and, with few exceptions, stays the hands of the police unless they have a search warrant issued by a magistrate on probable cause supported by oath or affirmation. And the law provides as a sanction against the flouting of this constitutional safeguard the suppression of evidence secured as a result of the violation, when it is tendered in a federal court." 335 U.S. at 453.

[33] Byars v. U.S., 273 U.S. 28 (1927); Lustig v. U.S., 338 U.S. 74 (1949); *Wong Sun*, note 8 *supra*; Bumper v. North Carolina, 391 U.S. 543 (1968).

one to possess or which constitute "the tools and instruments of crimes," would be immaterial even if it were based on reality. However, it is refuted by the history of the events in England, the colonies, and the states which resulted in the incorporation of the Fourth Amendment in the Constitution and by the words of the Fourth Amendment itself. These words decree that the right of the people to be secure in their persons, houses, and effects as well as in their papers against unreasonable searches and seizures shall not be violated.

The argument that the exclusionary rule has no deterrent effect, and does not prompt officers to obey the Fourth Amendment, is incompatible with events occurring at all times in all sections of the nation. Police departments, community colleges, and other institutions habitually teach newly recruited police and persons desiring to become police the exclusionary rule and the necessity for avoiding its consequence by obeying the Fourth Amendment. Federal and state appellate courts everywhere are replete with criminal prosecutions involving the rule. Indeed, the many cases on the subject reaching the Supreme Court refute the argument. Most noteworthy on this score is the revolution in the administration of criminal justice produced in the states by the ruling of *Mapp* that the Fourth Amendment applies to the states as well as to the national government. Before the *Mapp* decision, search warrants were virtually unknown and unused writs in many states having no exclusionary rules of their own. Now they engross a substantial part of the energy and time of the judicial and executive officers and the lawyers engaged in the administration of criminal justice in these states.

My three-score years at the bar have taught me that some judges, lawyers, and laymen call every law or constitutional principle they dislike "a legal technicality." Criminal prosecutions reveal that the exclusionary rule is successfully invoked because of deficiencies in applications and warrants in cases where the application fails to establish probable cause for the search or seizure or the warrants fail to describe the place to be searched or the person or thing to be seized. These deficiencies are not legal technicalities. They are of constitutional dimensions.

The argument that the exclusionary rule should be discontinued unless those who accept its validity demonstrate that "it serves its declared deterrent purpose and that the results outweigh the rule's heavy costs to rational enforcement of the criminal law" is most intriguing. The exclusionary rule is an essential ingredient of the Fourth Amendment. An express or implied command of the Constitution, I submit, does not become inoperative because those who accept it as such do not demonstrate that in its operation the constitutional command produces results pleasing to those who dislike it. I note without comment that a violation of the Fourth Amendment by a judicial or executive officer of the government is not a rational way to enforce the criminal law.

The argument that the rule "does nothing to punish the wrongdoing official" is completely beside the mark. The rule is designed to prevent unreasonable governmental searches and seizures and not to punish the officers making them for their individual misconduct.[34] For this reason, the Supreme Court declared in the *Weeks* case, "What remedies the defendant may have against [the wrongdoing officials] we need not inquire."[35]

I revere the Constitution because it creates for America the soundest system of government the earth has ever known, and because it establishes for Americans basic constitutional rights which must be respected by the government it creates if America is to endure as the land of the free. For these reasons, I have the temerity to make some additional unvarnished comments respecting the views of those who seek to abolish or modify the exclusionary rule. After all, they seek to twist awry the guaranty of the Constitution of my country that America shall not be converted from a land of liberty into a police state.

When a Supreme Court Justice succumbs to the temptation to nullify or modify the handiwork of the Founding Fathers, he impairs his capacity to see such handiwork steady and whole. Chief Justice Burger asserts that the exclusionary rule is unlike the implied constitutional rules that reject involuntary confessions violative of due process and compelled testimony violative of the Self-Incrimination Clause; that evidence obtained in violation of the Fourth Amendment is always true, whereas involuntary confessions and compelled testimony violative of the Self-Incrimination Clause are false at worst and dubious at best; and that the Constitution requires Courts to exclude involuntary confessions and compelled testimony violative of the Self-Incrimination Clause simply because of their false or dubious nature.

---

[34] Steagald v. U.S., 451 U.S. 204 (1981).
[35] 232 U.S. at 398.

The Chief Justice is in error. Many involuntary confessions and much compelled testimony violative of the Self-Incrimination Clause are true. The Constitution is not concerned with the truth or the falsity of this evidence or the evidence obtained in violation of the Fourth Amendment. On the contrary, the Constitution forbids the government to use such evidence in criminal prosecutions against persons aggrieved because it obtains the evidence by tyrannous practices that the Constitution outlaws.[36]

The arguments of the opponents of the rule justify a final comment. The Chief Justice makes this assertion in his concurring opinion in the *Stone* case:[37]

> A more clumsy, less direct means of imposing sanctions is difficult to imagine, particularly since the issue whether the police did indeed run afoul of the Fourth Amendment is often not resolved until years after the event. The "sanction" is particularly indirect when . . . the police go before a magistrate, who issues a warrant. Once the warrant issues, there is literally nothing more the policeman can do in seeking to comply with the law. Imposing an admittedly indirect "sanction" on the police officer in that instance is nothing less than sophisticated nonsense.

The Chief Justice misses the entire point of the matter. The Court is not imposing a sanction on a policeman. It is enforcing the second clause of the Fourth Amendment, which declares in plain words that "no warrants shall issue, but upon probable cause, supported by oath or affirmation, and particularly describing the place to be searched, and the person or things to be seized." Surely it is never "sophisticated nonsense" for a judicial tribunal to enforce a guaranty which was embodied in the Constitution to make America the land of the free.

---

[36] Involuntary confessions are not excluded "because such confessions are unlikely to be true but because the methods used to extract them offend an underlying principle in the enforcement of our criminal laws." Rogers v. Richmond, 365 U.S. 534, 540-41 (1961). "The constitutional privilege [against self-incrimination] was intended to shield the guilty and imprudent as well as the innocent and foresighted." Marchetti v. U.S., 390 U.S. 39, 51 (1968). "The restrictions upon searches and seizures . . . are not exclusionary provisions against the admission of kinds of evidence deemed inherently unreliable or prejudicial. The exclusion in federal trials of evidence otherwise competent but gathered by federal officials in violation of the Fourth Amendment is a means of making effective the protection of privacy." Jones v. U.S., note 20 *supra*, at 261. See also Ker v. California, note 32 *supra*, at 33; Silverthorne Lumber Co. v. U.S., note 29 *supra*. In short, constitutional provisions forbidding the acquisition of evidence in certain ways are not designed to protect the innocent from conviction, but are designed to protect the integrity of the judicial process against the use of evidence secured by government through tyrannous means.

[37] Note 15 *supra*, at 498.

C. PROPOSALS OF OPPONENTS OF THE EXCLUSIONARY RULE

Opponents of the exclusionary rule urge that it be abolished and that alternatives be established to take its place. There is, in reality, no alternative for the rule. This is true because the only effective way to make the Fourth Amendment effective is to deny government the power to use evidence obtained by its violation of the rule.

Nevertheless, some who dislike the rule have proposed that the rule be abolished in its entirety and that civil and criminal sanctions against offending officers be substituted for it. The lawbooks already declare that an officer who makes an unreasonable arrest, search, or seizure is subject to both criminal and civil liability for his unconstitutional act. But his lawbook liability is fictitious rather than pragmatic. Because they work in close collaboration and are dependent on each other, prosecutors simply do not bring criminal prosecutions against officers of the law whose zeal or ignorance prompt them to overstep Fourth Amendment bounds. And because the injuries of the persons aggrieved are largely emotional rather than pecuniary, juries in civil cases are not prone to award them substantial damages against officers of the law, whose wrongs are motivated by well-meaning overzealousness or ignorance of law rather than by malice. And even if the damages awarded be substantial in amount, they are usually uncollectible because of the indigency of the officer. For these reasons, the bench and bar know that as practical deterrents to Fourth Amendment violations the lawbook liabilities of offending officers are illusory and futile.

Chief Justice Burger believes "the rule need not be totally abandoned until some meaningful alternative could be developed to protect innocent persons aggrieved by police misconduct."[38] He urges that pending the consummation of that event the rule ought to be modified, and government ought to be permitted to use evidence obtained by it in violation of the Fourth Amendment if the officer seizing the evidence acted "in the good-faith belief that his conduct comported with existing law" and had "reasonable grounds for this belief."[39] The Chief Justice frankly admits that "private damage actions against individual officers" do not constitute an adequate alternative. He suggests that the doctrine of *respondeat superior* be made applicable

---

[38] *Id.* at 500. See also *Bivens*, note 14 *supra*, at 420 (Burger, C.J., dissenting).

[39] See Stone v. Powell, note 15 *supra*, at 501-02 (Burger, C.J., concurring). Chief Justice Burger notes that Justice White made this suggestion in his dissent in *Stone*, 428 U.S. at 538.

to government, federal or state, and that it be held responsible in damages for injuries inflicted on aggrieved persons by its officers "in a tribunal, quasi-judicial in nature and perhaps patterned after the Court of Claims."[40]

The proposal of the Chief Justice, I submit, is also illusory and futile. All tribunals would be reluctant to amerce innocent taxpayers for the sins of offending officers. Besides, the most grievous Fourth Amendment wrongs are perpetrated upon persons whose humble standings or limited means or unsavory reputations impair their capacity to obtain justice.

There is a repugnancy between the Fourth Amendment and the proposal that the exclusionary rule be modified to permit government to use evidence obtained in violation of the Fourth Amendment in criminal prosecutions against a person whose Fourth Amendment rights are violated if the police officer committing the violation acted in the good-faith belief that his conduct comported with existing law and he had reasonable grounds for his belief. This is true because the Fourth Amendment outlaws without exception or limitation all unreasonable searches and seizures. Besides, the adoption of the proposal would create an absurdity in our legal system. Ignorance of the law would not excuse the accused's commission of a crime, but ignorance of the Constitution would excuse the police officer's violation of it. If the United States is to be a free republic, the constitutional protections and rights of its people must be determined by the words of the Constitution and not by the understanding or lack of understanding of police officers respecting them.

D. WHAT THE FOURTH AMENDMENT REQUIRES

Some judicial and executive officers who are intellectually or physically lazy, and some judges, prosecutors, police, politicians, and others, who think it more important to convict and punish persons charged with crime than to observe constitutional guaranties of personal liberties, complain that the Fourth Amendment creates foolish obstacles to the rational administration of criminal justice. Their complaint is without solid foundation. While its application to the facts in particular instances may be difficult, the Fourth Amendment is plain and its requirements are simple. The Fourth

---

[40] *Bivens*, 403 U.S. at 421-24 (Burger, C.J., dissenting).

Amendment authorizes governmental searches and seizures which are reasonable and outlaws those which are unreasonable.

A search or seizure is ordinarily unreasonable and violative of the Amendment unless the officer making it acts under the authority of a valid search warrant.[41] But a warrant is not always required. There are certain carefully defined, limited, and exceptional cases in which the Amendment deems it reasonable for officers to make a search or seizure without a search warrant.[42] Before enumerating them, I will note that a search or seizure, with or without a search warrant, is unreasonable if it is not properly conducted and properly limited in scope,[43] and describe the requisites of a valid search warrant. A search warrant is valid under the Fourth Amendment if these things concur:

1. The officer seeking the warrant applies to a judge or magistrate, who must be neutral and detached, for the warrant by an application in writing, which is supported by oath or affirmation, and states the facts on which it is based.[44]

2. The judge or magistrate rightly determines from the facts stated in the application that there is probable cause for the search or seizure, and issues the warrant.[45]

3. The warrant describes with particularity the place to be searched and the persons or things to be seized.[46]

Under the Fourth Amendment, searches and seizures without search warrants are reasonable and constitutional in these carefully defined, limited, and exceptional cases:

1. An officer may search a person without a search warrant if such person voluntarily consents to the search.[47]

2. An officer may search private property without a search warrant if the person owning or lawfully possessing it voluntarily consents to the search.[48]

---

[41] Agnello v. U.S., note 29 *supra;* Johnson v. U.S., 333 U.S. 10 (1948); Jones v. U.S., note 29 *supra;* Chapman v. U.S., 365 U.S. 610 (1961); Vale v. Louisiana, 399 U.S. 30 (1970); Coolidge v. New Hampshire, 403 U.S. 443 (1971); Payton v. New York, 445 U.S. 573 (1979).

[42] U.S. v. Rabinowitz, 339 U.S. 56 (1950). See also cases cited in notes 44-48 *infra.*

[43] Terry v. Ohio, 392 U.S. 1 (1968); Chimel v. California, 395 U.S. 752 (1969).

[44] Berger v. New York, 388 U.S. 41 (1967); Whiteley v. Warden, 401 U.S. 560 (1971).

[45] Aguilar v. Texas, 378 U.S. 108 (1964); Camara v. Municipal Court, 387 U.S. 523 (1967); Chambers v. Maroney, 399 U.S. 42 (1970).

[46] Steele v. U.S., 267 U.S. 498 (1925); Marron v. U.S., 275 U.S. 192 (1927); Trupiano v. U.S., 334 U.S. 699 (1948); Lo-Ji Sales v. New York, 442 U.S. 319 (1979).

[47] Zap v. U.S., 328 U.S. 624 (1946); Katz v. U.S., 389 U.S. 347 (1967).

[48] Amos v. U.S., 255 U.S. 313 (1921); U.S. v. Mitchell, 322 U.S. 65 (1944); U.S. v. Jeffers, 342 U.S. 48 (1951); Chapman v. U.S., note 41 *supra;* Stoner v. California, 376 U.S. 483 (1964); Bumper v. North Carolina, note 33 *supra;* Schneckloth v. Bustamonte, 412 U.S. 218 (1973).

3. An officer may search the person of a party he arrests and the place of the arrest within the immediate possession and control of the party arrested without a search warrant if the arrest is lawful and the search is made at the time of the arrest.[49]

4. An officer may stop a moving vehicle, such as an automobile, a boat, or a wagon, and search it without a search warrant for stolen goods, contraband, or the tools of crimes if he has probable cause to believe it contains such materials, and it is not practicable to secure a search warrant because the vehicle may be quickly moved out of the locality in which the warrant must be sought.[50]

5. An officer may routinely stop and search without a search warrant and without probable cause travelers coming into the United States across an international boundary line because national protection reasonably requires one entering the country to identify himself as one entitled to admission and his belongings as effects which may be lawfully brought in.[51]

State courts, lower federal courts, and legal scholars suggest that the Supreme Court may recognize a limited number of additional exceptional circumstances justifying searches or seizures without search warrants if immediate emergencies require such action to prevent the hijacking of a plane, to enable officers to continue their hot pursuit of a fleeing criminal, or to save persons from imminent peril and the like.

III. ILLINOIS V. GATES

The Supreme Court decided *Illinois v. Gates*[52] on June 8, 1983. This decision requires comment.

The respondents, Lance Gates and his wife Susan, lived in Bloomingdale, Illinois. The police of that city received an anonymous letter charging in detail that Mr. and Mrs. Gates trafficked in drugs for a living. The police incorporated the anonymous letter with other data gathered by them in an affidavit, and applied on its basis to a magistrate

---

[49] U.S. v. DiRe, 332 U.S. 581 (1948); *Agnello,* note 49 *supra; Marron,* note 46 *supra;* Kremen v. U.S., 353 U.S. 346 (1957); *Ker,* note 32 *supra;* Fahy v. Connecticut, 375 U.S. 85 (1963); Preston v. U.S., 376 U.S. 364 (1964); *Stoner,* note 48 *supra.*

[50] Carroll v. U.S., 267 U.S. 132 (1925); Brinegar v. U.S., 338 U.S. 160 (1949); Cooper v. California, 386 U.S. 58 (1967); Dyke v. Taylor Implement Mfg. Co., 391 U.S. 216 (1968); *Chimel,* note 43 *supra;* Chambers v. Maroney, note 45 *supra;* Coolidge v. New Hampshire, note 41 *supra.*

[51] U.S. v. Martinez-Fuerte, 428 U.S. 543 (1976); U.S. v. Lovasco, 431 U.S. 783 (1977).

[52] 103 S. Ct. 2317.

for a search and seizure warrant covering the home and automobile of the respondents. Since the matters detailed in the affidavit and the incorporated anonymous letter shed no light on my objective, I refrain from reciting them.

Acting on the affidavit and its incorporated letter, the magistrate issued the search and seizure warrant requested. Pursuant to its authority, the police searched the home and automobile of the respondents and discovered marijuana in both of them. Illinois prosecuted the respondents in its courts for violation of its drug laws. On the timely motion of the respondents, the Illinois trial court suppressed the items discovered by the search, and its ruling was affirmed by the Illinois Appellate Court and the Illinois Supreme Court on the ground that the affidavit and its incorporated anonymous letter did not establish probable cause for the issuance of the search warrant. The Illinois courts based their ruling on the specific basis that the affidavit was defective under the "two-pronged" test established by the *Aguilar* and *Spinelli* cases, because it did not reveal the "basis of knowledge" of the writer of the anonymous letter or provide facts sufficient to establish his "veracity" or the "reliability" of his report.[53]

The Supreme Court granted certiorari to review the decision of the Illinois Supreme Court. After briefs had been filed and oral arguments had been made before it, the Supreme Court requested the parties to address this additional question: "Whether the rule requiring the exclusion at a criminal trial of evidence obtained in violation of the Fourth Amendment should to any extent be modified, so as, for example, not to require the exclusion of evidence obtained in the reasonable belief that the search and seizure at issue was consistent with the Fourth Amendment."[54]

Illinois v. Gates produced four opinions in the Supreme Court: a majority opinion by Justice Rehnquist joined by Chief Justice Burger and Justices Blackmun, Powell, and O'Connor; a separate concurring opinion by Justice White; a dissenting opinion by Justice Brennan joined by Justice Marshall; and a dissenting opinion by Justice Stevens joined by Justice Brennan.

The majority reversed the ruling of the Illinois Supreme Court. To do this, they decreed that the two-pronged test of *Aguilar* and *Spinelli* was improper and should be abandoned; that the proper test for

[53] Aguilar v. Texas, 378 U.S. 108 (1964); Spinelli v. U.S., 393 U.S. 410 (1969).
[54] 103 S. Ct. 436 (1982).

ascertaining whether probable cause for the issuance of a search warrant exists is the "totality of the circumstances" revealed by the affidavit; and that measured by this test the affidavit at issue established probable cause for the issuance of the warrant, that is, probable cause to believe that the contraband or evidence sought was located in the particular places designated in the affidavit and warrant.

Justice White asserted in his separate concurring opinion that there was probable cause for the issuance of the warrant for the search of the home and automobile of the respondents under the two-pronged *Aguilar-Spinelli* test and did not join the majority's opinion rejecting that test. Justice Brennan insisted in his dissenting opinion that the *Aguilar-Spinelli* rules constitute a sound test for determining whether probable cause exists for the issuance of a search warrant based on hearsay evidence and that the Illinois courts rightly ruled that the affidavit at issue did not establish probable cause. Justice Stevens insisted in his dissent that the affidavit failed to disclose probable cause for the search of the home of respondents, that there is a constitutional difference between searches of stationary houses and highly movable automobiles, and that the search of the automobile may have been valid if the police had probable cause to make it after the respondents drove it to Bloomingdale from Florida. He advocated vacating the judgment of the Illinois Supreme Court and remanding the case for determination of this question.

Apart from the request of the Supreme Court that the parties address the additional question drafted by the Court, *Illinois v. Gates* may be deemed a more or less "run-of-the-mine" case. This request, however, gave the prospective decision in the case a magnified anticipatory importance. The majority opinion announced that the Supreme Court would not address the issue whether the exclusionary rule should not be modified because it had not been presented to or decided by the court of Illinois. In so ruling, the majority could invoke orthodox precedents. Justice White insisted in his concurring opinion that the issue arose in the court of Illinois when the respondents invoked the exclusionary rule and criticized the majority for refraining to address the issue, and predicted it would be back another day. Justices Brennan, Marshall, and Stevens ignored the question in its entirety.

The only Justice who addressed the issue was Justice White, who maintained with vigor that the exclusionary rule should be modified so as to admit evidence obtained in violation of the Fourth Amendment when officers make a search or seizure "in the good-faith belief that their action comported with constitutional requirements."[55] To sustain his position, Justice White cites many nongermane decisions holding quite rightly that the exclusionary rule applies only in criminal trials against persons who have been subjected to unreasonable searches or seizures in violation of the Fourth Amendment. He also lifted out of context an inapposite quotation from *United States v. Peltier.*[56]

Justice White's separate opinion adds no argument of consequence to those previously made by the Chief Justice and himself to divorce the exclusionary rule and the Fourth Amendment. He indicates the difficulty attendant, however, on what they advocate by declaring "I would measure the reasonableness of a particular search and seizure only by objective standards."[57] Besides, he brings into doubt his opposition to the exclusionary rule insofar as the second clause of the Fourth Amendment is concerned by saying "in any event, I would apply the exclusionary rule when it is plainly evident that a magistrate or judge had no business issuing a warrant."[58] This statement is not antagonistic to the second clause which calls the exclusionary rule into operation only if the warrant is not issued "upon probable cause, supported by oath or affirmation, and particularly describing the place to be searched, and the person or thing to be seized."

The majority opinion quotes some *obiter dicta* from the *Calandra* case to the effect that "the exclusionary rule is a judicially created remedy designed to safeguard Fourth Amendment rights generally . . . and not a personal constitutional right of the party aggrieved."[59] As the Court stated in footnote 5 to *Calandra,* this question did not arise in that case: "We have no occasion in the present case to consider the extent of the rule's efficacy in criminal trials."[60]

The quoted statement is inconsistent with all the cases cited in note 12, which hold that the Fourth Amendment confers standing to invoke the exclusionary rule upon all victims of unreasonable searches and seizures in criminal cases where the government seeks to impose criminal sanctions upon them. I submit this creates a personal constitutional right. In those cases the purpose of the rule is to protect the victims against past unconstitutional police conduct—not to deter future unlawful police conduct.

---

[55] *Id.* at 2344.
[56] *Id.* at 2343, quoting U.S. v. Peltier, 422 U.S. 531 (1975).
[57] 103 S. Ct. at 2347.
[58] *Id.* at 2345.
[59] 103 S. Ct. at 2324, quoting U.S. v. Calandra, 414 U.S. 338, 348 (1974).
[60] *Calandra, id.* at 348 n.5.

The only issue before the Court in *Calandra* was whether a witness in a preliminary investigation before the grand jury can invoke the exclusionary rule. The Court adjudged he cannot, because "the grand jury does not finally adjudicate guilt or innocence, it has traditionally been allowed to pursue its investigative and accusatorial functions unimpeded by the evidential and procedural restrictions applicable to a criminal trial."[61]

I close my comments on *Illinois v. Gates* with these indisputable observations respecting the unanswered question the Supreme Court submitted to the parties:

1. The question is repugnant to the declaration of Article VI of the Constitution that "this Constitution . . . shall be the supreme law of the land."

2. The question implies that Supreme Court Justices possess sovereign power to confer on their violation by fallible police officers priority over the precepts of the Fourth Amendment.

IV. CONCLUSION

The exclusionary rule rests on the sound principle that it is better to permit a comparatively few guilty men to escape conviction and punishment than it is to deprive all men in whole or in part of their constitutional liberties. When it made blind obeisance to the law-and-order syndrome in 1970 and incorporated the subsequently repealed "no-knock" provision in the drug law of the nation,[62] Congress made it certain, as I predicted at the time, that some federal narcotic agents and some innocent householders would suffer violent deaths. The Supreme Court would make a similar calamity inevitable if it should succumb to the desire to maximize convictions in criminal cases and to that end nullify the Fourth Amendment in whole or in part. Moreover, Supreme Court Justices would defy, degrade, and defame the Constitution if they should adjudge that it authorizes the police to enforce criminal laws in the manner in which burglars ply their trade.

Because it is an essential ingredient of the Fourth Amendment, the Supreme Court has neither the constitutional power nor the moral right to ignore or nullify the exclusionary rule. As Chief Justice John

---

[61] *Id.* at 349.
[62] See D.C. Code, §23-591, P.L. No. 91-358, §210(a), 84 Stat. 630, repealed, P.L. No. 93-635, §16, 88 Stat. 2178 (1975).

Marshall made plain in *Marbury v. Madison*, the oath of a Supreme Court Justice to support the Constitution imposes on him a constitutional duty as well as a moral obligation to accept the Constitution as the absolute rule for his official conduct.[63] Bound by oath or affirmation to support the Constitution in its entirety, a Supreme Court Justice ought to accept as valid and enforce every provision in it as written, even though he may not approve of the handiwork of the Founding Fathers in some particular respect. After all it is not his function to amend, revise, modify, or nullify the Constitution.

In seeking to persuade their brethren to modify and thus nullify in part the exclusionary rule, Chief Justice Burger and Justice White are attempting to induce them to do what the Constitution forbids them to do, to wit, "to forgive the requirements of the Fourth Amendment in the name of law enforcement."[64] The Constitution is an intellectually honest document which speaks with finality. When it declares by the Fourth Amendment that "the right of the people to be secure in their persons, houses, papers, and effects against unreasonable searches and seizures shall not be violated," the Constitution means what it says, and the exclusionary rule alone makes what it says effective. The oaths of the Justices to support the Constitution deny them both the power and the right to convert the Fourth Amendment's guaranty against unreasonable searches and seizures into a false pretense by nullifying the exclusionary rule. Judicial usurpation is too high a price to pay for robbing the people of a free Republic, irrespective of their guilt or innocence, of the right to be secure in their persons, houses, papers, and effects from unreasonable searches and seizures.

I close on a pragmatic note. Advocates of its abolition or modification claim that multitudes of evildoers escape punishment for their crimes because the exclusionary rule bars the receipt by courts of evidence obtained by its violation. They delude themselves. As appears in a recently published column of Tom Wicker of the *New York Times*, entitled "Exploding a Crime Myth,"[65] court records reveal that conviction rates would be increased by less than one-half of one percent if the exclusionary rule was abolished.

---

[63] 1 Cranch 137 (1803).

[64] Berger v. New York, 388 U.S. at 62-63.

[65] NEW YORK TIMES, March 4, 1983, sec. 1, p. 31, col. 1; March 8, 1983, sec. 1, p. 31, col. 1.

ROBERT WEISBERG

DEREGULATING DEATH

I. Introduction

It is now more than a decade since the federal courts began their tortuous effort to contain capital punishment within the rule of law. This is a good time for a history of that effort, now that one important phase of it has ended.

In a startling quartet of cases handed down at the end of the 1982 Term, the Supreme Court essentially announced that it was going out of the business of telling the states how to administer the death penalty phase of capital murder trials.[1] In the two of those cases directly concerning the legal form of this penalty phase—which I shall call the "penalty trial"—the Court wanted to tell two state supreme courts that they could uphold death sentences even where the penalty trial seemed clearly to violate federal or state law.[2] To do so, the Court essentially had to undo a large part of the past decade's apparent doctrine building

Robert Weisberg is Assistant Professor of Law, Stanford University.

AUTHOR'S NOTE: My thanks to Robert Gordon, Thomas Grey, Samuel Gross, John Kaplan, and Mark Kelman for their comments on an earlier draft and to Douglas Schwartz for his research help. This article was written with the support of the Stanford Legal Research Fund, made possible by a bequest from the estate of Ira S. Lillick and by gifts from Roderick M. and Carla A. Hills and other friends of the Stanford Law School.

[1] The cases are Zant v. Stephens, 103 S. Ct. 2733 (1983); Ramos v. California, 103 S. Ct. 3446 (1983); Barefoot v. Estelle, 103 S. Ct. 3383 (1983), and Barclay v. Florida, 103 S. Ct. 3418 (1983). See Part IV *infra*. The most striking fact of the four important cases is that the Court upheld death sentences. In the previous seven years, since the Court constitutionally "restored" the death penalty in Gregg v. Georgia, 428 U.S. 153 (1976), in all but one of the fifteen fully argued capital punishment cases decided on the merits it had vacated or reversed the death sentence. The exception was Dobbert v. Florida, 432 U.S. 282 (1977) (no ex post facto violation to apply new procedural law to defendant who committed crime under old law).

[2] The two key cases, for my purposes, are Zant v. Stephens and Barclay v. Florida.

for the death penalty. The Court is uncertain whether it has abruptly changed its mind or instead has abruptly realized what it has mysteriously meant all along. In any event the Court has reduced the law of the penalty trial to almost a bare aesthetic exhortation that the states just do something—anything—to give the penalty trial a legal appearance. The new cases reveal the art of legal doctrine-making in a state of nervous breakdown.

A. THE DOCTRINAL DILEMMA AND THE PENALTY TRIAL

The penalty trial, the most interesting product of the past decade, is a curious new legal form in which the state prosecutes a convicted murderer[3] for the enhanced crime, or moral condition, of deserving the death penalty. The Supreme Court began fostering the development of the penalty trial in 1972. It issued an emotional and confusing ensemble of exhortations to the states that they create some legal form to cure the political embarrassment over the apparently lawless infliction of the death penalty.[4] The states responded with a variety of new legal rituals by which they would choose which murderers to execute.[5] The rituals which have survived the Court's scrutiny vary widely,[6] but one can very roughly describe their common denominator: In a regular criminal trial, the state applies its substantive criminal law to decide whether the defendant is "eligible" for the death penalty; in a secondary proceeding, the penalty trial, the judge or jury[7] finds and considers certain "aggravating" and "mitigating" facts about the defendant's crime or character and then sentences him to either execution or life imprisonment.[8] In some states, the law offers the

---

The Supreme Court has virtually prohibited the death penalty for any other crime than murder. Coker v. Georgia, 433 U.S. 584 (1977).

[4] Furman v. Georgia, 408 U.S. 238 (1972).

[5] In 1976, the Court struck down the capital punishment laws of those states which provided no penalty trial at all. Woodson v. North Carolina, 428 U.S. 280 (1976); Roberts v. Louisiana, 428 U.S. 325 (1976). The Court has also virtually required that the sentencer choose the defendant's penalty in a proceeding formally separate from the guilt trial. See note 16 *infra* and accompanying text.

[6] For a very helpful survey of the forty-odd death penalty schemes on the books in American jurisdictions, see Gillers, *Deciding Who Dies*, 129 U. PA. L. REV. 1, 13 n.48, 101-19.

[7] Twenty-seven states guarantee a capital defendant a binding jury determination in his penalty trial. In a few states, a jury makes a nonbinding recommendation of sentence to a sentencing judge, *e.g.*, Fla. Stat. Ann. §921.141 (West Supp. 1980), while in five states the judge has the sole power to decide sentence in the penalty trial, *e.g.*, Rev. Neb. Stat. §29-2520 (1979). See Gillers, note 6 *supra*, at 13-19.

[8] Even this minimal description does not fully account for such states as Texas, where the "aggravating" facts are essentially built into the narrow substantive liability law of murder. Jurek v. Texas, 428 U.S. 262, 270 (1976).

sentencer some modest guidance simply by mentioning these circumstances, while in others, it purports to control the sentencer's deliberation through a highly complex verbal formula.[9]

Since 1972, the Court has acted at times as if it wants systematically to educate the states in the legal science of administering the penalty trial. Certainly some of the lower federal courts have exercised their habeas corpus powers in a pedagogic way. But essentially the Court and the states have engaged in an ill-coordinated conversation about how to lend form to the penalty trial. The Court has spoken in a series of cryptic gestures and moral importunings, approving and disapproving various parts of the new state laws. The states have responded by trying to do every bit as much as, but little more than, the Court has vaguely asked for. As a result of this furtive conversation, by starts and stops the penalty trial in most states has become more formally sophisticated, combining pieces of doctrine from the substantive criminal law with a kind of delayed-reaction, Warren-Court jurisprudence of criminal procedure. By inducing, if not requiring, the states to refine the penalty trial, the Court has tried to dignify the once lawless death penalty with the reassuring symbolism of legal doctrine.

This doctrinal enterprise has proved very expensive for the federal courts. There has been economic expense, in accommodating a drastic increase in plausible new claims of doctrinal error, especially in habeas corpus petitions. And there has been intellectual expense, in the courts' strained efforts to maintain at least the appearance of doctrinal rigor on a subject stubbornly irreducible to rules of law. Suddenly, in the 1982 Term, the Supreme Court, perhaps finding these expenses unbearable, has largely reversed the enterprise.

A brief history of the decade's death penalty project might therefore also be a brief requiem for it. We can now examine how willing or able our legal institutions have been to tame capital punishment, or how much they have accommodated themselves to the futility of the task.

---

[9] Sentencing juries sometimes must answer a bewildering array of formal-sounding questions, phrased roughly as whether aggravating circumstances exist, whether mitigating circumstances exist, whether the aggravating circumstances themselves are sufficiently substantial to warrant the death penalty, whether the aggravating circumstances outweigh the mitigating circumstances, and whether the totality of the aggravating circumstances is sufficiently more substantial than the totality of the mitigating circumstances to justify the death penalty. See State v. McDougall, 308 N.C. ____ , ____ , 301 S.E.2d 308, 327 (N.C. 1981); Smith v. North Carolina, 103 S. Ct. 474 (1982) (Stevens, J., opinion respecting denial of certiorari) (describing possible jury interpretations of the North Carolina instructions).

Epigraphs often prove useful when one tries to set a theme for a historical account, and I offer two. The first is from the ironically prescient opinion of Justice Harlan in the 1971 case of *McGautha v. California:*[10]

> To identify before the fact those characteristics of criminal homicides and their perpetrators which call for the death penalty, and to express these characteristics in language which can be fairly understood and applied by the sentencing authority, appear to be tasks which are beyond present human ability.

The *McGautha* opinion was the Court's (soon unheeded) warning to itself that the entire enterprise of subjecting capital punishment to legal rules was hopeless and unnecessary. Justice Harlan's warning, sounding subtle questions of jurisprudence, is important for reasons beyond matters of federalism. To help address those questions, I want to add an epigraph from Norman Mailer, author of one of the two great modernist novels about the death penalty:[11] "Capital punishment is to the rest of all law as surrealism is to realism. It destroys the logic of the profession."[12] The "problem" of capital punishment is a simple twofold truth: Capital punishment is at once the best and worst subject for legal rules. The state's decision to kill is so serious, and the cost of error so high, that we feel impelled to discipline the human power of the death sentence with rational legal rules. Yet a judge or jury's decision to kill is an intensely moral, subjective matter that seems to defy the designers of general formulas for legal decision.

We can also view this decade's legalistic tinkering with capital punishment as an episode in the more general history of our ambivalent commitment to doctrinal rules, and to the illusions and delusions this ambivalence fosters in criminal law and other fields. The modern law of the death penalty is a wonderful study in how the manufacture of legal doctrine mitigates moral ambivalence and intellectual instability, and enables legal institutions to avoid confronting the stark issues before them.

B. McGAUTHA AS PROLOGUE

Justice Harlan's 1971 opinion in *McGautha v. California* receives brief mention in most summaries of capital punishment law as an

---

[10] 402 U.S. 183, 204 (1971).

[11] THE EXECUTIONER'S SONG (1977). The other is Albert Camus's THE STRANGER (1942).

[12] Mailer, *Until Dead: Thoughts on Capital Punishment*, PARADE, Feb. 6, 1981, at 6, 8.

obstinate final act of caution before the Court began its era of doctrinal creativity with the death penalty. But the *McGautha* opinion is now due for a bit of restorative interpretation, having proved partly prophetic in its technical holding, and generally prophetic in its skeptical philosophy.

Justice Harlan's opinion actually decides two cases—McGautha's from California and the case of one Crampton from Ohio.[13] Crampton had been sentenced to die under the capital murder scheme most common in the country at the time: a "unitary" proceeding in which the jury decided both whether the defendant was guilty of murder and, where necessary, whether he should be executed or be sent to prison for life.[14] McGautha had enjoyed a "bifurcated" trial in California—the jury first decided he was guilty of murder and then decided on his death sentence in a separate proceeding. Crampton argued that the unitary proceeding was unconstitutional, and both Crampton and McGautha argued that their death verdicts violated due process because in neither state did the court or legislature give the jury any guiding standards or criteria for deciding sentence.[15]

Justice Harlan's opinion for the court rejected both claims. His decision to uphold the unitary trial has essentially been overruled. Though the Court has never expressly required bifurcation, the states have read the Court's approving remarks on bifurcation as virtually requiring it.[16] Harlan's second and more famous holding, approving "standardless" sentencing, is the most obviously prescient now, because it comes close to capturing the position to which a prodigal Court has returned this Term. Nevertheless, both holdings contribute to Harlan's theme.

The problem with most of the old unitary capital trials was that the only evidence the jury would get on the question of sentence was whatever evidence the parties happened to have presented on the very different question of guilt.[17] The unitary trial therefore sometimes benefited the defendant on the sentencing issue, since the normal rules

[13] 402 U.S. 183, 185 (1971).

[14] Of the forty-one states that had death penalty laws at the time of *McGautha*, thirty-four had unitary procedures like Ohio, five had separate penalty proceedings like California, and two made death the automatic penalty for the most serious degree of murder. Project, *A Study of the California Penalty Jury in First-Degree-Murder Cases*, 21 STAN. L. REV. 1297, 1307 & n.10, 1432–38 (1969) [hereafter *California Penalty Jury*].

[15] 402 U.S. at 185.

[16] Gregg v. Georgia, 428 U.S. 153, 195 (1976) (plurality opinion) ("as a general proposition" the Court's concern with arbitrary death sentencing is "best met" by a bifurcated proceeding).

[17] See generally Knowlton, *Problems of Jury Discretion in Capital Cases*, 101 U. PA. L. REV. 1099, 1108–18 (1953). Since the defendant in *Crampton* pleaded not guilty by reason of insanity,

of guilt-phase evidence would not permit the state to introduce the defendant's earlier record—unless the defendant testified. The converse of that benefit was the basis of Crampton's claim. Crampton had wanted to get on the stand to plead for mercy and to offer evidence in mitigation of sentence. But that mitigating testimony might have actually hurt him on the guilt question by inviting the state to cross-examine or impeach him, particularly by bringing in his criminal record. In short, the unitary trial violated due process by "burdening" Crampton's privilege against self-incrimination.[18]

In rejecting the claim, Harlan does not stress that the state had any important interest in putting Crampton to this dilemma. Nor does Harlan say, as he does on the standardless sentencing issue, that the legislature would face any conceptual difficulties in writing a law to give Crampton the right he requested. Rather, Harlan seems perfectly willing to concede that Crampton's dilemma was unfair and even "cruel."[19] But he insists that a bit of reflection shows that all trials are in some ways unfair. The tone of the opinion is that life generally is unfair, and the law need be no fairer. Doctrinally, Harlan's argument is that the criminal defendant faces similar dilemmas in the guilt phase; the settled law of the Fifth Amendment requires the defendant in many cases to make "nice calculations" as to whether he will gain more from testifying than he will lose by inviting cross-examination or impeachment.[20] But Harlan does not simply rely on the conventional tools of precedent and analogy. He seems also to want to write a Burkean essay condemning the due process argument as romantic utopianism, a failure to achieve tragic wisdom.

Harlan recognizes that Crampton's claim reflects the "peculiar poignancy of the position of a man whose life is at stake, coupled with the imponderables of the decision which the jury is called upon to make,"[21] but he treats that "poignancy" as sentimentality. Harlan notes Crampton's argument that the guilt-phase law about self-incrimination is distinguishable because guilt decisions involve fact-finding, while capital sentencing involves imponderables. Harlan rejects the premise that outside capital sentencing criminal trials are free of imponderables.

---

the regular guilt-phase rules allowed him to introduce evidence of his troubled youth and drug and alcohol addiction. 402 U.S. at 191-95. For a further discussion of the unitary scheme, see notes 234-46 *infra* and accompanying text.

[18] 402 U.S. at 210-13.

[19] *Id.* at 214-15.

[20] *Id.* at 214-16.

[21] *Id.* at 216.

In noncapital sentencing "the sciences of penology, sociology, and psychology have not advanced to the point that sentencing is wholly a matter of scientific calculation from objectively verifiable facts," and he suggests that the guilt phase itself is not so free of imponderables as Crampton implies.[22] It is an illusion to think that any part of the law involves purely objective fact-finding.

As Harlan saw it, once one learns to accept the conventional cruel burdens of criminal trials, Crampton's case comes down to a complaint "that the death verdict will be returned by a jury which never heard the sound of his voice."[23] Having somewhat condescendingly treated Crampton's argument as symbolic, Harlan then dismisses it as just that—"largely symbolic."[24] Of course Harlan is unfair to Crampton here. Sometimes the only hope the defense has to defeat a death sentence is to "humanize" the defendant for the jury, to induce greater moral doubt in the jurors' minds by reminding them that they are deciding the fate of a person, not a legal abstraction. But Harlan's broader philosophical agenda impels him almost to mock and distort Crampton's claim.

Harlan's posture of Burkean skepticism is even more apparent in the second holding—that standardless jury sentencing does not violate due process. On that issue, Justice Brennan provides the perfect antagonist in the role of pedantic idealist—the Tom Paine to Harlan's Burke—so that the two can conduct a rhetorical debate on legal philosophy.[25] Brennan notes in moral outrage and disbelief Harlan's suggestion that the rule of law and the state's power to kill are in "irreconcilable conflict," and he then says somewhat obscurely that even if he took that cynical view himself, he would stand with the rule of law.[26] But Harlan has effectively deflated Brennan by saying that in a certain sense the rule of law and the death penalty are indeed in irreconcilable conflict, and that to the mature observer there is nothing very surprising or pernicious about the conflict.

---

[22] *Id.* at 217.

[23] *Id.* at 220.

[24] *Ibid.* Indeed, in the final cynical twist, Harlan says that Crampton's "symbolic" claim was vindicated anyway in the merely symbolic terms it merited. Ohio law afforded Crampton the common-law right of "allocution," the right to make a final personal plea for mercy. But under the common law, Crampton could make that plea only after the jury had returned its death verdict, and he could only plead to the judge, who had virtually no power to overturn the verdict anyway. *Id.* at 195.

[25] Compare PAINE, THE RIGHTS OF MAN (1792), to BURKE, REFLECTIONS ON THE REVOLUTION IN FRANCE (1790).

[26] 402 U.S. at 249-50 (Brennan, J., dissenting).

Harlan's famous statement that a comprehensive and intelligible death penalty law is beyond human ability bears careful reading in the context of the whole opinion. Harlan does not say that a jury's decision to kill is inevitably irrational. He says with some confidence that as jurors face so obviously awesome a decision they will naturally act with appropriate moral seriousness, guided by at least intuitive moral rationality.[27] Harlan says that we cannot mitigate our inevitable moral ambivalence about condemning people to death by dignifying our decision in the illusory language of legal science.

As constitutional doctrine, Harlan's holding on standardless sentencing is a simple matter of federalism: the Court is always reluctant to intervene in the substantive criminal law of the states, and in fact the state legislatures themselves rarely lay down strict criteria for sentencing of any kind. But more broadly, Harlan's opinion is an essay on the inevitable limits of legal doctrine-making and the pretenses of legal language. While Brennan declaims at length on the rational ideals of due process, Harlan demeans the moral and intellectual immaturity of due process romanticism. For him, a properly skeptical understanding of the law recognizes two things: first, that many legal decisions cannot be described in or reduced to precise legal language, and second, that those decisions are not for that reason alone arbitrary or irrational.

Harlan's skepticism more clearly extends beyond capital punishment when he summarizes the hapless history of legal efforts to reduce the state's decision to kill to the reassuring language of doctrine. At the beginning of that history is the common law of homicide itself. Since at common law, and under the early statutes, death was the automatic penalty for any felonious homicide, his study of capital sentencing gives him an opportunity to remark critically on the doctrinal history of homicide.[28] "Malice" and "premeditation" are two parts of the substantive law of crimes that induce even the most conventional legal scholars to look cynically on the follies of doctrine-making. In briefly noting the instability of those concepts, Harlan seems anxious to make the point that before we demand too much of legal doctrine in the peculiar area of capital sentencing, we should remember how tolerant we are of the limits of doctrine in the traditional law of liability.

---

[27] *Id.* at 207–08. Indeed, Harlan praises the California jury that condemned McGautha for rationally distinguishing McGautha's culpability from that of his accomplice, whose life it spared. *Id.* at 221.

[28] *Id.* at 197–99.

At the contemporary end of that history, Harlan reviews the ambivalent effort of the drafters of the Model Penal Code, the paradigm of modern rational criminal law doctrine, to write a death penalty statute. Despite its apparent formal complexity, the Model Penal Code's proposed capital sentencing law only minimally constrains the jury's discretion.[29] In the Code's handling of the death penalty, Harlan is able to treat the Code as a skeptical document itself, a confession of the finest artists of criminal law doctrine that they cannot devise an adequate rule of law.

In the end, Harlan concludes that, morally and intellectually, the Court has nothing to teach the states about capital punishment. One can of course dispute the truth of Harlan's central insight—that we cannot write a law of capital punishment in conventional legal language. Even if one accepts that truth, one can reject Harlan's inference from it—that the Court must leave the issue to the states. Indeed what follows *McGautha* is a struggle over both the truth and the significance of Harlan's assertion.

II. The General Doctrine of the Penalty Trial

In the most stinging of the four death penalty dissents he wrote in the 1982 Term, Justice Marshall complains that the Court has utterly contradicted what it has been saying since 1972.[30] Justice Stevens and Justice Rehnquist insist that the Court is at most clarifying what it has been saying all along.[31] The Court is thus engaged in a debate over the meaning of its own pronouncements. One side of the debate says that despite confusing signals and the appearance of contradiction, the Court has shown a steady commitment to formally disciplining the conduct of the state penalty trial, at least until this Term. The contending view is that the Court has never purported to do more than nudge the states into eliminating the most prejudicial injustices of the old lawless penalty scheme, while always acknowledging the impotence of constitutional law to make the penalty trial formally rational.

---

[29] The Code requires the jury to find at least one statutory aggravating circumstance before issuing a death sentence. Model Penal Code §210.6(2) (Proposed Official Draft, 1962), but once the jury does so, it can consider any aggravating or mitigating information, statutory or nonstatutory. *Ibid.*

[30] See Zant v. Stephens, 103 S. Ct. at 2758-61 (Marshall, J., dissenting).

[31] *Id.* at 2746-2752; see Part IV *infra.*

Of course the death penalty is hardly unique in this regard. Many lines of decisions, especially lines of plurality decisions, are fragile compromises among only partly overlapping legal agendas. The compromises may break down when Justices have different historical memories of the meaning of those decisions.[32] The Court may seem then to contradict itself, when in fact it has never spoken so clearly that we can accurately identify a contradiction. The death penalty cases are a good example of a sequence that may seem to be a series of contradictions, but is better seen as a consistently contradictory play for voices, a running doctrinal counterpoint. The competing historical accounts of the sequence are both perfectly true in the sense that the Court has at times fostered both of them, and in the sense that both have had important political effects.

To tell the history of the sequence is thus to tell it in more than one way. My first choice is to review a few of the major cases and to show how each fits into both historical accounts and how the first account, the one Justice Marshall claims to have believed, reflects a view of the Court's efforts that the Court found too expensive to maintain. But the history also deserves to be told from a perspective rarely noted in the literature—the actual conduct of penalty trials, as revealed in such texts as instructions and closing arguments. I should emphasize that I do not try to explain the cases by tracing the voting patterns of individual justices or the shifting coalitions of groups of justices. These are important matters, since death penalty cases rarely produce majority opinions, but they receive adequate treatment elsewhere.

A. THE FURMAN OPERA

One year after *McGautha*, the Court found that though it could not yet devise a doctrine to organize the penalty trial, neither could it accept Justice Harlan's wizened pessimism about legal doctrine-making. *Furman v. Georgia*[33] is the source of the competing histories of the death penalty cases. But the historical uncertainty over *Furman* is not so much about how to interpret the decision, but about whether there really ever was such a thing as a *Furman* decision at all.

For a decade, courts and commentators have invoked what may be called the *Furman* "trope": they decry a flaw in a death penalty statute

---

because it leads to the same arbitrariness "condemned in *Furman*."[34] But what *Furman* condemned is not very clear, at least in any legal sense. *Furman* may be a decision that in some way overruled *McGautha*, or *Furman* may be merely an exhortation to the states to solve a problem the Court could barely identify.

The Court had granted certiorari in *Furman* on the very vague question whether death sentences imposed under the typical state laws of the time violated the Eighth Amendment ban on cruel and unusual punishments.[35] Essentially, the Court chose to review the general scheme of standardless jury sentencing it had approved in *McGautha*. Getting around *McGautha*, of course, presented something of an artistic challenge, especially to the members of the *McGautha* majority, Justice Stewart and Justice White, who now wanted to go the other way. But the Justices could take advantage of the wonderful fiction that the Due Process Clauses and the Eighth Amendment might have very different things to say about standardless sentencing.[36] While the Due Process Clause did not directly condemn the "process" of the standardless schemes, the Eighth Amendment might still condemn the "products" of that process—the actual pattern of sentences it yielded. The Court was thus able to invoke the Eighth Amendment to nullify all death penalty schemes in the United States then in operation.

The problem, of course, is that there are nine separate opinions in *Furman*.[37] It is not so much a case as a badly orchestrated opera, with nine characters taking turns to offer their own arias. Justices Marshall and Brennan wrote long historical discourses on how the moral progress of civilization has categorically rejected the death penalty.[38] Those opinions are no longer important parts of the history of the Court's doctrine, though they do provide some of the normative language the Court uses later in selectively approving death penalty laws. The important opinions are those of Justices Stewart, Douglas, and White, which conditionally suspend the death penalty, and which are the source of the Court's later efforts in doctrine-making.

---

[34] *E.g.*, California v. Ramos 103 S. Ct. 3446 (vague sentencing standards might lead to the "arbitrary and capricious sentencing patterns condemned in *Furman*").

[35] 403 U.S. 952 (1971).

[36] Judges have an intriguing way of treating their earlier utterances as historical objects. Justice Stewart later conceded that *Furman* "is in substantial tension with a broad reading of *McGautha*'s holding." Gregg v. Georgia, 428 U.S. 153, 195-96 n.47 (1976) (plurality opinion); *cf.* Furman v. Georgia, 408 U.S. at 248 & n.11 (Douglas, J., concurring).

[37] All five justices in the majority and all four dissenters—the Chief Justice and Justices Blackmun, Powell, and Rehnquist—filed individual opinions, 408 U.S. at 375-470.

[38] *Id.* at 257 (Brennan, J., concurring); *id.* at 314 (Marshall, J., concurring).

Stewart and White both speak coolly and analytically, though with different notions of what is wrong with the results of standardless sentencing. Stewart assumes that random effects are inconsistent with the ideals of the rule of law. He can find no rational principle to distinguish those criminals the states have sentenced to death from those the states have spared.[39] White is less concerned with the formal demands of the rule of law than with the norm of functional rationality in criminal justice: assuming the states have legitimate retributional and deterrent goals in imposing the death penalty, they now execute too few people to achieve those goals.[40] In different and perhaps inconsistent ways, Stewart and White challenge the states to solve logical or functional flaws in the death penalty, though neither Justice suggests any particular legal forms for meeting the challenge.

The most dramatic opinion is that of Justice Douglas. Whereas Stewart and White pose intellectual and logistical challenges to the states, Justice Douglas essentially challenges the states to resolve his social and political discomfort over the products of the death penalty. The Douglas opinion is not so much a legal opinion as a cultural document, an emotive internal monologue of American political liberalism engaged publicly in moral self-criticism during the middle of the Vietnam era. It is a catalog of cultural embarrassments, not an analysis of legal error. Douglas dips briefly into textual and legislative history of the Eighth Amendment to find a source for complaint about unequal or unfair death sentencing, and then decries its infliction on the poor, minorities, outcasts, and the unpopular.[41] He cites provocative if ambiguous statistics on racial discrimination, and a penitentiary warden's lament about unequal treatment of the rich and the poor.[42] He jumps from a review of the mitigating facts in the cases technically being decided by the Court to a lurid and impassioned account of the seventeenth-century Bloody Assizes in England.[43]

The conscientious legislator who had no intention of satisfying Justices Marshall and Brennan might well have been vexed about how to satisfy the "decision" represented by Stewart, White, and Douglas: he encountered not a holding, but a declaration of social and political grievances to be redressed.

---

[39] *Id.* at 306, 309-10 (Stewart, J., concurring).
[40] *Id.* at 310, 311-14 (White, J., concurring).
[41] *Id.* at 241-45 (Douglas, J., concurring).
[42] *Id.* at 250-51.
[43] *Id.* at 252-55.

In the manner of literary criticism, one can extract unifying "themes" in the *Furman* opinions, such as the dangers of arbitrariness and discrimination, which support later decisions to impose specific formal constraints on the penalty trial. But because there really is no doctrinal holding in *Furman*, it has not logically impeded the Court from later claiming that it has never tried to impose such constraints.

The states responded with a variety of laws attempting to do whatever it was that *Furman* had required. Post-*Furman* statutes are often divided into two groups. The "mandatory" statutes mooted the problem of standardless sentencing by making the death penalty automatic for the highest degrees of murder.[44] The "guided discretion" statutes devised penalty trials, using some form of aggravating and mitigating circumstances to supply the intelligible criteria which Justice Harlan had warned were beyond our human powers. It is not necessary to review the details of these statutes here, but it is important to note for now that the "guided discretion" category includes a very wide variety of penalty trial schemes.[45] Some states retained their traditional categories of first-degree murder at the guilt phase and fine-tuned the penalty decision only with the new legislative "circumstances."[46] Others did much of the fine tuning at the liability stage by creating new enhanced crimes of "capital murder."[47] Some states devised detailed and apparently exhaustive statutory lists of all aggravating and mitigating circumstances,[48] while others described these circumstances only vaguely or suggestively.[49] Some statutes provided the sentencer with a formula for "processing" the aggravating and mitigating information and seemed to require a death sentence where the formula yielded a certain result.[50] Others did not tell the sentencer what to do with all the information, and made clear that the

---

[44] See Woodson v. North Carolina, 428 U.S. 280 (1976); Roberts v. Louisiana, 428 U.S. 325 (1976).

[45] For a concise chart of the elements of these statutes, see Gillers, note 6 *supra*, at 101-19.

[46] *E.g.*, Fla. Stat. Ann. §921.1412(b).

[47] *E.g.*, Tex. Code Crim. Proc. Ann. art. 37.071 (Vernon 1981). Some states have taken a middle approach, creating "special circumstances" for death eligibility, which the jury adjudicates after finding the defendant guilty of first-degree murder, but before deciding between life and death in a separate penalty trial. *E.g.*, Cal. Pen. Code §190.2 (West Supp. 1983).

[48] *E.g.*, Fla. Stat. Ann. §921.141.

[49] *E.g.*, Ga. Code Ann. §27-2503, 27-2534.1 (not enumerating mitigating circumstances); Cal. Pen. Code §190.3 (a)-(k) (West 1983) (listing eleven factors the sentencer must take into account but not labeling them as either "aggravating" or "mitigating").

[50] *E.g.*, Cal. Pen. Code §190.3 (West 1983) (sentencer "shall impose a death sentence if [it] concludes that the aggravating circumstances outweigh the mitigating circumstances"). For a discussion of these "quasi-mandatory" statutes, see notes 263-66 *infra* and accompanying text.

sentencer was free to give mercy regardless of how the aggravating information stacked up against the mitigating.[51]

B. THE TWO FACES OF GREGG

In its quintet of opinions in 1976, the Supreme Court selectively restored the death penalty in America by approving the "guided discretion" statutes enacted after *Furman*.[52] The terms of this approval, however, remain unclear. We can identify with certainty only two things that happened in the 1976 cases. First, in *Gregg*, the Court rejected the defense bar's categorical argument that capital punishment violates the Eighth Amendment, holding that some executions could comport with the enlightened moral development of our civilization.[53] Second, in *Woodson* and *Roberts*, the Court unequivocally rejected the new "automatic" death penalty statutes which made death the mandatory penalty for the most serious classes of murder.[54] Beyond that, the cases are subject to two competing interpretations—the "romantic" and "classical."

Under the romantic account, the crucial plurality in the 1976 decisions[55] viewed *McGautha* as a challenge to the powers of due process doctrine-making, and *Furman* as a moral injunction to try to meet that challenge. Harlan had warned that no rule of law could identify those criminals who deserved to die. In the romantic view, the Court's motto might be, "Harlan said it couldn't be done, but good old American know-how will prove him wrong."

Under the romantic view, *Woodson* and *Roberts* were merely the first and most obvious steps in designing a due process for death, striking down the most precipitous and brutish response to *McGautha* and *Furman*. *Gregg*, *Proffitt*, and *Jurek* represent the next step. They tentatively approve the more flexible statutes that yield at least some promise of solving the problem of capricious death sentences. Because death is qualitatively different from all other penalties, "there is a

---

[51] Ga. Code Ann. §27-2302.

[52] Gregg v. Georgia, 428 U.S. 153 (1976); Proffitt v. Florida, 428 U.S. 242 (1976); Jurek v. Texas, 428 U.S. 262 (1976); Woodson v. North Carolina, 428 U.S. 280 (1976); Roberts v. Louisiana, 428 U.S. 325 (1976).

[53] Gregg v. Georgia, 428 U.S. at 168-87 (plurality opinion).

[54] Woodson v. North Carolina, 428 U.S. 280 (1976); Roberts v. Louisiana, 428 U.S. 325 (1976).

[55] Justices Stewart, Powell, and Stevens joined with Justices Brennan and Marshall in striking down the automatic death penalty statutes of North Carolina and Louisiana, and joined with the Chief Justice and Justices White, Blackmun, and Rehnquist in upholding the "guided discretion" statutes of Georgia, Florida, and Texas.

corresponding difference in the need for reliability in the determination that death is the appropriate punishment in a specific case."[56] *Woodson* vaguely declares a normative goal for the penalty trial—to make a "reliable" decision about the propriety of death—and the Georgia, Florida, and Texas statutes at least have promising elements of substantive and procedural formality that might achieve that norm. But if the states want to retain the power to execute, they must be faithful to—and indeed refine—those formal elements.

Justice Stewart's opinion in *Gregg* is the key controversial text in the battle of historical interpretations.[57] If *Furman* was written in a rhetoric of lament and exhortation, Justice Stewart's opinion in *Gregg* is written in a rhetoric of subtle observation and approval. Running through *Gregg* is the theme that the constitutionally proper death penalty scheme should have certain features: a separate penalty trial, rigorous appellate review to check inequity among sentences, and, most important, a disciplined rational procedure to guide the sentencer in examining evidence at the penalty trial and applying it to a logical choice of sentence. The romantic account finds plenty of textual evidence to support this theme.

First, though no *Furman* opinion suggested any particular substantive or procedural rules, Stewart interprets *Furman* to show that the first step toward disciplining the death penalty has already been taken: "*Furman* mandates . . . that discretion must be suitably directed and limited" to preclude arbitrary sentencing.[58] Stewart then lauds the general idea of a separate penalty trial, stressing that a bifurcated scheme can make penalty decisions "consistent" and "rational."[59] He notes with approval that bifurcation offers the sentencer the wide range of evidence it needs, but he stresses that the information will only be useful to the jury if "it is given guidance regarding the factors about the crime and the defendant that the State . . . deems particularly relevant to the sentencing decision."[60] Stewart emphasizes that juries must receive "careful instructions on the law," and must be "carefully and adequately guided in their deliberations."[61] The opinion is vague enough to avoid committing the Court to any specific constitutional requirements, but it supplies a wealth of

---

[56] Woodson v. North Carolina, 428 U.S. at 305.

[57] See Part IV *infra*.

[58] 428 U.S. at 189.

[59] *Id.* at 189-91.

[60] *Id.* at 192.

[61] *Id.* at 193.

dignified phrases about legal formality that will help the defense bar fight later due process battles.

Courts and commentators who have relied on the romantic account have identified two important subthemes in *Gregg*. One is that the states must not merely throw the aggravating and mitigating information at the jury, but must guide the jury in a relatively formal process of comparatively weighing aggravating and mitigating circumstances.[62] The other is that the state must use statutory lists of factors—at least on the aggravating side—to discipline the jury's use of the information it hears.[63] Stewart gives equivocal support to both these subthemes by his canny description of two statutes. The first of these statutes is, ironically, the very Model Penal Code proposal for a death penalty scheme which Harlan had used for the opposite purpose. Stewart offers the Model Penal Code as proof that what Harlan said could not be done had indeed been done. Relying on the drafters' comments more than on the proposed rule itself, Stewart treats the Code as mandating a rational comparative weighing formula for treating aggravating and mitigating information.[64] The second is the Georgia death penalty statute itself, which forbids a jury to hand down a death sentence unless it finds at least one statutory aggravating circumstance. Stewart reviews the provisions of the statute in detail, repeating congratulatory incantations about consistency and rationality.[65]

The "classical" account of the 1976 cases would stress the very little that the Court did, as opposed to the great deal it appeared to say.[66] It

---

[62] E.g., Hertz & Weisberg, *In Mitigation of the Penalty of Death: Lockett v. Ohio and the Capital Defendant's Right to Consideration of Mitigating Circumstances*, 69 CALIF. L. REV. 317, 320; Radin, *The Jurisprudence of Death: Evolving Standards for the Cruel and Unusual Punishments Clause*, 126 U. PA. L. REV. 989 (1978); cf. Coker v. Georgia, 433 U.S. 584, 589-91 (1977) (plurality opinion) (Georgia death penalty juries must comparatively weigh aggravating and mitigating circumstances).

[63] E.g., Henry v. Wainwright, 661 F.2d 56, 59-60 (5th Cir. 1981); Hertz & Weisberg, note 62 *supra*, at 374.

[64] 428 U.S. at 193 (citing Model Penal Code §201.6, Comment 3, at 71 (Tent. Draft No. 9, 1959)).

[65] Stewart says that because the jury must find at least one statutory aggravating circumstance, "[n]o longer can a Georgia jury do as *Furman*'s jury did: reach a finding of the defendant's guilt and then, without guidance or direction, decide whether he should live or die." *Id.* at 197. The jury's discretion is "controlled by clear and objective standards so as to produce non-discriminatory application." *Id.* at 198 (quoting Coley v. State, 231 Ga. 829, 834, 204 S.E.2d 612, 615 (1974)). Especially when reinforced by rigorous appellate review, the jury's discretion is "channeled"; indeed it is "always circumscribed by legislative guidelines." 428 U.S. at 206-07.

[66] For a rigorously unromantic view of *Gregg* written before the new decisions from the 1982 Term, see Ledewitz, *The Requirement of Death: Mandatory Language in the Pennsylvania Death Penalty Statute*, 21 DUQ. L. REV. 103, 119-128 (1982).

would treat the 1976 decisions as a minimal response to the state's modest achievements in redressing the worst prejudicial defects of the pre-*Furman* laws. Under this view, *Woodson* and *Roberts* represent the only clear constitutional constraint on the penalty trial the Court intended; *Gregg* and the other cases do little more than confirm that the Court may permit almost any scheme except the kind that *Woodson* expressly forbids.

The often overlooked but very obvious point about *Gregg* is that all it did as a matter of law was to uphold a statute. *Gregg* cannot logically require anything, because it affirms a death sentence. Nothing the opinion says about the Model Penal Code is very significant legally. First, to the questionable extent that the Code creates formal rules for penalty trials, Stewart's discussion of them is pure dictum in a case about a different statute. Second, despite Stewart's optimistically selective citation of the Code, the drafters, as Harlan noted, took an utterly skeptical, unromantic view of the whole enterprise of creating such roles.[67]

Moreover, underneath all the rhetoric about "guidance," the Georgia statute itself represents only the most modest advance toward formality over the old pre-*Furman* statute.[68] The threshold requirement of a statutory aggravating circumstance somewhat narrows the grounds of substantive criminal liability that make a defendant eligible for the death penalty. But beyond that, the statute essentially does just two things. It ensures that the jury will hear more information than it would have heard in a unitary trial. And, through the rhetoric of a formal-sounding but nonbinding list of aggravating circumstances, it vaguely encourages the jury to act with appropriate moral seriousness.[69]

---

[67] The Model Penal Code, like the Georgia statute, permits the sentencer to consider a wide range of aggravating evidence that does not fall within statutorily enumerated factors. The proposed statute itself does not require the sentencer to weigh aggravating against mitigating factors, though it does forbid a death sentence unless the jury finds at least one aggravating circumstance and further finds that there are "no substantial mitigating circumstances." Finally, contrary to Justice Stewart's suggestion, the Code does not require the sentencer to specify the factors on which it relied. Model Penal Code §201.6 (Tent. Draft No. 9, 1959).

[68] Though the statute does require the jury to find at least one statutory aggravating circumstance from a list of ten, once the jury gets past that threshold it can rely on virtually any aggravating evidence the prosecutor offers, regardless of its fit with statutory categories, and the statute does not even purport to give examples of mitigating circumstances. More important, the jury is never told to weigh the aggravating or mitigating information comparatively, or indeed to do anything at all with it other than to "consider" everything it hears. 428 U.S. at 162-68. In an important passage few courts or commentators ever mention, the *Gregg* plurality fully acknowledges the formlessness of the Georgia penalty trial. See *id.* at 203-04.

[69] Though the opinion lauds the availability of appellate review, the informality of the procedures in the penalty trial ensures that there is not a great deal of legal error for the appellate court to correct.

In the end, under the classical view, all the rhetoric about "guidance" and "channeling" interwoven through Stewart's summary of the statute amounts to little more than judicial sighs of relief over how Georgia has allowed the Court to escape gracefully from the responsibility it posed for itself in *Furman.*[70] One can say little with certainty about *Gregg v. Georgia* except that it makes a great many things constitutionally significant, but makes nothing either constitutionally necessary or clearly constitutionally sufficient.

C. MAKING SENSE OF LOCKETT

Under the "classical" view of *Gregg*, the states had categorically refuted *McGautha* and satisfied *Furman.* The Court had found enough formal rationality in the new laws to settle the issue forever. But under the romantic view, *Gregg* was only a conditional grant of power to the states. The guided discretion statutes had made reasonable promises of formal rationality, but they had not yet delivered on those promises.[71] The defense bar's strategy was now clear. Its short-term goal was to prevent or overturn as many death sentences as possible. Its long-range goal was simultaneously to encourage the development of the romantic approach to the penalty trial and to make it as burdensome as possible to sustain. The ultimate goal was to make the courts, if not the legislatures, realize the administrative and intellectual futility of the experiment with the rule of law. The defense bar's most striking victory toward these goals was *Lockett v. Ohio.*[72] In *Lockett*, the defense bar directly exploited the instability of the Court's effort at formal rationality by inducing the Court to recognize that formal rationality was an incomplete solution to the death penalty.

---

[70] Usually treated as footnotes to the expansive discourse in *Gregg*, the companion plurality opinions in Proffitt v. Florida and Jurek v. Texas nicely help foster the double history of the 1976 decisions. The Florida death penalty statute is somewhat more formal than either the Georgia statute or the Model Penal Code provision, enumerating both aggravating and mitigating factors and expressly requiring the sentencer to weigh these factors comparatively. Proffitt v. Florida, 428 U.S. at 247-51. Thus, the Court's approval of this statute is at least consistent with the romantic account of the Court's doctrine. On the other hand, the Court seems to acknowledge that Florida might be able to place some nonstatutory aggravating factors on the state's side of the balance. *Id.* at 250 n.8. Ironically, the petitioner in *Proffitt* objected that the weighing formula was not rational, "since the state law assigns no specific weight to any of the circumstances." *Id.* at 257. The Texas statute upheld in *Jurek* might seem to be an ultraformal law since it asks the jury to resolve purportedly specific questions about the defendant's mental state at the time of the killing and his proclivity to violence. But to ensure that the statute satisfies *Woodson*, the Court has treated it as permitting a broad normative inquiry into the defendant's desert. See Hertz & Weisberg, note 62 *supra*, at 328-41.

[71] Zant v. Stephens, 456 U.S. 410, 413 (1982) (*per curiam*) (certifying question to Georgia Supreme Court concerning meaning of Georgia death penalty statute).

[72] 438 U.S. 586 (1978).

In *Gregg*, the Court had purported to demonstrate that the death penalty decision was indeed susceptible to the discipline of legal form. But in *Woodson*, the Court had tried to accommodate Harlan's view that the death decision is a moral judgment based on imponderables as well as facts. The Court thus required some form of "individualized" penalty trial, because all death cases are in some sense potentially different from all others.[73] *Woodson* therefore prohibited the states from executing a defendant solely because he had violated a general criminal law. The state had to provide some extra ritual or moral scrutiny at which the defendant could show he was different from other people who had violated the same law. To make a moral decision about a defendant is to treat him as a unique being. And the state cannot treat him as unique under a substantive criminal law, since a criminal law is necessarily a generalization about human behavior and moral desert. Of course, the guided discretion statutes approved in *Gregg* enable the sentencer to examine the defendant and his behavior with the help of more precise and subtle rules—the aggravating and mitigating circumstances. But statutory descriptions of behavior, however finely drawn, are still generalizations. A death penalty law must contain intelligible generalizations if the law is to meet Harlan's challenge in *McGautha*. But no generalization can permit the moral sensitivity which the death penalty decision requires—at least on the side of mercy. The Court faced this problem in *Lockett*, and ended by subverting its own efforts at doctrinal generalization.

In *Lockett*, the defendant was convicted of felony murder for her role as the getaway driver in a robbery. The Ohio sentencing judge heard some impressive mitigating evidence. Lockett had neither intended nor physically caused the victim's death; she was only twenty-one, had committed no major crimes before this one, and showed good prospects for rehabilitation.[74] But the Ohio law enumerated only three mitigating circumstances, and the impressive mitigating evidence was relevant to none of them.[75] Thus, despite *Woodson*, though Ohio permitted the sentencer to hear a wide range of evidence, it guided the sentencer's decision with restrictive legal generalizations.

---

[73] Woodson v. North Carolina, 428 U.S. at 303-04 (plurality opinion).

[74] 438 U.S. at 592, 594, 608.

[75] The mitigating evidence did not show that the victim had contributed to his own demise, that the defendant had acted under duress or provocation, or that the crime resulted from the defendant's mental impairment. *Id.* at 607.

The Court could have protected its efforts to create rational doctrinal rules for the death penalty, but only by sacrificing or limiting the moral principle that every defendant is unique and that no legal generalization can capture that uniqueness. While faithful to the legalist rhetoric of *Gregg*, the Court felt imprisoned by the moral demands of *Woodson*. It therefore concluded that the state could not categorically use legal generalizations to constrain the sentencer's power to identify mitigating factors.[76]

The most immediate problem of doctrine-making in *Lockett* is to define "mitigating circumstances." *Lockett* speaks in the double-talk typical of the major capital cases, shifting between hints of bounded rules and rhetoric of broad constitutional norms. The state cannot preclude the sentencer's considering as an independent mitigating factor "any aspect of a defendant's character or record or any of the circumstances of the offense that the defendant proffers as a basis for a sentence less than death."[77] And the state cannot use definitions of mitigation that "create the risk that the death penalty will be imposed in spite of factors which may call for a less severe penalty."[78]

Even if this language restricts "mitigating circumstances" to facts relevant to the particular defendant's character, record, and offense,[79] it does not exclude very much.[80] Beyond obliterating the distinction between status and conduct, *Lockett* may more broadly offer a

---

[76] *Id.* at 604, 608.

[77] *Id.* at 604.

[78] *Id.* at 605; *cf. id.* at 608 (unconstitutional to "preclude consideration of relevant mitigating factors").

[79] The Chief Justice's opinion notes hopefully that the states can continue to apply traditional rules of relevancy to exclude matters not bearing on the defendant's character, record, or offense. *Id.* at 604 n.12.

[80] Judicial attempts to define "mitigation" have proved vapid or circular. *E.g.*, Coker v. Georgia, 433 U.S. 584, 591 (1977); State v. Irwin, 304 N.C. 93, 104, 282 S.E.2d 439, 446-47 (1981). If a mitigating circumstance is any fact the defendant proffers in mitigation, *Lockett* would seem to require admission of any fact about the defendant's character, record, or offense. First, and most obvious, the defendant is not limited to evidence that might reduce his culpability for murder under the substantive criminal law. Eddings v. Oklahoma, 455 U.S. 104, 126 (1982). The penalty trial thus becomes the depository of all the determinist explanations of the defendant's behavior which lie outside the normal rules of insanity, diminished capacity, or provocation. The classic grounds of mitigation are that the defendant was abused or neglected as a child, or is psychologically impaired though not insane, or took drugs or alcohol before the crime. See SOUTHERN POVERTY LAW CENTER, TRIAL OF THE PENALTY PHASE 15 (1981) [hereafter TRIAL OF PENALTY PHASE]. Second, virtually any evidence of redeeming character falls within the "narrow" definition of *Lockett*, even if it arises after the murder for which the defendant is being sentenced. Thus the sentencer must hear that the defendant has shown remorse, State v. Arnett, 125 Ariz. 201, 204, 608 P.2d 778, 781 (1980), or has behaved admirably in prison after the crime, State v. Schad, 129 Ariz. 557, 573, 633 P.2d 366, 382 (1981), or, that the defendant has been born again and has begun a Christian mission from his prison cell, TRIAL OF PENALTY PHASE, *supra*,

normative definition of mitigation, permitting the defendant to introduce any facts peculiar to his case, but not really bearing on his character, record, or offense, which might inspire the sentencer to mercy.[81] And the courts have begun addressing the still broader reading of *Lockett*—that the defendant may introduce any general evidence or arguments against the utility or morality of capital punishment.[82] The penalty trial can become not only a trial of the personality and soul of the defendant but also an adversarial morality play in which the law itself stands trial. *Lockett* seems inherently to subvert any pretenses of doctrine-making.

Assuming that *Lockett* does grant some very broadly defined right to introduce mitigating circumstances, how can we fit it into the competing historical accounts of the Court's struggle to contain the death penalty? The romantic account would seem to have a hard time accommodating *Lockett*. *Lockett* restores a large part of the jury discretion that the Court has purported to restrain. Since the romantic account views *Gregg* as controlling the prosecution case by statutory directive,[83] it faces the problem of asymmetry. Under even the "narrow" view of mitigation, the defense seems far less inhibited in communicating with the sentencer than is the prosecution.

There have been two types of efforts in the commentary to accommodate *Lockett* to the romantic account. One effort is to argue that *Lockett* is really consistent with the romantic account. This effort involves two very questionable rationalizations of *Lockett*. The first

---

at 129-31 (transcript of penalty phase evidence in Georgia v. Lamb). Nor does the state seem to have a conceptually defensible way to exclude mitigating factors which seem trivial, *e.g.*, State v. Arnett, 125 Ariz. 201, 204, 608 P.2d 778, 781 (1980); or which seem morally equivocal, compare Washington v. Watkins, 655 F.2d 1346, 1375 (1981) with *id.* at 1379 (Coleman, J., dissenting). Thus, no legal rule can predict what evidence of character, record, or offense a sentencer might find mitigating. For a thorough discussion of this issue, see Ledewitz, note 66 *supra*, at 136-57.

[81] The defendant can offer evidence that he has a loving family that will suffer terribly if he dies, *e.g.*, Cofield v. State, 247 Ga. 98, 110, 274 S.E. 2d 530, 542 (1981), or that he had an equally culpable accomplice who was offered a plea to a noncapital charge, *e.g.*, Stokes v. State, 403 So.2d 377 (Fla. 1981); State v. Goodman, 298 N.C. 1, 257 S.E.2d 569 (1979). The argument can run still further. One suggested definition of mitigating evidence is evidence which shows that the execution of the particular defendant will not serve any of the legitimate goals of capital punishment. Liebman & Shepard, *Guiding Capital Sentencing Discretion Beyond the Boiler Plate: Mental Disorder as a Mitigating Factor*, 66 GEO. L. J. 757, 810-19 (1978).

[82] Defense lawyers have argued that no sentencer can decide whether death is the appropriate punishment in a particular case unless it knows how executions work, and what social function they serve. See generally TRIAL OF PENALTY PHASE, note 80 *supra*, at 17-20; Gall v. Commonwealth, 607 S.W.2d 97, 112 (Ky. 1980) (psychologist and sociologist testify that death penalty not a deterrent; journalist testifies about 22 gruesome electrocutions he has witnessed).

[83] See note 63 *supra* and accompanying text.

rationalization is that *Lockett* is really quite consistent with a formalist reading of *Gregg*, because it introduces unguided discretion *only* on the side of mitigation. So long as all defendants sentenced to death deserve to die according to state definitions of capital murder and aggravating circumstances, there is nothing unconstitutionally arbitrary about sparing some of those defendants.[84] Some language in *Gregg* supports this view,[85] but that may simply show that the Court was speaking incoherently even before *Lockett*. If we compare two capital defendants and cannot explain according to rules of law why one is sentenced to death and the other not, we have cast doubt on the rule of law. The state might be giving people fair notice of the worst sanction they can suffer for murder, but not very good notice of the sanction they are most likely to suffer. And it will not be treating similarly situated criminals in a similar way under explicable criteria.[86]

The second part of the rationalization is that some asymmetry is inherent in the criminal law. Because we want to throw the risk of erroneous conviction on the state we use asymmetrical doctrines like burden of proof and double jeopardy to favor the defendant.[87] These doctrines do show that the criminal law generally gives the benefit of the doubt to defendants, but the analogy between these guilt-phase doctrines and capital punishment rules is imperfect. *Lockett* seems to show that there is no objective definition of which defendants, at least relative to each other, deserve to die. If so, it is hard to speak of distributing the risk of error in a penalty trial, because it is hard to tell when a death sentence is erroneous.[88]

The doctrine of double jeopardy—specifically the rule that the state can never appeal an acquittal—suggests another basis for asymmetry relevant to capital sentencing. A court cannot reverse a jury acquittal on the ground that the jury committed clear legal error, because the juries may reject or "nullify" the law—though only in favor of the defense. In that sense, *Lockett* is simply a rule of jury nullification, but the analogy is troublesome. Though the history of jury nullification is

---

[84] Hertz & Weisberg, note 62 *supra*, at 374–76; see Goodpaster, *The Trial for Life: Effective Assistance of Counsel in Death Penalty Cases*, 58 N.Y.U. L. REV. 299, 315 (1983).

[85] 428 U.S. at 199 (neither *Furman* nor other cases forbids selective discretion to afford mercy).

[86] Indeed, as David Gillers has said, if the state reduces the jury's sentencing discretion to a narrow pool of the perpetrators of the most serious murders, different sentences for defendants within that pool may seem all the more capricious. Gillers, note 6 *supra*, at 28.

[87] Hertz & Weisberg, note 62 *supra*, at 376.

[88] For a fuller discussion, see notes 158–62 *infra* and accompanying text.

complicated, the law has settled into a clear but paradoxical compromise: A jury has unreviewable power to acquit "in the teeth of the law," but neither the court nor the defense may tell the jury it has that power.[89] Jury nullification is a power, but not a right. It is not a part of the law, but a subversive act tolerated by the law.

If *Lockett* is a rule of jury nullification, it violates that compromise and demonstrates its irrationality. If the defense can urge the capital sentencer to give mercy for almost any reason, it can essentially tell the sentencer that it is permissible to nullify the law. Even if consideration of the legally defined aggravating and mitigating circumstances logically leads to a death sentence, the jury can reject the result. Under *Lockett*, jury nullification is not a secret power tolerated by the law, but a constitutional element of the law.

The other type of effort to fit *Lockett* into the romantic account is quite simply to accept *Lockett* as a flat contradiction of the Court's project in *Gregg*.[90] Under this view, the Court had indeed begun an experiment in imposing rational form on the penalty decision. But there is no point in pretending that *Lockett* is consistent with that experiment. Rather, *Lockett* is the Court's first confession of the failure of that experiment. The Court had put itself between a rock and a hard place. *Furman* demanded horizontal equity among capital murderers, thereby calling for formal rules of law governing their sentences. Similar people and crimes must be treated similarly. But a rule that treats similar people similarly is a categorical generalization which cannot account for uniqueness. A person cannot be both "unique" and "equal." The Court would then have to realize that it has three choices: first, reverse *Lockett* and fully commit itself to very formal rules for the penalty trial; second, return to Justice Harlan's position in *McGautha*, except perhaps for requiring a separate penalty hearing; third, finally declare the entire experiment a failure and end the death penalty forever.[91]

There remains finally the question of accommodating *Lockett* and the classical account. This is not very difficult. The classical account would readily acknowledge that *Lockett* gives the sentencer unguided

---

[89] See United States v. Dougherty, 473 F.2d 1113 (D.C. Cir. 1972). See generally KADISH & KADISH, DISCRETION TO DISOBEY 47-48, 54-55 (1973); Scheflin, *Jury Nullification: The Right to Say No*, 45 S. CAL. L. REV. 168, 169-77 (1972).

[90] Ledewitz, note 66 *supra*, at 156-57; Radin, *Cruel Punishment and Respect for Persons: Super Due Process for Death*, 53 S. CAL. L. REV. 1143, 1148-55 (1980).

[91] Ledewitz, note 66 *supra*, at 156-57; Radin, note 90 *supra*, at 1155, 1180-85.

discretion on the side of mercy, but it would find no disturbing asymmetry there at all, because the Court had never very seriously constrained the penalty decision on the aggravation side anyway. The Georgia statute upheld—if somewhat mischaracterized—in *Gregg* requires the sentencer to "convict" the defendant of the crime of "first-degree murder-plus-one-statutory-aggravating-circumstance."[92] But the sentencer then has discretion to consider any aspect of the defendant's character, record, or offense which calls for the more severe penalty. The Court has never pretended to require anything more than a separate penalty ritual in which the sentencer can decide on the penalty in the light of all relevant information, unconstrained by the evidentiary restraints of the guilt trial.

Lockett may be the Court's failure of nerve in its rebuttal to Justice Harlan, or it may confirm that since 1976 the Court has largely agreed with Justice Harlan.

III. DEATH PENALTY DOCTRINE-MAKING

I have now considered differing accounts of the Court's major cases developing Eighth Amendment doctrine. But the romantic account finds support in the development of less abstract doctrines. Whatever these cases have said or meant, they have induced courts and legislators to participate in an experiment investing the penalty trial with greater rational formality. The "methodology" of the experiment has taken two forms. First, courts and legislatures have adapted the intellectual structure of the substantive criminal law to the penalty trial and created new codes of enhanced murder liability. Second, the courts and legislatures have increasingly shaped the penalty trial with the forms of criminal procedure borrowed from the guilt trial. On both substance and procedure, the Supreme Court has effectively inspired new growth industries in legal doctrine-making, often with ironic results.

A. A NEW PENAL CODE OF AGGRAVATION

As Justice Harlan recognized, the difficulties in reducing the death penalty to the rule of law derive in part from historical difficulties in creating a rational substantive law of homicide.[93] Before *Furman*, the

---

[92] See note 68 *supra.*
[93] See notes 28-29 *supra* and accompanying text.

criminal law relied on two of its least stable categories, premeditation and felony murder,[94] to create a large pool of death-eligible defendants and attempted no further doctrinal regulation of the process of identifying those so culpable that they deserve to die. More specifically, the substantive criminal law has been at once too broad and too narrow to deal with the issues that have proved relevant to capital sentencing. First, the law of homicide focuses only on the fact of the killing and a few general questions about the defendant's state of mind with regard to the killing. It avoids subtler questions about the motives behind the killing and its social consequences. Second, the law of homicide, like the criminal law generally, narrowly focuses on the immediate act and state of mind of the defendant and thus rejects a broad inquiry into the defendant's background and character.[95]

Stimulated by the Supreme Court, the states have created what are in effect new laws of murder for the penalty trial, with aggravating and mitigating circumstances playing the roles of new crimes or elements of crimes and new defenses. These laws address both the broader and narrower questions that the traditional law of homicide avoids, while attempting to reduce the elements of capital culpability to rule-like form for use at the penalty trial. But in breaking out of the conceptual limits of the substantive criminal law, the courts and legislatures have encountered all the problems the substantive criminal law has always faced in trying to maintain rule-bound clarity.[96]

Most of the common aggravating circumstances try to identify special indicia of blameworthiness or dangerousness in the killing. Aside from the almost universal circumstance that the killing was committed in the course of another dangerous felony,[97] which significantly overlaps the felony murder rule, the common ones are that the murder was committed for hire or for pecuniary gain, or for the purpose of avoiding or preventing a lawful arrest or effecting an

---

[94] See FLETCHER, RETHINKING CRIMINAL LAW 253-56, 274-321 (1978); CARDOZO, LAW AND LITERATURE 100 (1931). The Model Penal Code abolishes the premeditation formula and uses the commission of an independent dangerous felony only to create a rebuttable presumption that the defendant acted with extreme recklessness. §210.2 (Official Draft 1962).

[95] As Mark Kelman has argued, the substantive criminal law relies on a few basic "interpretive constructs" that narrow the range of inquiry into the defendant's character and behavior at a criminal trial. Kelman, *Interpretive Construction in the Substantive Criminal Law*, 33 STAN. L. REV. 591 (1981).

[96] On the problems of making rational doctrine for a broad range of mitigating circumstances, see notes 77-82 *supra* and accompanying text.

[97] E.g., Fla. Stat. Ann. §921.141(5) (d) (Suppl. 1983), (enumerating robbery, rape, arson, burglary, kidnapping, aircraft piracy, or use of explosives).

escape from lawful custody, or to disrupt or hinder the lawful exercise of any government function or the enforcement of laws,[98] or to conceal the commission of a crime or the identity of the perpetrator,[99] or that the victim was either a witness to the defendant's independent crime[100] or a law enforcement officer engaged in the performance of his duties.[101]

These circumstances are in one sense the states' main contribution to helping the Supreme Court prove Justice Harlan wrong. On their face, they have the reassuring clarity, precision, and thoroughness of model criminal laws. One might describe them in the aggregate as a model penal code of aggravation. But some of their legal virtues have proved illusory.

This laundry list of enhancing facts may derive from some of the same social impulses that underlie the felony murder rule. Some murders are especially blameworthy for reasons beyond society's terror at the extinction of a life, because they cause or threaten a wider social or legal disruption. People may commit premeditated murder for nonrecurring personal reasons. But murders committed in the course of other serious crimes portend more victims or more crimes, and often provoke responses from victims, bystanders, and police so as to generate a widening circle of violence and disorder.

The courts, however, have had considerable difficulty in discovering or implanting rational act and state-of-mind elements in the circumstance statutes. The difficulties arise in part because the legislatures have done a poor job in keeping these apparently very particularized elements discrete from each other and from grounds for murder liability. In operation, these circumstances often prove to describe the same aspects of the crime in different ways.

The overlap has taken two forms. First, whenever the state wins a murder conviction on a felony murder theory, it thereby benefits from the presence of the independent felony. If it then tries to use the independent felony as an aggravating circumstance, it is effectively double-counting. The irony of this is that it makes felony murder a more heinous crime than premeditated murder, regardless of the felony murderer's state of mind with regard to the killing: unlike the premeditating murderer, every felony murderer will enter the penalty

---

[98] E.g., id. §921.141(5) (e)-(g).
[99] E.g., Neb. Rev. Stat. §29-253(1) (b) (1979).
[100] E.g., Ill. Ann. Stat. ch. 38, §9-1(b) (7) (Smith-Hurd 1979).
[101] E.g., id. §9-1(b) (1).

trial with an automatic aggravating circumstance racked up on the state's side.[102] But it is a second problem of double-counting that exposes the serious interpretational problems with the new doctrine of aggravation. This second type arises wholly within the penalty phase, after the defendant is convicted of a murder that involves an independent felony, whether or not the conviction was grounded in felony murder. Virtually any murder related to another felony entails plausible application of two or more of these new circumstances.[103]

Some courts have simply held it unfair for the state to gain two aggravating circumstances from one aspect of the crime. Where by their language two circumstances apply to the same aspect, the court simply permits the state only one.[104] Other courts, however, have generated intriguing new interpretive doctrines to keep these circumstances distinct. But these doctrines sometimes merely revive some of the most questionable interpretational devices from some of the hoarier issues of the traditional substantive criminal law.[105]

One of the best examples is the overlap between the circumstance that the murder arose from an independent larceny-based felony—robbery or sometimes burglary—and the circumstance that the murder

---

[102] State v. Cherry, 298 N.C. 86, 113, 257 S.E.2d 551, 567 (N.C. 1979). Some courts have vaguely perceived an injustice here, and have struck the circumstance without finding a legal category to explain what they are doing. *E.g.*, Bufford v. State, 382 So.2d 1162, 1173 (Ala. Crim. App. 1980). But see, *e.g.*, State v. Cherry, *supra*, 298 N.C. at 113, 257 S.E.2d at 567-68 (striking circumstance on grounds of common law merger and double jeopardy).

[103] For example, any robber-murderer who kills his robbery victim arguably "commits" not only the circumstance of the independent felony but also murder for pecuniary gain (the property robbed) and murder of witness to a crime (the robbery victim). Where the defendant kills a robbery victim or bystander, he also "commits" murder to conceal the commission of the crime or the identity of the perpetrator (since silencing any witness accomplishes these things). If the victim of the killing, whether he is the victim of the robbery or a bystander, tries to restrain or capture the killer, the murder may also entail murder to avoid lawful arrest or escape from lawful custody as well, and if the victim is a police officer who has come upon the scene, the defendant is arguably liable for all the above circumstances as well as murder of a police officer and murder to hinder the lawful exercise of the enforcement of the laws.

[104] *E.g.*, Provence v. State, 337 So.2d 783 (Fla. 1976).

[105] One common statutory aggravating circumstance, that the defendant "knowingly created a great risk of death to many persons," Model Penal Code §210(6) (3) (d), has served mainly to dredge up one of the most stubborn old conceptual problems in the substantive criminal law, the problem of "attempted recklessness." The traditional doctrine treats all inchoate crimes as intentional. Thus, if a person acts very recklessly, as by throwing a heavy object from a rooftop to a crowded street, but if by luck the reckless act harms no one, the criminal law has found it conceptually impossible to treat this as a crime of attempt. *E.g.*, Merritt v. Commonwealth, 164 Va. 653, 660-61, 180 S.E. 395, 398-99 (1935). Though some legislatures have sensibly created crimes of reckless endangerment, courts have sometimes adopted disingenuous fictions as that "wanton and reckless disregard for human life ... would supply the intent necessary to a conviction of assault with intent to murder." Easley v. State, 49 Ga. App. 275, 175 S.E. 23 (1934). See KADISH, SCHULHOFER, & PAULSEN, CRIMINAL LAW AND ITS PROCESSES 466-70 (4th ed. 1983).

was committed for "pecuniary gain." Several courts have given distinct meaning to the "pecuniary gain" circumstance by holding that it only applies to cases such as murder for hire, or murder to obtain insurance proceeds or inheritances or bequests.[106] The rationale is that in those cases the defendant is "motivated primarily" by the hope for gain.[107] Thus the court treats the circumstance as trying to identify an aggravating "motive" beyond the state of mind inherent in robbery or larceny-based burglary, though those crimes require "intent" to take property of another. The concept of "motive" is not really a term of art in modern criminal law, but courts use it to try to give rational rule-like form to this intuition of an aggravating state of mind. It is not clear why the standard robber-murderer does not have this motive when he intentionally kills the robbery victim or a bystander to ensure that he obtains or escapes with the property he steals. The courts essentially rely on one of the more questionable of interpretive devices in the criminal law, the distinction between "primary" and "secondary" intent.[108] In both the murder for insurance proceeds and the standard intentional robbery murder, the killer would presumably be just as happy to obtain the money without killing, but finds he must kill to get or enjoy the money.[109]

A similar problem arises when a robber kills his robbery victim or a passerby and the state proffers the circumstance that the murder was committed to avoid or prevent unlawful arrest. Some state courts hold this circumstance applies only where the defendant kills an authorized officer engaged in making an arrest, because this circumstance is designed to protect a special class of victims.[110] But if that is its purpose, the circumstance stumbles over another circumstance that often appears in the same state's law—murder of a peace officer in the performance of his duties. One might therefore just as well interpret

---

[106] *E.g.*, State v. Simants, 197 Neb. 549, 567, 250 N.W.2d 881, 891 (Neb. 1977).

[107] *Ibid.*

[108] This distinction arises in the commentary on the wonderfully academic doctrine of "impossible" attempts. The permutations of "legal" and "factual" impossibility are numerous and confusing, but many commentators have offered purportedly bright-line rules by distinguishing levels of intent. The best example is Perkins, *Criminal Attempt and Related Problems*, 2 U.C.L.A. L. REV. 319, 330-32 (1955). Kelman demonstrates how such other important criminal law scholars as LaFave, Scott, and Fletcher also arbitrarily choose broad and narrow views of a person's "primary intent" to distinguish among the various types of impossible attempts. Kelman, note 95 *supra*, at 620-24.

[109] The courts do not handle these subtle distinctions among levels of intent with great sophistication. See, *e.g.*, State v. Oliver, 302 N.C. 28, 274 S.E.2d 183, 204 (1981).

[110] *E.g.*, *Ex parte* Johnson, 399 So.2d 873, 874 (Ala. 1979).

the circumstance as identifying an aggravating motive, not a type of victim.[111] But if so, as some courts have suggested, the circumstance logically applies whenever a robber-murderer shoots a robbery victim or civilian passerby who might have called the police and thereby made an arrest possible.[112]

There is one final irony in these legislative and judicial efforts at capturing the public's concern with socially disruptive violence in rule-like form. The majority of the states, after listing such circumstances, conclude their lists with the infamous aggravating circumstance that the murder was "especially heinous, atrocious, or cruel." Having attempted rule-like formality, these statutes then undermine their efforts with this paradigmatic anti-rule-like moral standard. On the authority of *Godfrey v. Georgia*,[113] the state courts must then haplessly try to restore the principle of legality by developing a common law of rule-like indicia to give shape to this remarkable provision.[114]

In creating these new criminal laws, the courts and legislators are essentially looking for sources of law to fill the gap of lawlessness exposed by *Furman*. Their major source has been the pool of doctrinal forms in the substantive criminal law. In that sense, they have tried to

---

[111] One state court has taken this view, but to the state's benefit. The defendant killed two policemen who were investigating a disturbance he was involved in. The state offered two aggravating circumstances—the murder was committed for avoiding a lawful arrest and the victim was a police officer engaged in the performance of his duties. The court upheld both circumstances as independent, because the former looked to the defendant's "subjective motivation," while the latter looked to the "underlying factual basis . . . of the crime." State v. Hutchins, 303 N.C. 321, 355, 279 S.E.2d 788, 809 (1981).

[112] Some courts have inclined toward this view, but have tried to avoid applying the circumstance to all killings of people who witness crimes. They permit application of the circumstance where the victim is a civilian witness to the crime, but require some specific proof that the defendant was thinking of the risk of identification or arrest when he pulled the trigger. Riley v. State, 366 So.2d 19, 22 (Fla. 1979); Menendez v. State, 368 So.2d 1278, 1282 (Fla. 1979); Demps v. State, 395 So.2d 501, 506 (Fla. 1981). On the interpretive device of shifting between broad and narrow views of the criminal transaction, see Kelman, note 95 *supra*, at 616-18, 633-40.

[113] 446 U.S. 420 (1980) (plurality opinion) (state courts must narrowly construe "heinousness" circumstance to draw rational distinctions among levels of depravity in murder).

[114] Florida has tried harder than many states. The Florida Supreme Court has held that the "heinous, atrocious, and cruel" circumstance requires that the "horror of the murder is 'accompanied by such additional acts as to set the crime apart from the norm.'" Copper v. State, 336 So.2d 1133, 1141 (Fla. 1976). It has attempted to carry out this nebulous standard by requiring proof that the killing was "unnecessarily torturous to the victim." State v. Dixon, 283 So.2d 1, 9 (Fla. 1973). Compare, *e.g.*, Welty v. State, 402 So.2d 1159 (Fla. 1981), with *e.g.*, Kampff v. State, 371 So.2d 1007 (Fla. 1979), and Halliwell v. State, 323 So.2d 557 (Fla. 1975). The circumstance does not apply simply because the killing was "premeditated, cold, and calculated," Lewis v. State, 398 So.2d 432, 438 (Fla. 1981), or because the defendant killed the victim in the presence of the victim's family, Riley v. State, 366 So.2d 19, 21 (Fla. 1978).

overcome the somewhat illogical separation of liability law and sentencing policy. The ironic result has been that death penalty laws have been as much infected as enriched by substantive criminal law doctrine.

The difficulties with this effort at integration from the opposite perspective are demonstrated in the important case of *Enmund v. Florida*, where the Supreme Court partly barred the states from using the felony murder rule as a basis for capital punishment.[115] In *Enmund*, the Court discovered that any effort at designing a rational law of capital punishment may founder on the doctrinal confusion of substantive homicide law.[116] Under the rubric of "proportionality," the Court tried to use its Eighth Amendment powers to prod some reform in state homicide law.[117] Struck by the incoherence of the felony murder rule,[118] the Court tries to draw a bright rational line through homicide doctrine to determine the minimally culpable kind of murder that can merit the death penalty. The Court fails miserably at this task, getting entangled in, rather than reforming, the hierarchies of blameworthiness.[119] Further, *Enmund* invites, indeed requires, the states to participate in the rulemaking at which it has proved so hapless,

---

[115] 102 S. Ct. 3368 (1982). On the felony murder rule, see generally LaFave & Scott, Handbook on Criminal Law 545-61 (1972).

[116] The defendant in *Enmund* was the classic felony murder wheelman. Apparently, though he had agreed to keep the getaway car running while his cohorts perpetrated a robbery, he neither agreed nor had reason to foresee that the cohorts would shoot the victims. But he was "constructively present aiding and abetting the commission of the robbery" resulting in death. 102 S. Ct. at 3371 (quoting Enmund v. State, 399 So.2d 1362, 1370 (Fla. 1981)).

[117] The Court holds that execution of a defendant with no greater culpability than Enmund's is cruel and unusual punishment because it is disproportionate to the severity of his crime. There was not much constitutional law on which to hang this judgment. Compare 102 S. Ct. 3375, 3378-79 with *id.* at 3388-89 (O'Connor, J., dissenting).

[118] Felony murder works as a conclusive presumption that participating in a felony entails highly blameworthy risk taking about death. Like all conclusive presumptions, it gives the state a readily administerable rule at the cost of ignoring significant nuances of conduct and state of mind. It catches within the net of capital murder people who at worst may have been mildly careless about the remote possibility that someone might get killed. The Court thus holds that execution of this least culpable type of murderer serves neither general deterrence nor retribution. 102 S. Ct. at 3378.

[119] There are at least three ways to read *Enmund*, and a lower court's choice depends entirely on its view of fundamental criminal law questions which are exposed but unanswered by *Enmund*. First, the case may hold that it is unconstitutional to execute a criminal who is no more culpable than Enmund was. The felony murder rule in Florida had freed the state from proving *anything* specific about Enmund's own state of mind with respect to the killings. Thus, a state might satisfy *Enmund* simply by showing that the defendant personally exhibited *some* culpable mental state, even mere negligence, so long as it does not draw any automatic inferences from the defendant's participation in the felony. The Court, however, suggests a broader reading in the way it explicitly frames the question on appeal: whether the death penalty is permissible "for one who did not kill or attempt to kill, and did not intend the death of the victim." 102 S. Ct. at 3376. Under this reading, the death sentence is legal so long as the defendant *either* performed the

and within one year has inspired a minigrowth industry of state doctrinal reform of homicidal mens rea.[120] The Court may soon recognize the perils of attempting to make rational rules for murder.

B. TRIALS WITHIN TRIALS WITHIN TRIALS

The new death penalty laws encounter other difficulties when they examine the broader questions about the defendant's background and character that the traditional law of homicide ignores. The new laws of aggravation and mitigation make the defendant's whole career and soul the subject of the penalty trial. The unbounded inquiry into the defendant's life is more obvious on the side of mitigation: the common statutory mitigating circumstances are essentially expansions of the determinist defenses sharply limited at the guilt trial.[121] But the innovation of the penalty trial is more striking on the side of aggravation. Like the court deciding on prison terms and probation, the sentencer in the penalty trial can consider evidence of the defendant's background and record. But because the courts have attempted to invest the sentencer's consideration of aggravating evidence with the dignity of legal formality, the penalty trial has taken on doctrinal complexity wholly foreign to noncapital sentencing.

The state chiefly benefits from this freedom of inquiry by introducing as an aggravating circumstance the defendant's "priors," often earlier capital crimes or violent felonies, to argue for his execution. Traditionally, the evidence rules for criminal trials forbid

---

physical act of killing or abetted the criminal transaction with the intent that life be taken. The classic single felony murderer, who kills carelessly but unintentionally in perpetrating an independent felony, could still be put to death. But the amazingly careless language of the opinion explicitly suggests a broader reading still. In its effort to find the level of moral blameworthiness proportional to the death penalty, the Court indicates several times that only intentional killers can merit execution. Indeed, in trying to identify the type of killer whose execution might serve general deterrence, the Court even suggests "deliberation and premeditation" as the minimum state of mind for capital murder. 102 S. Ct. at 3377 (citing Fisher v. United States, 328 U.S. 463, 484 (1946) (Frankfurter, J., dissenting)). If so, the Court has banned capital punishment whenever conviction rests on felony-murder grounds, for triggermen and wheelmen alike.

[120] See, *e.g.*, Johnson v. Zant, 249 Ga. 812, 816-17 (1982); *Ex parte* Raines, 429 So.2d 1111 (Ala. 1982). The state courts have struggled to identify an elusive category of "active involvement" in the felonious acts for nontriggermen who did not clearly intend death to occur.

[121] Thus, the death penalty offers residual versions of the doctrines of provocation and diminished capacity, and the defenses of duress, justification, imperfect self-defense, and insanity. The Model Penal Code is representative. See §210.6(4) (Official Draft 1962). While the substantive criminal law generally forbids evidence of the defendant's postcrime conduct to relieve him of liability, see Kelman, note 95 *supra*, at 611-14, under statutory law and *Lockett*, the penalty trial expands forward from the moment of the crime to consider the defendant's conduct or remorseful attitude that may partly redeem, if not explain, the murder.

the state to introduce the defendant's earlier crimes.[122] The criminal law thus purports to assume that we cannot predict actions from past actions, and that character and action are separate things. Yet as if to concede that these principles are dubious, the law offers some generous exceptions.[123] Most important, the court itself can consider any earlier actions of the defendant in conventional discretionary sentencing, where it determines the actual consequences of his criminal liability. Perhaps fearful that issues of character cannot be reduced to legal rules, we allow character evidence in the one phase of the trial we have largely released from the constraints of legal rules.

The capital punishment laws give the sentencer the same information that the noncapital sentencing judge receives in a probation report. But now the criminal record becomes the subject of the adversarial penalty phase: The capital defendant faces a "trial" of the new "crime" of having previously committed violent crimes. As a result, state courts have had to create new substantive and procedural doctrines, erratically trying to constrain the state's effort to use this new trial form to lay out a raw narrative of aggravating facts.[124]

A few states have chosen the apparently informal approach of permitting evidence of previous crimes of which the defendant was never convicted.[125] In order to pay fealty to constitutional principles of legality, these states generally require the state to prove the old crime to the new penalty jury beyond a reasonable doubt.[126] The law thus redeems the informality of the substance of the aggravating circumstance with the formality of a trial. But the defendant hardly benefits from this quasi-constitutional right to a fair trial on the unadjudicated old crime, because the jury for this new minitrial will have a hard time being impartial, having already convicted the defendant of capital murder.[127] In a normal guilt trial of the old crime,

---

[122] See MCCORMICK'S HANDBOOK OF THE LAW OF EVIDENCE (Cleary ed. 1972), §190, at 447.

[123] The state can introduce other crimes for which the defendant is not on trial if they are closely enough connected to the immediate crime to help prove he did it. And the defendant's general character becomes fair game when he "puts it in issue" by offering good character evidence or by testifying and thereby implicitly asserting his honesty. *Id.* at 447–59.

[124] Formal rules permitting priors as aggravating circumstances somewhat resemble habitual offender or recidivist statutes, which subject a defendant to an enhanced statutory sentence upon the conviction for a particular crime if the state can simultaneously prove that the defendant had previously been convicted of other similar or serious crimes. See generally RUBIN, LAW OF CRIMINAL CORRECTION 453 (2d ed. 1973). The Supreme Court has sustained such statutes against various constitutional challenges. See, *e.g.,* Spencer v. Texas, 385 U.S. 554, 560, 565–69 (1967).

[125] *E.g.,* Ark. Crim. Code §41-1303(3) (1977); Cal. Pen. Code §190.3(b) (1983).

[126] *E.g.,* People v. Haskett, 30 Cal.3d 841, 640 P.2d 776 (1982).

[127] For this reason, two state courts have struck down provisions of their states' death penalty

the state could never strengthen its case by offering proof of the capital crime.[128]

Even where the statute purports to reduce the narrative of violence to the cold formality of a conviction record, the state wants to exploit the more dramatic form of the "minitrial" on the old crime. The problem results from the uncertain relationship between a violent deed and a formally defined crime of violence. Some state courts have tried to exclude from the category of "violent crimes" those which do not contain violent acts or threats as an element of the crime and which, as a practical matter, rarely involve harm to a person.[129] But the state courts have confronted an intermediate class of crimes, such as burglary or arson, which do not include violence to the person as an essential legal element, but which some criminals nevertheless commit in a manner involving physical violence. Defendants have argued that the aggravating circumstance provision of "prior felonies involving the use or threat of violence to the person" must be construed with rule-like rigor, including only those felonies that are inherently violent as a legal matter. The defense claim here is ironically reminiscent of the rather elusive doctrine of second-degree felony murder, which permits the state to use only felonies which are "inherently dangerous in the abstract."[130] The "abstractness" rule ignores the particular danger to life with which a person commits a felony to preserve the distinct rule-like form of the felony murder doctrine.[131] The rule-like form has not fared so well in the penalty trial, where some state courts now permit the state to hold a minitrial of the old crime to prove that the capital defendant had committed the earlier crime in a particularly violent way.[132]

---

laws allowing introduction of unadjudicated earlier crimes. State v. McCormick, 397 N.E.2d 276, 280-81 (Ind. 1979); State v. Bartholomew, 654 P.2d 1170, 1184 (Wash. 1982).

[128] State v. McCormick, 397 N.E.2d 276, 280-81 (Ind. 1979). Even where the statute requires proof that the defendant has been convicted for the earlier crimes, the states have taken an expansive view of what constitutes an earlier crime. See, *e.g.*, Jones v. State, 381 So.2d 983, 994 (Miss. 1980) (permitting use of conviction obtained before capital trial for crime committed after capital crime).

[129] *E.g.*, State v. Gill, 273 S.C. 190, 192-93, 255 S.E.2d 455, 457 (S.C. 1979) (statutory rape); Lewis v. State, 398 So.2d 432 (Fla. 1981) (breaking and entering, escape, grand larceny, possession of firearm by felon not inherently dangerous).

[130] *E.g.*, People v. Phillips, 64 Cal.2d 574, 414 P.2d 353, 51 Cal. Rptr. 225 (1966) (grand larceny not dangerous to life in abstract); People v. Satchell, 6 Cal.3d 28, 489 P.2d 1361, 98 Cal. Rptr. 33 (1971) (carrying concealed weapon by ex-felon not dangerous).

[131] FLETCHER, note 94 *supra*, at 295.

[132] State v. McDougall, 308 N.C. 1, ___ , 301 S.E.2d 308, 318-19 (N.C. 1983); State v. Moore, 614 S.W.2d 348, 351 (Tenn. 1981).

On the other hand, crimes such as rape and armed robbery include violence to the person as an essential legal element, so the state need not demonstrate the particular violence with which the defendant committed the old crime. But rather than rely on the cold formality of the conviction record, the state nevertheless tries to exploit the dramatic form of the minitrial to impress the sentencer with the colorful underlying facts of the old conviction. The defendant frequently tries to "plea-bargain" his way out of this minitrial by stipulating to the conviction for the old violent crime. But some state courts have permitted the state to hold the minitrial anyway, partly for the ironic reason that the minitrial requires the state to prove the aggravating circumstance beyond a reasonable doubt. But in an infinite regress of the penalty trial, they also permit the defendant to put on evidence specifically mitigating the old crime.[133] The penalty trial then contains a mini-guilt trial which contains elements of a mini-penalty trial.[134]

C. DUE PROCESS DETAILS FOR THE PENALTY TRIAL

The "growth industry" in procedural doctrine has imposed on the penalty trial the constitutional due process model of the guilt trial. The Burger Court itself has been active in designing the penalty trial, reaching back to borrow from the Fifth and Sixth Amendment criminal procedure doctrines generated by the Warren Court. The list of defense victories on this score has been impressive. Since *Gregg*, the capital defendant has gained, among other things, a confrontation right to rebut state evidence,[135] a compulsory process right to introduce favorable penalty phase testimony regardless of the constraints of state evidence law,[136] application of the privilege against self-incrimination to evidence used only in the penalty trial,[137] and a right to preclude double jeopardy where the defendant has won a "life sentence" verdict.[138] As of the 1982 Term, the courts were still addressing other

---

[133] Elledge v. State, 346 So.2d 998, 1001 (Fla. 1977); State v. Taylor, 304 N.C. 249, 278-79, 283 S.E. 761, 780 (1981). Sometimes, it is the defendant who requests the minitrial. See, *e.g.*, State v. Hamlette, 302 N.C. 490, 276 S.E.2d 338, 347 (1981).

[134] Some courts have tried to put an end to this by creating nebulous doctrine about the trial judge's authority to "ban unduly repetitious and argumentative questions," or to bar "inquiry into matters of tenuous relevance." State v. McDougall, 301 S.E.2d at 321. See also State v. Taylor, 304 N.C. 249, 283 S.E.2d 761, 780 (1981).

[135] Gardner v. Florida, 430 U.S. 349 (1977).

[136] Green v. Georgia, 442 U.S. 95 (1979) (*per curiam*).

[137] Estelle v. Smith, 451 U.S. 454 (1981).

[138] Bullington v. Missouri, 451 U.S. 430 (1981).

important procedural issues, including the right to a jury at the penalty trial, the right to a reasonable-doubt instruction, and the right to effective penalty trial counsel.[139]

In examining the new procedural doctrine of the penalty trial, I am less concerned with specific issues than with the doctrinal rhetoric the courts have used in adapting procedural rights originating in the guilt phase to the very different matter of penalty: the penalty trial is both a very compelling and a very inapposite place to apply rights of criminal procedure.[140]

In *Gardner v. Florida*, the penalty trial judge had reviewed a presentence report on the defendant, but the defense was never allowed to see the whole report or to contest its accuracy.[141] The State offered a "practical" argument: keeping the report secret encouraged otherwise hesitant social workers and probation officers to provide the court full and sensitive information.[142] The defendant had the counterargument that keeping the report secret might increase the quantity of the information at the cost of its quality and truth.[143] In addition, of course, the defendant had the intuitive argument that keeping the information from him was simply unfair. But the key issue in *Gardner*, as in all the procedural cases, is one of characterization.

The State's case essentially came down to the argument that trial-type due process is inapposite to sentencing because sentencing is different from a trial. The defendant thus had to persuade the Court that death penalty sentencing, at least, really is like a trial. In holding for Gardner, the plurality used what has become a sort of rhetorical formula for procedural death penalty doctrine. It cited *Gregg* and *Furman* for the principle that death is different from other punishments,[144] and said that in earlier cases the Court had recognized that trial-type rights may apply at sentencing.[145] In short, the defendant won the battle of characterization by invoking a developing common law of characterization.

---

[139] See notes 160, 161, 224 *infra*.

[140] In this sense, the penalty trial resembles juvenile dependency or delinquency proceedings, where due process is an attractive but in some sense misplaced concept. See Katz & Teitelbaum, *PINS Jurisdiction, the Vagueness Doctrine, and The Rule of Law*, 53 IND. L. J. 1 (1977).

[141] 430 U.S. 349, 352-53 (1977) (plurality opinion).

[142] *Id.* at 358-59. The state also argued that disclosing the report would unduly delay the penalty decision and that full disclosure of presentence reports generally disrupts rehabilitation. Neither argument was very persuasive in a death penalty case. *Id.* at 359-60.

[143] *Id.* at 359.

[144] *Id.* at 357.

[145] *Id.* at 358 (citing Mempa v. Rhay, 389 U.S. 128 (1967); Specht v. Patterson, 386 U.S. 605 (1967)).

Predictably, the court carefully denied any implication that the "entire panoply" of criminal procedure rights applies to the penalty trial.[146] But it is very hard for the Court to stop the momentum of characterization that it enhanced by its holding. In future cases, the defense could cite *Gardner* for the proposition that because death is different, the Court has increasingly recognized that trial-type due process applies to the penalty decision.[147]

Justice White recognizes this problem and tries to solve it with a different strategy of characterization: *Gardner's* right to see the report derives not from the Due Process Clause, but from the Eighth Amendment requirement of "reliability" and full consideration of the character and record of the individual offender in the penalty trial.[148] Thus if we do not call it a due process case, we reduce the risk of implicating the "entire panoply" of due process rights. The irony of Justice White's solution, however, is that on such other issues as the right to a jury and the right to a reasonable doubt instruction at the penalty trial, the Eighth Amendment rhetoric has if anything strengthened defense arguments for trial-type rights which would otherwise seem inapposite to sentencing.[149] Precisely when the state argues that sentencing is different from trial, the defense can cite the Eighth Amendment for the principle that the unique nature of the death penalty decision—distinguishing it from both the guilt trial and noncapital sentencing—enhances the need for procedural fairness.[150]

Perhaps the most revealing case for death penalty procedure doctrine is *Bullington v. Missouri*, in which the jury convicted the defendant of capital murder, but, under the relatively formal procedure of the Missouri penalty trial, fixed the punishment at life rather than death.[151] Bullington then won a new trial on the murder charge after proving improper jury selection, and the question was whether the double jeopardy clause permitted the state to seek the death penalty again if it won a second conviction.[152]

---

[146] 430 U.S. at 358 n.9.

[147] See, *e.g.*, Estelle v. Smith, 451 U.S. 454, 463 (1981); Bullington v. Missouri, 451 U.S. 430, 446 (1981). *Cf.* Brown v. Wainwright, 392 So.2d 1327 (Fla. 1981).

[148] 430 U.S. at 362-64 (White, J., concurring in the judgment, quoting Woodson v. North Carolina, 428 U.S. 280, 304-05 (1976)).

[149] See notes 160-61 *infra*.

[150] See Beck v. Alabama, 447 U.S. 625, 637-38 (1980) (capital defendant's unique right to lesser-included-offense instruction.

[151] 451 U.S. 430, 431-35.

[152] *Id.* at 435-37.

The Court had long before held very clearly that if a defendant who was convicted and then sentenced to life imprisonment won reversal of his conviction, the state could seek the death penalty again in the retrial.[153] The Court distinguished that old case because it involved a unitary trial in which the sentencer had full discretion to choose sentence, wholly unguided by legislative standards.[154] By contrast, the penalty phase under contemporary Missouri law is a separate trial-type proceeding in which the State must prove certain legislatively defined aggravating facts, and the jury must follow statutory rules in considering the evidence.

The Court also distinguished the death penalty trial from noncapital sentencing. Normally, the Fifth Amendment bars the state from seeking retrial on a criminal charge where the jury or judge in the first trial has shown by acquittal that the state has "failed to prove its case."[155] This rule cannot apply in noncapital discretionary sentencing to bar the state from seeking a longer prison term after a second conviction; given the court's discretion to choose from a wide range of sentences, there is no definable "case" for the state to prove.[156] The formal penalty trial does resemble a guilt determination, however, and the substantive standards governing the penalty jury do, in effect, require the state to "prove its case" for death. The jury's choice between life and death at the penalty trial thus resembles the choice between innocence and guilt more than a choice from a range of noncapital sentences.

Technically, *Bullington* did not require the states to impose trial-type controls on the penalty phase. One can read it narrowly to hold that where a state has chosen trial-type formalities, like the reasonable-doubt requirement in the Missouri statute, it must accept the consequences of the trial model—including double jeopardy. Could a state then avoid *Bullington* by repealing its statute's trial-type formalities? The difficulty is that despite this technically plausible reading, *Bullington* adds to the momentum of the due process characterization. If after *Bullington* a state did try to remove formal controls on the sentencer, the defense could readily cite *Bullington* for the view that "the Court has increasingly recognized that the penalty phase resembles a trial to which due process principles apply. . . ."[157]

---

[153] Stroud v. United States, 251 U.S. 15 (1919) (defendant was the "Birdman of Alcatraz").

[154] 451 U.S. at 439.

[155] Burks v. United States, 437 U.S. 1 (1978).

[156] 451 U.S. at 442-44; see North Carolina v. Pearce, 395 U.S. 711 (1969).

[157] 451 U.S. at 444-46.

Justice Powell's dissent in *Bullington* goes to the heart of the doctrinal problem. He attacks the conceptual analogy that by giving the defendant a life sentence the first penalty jury "acquitted" him of the death penalty. Powell recognizes two grounds for the double jeopardy rule barring retrial after acquittal: to spare the defendant expense and anxiety, and to avoid the risk of error in the second trial. Powell quickly dismisses the first,[158] because his view of the second ground captures the chief weakness of the trial analogy. A guilt trial, he says, aims to determine objective facts. The first trial might be right, and the second wrong. But we cannot speak coherently of risk of error in a penalty trial, because whether the defendant deserves to die is not an objective factual question.[159] A death sentence in the second penalty trial may be just as "correct" as a life sentence in the first. If made with proper moral seriousness, both judgments are correct at the moment they are made. Powell believes the Court has been seduced by a metaphor, and wants to prove the metaphor inapt by emphasizing the subjectivity of the death decision. But once the Court has invested in the trial metaphor, it has made it very hard for the state in future cases to offer arguments based on the practical differences between guilt and sentencing decisions. The rhetoric of defense argument on such unresolved procedural issues as the right to a reasonable-doubt instruction[160] and the right to jury sentencing[161] provides ample

[158] *Id.* at 448-51 (Powell, J., dissenting).

[159] *Id.* at 450-51.

[160] Though many states have imposed some sort of requirement that the state prove its case for the death penalty beyond a reasonable doubt, defendants frequently request reasonable-doubt instructions on constitutional grounds. The reasonable doubt standard can be applied not only to the ultimate question whether the defendant should die, but also to the purportedly formal intermediate questions juries must ask in some states, *e.g.*, whether aggravating circumstances outweigh mitigating circumstances, or whether aggravating circumstances by themselves are sufficiently substantial to warrant death. See note 9 *supra*. The arguments on this issue are predictable enough. The defense argues that the Fifth Amendment requires proof of guilt beyond a reasonable doubt, and, of course, that the Court has increasingly recognized the similarity between the penalty trial and the guilt trial. Even if the direct analogy to a criminal trial does not hold, the defendant can rely on the flexible due process balancing principle, which adjusts the standard of proof in a proceeding according to the relative weights of the state and individual interests. Addington v. Texas, 441 U.S. 418 (1979) (civil commitment). On the other hand, if the death penalty decision is of much greater moral gravity than noncapital decisions, the Eighth Amendment itself may require the highest possible standard of proof to ensure greater "reliability" and to prevent arbitrary decisions. Woodson v. North Carolina, 428 U.S. 280, 305 (1976). The state has no very specific affirmative arguments for a lower standard of proof. Rather, it must argue that the whole concept of standard of proof is designed to distribute the risk of factual error, and is therefore inapposite to the penalty trial, which does not involve objective questions of fact.

[161] Without specific constitutional requirement, states have imposed on the penalty trial many of the formal elements of the criminal guilt trial. The Supreme Court, partly relying on the trial model created by the states, has increasingly recognized the similarity between the modern

illustration. The death decision is like the guilt decision, precisely because the metaphor says so.[162]

IV. THE NEW DEREGULATION OF THE PENALTY TRIAL

In its quartet of death penalty decisions handed down at the end of the 1982 Term, the Court largely refuted the romantic account of its efforts at death penalty doctrine-making. Two of the quartet, *Barefoot v. Estelle* and *California v. Ramos,* are relatively accessible decisions and are likely to receive the most public notice. They merit brief summary here as background for the complex and obscure decisions in *Zant v. Stephens* and *Barclay v. Florida.*

Barefoot very explicitly declares the overtly political theme of the Term: the federal courts are to sharply reverse their use of the habeas corpus jurisdiction in death penalty cases. Specifically, *Barefoot* holds that the federal circuit courts need not protract death penalty cases by granting stays or giving full-merits treatment to a capital defendant who appeals a district court's denial of federal habeas corpus.[163] It thereby puts a bizarre twist on the rhetorical trope that "death is different" from all other sanctions, though the new rhetorical maneuver in fact very nicely summarizes the Court's new position: capital defendants ritually argue that death is different because denial of a stay pending full consideration of a capital appeal rather obviously

---

penalty decision and a criminal trial. The right to a trial by jury follows almost ineluctably from this sequence of characterization. And see Gregg v. Georgia, 428 U.S. at 173.

[162] Ironically, the subjectivity of the death decision might make it easier to argue a due process claim in a penalty trial than in a guilt trial. Precisely because there is no coherent concept of "error" in the penalty trial, the state cannot logically rely on an argument that often supports the denial of a due process claim in the guilt trial—that the procedural right at issue is not necessary to reduce the risk of error in fact-finding. *E.g.,* United States v. Ash, 413 U.S. 300 (1973) (no right to counsel at pretrial photographic display).

[163] *Barefoot* says that when a capital petitioner presents a nonfrivolous federal claim in appealing a district court denial of habeas corpus, the circuit court need not grant a stay of execution in order to decide the appeal according to its full briefing and argument procedures. 103 S. Ct. 3383. It can summarily decide the appeal at the moment it considers and denies a defendant's request for a stay of execution, so long as in the summary procedure the circuit court addresses the merits of the federal claim and permits the petitioner some notice and opportunity for argument. In Barefoot's case, the circuit court had addressed the merits of the petitioner's substantive claim when it rejected his request for a stay, on the ground that there was no likelihood he could prevail on the merits. The Supreme Court decided that the Court of Appeals' only procedural error was the trivial one of failing to state explicitly that it was affirming the District Court's judgment. *Id.* at 3392-93. The Court advised the circuits to devise local procedures for summarily deciding the merits of death penalty appeals on motions for stay of execution. *Id.* at 3393-95. Normally, when a District Court believes that a rejected claim is "nonfrivolous," it will issue a "certificate of probable cause." *Ibid.* If it does not issue the certificate, the Court of Appeals need not even meet the modest requirements of *Barefoot.*

may moot the petitioner along with the appeal. In the Court's view, death is a unique sanction because the state rather obviously cannot begin to exercise its right to carry out the sentence while the petitioner is litigating the appeal.[164] So because death is different, capital petitioners have less time, not more time, to plead their appeals.

Barefoot also decided a substantive issue. The Court held that the state may introduce expert psychiatric testimony that the defendant is likely to commit acts of criminal violence in the future if he is not executed.[165] The defense had argued that because expert predictions of violence are demonstrably unreliable, such evidence distorts the penalty trial by inducing the jury to engage in unfounded speculation.[166] In rejecting the claim, the Court sounded the second, more subtle theme of the 1982 Term: the federal courts will no longer regulate what a penalty jury hears, except to approve the procedures by which the jury gets to hear as much as possible.

Ramos sounds this second theme as well, in upholding a unique element of the California death penalty statute. The so-called Briggs instruction requires the penalty trial judge to tell the jury that "life without possibility of parole"—the only alternative to death at the penalty trial—does not mean exactly what it says, because the governor can commute an "LWOP" sentence to life with the possibility of parole.[167] Ramos claimed that the Briggs instruction was unfair and misleading.[168] He also argued that, like the psychiatric testimony in

---

[164] *Id.* at 3391.

[165] Essentially, the Texas death penalty statute in *Barefoot* asks the penalty jury whether "there is a probability that the defendant would commit criminal acts of violence that would constitute a continuing threat to society." Tex. Code. Crim. Proc. Ann. §37.071(b) (2) (Vernon 1981). In *Jurek* the Court had held that the infamous question number two in the Texas scheme did not introduce an impermissibly speculative factor into the penalty decision. Jurek v. Texas, 428 U.S. 262, 274-76 (1976) (plurality opinion). In Estelle v. Smith, however, the Court held, without addressing the general question of psychiatric testimony, that the defendant had a right to counsel and *Miranda* warnings before a state psychiatrist could examine him in preparing to answer question number two at the penalty trial. 451 U.S. 454 (1981).

[166] 103 S. Ct. at 3395-96.

[167] California v. Ramos, 103 S. Ct. 3446. The mere fact that the Court voted to hear *Ramos* illustrates its overtly political agenda. There is something gratuitous about the Court's taking a case where a state court has benefited capital defendants by striking down a unique state statute, especially when twenty-five of the twenty-eight other state courts that have addressed the issue have condemned jury instructions mentioning the possibility of commutation or parole. Since no state would have been found to follow California, Justice Stevens, in angry dissent, suggests that the only reason for granting certiorari in *Ramos* was to speed up executions in America. *Id.* at 3468 (Stevens, J., dissenting).

[168] Under California law, the trial judge does not tell the jury that the governor can also commute a death sentence. Ramos therefore argued that the Briggs instruction misled the jury into thinking that a death sentence, unlike life without parole, would ensure that the defendant would never reenter society.

Barefoot, the commutation issue raised irrelevant and speculative questions about the defendant's future that "deflect" the penalty jury from its central task of considering the defendant's character, record, and offense.[169] In rejecting these claims, the Court explains that the penalty trial is not an exercise in objective fact-finding, so there is no determinate "central task" from which the jury might be deflected.[170] The Court thereby forthrightly announced that it wants to reverse its ambivalent, decade-long commitment to the metaphoric bond between the penalty trial and a real trial.[171]

A. ZANT, BARCLAY, AND THE UNDOING OF DOCTRINE

If *Barefoot* and *Ramos* announce that the courts should stop regulating the penalty trial as if it were a guilt trial, *Zant* and *Barclay* attempt to dismantle the entire doctrinal basis for the trial metaphor.

In both cases, the trial court in the penalty phase had improperly admitted certain aggravating evidence under the rubric of a statutory aggravating circumstance, and in both cases the state appellate court nevertheless refused to vacate the death sentence and remand the case to the jury for a new and errorless penalty trial. At least in a general sense, *Zant* and *Barclay* simply presented the Court with yet one more of the procedural issues in the line of the *Gardner* and *Bullington* cases—in this instance, the issue of harmless error.[172]

Though the Court seems reluctant to treat the issues in those terms, the concept of harmless error helps explain why these cases prove such effective instruments for the Court's drastic reversal of penalty trial

---

[169] The problem of relevancy and deflection may arise in a guilt trial where the "central task" is proving the factual elements of the crime. See Beck v. Alabama, 447 U.S. 625 (1980) (absence of lesser-included-offense instruction distorts decision on murder liability).

[170] 103 S. Ct. at 3455. There is only the general concern that the penalty be tailored to the individual defendant and the offense. This amorphous concern invites consideration of "myriad," indeed "countless" factors. *Id.* at 3456-57. Where anything can be a factor, no factor is irrelevant or overly speculative. *Barefoot* and *Ramos* thus confirm the "classical" reading of Lockett v. Ohio.

[171] In deregulating the penalty trial, the Court thus has rehabilitated the state law that has been a persistent anomaly in the Court's earlier purported effort at regulation. See Black, *Due Process for Death: Jurek v. Texas and Companion Cases,* 26 CATH. L. REV. 1, 13-16 (1976), Hertz & Weisberg, note 62 *supra,* at 332-41.

[172] It is a bit misleading to speak so generally about harmless error, since harmless error doctrine varies according to the nature of the error. In *Zant,* the error is technically one of federal constitutional law, at least if we accept the Georgia Supreme Court's view of the invalid aggravating circumstance, see note 178 *infra,* while in *Barclay* the error seems clearly one of state law.

doctrine-making. It also helps explain why *Zant* and *Barclay*, while politically transparent, are doctrinally almost incomprehensible.

The question of harmless error in a penalty trial underscores the difficulties of conceiving the penalty trial within traditional legal categories. If Justice Powell was right in *Bullington*, and if we cannot speak sensibly of a death penalty decision being "correct" or "incorrect," then it seems intuitively wrong to speak of "error" in the penalty trial in the first place. But that view would seem to prove too much, at least once the Court has committed itself to the trial metaphor.

If the penalty phase is indeed a trial, the defendant deserves at least as much protection as he receives under the guilt-phase harmless error doctrine of *Chapman v. California*.[173] Moreover, the presumption that a legal error—at least a constitutional error—has tainted the trial decision should be even greater in the penalty trial, since the "back-up" Eighth Amendment doctrine demands the greatest possible "reliability" when the defendant's life is at stake. On the other hand, even if *Ramos* correctly disjoins the penalty trial from its metaphoric tie to the guilt trial, the case against finding error harmless is strong. Logically, we can only find error harmless when we can reconstruct the jury's likely reasoning to determine whether changing one variable in the trial would or might have changed the result. If a penalty decision is a subjective one involving "myriad" and "countless" factors, however, an appellate court can never be sure that adding or subtracting any one factor could not possibly have affected the result.[174]

Despite the conceptual difficulties in applying harmless error to the penalty trial, it is an especially useful instrument for carrying out the Court's political agenda. The federal courts face a great number of plausible claims of legal error because they have generated so much substantive and procedural doctrine under which penalty trials must be conducted. If the Court can devise a special harmless error doctrine for capital cases, it might be able to reduce the administrative cost of hearing these claims, while cheating on the intellectual cost of undoing the great doctrinal structure it has helped create.

---

[173] 386 U.S. 18 (1967).

[174] For one colorful view, see People v. Hines, 61 Cal. 2d 164, 169, 390 P.2d 398, 402, 37 Cal. Rptr. 622, 626 (1964) (jury's decision process an unknowable "dark ignorance").

B. ZANT AND THE BATTLE OF METAPHOR

Justice Stevens's opinion in *Zant v. Stephens* requires very careful parsing, but parsing the opinion will not produce intellectually satisfying results: the exercise simply confirms the sense that one receives from a superficial reading—that the opinion is a series of rationalizations and non sequiturs. Essentially, Justice Stevens seems uncertain of the moral propriety and the doctrinal correctness of applying the harmless error doctrine in a death case. He therefore takes on a far bigger matter than the case originally seemed to raise. He has to revoke the romantic due process view of the penalty phase as a criminal trial.

In *Zant*, the jury had expressly found three statutory aggravating circumstances.[175] While Stephens's appeal was pending, the Georgia Supreme Court struck down as unconstitutionally vague one of those statutory circumstances—that the defendant "has a substantial history of serious assaultive criminal convictions."[176] The State Supreme Court nevertheless held that Stephens's death sentence could stand on the basis of the other, valid statutory aggravating circumstances.[177]

Assuming that the Georgia trial court error was indeed federal error—an issue on which the Justices are rather coy[178]—the Supreme Court had to choose from among three lines of doctrine. All three lines are forms of "harmless error" principle, though only one of them is actually associated with that name.

The first line of doctrine is what might be called the "*per se* harmful*" error rule derived from *Stromberg v. California*.[179] Stromberg was charged with violating a state statute that prohibited displaying a flag with an emblem opposing organized government and using the flag to invite anarchy and aid seditious propaganda. He was convicted on a general verdict. The Supreme Court held that the first statutory ground impermissibly punished protected speech. Since the general verdict of guilt might have rested wholly on the invalid ground, the Court reversed the conviction.

---

[175] The jury found that the defendant had a prior conviction for a capital murder and a "substantial history of serious assaultive criminal convictions," and that he had escaped from lawful confinement at the time of the killing. Zant v. Stephens, 103 S. Ct. at 2737-38.

[176] Arnold v. State, 236 Ga. 534, 540, 224 S.E.2d 386, 391 (1976).

[177] 103 S. Ct. at 2738.

[178] Compare *id.* at 2738 with *id.* at 2752-53 & n.2 (Rehnquist, J., concurring in the judgment). Since *Zant* seems irreducibly obscure in any event, one could plausibly read the whole affair as a pretext for overturning the state court decision on the vagueness issue.

[179] 283 U.S. 359 (1931).

Stromberg was extended slightly in *Thomas v. Collins*[180] and *Street v. New York.*[181] In those cases, as in *Stromberg*, a defendant was charged with two or more statutory violations, one of which was invalid under the First Amendment. But in *Thomas* and *Street*, unlike *Stromberg*, the appellate courts had some basis to believe that the judgment rested at least in part on one of the valid statutory grounds.[182] The Court nevertheless reversed both judgments, since they may have rested on some combination of the valid and invalid grounds, and so were still tainted by the constitutional error.

The second type of harmless error rule, the one associated with the phrase "harmless error," is that of *Chapman v. California.*[183] *Chapman* requires reversal of a criminal judgment for any federal constitutional error unless the appellate court concludes beyond a reasonable doubt that the error did not affect the result. Significantly, *Chapman* is never mentioned in any of the major opinions in *Zant* and *Barclay*.

Finally, the Court had before it another line of "harmless error" cases not associated with that phrase, and concerned essentially with sentences and not guilty verdicts. The principle derived from *Claassen v. United States*, which might be called the *per se* harmless error rule, applies where a defendant has been convicted on several counts of a multicount indictment, and one of those counts proves invalid on appeal.[184] The question arises whether the appellate court can uphold the sentence, normally a prison sentence, despite the invalid count. The *Claassen* principle is that the appellate court will normally uphold the sentence so long as at least one of the original counts remains valid, and so long as the sentence does not exceed the maximum legal sentence for any single valid count. Strictly speaking, the *Claassen* rule is as illogical as the *Stromberg* rule is logical, because it is perfectly possible that the judge based the sentence on the aggregation of several counts, including the invalid one. *Claassen* simply creates an irrebuttable presumption that the entire sentence rested on the valid counts. The Court has essentially designed an administrative device to avoid endless review of sentences. If the Court were forced to reconcile *Claassen* with *Stromberg*, it would probably say that noncapital sentencing is a discretionary process involving so many

---

[180] 323 U.S. 516, 528-29 (1945).
[181] 394 U.S. 576, 586-88 (1969).
[182] See *Thomas*, 323 U.S. at 528 n.14, *Street*, 394 U.S. at 589.
[183] 386 U.S. 18 (1967).
[184] 142 U.S. 140 (1891); accord, Barenblatt v. United States, 360 U.S. 109 (1959).

factors that one cannot logically reconstruct the judge's reasoning as *Stromberg* would require.

The *Zant* Court had to decide which line, if any, to apply. Justice Stevens admits that he finds the choice bewildering.[185] He first must reexamine the nature of the error and the nature of the proceeding the error allegedly harmed.

The State of Georgia had first appealed *Zant* in the 1981 Term, and the Court, as if unable to figure out how to fit the Georgia penalty phase into the available harmless error tests, took the unusual step of requesting help from the Georgia Supreme Court. It certified a question to that court requesting an explanation of the state-law basis for that court's "harmless error" judgment.[186]

The Georgia Supreme Court's answer to the certified question is the heart of Justice Stevens's final opinion for the Court in *Zant*, and it is a remarkable document.[187] One must recall that the Court's rhetorically elusive characterization of this very Georgia death penalty statute was the key to the *Gregg* decision in 1976 restoring the death penalty to constitutional respectability. In one sense, the Georgia court's answer simply and correctly restates the few procedural steps in the Georgia statute, the very ones noted by *Gregg*. The jury must find at least one aggravating circumstance from a statutory list, and then must consider all legal aggravating circumstances and all mitigating circumstances to determine the defendant's fate. But if the *Gregg* Court had somewhat dressed up these simple steps in the rhetoric of "guided discretion" and "specific criteria," the Georgia Court now casts the statute in an imaginative new way that utterly severs the statute from the trial metaphor that *Gregg* had fostered.

The Georgia Supreme Court breaks down the trial metaphor by expressly offering a countermetaphor.[188] The State's death penalty scheme is a pyramid. It is as if the state court had hired Dante to give aesthetic, if not legal, form to the death penalty scheme. The pyramid is cut by three horizontal planes, and so has four levels. In the bottom level, just above the base, are all people guilty of homicide. A person rises through the first plane into the second level if his homicide is first-degree murder. Thus all people in the second level must face a penalty trial. These capital defendants cross the second plane into the

---

[185] 103 S. Ct. at 2746 (finding the matter a "difficult theoretical question").
[186] Zant v. Stephens, 456 U.S. 410 (1982) (*per curiam*).
[187] 250 Ga. 97, 99–100, 297 S.E.2d 1, 3–4 (1982); see 103 S. Ct. at 2739–41.
[188] *Ibid.*

third level only if the prosecutor proves at least one statutory aggravating circumstance in the penalty trial. If so, the sentencing jury can then exercise virtually unguided discretion to determine the defendant's fate, relying on any aggravating and mitigating evidence it finds useful. If it chooses a death sentence, the defendant then crosses the third plane into the fourth level, reserved for those the state will execute.[189] It is a wonderful metaphor, much more colorful than the trial metaphor. It is a Dante's hell of criminal procedure turned on its head, the most heinous killers rising to the top and disappearing into the nonspace of the apex.

The third plane of the metaphor is the key element, identifying an unregulated final stage of the penalty trial in which the formal statutory character of the aggravating circumstances plays no role at all. Whether an aggravating circumstance is "statutory" only helps push a case through the second plane, into the third level. Once a defendant is in the third level, the formal statutory rubric does not even guide—much less restrain—the jury.

This imaginative but technically correct reading of the Georgia statute essentially negates the romantic due process view of the penalty trial. That historical account, always shaky on the facts, generally ascribed two elements to the penalty trial. First, the sentencer's consideration of aggravating circumstances was firmly constrained by statute, even if the sentencer's reference to mitigating circumstances was not. Second, the sentencer had to follow some objectively describable reasoning process in translating the aggravating information and mitigating information into a sentencing decision, usually conceived as a weighing or balancing process.[190] Georgia's reading of its statute essentially breaks down the romantic account on both grounds.

Justice Stevens is justly grateful for the Georgia court's new metaphor, since it greatly relieves his troubles in testing the death judgment for harmless error. The new metaphor helps him not only to recharacterize the constitutional error as trivial, but also to recharacterize the Georgia penalty trial as a proceeding largely immune to error anyway.[191]

---

[189] In its brief and argument during the first round of *Zant*, the state tried yet another metaphor, describing the finding of one statutory aggravating circumstance as "a bridge" that takes the jury from the general class of murderers to the smaller group that may deserve death. 456 U.S. at 416.

[190] See notes 62-63 *supra* and accompanying text.

[191] Ironically, the first Supreme Court opinion in *Zant* asked the Georgia Supreme Court to

According to Justice Stevens, *Stromberg* does not apply to this death judgment, because the penalty jury, rendering a sort of special verdict, specifically found two valid statutory aggravating circumstances.[192] Thus, the defendant legally rose to the second-highest level of the pyramid, and the constitutional error thus could only have harmed him as he crossed the third plane into the top level. But the defendant had an interesting argument, here, that at the third plane he suffered harmful error under *Collins* and *Street*. In the final, discretionary phase of the penalty decision, the jury had clearly but incorrectly believed that the defendant's criminal record constituted a statutory aggravating circumstance. That invalid statutory circumstance might well have combined with the valid statutory circumstances in the jury's mind to persuade the jury that he deserved to die. Justice Stevens admits that he finds the analogy to *Thomas* and *Street* attractive but puzzling.[193] But in a final act of recharacterization, he explains how the entire *Stromberg* line is inapposite.

The Georgia Supreme Court may have found the "substantial history of serious assaultive criminal convictions" circumstance void for vagueness. But *Stromberg, Thomas,* and *Street* only apply where a judgment is tainted by a provision of state law that punishes constitutionally protected conduct.[194] The "conduct" for which the defendant in *Zant* was "punished" under the invalid circumstance was a sequence of violent crimes, not First Amendment self-expression. Even if the statutory provision was unconstitutionally vague, nothing in the Bill of Rights forbids introduction of the evidence—the record of violent crimes—which supported the statutory circumstance. Introducing a defendant's "priors" in the penalty trial is not like a *Miranda* or Fourth Amendment violation.[195]

The sentencing jury did not hear any evidence that was impermissible under state or federal law. The only illegal information they received was the "information" that the Georgia legislature had

---

explain the statute provisionally upheld in *Gregg,* so the Supreme Court could determine whether the statute had fulfilled its promise of preventing capricious death sentencing. Zant v. Stephens, 456 U.S. 410, 416-17 (1982) (*per curiam*). One reading the Georgia pyramid metaphor in light of the first *Zant* opinion might logically have predicted that it would convince the Court that the entire Georgia statute violated the Eighth Amendment.

[192] 103 S. Ct. at 2746.

[193] *Ibid.*

[194] *Ibid.*

[195] Justice Stevens says the Court is reserving the question whether reversal would be necessary where the information underlying the aggravating circumstance was "materially inaccurate or misleading," *id.* at 2748 n.24, though it is not clear how that sort of question of fact could create constitutional error.

placed a special legal imprimatur on the defendant's criminal record.[196] That error in labeling would require reversal if the invalid statutory circumstance were the only one in the case. In that event, the defendant would never have risen from the second level of the pyramid to the third. But in the later or higher phase where it applied, the incremental weight of the incorrect statutory imprimatur could have had only an "inconsequential impact" on the jury's thinking.[197]

Justice Stevens thus reached the end of his tortuous effort to prove the error harmless under *Street* and *Thomas*. And at the same time, without ever mentioning *Chapman v. California*, he manages to remove the *Chapman* issue as well: once we recharacterize an error so as to prove it inconsequential, we can readily conclude that we are sure beyond a reasonable doubt that it did not affect the result. The only remaining harmless error doctrine is that of *Claassen*.

The Stevens strategy seems to have produced a grandiloquent non sequitur. Even if the jury was never required to look at the statutory list of aggravating circumstances and even if the jury did not have to "formally" weigh aggravating against mitigating evidence, the jury had to do something with the information it received. A jury facing a difficult moral judgment on the basis of lots of raw evidence is likely to be somewhat affected by the idea that the legislature had placed a special imprimatur on the defendant's criminal record, especially when, contrary to Stevens's elegantly serial view of the proceeding, the jury considers statutory and nonstatutory aggravating circumstances all at once.

In treating the imprimatur as trivial, Stevens derogates the very notion of doctrinal form having any heuristic value for juries. *Zant* is a case of doctrine at war with the significance of doctrine. Though Stevens, unconvincing and perhaps unconvinced, is hesitant to admit it,[198] he has placed the penalty phase in the *Claassen* category of harmless error. To do that is, of course, to call off the trial metaphor and to look to conventional noncapital sentencing as the better analogy for the penalty phase. More important, it is to adopt the implicit conceptual and political premises of the *Claassen* line: that it is too

---

[196] The Fifth Circuit, whose decision was reversed in *Zant*, missed this subtlety on its first try. Stephens v. Zant, 631 F.2d 397, 406 (5th Cir. 1980). It then corrected itself. Stephens v. Zant, 648 F.2d 446 (5th Cir. 1980) (*per curiam*) (modification of opinion on petition for rehearing).

[197] 103 S. Ct. at 2749.

[198] *Id.* at 2746 (*Zant* issue "not precisely the same" as *Claassen* issue). Justice White draws the analogy very explicitly. *Id.* at 2750-51 (White, J., concurring in part and concurring in the judgment).

expensive—even in death cases—to reopen sentencing judgments, and that there are so many unmeasurable factors in a sentencing decision that we cannot know whether under slightly different conditions the sentence would have been different. But the Stevens opinion is too hesitant to acknowledge that it has joined the death penalty to the *Claassen* principle, perhaps because to do so would be to frankly acknowledge the inscrutability of the death judgment.

On this issue, Justice Rehnquist provides the perfect rhetorical counterpoint.[199] About the only conceivable purpose of the Rehnquist concurrence is to criticize Stevens for a failure of nerve, and to draw out the doctrinally nihilistic implications of Stevens's opinion. Unconcerned with fastidious adherence to legal formality, Rehnquist sounds one central theme—unlike a jury deciding guilt, the penalty jury rests its decision on "literally countless" factors. He repeats this hyperbole of infinity several times[200] to establish the penalty judgment as an ineffable, subjective decision to which all quixotic due process ideals and all formal "modeling" are irrelevant.[201] In a sense, Rehnquist is discovering and asserting Justice Powell's view in *Bullington:* the penalty trial is an existential moment of moral perception, neither right nor wrong, and therefore largely unreviewable.

Justice Marshall's dissent in *Zant* is full of the outrage of one who has been cheated and lied to.[202] He speaks in disbelief over whether his *Gregg* and *Furman* decisions are the same as Justice Stevens's *Gregg* and *Furman* decisions. Justice Marshall speaks as one who has accepted the romantic due process account and now is bewildered as the Court reads it out of its own historical memory. But the Court has simply proclaimed the minimal account of *Gregg* to be the correct one. All a state must do is to narrow somewhat the group of murderers eligible for death by requiring at least one statutory aggravating circumstance, and then to provide appellate review to check the most irrational excesses of the jury's discretion. Justice Marshall angrily complains

---

[199] *Id.* at 2751 (Rehnquist, J., concurring in the judgment).

[200] See, *e.g., id.* at 2755 (evidence admitted on "literally countless subjects"); *ibid.* (jury weighs "countless considerations"); *ibid.* (jury considers "literally countless factors"); *id.* at 2756 (sentencing decisions rest on "countless facts and circumstances").

[201] Justice Rehnquist points out the few exceptions to *Claassen* in noncapital sentencing, but they are exceptions that prove the rule. In United States v. Tucker, 404 U.S. 443 (1972) and Townsend v. Burke, 334 U.S. 736 (1948), the record explicitly showed that the sentencing judge gave specific attention to the impermissible ground for sentencing. A sentence loses its immunity under *Claassen* when the judge makes the mistake of leaving a record of his reasoning, and therefore surrenders the shield of "inscrutability." See 103 S. Ct. at 2756-57.

[202] 103 S. Ct. at 2757 (Marshall, J., dissenting).

that the Court has asked virtually nothing of the states that they were not doing before *Furman*, and essentially he is right.[203] It is as if the constitutional strictures on the death penalty are merely a matter of legal aesthetics. The state will satisfy the Court if it can describe its penalty scheme according to some rational-looking form—indeed some metaphor of rational form.

C. BARCLAY AND LEGAL DISORDER

The Court granted certiorari in *Barclay v. Florida* on the question whether a death sentence could rest on a combination of statutory and nonstatutory aggravating circumstances.[204] It would seem that *Zant* settled that question, since under the pyramid metaphor the Georgia jury had unregulated discretion to consider raw aggravating evidence.

Florida's death penalty law pretends to much greater formality than Georgia's. The sentencing judge or jury may look only to statutory aggravating circumstances, and may not hand down a death sentence unless the statutory aggravating circumstances are at least as weighty as the mitigating circumstances and, taken by themselves, are sufficiently weighty to justify execution.[205] On its face, the Florida statute is if anything more constitutionally sound than that of Georgia. If a Florida sentencer violated this formal scheme by relying on nonstatutory aggravating circumstances, the substantive error would clearly seem to be one of state law alone, while the error in *Zant* was arguably federal.

At least after *Zant*, the defendant in *Barclay* had only one hope—a sort of Eighth Amendment "entitlement" theory. Where a state does enact formal rules governing the penalty trial, it induces people to rely on that rule's being fairly and consistently applied.[206] The obvious problem with this view is that it essentially collapses state law into federal law, and invites the state to avoid the "federal" violation in the future simply by removing the state law protection. Nevertheless, one can imagine this otherwise questionable principle's having some special valence in capital punishment. The ever-versatile Eighth

---

[203] *Id.* at 2758-60.

[204] Barclay v. Florida, 103 U.S. 3418.

[205] Barclay v. Florida, 103 S. Ct. 3420 (1983) (plurality opinion); see Proffitt v. Florida, 428 U.S. at 248-51 (1976).

[206] *Cf.* Hicks v. Oklahoma, 447 U.S. 343 (1980). That reliance is similar to the "new property" entitlement that has invoked due process protection in noncriminal cases, *e.g.*, Board of Regents v. Roth, 408 U.S. 564 (1972).

Amendment rhetoric denouncing arbitrary infliction of the death penalty at least vaguely suggests that states are constitutionally required to apply their penalty schemes fairly and consistently, whatever form those schemes take.[207] And the Court's emphasis in *Gregg* and *Proffitt* on the importance of careful appellate review vaguely suggests an Eighth Amendment requirement that the states carry out their statutory promises.[208]

Barclay presents a perfect case for this approach. The bizarre, gratuitous violence of the killing[209] seems to have invoked in the Florida judiciary a desire to perform similar violence to the formal pretenses of the statute. *Barclay* almost seems chosen for literary purposes to reflect the Court's new disbelief in the feasibility of treating capital sentencing under the niceties of the rule of law.[210] The *Barclay* case is as much a literary as a legal phenomenon, a narrative of the breakdown of the civility of law by both the defendant and the trial and appellate processes.

The advisory sentencing jury recommended a life sentence for Barclay. Despite the statutory presumption in favor of upholding that recommendation,[211] the trial judge committed random, casual error, and the Florida Supreme Court upheld the trial judge without even acknowledging error. Perhaps as a result, the Supreme Court finds it difficult even to identify the specific legal category of the errors before it.

The most important error concerns the trial judge's reliance on Barclay's prior crimes, the worst of which was breaking and entering with intent to commit grand larceny.[212] *Zant* made clear that there was no constitutional problem in admitting evidence of priors in the

---

[207] This was the view of the Fifth Circuit in the case that squarely presented the key issue in *Barclay* and which *Barclay* was effectively designed to reverse. Henry v. Wainwright, 661 F.2d 56, 59-60 (5th Cir. 1981).

[208] *E.g.*, Zant v. Stephens, 456 U.S. 410, 413 (1982) (*per curiam*).

[209] Barclay and his accomplices formed a Black Liberation Army and chose their white victim, a hitchhiker, at random with the professed goal of starting a revolution by threatening the widespread killing of whites. After the murder, they sent tape recordings to the victim's mother and to television stations, giving lurid details of the killing and calling for an urban guerilla revolution. 103 S. Ct. at 3420-21.

[210] Justice Blackmun, who voted with the majority in *Zant*, dissented in *Barclay*. He expressed offense at the killing, but said he was also offended because the Florida courts had made a "mockery" of the Florida statute. *Id.* at 3445 (Blackmun, J., dissenting).

[211] The judge has the ultimate sentencing power in Florida, but is not supposed to reject a jury's recommendation of mercy unless "the facts suggesting a sentence of death [are] so clear and convincing that no reasonable person could differ." Proffitt v. Florida, 428 U.S. at 249 (quoting Tedder v. State, 322 So.2d 908, 910 (Fla. 1975)).

[212] 103 S. Ct. at 3421.

penalty trial. But Florida's restrictive statutory list of aggravating circumstances referred only to prior crimes of violence, and the Florida Supreme Court had held that breaking and entering did not fall within the circumstance.[213]

Nor is it clear that the admission of the priors is the only error under review. The trial judge had found several other statutory aggravating circumstances with no very clear basis in the facts or in state law.[214] And, in overruling the jury's call for mercy, the trial judge measured Barclay's crime against his own purported experience with racial violence in World War II.[215] The Justices seem vaguely to appreciate the danger of caprice when the sentencer so explicitly relies on matters of personal experience. But they seem uncertain whether to treat this matter as evidence of statutory circumstances,[216] or as another nonstatutory aggravating circumstance, or not as a circumstance at all but simply as an aspect of the judge's process of moral reasoning.[217]

Barclay's penalty trial was thus a farce of errors. The federal character of the errors nonetheless remains elusive after *Zant*, unless the Eighth Amendment permits the Court to take a "systemic" view of a state penalty scheme and strike down a death sentence where the state courts virtually mock their own law.

Justices Stevens and Rehnquist again write the key opinions in the case and present the same contrast in tone and rhetoric as they did in *Zant*. This time, Rehnquist writes for the plurality, and simply recurs

---

[213] 103 S. Ct. at 3422; Lewis v. State, 398 So.2d 432, 438 (Fla. 1981). Even assuming this error had constitutional significance, the Florida Supreme Court in earlier cases had addressed this very issue and had fashioned a sort of harmless error doctrine for it. See 103 S. Ct. at 3426-7; notes 222-23 *infra* and accompanying text. Thus, if anything, the constitutional question here would not concern the error itself, but the state harmless error test as applied to it.

[214] The trial judge found the circumstances that Barclay knowingly committed a great risk of death to many persons, that he committed the murder in the course of the kidnapping, and that he was under sentence of imprisonment at the time of the murder. The first of these findings was an error of state law. The second had a weak factual basis, and the third had none. See 103 S. Ct. at 3422-23. The trial judge had a very consistent record of sentencing defendants to death over jury recommendations of mercy, and of finding this litany of aggravating circumstances in most of his capital cases, regardless of the facts.

[215] Justice Rehnquist quotes extensively from the judge's emotional discussion in his sentencing order. 103 S. Ct. at 3423-24 n.6 (plurality opinion). Unfortunately, the trial judge had repeated the litany of his personal experiences in very similar words in all his previous death orders. *Id.* at 3440-41 n.12 (Marshall, J., dissenting).

[216] Justice Rehnquist suggests that the trial judge's citation of his experiences supports the circumstances that Barclay had committed a great risk of death to many persons, or had disrupted the lawful exercise of governmental functions, or that the murder was especially heinous, atrocious, or cruel. *Id.* at 3424 (plurality opinion).

[217] Justice Stevens suggests that the judge was merely doing what a jury would do—bringing his personal experiences and moral principles to bear on the facts. *Id.* at 3435 (Stevens, J., concurring).

to the nihilistic view of the penalty trial that he expounded earlier. He asserts in an abrupt, conclusory manner that none of the errors of state law made the trial so arbitrary or capricious as to violate the Constitution.[218] He makes a few specific legal points,[219] but the opinion reads mostly like a laconic expression of annoyance that anyone could seriously imagine the Court's being concerned with violations of the procedural niceties of Florida law. For him the doctrines of the penalty trial having been deconstructed in *Zant*, *Barclay* requires barely more than a summary affirmance.

Justice Stevens expresses distress over Rehnquist's repeated casual nihilism.[220] But the disagreement is again one of attitude rather than of law. Stevens's doctrinally fastidious effort to rationalize *Barclay's* penalty trial severs the penalty phase from the formalities of the trial metaphor just as effectively. Ultimately, Stevens, like Rehnquist, relies on the strong if Delphic authority of *Zant* to declare *Barclay's* claims worthless. But he first takes excruciating pain to describe the procedural complexity of the Florida penalty decision, accomplishing little more than self-contradiction.

Stevens sets out to do for the Florida statute what the Georgia Supreme Court did for its own in *Zant:* he draws an aesthetically complex chart of the elements of the penalty decision in Florida,[221] but accomplishes little more than to set up his final non sequitur—his admiring description of Florida's harmless error rule.

After *Zant* it should not matter to Stevens whether Florida has a harmless error rule. And in any event, whatever the value of that rule, the Florida Supreme Court ignored it in *Barclay's* case. But if Stevens simply wanted to show his general appreciation for Florida's appellate review, his explanation of Florida's harmless error rule underscores its illogic. The rule seems to be that reliance on a nonstatutory aggravating factor is harmless error where there remains at least one valid statutory aggravating circumstance and where the case presents no mitigating circumstances.[222] In those cases, of course, the valid

---

[218] *Id.* at 3424 (plurality opinion).

[219] Rehnquist cursorily notes that *Zant* approved the introduction of the defendant's criminal record in aggravation. *Id.* at 3245 n.8.

[220] Stevens criticizes Rehnquist for speaking with unnecessary and inappropriate breadth, and for suggesting that the Eighth Amendment merely asks whether the state court decision has been "so unprincipled or arbitrary as to somehow violate the United States Constitution." *Id.* at 3429.

[221] See *id.* at 3429-32.

[222] 103 S. Ct. at 3434-35 (Stevens, J., concurring); see *e.g.*, Elledge v. State, 346 So.2d 998 (Fla. 1977).

aggravating circumstance will always win the weighing contest. But by Stevens's own description of Florida law, in the third stage the sentencer also asks whether the statutory aggravating circumstances viewed, without regard to mitigation, are sufficiently substantial to justify the death sentence.[223] Stevens thus has unwittingly proved that the nonstatutory aggravating circumstance is likely to taint this final stage of the sentencer's decision. Stevens's logic dissolves because he is unwilling to admit that the consequences of the trial metaphor are too great for the death penalty system to bear.

D. THE DOCTRINAL FUTURE

The Court's experiment in reducing the death penalty to the rule of law has devolved to a merely aesthetic requirement: the states must have some sort of penalty trial law on their books to fill the embarrassing gap created by *Furman*. The law must somehow identify a class of death-eligible murderers smaller than the class of all murderers, must give some sentencer some discretion about choosing which of the eligibles to execute, and must grant defendants a fairly broad opportunity to make a case for mitigation. Beyond that, the rule may be of any kind, and the Court will not monitor its enforcement.

If *Zant* and *Barclay* announce the federal deregulation of the penalty trial, they do not mean that the Court will stop reviewing death sentences. If the Court discovers a new disequilibrium in the death penalty, there will still be constitutional doctrine consistent with *Zant* and *Barclay* which the Court can use in any effort at regulation.

Zant and *Barclay* essentially grant the stakes a *Lockett* right: the penalty trial is to be a free market in information. The Court will permit the state to introduce virtually any evidence in aggravation, without the constraint of legal categories. But it is likely to show continued or renewed vigor in ensuring that the defendant can introduce any mitigating evidence that might lead a sentencer to give mercy.[224]

---

[223] 103 S. Ct. at 3431 (Stevens, J., concurring); see, *e.g.*, Lewis v. State, 398 So. 2d 432, 438-39 (Fla. 1981). Ironically, Barclay did indeed proffer some mitigating circumstances. 103 S. Ct. at 3433 n.13 (Stevens, J., concurring); *id.* at 3438 n.2 (Marshall, J., dissenting).

[224] For a discussion of how a variety of state evidence laws may be preempted by *Lockett*, see Kaplan, *Evidence in Capital Cases*, 11 FLA. ST. L. REV. 369, 373-76 (1983). The knotty problem of creating constitutional doctrine to measure the ineffectiveness of defense counsel arises with special force in death penalty cases. Perhaps the most crucial job a defense lawyer faces in a capital trial is taking full advantage of *Lockett* by discovering and generating as much mitigating

The Court has also left itself generous room for expanding Eighth Amendment doctrine: it will simply have to focus on points in the system of death penalty decisionmaking other than the moment of decision by the sentencer. First, it can continue or refine its effort to integrate capital sentencing with substantive criminal law, putting more pressure on the legislative definition of murders and murderers who must face a discretionary penalty trial.[225] The Court can extend the reach of *Edmund v. Florida* and *Godfrey v. Georgia* to ensure that merely "ordinary" murderers identified by first-degree murder doctrine are not eligible for death.

Second, if the states can give the sentencer virtually unlimited discretion to decide which eligible murderers should die, the Court may reexamine who that unrestricted sentencer may be. *Zant* and *Barclay* may signal the Court's intention to let the states determine both the mode of sentencing and the identity of the sentencer. But the Court could decide that if the defendant is to suffer the unguided discretion of a sentencer, he is entitled to the unguided discretion of a jury,[226] and indeed to a jury no more inclined to consider issuing a death sentence than the society from which it is drawn.[227]

Finally, the Court could refine its apparent requirement of vigorous state appellate review, but that review will concern the products, not the processes, of death penalty decisions. If each penalty decision is inherently ineffable, perhaps the state courts need not try to reconstruct how the sentencer reached it. But under the rubric of

information as possible. The Court will have to decide how good a job the Constitution requires the lawyer to do. Washington v. Strickland, 693 F.2d 1243 (5th Cir. 1982) (Unit B *en banc*), *cert. granted*, 103 S. Ct. 2451 (1983).

[225] *Zant* gives some vague force to its apparent requirement that the state prove at least one statutory aggravating circumstance before subjecting the defendant to a discretionary penalty trial. It reads *Furman* as requiring that an aggravating circumstance "genuinely narrow the class of persons eligible for the death penalty and . . . reasonably justify the imposition of a more severe sentence on the defendant compared to others found guilty of murder." Zant v. Stephens, 103 S. Ct. at 2742. (footnote omitted). If, as is now clearer than under *Gregg*, the formality of the threshold statutory aggravating circumstance must bear the major burden of satisfying the Eighth Amendment prohibition of arbitrary sentencing, then the Court will essentially have to induce further reform in the substantive criminal law of murder.

[226] See note 161 *supra*.

[227] Under Witherspoon v. Illinois, 391 U.S. 510 (1968), the prosecution may not challenge for cause a potential juror who expresses opposition to the death penalty but who does not categorically state that he will refuse to vote for a death sentence in any case. The Court may be disinclined to deny the state the power to exclude at least those jurors who would absolutely refuse to vote for death, but it may have to confront the emerging question whether a jury "death qualified" for the sentencing phase may be unfairly biased against the defendant at the guilt phase. See Grigsby v. Mabry, 569 F. Supp 1273 (E.D. Ark. 1983) (relying on extensive empirical evidence to hold that death qualification under *Witherspoon* denies capital defendants the right to a jury representative of society, and creates juries that are unfairly conviction prone).

"proportionality" review, the state appellate courts can at least take an Olympian view of the results of numerous death penalty decisions, demanding of the trial courts as a whole some sort of coherent and nondiscriminatory pattern.[228] In short, the state courts may have to recur to the minimal message of *Furman*—to prevent the worst arbitrary and discriminatory effects of discretionary death penalty decisions.

What the Court will probably not do is dictate any formulas for the process by which the sentencer must use the variety of information it is likely to hear. Whether this deregulation will actually change the way judges and juries make death penalty decisions is very hard to predict. The states may not take full advantage of the Court's invitation to abjure their complex formula for processing information. Nor is there a certain way to tell how much these formulas actually have controlled sentencer discretion in the first place. A jury told that it has unlimited discretion must do something with the aggravating and mitigating information it hears, probably some intuitive form of comparative weighing. A complex, formal instruction speaking in legalistic terms about comparative weighing may make less difference than the legislatures have assumed. What *will* change, of course, is the chance of the defendant's winning appellate reversal because of some error in applying constitutional or statutory doctrine. Defense lawyers may have to focus their efforts more on willing life verdicts than on preserving issues for appeal.

V. GIVING VOICE TO DOCTRINE: A DOCUMENTARY REVIEW

A. LEGAL VOICES AND THE LAW

If we are concerned with the actual "accomplishments" of the decade of Eighth Amendment doctrine canvassed above, we must examine the history in more specific terms, the terms in which the doctrine is actually communicated to the sentencer. That examination supplies a more concrete sense of the effects of the due process romanticism of the decade, and derives from a look at the texts of some jury instructions and attorney arguments as they have evolved through the decade. I make no pretense of an empirical study of the operation of the death penalty here, but the documents strikingly demonstrate the bite of formula.

---

[228] See Harris v. Pulley, 692 F.2d 1189 (9th Cir. 1983), *rev'd*, 104 S. Ct. _____ (1984).

Since these texts cover several stages of legal development, note what they have in common. The goals of the prosecution and the defense at the penalty stage have not changed. There are certain types of information or messages that the prosecutors generally want to convey and other types of information or messages that the defense will generally want to convey. The interesting thing is how the two sides have been aided or thwarted in achieving these goals by the different legal structures imposed on them at different times.

A prosecutor demanding the death penalty wants to convey and reinforce the most damning facts about the crime for which the penalty is sought. He wants to bring out the criminal record of the defendant to paint a portrait of an irredeemably evil person. Where there is evidence of good character, he wants to stress the crime, and where there is evidence of bad character, he wants to stress that. Finally, he wants to stress the jury's responsibility or opportunity to heal and prevent social disruption through execution, and the need to match the harm suffered by the victim with a commensurate harm for the defendant.

The defense, where possible, may want to cast doubt—even after conviction—on the defendant's actual guilt, underscoring the danger of making a mistake as to guilt irreparable.[229] But often his only strategy is to have the defendant confess to the crime, or have witnesses, in effect, confess for him, and thereby offer a plea in avoidance of penalty.[230] Where the defendant has evidence of good character, the defense wants to plead that the crime was an aberration. In most cases, the defense wants to proffer a causal, determinist explanation of the crime, often showing a history of child abuse or neglect and thereby putting the defendant's family on trial. And it wants to use any evidence of the defendant's drug or alcohol abuse as a residual "diminished capacity" defense. The overall goal of the defense is to present a human narrative, an explanation of the defendant's apparently malignant violence as in some way rooted in understandable aspects of the human condition, so the jury will be less inclined to cast him out of the human circle.

The defense case has its roots in the premodern model of the death penalty, where the trial and execution were ritual ordeals to extract the

---

[229] Coordinating the guilt phase defense with the mitigation case in the penalty trial is a difficult matter. See generally Goodpaster, *The Trial for Life: Effective Assistance of Counsel in Death Penalty Cases*, 58 N.Y.U.L. REV. 299, 328-34 (1983).

[230] For a general summary of defense strategy in the penalty phase, see *id.* at 334-39.

truth from the defendant to force him to participate in a ceremony of celebrating the power of the sovereign.[231] In the modern death penalty, the defense essentially tries to give the state its moral victory by acknowledging his crime but by trying to persuade the jury that it can accommodate the crime into the assumptions of social order it wants to reaffirm. In addition, and especially when these other strategies are not available, the defense often wants to put the death penalty itself on trial by rebutting the legitimacy of the retributional, incapacitative, and deterrent justifications.[232]

On the whole, the development of capital punishment law has helped both sides to achieve their goals by creating a new, independent penalty trial, thereby freeing the sentencing determination from the restrictions of the guilt determination. But the penalty trial has also become more formal, more like the guilt trial. The increasing formality has had some surprising effects, indeed some very ironic effects, for the defendants it was largely designed to protect.

There is a continuum of "types" of death penalty schemes, ranging from the most informal to the most legally sophisticated. The most informal type is the pre-*Furman* unitary trial. In the middle is an independent but only mildly regulated penalty trial, which was available in a few states before *Furman*. At the end of the continuum is the formal, trial-like penalty phase that has evolved in the last decade. But to this continuum there are two caveats.

First, the continuum represents abstract types, not a historical progression, even if the most formal type seems to have emerged in recent years at the Supreme Court's encouragement. Before *Furman*, the states varied widely in the way they ran the death penalty decision; they still run it differently, despite the development of federal constitutional doctrine. A major determinant of the way the death penalty decision operates is what one might call the local criminal law "culture." The criminal law bars of the states vary widely in their legal sophistication, financial resources, and oratorical traditions, and these factors affect the conduct of the penalty trial as much as the legal doctrine handed down by appellate courts. Thus the penalty trial in some states today has aspects of the informal model, while in other states the penalty trial has always had more modern, formal elements.

---

[231] See FOUCAULT, DISCIPLINE AND PUNISH 35-44 (Sheridan trans. 1979).
[232] See note 82 *supra* and accompanying text.

The second caveat is that once again I am addressing jury sentencing. The trend toward formality also affects the conduct of judicial sentencing in capital cases, but in different ways.[233]

B. THE INFORMAL SCHEME

The following exchange comes from a late 1930s case from Ohio under the unitary scheme upheld decades later in *McGautha v. California*. The judge gave the jury the following standard instruction on the death sentence:[234]

> And now, ladies and gentlemen of the jury, if after a fair, careful, and impartial consideration of all of the evidence in this case you find that the defendant has been established guilty of murder in the first degree, then you will have one further duty to perform, and that is, you will determine whether or not you will extend or withhold mercy. . . . In that connection whether you recommend or withhold mercy is a matter solely within your discretion, calling for the exercise of your very best and most profound judgment, not motivated by considerations of sympathy or as a means of escaping a hard or disagreeable duty, but must be considered by you in the light of all the circumstances of the case with respect to the evidence submitted to you and the other circumstances surrounding this defendant.

After deliberating for some time, the jury returned to pose the following question:[235]

> The Foreman: What are grounds for granting mercy?
> The Court: That rests solely and wholly in your sound discretion. You should determine whether or not in your discretion mercy should be granted from a consideration of the evidence, the character of the crime and the attending circumstances. Are there any other questions which you have?
> The Foreman: No, I don't think so. I beg your pardon. We have another question or two. What are extenuating circumstances? Are they something which we can determine in our own judgment alone?

---

[233] In jury sentencing, the jury instruction is of course a major medium for conveying legal doctrine, and becomes a major text to be reviewed on appeal. In judge sentencing, the key text is the summary of facts and law supporting the sentencing order. Since the judge, unlike the jury, normally explains what facts he relied on and how he applied the law to the facts, a mild legal error in his explanation can invalidate the sentence. See, *e.g.*, Eddings v. Oklahoma, 455 U.S. 104, 109; *id.* at 124 (1982) (Burger, C.J., dissenting).
[234] State v. Caldwell, 135 Ohio St. 424, 425-27, 21 N.E.2d 343, 344 (1939).
[235] *Ibid.*

> The Court: No, if there are any, you must determine them from the evidence . . .
>
> The Foreman: Well, then, may we consider sociological matters and environment in determining this question of granting mercy?
>
> The Court: No—they have nothing whatever to do with this case.

This exchange shows the guidance, or lack of guidance, that the pre-*Furman* law generally conveyed to the jury, and so illuminates the State's conception of the penalty decision. The instruction is a noninstruction, almost an anti-instruction. It impresses on the jury the moral gravity of its task by telling the jury that the decision comes unaided by the State. It describes the decision as a question about mercy but warns the jurors not to be affected by sympathy. Why this simultaneous invitation to subjectivity and constraint on "sympathy"? The instruction ends by referring the jury to "the evidence." One must remember that in the unitary trial, the jury would normally hear no evidence on the question of punishment, except whatever evidence happened to be thrown up by issues in the guilt phase that might coincidentally be relevant to punishment.[236] In fact, the states were often lax about this practice. They erratically permitted evidence of good character and of prior crimes.[237] But Ohio law severely restricted penalty evidence. For decades, Ohio courts were faithful to the principle that it was not only unnecessary but indeed illegal for the judge to give the jury any guidance whatsoever on the penalty phase.[238] The law thus aggressively reinforced the notion that the jury could not look to the law for any relief from the moral question of the death sentence. The jury was left in a discomforting legal limbo, as this exchange shows. It may seem puzzling that the courts would not tell the jurors they could consider "environmental and sociological matters"; so instructing them would be consistent with the principle that there are no formal legal rules governing their decision. But to give this instruction might invite the lawyers to discuss "environmental and sociological matters" in their arguments. The State's position seems to be that the jurors are not to hear any advice on the penalty decision from any professional legal voice,[239] lest they believe they were

---

[236] See notes 17-18 *supra* and accompanying text.

[237] Knowlton, note 17 *supra*, at 1111-18.

[238] *E.g.,* Ashbrook v. State, 49 Ohio App. 298, 302, 197 N.E. 214, 216 (1935).

[239] Under old Ohio law, the defense could not challenge for cause a juror who said he would automatically vote for the death penalty if he found the defendant guilty, even though the jury

receiving legal guidance. In this early stage of the death penalty, the law was relentlessly antilegal.

The jury, of course, gets its legal signals from the closing arguments as well as from the judge's instructions. The typical rhetorical style of the arguments in the pre-*Furman* unitary trial bears an interesting relationship to the rhetoric of judicial instruction. It is very hazardous to generalize about the forms of prosecution argument, depending as they do on local and individual styles. But the restrictions on evidence and the anti-instructional nature of the jury instructions in the unitary trial presented a common problem to the lawyers. The trial left them with virtually nothing of any tangible legal nature to talk about with respect to the punishment.

The prosecutor could rely on the available material—the guilt-phase facts about the crime—and could rehearse those facts in all their luridness. But having little further tangible subject matter to discuss, the prosecutor essentially had to "personalize" the argument, speaking of his own role and responsibility and asking the jury to share it. Here is one example from a Texas capital rape case:[240]

> I am not in this case to make any kind of a reputation. I have been in this game for thirty-five years, too long for me to be trying to do something to make a reputation. My reputation, good or bad, has been established a good while.
>
> Gentlemen, I am going to tell you from the depths of my heart that I have always dreaded the day ever coming when a crime of this kind is committed. I have had a horror of it ever since I have been practicing law, and ever since I have been prosecuting attorney, which started back in 1933.

Also, since he could not refer to very much evidence specific to this defendant's punishment, the prosecutor would make a general plea about the necessity of a death sentence to affirm the value of law and order. From the same trial:[241]

> We still haven't reached the point—although sometimes I think we are getting close to it—to where the ninety-three per cent of

---

had discretion to recommend mercy on the facts of the particular case. The court essentially explained that the question of sentence was not really a legal question on which a juror need be impartial. State v. Ellis, 98 Ohio 21, 31, 120 N.E. 218, 219 (1918).

[240] The quotes are from the trial in Branch v. Texas, 447 S.W.2d 932 (Tex. Ct. Crim. App. 1969), which was reversed as a companion case to Furman v. Georgia, 408 U.S. 238 (1972) (transcript on file with author).

[241] *Ibid.*

good citizens are at the mercy of the seven per cent criminal law violators in our country, and that is what our statistics show at this time. We have got no place for that in this country. It's here. I know it's here, and in certain places they are having hell, but I still tell you we have no place for that in our society, but I tell you that any man that breaks into a widow's house where she has no protection, and rapes her by force should be sent to the electric chair to tell the whole world and anyone who is inclined to want to go and do likewise that if you do and we catch you, we will kill you.

There are few reported appellate decisions examining the excesses of prosecution argument.[242] It is as if the law, having constrained the prosecutor by denying him specific aggravating evidence, allowed him to fill the gap with his own rhetorical invention. The defense in the pre-*Furman* unitary trial faced the same, if not a greater, problem. He had often no specific mitigating evidence to argue about. But once the prosecution had turned the trial into an emotional and oratorical free-for-all, the defense lawyer could at least try to compete in terms. The defense would inveigh generally against the idea of punishment, offer whatever good character testimony had been proffered as a result of the guilt issues, and denounce revenge. Where possible, he might try to cast doubt on the defendant's guilt, and stress the danger of mistake. But also, mimicking the prosecutor, he would make himself the subject of the argument and offer himself as a personal medium of empathy between the jury and the defendant. He would speak of his own humility before the task, impressing on the jury the fearful responsibility of dealing in life and death:[243]

> I wish that I were smart enough to get up here and be able to sway you with eloquence, with fancy talks with quotations from the Bible or books, great men, but I am not. All I can do is to try and go over the facts of this case with you, which is my right and my privilege, and maybe, in some way, clarify the hard road you have.

The oratorical/emotive style of counsel argument continues today in some Southern states as the one aspect of the penalty phase most unchanged by modern law. The prosecutors in states such as

---

[242] The only very common restraint was that prosecutors were not supposed to argue to the jury that if the defendant were not executed he might one day be paroled and return to endanger society, but courts often held any such remarks harmless error. Knowlton, note 17 *supra*, at 1119. *Cf.* State v. Watson, 28 Ohio St.2d 15, 26, 275 N.E.2d 153, 160 (1971).

[243] This quote is also drawn from the *Branch* trial, note 240 *supra*.

Kentucky[244] and Georgia[245] often take little advantage of the more specific penalty evidence or formalities of the statutory aggravation. They rely instead on unabashed emotional and religious themes, and the defense lawyers respond in kind.[246]

C. THE MIDDLE TYPE

There is a second, intermediate type of death penalty scheme, in which the penalty issue at least receives the legal dignity of a separate proceeding. The best example of this middle type is the California penalty trial as it was conducted from the mid-1950s until the California Supreme Court anticipated *Furman* by one year and struck down the state capital punishment law.[247] In this middle-type scheme, the court permitted both sides to introduce a wide range of evidence specifically relevant to the penalty question, but regulated the evidence to exclude incompetent and prejudicial matters.[248] However, even if legal doctrine determined what evidence the jury heard, it played no role in the jury instructions, since the jury was never told how to process the evidence. This form of the death penalty is especially notable, because it is very close to the new, reduced constitutional model of the penalty phase to which the Supreme Court has apparently returned.

---

[244] *E.g.*, the penalty trial of Randy Lamb, transcribed in TRIAL OF PENALTY PHASE, note 80 *supra*, at 156, 168.

[245] See Hance v. Zant, 696 F.2d 940, 952 (11th Cir. 1983). The court held that the prosecutor's remarks were so prejudicial as to render the death sentence unconstitutional, but they only mildly exaggerate the kind of argument frequently made in Georgia: "I'm going to sleep well tonight, having [recommended Hance's electrocution] to you. As a matter of fact, I'm going to sleep better and safer in my home with my family if you come back with a sentence of death. . . . How many times have you said to yourself as you pick up your morning newspaper or turn on your radio or television newscast, has the whole world gone crazy, when you read about a crime like this, has the whole world lost its mind? . . . When have you said to yourself, what can I do, just one citizen, just one individual, to stop this? . . . Well, it's time for somebody to do something. . . . You're in the batter's box, so to speak . . . it's a matter of fish or cut bait, because we're right down to it, we're right down to it. Frankly, the one thing I look for in selecting jurors in this case, the one characteristic, . . . I looked for courage . . . You know, we've had three wars in this Country just in my lifetime, World War II, war in Korea, war in Vietnam. In each of those wars we drafted young men, take them out of civilian life, train them, equip them, sent them to fight for us, young as seventeen, perhaps some as young as sixteen years of age. And we've sent them off to some land halfway across the world, and we've pointed them at some individual that they didn't even know, and we've said, this person is the enemy, they are trying to destroy our way of life, when you see this person, kill him. . . . Do we ask any less of you in this situation?"

[246] See the end of the closing argument in the penalty trial of Randy Lamb, TRIAL OF PENALTY PHASE, note 80 *supra*, at 185-87.

[247] People v. Anderson, 6 Cal. 3d 628, 493 P.2d 880, 100 Cal. Reptr. 152, *cert. denied*, 406 U.S. 958 (1972).

[248] See *California Penalty Jury*, note 14 *supra*, at 1312-14.

During this era, California penalty juries received an instruction such as the following:[249]

> The jurors should understand that it is their duty to conscientiously consider all the evidence in the case in arriving at their decision but that it is not essential to their choice of either penalty that they find palliating or mitigating circumstances on the one hand or evidence in aggravation of the offense on the other hand; that insofar as selecting the penalty is concerned (as between the two alternatives) the law does not itself prescribe, nor authorize the court to innovate, any rule circumscribing the exercise of their discretion, but, rather, commits the whole matter of its exercise to the judgment and the consciences of the jury; that in deciding the question whether the accused should be put to death or sentenced to imprisonment for life.
>
> . . . [I]t is your discretion alone for you to determine, each for yourself, how far you will accord weight to the consideration of the several objectives of punishment, of the deterrence of crime, of the protection of society, of the desirability of stern retribution; or of sympathy, as well as revulsion against the defendant for his crimes, or clemency, of age, as well as experience, sex, human passion, as well as ability to carefully deliberate and plan, ignorance . . . or weakness, as well as strength, or of the presumptions concerning, or possible uncertainties attaching to, life imprisonment, or of the irrevocableness of an executed sentence of death . . . .

In one case from this era, the jury returned from the jury room with the following question:[250]

> The Foreman: . . . We have a question of a point of law and we feel it would be helpful to us in determining a verdict. . . . What we wish to know is is there an interpretation of the law which may aid the jury in determining whether the punishment should be a life sentence or the maximum penalty in a verdict of first degree murder, that is, does the law consider any legal mitigation in this respect? If it does, may we be made available of such?
>
> The Court: The only thing I can tell you is that it is entirely up to you folks. I will ask you a question: Do you find any mitigating circumstances?
>
> The Foreman: I am of the opinion that there are circumstances which . . . may be considered to be in mitigation. I am not sure how the law defines mitigating and I don't know what Webster says on it either, frankly.

---

[249] *E.g.*, People v. Friend, 47 Cal.2d 749, 767–68; 306 P.2d 463, 474–75 (1957); People v. Lane, 56 Cal.2d 773, 786–87, 366 P.2d 57, 65, 16 Cal. Rptr. 801, 811 (1961) (emphasis omitted).
[250] People v. Friend, 47 Cal. 2d 749, 760–61, 306 P.2d 463, 470 (1957).

> The Court: Get me the dictionary and I will read it to them. . . .
> Webster's New International Dictionary, Second Edition, . . .
> defines mitigate as follows: . . . .

The judge proceeded to quote the dictionary definition at some length and concluded:[251]

> The only thing I can say to you, ladies and gentlemen, is that you heard the evidence; you are the sole judges as to what the penalty or punishment is to be in this case. That is up to you. I can't tell you what to do. I gave you all the instructions. You have the instructions with you and if you can find any mitigating circumstances in the case, why, if that is what you are looking for, why it is up to you to find them. I can't tell you anything about them. If you want to argue some more about it I will let you go back; if you don't want to I will put you to bed. What do you want? In my opinion there is absolutely no reason why you shouldn't arrive at a verdict.

As in the Ohio case above, the jury instruction here is a sort of opaque anti-instruction, reminding the jurors anxious for guidance that the law refuses to give them any guidance. But it is a more eloquent anti-instruction, a sort of essay on the aspects of the human condition that surround violence. In a sense, it lists factors for the jury to consider, but it wholly avoids investing these factors with any formal legal status or dignifying them with any legal language. It merely reminds the jurors of the inevitable questions about crime and character that they must think of in making so momentous a decision, and it insists that they are wholly free—and thus wholly alone—in deciding how to weigh the factors before them. There are no presumptions or burdens of proof to help decide close cases. Indeed, though the lawyers might speak in terms of "aggravating" and "mitigating" circumstances, the jury is free to choose death without identifying an aggravating factor or to choose life without identifying a mitigating factor.

When the jury haplessly asks for an "interpretation of the law," all the judge can give them is a nonlegal, dictionary definition. Instead of a litany of legal factors, the jury hears a list of synonyms for mitigation which might remind the jurors of the elements of commonsense morality they ought to consider. Unlike Ohio law, California law gave specific legal instructions that the jury make a nonlegal judgment, "a complete and careful analysis of [the defendant] as a human composite of emotional, psychological and genetic factors."[252]

---

[251] *Ibid.*

[252] People v. Morse, 60 Cal. 2d 631, 647, 388 P.2d 33, 43, 36 Cal. Rptr. 201, 211 (1964).

During this era, the California courts generated a great deal of doctrine governing the penalty trial.[253] The legislature allowed both the State and the defense to introduce almost any evidence relevant to the defendant's character, record, or offense. The courts backed this legislation up by granting the defendant rights of confrontation and compulsory process, but qualified it by enforcing the conventional guilt-phase rules against hearsay. The courts also strictly forbade the parties to use the penalty trial to debate the general legislative questions concerning the efficacy or moral propriety of the death penalty, and the prosecution was forbidden to warn the jury about the possibility of parole in order to win a death verdict.[254] Finally, the prosecutor could not remind the jury that the Governor had power to commute a death sentence, or that the law required the California Supreme Court to review every death sentence. As that court explained, a jury that considered the possibility of commutation or of reversal on appeal might feel a diminished sense of moral responsibility in making the death penalty decision.[255]

Thus, the California courts created doctrine to regulate the penalty trial, but virtually none of that doctrine was ever communicated to the jury. Rather, the purpose of the doctrine was to create a sort of pure laboratory condition in which the jury had no choice but to exercise its moral discretion, possessed of all relevant and reliable information, undistracted by prejudicial information, and utterly unaided by any legal formula. The law had carefully constructed the penalty trial to be a "legal vacuum."[256]

It is difficult to obtain transcripts of lawyers' arguments from this era, but my discussions with California criminal lawyers who litigated death penalty cases in the 1950s and 1960s report that the arguments were often very emotional. They lacked the religious, oratorical bombast of the Southern tradition, and the California courts, unlike the Southern courts, did impose some stern restrictions on the most

---

[253] For detailed summaries of the California law described in the text, see *California Penalty Jury* note 14 *supra*, at 1311-15; Project, *The Death Penalty Cases*, 56 CALIF. L. REV. 1268, 1366-69, 1404-42 (1968).

[254] The trial judge had to instruct the jury to assume that if the defendant received a life sentence, the parole authorities would not release him into society unless and until he ceased to pose any danger. People v. Morse, 60 Cal.2d 631, 648, 388 P.2d 33, 43-44, 36 Cal. Rptr. 201, 211-12 (1964).

[255] *Id.* at 649-53, 388 P.2d at 44-47, 36 Cal. Rptr. at 212-15.

[256] People v. Terry, 61 Cal.2d 137, 154, 390 P.2d 381, 392, 37 Cal. Rptr. 605, 616 (1964).

prejudicial and inflammatory arguments.[257] Moreover, the prosecution and defense counsel in California, unlike those operating under the unitary system in other states, at least had some specific subject matter they could discuss in arguing punishment. They could review the aggravating and mitigating facts they had presented in the penalty trial. But because the statute offered the jury no formal legal guidance in how to treat these punishment facts, the lawyers could not couch their arguments in very legalistic terms.

D. THE FORMAL TYPE

The last type on the continuum is, of course, the formal, trial-type penalty proceeding. In one sense, this proceeding is more open than the California type, since normally the hearsay rules do not apply to keep out relevant evidence.[258] But the major difference is that in many states the court specifically instructs the jury in treating the evidence, using formal legal language about aggravating and mitigating circumstances, and offering a purportedly systematic formula for comparatively weighing the legal circumstances.

The new instruction in California, typical of the formal schemes, runs through all the statutory circumstances in some detail, even where the parties have proffered evidence only bearing on some of the circumstances.[259] The court instructs the jury to take account of and be guided by the aggravating and mitigating circumstances, and is told that if it finds the aggravating outweigh the mitigating it must choose a death sentence.

---

[257] Both before and after *Furman*, the California rules defining prosecutorial misconduct during argument in the guilt phase of the trial were applicable to the penalty phase. The prosecutor had to base his closing argument solely on factual matters which had been the subject of evidence received at trial "or of which no evidence need ever be introduced because of their notoriety as judicially noted facts." Counsel "may state matters not in evidence that are common knowledge, or are illustrations drawn from common experience, history, or literature." People v. Love, 56 Cal.2d 720, 730, 16 Cal. Rptr. 777, 782, 366 P.2d 33, 38 (1961). The prosecutor could not assert as facts matters not in evidence or excluded as inadmissible, People v. Kirkes, 39 Cal.2d 719, 724, 249 P.2d 1, 4 (1952); use evidence offered for a special purpose, such as credibility or state of mind, to argue inferences for which the evidence is inadmissible, People v. Purvis, 56 Cal.2d 93, 99, 13 Cal. Rptr. 801, 804-05, 362 P.2d 713, 716-17 (1961); argue his own belief in the defendant's guilt, People v. Kirkes, 39 Cal. 2d 719, 724, 249 P.2d 1, 4 (1952); use argument calculated to mislead the jury, People v. Purvis, 52 Cal.2d 871, 886, 346 P.2d 22, 30-31 (1959); or use arguments or evidence that appealed primarily to passion or prejudice, People v. Love, 53 Cal.2d 843, 856, 3 Cal. Rptr. 665, 672-73, 350 P.2d 705, 712-13 (1960).

[258] See Green v. Georgia, 442 U.S. 95 (1979) (*per curiam*).

[259] The California list of circumstances is unusual, because it blends aggravating and mitigating circumstances into a single list without distinguishing them. Cal. Pen. Code §190.3 (West 1983). Nevertheless, the jury instructions assume that the jurors can tell aggravating and mitigating factors apart. The standard instruction tracks the statute.

On December 15, 1982, a jury in Placerville, California, had to choose between death and life without parole for a defendant named Neely. The jury received the regular California instruction, along with a new boilerplate instruction about telling the jury to consider sympathy but not prejudice. Again, the jury asked the judge for more help:[260]

> The Court: Good morning ladies and gentlemen. I have a note from Mr. Crill.
>
> Now, we have a note that reads as follows:
>
> "On this page the instructions state, 'If you conclude that the aggravating circumstances, et cetera you shall impose a sentence of death.' Does this mean we have to, or see Page 22."
>
> The note attached to that, "May we show mercy and give life without possibility even though we feel aggravating outweighs mitigating?"
>
> I will answer that question as follows: I am going to now direct your attention to Page 17 of those instructions, which has been previously read to you, which you now have with you in the jury room.
>
> That page reads as follows: It is now your duty to determine which of the two penalties, death or confinement in the State Prison for life without possibility of parole, shall be imposed upon defendant.
>
> After having heard all of the evidence, and after having heard and considered the arguments of counsel, you shall consider, take into account, and be guided by the applicable factors of aggravating and mitigating circumstances upon which you have been instructed.
>
> If you conclude that the aggravating circumstances outweigh the mitigating circumstances, you shall impose a sentence of death. However, if you determine that the mitigating circumstances outweigh the aggravating circumstances, you shall impose a sentence of confinement in the State Prison for life without possibility of parole.
>
> Before you may consider a particular aggravating circumstance to be true, you must be satisfied of the existence of that aggravating circumstance beyond a reasonable doubt.
>
> Page 22 of the jury instructions, which you sent back to me, allows the jury to consider pity, sympathy, and mercy as those factors may constitute a mitigating circumstance within the Defendant's background. The language should not be interpreted as providing anything contrary to Page 17 of your instructions.
>
> I will return the instructions with the Bailiff so you may take them into the jury room with you.

---

[260] People v. Neely, No. 40424 (Cal. Super. Ct. El Dorado Cty., Dec. 15, 1982). Transcript of Proceedings at 204 (on file with author). A remarkably similar exchange occurred in State v. Smith, 292 S.E.2d 264, 274–75 (N.C.). (1982).

Two hours after this exchange, the jury sentenced Neely to death.

Both the question and answer are remarkable, and neither could have occurred in a penalty scheme in one of the earlier stages of death penalty law. The question here is remarkable because, unlike the previous exchanges, the jury asks not for formal legal guidance, but for release from the strictures of legal guidance. Theoretically, after *Lockett*, the jury has a broad, perhaps unrestricted right to identify mitigating circumstances. *Lockett* virtually forbids a legal definition of mitigation. A jury can thus rely on almost anything as a mitigating circumstance, and can certainly "weight" a mitigating circumstance as heavily as it wishes. It seems odd that a jury, whose power to give valence to mitigating circumstances is almost unrestricted, could get itself into the dilemma of believing that the mitigating circumstances have less aggregate weight than the aggravating circumstances and yet still believe that death is an inappropriate sentence.[261] The jurors must have engaged in a two-step process. First, they articulated some mitigating circumstances in express or legal terms. Second, they intuited some other reason that made them reluctant to choose a death sentence, but even though that reason probably derived from their image of Neely's character, record, or offense, they were unable to articulate it as a mitigating circumstance.[262] The jurors may have learned rather clumsily to think in legal categories. Having received a formal instruction from the judge, they became confused because they could not capture in legal language their own ideas or sentiments about the defendant's just deserts.

Unlike the judges in the previous exchanges, the judge in Neely's penalty trial is ready to offer the jury legal help. Yet in a sense he does exactly what the other judges did: he simply repeats the major instruction. The judge, like the jury, confronts the somewhat contradictory language of the standard instruction, which seems at once to forbid and to encourage the exercise of subjective compassion. Whether the contradiction is inadvertent or reflects the courts' and

---

[261] One possible explanation is that at that time the California statute on its face violated *Lockett*. The last statutory circumstance provision refers to "[a]ny other circumstance which extenuates the gravity of the crime even though it is not a legal excuse for the crime." Cal. Pen. Code §190.3(k) (West 1983). If the judge gives no other instructions on mitigating circumstances, the jury might think it could not consider mitigating facts about the defendant's character which do not bear directly on his responsibility for the murder. The California Supreme Court has since directed trial courts to give capital juries a broad mitigation instruction consistent with *Lockett*. People v. Easley, 34 Cal. 3d 858, 878-79 n. 10 (1983).

[262] For an excellent discussion of why jurors may intuit perfectly legitimate mitigating circumstances which they cannot articulate, see Ledewitz, note 66 *supra*, at 152-56.

legislature's ambivalence about the relationship of law and ethics, the judge offers to relieve the jury of its dilemma by asserting that the legal category is paramount.

This very concrete instance of a jury's dilemma reflects one of the most important doctrinal issues that has arisen in recent appellate litigation—the issue of the "quasi-mandatory" death penalty statute. In *Woodson*, the Court prohibited an automatic death penalty law which effectively required the jury to sentence a defendant to death if it found him guilty of the highest degree of murder.[263] In *Lockett*, the Court removed another "mandatory" aspect of the death penalty: the states could not require the jury to choose a death sentence when formal statutory mitigating circumstances were insufficient to overcome aggravating circumstances, regardless of the jury's perception of other mitigating circumstances.[264] But *Woodson* and *Lockett* do not clearly forbid a state to devise a more complex and purportedly sensitive formula for the penalty trial and to instruct the jurors that if that formula yields certain factual conclusions, they must choose a death sentence.[265] *Zant* and *Barclay* certainly permit schemes without such mandatory aspects, but by themselves they do not forbid anything at all.

If the courts want to invalidate these "quasi-mandatory" statutory provisions and instructions, they can easily look to the generously amorphous rhetoric about "reliability" and "individualized" sentencing in *Woodson* and *Lockett* for doctrinal support. But the interesting question is why this dialectic between formality and informality has constantly arisen in the death penalty. The defense bar has continually called both for more law for capital punishment and for less. Before *Furman*, the juries simply had to decide whether, in visceral and moral terms, the defendant deserved to die. The courts then transformed that question into a variety of legal formulas, the defense bar often challenging those formulas for insufficient adherence to the rule of law. But as those formulas become more legalistic, the defense bar has had to remind the courts that the jury still must conceive the issue

---

[263] See note 54 *supra* and accompanying text.

[264] See notes 77-82 *supra* and accompanying text.

[265] For a discussion of "quasi-mandatory" statutes, see Ledewitz, note 66 *supra*, at 103-13. The "quasi-mandatory" instruction has now been obliquely restricted, though not declared unconstitutional, in *Easley*, 34 Cal. 3d at 875-85. The instruction has its greatest effect where the defense offers no specific mitigating evidence whatsoever, relying simply on a general appeal to mercy.

consciously and explicitly in terms of whether the defendant deserves to die. Due process romanticism turns back to haunt the defendant.

It seems useful again to treat the issue in terms of jury nullification. Criminal trial juries always have the power to nullify the demands of the rule of law. But we adhere to the rule of law by never telling the jury they have this power.[266] The penalty jury in the *Neely* case need never have asked the judge the question it did. It could have decided on a life sentence even if it thought the legal formula demanded otherwise. No appellate court could ever have upset that decision. Nor would the public very likely have been able to condemn the jurors for acting contrary to the law and the facts as it might in the case of a guilt trial, because the penalty trial does not offer the public any clear image of the law and the facts. But the jury took the formula very seriously, and the defense must argue that, in the case of the death penalty at least, the power to nullify the law must become an express part of the law itself.

In that sense, the defense bar cannot wholly disagree with the view of the penalty decision expressed by the Supreme Court in *Ramos* and by Justice Rehnquist in *Zant* and *Barclay*.[267] Weighing and balancing legally defined factors may be useful in helping the jury frame the issue, but the penalty decision is ultimately irreducible to legal terms. With enhanced rules of murder liability and aggravating circumstances about the defendant's crime and criminal record, the law perhaps can sensibly screen out those defendants who do not deserve to die. But that leaves no legal theory about which defendants *do* deserve to die.

The most striking change from previous versions of the penalty trial is the change in the tone and rhetoric of the prosecution's closing argument, which frames and interprets the instructions for the jury. Even in California, under the pre-*Furman* statutory scheme, prosecutors relied on emotional exhortation to win death sentences. But unlike prosecutors in many other states, they have now taken full advantage of the doctrinal formality of the penalty trial to make the case for death in the most lawyerly, legalistic, dispassionate form. The prosecutor often reinforces the judge's instructions that if the formula of fact-finding produces a certain result, the jury has a duty to vote for death. But the prosecutor does not emphasize legal duty as such, but

---

[266] See note 89 *supra* and accompanying text.
[267] See notes 199-201, 218-19 *supra* and accompanying text.

rather legal duty as a reassuring escape from the anxiety of moral choice. The prosecutor's job is essentially to help the jurors realize that their apparently painful choice is no choice at all—that the law is making it for them.

The prosecutor often begins his argument in a manner literally the opposite of the old emotive style:[268]

> Ladies and gentlemen, it's not with any great passion that I will argue to you this morning. It's not my purpose or intent to arouse you or cause you to make a decision based upon anything other than what is reasonable and what is required under the law and the evidence.

The prosecutor then follows a fairly fixed ritual. He explains that the penalty phase law is simple and straightforward, and reassuringly directive:[269]

> . . . . When you rendered your [guilt] verdict on Friday and you went home, I suspect that many of you thought about what you were going to have to do when you came back here and you considered the death penalty, and how you felt about it and those kind of things.
>   But you didn't have any roadmaps, you didn't have any guidelines for knowing what you were supposed to look at in judging whether or not the appropriate sentence in this case is death. But the judge just gave you those.

The prosecutor then proceeds through what might be called the litany of circumstances, or the penal arithmetic.[270]

> Basically what happens there are 11 factors that you have to consider.
>   And I'm going to read those 11 factors just for once so that you can hear them and get the general picture.
>   Then I'll tell you the significance of them.
>   And then we're going to go through the factors one by one and talk about them.

He methodically runs through all the circumstances in the California statute, briefly explains their significance, and, where the evidence

---

[268] People v. Wade, No. SCR-38259 (Cal. Super. Ct. San Bernardino Cty., 1982) Transcript Vol. 31, at 6452 (on file with author).

[269] People v. Jones, No. 11015 (Cal. Super. Ct. Merced Cty., June 18, 1982) Transcript Vol. 11, at 864-65 (on file with author).

[270] People v. Bittaker, No. 196434 (Cal. Super. Ct. Los Angeles Cty., Feb. 23, 1981) Transcript at 2546 (on file with author).

supports an aggravating circumstance, carefully ties the raw evidence to the statutory category:[271]

> The third consideration is the presence or absence of any prior felony convictions.
> This third guideline was satisfied through evidence presented by the people yesterday. The defendant does in fact have two felony convictions. One is for—is related to the escape back in Kentucky in 1973. The second is with respect to the robbery in 1977. So again we have more aggravating factors to be considered in this case.

Perhaps the most devilishly legalistic part of this rhetorical exercise is to stress the importance of a statutory mitigating category where there is no evidence to support it. The prosecutor is able to cite a mitigating circumstance and take advantage of the proof of a negative:[272]

> The fourth consideration is whether or not the offense was committed while the defendant was under the influence of extreme mental or emotional disturbance. There is no such evidence in this case. With respect to number four, it simply doesn't apply in this case.
> Guideline number five, whether or not the victim was a participant in the defendant's homicidal conduct or consented to the homicidal act. All right, this is clear it has no application to what the defendant did on September 5th of 1980.

The legal category has fully triumphed over the raw facts of aggravation and mitigation. The prosecutor uses the statutory categories to create a portrait of the hypothetical killer who deserves mercy, and the defendant's failure to match the statutory portrait condemns him.

In the end, the prosecutor reviews the aggravating and mitigating circumstances and literally performs legal arithmetic, adding them up on the board, and showing that the aggravating outweigh or outnumber the mitigating. The prosecutor then calmly summarizes the result:[273]

> You have a scale in front of you. One is for aggravation and one is for mitigation. If the scale tips towards mitigation, then you are

---

[271] People v. Hamilton, No. 25591 (Cal. Super. Ct. Contra Costa Cty., Sept. 30, 1981) Transcript Vol. 19-B, at 8 (on file with author).

[272] *Id.* at 9.

[273] *Id.* at 14–15.

bound by law to impose the sentence of life without possibility of parole. But if on the other hand that scale tips at all towards the factors in aggravation outweighing the circumstances in mitigation, then you are bound by law to impose the sentence of death in this case.

Throughout this rhetorical exercise, the prosecutor stresses that the jury need not exercise any personal judgment at all. Thus, he does not simply reinforce the judge's "quasi-mandatory" instruction; indeed the prosecutor might be able to use this strategy even without the aid of a quasi-mandatory instruction. He simply wants to reassure the jurors that there is available to them a legal formula which logically calls for a death sentence:[274]

> It's never easy for someone to ask for another man's life. But your burden is lightened in this case because of the law.
> The way the law is set up, as I'll explain it to you, the weighing process that you go through and the fact that if the aggravating circumstances outweigh the mitigating circumstances, you shall return a verdict of death.
> It's just that simple. The law lightened your burden in that regard, in the analysis that you go through. . . .
> The way the criminal justice system is set up, it's set up that every individual's rights are protected, and this defendant's rights have been protected.
> You have no worry there. . . .

Or:[275]

> All you are going to hear is you are to consider these factors and you are then to return a verdict of death, a verdict of life without parole. That is all you decide. You decide what the verdicts are. You don't gas anybody. . . .

Or:[276]

> Now, in this respect, if you try to do, what is in your own mind, justice or try to impose what is, in your own mind, truth, in this particular case, you're not required. A burden that is personal to

---

[274] People v. Guzman, No. 38466 (Cal. Super. Ct. El Dorado Cty. 1981) Transcript Vol. VI, at 1566-67 (on file with author).

[275] People v. Warren, No. A616720 (Cal. Super. Ct. Los Angeles Cty. 1981) Transcript Vol. 15, at 3698 (on file with author).

[276] People v. Milner, No. 74854 (Cal. Super. Ct. Santa Clara Cty. 1982) Transcript Vol. 12, at 3403-04 (on file with author). *Cf.* United States v. Dougherty, 473 F.2d 1113 (D.C. Cir. 1972) (instructing jurors of their power to nullify law would cause them undue anxiety).

you, but ladies and gentlemen, I submit to you you're not to do or arrive at what you, as individuals, feel is just or true in this particular case, based upon your own standards, because if you do so, you're taking upon each one of you individually a burden that the law does not require.

Now, if you get away from these factors and interpose your own personal feelings or prejudices concerning this, and you are truly stepping outside of the law and taking personal responsibility for your decision.

The prosecutor essentially tells the jurors that even if they have the power to nullify the law, they should not exercise it and thereby yield the moral comfort that the legal formula offers them.

The modern prosecutor thus relies on roughly the same range of evidence available to him in the earlier California bifurcated procedure, but now recasts it into a language of legalism. He thereby sets the rhetorical agenda of the arguments as a legalistic and not an emotional one. And where the medium of discourse is legalism rather than emotion, the defense is at a disadvantage. There may be some cases where the defense can stress statutory mitigating circumstances to make a legalistic argument for mercy, but those cases are probably rare, given sensible prosecutorial case selection. One other approach has been to request the judge to include in the instructions a detailed listing of nonstatutory mitigating circumstances proffered by the defense, hoping that these circumstances will thereby at least receive some legal status in the mind of the jurors equal to that of the statutory aggravating circumstances.[277] But the more promising, sometimes the only promising, strategy of the defense in the argument phase is to try to reverse the legalistic tone of the discourse. This is a difficult strategy, because an overly emotional approach may not sit well with a jury impressed by the formal dignity of the prosecution argument. An emotional argument may seem by comparison like a confession that the defense has no argument at all.[278] So the defense strategy in reversing the rhetoric of the penalty arguments must be subtle.

The very beginning of the defense argument is crucial in breaking the mood of the jury. The defense counsel often begins in a tone of measured emotional intensity, and his very first goal is somehow to "delegalize" the tone of the penalty trial. Often the lawyer does this by

---

[277] Washington v. Watkins, 655 F.2d 1346, 1373-77 (5th Cir. 1981).

[278] The defense lawyer often prepares the jury for his counterargument at pretrial voir dire, by telling prospective jurors that no matter what evidence or argument they hear at trial, they will retain discretion to show mercy.

making personal reference to himself, but in a way designed to impress the jury that legal formalism is useless to the task before them. He therefore begins in gesture of professional humility, if not self-abasement:[279]

> Good morning, ladies and gentlemen. I would like to tell you that I have been a public defender for about six years, and practiced law criminally and civilly for a few years before that. I have never done this before.
>
> I have never appeared before a jury who has a decision whether to vote for the death penalty or life without possibility of parole, and it is not, obviously, the life without possibility of parole that makes me feel so shaken. It is because we are talking about the death penalty.
>
> It is, I feel, an awesome responsibility that I have, but my responsibility is nothing, nothing at all compared to the responsibility that you bear, and I appreciate that, and I feel that, you know, we have been together in this trial about five weeks. . . .

Or:[280]

> Ladies and Gentlemen, when I was preparing for final argument, I thought how woefully inadequate my legal training has been, because I was never in anyplace in law school or anyplace else to argue life versus death.

In debasing the relevancy of his professional training and status, counsel is of course telling the jury that the law itself, contrary to the prosecution's suggestion, does not provide guideposts and relief here. This sort of introductory flourish sets up the main theme of the argument: that the decision over penalty is not a question of penal arithmetic, and that it is a grave, agonizing moral decision that each juror must face alone. Where the prosecutor reassured the jurors that the law offers them protection from the anxiety of personal responsibility, the defense tells them that that offer of protection is an illusion:[281]

> What does the law tell you? What kind of guidelines are provided here? First, as you know the law does not tell you that

---

[279] People v. Hendricks, No. 105415 (Cal. Super. Ct. San Francisco Cty., Nov. 20, 1981) Transcript Vol. XXI, at 32 (on file with author).

[280] People v. McDonald, No. A-020403 (Cal. Super. Ct. Los Angeles Cty., Mar. 3, 1981) Transcript Vol. VI, at 1169 (on file with author).

[281] People v. Cummings, No. 81041 (Cal. Super. Ct. Santa Clara Cty., Jan. 10, 1983) Transcript at 2818-19 (on file with author).

anybody who has committed two murders in the first degree must be killed. If that were the case, your job would be simple and straightforward. You arrived at your decision; therefore death must follow. . . . Were that the case, were it a matter of addition, then all the law would have to do would say in circumstances such as this where two murders in the first degree have been proved and X number of other assaults, you must therefore return the death penalty. The law recognizes, as you do, that, even in this case, the law does not say that you must return the death penalty. It is a decision which each and everyone of you will have to make. And unless each and everyone of you make it, Mr. Cummings will not be killed in the gas chamber. The law does not say that you must do so. The law does not say that. You shall do so.

The defense lawyer will make what use of the evidence about the murder itself he can. He may review it to prove that the defendant's vicious acts suggest involuntariness—that the random, gratuitous violence of the murder in question or a prior crime suggests a person who cannot fully control his actions. Defense counsel then interweaves this reinterpretation of the aggravating facts with whatever mitigating facts are available to suggest a determinist theory of the defendant's behavior. The artful defense lawyer describes a narrative chain from a childhood of abuse, neglect and family turmoil, to a youth in social or penal institutions and an introduction to brutality and crime, up to the present murder. An especially skillful version of such narrative shows how it can be done with almost entrancing Faulknerian rhythm, "humanizing" the defendant without expressly appealing to sentiment:[282]

Donald Cummings, who at the age of three in a home of alcoholics and people who locked him and his siblings into their house when they would go downtown to drink, who wasn't fed, who wasn't clothed, who lived in dirt, who lived in filth and who lived in squalor, at the age of three when a sibling was taken from him through pneumonia, through neglect, he was present, he must have seen that. Donald Cummings, who a year later was there when, presumably was there, when his mother said to the Department of Social Services, "Take this one. I can't stand the sight of him," who a year later another sibling died of neglect in the house, who lived in filth, who lived in squalor. "My neck hurts. My father's been squeezing my neck. I can't hear out of an ear." The

---

[282] *Id.* at 2836-37. Experienced defense lawyers suggest that one lawyer should do both the entire guilt trial and the entire penalty phase. Counsel thereby conveys his personal bond with his client in order to induce the jury to develop some personal feeling for the client as well.

sister engaged in some sex plays with others, not toilet trained who lived in filth, who lived in squalor, who lived in neglect, who was locked in the house and left alone. What happened to the so misshapen spirit on some primordial level at an age beyond control, at an age before reason, at an age when he didn't have a choice? Human frailty. Look at the offenses. Something happened. And it happened then, and you know it. Human frailty. He has lived a life that is different from the lives everyone of you have lived, has been subjected to the influences that none of you have felt in that way, who has seen and experienced at an age of the utmost importance things that are unimaginable to us. "I saw bloody brains on the sidewalk."

The defense lawyer's key theme is that contrary to the prosecutor's reassurance, the decision to execute is not a matter of following a legal formula; it is a painful moral decision, and it is a decision whether to kill:[283]

It's not like you were going to the produce section in the supermarket and want to find out how many pounds of tomatoes you are going to get or what the bananas weigh. . . . How do you do that? The law does not tell you. It is a subjective judgment on your part, on the part of each and everyone of you. There is no salvation by referring your decision to an effective standard beyond your control, it is a subjective evaluation for each and everyone of you. And that is inescapable. So, you must decide what the weight is and how that weight compares in the balance, something that the law does not tell you how to do. And how on earth do you do that?

We are talking about whether or not Mr. Cummings is going to be destroyed, is going to be strapped in a seat in a gas chamber in San Quentin, when cyanide is dropped in sulphuric acid and he chokes because he does not want to breathe and he does. And he turns purple and his eyes . . . I know you take this matter seriously. There is no more serious decision that you will ever have to make in your entire life. And it is a decision that you will live with for the rest of your life.

Though a skillful defense lawyer can use these devices to counter the prosecutor's rhetorical strategy, some defense lawyers operating under the new formal penalty trial scheme in California believe the defendant had a better chance for mercy under the older, unregulated scheme.[284] When the prosecutor must largely appeal to emotion in his

---

[283] *Id.* at 2827.

[284] I base this conclusion on conversations with several California defense lawyers who have litigated death penalty cases under both the old and new schemes.

argument, he is fighting in territory where the defense lawyer is comfortable. The formal, legalistic image of the law of capital punishment that the jury now receives from the court and the prosecutor is often a great advantage to the state.

VI. SOME PERSPECTIVES ON DOCTRINE: ITS CAUSES AND EFFECTS

The recent doctrinal history of the death penalty reveals a singular example of prolific generation of doctrine followed by its sudden and apparently drastic undoing. The documentary history of the penalty trial offers some colorful examples of how abstract doctrine may trickle down to the actors who decide real cases. The implications of these histories help to animate the causes and effects of doctrine. Why did the courts create or induce the creation of legal forms to guide or constrain the moral choices of sentencers? How are sentencers affected when legal forms are imposed on or are made available for their choices?

A. THE SOCIAL VALUE OF MAKING DOCTRINE

Beginning a decade ago, the problem of the death penalty induced in our legal institutions the abundant manufacture of legal doctrine on an issue where there had previously been no law at all. The death penalty is thus a very tempting subject for those inclined to offer theories about the social role of doctrine. The temptation is especially strong where so much of the doctrine involves the rhetoric of due process rights, which some critical scholars view as essentially ideology designed to obscure social injustice.[285]

The court decisions approving the contemporary death penalty have dignified the penalty decision with the structure and language of substantive and procedural doctrine, at the same time subverting the state's efforts to carry out the death penalty by providing innumerable doctrinal grounds for appeal. This apparently contradictory pattern suggests at least a superficial resemblance to the operation of the death penalty in eighteenth-century England, described in Douglas Hay's famous and controversial essay.[286] Hay's study attempts to explain the

---

[285] See Sumner, *The Ideological Nature of Law*, in MARXISM AND LAW 255-61 (Beirne & Quinney eds. 1982).

[286] Hay, *Property, Authority and the Criminal Law*, in HAY, LINEBAUGH, RULE, THOMPSON, & WINSLOW, ALBION'S FATAL TREE: CRIME AND SOCIETY IN EIGHTEENTH-CENTURY ENGLAND 17-63 (1975).

puzzling presence of three phenomena in that period: the great and increasing number of laws making death the automatic penalty for common property crimes, the formal complexity of pleading and proof that often saved capital defendants from conviction, and the numerous but unpredictable pardons offered through executive or royal grace or the forgiveness of private victims. Hay suggests that this odd combination of phenomena represents, not the paralyzing contradiction of criminal justice, but a very efficient scheme of social control through ideology. The criminal law terrified the lower classes by the sheer number of laws that threatened execution. But it also dignified itself as an instrument of disembodied natural justice rather than class domination, and inspired gratitude for its gifts of mercy.

Hay's theory of criminal justice raises general questions about legal doctrine as an ideology designed to persuade the populace of the legitimacy of political and economic power. Even before we address the difficult question whether the general populace is persuaded by legal ideology,[287] Hay's form of "legitimation" theory assumes at the very least that legal doctrines and rules are actually communicated to the general populace.[288] Hay's theory seems especially plausible for the period he studied simply because the English criminal law of the eighteenth century had a very obvious means of communicating with the populace. So many common crimes were capital that the capital sanction directly threatened many poor people, and capital prosecutions at least indirectly touched the lives of even more. In modern America, only a minuscule part of the citizenry ever commits or considers committing a capital crime or is ever so personally involved with murderers or their victims as to learn very much about the law of capital punishment. Most Americans are probably only barely aware how capital punishment operates or fails to operate, much less how the law of capital punishment has developed.[289]

Modern capital punishment law is more conducive to a narrower legitimation theory. Professional actors in legal institutions rely on

---

[287] For a detailed criticism of Hay's view of the socially legitimating power of the criminal law, see Langbein, *Albion's Fatal Flaws*, PAST & PRESENT (Feb. 1983, No. 98), at 96.

[288] See Hyde, *The Concept of Legitimation in the Sociology of Law*, 1983 WISC. L. REV. 379 (1983); Tushnet, *Perspectives on the Development of American Law: A Critical Review of Friedman's "A History of American Law,"* 1977 WISC. L. REV. 81, 92.

[289] An impressive empirical study of public opinion about the death penalty reveals that for most Americans capital punishment is an abstract social symbol rather than a seriously examined political issue. See Ellsworth & Ross, *Public Opinion and Capital Punishment: A Close Examination of the Views of Abolitionists and Retentionists*, 29 CRIME & DELINQUENCY 116 (1983).

doctrine to reassure themselves that the sanctions they inflict follow inevitably from the demands of neutral, disinterested legal principles, rather than from their own choice and power.[290] In fields of law fraught with hard social questions, legal actors—especially judges—may experience moral anxiety when they perceive a conflict between the apparent commands of the positive law, on the one hand, and the demands of natural justice or personal ethics on the other.[291] For many judges capital punishment poses, if not the moral anxiety of enforcing an evil law, at least the intellectual and cultural discomfort of issuing the worst of sanctions without the reassuring symbolic compass of objective facts and clear rules. The "lawless" death penalty before *Furman* may well have been a disorienting experience for judges temperamentally inclined to look for doctrinal rationalizations for their decisions.

Judges on all levels have therefore contributed to inventing complex law to fill the gap where there had been no law. And of course, the most attractive source for this gap-filling doctrine became the substantive and procedural formality of the criminal trial. Half a century ago, without relying on the formal anthropology of social ritual or Marxist theories of the relative autonomy of the law, Thurman Arnold tried to describe the phenomenon of the criminal trial in these terms.[292] The criminal trial is in part a representational medium that accomplishes what legislation and discourse cannot—it can capture and express contradictory beliefs simultaneously. The substantive and procedural doctrine of criminal law serves as a grammar of social symbols that help us represent to ourselves the ideals we cannot logically reconcile with our conduct. The criminal trial is a "miracle play" of government in which we can carry out our inarticulate beliefs about crime and criminals within the reassuring formal structure of disinterested due process.[293] Arnold's view of the trial as a stabilizing social ritual probably greatly exaggerates the practical political importance of law in general society. But it nicely expresses the view that judges have of the political value of formal legal ritual in resolving social disorder, and helps explain why American

---

[290] Tushnet, note 288 *supra*, at 93.

[291] As Robert Cover has observed among the antebellum judges deciding slavery cases, judges often resolve this conflict by retreating to highly formal characterizations of the issues so they can treat their morally ambivalent decisions as if they were choiceless deductions from fixed legal rules. COVER, JUSTICE ACCUSED 229-38 (1975).

[292] ARNOLD, THE SYMBOLS OF GOVERNMENT 128-48 (1935).

[293] *Id.* at 130-47.

judges have persistently dealt with the death penalty by borrowing from the doctrinal symbolism of the trial. Doctrine will be generated when judges find it important, even if the populace does not.

But there is another, less abstract explanation of the social role of doctrine-making in the death penalty. Judges may manipulate legal doctrine with an eye toward the populace, not to mystify them with images of legitimate authority, but simply to help achieve the number of executions which they think the populace wants and demands. There may never be a social consensus on the role of capital punishment, but a social engineer might try to identify a sort of culturally optimal number of executions that would best compromise among the competing demands made by the different constituencies of the criminal justice system.

The most obvious approach is to have some executions, but not very many. A small number of executions offers a logical, if crude, compromise between the extreme groups who want either no executions or as many as possible. It would also satisfy those who believe that execution is appropriate only for a small number of especially blameworthy killers, at least if the right ones are selected. It might further satisfy those who do not believe there is a discernible and small category of most blameworthy killers, but who believe that a small number of executions might adequately serve general deterrence and make a necessary political statement about society's attitude toward crime. But our hypothetical social engineer would want to consider other points of view or factors as well in designing his culturally optimal number. Too many executions would inure the populace to the fact of state killing and thereby deprive the death penalty of its value as a social symbol. Or too many executions might have the opposite effect of morally offending people with the spectacle of a bloodbath. On the other hand, if the number were too low in comparison with the number of murders, capital punishment might not serve general deterrence. Or if we execute too few people, we may not produce a big enough statistical sample to prove that the death penalty meets any tests of rationality or nondiscrimination.

We might therefore imagine a socially stabilizing design for the death penalty which leads to just the right number of executions to keep the art form alive, but not so many as to cause excessive social cost. It is, of course, fanciful to imagine any political institution having the skill or authority to take such a systemic approach to executions. Under the current capital punishment laws, judges have some opportunity to manipulate the rate of execution. Legislators theoretically can affect the execution rate by changing the substantive laws of murder and punishment. But between the constitutional restrictions on death sentencing and the voters' general demand for capital punishment, legislators in most states probably do not have a great deal of room to maneuver. A prosecutor can ensure that any given murder defendant will not face execution, but because he cannot control the jury or judges he can never guarantee that a defendant is executed. A juror can at best control the rate of execution in one case. But judges, especially appellate judges, have a good deal of freedom to control the number of executions within the pool of capital claimants who come before them.

Viewing the statistics of the last decade, one might imagine that in a rough, systemic way, judges have indeed manipulated death penalty doctrine to achieve a culturally optimal number of executions. That number is very close to zero, but it must be viewed in light of a very different number—the number of death sentences.[294]

If we somewhat fancifully treat the judiciary as a single and calculating mind, we could say that it has conceived a fiendishly clever way of satisfying the competing demands on the death penalty: We will sentence vast numbers of murderers to death, but execute virtually none of them. Simply having many death sentences can satisfy many proponents of the death penalty who demand capital punishment, because in a vague way they want the law to make a statement of social authority and control. It will also satisfy jurors who want to make that statement in specific cases with the reassurance that the death sentence will never really be carried out. And we can at the same time avoid arousing great numbers of people who would vent their moral and political opposition to capital punishment only on the occasion of actual executions. Once a murderer enters the apparently endless appellate process, much of the public ceases to pay attention.

---

[294] Since *Furman,* the states have sentenced over two thousand people to death, a rate over two hundred per year. Greenberg, *Capital Punishment as a System,* 91 YALE L. J. 908, 917-19 (1982). That rate is, in absolute numbers, higher than the rate in the fifties and sixties. While the percentage of criminals sentenced to death before *Furman* who were actually executed ranges as high as 80 percent in some jurisdictions, SELLIN, THE PENALTY OF DEATH 69-74 (1980), since *Furman* the courts have effectively reduced that percentage to something less than half of one percent. At least 60 to 75 percent of defendants sentenced to death win some sort of formal reversal of sentence at some point in their appeals, roughly ten times the rate for federal criminal appeals, and almost one hundred times the reversal rate for general felony convictions in the California state courts. Greenberg, *supra,* at 918.

If the death penalty system has achieved any stability in the decade since *Furman*, it has thus been a wonderfully paradoxical stability. In this sense, the death penalty resembles plea bargaining. The courts have invested the criminal trial with so many formal protections for the defendant that it is now too expensive for the prosecution to allow the defendant to exercise those rights. The result is a public declaration of legal rights which few criminals actually enjoy. By ironic contrast, the courts have essentially permitted the states an abstract right to execute which they almost never exercise.

How do these perspectives bear on the Court's abrupt drastic reversal of its commitment to penalty trial doctrine? One can imagine the Supreme Court responding to the complaints of some constituents that the drastic disjuncture between death sentences and executions and the protraction of appeals is intolerable. It is not clear that the political demand for more executions is all that strong, or that the Court would react to it so abruptly. The constituency the Court is most concerned with is most likely the judiciary itself.[295] *Barefoot* and *Ramos* express impatience with the delaying tactics of capital defendants. *Zant* and *Barclay* express fatigue and mental strain as well. For several years the courts have benefited more from the moral comfort of dignifying the death penalty than they have suffered in trying to make the doctrine appear rational. Now things have changed.

B. MORAL CHOICE AND LEGAL FORM

The availability of the sort of legal formulas that the Supreme Court has encouraged—at least until this Term—may cause some jurors to vote for the death penalty where they might otherwise be inclined to afford mercy. That the new, more formal penalty trial might increase the chances of a death sentence for particular defendants does not prove that the law has not achieved its goals. An increase in executions might actually help justify the death penalty according to at least two of the opinions in the *Furman* majority: more executions may help solve the problems of the horizontal inequity or the disutility of the

---

[295] In a speech before the Eleventh Circuit on May 9, 1983, shortly before the Court handed down its new death penalty decisions, Justice Powell addressed this issue very candidly. He lamented that the Court receives a great number of certiorari petitions in capital cases, as well as applications for stay of execution at a rate of almost one a week. He suggested that if the courts and Congress do not restrict the defense bar's opportunities for protracted federal appeals, the states ought to consider simply abolishing capital punishment. LOS ANGELES DAILY JOURNAL (May 12, 1983).

penalty.[296] Moreover, one cannot assume that a juror's unguided moral instinct to show mercy is "right," or that legal formulas that deflect that instinct are wrong.

Nevertheless, so long as one cannot confidently articulate a very rigorous legal theory about which criminals deserve to die, the chance that the law might permit a sentencer to rationalize a death sentence which his moral sentiments oppose is disturbing. The Supreme Court haplessly but repeatedly recurs to the idea that, at least in the absence of racial prejudice, jurors may legitimately exercise their conscience or conventional moral judgment in choosing which murderers to execute. But to demonstrate that legal rationalization unfairly distorts the choice of penalty, one would have to know what kind of judgment the civilized, nonracist juror "naturally" makes in sentencing a criminal to death. There is very little knowledge of what jurors actually think about when they make death penalty decisions. The constitutional cases contain much discussion about the penological purposes that generally justify the death penalty.[297] But this ignores the more concrete question of what purposes jurors have in mind when they vote for death.

One possibility is that jurors think about whether executing the defendant before them will deter other people from committing murder. But it is not clear as a logical matter how jurors could do this, so long as we assume that they follow the minimal court instruction to consider the individual aggravating and mitigating circumstances of the particular defendant's case. How does one logically decide that the execution of a particular defendant will serve general deterrence, more than the execution of other defendants? The answer from the Court and some commentators is that we serve general deterrence by issuing a death sentence for the type of crime or killer who is himself the most deterrable. Thus, it makes sense to execute the cold, deliberative killer, because the people who are most likely to be deterred by his execution are the cold deliberative potential killers who will identify with him. There is nevertheless something suspicious about the logic of a theory that would execute a paradigmatically "deterrable" killer who by hypothesis was not deterred. Even if the most deterrable killer is the

---

[296] See notes 39-40 *supra* and accompanying text.

[297] *E.g.*, Radin, note 90 *supra*, at 1164-73; *Commentary: The Death Penalty: A Critique of the Philosophical Bases Held to Satisfy the Eighth Amendment Requirements for Its Justification*, 34 OKLA. L. REV. 567 (1981).

calculating one, he may well be deterred by execution for murder.[298] Moreover, the modest empirical research on the subject suggests that juries are not inclined to choose the most calculating killers anyway;[299] they are quite willing to give death sentences to psychologically impaired defendants who are the most obviously undeterrable themselves.

A more plausible theory is that jurors think about whether the defendant would commit violent crimes again if he were ever released into society. It is hard to tell how much jurors think about this. In the majority of states right now, the prosecutor cannot explicitly raise the issue of possible parole,[300] and probably few jurors are concerned that a defendant will commit violent crimes in prison against other inmates. Some empirical data at least cast doubt on whether penalty jurors who vote for execution do so to incapacitate the defendant.[301]

Then there is the much-abused category of retribution. The commentators examining the general justifying theories of punishment have noted that "retribution" actually is used as a name for several different theories of punishment, some which view punishment as a good in itself, and others which view it as an instrument of social policy.[302] The purest form is simple moral retributivism, the straightforward idea, rooted in religious belief or moral instinct, that certain crimes by their very nature merit death. To assume that jurors act out of pure moral retribution is to assume that they focus on the crime more than the criminal, and hence rely chiefly on the aggravating circumstances. Certainly the presence of very serious aggravating factors makes the defendant a strong *prima facie* candidate for death. But if jurors pay at least some attention to mitigating

---

[298] The public may pay less attention to the details about the state of mind of a particular executed killer than to the simple fact that a killer was executed. Moreover, to execute an impulsive killer who might have a plausible argument for defense or mitigation could deter a calculating killer who would otherwise hope to contrive such a defense. HART, PUNISHMENT AND RESPONSIBILITY 18–20 (1968).

[299] See *California Penalty Jury*, note 14 *supra*, at 1426; Baldus, Pulaski, Woodworth, & Kyle, *Identifying Comparatively Excessive Sentences of Death: A Quantitative Approach*, 33 STAN. L. REV. 1, 27–28 (1980).

[300] In twenty-five of the twenty-eight states where the issue has arisen, the courts have forbidden the prosecutor and judges to raise the possibility of commutation or parole with the sentencing jury. California v. Ramos, 103 S. Ct. at 3466 (Marshall, J., dissenting). It is of course, unclear whether these state courts will change their views now that *Ramos* has found no federal constitutional bar to instructing the jury on parole and commutation. See notes 167–71 *supra* and accompanying text.

[301] See *California Penalty Jury*, note 14 *supra*, at 1427–28.

[302] See Radin, note 90 *supra*, at 1164–73; Commentary, note 297 *supra*, at 585–97; *cf.* Lempert, *Desert and Deterrence: An Assessment of the Moral Bases of the Case for Capital Punishment*, 79 MICH. L. REV. 1177, 1181–87, 1225–31 (1980).

evidence, they would not seem to be acting out of pure moral retribution. If the jurors do assess the defendant's general character, or the excuses he offers for the murder, at best we can say that they will act out of moral retribution when the crime is otherwise unredeemed by the defendant's good qualities or excused by psychological causes.

My own rough guess is that many jurors vote to execute when they are repelled by the defendant, because he presents the threatening image of gratuitous, disruptive violence that they cannot assimilate into any social or psychological categories they use in comprehending the world. Jurors can probably give mercy to even the most vicious killers if they can somehow understand what might cause this person to be a killer, or if they see so much of the normal or the good in the killer that they can rationalize his crime as an aberration. In that sense, the decision to execute, individual or collective, is related to what moral philosophers call vindictive utilitarianism, or the "hedonistic" retributivism.[303] A juror votes to expel the defendant who presents an image of violence he or she cannot assimilate into any stabilizing categories, and who thereby threatens his or her sense of comfortable order in the world.

If the death penalty decision contains these moral and psychological elements at least to some degree, then one could indeed sensibly say that the legal formulas "distort" the decision. If the decision to kill is indeed fraught with personal moral intensity, arousing the sentencer's most intense fears and anxieties, then it may be a harmful illusion for the juror to believe that he or she is choiceless.

The empirical studies of jury conduct shed little light on this question whether jurors artificially distance themselves from choices by relying on legal formalities.[304] But the controversial Milgram experiments in social psychology show how the dignifying formalities of another profession—experimental science—do serve a similar function in a chillingly similar situation.[305]

In Stanley Milgram's study, people volunteered to participate as "teachers" in a study of learning behavior.[306] The volunteer's job was

---

[303] Commentary, note 297 supra, at 574; Feinberg, Punishment, in PUNISHMENT 2, 8 (Feinberg & Gross eds. 1975).

[304] But cf. KALVEN & ZEISEL, THE AMERICAN JURY 427 (1966) (where jury follows its own sentiments rather than legal instructions, it rationalizes decisions "under guise of resolving issues of evidential doubt").

[305] MILGRAM, OBEDIENCE TO AUTHORITY (1974).

[306] For the basic design of the experiments, see id. at 13-26.

to subject a "volunteer" learner to electric shock as negative reinforcement in a learning exercise. In fact, the electric shock device was a harmless fake, and the volunteer learner was a knowing member of the team that designed the experiment. But none of this was known to the volunteer teacher, who actually thought the device inflicted great pain. The astounding results of the Milgram experiments quickly became famous and infamous. Otherwise perfectly civilized volunteer teachers proved themselves willing and able to inflict apparently severe and even excruciating pain on the learners. When the learners feigned agony and screamed for the shocks to stop, many of the volunteer teachers asked the supervising scientist at their side what to do. The scientist would say in a mechanical voice that "the experiment says you must go on," and most of the volunteer teachers did so.[307] When some volunteers asked the scientist if he would "take responsibility" for any harm, he would agree to do so, and the volunteers would inflict still higher "voltage."[308]

Milgram concluded that the key factor in the volunteers' readiness to abdicate normal moral responsibility for their acts was the reassuring professional authority of the scientist, as expressed by his language and his appearance, and the generally formal atmosphere in which the experiment was conducted.[309] Finding himself in a novel and disorienting situation that posed for him a distressing moral dilemma, the volunteer sought a professional, symbolic interpretation of the situation to reorient him—not he, but science, chose to inflict harm.[310] The Milgram experiment bears an eerie similarity to the situation of Neely's penalty jury in Placerville, California. The jury in that case asked the judge what personal moral responsibility it had over the defendant's life. The judge responded with the nonanswer of repeating the most legalistic of the technical jury instructions, essentially telling the jury it had no responsibility. In the very special situation of the criminal courtroom and the death penalty trial, it seems fairly plausible that a lay jury exposed to the mystifying language of legal formality may indeed allow its moral sense to be distorted.[311]

In another context, Robert Burt has argued against the wisdom of providing clear legal rules to answer intractably moral questions.[312]

---

[307] *E.g., id.* at 73–74.
[308] *E.g., id.* at 75–76.
[309] *Id.* at 138–43.
[310] *Id.* at 144–48.
[311] *Cf.* text at notes 287–93 *supra.*
[312] See generally BURT, TAKING CARE OF STRANGERS (1979).

Burt focuses on two issues, civil commitment and informed consent to terminate medical treatment, in which lawyers, doctors, and lay people have an opportunity to choose whether to terminate the freedom or life of another. He argues that these situations pose painful dilemmas to the people deciding the issues by arousing their natural insecurity about madness, or helplessness, or death.[313] People escape the dilemma when the law offers them the "choice to be choiceless" through a mechanical formula of decision cloaked in the rhetoric of professional authority. The person with the power of choice over others achieves artificial distance from his object by achieving artificial distance from himself. Burt argues that the legal system should decline the invitation to resolve these problems with clear legal rules, because any rule-like solution is an illusion.[314] If we suppress our moral ambivalence, it will simply arise in another form.

In the case of the death penalty, the law has sometimes offered the sentencer the illusion of a legal rule, so that no actor at any point in the penalty procedure need feel he has chosen to kill any individual. But our ambivalence has simply manifested itself in the clumsy administrative and legal complexities with which we have undone the innumerable death sentences that we have generated. The due process romanticism of the penalty trial has enabled us to avoid acknowledging the inevitably unsystematic, irreducibly personal moral elements of the choice to administer the death penalty.

One inevitably returns to *McGautha v. California*, and Justice Harlan's warning that it is neither feasible nor wise to try to design legal formulas for the morally complex question whether to sentence a criminal to death. When we read Harlan's opinion from the perspective of the doctrinal and documentary history I have described, we see that his warning raises broader questions about the wisdom of prescribing rules for moral action, questions that lie at the heart of contemporary moral philosophy.[315]

Harlan's opinion invokes the traditional liberal view that in a culture of plural values, moral choice—even the choice of an individual—

---

[313] *E.g., id.* at 47.

[314] *E.g., id.* at 162-73.

[315] Such otherwise very different writers on moral philosophy as Bernard Williams, Robert Nozick, John Rawls, Amartya Sen, and the British intuitionist writers C. D. Broad and W. D. Ross reveal a common concern, similar to Harlan's, with the question of rational formulas for moral choice. In different ways, they recognize the futility or danger of designing a mechanical decision procedure for moral reasoning, while they believe and try to demonstrate that moral agents can nevertheless generate their own rational forms in moral choice.

entails the sacrifice of at least some values.[316] Moral or legal formulas cannot change that. Conflict of value is not a pathology of culture, but a natural aspect of the very phenomenon of having values.[317] Of course, even if we cannot avoid sacrificing some value in a moral decision, we might seek a formula that ensures that we do not sacrifice the greater value to the lesser. But a formula for moral choice can at best instruct a person to identify the different values or factors that support the alternative courses of action, and to choose the alternative whose supporting values are strongest. Indeed, the modern model for making death penalty decisions takes just this form, with aggravating and mitigating circumstances serving as the differing and competing values.

However, a moral formula cannot even achieve this goal, so long as we cannot translate differing and competing values into a "universal currency" for comparative measurement.[318] As Robert Nozick has nicely put it, a rational formula for comparatively "weighing" values is impossible, because we cannot devise a mechanical, verifiable process for "weighting" the values—that is, assigning them valences in the first place.[319]

Even if such a mechanical formula were possible, it would represent the "total reduction of the moral life to rules of efficient behavior," and so nullify all moral experience.[320] Moreover, a perfectly rational moral algebra may not be necessary to satisfy the demands of formal logic or the normal individual desire for a sense of moral coherence.[321] Without acknowledging the similarity of their ties to the modern school of intuitionism,[322] both Nozick and Williams argue that the impossibility

[316] WILLIAMS, MORAL LUCK 71-72 (1981); see generally BERLIN, FOUR ESSAYS ON LIBERTY (1970).

[317] WILLIAMS, note 316 *supra*, at 72.

[318] *Id.* at 77. Williams's chief antagonist in his campaign against moral algebras is utilitarianism. See SMART & WILLIAMS, UTILITARIANISM: FOR AND AGAINST (1973). He assumes that the only "plausible candidate" for a universal currency of value comparison is Benthamite utility. WILLIAMS, note 316 *supra*, at 78; *cf.* Sen, *Rational Fools: A Critique of the Behavioral Foundations of Economic Theory*, 6 PHIL. & PUB AFFRS. 317 (1977).

[319] NOZICK, PHILOSOPHICAL INVESTIGATIONS 294 (1981). See DONAGAN, THE THEORY OF MORALITY 23-24 (1977); RAWLS, A THEORY OF JUSTICE 34, 39, 416 (1971). Nozick does make one very long and playful, if technically abstruse, attempt at a mathematical model for moral choice, NOZICK, *supra*, at 474-504, but he acknowledges that the whole model simply assumes that we can agree on numerical values for moral weights, *id.* at 491.

[320] WILLIAMS, note 316 *supra*, at 75. Nozick may be similarly concerned with the danger, as opposed to the futility, of seeking mechanical moral formulas. *Cf.* NOZICK, note 319 *supra*, at 291-316.

[321] WILLIAMS, note 316 *supra*, at 72, 81-82.

[322] A useful summary of the intuitionist school of moral philosophy is DONAGAN, note 319 *supra*, at 17-25. Intuitionism deserves mention in this discussion because the moral philosophy

of objectively "weighting" and comparing values does not condemn the moral life to entropy. Once we recognize moral choice as more art than science, we can achieve a reasonable amount of harmony and consistency in the course of our moral choices, so that at least in retrospect we can say we have acted in some sense "rationally." The call for something more reassuring—a verifiable formula of moral decision that prescribes future choices—comes not from moral philosophy, but from the need of the "public order" for political symbols of rationality.[323]

One can hardly criticize the defense bar for its contribution to the romantic formalism of the death penalty. Lawyers, especially death penalty lawyers, must try to win individual cases, and one can only win an appellate reversal of a death sentence by pointing to some legal constraint on capital sentencing that the state has violated. Nor is there any empirical proof that the formal model of the penalty trial results in more executions than the less formal model, though one can identify some cases where the degree of legal formality may be the key variable in explaining a death sentence. The development of the formal model, at least in the long run, suppresses more than it answers the moral and political questions that ought to be addressed before we execute people. A penalty trial that looks legally sophisticated offers some comforting illusions about the moral order of our public law, and might thereby earn for the death penalty at least some grudging political respect it does not deserve.

In its own clumsy and often dishonest way, and perhaps for illegitimate reasons, the Supreme Court seems to have decided that it no longer wants to use constitutional law to foster legal formulas for regulating moral choice at the penalty trial. In this sense, Justice Marshall is right when he says the Court has returned to its pre-*Furman* view of the penalty decision. It has come very close to restoring as the minimal constitutional model the middle-stage California scheme—the bifurcated proceeding in which the jury gets all the information in which it can have any legitimate interest, but the law offers it no illusory guidance on the decision to kill. One is tempted to speak of the existential death penalty: no actor in the legal system can say he had no choice.

---

of the modern intuitionist closely resembles the Court's new minimal constitutional requirements for the penalty trial.

[323] B. Williams, note 316 *supra*, at 81–82.

GAYLE BINION

"INTENT" AND EQUAL PROTECTION: A RECONSIDERATION

I. INTRODUCTION

During the past decade the Supreme Court of the United States has developed a requirement of intent in equal protection juris-prudence. The requirement that plaintiffs prove that the government intended to discriminate against them has become a formidable obstacle to invalidation of public policies that are alleged to violate the Equal Protection Clause of the Fourteenth Amendment. The intent rule has been most important in cases challenging the constitutionality of facially "neutral" laws which either effect segregation or disproportionately disadvantage blacks, hispanics, or women. From *Jefferson v. Hackney*[1] through *City of Memphis v. Greene*[2] the Court has responded to these challenges by erecting a progressively more impenetrable barrier of "intent."[3] Unless plaintiffs are able to demonstrate that the segregative or unequal consequences of the law were themselves intended by the responsible decisionmakers, the Court will examine only the facial classifications of the law and will do so under the deferential "mere rationality" standard of review. When faced with conflicting claims on the motives behind the policy in question, the Court has adapted the principle of *McGowan v.*

Gayle Binion is Associate Professor of Political Science, University of California, Santa Barbara.

AUTHOR'S NOTE: I thank Professors Thomas S. Schrock, Stanley V. Anderson, and C. Herman Pritchett for their extremely helpful comments on an earlier draft of this paper, and the Regents of the University of California, whose generous financial support made my research possible.

[1] 406 U.S. 535 (1972).

[2] 451 U.S. 100 (1981).

[3] The Court has brought the Thirteenth Amendment under the intent rule in City of Memphis v. Greene, *id.* The Fifteenth Amendment was subjected to the rule in Mobile v. Bolden, 446 U.S. 55 (1980).

Maryland.[4] as long as the Court is able to imagine that a legitimate motive existed for the passage of the law in question, it will assume that that motive explains the existence of the law. Through reliance on various unexamined premises, the Court has rationalized the assumption that the strictures of the Equal Protection Clause attach primarily to the process by which official decisions are made and not independently to the effects and consequences of these decisions.

My thesis is that the intent rule is not dictated by the Constitution, by the weight of precedent, or by rules of sound constitutional exegesis. The alternative of a "state responsibility" model will be offered. Under this approach to equal protection, the state should be accountable for what it has done and not for the motivations of its officials. Public policies which disproportionately disadvantage protected groups[5] would be subjected to serious scrutiny. The challenged policy should be upheld only upon proof that the legitimate consequences of the law were not attainable with less discriminatory by-products.

A. THE DEVELOPMENT OF THE INTENT RULE

The case law on equal protection of the laws developed substantially during the 1950s and 1960s. During this time the major distinction drawn was between segregation and discrimination which was *de jure* and that which was apparent but not thought to have been caused by government. The latter was called *de facto*. The major questions of the period were whether government was responsible for the acts in question and whether these acts constituted a violation of the Equal Protection Clause. The decisions of the 1950s focused primarily on the latter question. Important precedents laid the groundwork for a new constitutional commitment to equality under which the government was prohibited from disfavoring individuals on the basis of race.[6]

The 1960s were marked by cases on implementation of the civil rights principles of the 1950s, again, primarily with respect to racial

---

[4] 366 U.S. 420 (1961).

[5] The concept of a "suspect classification" stems from the tradition of discrimination, public and private, intentional and unintentional, that has disadvantaged these people, as well as from the ascriptive, involuntary, and largely unchangeable quality of the statuses. The final distinguishing mark of "suspect classifications" is the basic irrationality of the stereotypes that underlie the prejudices against them. The Supreme Court has been consistent only in its treatment of race as a "suspect classification." I use the term "protected groups" to include disadvantaged racial, religious, and ethnic minorities and women.

[6] See, for example, Brown v. Board of Education, 347 U.S. 483 (1954), Mayor of Baltimore v. Dawson, 350 U.S. 877 (1955), Gayle v. Browder, 352 U.S. 903 (1956), and Holmes v. Atlanta, 350 U.S. 879 (1955).

equality.[7] During this decade the questions of *de jure* versus *de facto* discrimination became sharpened, especially in the "state action" cases. When it became clear to governmental officials that the Constitution no longer permitted overt official racism, the responsibility for enforcing the customs of Jim Crow—no longer enforceable through law—fell to the private citizenry. The civil rights decisions of this era, beginning with *Burton v. Wilmington Parking Authority*,[8] however, invalidated those acts of private discrimination which were unduly infected with officialdom. Through "sifting facts and weighing circumstances"[9] the Court, in numerous cases through the 1960s and into the 1970s, held the state constitutionally responsible for actions of private parties with which it was sometimes only passively associated.[10] What is significant is that the equal protection cases and issues of the 1950s and 1960s, especially the state action/*de jure–de facto* questions, did not revolve around the question of discriminatory intent; they were resolved on the basis of whether official power (that is, the state) was responsible, regardless of intent, for the apparent disfavored treatment of blacks. Perhaps racism was so ubiquitous and so manifest in all areas of social life that the question of intent did not need to be asked, but what is arguably more critical is that the line between *de jure* and *de facto* discrimination during these decades was between that which the government had caused and that which was privately perpetrated or for which the cause was not known.

During the 1970s a significant growth and redirection in the law of equal protection took place. The problem of implementing the principles of desegregation developed in the 1950s continued, especially in education and housing.[11] From the end of the Warren era on, the interests of groups other than blacks have been litigated frequently under the Fourteenth Amendment, although with inconsistent continuity of protection for the poor,[12] for women,[13] for

[7] See, for example, Burton v. Wilmington Parking Authority, 365 U.S. 715 (1961), Loving v. Virginia 387 U.S. 369 (1968), Green v. County School Board, 391 U.S. 430 (1968), Peterson v. City of Greenville, 373 U.S. 244 (1963), Watson v. City of Memphis, 373 U.S. 526 (1963), and Hunter v. Erickson, 393 U.S. 385 (1969) for a small sample of the important developments in the law of racial equality under the Equal Protection Clause during the 1960s.

[8] 365 U.S. 715.

[9] *Id.* at 722.

[10] See, especially, Reitman v. Mulkey, 387 U.S. 369 (1967).

[11] See, for example, Keyes v. Denver, 413 U.S. 189 (1973), Pasadena Board of Education v. Spangler, 427 U.S. 424 (1976), Hills v. Gautreaux, 425 U.S. 234 (1976), and Village of Arlington Heights v. Metropolitan Housing Development Corp., 429 U.S. 252 (1977).

[12] See, for example, Shapiro v. Thompson, 394 U.S. 618 (1969); Dandridge v. Williams, 397 U.S. 471 (1970); James v. Valtierra, 402 U.S. 137 (1971); Boddie v. Connecticut, 401 U.S. 371 (1971); U.S. v. Kras, 409 U.S. 434 (1973).

[13] See, for example, Reed v. Reed, 404 U.S. 71 (1971); Frontiero v. Richardson, 411 U.S. 677

aliens,[14] for illegitimate children,[15] and for homosexuals.[16] During the 1970s demands from minority groups on the political and legal systems became twofold. First, they argued, the law should be cleared of any overt group distinctions disadvantageous to protected classes. This was a demand simply to extend to, for example, head and master laws, antisodomy laws, and child inheritance laws the principles of nondiscrimination which had already been applied to laws on racial segregation and antimiscegenation. The crux of this first demand, and of the substantive antidiscrimination principle more generally, is the irrelevance to public policy of the classification employed.[17] The decisions of the 1950s and 1960s had held that race may not be a criterion of selection.[18] Women, gays, and illegitimate children began to ask for the same classificatory irrelevance.

The second demand of the past decade, reflecting primarily the status and experience of blacks, hispanics, and women, has proven more problematic. It is that the impact of public policy be equitable to minority groups either in their exercise of constitutional rights (such as voting) or in their enjoyment of gratuitous goods and discretionary benefits. An argument suggested in litigation and advanced here is that the Equal Protection Clause is violated whenever governmental policies unnecessarily effect segregation or disproportionately disadvantage protected minority group members.[19]

There have been two prominent means advanced to remedy the consequence of group disadvantage. One is the type of affirmative

---

(1973); Rostker v. Goldberg, 453 U.S. 57 (1981); Michael M. v. Sonoma County Superior Court, 450 U.S. 464 (1981).

[14] See, for example, Graham v. Richardson, 403 U.S. 365 (1971); *In Re* Griffiths, 413 U.S. 717 (1973); Sugarman v. Dougall, 413 U.S. 634 (1973); Foley v. Connelie, 435 U.S. 291 (1978); Ambach v. Norwick, 441 U.S. 68 (1979).

[15] See, for example, Levy v. Louisiana, 391 U.S. 68 (1968); Labine v. Vincent, 401 U.S. 532 (1971); New Jersey Welfare Rights Organization v. Cahill, 411 U.S. 619 (1973); Mathews v. Lucas, 427 U.S. 495 (1976); Lalli v. Lalli, 439 U.S. 259 (1978).

[16] Doe v. Commonwealth's Attorney for City of Richmond, 425 U.S. 901 (1976).

[17] See Brest, *Foreword: In Defense of the Antidiscrimination Principle*, 90 HARV. L. REV. 1 (1976); and Ely, *Legislative and Administrative Motivation in Constitutional Law*, 79 YALE L. J. 1205, *passim* (1970).

[18] Race may not be a criterion of selection unless the government is able to demonstrate that the use of the classification is in service of a "compelling state interest." See, *e.g.*, *Loving; Shapiro.*

[19] The term "unnecessarily" is used to signify that there has not been, to my knowledge, a serious claim made that disproportionately disadvantageous impacts should always be unconstitutional. All that critics have demanded is that government meet varying levels of scrutiny of their "need" for the challenged policy. This has ranged from proving only that the policy is actually rational to demonstrating that it has a compelling need for the policy in question.

action program[20] which applies different criteria of selection to minorities or to women so as to effect a more equitable result.[21] This affirmative action approach has fared moderately well in the courts, despite the legal claim by plaintiffs of "reverse discrimination."[22] But affirmative action programs of this type must be encouraged piecemeal through policy channels, engender much public misunderstanding and resentment, and cannot effect significant changes in many areas of disadvantage. And, perhaps most important, affirmative action programs of this type leave intact the legitimacy of the often-unexamined, usual criteria of selection, implying the inferior status or worth of the beneficiary of the alternate, affirmative action criteria.

The Equal Protection case law of the 1970s into the 1980s has, therefore, been prominently marked by the second agenda, the attempt by blacks, hispanics, and women to convince the Supreme Court to apply some serious measure of scrutiny to criteria of selection which lead—often inevitably—to severe disadvantage for members of these groups. In contrast with the Court's passive willingness to uphold moderate affirmative action programs—adopted through policy channels—the Court has refused to exercise aggressive judicial review over the arguably inequitable consequences of allegedly "neutral" criteria of selection. What the Court has done, in effect, is to move the line defining *de jure* discrimination from that which has been caused by law to that which has been intentionally caused by law. Consequently, one must demonstrate that the arguably benign classification, which has caused the disadvantageous results, was adopted or maintained in order to discriminate against those who have been disadvantaged by the law. If not, the Court will apply only "mere rationality" scrutiny, and it will apply it only to the classification

---

[20] There are various types of so-called affirmative action policies. They have in common the intentional goal of increasing the representation of underrepresented groups in the institution. This may be accomplished in some cases simply by hiring in an openly competitive manner or by advertising that women and minorities are welcome to apply for jobs. At the other end of the spectrum are those policies which set hard quotas for minority representation by setting aside specific "slots" for which the minority group members compete only among themselves. It is this form of affirmative action to which I refer in the text.

[21] For example, a school board might agree to waive residency (in an attendance zone) requirements for attending a particular school. A police department may agree to hire women who are only five feet six inches while a man needs to be five feet eight inches. Or a medical school may set aside certain places in its freshman class for disadvantaged minorities whose MCAT scores are below those ordinarily required for admission.

[22] See, for example, Regents of the University of California v. Bakke, 438 U.S. 265 (1978) (upholding a modified principle of affirmative action); Steelworkers v. Weber, 443 U.S. 193 (1979); Fullilove v. Klutznick, 448 U.S. 448 (1980). Each of these cases was decided by a very divided Supreme Court.

facially employed in the legislation. As the Court averred in *Personnel Administrator of Massachusetts v. Feeney,*[23] "uneven effects upon particular groups . . . are ordinarily of no constitutional concern."[24]

It is important to note that *Feeney* involved a challenge to a lifetime veterans' preference law. Any veteran who passed the Massachusetts civil service examination was given priority over all other, nonveteran test takers. Because women constitute fewer than 2 percent of veterans, the Massachusetts law effectively prevented their entry into any but the least competitive positions. Neither this impact nor its origin in the discriminatory recruitment policies of the military was deemed to be of any relevance to the Equal Protection Clause. As the Court suggested in *Feeney* and subsequently repeated in *City of Mobile v. Bolden,*[25] a public policy does not contravene the Equal Protection Clause unless it was adopted, at least in part, because of and not just in spite of the foreseeable adverse impacts.[26]

The Court has placed the burden of proof squarely on plaintiffs to demonstrate that a secret nefarious agenda, and not the public justification for the challenged law, really explains its adoption. The Court is otherwise inclined to assume that facial neutrality toward protected groups is evidence of neutrality in fact. This assumption by the Court often rests on very narrow thinking and restrictive conceptions of classifications. In upholding California's disability plan for public employees, which exempted pregnancy from its coverage, for example, the Court in *Geduldig v. Aiello*[27] reasoned that the policy was gender neutral. In the Court's view, if the policy created any classification, it was between pregnant women and all other people.[28] This, the Court reasoned, was not equivalent to discrimination based on gender because not all women are pregnant women.[29] Because plaintiffs could not meet the burden of demonstrating that the economic benefit was but a pretext for discrimination, the Court would not apply more than "rationality" scrutiny. The plaintiff's

---

[23] 442 U.S. 256 (1979).

[24] *Id.* at 272.

[25] 446 U.S. 55 (1980).

[26] 442 U.S. at 274, 279; 446 U.S. at 71-72 n.17.

[27] 417 U.S. 484 (1974).

[28] *Id.* at 496 n.20.

[29] The Court's conceptualization of classifications is not always consistent. In *Geduldig,* only pregnant women were classified for disadvantageous treatment; in *Bakke* only disadvantaged minorities were favored. In the former case, the Court denied that the larger classification (that is, gender) was at work, but in the latter it assumed that the larger classification (race) was employed.

argument, that the State should have to find a route to economy that is less discriminatory in its impact, irrespective of intent, was, therefore, rejected by the Court.

In the past ten years the intent rule has been dispositive of more than a dozen important cases. It has had significant ramifications for the legal interests of blacks, hispanics, and women and has been an important factor in the case law governing school and housing segregation, jury composition, employment opportunity, electoral power, and welfare benefits. But why has it been adopted by the Court? What explains its appeal and its popularity?

B. THE APPEAL OF THE INTENT RULE

The intent rule has been supported to varying degrees by every member of the contemporary Court.[30] It has also had enthusiastic support from some legal scholars[31] and modified approval from others.[32] There appear to be three categories of reasons for supporting the intent rule: a preoccupation with process-based theories of democracy, an apprehension about the perceived alternative, and a concern about potential, far-reaching judicial remedies.

1. *Preoccupation with process-based theories.* Professor Laurence Tribe has observed that courts possess a view of democracy and are inclined to measure the constitutionality of political processes by their approximation of these democratic process values.[33] In the realm of equal protection the Court appears to be concerned with only the cleanliness of the process by which policy choices have been made and not independently with the substance and consequences of these

---

[30] The Justices have demonstrated very different voting patterns in the cases, due to their individual conceptions of what constitutes discriminatory intent and their differing assessments of the constitutional sufficiency of the illicit intent that had been demonstrated. Even Justice Stevens, who has expressed extreme distaste for the concept of "intent" in equal protection cases in Rogers v. Lodge, 102 S. Ct. 3272, 3283 (1982), has nevertheless supported the reliance on the concept in Personnel Administrator of Massachusetts v. Feeney and Memphis v. Greene.

[31] See, for example, Ely, note 17 *supra*; Simon, *Racially Prejudiced Governmental Action: A Motivation Theory of the Constitutional Ban against Racial Discrimination*, 15 SAN DIEGO L. REV. 1041 (1978); and J. Morris Clark, *Legislative Motivation and Fundamental Rights in Constitutional Law*, 15 SAN DIEGO L. REV. 953 (1978).

[32] See, for example, Brest, *Palmer v. Thompson: An Approach to the Problem of Unconstitutional Legislative Motive*, 1971 SUPREME COURT REVIEW 95; Eisenberg, *Disproportionate Impact and Illicit Motive: Theories of Constitutional Adjudication*, 52 N.Y.U. L. REV. 36, 140 (1977), with respect to individual claims of discrimination; Boyd, *Purpose and Effect in the Law of Race Discrimination: A Response to Washington v. Davis*, 57 U. DET. J. URB. L. 707 (1980), endorses intent as an independent ground for unconstitutionality.

[33] Tribe, *The Puzzling Persistence of Process-based Constitutional Theories*, 89 YALE L. J. 1063, 1077 (1980).

choices. When laws are challenged as racist or sexist, a preoccupation with process values explains the tendency to ask whether this result motivated the decisionmakers, that is, whether the process of decisionmaking was perverted by a discriminatory intent.

Professor Paul Brest noted more than a decade ago that there was an absence of any serious attention to why official intent should be subject to judicial scrutiny. He concluded that the lack of serious attention to the question reflected the simplicity of the principle protected by such scrutiny: that government should not pursue illicit objectives.[34] Professor Michael Perry similarly views the intent rule as reflecting what he takes to be the central prohibition of the Equal Protection Clause, that government should not deliberately use race as a criterion of selection.[35]

Whereas for Brest and Perry the process-based conception of equal protection is virtually "by definition"—the Clause prohibits government from considering discriminatory goals in its decisionmaking process—Professor Larry Simon has been more concerned with process distortion. Decisions based on racially discriminatory goals violate the Equal Protection Clause, in Simon's view, because illicit considerations distort the process of decisionmaking that would, by hypothesis, otherwise take place.[36]

The two variants of the process approach define the Equal Protection Clause as prohibiting legislatures from making decisions which are the product of illicit motivations. Why this is thought to be the central, let alone the only, prohibition of the Clause—thereby necessitating the demonstration of illicit intent—is not satisfactorily explained. The process approach to the Equal Protection Clause does not, therefore, provide proof of its correctness.

2. *Apprehension about the perceived alternative.* The intent rule has also proven attractive because of fear of the perceived alternative of an impact rule for equal protection cases. As Professor Robert Schwemm observed in his critique of the *Washington v. Davis*[37] decision, "[T]he Court chose to focus on discriminatory purpose not so much because of the inherent merits of this standard . . . but because the alternative was seen as unacceptable."[38]

---

[34] Brest, note 32 *supra*, at 115.

[35] Perry, *The Disproportionate Impact Theory of Racial Discrimination*, 125 U. PA. L. REV. 540, 548 (1977).

[36] Simon, note 31 *supra*, at 1054.

[37] 426 U.S. 229 (1976).

[38] Schwemm, *From Washington to Arlington Heights and Beyond: Discriminatory Purpose in*

Justice White, in *Washington*, assumed not only that eschewal of the intent rule would necessitate scrutiny of all uneven impacts of public policy on minorities and the poor, he assumed as well that these impacts would necessarily be invalid.[39] The same concern about impact analysis also explains the Court's disposition of *Jefferson v. Hackney, Village of Arlington Heights v. Metropolitan Housing Development Corporation*,[40] *Personnel Administrator of Massachusetts v. Feeney*, and *City of Mobile v. Bolden* because in each case the Court equated scrutiny of unequal consequences with a finding of their unconstitutionality.[41]

A variation on the theme rests on the assumption that group impact theory could completely supplant intent theory and in so doing eliminate a cause of action for disparate treatment. Opponents of affirmative action, for example, may legitimately fear a view of equal protection concerned solely with group-based results. Persons seeking public employment or admission to professional school who are given disfavored treatment because their acceptance will not advance a minority quota might imagine that they would have no legal claim. As long as their group is not statistically underrepresented in the results of the recruitment, they fear, they would be without an equal protection claim against the disparate treatment that they experience.

Although it is speculative, it is indeed possible that concern about the eschewal of the intent rule—in favor of the assumed alternative of an impact rule—also reflects a fear of loss of privilege. While stereotypical affirmative action programs are constitutionally vulnerable to the charge of disparate treatment (in the service of equal results), a redefinition of merit and of criteria of selection may permit both equal treatment and equal group impact. An impact approach to equal protection that encourages the political decisionmakers to consider the equity of results may lead to a new, integrated meritocracy, reflecting new criteria of selection.[42] More fully integrated schools might develop if preexisting attendance zones were no longer the single criterion of school assignments. Those classes of

---

Equal Protection Litigation, 1977 U. ILL. L. F. 961, 1050. The conclusion was also reached by Eisenberg, note 32 *supra*, at 113.

[39] 426 U.S. at 248. But see Eisenberg's rebuttal to these assumptions, note 32 *supra*, at 113.

[40] 429 U.S. 252 (1977).

[41] On this point, see discussion in Section II-E2, *supra*.

[42] On this point, see the rebuttal of Lerner, *Employment Discrimination, Adverse Impact, Validity and Equality*, 1979 SUPREME COURT REVIEW 17, 43.

people most prone to score well on LSAT exams, or to live in all-white school attendance zones, or to be veterans with civil service priority, would not be served by the adoption of new classification schemes. Although policymakers are already free to adopt new, more equitable criteria of selection, so long as the intent rule is intact they are not constitutionally obliged to do so. The intent rule may, therefore, protect socioeconomically privileged classes whose interests are represented in legislative and administrative policy from judicial interference, with their resulting, often unquestioned, advantages. Despite the speculative quality of this explanation for support of the intent rule, it is intuitively persuasive and well within the principles and assumptions of interest-group politics.

3. *Concern about potential, far-reaching judicial remedies.* Significant support for the intent rule stems from concern about potentially far-reaching judicial remedies. There is concern about both the extensiveness of the remedies that would be necessary and the frequency with which they would be sought.[43] It has been suggested that the intent rule is viewed as an effective way to limit the role of the judiciary vis-à-vis the authority of the executive and legislative branches and thereby to maximize flexibility in decisionmaking.[44] The Court itself has acknowledged anxiety that far-reaching remedies might be routine if intent analysis were abandoned in equal protection cases.[45] In each of the disparate impact cases, therefore, the Court has consciously limited its authority over the inequality of effects. In *Feeney* the Court observed that "calculus of effects . . . is a legislative and not a judicial responsibility."[46] More specifically, the Court's disposition of *Milliken v. Bradley*[47] may be understood as utilizing intent theory directly as a curb on judicial remedies. The Court was clearly reluctant to "punish" arguably "innocent" suburbs by involving them in a desegregation plan, no matter what the

---

[43] See, for example, Perry, note 35 *supra* at 565-66.

[44] On this point, see Note, *Discriminatory Purpose and Disproportionate Impact: An Assessment after Feeney*, 79 COLUM. L. REV. 1376, 1378, 1384 (1979); Brest, *Reflections on Motive Review*, 15 SAN DIEGO L. REV. 1141, 1142 (1978); Sellers, *The Impact of Intent on Equal Protection Jurisprudence*, 84 DICK. L. REV. 363, 387 (1980). See also Note, *Toward a Redefinition of Sexual Equality*, 95 HARV. L. REV. 486, 491 (1981) (arguing that when the courts fear a particular remedy they simply deny that equal protection has been violated). For another point of view, see Sager, *Fair Measure: The Legal Status of Underenforced Constitutional Norms*, 91 HARV. L. REV. 1212 (1978).

[45] See, for example, Justice White, writing for the Court in *Washington*, and noting the concern about far-reaching decisions, 426 U.S. at 248.

[46] 422 U.S. at 272.

[47] 418 U.S. 717 (1974).

consequences for the interests of plaintiffs. Finally, Justice Blackmun's concurrence in *City of Mobile* expressed the most unabashed concern about remedies. Even though Blackmun was satisfied that nefarious intent had been demonstrated in the case, he was nevertheless not convinced of the propriety of the remedy ordered by the trial court. The trial court had ordered the adoption of the mayor-council form of government. Blackmun would have considered a remedy with less extreme judicial intrusion into the political structure of Mobile.[48]

While concern about far-reaching judicial remedies is always a legitimate issue in public law, its relation to the intent rule is particularly problematic. As a general proposition, constitutional rights ought not to be defined by the availability of a judicial remedy; they certainly should not be determined by the advisability of a judicial remedy.[49] But this is what the intent rule tends to do. In the service of judicial restraint the rule leads to narrow definitions of the rights protected by the Fourteenth Amendment. The judicial restraint justification for the intent rule is especially restrictive of "suspect classification" analysis and of the protections for these groups under the Fourteenth Amendment. The concept of suspect classification represents a judicial recognition of the constitutional relevance of a long history of discrimination, private and public, that has disadvantaged members of particular minority groups. While one may demand of governments that they demonstrate "clean hands" with respect to their motivations toward suspect classes, the judicial role involves more. It involves an obligation to "render whole" the aggrieved parties whom governments have, as a class, disadvantaged. Governments thus have a positive obligation to undo the harm that their involvement in a tradition of discrimination has wrought. While we may not know with any certainty what a condition of "wholeness" would be,[50] such an understanding of suspect classification demands, *a fortiori*, that courts prevent further official impositions of racial or gender-based

---

[48] 446 U.S. 55, 80-83 (1980).

[49] See Sager, note 44 *supra*.

[50] I certainly do not mean to imply that all remnants of racial discrimination are traceable to the history of governmental racism. While invidious discrimination has strong social roots as well, it is important to note that official involvement in various forms of discrimination added to their legitimacy and their staying power. In Diamond's terms, law buttresses social forces and thereby adds to their strength. See Diamond, *Rule of Law versus the Order of Custom*, 38 SOC. RESEARCH 42 (1971). But see Eisenberg, note 32 *supra*, at 66-68 (arguing that one must demonstrate that past discrimination is the proximate cause of the discriminatory impact of a challenged policy).

disadvantage. Rendering whole involves compensation[51] and not only a prohibition on the continuation of unconstitutional practices. The intent rule thus leaves judges two steps removed from "rendering whole": it allows judicial intervention only when the continuation of officially imposed disadvantages on protected groups is by design.

There is a further but related problem in the association between the intent rule and judicial restraint. Concern about judicial remedies not only supports the reliance on the rule; more important, it encourages a judicial reluctance to acknowledge illicit intent that has actually been demonstrated. The argument can be advanced that the Court's self-restraint is manifest not in the intent rule itself but rather in its almost uniform unwillingness to conclude that the rule has been satisfied. The intent rule itself would not reflect judicial restraint unless it significantly reduced either the opportunity or the need for judicial intervention in the policymaking process. The Court's formulation and application of the intent rule appear designed to serve a gatekeeper function.

Support for the intent rule thus stems from at least three types of concerns. While the process approach is a constitutionally grounded justification for the intent rule, it is ultimately tautological and conclusory. It defines the Clause as prohibiting only those policies that result from the deliberate, therefore intentional, consideration of race or other protected classifications in the decisionmaking process. It offers no external argument for the virtue of this antidiscrimination principle. To be sure, apprehension about the perceived alternative to intent theory and concern about potentially far-reaching judicial remedies are both pragmatic, independent justifications for the mediating principle of illicit intent. In concert they explain much of the Court's decisionmaking on the subject. Less satisfactory, however, is their value in persuading skeptics that the Court ought to use the intent rule to resolve these concerns.

II. OBJECTIONS TO THE PRINCIPLE OF INTENT

Despite recent judicial adherence to the intent rule, serious objections may be raised to it. While objections to the rule may rest on a concern that the intent behind official actions is simply not knowable or may reflect skepticism about the motives of the Court that has

---

[51] A doctrine of the obligation of governments to compensate for past discrimination which has continuing effects may, for example, justify affirmative action programs.

erected it, I will assume, *arguendo*, that official intent is at least potentially knowable and that the motives of the Court are not of any inherent legal significance. One may, nevertheless, reach the conclusion that governmental intent is a constitutionally irrelevant consideration which has been inappropriately raised to primary importance in equal protection litigation. By assuming that the strictures of the Equal Protection Clause attach primarily to the process by which decisions are made and not independently to the substance and consequences of those decisions, the Court has endorsed a kind of legal alchemy: the recipe for equal protection involves avoiding impure thoughts while stirring the legislative pot. While this may be good legal alchemy it does not conform to sound constitutional exegesis. It is not required by the Constitution. It is not supported by the weight of precedent. It is not suggested by analogy to other constitutional rights; and it is not dictated by considerations of justice or fairness. In addition to all of these objections based on constitutional principles are a host of pragmatic concerns which argue strongly against reliance on the intent doctrine.

A. THE EQUAL PROTECTION CLAUSE

The most obvious objection to the intent rule is that the Constitution includes no reference to intent. The Equal Protection Clause states, "[N]or shall any State . . . deny . . . the equal protection of the laws."[52] The words themselves cannot be the source of the intent rule, nor is it implied by the words of the Equal Protection Clause. The conclusion is readily reached by even the casual reader of the Constitution that the rule must be the result of quite subtle interpretation. Because of the great importance of the rule, one is entitled to expect a persuasive judicial exposition and proof, but little has been forthcoming.

B. CONTRARY PRECEDENT

The Court's uncritical reliance on the intent rule in *Washington v. Davis*[53] has been questioned by most legal scholars who have analyzed the case; others were simply surprised by the pronouncement.[54] The

---

[52] U.S. Constitution, Amend. XIV, sec. 1.

[53] *Washington* was not the first equal protection case to stress the intent rule. The Court had already done so in Jefferson v. Hackney, Keyes v. Denver, and Milliken v. Bradley. *Washington* was, however, the first case to be decided squarely on the failure to demonstrate illicit intent.

[54] See Eisenberg, note 32 *supra*, at 46; Schwemm, note 38 *supra*, at 972-73; Perry, note 35 *supra*,

opinion of the Court treated intent as an obvious component of an equal protection violation, too apparent to require proof. In contrast with the Court's disposition of *Washington*, every circuit court of appeals that had already faced the question had rejected the necessity of demonstrating intent, focusing instead on the effects of public policies.[55] The Supreme Court summarily rejected these decisions from lower courts as inapposite,[56] and contrary authority in the Court's own precedents was largely ignored.

But significant decisions on equal protection and on constitutional rights generally had not been based on the motivation of decision-makers. In fact, it was not entirely clear that legislative motives could be scrutinized by the Court.[57] *A fortiori*, it was even less clear that illicit intent could be assumed to be a necessary element of a constitutional violation. Whereas precedents had questioned the use of illicit motivation as an independent ground for invalidating an otherwise constitutional policy, in contrast, the question raised by the recent equal protection cases, including *Washington*, is whether a potentially unconstitutional policy is immune from serious scrutiny because of the absence of a nefarious motive. With little examination of the issue, the Court ruled that it is.

It is clear that not all of the Court's earlier decisions on equal protection can be forced into the "illicit purpose" mold.[58] In contrast with scholars who note the lack of uniform history of motive review, I am persuaded that a substantial weight of equal protection precedent focuses on effects rather than on intent, and in those cases noting intent, the intent either was too apparent to escape judicial comment or was assumed from the impact of the policies challenged. The Court's assumption in *Washington*, its precursors and its progeny, that intent

---

at 544; Boyd, note 32 *supra*, at 716-17. One of the reasons for scholarly surprise at the Court's disposition of *Washington* is that the defendant did not even challenge impact theory.

[55] See Brest, note 17 *supra*, at 24; Schwemm, note 38 *supra*, at 972-73; MHDC v. Arlington Heights, 517 F.2d 409 (7th Cir. 1975); Kennedy Park Homes Assn. v. Lackawanna, 436 F.2d 108 (2d Cir. 1970), *cert. denied*, 401 U.S. 1010 (1970); Otero v. New York City Housing Authority, 484 F.2d 1122 (2d Cir. 1973); Cisneros v. Corpus Christi Independent School District, 467 F.2d 142 (5th Cir. 1972), cert. denied, 413 U.S. 920 (1973); Douglas v. Hampton, 512 F.2d 976 (D.C. Cir. 1975); Chance v. Board of Examiners, 458 F.2d 1167 (2d Cir. 1972); Hawkins v. Town of Shaw, 437 F.2d 1286 (5th Cir. 1971); Carter v. Gallagher, 452 F.2d 315 (8th Cir. 1972); Southern Alameda Spanish Speaking Organization v. Union City, 424 F.2d 291 (9th Cir. 1970); Harper v. Mayor of Baltimore, 359 F. Supp. 1187 (D. Md. 1973), aff'd in part sub. nom. Harper v. Kloster, 486 F.2d 1134 (4th Cir. 1973); Castro v. Beecher, 459 F.2d 725 (1st Cir. 1972).

[56] 426 U.S. 229, 244-45 (1976).

[57] See, for example, Eisenberg, note 32 *supra*, at 39; Bailey v. Drexel Furniture Co., 259 U.S. 20 (1922); Veazie Bank v. Fenno, 8 Wall. 533 (1869).

[58] See Boyd, note 32 *supra*, at 716-17; Schwemm, note 38 *supra*, at 93.

is a necessary element of an equal protection violation is simply not supported by the significant decisions on the subject. Cases involving voting, welfare, education, and public facilities belie the Court's conclusion.

1. *Voting.* The case law on reapportionment cannot be understood as based on the importance of demonstrating nefarious intent. From the decisions on justiciability[59] through those governing single-function districts,[60] the focus has been almost exclusively on the existing electoral systems and not on the reasons for their adoption or perpetuation.[61] The Court has, in fact, left virtually no room for governments to effect any goals, including laudatory ones, in their apportionment systems, if these considerations would result in other than roughly equal electoral power per voter.[62] Nevertheless, Justice Stewart's opinion in *City of Mobile v. Bolden*, which ignored the precedential authority of the reapportionment cases, required plaintiffs to demonstrate that the at-large electoral system in Mobile, Alabama, was adopted in order to dilute black electoral strength. Ironically, the only case cited by Stewart in support of the intent rule was *White v. Regester*,[63] which was clearly based on effects and not intent. In *White*, which, like *Mobile*, challenged multimember electoral districts, the Court had held: "The plaintiffs' burden is to produce evidence . . . that its members had less opportunity than did other residents in the district to participate in the political processes and to elect legislators of their choice."[64] *White* required no evidence that the dilution of black electoral power was by governmental design; *Mobile* demands conclusive evidence of it.[65]

Beyond reapportionment, other earlier decisions on equality in the franchise had similarly rested on the effects of governmental policies and not the intent behind their adoption or retention. While students of civil rights know that the poll tax in the South and the redrawing

---

[59] Baker v. Carr, 369 U.S. 186 (1962).

[60] Hadley v. Junior College District of Kansas City, Mo., 397 U.S. 50 (1970); *cf.* Salyer Land Co. v. Tulare Lake Basin Water Storage District, 410 U.S. 719 (1973).

[61] See, for example, Reynolds v. Sims, 377 U.S. 533 (1964); Davis v. Mann, 377 U.S. 678 (1964); Roman v. Sincock, 377 U.S. 695 (1964); and Lucas v. 44th General Assembly of Colorado, 377 U.S. 713 (1964).

[62] But see Brown v. Thomson, 103 S. Ct. 2690 (1983), which suggests that the Court will now uphold at least some apportionment plans based on the integrity of county lines.

[63] 412 U.S. 755 (1973).

[64] *Id.* at 766.

[65] The Court's rather surprising resolution of Rogers v. Lodge, note 30 *supra*, while suggesting futher the inconsistencies that are possible in "intent" cases, nevertheless continues to rely on the necessity of demonstrating illicit intent.

of the boundaries of the city of Tuskegee were both racially motivated, it is equally clear that the Court's decisions invalidating both were based on the effects of the challenged laws. *Harper v. Virginia Board of Elections*[66] was decided not on the basis of the racial motivation behind poll taxes but rather on the irrationality of the effect—people unable to pay the tax were denied the franchise. Similarly, *Gomillion v. Lightfoot*[67] was decided on the basis of the "essential inevitable effect"[68] of the challenged law—to wit, the removal of nearly every black voter from the city of Tuskegee.

2. *Welfare.* Neither is support for the intent rule to be found in the cases on welfare funding, or in segregation of education and public facilities. In *Dandridge v. Williams*[69] the Court upheld Maryland's maximum welfare benefit law, at least in part because of the absence of a discriminatory pattern of effects: "It is important to note that there is no contention that the Maryland regulation is infected with a racially discriminatory purpose *or* effect such as to make it inherently suspect."[70] This observation, although alluding to purpose scrutiny as well as effects scrutiny, clearly rejects the proposition that plaintiffs must demonstrate an illicit intent in order to prevail in an equal protection suit. *Dandridge* endorses the proposition that either an illicit motivation or an illicit result is subject to strict scrutiny. One need not demonstrate both. It is, therefore, rather odd that only two years after *Dandridge*, in *Jefferson v. Hackney*, the Court was to uphold a welfare-funding policy which, in discriminating against those in the AFDC category,[71] disproportionately disadvantaged blacks and hispanics.[72] Justice Rehnquist cited the finding of the court below that "defendants did not know the racial makeup of the various welfare assistance categories."[73] The classification adopted could not, therefore, have been motivated by racism. Because the Court assumed that official illicit intent must be shown and could not be shown in this case, it would not subject the funding program to "strict" scrutiny. Footnote 17 in *Dandridge* was simply ignored.

---

[66] 383 U.S. 663 (1966).

[67] 364 U.S. 339 (1960).

[68] *Id.* at 341.

[69] 397 U.S. 471 (1970).

[70] *Id.* at 485 n.17.

[71] Under the challenged policies the AFDC program was funded at 75 percent of established need, whereas the other welfare programs were funded at 95 percent of established need.

[72] Blacks and hispanics constituted 87 percent of AFDC recipients; they were approximately 40 percent of the recipients in other aid categories.

[73] 406 U.S. at 547.

The decisions of the Court in *Shapiro v. Thompson*[74] and *Memorial Hospital v. Maricopa County*,[75] both challenging welfare funding restrictions on states' new residents, were also based on the effects of the challenged policies. The crux of the Court's ruling in each was that the one-year residency requirement for eligibility abridged (unequally) the privilege and immunity of interstate travel. The primary purpose of each law was clearly economy and, arguably, not the prevention of interstate migration, but the effects of the law violated equal protection. It is worthy of note that the opinion in *Memorial Hospital* stressed that one need not be deterred from exercising a right for it to be abridged: one need be only "penalized" by its exercise.[76]

One might argue that some of the equal protection cases discussed above (on voting rights and interstate travel) are inapposite because they involve other substantive rights, the unequal denial of which is subject to strict scrutiny. This is not, however, a persuasive objection. First, even if one were to concede that unequal abridgments of fundamental rights are worthy of treatment different from that applicable to all other equal protection cases, the argument that the relevant equal protection precedents eschewed intent analysis may nevertheless be sustained. *Mobile* and *Jefferson* were direct analogues of, respectively, *White* and *Dandridge*. While *White* involved voting rights, *Dandridge* involved only the "gratuity" of welfare. The effects test as applied in *White*, and endorsed in *Dandridge*, should have been applied in *Mobile* and *Jefferson*, because the constitutional questions were the same as in the antecedent of each. But one ought not to concede that cases involving the unequal enjoyment of fundamental rights are necessarily different from those involving discrimination against protected classes, nor that an appropriate distinction may be located on the issue of intent.

It must be remembered that strict scrutiny, under which the challenged law may be sustained only upon a showing of "compelling need," is equally applicable to suspect classifications and abridgments of fundamental rights. If strict scrutiny must be applied to policies with uneven denials of fundamental rights as consequences, then strict scrutiny must be applied to policies with uneven effects on "suspect" classifications. If application of strict scrutiny to fundamental rights cases is not subject to an intent rule, it ought not be assumed that its

---

[74] 394 U.S. 618 (1969).
[75] 415 U.S. 250 (1974).
[76] 415 U.S. at 257-59.

application to suspect classifications is subject to this determination. One may or may not be prepared to demand a test of strict scrutiny for either unequal infringements of fundamental rights or discrimination against suspect classes, but there is no particular merit to assuming, a priori, that strict scrutiny shall apply to the former in all cases but to the latter only when illicit intent has been demonstrated. The equal protection precedents on voting rights and on interstate travel are therefore as authoritative on the intent issue as are cases involving racial disparities in the distribution of what Dean Ely terms "gratuitous goods."[77]

3. *Education*. Contrary to the Court's dicta in *Keyes*[78] and subsequent school desegregation decisions,[79] analysis of impact and not of intent has played a key role in the school desegregation decisions of the Warren Court and of the early years of the Burger Court. *Brown v. Board of Education*,[80] it must be remembered, was primarily and most importantly a decision focusing on the effects of—and not the intent behind—governmental segregation of public schools. What made segregation unconstitutional were the effects of racial separation on black students: on their self-esteem, their ability to learn, and their potential for success in later life.[81] While white segregationists clearly wanted to maintain their distance from blacks—and segregation ensured this for their progeny—it was not at all clear that they wanted to disadvantage blacks educationally, intellectually, or psychologically, the injuries upon which the violation of equal protection rested. In rejoinder, some may point to the obvious, that the educational separatism was itself intentional as it was prescribed by law. This is true, but separatism was not an unconstitutional governmental goal prior to *Brown* or because of *Brown*. *Brown* ruled only that the effects

---

[77] Ely, *The Centrality and Limits of Motivation Analysis*, 15 SAN DIEGO L. REV. 1155, 1160-61 (1978).

[78] 413 U.S. 189 (1973).

[79] See, for example, Austin Independent School District v. U.S., 429 U.S. 990 (1976); Dayton Board of Education v. Brinkman, 433 U.S. 406 (1977); School District of Omaha v. U.S., 433 U.S. 667 (1977); Brennan v. Armstrong, 433 U.S. 672 (1977).

[80] 347 U.S. 483 (1954).

[81] "Does segregation of children in public schools solely on the basis of race . . . deprive the children of the minority group of equal educational opportunities?" *Id.* at 493. "To separate them . . . generates a feeling of inferiority [that] may affect their hearts and minds in a way unlikely to be undone." *Id.* at 494. The Court stressed further the importance of education for the adoption of cultural values with respect to later professional training and the ability to adjust to one's environment. *Id.* at 493. Because of these effects of segregation on black children, the Court decided the following, "We conclude that in the field of public education the doctrine of separate but equal has no place." *Id.* at 495.

of an otherwise constitutional goal of "separate but equal" made it inherently unequal when applied to education. It was therefore a surprise to many constitutional scholars when the Court, one year after *Brown,* issued a series of *per curiam* decisions suggesting that separatism was itself an unconstitutional governmental goal.[82]

Just as *Brown* invalidated educational segregation in the public schools because of its effects, the cases implementing *Brown* similarly turned on the impact of governmental policies on the dismantling of the dual school system. The "freedom of choice" plans of the 1960s were invalidated by the Court because they failed to bring about desegregation.[83] Had the school boards involved demonstrated noble, color-blind intentions, the plans would, nevertheless, have been rejected by the Court. The same conclusion may be reached with respect to *Cooper v. Aaron*[84] in which the Court would not delay a desegregation order despite the presumed clean hands and good faith of the responsible school board members.[85] Most important, in *Wright v. City of Emporia*[86] and *United States v. Scotland Neck*[87] the Court declared that the only consideration in measuring the action of school boards in desegregation cases is the "effect on desegregation"[88] of the challenged official acts. More to the point, Justice Stewart averred, "[t]his 'dominant purpose' test [mistakenly applied by the 4th Circuit Court of Appeals] finds *no* precedent in our decisions."[89] Finally, even *Palmer v. Thompson,*[90] which civil rights plaintiffs had lost before the Court only one year prior to *Emporia,* rested on the relative unimportance of segregative intent. Observing that "[i]t is difficult or impossible for any court to determine the 'sole' or 'dominant' motivation behind the choices of a group of legislators,"[91] the Court noted that the *O'Brien*[92] decision "explained well the hazards of declaring a law unconstitutional because of the motivation of its

---

[82] See note 6 *supra.*

[83] See, for example, Green v. County School Board, 391 U.S. 430 (1968); Raney v. Board of Education of Gould School District, 391 U.S. 443 (1968); Monroe v. Board of Commissioners of Jackson, Tenn., 391 U.S. 450 (1968).

[84] 358 U.S. 1 (1958).

[85] *Id.* at 14–15.

[86] 407 U.S. 451 (1972).

[87] 407 U.S. 484 (1972).

[88] 407 U.S. 451, 462 (1972).

[89] *Id.* at 461. See also North Carolina State Board of Education v. Swann, 402 U.S. 43 (1971) (suggesting that color-blindness cannot work in segregated districts).

[90] 403 U.S. 217 (1971).

[91] 403 U.S. at 225.

[92] U.S. v. O'Brien, 391 U.S. 367 (1968).

sponsors."[93] Even Justice Douglas, dissenting in *Palmer*, eschewed intent analysis, focusing instead on the consequences of the city's action.[94]

In sum, the intent rule attached to the Equal Protection Clause by the contemporary Supreme Court is dictated neither by the substance of the Clause itself nor by the weight of precedential authority on the subject.

C. THE UNIQUENESS OF EQUAL PROTECTION

A basic question, ignored by the Court and unsatisfactorily answered by scholars addressing it, is why equal protection ought to be treated as unique among constitutional rights and liberties.[95] No other guarantee of the Constitution is subjected to the necessity of proof that the violations alleged were by governmental design. To the contrary, the violation of any other constitutionally protected right is demonstrated by evidence that the law or practice challenged infringes upon the right in question. It is always sufficient to challenge what the law does, its substance, and its consequences for constitutionally protected rights. Decisions governing the Bill of Rights suggest, furthermore, that governments may have an affirmative duty to protect provisions of these Amendments and may also be held accountable for consequences of their policies which result from volitional private behavior. The scrutiny applied to these arguably unintended by-products of public policies is as strict as that applicable to intentional abridgments of constitutional rights.

1. *The First Amendment.* Professor J. Morris Clark has argued that the First Amendment, like the Equal Protection Clause, may be understood as reflecting suspicion about the motives of legislators. He is thus persuaded that considerations of illicit purpose are as relevant to First Amendment cases as they are to equal protection cases.[96] While Professor Clark is correct that the First Amendment reflects a concern about the temptation of those in power to silence their critics or to censor the expression of unpopular beliefs, he has confused the origin

---

[93] 403 U.S. at 224.

[94] *Id.* at 235–39.

[95] See, for example, the Court's argument in San Antonio Indep. School Dist. v. Rodriguez that "[i]t is not the province of this Court to create substantive constitutional rights in the name of guaranteeing equal protection of the laws." 411 U.S. 1, 33 (1973). See Ely, note 17 *supra*, at 1160–61, but see Westen, *The Empty Idea of Equality*, 95 HARV. L. REV. 537, 565 (1982).

[96] Clark, note 31 *supra; cf.* Island Trees Union Free School District v. Pico, 457 U.S. 853 (1982).

of the right with the protections of it. Not only does the individual not have to prove nefarious intent in First Amendment cases, the evidence of even a benevolent motivation cannot save a law the effects of which infringe upon the Amendment. This is true even in the area of commercial speech, an area of First Amendment rights with the most limited protections and the greatest latitude for governmental control. Witness the unanimous decision of the Court in *Linmark v. Township of Willingboro*.[97] Willingboro had sought to prevent white flight and racial block-busting by prohibiting the display of "for sale" signs on residential properties. The Court was not unsympathetic to the intent of the town: the intent behind the law was simply irrelevant to the First Amendment issue.[98]

In First Amendment cases, generally, the judicial tests and principles applied measure the substance, effects, and consequences of the challenged policies. One needs to demonstrate only that First Amendment liberties are curtailed—for whatever reasons—and the judiciary will determine independently whether such infringements are constitutionally permissible under the conditions it finds to exist. Why the legislators adopted the law is not dispositive of the constitutional question. Second, the Court will apply very serious scrutiny even to those laws that curtail First Amendment rights not because of what the law actually does but because of the reactions of individuals to the law. Under the concept of "chilling effect," the Court will reject statutes and practices which could bring about the loss of First Amendment freedoms if persons overreact to them. In such cases the argument is easily advanced that not only is there no conclusive evidence that the state intended to restrict freedom of speech but that it is not even clear that the state should be held responsible for the interpretations and apprehensions of individuals. Despite the absence of official illicit motivation and despite the mootness of official responsibility, the Court has scrutinized even the potential and collateral impacts of policies on First Amendment rights. This concern with self-censorship rationalizes the Court's landmark decisions on libel, on legislative investigation, on privacy of association, and also on the very broad category of First Amendment cases under the rubric "void for vagueness." If the state is to be held

---

[97] 431 U.S. 85 (1977).

[98] Compare *Linmark* with Pittsburgh Human Relations Commission v. Pittsburgh Press, 413 U.S. 376 (1973), in which the practice advertised was itself illegal. The vote of the Court upholding the ban on gender-based job ads was, nevertheless, only five to four. Compare with Bigelow v. Virginia, 421 U.S. 809 (1975).

responsible for the unintended, privately caused infringements on freedom of speech or press, which may be by-products of official policies, ought it not to be held responsible for the direct impacts of state policies over which individuals have no discretionary reactive powers and which raise questions under the Equal Protection Clause?

It may be objected that the religion clauses of the First Amendment are constitutional provisions the breach of which may be a function of the official intent behind the challenged policy. But two factors must be clarified. First is that the popular religion "test" embodying intent creates two independent bases for invalidation, purpose or effect. One need not demonstrate both.[99] Second is that the purpose or primary effect test was designed to satisfy, simultaneously, the strictures of both the Free Exercise and Establishment Clauses. The "purpose" option was probably meant to allow one to challenge practices which suggest establishment but which have no discernible effects, such as religious resolutions.[100] Free exercise cases, however, rest almost exclusively on a determination of the effects of the challenged policies, even the unintended ones. Perhaps the clearest example is *West Virginia v. Barnette*,[101] in which mandatory flag salute was held to infringe upon the freedom of conscience of a Jehovah's Witness. The challenged policy had no particular religious purpose, either in support or denigration thereof. It was nonetheless unconstitutional as applied. One can also point to *Sherbert v. Verner*[102] in which the Court held that a "neutral" unemployment compensation law was unconstitutional insofar as it denied eligibility to a Seventh-Day Adventist who would not work on Saturdays.

It should also be noted that in the "purpose or primary effect" test the "primacy" of an effect has not been a serious limitation. One is able to attack governmental policies successfully if one of the direct effects is either an establishment of religion or an abridgment of free exercise. The educational funding decisions of the 1970s are comprehensible only as evidence that all direct—even potential—consequences of the laws in question will be scrutinized to determine if there has been "undue entanglement" between government and religion.[103] Laws

---

[99] See, for example, Abington v. Schempp, 374 U.S. 203 (1963).

[100] Prayer in the public schools, for example, has no discernible secular purpose. One need not demonstrate unconstitutional effects beyond the practice itself.

[101] 319 U.S. 624 (1943).

[102] 374 U.S. 398 (1963).

[103] See, for example, Walz v. Tax Commission, 398 U.S. 664 (1970), from which the standard

designed to assist schools in the nonsectarian aspects of their education programs have been reviewed to discern if assumedly unintended consequences, such as the diversion of funds to religious ends, were possible.[104]

2. *Amendments 4 through 8.* The rights guaranteed by Amendments 4 through 8 of the Bill of Rights, those focusing primarily on the rights of defendants in criminal cases, are also not defined by the intent behind the official behavior. The case law on the Fourth and Fifth Amendments is replete with examples of constables blundering and evidence being excluded or convictions being overturned. The range of unintentional blundering runs from simple ignorance of Fourth and Fifth Amendment principles, to mere oversight, to good faith interpretations of the Constitution which are subsequently rejected by the courts. The responsibility of the courts in any of these situations is to reach an independent judgment whether the official treatment of the accused resulted in a denial of his or her procedural rights. The reasons this state of affairs came about are ordinarily of no constitutional significance.[105]

Perhaps the closest analogy to an effects approach to equal protection is evident in the Court's disposition of *Furman v. Georgia.*[106] Not only does there not have to be illicit intent for the Eighth Amendment to be violated but a violation may rest on aggregate data. The unconstitutionality of the death penalty as applied was due in large measure to the history of disproportionate number of blacks and poor people among those subjected to it. There was no suggestion in the case that any particular prosecutor, judge, or jury was negatively predisposed toward a defendant because of his or her race. No evidence was amassed to demonstrate conscious illicit intent.[107]

---

comes. See also Lemon v. Kurtzman, 403 U.S. 602 (1971); Meek v. Pittenger, 421 U.S. 349 (1975); Levitt v. Committee for Public Education, 413 U.S. 472 (1973).

[104] For two very provocative views on the relationship between legislative neutrality as it affects race, etc., and neutrality as it affects religion, see Eisenberg, note 32 *supra*, at 165, and Ely, note 17 *supra*, at 1313-27.

[105] While Wyman v. James, 400 U.S. 309 (1971), notes an absence of illicit governmental intent, this observation was dictum. In Michigan v. DeFillippo, 443 U.S. 31 (1979), and Rhode Island v. Innis, 446 U.S. 291 (1980), both "good faith" cases, "good faith" was defined with respect to foreseeability and not to motives.

[106] 408 U.S. 238 (1972).

[107] See, for example, Zeisel, *Race Bias in the Administration of the Death Penalty*, 95 HARV. L. REV. 456 (1981). Imputing race bias to jurors as individuals is rather risky as each case and jury is like another roll of the dice. There is no control from which to compare cases and measure bias. One can, however, conclude that the system may work better for white defendants than for black in the aggregate. But that is a different conclusion from one claiming illicit intent.

Finally, with respect to other provisions of the Bill of Rights, the case law on the Sixth Amendment right to counsel constitutes an example of the affirmative state responsibility model. From *Powell v. Alabama*[108] through *Gideon v. Wainwright*[109] to *Argersinger v. Hamlin*[110] the Court has overturned convictions and sentences in criminal cases in which defendants had not enjoyed the assistance of counsel. The constitutional infirmity in each was the failure of the state to provide counsel without charge to indigent defendants. Not only was there no evidence of official intent to deprive the accused of his or her Sixth Amendment rights, but it was questionable that the state was responsible for the deprivation suffered. It was inaction of government, inattention to the defendant's need for counsel, that constituted the relevant state action. The affirmative responsibility model applied in the Sixth Amendment cases is precedent for the suggestion that when states make policy choices, such as how to spend public funds, certain priorities are constitutionally mandated. The application of an affirmative responsibility to equal protection cases, to be discussed below, would reflect the constitutional priority of integration and of not unnecessarily disadvantaging the disadvantaged. The states would be expected to consider these priorities, as they must consider the cost of free counsel, when they make policy choices.

The current state of constitutional law renders the Equal Protection Clause unique. The enjoyment of no other constitutional right is protected from only intentional intrusion by government. Under the First Amendment the government is responsible for the substance and consequences of laws as well as for the potential consequences of individuals' voluntary reactions to laws curbing freedom of speech, press, and association. Under the religion clauses, although a law may be unconstitutional because of motivation, the state is similarly responsible for all direct consequences of its laws as they affect free exercise and establishment. The amendments protecting the rights of the accused in criminal cases protect the conditions under which the criminal law is applied. The state is responsible not only for what it has done but as well for what it has failed to do to protect defendants' rights. Aside from the Court's assumption that the intent rule is necessary "by definition," it has offered no persuasive evidence why the intent rule ought to attach to only the Equal Protection Clause.

---

[108] 287 U.S. 45 (1932).
[109] 372 U.S. 335 (1963).
[110] 407 U.S. 25 (1972).

D. THE NATURE AND EXTENT OF THE INJURY

If precedents from litigation over equal protection and the Bill of Rights provide little support for the constitutional necessity of demonstrating illicit intent, considerations of the nature and extent of the injury suffered argue against its inherent logic. One of the major problems associated with the intent rule is that it suggests that the locus of the denial of equal protection is in the process of decisionmaking, specifically in the desire of those in power to segregate or otherwise disadvantage the aggrieved. It is similarly assumed that the extent of the injury suffered is commensurate with the extent of the illicit intent. Support for this view rests on one or more of three perceptions: that the substance of the injury to equal protection is the distortion of the process of decisionmaking[111] caused by paying attention to legally irrelevant considerations, that the harm suffered is dignitary harm,[112] or that the social contract, obligating government to think all citizens equally worthy, has been violated.[113]

The assumption that the injury suffered is a function of the intentional quality of the disadvantage perpetrated fails to hold up on examination. First, the argument that the constitutional violation suffered is "process distortion" may be rejected on three counts. The constitutional infirmity of distortions in the decisionmaking process is more properly decided under the Due Process Clause and is not particularly relevant to equal protection. The second objection to the process-distortion theory is in a sense parasitic upon the first: distortions in the political process are suffered by all and are not therefore uniquely injurious to those disadvantaged by the law. This further suggests that process distortions are not intrinsically an affront to equal protection. Finally, there is no reason to assume that discriminatory intentions necessarily distort the policy system. There is no necessary relationship between the extent of the racism present and the degree to which policies are perverted by it. As the discussion of quantum of intent below will suggest, the Court has adapted the process-distortion logic to the end of disallowing only those policies which would not have passed but for the discriminatory intentions.[114] Process distortion is clearly one of the potential dangers of illicit

---

[111] See Simon, note 31 *supra*, at 1054.

[112] See, for example, Perry, note 35 *supra*, at 557; Brest note 17 *supra*, at 8-9; Simon, note 31 *supra*, at 1054-55; Clark, note 31 *supra*, at 966-67.

[113] Clark, note 31 *supra*, at 965-66.

[114] See *Arlington Heights*, 429 U.S. at 270-71 n. 21.

motivations, but rather than representing the underlying danger against which equal protection "protects," it serves as the only consequence of illicit motivation which the Court finds unconstitutional.

The second assumed injury rationalizing the focus on intent, that of dignitary harm, is a more substantial equal protection interest. While the Equal Protection Clause should be understood to protect individuals from dignitary harms, the relevant question is whether the intent rule necessarily isolates and furthers this value. There is, no doubt, a dignitary harm to minority groups who have suffered intentional discrimination, but it is more critical that they believe that the act was intentional than that it actually be so. In *Brown v. Board of Education*, the Court noted, *inter alia*, the psychological harm to black students resulting from *de jure* segregation. While the Court suggested that the weight of law behind this segregation was critical, in more modern times, students in segregated schools believing, even inaccurately, that the school board intentionally fostered segregation are no less injured. In brief, the perception of illicit intent and not its reality is what causes dignitary harm.[115]

The final justification for intent theory rests on the principle that the right to be considered "equal" is inherent in the social contract. Intentional discrimination represents a violation of the assumption of equal virtue and worthiness. The shortcomings of this justification are twofold. The hypothesis that the social contract obligates government to consider each citizen to be equally worthy is also transgressed by a decisionmaking process which simply ignores minority interests. While intentional discrimination may be more intensely violative of the social contract than is simple neglect, either is reflective of unequal worth. Second, one might argue rather persuasively that the commitment of government to the equal value of each of its citizens is measured by what government does. The intentions of government are no more indicative of a human devaluing than are its policies and their impact.

The three major justifications for locating the injury to equal protection in the process behind governmental decisionmaking are either not particularly germane to equal protection or to intent, or if

---

[115] The Court does not, however, recognize a common perception of intentional racism as unconstitutional. It must be convinced of the racial intentions behind the official acts. See Crawford v. Board of Education of Los Angeles, 102 S. Ct. 3211 (1982), upholding California's Proposition 1, and Washington v. Seattle School District, 102 S. Ct. 3187 (1982), invalidating Washington's Initiative 350.

germane are not uniquely linked to the reality of the intent behind the official behavior.

Also ignored by approaches to equal protection which focus on the decisionmaking process as the locus of the violation are the material and status injuries[116] that are a function of what the law actually does. Thus, the focus on intent simply does not measure the full extent of injuries to equal protection. As the Court itself acknowledged in *Burton v. Wilmington Parking Authority*, "[i]t is of no consolation to an individual denied the equal protection of the laws that it was done in good faith."[117] William Silverman has similarly concluded,[118]

> From the point of view of the victim of discrimination, it matters little whether the root of the problem is racists acting with an intent to cause racially discriminatory impact or nonracists acting with no such purpose but causing the same discriminatory result. The black person is denied an education, a job, or a house just the same.

While one does not have a constitutionally protected right to an education, to a job, or to a home, actions of government which render minorities unequally capable of securing these necessities should be recognized as status injuries. This proposition does not answer the question, taken up in the last section of this paper, of the extent of the governmental obligation to avoid inflicting injury, but it is important to note that an injury has occurred when one experiences (involuntarily) segregation in education, housing, or employment or an inequality of access to them.[119] When it has been brought about by government, irrespective of the reason for its occurrence, a constitutionally relevant injury has occurred. It might further be suggested that the material injury involved in segregated or unequal education, housing, and employment or nonmaterial injury in unequal political power contribute to a cycle perpetuating the negative stereotypes of minority groups. In short, status harms not only are injuries in themselves but also communicate messages of assumed inferiority and therefore are not entirely separable from dignitary harms. But status harms ought to be recognized as injuries in and of themselves.

---

[116] Fiss, *Groups and the Equal Protection Clause*, 5 PHIL. & PUB. AFF. 107, *passim* (1976).

[117] 365 U.S. 715, 725 (1961).

[118] Silverman, *Equal Protection, Economic Legislation, and Racial Discrimination*, 25 VAND. L. REV. 1183, 1183 (1972).

[119] Sullivan, *The Intent Requirement in Desegregation Cases: The Inapplicability of Washington v. Davis*, 10 J. L. & EDUC. 325, 330 (1981).

E. THE DEFINITION OF INTENT

There are a rich history and literature, in both case law and commentary, which suggest the pitfalls of analysis of legislative intent. In highlighting the futility of the enterprise, Joseph M. Sellers has noted the burdensome nature of intent analysis, the Court's inability to evaluate states of mind, and the web of legislative events that must be scrutinized.[120] Professor Abram Chayes has noted this fundamental problem and has suggested that common-law principles are not easily applied to contemporary public law. "Indeed, in dealing with the actions of large political or corporate aggregates, notions of will, intention, or fault increasingly become only metaphors.[121]

In equal protection cases, the Court has chosen nevertheless to make a glaring exception to its usual trepidation about assessing legislative intent. It has simply ignored the uncertainties and ambiguities inherent in determining what were the intended consequences of the numerous responsible decisionmakers. It has confidently, and almost uniformly, concluded that sufficient illicit motivation had not been demonstrated. The problem, as defined by Professor Eisenberg, is that the Court does not know when it actually knows or is able to know legislative motives.[122] Even simple public policies often have multiple and complex effects. Consequently, support for a given policy may be consistent with a variety of legislative motives. The Court has not acknowledged this limitation on its ability to know which motivation was determinative.

One manifestation of the Court's intolerance for the uncertainties inherent in intent analysis is its tendency to assume the existence of unproved states of affairs or to speculate about plausible explanations for official actions. To "explain" Texas's policy funding AFDC at only 75 percent of established need while AABD (among other programs) was funded at 95 percent of need, the Court speculated that "the State may have concluded that the aged and infirm are the least able of the categorical grant recipients to bear the hardships of an inadequate standard of living."[123] It is of course possible that the

---

[120] Sellers, note 44 *supra*, at 374–75.

[121] Chayes, *The Role of the Judge in Public Law Litigation*, 89 HARV. L. REV. 1281, 1296 (1976).

[122] Eisenberg, note 32 *supra*, at 105. See also Brest, note 44 *supra*, at 1145, where he criticizes not only the Court's failure to define the procedures for review of motive but also its failure to define more precisely what motives are constitutional.

[123] 406 U.S. 535, 549 (1972).

responsible administrators did indeed base their decision on that which the Court has imagined. It is equally possible that the policymakers were personally repulsed by the predominantly minority welfare mothers and children and the cycle of poverty that they represented. (Although the Court was satisfied that the decisionmakers did not know the precise ethnic representations in the various aid categories, it is not possible that they did not know that ADFC recipients were overwhelmingly minority.) The relevant point is that the Court did not know what the motivation was behind the disparate treatment of the welfare categories. It simply substituted speculation on intent for evidence of intent. Similarly, in *City of Memphis v. Greene* the Court disposed of the allegation that the Hein Park street closure was racially motivated by observing that it was unlikely that the residents would have welcomed white traffic either.[124] Not only was this assumption untested, but, more to the point, it was relied upon as evidence of racial neutrality, which it is not.[125]

The same logical weakness was evident in the Court's opinion in *Feeney*. The Court concluded that "too many men are [negatively] affected"[126] by the challenged veterans' preference statute for it to be understood as a "pretext" for preferring men over women. While the law effectively disqualified a substantial percentage of men from the desirable civil service jobs, more significant was its simultaneous disqualification of virtually all women (more than 98 percent). The datum cited by the Court does not demonstrate the absence of antifeminism. The effect on men may simply represent overkill or an undesired consequence. A legislature intent on keeping women out of high official places could find no more efficient surrogate for a men-only policy than a veteran preference. Massachusetts may or may not have intended to disadvantage women, but the simultaneous disqualification of a large number of men—leaving eligibility to a universe of only some men—does not constitute evidence of an absence of discriminatory intentions concerning women.

Finally, in *Arlington Heights* the Court assumed that plaintiffs had failed to prove illicit intent in the Village's rejection of the housing

---

[124] "The record plainly does not support a conclusion that the residents of Hein Park would have welcomed the heavy flow of transient traffic through their neighborhood if the drivers had been predominantly white. It is unlikely that a mother who finds herself 'rushing to the window when I hear screeching brakes,' . . . is concerned about the race of the driver of the vehicle." 451 U.S. at 116-17 n.27. Emotional appeals aside, the question is not whether white drivers would have been welcomed, but whether the same extreme action would have been taken.

[125] The relevant question is why the city closed only this street.

[126] 422 U.S. at 275.

development. The Court, however, paid little attention to the record demonstrating that the plaintiffs had been forced by the trial court to focus on the effects of the challenged action and not on the motives behind it.[127] The Court's conclusion that the plaintiffs had failed to prove illicit intent was based on the assumption that the plaintiffs had waived their right to do so rather than on the fact that they had not had the opportunity to pursue this evidence in the trial court.[128]

One could cite other examples of the Court's tendency to decrease ambiguity and uncertainty by assuming the existence of questionable states of affairs or to use data to "prove" that which they do not prove, but there are two more general conceptual problems in the Court's handling of intent analysis. These are its definition of whose intent is relevant and its determination of how much illicit intent must be demonstrated to trigger scrutiny more strict than mere rationality. In answering each of these questions in the cases of the past decade, the Court has been inconsistent, and, in making the intent barrier progressively more impenetrable, it has upheld official actions which plausibly reflected actual discriminatory intent of a significant sort.

1. *Whose intent is relevant?* If nefarious intent must be demonstrated for the discriminatory effects of laws to be deemed unconstitutional, then one must know whose intent must be scrutinized. Even if one assumes that each governmental body has within it a unified knowable intent, one must nevertheless determine which body's decisionmaking motivation shall be deemed determinative on the intent question. This raises questions of constitutional responsibility in terms of time frame, jurisdictional boundaries, and the role of the citizenry vis-à-vis government. While the Court has not rejected the principle that governments are corporate bodies independent of the individuals who occupy official positions, it has treated governmental units as equivalent to persons. The Court has used the question of whose intent is relevant to an equal protection violation not only to determine if an injury has occurred but also, as in the criminal law, to identify the wrongdoer. And a concomitant purpose of the "who" inquiry is to circumscribe the governmental bodies which may be obligated to remedy the abridgment.

a) Time Frame. If a challenged policy is not new, must the illicit intent reside with the governmental body as constituted when the

---

[127] Schwemm, note 38 *supra*, at 1012-33.
[128] *Id.*

policy was adopted or with the body which has failed to alter it? The Court has provided no clear answer to this question. In *Keyes* the Court held that segregation is illegal if it is either "brought about *or* maintained by intentional state action,"[129] and the Court suggested as well that remoteness in time does not disprove discriminatory intent.[130] But in two more recent decisions the Court has cast doubt on its facility for scrutinizing illicitly motivated retentions of public policies. In the earlier of these two cases, *Mobile v. Bolden*, the Court displayed a reluctance to focus its scrutiny on retention, and in the more recent decision, *Rogers v. Lodge*,[131] it displayed a serious confusion about what constitutes evidence of illicit motivation in the retention of a law. The inconsistency apparent in the resolutions of *Mobile* and *Rogers* invites questions about the value of the intent rule.

In contrast with the *Keyes* principle, the plurality opinion in *Mobile* deflected focus away from the district court's finding that retention of at-large districts served a discriminatory purpose. The Court held that "[i]f the District Court meant . . . that the existence of the at-large electoral system was . . . unexplainable on grounds other than race, its inference is contradicted by the history of the adoption of that system in Mobile."[132] The Court's suggestion that "history offers another explanation" is rather obtuse, as history, or the Court's recounting of it, points to no particular explanation of official motivation.[133] As important, the Court did not successfully refute the findings on retention of the system, the issue addressed by the trial court.[134] The Court's disposition of *Mobile* is significant for the apparent reluctance to scrutinize the inaction of contemporary officials who have retained the policies that have resulted in inequities.

In stark contrast to Mobile is the recent decision of the Court in *Rogers v. Lodge* which challenged the electoral system of Burke County, Georgia. Like the electoral system of *Mobile*, Burke's electoral system had been at-large since 1911, and in neither jurisdiction had

---

[129] 413 U.S. at 198.

[130] *Id.* at 210-11.

[131] 102 S. Ct. 3272 (1982).

[132] 446 U.S. at 71-2 n.17.

[133] See, for example, J. Morgan Kousser, *Voting Rights, Yes, No, Maybe: Obstructionists Threaten to Undo 16 Years of Effort*, LOS ANGELES TIMES, February 7, 1982, sec. 4, at 5, col. 3-5. Professor Kousser, an expert witness in a case similar to *Mobile*, in Birmingham, points out that evidence of discriminatory intent behind the adoption of the electoral process for local government in 1901, in Alabama, was simply ignored by the trial court.

[134] See Justice White's dissenting opinion in *Mobile*, in which he recites the findings of discriminatory purpose by the trial court. 446 U.S. at 99-103. These findings were thought to be insufficient by the majority of the Supreme Court.

black candidates ever been elected to public office. In each case the argument had been made by plaintiffs that blacks were effectively prevented from acquiring political power and that their (group) interests were ignored by the white political power structure. It was further averred in each that the retention of the at-large system was in service of discriminatory goals. In an opinion that lacks persuasiveness, the Court concluded that the at-large electoral system in Burke County—in contradistinction to that upheld in *Mobile*—"was being maintained for the invidious purpose of diluting the voting strength of the black population."[135] The major shortcoming of the *Rogers* ruling was not the invalidation of the electoral system—a decision with which I agree—but rather the Court's assumption that there was evidence that racial animus explains the failure of the County to switch to a district-based electoral system.[136] Not only does one have to suspend disbelief to accept the conclusion of the Court on the "intent" behind the retention of the system, the decision does not successfully distinguish the case from *Mobile*. Whether *Rogers* represents a shift in the Court's approach to the intent rule or will prove to be an oddity cannot, of course, be known at this time.

The second relevant element of the *Keyes* doctrine, that remoteness in time is not a bar to constitutional scrutiny, raises a more fundamental and, surprisingly, controversial question. Ought the Court to issue judgments against current governmental officials because of the intentional acts of discrimination of earlier officials? Public policies passed long ago may continue to disadvantage minorities or maintain segregation. If contemporary governmental bodies (for arguably benign reasons)[137] do nothing about the continuing effects of past behavior, are they therefore to be held responsible for these policies? Professor Eisenberg has noted the dilemma by arguing in favor of restricting the use of benign policies which are infected with discriminatory intent from the past, but simultaneously questioning the fairness of holding current officials responsible for the intentional acts of their (often temporally distant) predecessors.[138] Professor Edmund Kitch is an even stronger critic on the latter point, arguing

---

[135] 102 S. Ct. at 3278.

[136] *Id.* at 3278–81.

[137] This differs from the previous example where retention was for discriminatory purposes. In this example the original act may have been motivated by racism but its continued existence is not. In the former instance the argument is that, but for racism, the policy would have been changed; the argument in the latter is that racism caused the policy to come about but that it now may have other justifications.

[138] Eisenberg, note 32 *supra*, at 54–55.

that intentionally racist acts, such as that challenged in *Plessy v. Ferguson*,[139] were legal when promulgated and enforced and should not, therefore, create obligations on future governments to remedy their effects.[140] Kitch is especially concerned about judicial remedies which "punish" the wrong parties.[141]

The predominant view within the Supreme Court is that the state is a corporate body which as such is accountable for constitutional transgressions irrespective of changes in official personnel. The concept of "government of laws and not of men" has this second meaning. While the Court is reluctant to find illicit intent in past behavior and is extremely unlikely to hold overt discrimination of the past actually responsible for contemporary inequalities,[142] it has not refused to fashion remedies for continuing abridgments of equal protection just because the imposition of the intentional discrimination was by those no longer in power. The Court's disposition of *Dayton II*[143] and *Columbus*,[144] and more generally its decisions dismantling *de jure* segregation in the South, all rest on the notion of governmental continuity. To espouse the contrary view is to analogize constitutional law to the criminal law or to the law of intentional torts, and to assume that the effectuation of constitutional rights is a punishment to which only guilty individuals officials of the government ought to be subjected. Just as the policeman has not been punished by the exclusionary rule, individual state officials are not punished by orders to redress constitutional wrongs.[145] They are not thereby forced, in any personal way, to compensate victims of discriminatory acts by their predecessors.

b) Jurisdictional Boundaries. The Supreme Court has eschewed the individualistic criminal law model in holding governmental structures responsible for the intentional acts of their past officeholders. It has,

---

[139] 163 U.S. 537 (1896).

[140] Kitch, *The Return of Color Consciousness to the Constitution*, 1979 SUPREME COURT REVIEW 1, 10-11.

[141] "The young family, the student or worker [is disadvantaged while] the individuals responsible—the former school board officials, the former members of craft unions, the former members of the Court itself—remain unaffected, protected by the scope of their official immunities or the passage of time." *Id.* at 11.

[142] The Court will not, for example, hold the history of housing segregation and educational segregation responsible for the higher rate of failure of blacks on standardized tests, such as that administered to recruits to the Washington, D.C., police force.

[143] 443 U.S. 526 (1979).

[144] 443 U.S. 449 (1979).

[145] See, for example, Schrock & Welsh, *Up from Calandra*, 59 MINN. L. REV. 251, 356-60 (1974), for an excellent discussion of this question.

however, treated each governmental unit as analogous to a separate individual in cases involving more than one governmental jurisdiction. It has held that the intentional acts of segregation or other minority disadvantage by one governmental unit generate no obligation on the part of other jurisdictions, either to participate in a remedy for the discrimination or to avoid aggravating it by incorporating the discriminatory scheme into its own, arguably benign, policies. The Court's commitment to strict jurisdictional autonomy and differentiation has been applied to separate governmental bodies within states and to the states versus the federal government.

With the possible exception of *San Antonio Independent School District v. Rodriguez*,[146] no decision of the Supreme Court has been as supportive of the autonomy of local governmental units as *Milliken v. Bradley*. The public school system of the City of Detroit was found to have intentionally segregated students on the basis of race. The trial court concluded that the only effective way to remedy the segregation was with a metropolitan area desegregation plan involving the suburban school districts of Wayne County. The Supreme Court's rejection of the metropolitan plan suggests a troubling component of the intent rule. The Court assumed that desegregation plans are a "punishment" to which only "guilty" governments and citizenry ought to be subjected.[147] The suburban districts, not parties to the suit, were presumed to be innocent of any intentionally segregative actions vis-à-vis the Detroit city school district. They were, therefore, not wrongdoers and should not be party to the remedy. The message of *Milliken* is that if an intentional abridgment of the Equal Protection Clause can be remedied only by a plan that crosses into an "innocent" jurisdiction, then an effective remedy may be denied. Gone was the language of earlier equal protection decisions, the language of individual rights and governmental responsibilities. In its place were the concepts of the criminal law: intent, guilt, punishment. The intent rule became the means not only to determine if a denial of equal protection had occurred but as well to identify the wrongdoer and coincidentally to limit the appropriate remedy.[148]

---

[146] 411 U.S. 1 (1973).

[147] 418 U.S. at 742-45.

[148] An alternate approach to Milliken v. Bradley would have been the state responsibility approach: that the Constitution makes no provision for the recognition of the subdivisions of the states. A strict approach might hold the states responsible for the actions of their subdivisional governments. Detroit had been found to have practiced intentional segregation in its schools; Michigan could have been ordered to correct this condition through the means available to the

The Burger Court has not yet tackled the questions involving functionally discrete but geographically coincident or overlapping governmental units. The Court would not force suburban school districts to participate in the desegregation of inner-city schools (in *Milliken*) in part because there was no evidence that they had engaged in acts of intentional segregation affecting the inner-city district. It is also not at all clear that the Court would expect a school district to desegregate its schools if the racial patterns have resulted from housing segregation, intentionally imposed by state or local housing authorities. Although the Court has not faced this question directly,[149] extrapolation from the school desegregation decisions in which the equitable jurisdiction of the federal courts was limited to remedying only the effects of the intentionally segregative acts of the defendant school districts suggests that the jurisdictional component is controlling.[150] Is it reasonable for the Court to view the acts of each jurisdiction in a separate vacuum, immune from the potential necessity of participating in remedies which only "innocent" governmental jurisdictions may be able to effect? The focus on the intent behind the behavior of each separate jurisdiction also precludes attention to the possible abridgment of equal protection which may result from "benign" reliance on the intentionally discriminatory decisions of other governmental bodies. School boards may naively adopt neighborhood boundaries reflecting discriminatory housing policies. A city may require residency status for public employment while the state or local housing authorities have promoted racial homogeneity within its borders.

Perhaps the most striking and extreme example of the phenomenon of "benign reliance" is the Court's approval of state laws granting to veterans a total lifetime preference in public employment. In *Personnel Administrator of Massachusetts v. Feeney,* the Court upheld this preference on the assumption that the desire to help veterans motivated that state, and not the desire to disqualify most women from

---

state. If one were to take this approach, then the concept of subdivisional autonomy, so important to the resolution of *Milliken*, would have paled in significance.

[149] See Justice Douglas's dissent in Spencer v. Kugler, 404 U.S. 1027, 1029-30 (1972); *cf.* Justice Stewart concurring in Bradley v. Milliken, 418 U.S. 717, 755 (1974). Perhaps the most narrow perspective on this question comes from Justice Rehnquist, dissenting from denial of certiorari in Cleveland Board of Education v. Reed, 445 U.S. 935 (1980).

[150] As the Court has ruled with respect to *Dayton, Omaha,* and *Austin,* the remedy should be only as broad as the intentional segregation caused by the school district. Justices Douglas and Powell each took a very different view in *Keyes,* 413 U.S. 189, 214-36 (1973). Note also the disclaimer of the Court in Swann v. Charlotte-Mecklenburg Board of Education, 402 U.S. 1, 23 (1971).

competitive civil service positions. Because the Court viewed such assistance to veterans as rationally related to a legitimate state objective, it would not upset the policy. The inability of women to compete for Massachusetts's state jobs—or those of any other state with a similar policy—is directly attributable to the recruitment policies of the military which are overtly and intentionally gender based. Even if one accepts the Court's view that the intent of Massachusetts was itself benign,[151] there is nevertheless no question but that the discriminatory impact of the law is a result of intentional gender-based policies of the federal government. In response to this observation, the Court simply replied, "But the history of discrimination against women in the military is not on trial in this case."[152] The failure of the Court to hold the State accountable for its, arguably benign, use of the intentionally discriminatory classification scheme of the federal government is reminiscent of the "silver platter" doctrine of decades past: while one jurisdiction acts with discriminatory intent, another may harvest the fruits of the classification scheme, provided that some behavior is not tainted with illicit motives. As in the Fourth Amendment cases of the silver platter era, the intent cases under equal protection rest on the importance of the clean hands of the second actor. In the Fourth Amendment cases, the Court acknowledged the folly of this fiction. The same awareness ought to be applied to the Equal Protection cases.

c) Government versus Citizenry. Finally, and perhaps the most troublesome element of the Court's approach to whose intent is dispositive of the intent question, is its bifurcation of governmental officials and citizens. In *Memphis v. Greene* the Court upheld the ceding and closure of a street which connected an upper-middle-class white neighborhood and a black neighborhood. Evidence was introduced at trial in support of the contention that the community activists (demanding closure of the street) were motivated by the desire to limit black vehicular traffic through their neighborhood. Justice Stevens concluded for the Court that the intentions of the citizenry were irrelevant because it was public officials of Memphis who were sued and not the residents of Hein Park. "Therefore we must focus on the decisions of these public officials, and not on the actions of the residents of Hein Park, in determining whether respondents have

---

[151] But see Justice Marshall's dissent at 442 U.S. 256, 284–85 (1979).

[152] *Id.* at 278. The Court has subsequently upheld the male-only registration system for the draft in Rostker v. Goldberg, 453 U.S. 57 (1981), on the logic that a male-only combat law (assumed to be constitutional) rationally supports a male-only draft registration system.

proved their claim."[153] As it had done in previous cases, in *Memphis* the Court narrowly defined whose intent was relevant and by so doing identified the wrongdoer and limited the possibility of recovery. While there has been disagreement among scholars on the responsibility of governments for the actions of their citizenry,[154] the Court's resolution of this issue has at least three weaknesses. It is contrary to principles and practices of democracy, to precedent, and to common sense.

The Court's bifurcation of governmental officials and citizens on the question of intent conflicts with basic principles of democracy as we know them. Under one theory of majoritarian representative government, official decisionmakers ought to respond reflexively to the demands of their constituents. Their intent should be either irrelevant or identical to that of a majority of the citizens. The Court's assumption that the separate intentions of those empowered to make official decisions must themselves be illicit suggests its rejection of this basic conception of representative government. Put in a slightly different and more empirical light, in any given case the Court ought to ask—at minimum—whether the challenged policy would have been made without support from at least some segments of the public. Even if public input only influenced the making of the policy, which it nearly always does, the motivation behind it must be scrutinized if any motive analysis is to be required. To hold otherwise is to ignore the question which the Court purports to answer, to wit, why the challenged policy was made. In the *Memphis* case, more specifically, the challenged municipal action was initiated by and continuously pressured for by the residents of Hein Park. To dismiss their intentions as irrelevant because they were not the defendants in the suit is to undermine whatever virtue might otherwise attach to the intent rule. We are supposed to know whether official governmental authority was used for illicit ends. What is in the hearts and minds of those who fill official positions may tell us little or nothing about why decisions were made. Elected representatives may simply want to be reelected. They may respond to pressure from influential citizens, as often as not having no interest in particular policy choices. The Court's reluctance to scrutinize mass motives is understandable given the great difficulty of ascertaining such. Except in those cases in which official decisions

---

[153] 451 U.S. at 114 n. 23.

[154] On this point, see, for example, Alexander, *Introduction: Motivation and Constitutionality*, 15 SAN DIEGO L. REV. 925, 946 (1978), and Eisenberg, note 32 *supra*, at 49.

are made independently of public attitudes and pressure, it is not persuasive to ignore them, not if one is to comprehend fully why the official decisions were made.

In addition to the antidemocratic nature of the Court's refusal to scrutinize unofficial motives, it is also contrary to precedent. On various occasions, the Court has held the state responsible for allegedly "private" motives when the state has been unduly entangled with those motives or with the resulting behavior of the private actors. This proposition underlies all of the "state action" cases and (if anyone's intent must be demonstrated) is the means by which the illicit behavior of private parties becomes the responsibility of government. *Burton v. Wilmington Parking Authority* and *Gilmore v. City of Montgomery*[155] are but two examples of cases in which the intentionally discriminatory acts of private parties were at issue and not the intentions of the governmental parties sued. It mattered little in either case whether the local officials responsible for the contractual arrangements with the private parties were supportive of racial segregation. It mattered only that official power, after "sifting facts and weighing circumstances," was found to be unduly associated with the resulting discriminatory behavior.

A similar view may be taken of *Reitman v. Mulkey*.[156] The respondents in the cases were landlords who were accused of racial discrimination in their rental decisions. In their defense, the landlords cited the (then) recently passed Proposition 14 which protected their right to make any decisions, even racially motivated ones, governing the sale or rental of their real property. The relevant aspect of the ruling of the Supreme Court in *Reitman* was its scrutiny of the environment within which the passage of Proposition 14 occurred. This was probative, not of the motivation of the defendants in the case at bar, but rather of the populace responsible for the passage of Proposition 14. Footnote 23 in *Memphis* suggests that the Court must scrutinize the motives of only the defendants in the case before it. *Reitman* suggests otherwise. The public, environmental considerations so critical to the resolution of *Reitman* were considered to be largely irrelevant in *Memphis*.

The third weakness of the bifurcation of officials and citizens on the question of intent is that it is contrary to common sense and, implicitly, to justice. The Court stressed in *Memphis* that the relevant intention is

---

[155] 417 U.S. 557 (1974).
[156] 387 U.S. 369 (1967).

that of the parties sued, but from whom can appropriate remedy be had? Only the city had the power to close the street. Only the city had the power to reopen and maintain it. Ultimately, it was the city which allowed official power to be used for allegedly discriminatory purposes. The residents lobbied for the street closure, but they were not themselves responsible for the misuse of governmental power. More important, the Court ought to recognize that the residents' political activities are protected by the First Amendment. It would be dangerous indeed for the courts to award damages against citizens for the content of their political wants. The strictures of the First Amendment, the responsibility for the actual use of official power, and the consideration of appropriate remedies all combine to suggest the inappropriateness of the Court's rigid perspective.

2. *How much illicit intent must be demonstrated?* A critical question raised by the Court's formulation of equal protection is, How much illicit intent is necessary to constitute a constitutional violation? The issue of quantum of intent is important, because to ignore it is to assume that all of the responsible decisionmakers in the policymaking process are identically disposed and that there is always but one goal motivating them. It is to the Court's credit that the question has been addressed, but the Court's answer is not entirely satisfactory. As in its response to the question of whose intent is relevant, the Court has answered the question with inconsistent formulations. The Court has also assumed that it has adequate tools to measure intent. And finally, it has failed to ask the correct equal protection question, that is, How much illicit intent is needed to trigger scrutiny more strict than mere rationality? The Justices have assumed that illicit intent sufficient to invalidate a law must be demonstrated.

The misconception of the relevant question, the assumptions about the explanatory weight of various causative factors, and the Court's own sense of confidence about what has been demonstrated all suggest that the Court has simply adapted the *McGowan* approach, measuring not what does explain the challenged policy but rather what could explain it. In so doing the Court has met—if crudely—the "futility" objection to intent analysis (that is, that the same policy could be reenacted, stating licit goals):[157] if the policy in question in an equal protection case could be passed for legitimate reasons, the Court will assume that those reasons existed and that they explain the adoption of

---

[157] See, for example, Palmer v. Thompson, 403 U.S. 217, 225 (1971).

the policy.[158] Thus, in determining the role of the quantum of demonstrated intent, the Court has not protected members of suspect classes from being disproportionately disadvantaged by policies designed to injure them. They are potentially protected from only those disadvantageous policies which could not possibly be a function of any other goal but that of discrimination.[159] Even if one grants the constitutional relevance of intent analysis, the Court's formulation provides inadequate protection from intentional racism or sexism.

Despite the Court's suggestion that a public policy has only one discernible goal,[160] the Justices have nevertheless acknowledged the possibility that the desire to effect discrimination might be but one of the multiple purposes of legislation. The problem is that the Court has not been consistent in its statement of how much of the explanatory intent must be illicit, and it has set uneven obstacles to demonstrating sufficient illicit intent to warrant some level of scrutiny more serious than mere rationality. In almost all cases, the Court has demanded that the illicit intent be more responsible for the disputed policy than the Court has found it to be.

A clear statement of the "clean hands" approach, under which government must demonstrate that discrimination played no part in its decisions, is found in *Keyes*. Justice Brennan, writing for the Court, held that defendants must demonstrate that "segregative intent was not among the factors that motivated their actions."[161] In dicta, the *Feeney* Court said, similarly, that the policy must have been "at least in part" for discriminatory reasons.[162] Had the Court seriously applied this test in cases subsequent to *Keyes*, different results would have been likely. Instead, the Court switched to a test requiring proof that, save for the

---

[158] Ely has been most concerned about meeting the "futility" objection to intent analysis, see Ely, note 17 *supra*, at 1279-80. For a different view, one that I might share were I an exponent of intent analysis, see Brest, note 32 *supra*, at 125-27. Brest does not think that the Court ought to uphold a policy resulting from discriminatory motives simply because it might be passed again for good motives.

[159] The one noteworthy exception to this rule appears to be the recent decision of the Court in *Rogers*, in which it is difficult to imagine that retention of at-large voting in Burke County, Georgia, was the result of only the intent to discriminate.

[160] In *Davis* and in *Arlington Heights*, the Court suggested that the plaintiffs would have to disprove the professed motive in order to maintain the argument that there was an illicit motive. In *Feeney*, the Court suggested that one would have to disprove the pro-veteran motivation in order to argue that there was a sexist intention. Each of these cases implies that the Court acknowledges only one controlling motive as accounting for a given policy, and its use of terms such as "pretext" suggests its insensitivity to the possibility of multiple, simultaneous causative factors.

[161] 413 U.S. at 210.

[162] 442 U.S. at 276.

desire to effect discrimination, the challenged policy would not have been adopted. The Court has rejected the view of Professor Brest and others who have argued that any nontrivial evidence of discriminatory purpose ought to trigger strict scrutiny,[163] and has instead turned the intent rule into an almost insurmountable barrier to equal protection scrutiny. A crucial footnote in *Arlington Heights*, often overlooked, is quite explicit. Policies disproportionately disadvantageous to minorities, adopted even in substantial part to effect this disadvantage, and even acknowledged as such, are neither per se unconstitutional nor must they be subjected to strict scrutiny. They are invalid only if the Court determines that minus the quantum of illicit intent present the policy would not or could not have been adopted.[164] But the Court never had to reach this point in *Arlington Heights*, because it held that plaintiffs had failed to show that segregation was a factor in the decision of the Village to reject the proposed housing development.

The Court's resolution of *Arlington Heights* was curious, although not unparalleled insofar as the Court exhibited confidence in its ability to know and to weigh the relative explanatory importance of the "causes" of public policies. The reader is not always as confident as is the Court on these questions. The Court concluded that the plaintiffs had not demonstrated illicit intent. But does the Court know this? Despite voluminous circumstantial evidence of illicit purpose, the *Arlington Heights* case was decided in the court below on the basis of effects. Two factors explain this. Precedents from lower federal courts suggested to the trial court the propriety of an effects approach, and the trial court ruled that the responsible decisionmakers were entitled to privilege on the question of intent. More important, perhaps, the Court either did not understand or misportrayed the factual situation concerning the zoning issue. While the Court viewed the desire to preserve substantial R-1 space as a legitimate community interest, it did not acknowledge as legally significant the freezing effect of such zoning practices. Many communities downzone all or nearly all vacant land in order to retain discretion over how and by whom the land will later be used. It is not simply that this may result in disadvantage to minorities and the poor. It may be designed, at least in part, for that purpose. One who is committed to discerning intent in equal protection cases must, therefore, be prepared to assess the relevant data. The Court presumed to do so in *Arlington Heights* but displayed

---

[163] Brest, note 32 *supra*, at 130–31.
[164] 429 U.S. at 270–71 n. 21.

substantial ignorance about what needed to be measured. The Court was confident of the legitimacy of the decision not to rezone the land in question. It was consistent with the village's stated policy. It was not, however, necessarily consistent with the village's actual practices, under which, for example, land surrounding high schools was routinely rezoned for multiple-unit housing.[165] The MHDC project was adjacent to a high school but was assumed by the Court to fall under the stated policy of R-5 zoning "to serve as a buffer" between commercial/industrial land and R-1 lots.[166] In short, if the Court had perceived the situation correctly it would have asked whether this unsuccessful rezoning, in comparison with other successful rezonings, was explainable on the basis of race.

Uniqueness was an even more critical feature in *Memphis v. Greene* and *National Education Association v. South Carolina.*[167] In *Memphis*, the Court assumed that the city had ceded and closed the street in question for traffic control purposes. It was not inclined to question why this street was closed when the City of Memphis had never before closed a street for traffic control purposes and in this case had done so without meeting fully its own procedural rules.[168] In *NEA v. South Carolina*, the Court sustained the use of the National Teachers' Examination for hiring teachers and setting salaries in South Carolina. Reliance on this test disqualified 83 percent of black applicants but only 17.5 percent of white applicants.[169] Despite the grossly disproportionate racial impact, the Court summarily affirmed the finding of the district court that "plaintiffs failed to prove a racially discriminatory purpose."[170] But if the test was not serving a discriminatory purpose, why was it being used and why was it needed? "The District Court here held that no other measures would satisfy the State's interest in obtaining qualified teachers and paying them fairly."[171] As the dissenters in *NEA* were quick to note, only two other states relied on the National Teachers' Examination to select teachers

---

[165] Schwemm, note 38 *supra*, at 1032.

[166] As Justice Powell noted, approvingly, in *Arlington Heights:* "[T]he Village's apartment policy . . . called for R-5 zoning primarily to serve as a buffer between single-family development and land uses thought incompatible, such as commercial or manufacturing districts. Lincoln Green did not meet this requirement, as it adjoined no commercial or manufacturing district." 429 U.S. at 258.

[167] 434 U.S. 1026 (1978).

[168] See Justice Marshall's dissent in Memphis v. Greene, 451 U.S. at 142-43.

[169] 434 U.S. at 1027.

[170] *Id.*

[171] *Id.* at 1028.

and only South Carolina used the test to determine pay.[172] The relatively limited reliance on the National Teachers' Examination ought to have opened to question its assumed utility and in turn perhaps raised at least some question about the State's purposes. The trial court, like the Supreme Court, had before it evidence that the test in question was a reliable measure of only familiarity with teaching materials and did not predict job performance.[173] The willingness of the Supreme Court to accept the trial court's conclusion that South Carolina could find no substitute for the test is, therefore, especially perplexing. As in *Memphis* and *Arlington Heights*, the Court was concerned primarily with what could or might explain the challenged policy. The combination of the Court's *McGowan*-like approach to assuming the existence of states of affairs and its facile assumptions about the relative weights of causative factors has made the Court rather less concerned than it might otherwise have been with evaluating what actually explains racially disadvantageous policies. To do so the Court would have to assess more seriously circumstantial evidence and official patterns and practices over time. Except in the area of school segregation, the Court has consistently refused to do so.[174]

One of the most striking examples of the Court's deference to local government and its satisfaction of the futility objection to intent analysis was its resolution of *City of Richmond v. United States*.[175] The Court acknowledged that the annexation of a section of Chesterfield County by the City of Richmond, Virginia, was done for the purpose of diluting the black vote.[176] It reasoned, nevertheless, that the annexation might stand if the city could offer some post hoc nondiscriminatory justification for its actions.[177]

---

[172] *Id.*

[173] *Id.* at 1027. Even Justice White, the author of Washington v. Davis, thought that that case left intact the requirement that there be a connection between training and the job that one is to hold.

[174] See, for example, Justice Marshall's dissent in Memphis v. Greene, 451 U.S. at 143-44; *Feeney*, 442 U.S. at 280 n.27; *cf.* Marshall's dissent, *id.* at 285. See also the comment of the Court, "But past discrimination cannot, in the manner of original sin, condemn governmental action that is not itself unlawful. . . . More distant instances of official discrimination in other cases are of limited help in resolving [the] question." *Mobile*, 446 U.S. at 74. Ironically, on the one occasion not involving school segregation that the Court appeared to look at patterns of behavior over time, they were not germane to the question. See *Rogers*, note 131 *supra*.

[175] 422 U.S. 358 (1975).

[176] The U.S. Commission on Civil Rights quoted Mayor Bagley of Richmond, Virginia, as saying, " 'As long as I am Mayor of the City of Richmond the niggers won't take over this town.' " UNITED STATES COMMISSION ON CIVIL RIGHTS. THE VOTING RIGHTS ACT: TEN YEARS AFTER 302 (1975).

[177] 422 U.S. at 375.

The pattern of the Court's resolution of these cases suggests that while the Court has offered inconsistent dicta, it has ultimately applied a "same decision" rule. The problem is that the Court displays entirely too much confidence in its ability to know whether the challenged policy would have been adopted had there been no illicit intent. If it can imagine a legitimate rationale or if one is involved in part, the Court will assume that it was controlling. Its decision in *Richmond* is particularly troublesome, because it suggests that government will be forgiven its intentional misdeeds if it can subsequently manufacture another sanitized justification for the same action. While it may be argued that *Richmond* was a very special case because of the compromise that had been reached between the City and the Department of Justice under the Voting Rights Act, it nevertheless establishes bad authority easily applied to other equal protection cases. The *Richmond* decision is but the logical rebuttal to the futility argument against intent analysis. It does not, however, protect individuals from purposeful acts of disadvantage due to race, ethnicity, or sex. It protects them from only those acts for which a new rationalization, even after the fact, cannot be imagined. Even if one were inclined to adopt the intent rule, the Court's "minimum" fails to protect individuals from the very abridgments that the theory of intent is ostensibly meant to prevent, that is, from the disadvantageous consequences of laws which, while facially neutral, are infected with discriminatory intent.

A major problem with the Court's calibration of the quantum of illicit intent is that the Court has substituted the question of what violates the Constitution for the appropriate equal protection question of what triggers scrutiny stricter than mere rationality. Consequently, the debate between the Court and its critics is an uneven one in that the critics almost uniformly question whether intent rather than discriminatory effects ought to trigger serious scrutiny of the challenged governmental policy. Because the Supreme Court has preempted any consideration of the state's interest in a policy— whether through balancing, intermediate scrutiny, or strict scrutiny— it has instead set a very high threshold of intent beyond which it will simply invalidate the challenged policy. The Court's self-restraint has been manifested inappropriately in denying that an injury has occurred rather than in carefully considering the competing interests and in judiciously using its remedial powers.

F. UNDESIRABLE CONSEQUENCES OF THE INTENT RULE

A most serious consequence of the intent rule, especially in the Court's formulation of it, is that policies actually designed to foster discrimination may easily escape judicial remedy. Not only is the process of litigation one of post hoc reconstruction and rationalization of what decisionmakers have done, but if any other motive could explain the challenged policy the Court will assume that it does. And, as Professor Kenneth Karst has noted, the Court has placed the burden on the wrong side.[178] Policies that result in gross disadvantage to minority groups ought, at minimum, to create a presumption that such disadvantage was intended. Intent theory also renders decisions made through the electoral and referendum processes relatively immune from scrutiny. As Professor Lawrence Sager has noted, elections are by design opaque as to motives.[179] There is a further irony in the Court's adoption of the intent rule. Although considerations of institutional self-restraint and respect for the other branches and levels of government may explain the Court's attraction to the intent rule, these considerations may also be responsible for the Court's virtual refusal to find the rule satisfied. And in *Rogers*, the only noneducation case in which the Court found the intent test satisfied, there was no reasonable evidence that the Court's own announced standards had been met. The alleged virtues of the rule appeared to be outweighed by the weaknesses in its philosophical premises, its application, and its pragmatic consequences.

1. *Process of identifying intent is unseemly and counterproductive.* The cases challenging the impact of policies affecting minorities typically involve the profession by government of a benign motive for its acts, whether it is veterans' preference laws, exclusion of pregnancy from disability plans, screening tests for police personnel, preserving neighborhood schools, or controlling the flow of traffic. In order to challenge successfully the impact of these policies it must be demonstrated, not only that the professed motives were not the real ones, but that illicit ones were the most significant in bringing about the policies in question. Plaintiffs may succeed only by demonstrating the pervasiveness of a "secret" agenda. Because it must be shown that the decisionmakers were motivated by that which they deny, the

---

[178] Karst, *The Costs of Motive-Centered Inquiry*, 15 SAN DIEGO L. REV. 1163, 1165 (1978).
[179] Sager, *Insular Majorities Unabated: Warth v. Seldin and City of Eastlake v. Forest City Enterprises*, 91 HARV. L. REV. 1373, 1421 (1978).

plaintiffs must prove them to be liars. This necessarily involves the courts in an unseemly review of the behavior and attitudes of legislators and other official decisionmakers, a process necessarily characterized by innuendo, gossip, and suspicion. The Court is not unaware of the legal and political implications of judicial resolution of cases finding illicit intent. This may explain its almost uniform rejection of findings of unconstitutional intent by lower courts.[180] Another problem related to the Court's unwillingness to find illicit intent is that it has not resolved the question of "privilege." It is indeed likely that the Court would uphold the immunity of members of Congress from disclosing their motives under the Speech and Debate Clause of the Constitution. At least one trial court has found such a privilege to exist under state law.[181]

The process of identifying and proving illicit intent is not only unseemly, but the consequences of the process are also counterproductive. Enmity is likely to be engendered between legislators and courts,[182] and the name-calling that pervades such cases poisons the political atmosphere within which constructive resolution of public questions ideally takes place. Is a group such as the NAACP capable of lobbying for the interests of blacks after waging a legal battle which, by necessity, must impugn the character of the responsible decisionmakers?[183] It is not just a matter of legislators being angered by an accusation of intentional racism. There is also the problem that "racial attitudes often operate at the margin of consciousness."[184] Legislators may truly *believe* that their motives are pure. Injured groups are convinced otherwise. Is there a substantial reality to be discerned? Under the intent rule can the courts serve any fruitful purpose?

2. *Official adaptation to intent rule may itself disadvantage minorities.* The Court has paid little attention to the possible reactions of legislators under the intent rule. Defensiveness is a very real phenomenon in public institutions, and one should be mindful of the adaptive behavior that is likely among legislators faced with the intent rule. First, the legal alchemy inherent in intent analysis puts a premium on ignoring the problems of women and minority groups. If no

---

[180] See, for example, *Mobile, Arlington Heights,* and *Memphis,* in which painstaking analysis of intent suggested to the lower courts that there was discriminatory motivation. The Court rejected these findings.

[181] Schwemm, note 38 *supra,* at 1013.

[182] Brest, note 32 *supra,* at 128–30.

[183] Karst, note 178 *supra.*

[184] *Id.*

attention is paid to these interests, it is unlikely that illicit intent could be demonstrated. At most, minorities might demonstrate that they had been ignored. There is little indication in Court opinions, especially after *Mobile*, that this would be deemed equivalent to active illicit intent under the Equal Protection Clause.[185] Second are the problems associated with the appropriate role that race or gender may play in the formulation of public policy. Dean Ely has endorsed the intent rule as a way to preserve "color-blindness" in official decisionmaking.[186] But what is the effect of this approach on the public value of integration? Should the state be immune from judgments against it if it does not think about race; is it similarly foreclosed from considering the effect of various policy options on integration? Does neutrality among races—or between genders—necessitate neutrality as between segregation and integration? Will legislators not steer wide of the "intent" mark by avoiding such considerations? Finally, has the Court's focus on discriminatory intent seriously deflected debate over the meaning of equal protection? As Professor Karst has suggested, the judicial preoccupation with intent has ignored the real social problem, which is racial inequality.[187] Legislators are under no obligation, in fact have been given a strong disincentive, to consider what equal protection means beyond its narrowest procedural meaning. The Court has provided no substantive framework within which to debate fundamental questions of equality in the distribution of public resources and in the public rules governing access to private resources.

3. *Intent theory deflects state responsibility for state actions.* Perhaps the most profound consequence of intent theory is that it shifts constitutional law away from its focal attention on state responsibility for state actions. It distorts the law by holding states constitutionally responsible for what they intended to do and not for what they have done. Even if one accepts, for the sake of argument, that a state's motives are knowable and that it has had only "clean" motives, that does not relieve the state of responsibility for actions that may have exacerbated racism or sexism or unwittingly contributed to private organized efforts as such. Professor Sellers has therefore noted that the intent rule is most unsatisfactory for its inability to measure accurately

---

[185] For a very persuasive argument that one of the major facets of racism is "racially selective sympathy," see Brest, note 17 *supra*, at 7-8.

[186] Ely, note 17 *supra*, at 1260.

[187] Karst, note 178 *supra*.

the state's involvement in the perpetuation of racial disparities.[188] The long line of state action cases had made the state legally responsible for racial discrimination which it, even unintentionally or unwittingly, encourages, causes to happen, or with which it is too entangled. *Shelley v. Kraemer*[189] is the most obvious example of this phenomenon. The state was nothing more than a neutral referee in a suit over a restrictive covenant. It was nevertheless responsible for providing the means by which a private act of segregation could be carried out. The state action cases, it must be recalled, were not decided on the basis of official intentions. They were decided on the basis of what states of affairs the state had participated in establishing and maintaining. A major shortcoming of intent analysis, in contrast with state action precedents, is that the state is not held accountable for all of the states of affairs that it has brought about. While not all public policies that disproportionately disadvantage minorities and women are necessarily unconstitutional, they are consequences for which the state ought to be held accountable and to which the courts ought to apply careful scrutiny.

III. Reformulations of the Intent Rule

Dissatisfaction with the Court's formulation of and reliance on intent theory has led numerous critics to suggest different approaches, including that the quantum of illicit intent be lowered to render constitutionally relevant any or any substantial showing of illicit intent,[190] or that the Court redefine intent to include institutional intent.[191] In contrast with the preoccupation of the Court with determining who intended what when decisions were being made, the institutional approach would ask whether the decisions of the official body in question suggest that they acted "as if" segregation or other minority disavantage were among its goals. Yet another approach is to broaden the concept of illicit intent to include any attempt to devalue the needs or ignore the interests of members of minority groups.[192] The

---

[188] Sellers, note 44 *supra*, at 383.

[189] 334 U.S. 1 (1948).

[190] See, for example, Note, *Discriminatory Purpose*, note 44 *supra*, at 1385; Brest, note 32 *supra*, at 125-27.

[191] See, for example, Note, *Reading the Mind of the School Board: Segregative Intent and the De Facto/De Jure Distinction*, 86 YALE L. J. 317, 352 (1976); Simon, note 31 *supra*, at 1097; Note, *Discriminatory Purpose*, note 44 *supra*, at 1408.

[192] See, for example, Brest, note 17 *supra*, at 6, 8; *cf.* Fiss, note 116 *supra*, at 153-54; Judge Wright in Hobson v. Hansen, 269 F. Supp. 401, 497 (D.D.C. 1967); Clark, note 31 *supra*, at 966-67.

most liberal redefinition of the intent rule would hold government accountable for the reasonably foreseeable consequences of its actions.[193] Each of these proposed reforms is nevertheless subject to one or more of the criticisms leveled at intent theory, especially the criticism that they focus the concern of equal protection almost exclusively on the process by which decisions are made.

The disproportionately disadvantageous impact on minorities of government policies is often predictable in advance. It has, therefore, been suggested that a foreseeability approach may be tantamount to an effects approach.[194] While a foreseeability approach to intent may be virtually as protective of minorities as is an effects approach, there are several problems with a foreseeability approach. First, like other concepts of intent, it focuses on the process of decisionmaking for the locus of the injury. Second, it assumes that the responsibility of government is only to be careful, whereas constitutional law creates an obligation more analogous to absolute liability than to a standard of negligence. Third, one could argue that a foreseeability approach is not "necessary" because, as Professor Chayes has observed, public law litigation is largely prospective.[195] That is, decisions in constitutional law are more significant for the guidelines they set for future behavior of governments than they are for condemning or punishing past behavior. While the judiciary often fashions creative equitable remedies in constitutional cases, the most fundamental remedy is stopping the unconstitutional behavior in question. Those policies that have unpredictably resulted in disproportionate disadvantages for minority group members will predictably continue to have these effects. It may, therefore, be argued that the retention of such policies constitutes a future, foreseeable abridgment of equal protection of the laws. A justification of a foreseeability standard that rests on determining "guilt" is inappropriate to constitutional law. A justification resting on avoiding chaos is easily preempted by future-oriented remedies. There should, therefore, be little concern that chaos need result from holding states accountable even for that which they did not foresee at the time of the adoption of the challenged policy.

The reformulations of the intent rule have the virtue of overcoming some of the inconveniences of the rule as presently applied by the

---

[193] See, for example, Boyd, note 32 *supra*, at 740-41, 750; even Ely, note 17 *supra*, at 1265, sees some virtue in this approach.

[194] Eisenberg, note 32 *supra*, at 50 n. 76.

[195] Chayes, note 121 *supra*, at 1296.

Supreme Court. They do not, however, succeed in refuting the arguments outlined above that evidence of discriminatory intent is not mandated by the Constitution, by the weight of precedent, or by sound rules of constitutional interpretation. It was further suggested that the way in which the Court has enforced the intent rule does not even protect individuals from that which it purports to protect them. In sum, if the Equal Protection Clause has been violated, it is because of what the law does and not what it was intended to do. A responsible theory of equal protection, like a responsible theory of the First Amendment, recognizes that laws may simultaneously do many and varied things. Some of the consequences may have been intended, some may be only tolerated, and others may have been entirely unexpected. It should be of little constitutional significance into which category a consequence falls. An adequate test of constitutionality must, therefore, distinguish the legitimate consequences of state lawmaking from those that are constitutionally suspect. It is, in any case, the substance and consequences of laws that must be assessed and not the intentions behind them. The question is, therefore, not whether practices which disproportionately disadvantage racial, ethnic, or gender groups ought to be scrutinized, but whether they ought to be subject to scrutiny as strict as would be applied to such facial classifications in the law. This does not mean that these impacts are necessarily unconstitutional. The critical question, the one eclipsed by the Court's approach to the question, is, What is the appropriate level of scrutiny?

A number of critics of the intent rule, who are prepared on some occasions to scrutinize effects, have recommended that the courts apply "flexible review" to disproportionately disadvantageous policies. These are basically balancing tests. Professor Eisenberg has suggested that if race is shown to be both the proximate cause and the cause in fact of the disadvantage suffered, then the courts ought to balance the interests of the individual with the needs of the state. Under Eisenberg's formulation, the court would weigh the degree of unevenness of the impact, the importance of the subject area to the plaintiff, the need for legislative freedom, the existence of alternatives, and the state's willingness to take remedial action.[196] Professors Boyd[197]

---

[196] Eisenberg, note 32 *supra*, at 73.

[197] Boyd's balance would consider degree of impact, level of culpability of government for the pattern of impact, societal need for the policy. Boyd, note 32 *supra*, at 742.

and Perry[198] have suggested similar multivariable balancing schemes for effecting a compromise between the legitimate interests of the state and those of disadvantaged groups.

While balancing has the virtue of considering all of the affected interests and is, therefore, attractive to one's sense of fairness, it does have drawbacks. In disproportionate impact cases, its use compensates for either a failure to define and thereby circumscribe the meaning of disproportionate impact or a failure to identify the impacts for which the state ought to be held responsible. It is a general compromise which is ad hoc and, as is the case of balancing generally, fails to specify the weight that must be attached to each element worthy of balance and to justify the weight that is assigned. It is also not always clear that the elements to be balanced are accurately identified. For example, Perry has concluded that "balancing" would have led to the same conclusion as that reached by the Court in *Jefferson v. Hackney* because of the importance to the state of autonomy over the allocation of scarce welfare funds.[199] Is the issue not the importance to the state of the decision it has actually made? Are not arguments from "autonomy" ultimately arguments against judicial review and therefore against judicial balancing? Even if in some circumstances autonomy legitimately enters the balance, it is difficult at best to understand why this should be assumed in welfare funding cases.

IV. THE STATE RESPONSIBILITY ALTERNATIVE: SERIOUS SCRUTINY

Serious scrutiny of disproportionately disadvantageous impacts is preferable to ad hoc balancing. States should be held accountable for all of the consequences of their actions, and those consequences which are particularly injurious to protected groups must be seriously scrutinized. The courts should invalidate the challenged disproportionately disadvantageous policy unless it is shown to be essential to the substantial effectuation of the significant legitimate consequences of the challenged policy. In brief, if the state is able substantially to bring about the legitimate consequences of the law without the degree of relative disadvantage that it has caused, it should be constitutionally obligated to do so. If a significant and legitimate state interest, which

---

[198] Perry would consider in his balance the degree of disproportionality, the nature of the private interest disadvantaged, efficiency and availability of governmental alternatives, and the nature of the governmental needs advanced. Perry, note 35 *supra*, at 560.

[199] *Id.* at 564–65.

is actually being furthered by the challenged policy, cannot be served by a less discriminatory means, then the courts ought to uphold the policy.

A. VIRTUES OF SERIOUS SCRUTINY

Perhaps the most significant virtue of serious scrutiny, a virtue shared by all theories testing the effects of public policies, is that it takes account of habitual institutional behavior with discriminatory impacts. It acknowledges that serious social, political, and economic inequalities are traceable to the actions of public institutions, no matter what the actual motives and no matter what the motives that are provable in a court of law. It further acknowledges that, while society need not be structured so as to render each person materially equal, the state ought not to be a contributor to inequalities on the basis of race, ethnicity, or gender. The test of serious scrutiny is a rather conservative way of achieving this goal. It prohibits government only from unnecessarily disadvantaging groups that are already disadvantaged—groups whose relative disadvantage is traceable, at least in part, to a history of governmental discrimination and stereotyping. The approach also takes account of the fact that there are often many ways to achieve various social and political goals. When the state makes policies it has made choices, choices of goals and choices of means to effect them. The test of serious scrutiny deprives the state of none of its otherwise constitutional powers of choice, except that it must choose the least discriminatory means of effecting the chosen goals.

Serious scrutiny identifies racial, ethnic, and gender-based equality as a public value. It similarly acknowledges integration as a public value. There has been much attention paid to the disadvantages inherent in segregated education. Serious scrutiny would attach similar concern to officially caused segregation in employment, housing, and juries. Justice Powell made an eloquent plea for an affirmative duty with respect to school integration in *Keyes*.[200] Serious scrutiny would identify an affirmative, although limited, responsibility on behalf of government in all areas of public policy. As it involves a concern about integration, the state-responsibility model and the serious scrutiny attached to it reject the assumption that educational segregation is *sui generis*. The state would be expected to promote its goals with

---

[200] 413 U.S. at 226–28.

segregative consequences as minimal as possible. While imposing on the states a positive obligation to minimize the segregative and other minority-disadvantaging impacts of their policies, serious scrutiny is particularly sensitive to the existence of other public goals besides those of integration and proportionate equity for disadvantaged groups. "Strict scrutiny," applied by the Court to cases of overt racial classification, unlike the concept of serious scrutiny as offered here, requires that the state demonstrate that its countervailing interest is "compelling." Serious scrutiny requires only that the countervailing interest be significant and legitimate. For example, the need to have randomness in the selection of jurors is a significant public interest. While the state would therefore be obligated to structure its jury selection system to maximize the proportionate representation of minority groups on the jury rolls, its interest in randomness of selection would mitigate against refining the process of selection to ensure representation of minorities on each individual jury.

Perhaps the most important virtue of serious scrutiny is that it puts concern for equal protection on a par with the concern for other important constitutional rights. Despite Justice Stewart's contention to the contrary,[201] the expectation that the state will accomplish its legitimate interests using the "least restrictive alternative," with respect to impact on constitutionally protected rights, has a respectable history. It has often been applied to equal protection cases as well.[202] Serious scrutiny is a modified version of the minimal review applied in First Amendment cases. The state must identify its legitimate, significant interest. If the challenged policy is found to impinge on freedom of speech, press, or religion, the state will be expected, at the very least, to use carefully drawn statutes to effectuate only the legitimate goals and not to abridge unnecessarily the countervailing interests in civil liberties. In sum, serious scrutiny in equal protection law would simply give to the Clause a consistent concern that is similar to that attached to other constitutional provisions protecting civil rights.

B. ANTICIPATED CRITICISMS OF SERIOUS SCRUTINY

1. *Equal protection protects only equality of treatment.* The proposition that equal protection applies to only the treatment of

---

[201] "Invidious discrimination does not become less so because the discrimination accomplished is of a lesser magnitude." 422 U.S. 256, 277 (1979).

[202] See, for example, Shapiro v. Thompson, Memorial Hospital v. Maricopa County, and Shelton v. Tucker, 364 U.S. 479 (1960).

individuals by the state and not to the results of that treatment is a seductively simple principle. It comports with our sense of "equality before the law" and our belief in treating people as separate, worthy individuals. Even Professor Eisenberg, who supports at least a limited effects approach to equal protection, worries about the possibility that a commitment to proportionate results will eclipse our commitment to judging individuals on their own merits.[203] This result would not necessarily occur. It is possible to preserve equality of treatment while incorporating a group disadvantaging principle into our understanding of the Equal Protection Clause. If one starts from the premise that individuals should have an equal right to compete for public gratuities, to take advantage of the public "goodies" such as jobs, good schools, political power, and so on, then one must ask whether classifications are skewed to give a certain class of persons a competitive edge. Professor Owen Fiss has argued rather persuasively that, by hypothesis, if the interests of disadvantaged groups were seriously considered in the policymaking process, "other" values (than those currently advanced) would be incorporated into public policies.[204] While Professor Fiss's position is intuitively persuasive, it remains hypothetical. Perhaps more important is the fact that disadvantaging results are a function of classificatory schemes such as veteran status, pregnancy-based disability, ability to pass Test 21, welfare aid categories. A commitment to an effects approach is simply a commitment to the legal relevance of the reality that some classification schemes embody more than their facial classifications. The state is, therefore, to be held responsible for all of the "other" classifications which it may have, even unknowingly, incorporated into public policy.

Seen in this perspective, scrutiny based on effects is not different in kind from routine equal protection scrutiny, scrutiny of the classification schemes which are "procedural" only to the extent that they determine to whom and under what conditions the law is to be applied.[205] But it also cannot be emphasized too strongly that one need not make a choice between equality of treatment and equality of

---

[203] Eisenberg, note 32 *supra*, at 42.

[204] Fiss, note 116 *supra*, at 154.

[205] Professor Westen has stated so eloquently what seems to have been overlooked by some scholars of equal protection: the concept of equality that requires that "likes" be treated "alike" has no inherent meaning. It is the law that defines what the likenesses are that make like treatment appropriate, and one cannot therefore measure the constitutionality of laws by this maxim. Westen, note 95 *supra*, at 551.

results. Serious scrutiny asks whether the state might not meet its legitimate interests through the formulation and application of a different classification scheme, which when equally applied effects less disproportionate results. Equality of treatment ought to be preserved as a value under the Equal Protection Clause, but it need not, and should not, be accompanied by gross inequality of results. And scrutiny of results is really nothing more than scrutiny of classification schemes, a scrutiny that takes into account all of the classifications which may simultaneously be at work.[206]

2. *Are there no limits to the effects for which the state ought to be held responsible?* Holding the state responsible for racial, ethnic, or gender-based outcomes and effects of public policies, it must be remembered, only triggers serious scrutiny of these policies. It does not prohibit the states from exercising legitimate authority and promoting substantial goals. This does not mean, however, that the state must be held accountable for outcomes of policies and laws for which it is not actually responsible. An important distinction must be drawn between consequences of policies that follow inextricably and those that result from the volitional acts of private parties. One can thus easily differentiate pre-employment tests or welfare-funding policies that disproportionately disadvantage minorities from, for example, criminal arrest or conviction statistics or the outcome of elections. In the former situations, minorities are arguably only passive victims of the challenged policies and are not immediately capable of altering their impacts, but in the latter cases it is not at all clear that the group disadvantage did not result from voluntary actions of private individuals. To adapt Eisenberg's formulation, it is not obvious in the latter cases that the state is the cause in fact of the alleged injury.[207] In such cases the state must have the opportunity to disprove its responsibility for the outcomes.

Consider the not-too-hypothetical example of capital punishment. Assuming that such punishment does not violate the ban on cruel and unusual punishment in the Eighth Amendment, is the Equal Protection Clause violated by a likelihood that blacks disproportionate-

---

[206] Those who find this equating of effects with treatment too large a leap might consider the mediating principle of "equality of opportunity," which has been very popular in our constitutional mythology. Is a minority group offered equal opportunity to compete for public gratuities if the selection criteria unnecessarily disqualify them from the opportunity to compete? Another approach worth considering posits that equality of effects is a penumbral right radiating from the Equal Protection Clause, without which the concept of equality of treatment and opportunity—the traditional notions of equal protection—cannot be meaningful.

[207] Eisenberg, note 32 *supra*, at 64–66.

ly will be sentenced to death? Under the state responsibility model, the death penalty would be subjected to serious scrutiny and disallowed unless the state demonstrated that its use was essential to the realization of the legitimate benefits that actually result from its use. But the state must also have the opportunity to disprove its responsibility for the pattern of sentences: it must be allowed to demonstrate that the volitional behavior of blacks bears the actual responsibility. This would require that the state demonstrate that blacks actually commit a similarly disproportionate share of the heinous, aggravated murders that are subject to capital punishment. In contrast with intent theory, this formulation asks, not if juries are "racist," but rather whether private individuals' choices or the criminal justice system is to be held accountable for the apparent disparities. Satisfying the burden of proof in such cases may indeed prove difficult for states, but the important point is that states would be provided the opportunity to disprove the *prima facie* assumption of their responsibility for the outcomes and effects of their policies.

The nature of the state's responsibility for the challenged impact of public policies is also problematic in cases challenging at-large electoral systems, challenges such as those waged in Mobile, Alabama, and Burke County, Georgia. These suits were premised not on the nonelection of blacks to public office but on their nonelectability under the at-large systems. This may seem a semantic point, but it is not. A distinction must be made between election results reflecting only voter preferences and those where such preferences are potentially thwarted by systemic features. Thus, even a predominantly black district that elects Caucasians to office fails to attain proportional representation by race. The failure to elect blacks is not, however, an effect of the electoral process for which the state ought to be held accountable. The electoral system did not preclude the possibility of such proportional representation. In contrast, voluminous evidence suggests that, in communities with racial polarization, at-large electoral systems preclude not only the election of minorities to office but perhaps more importantly immunize elected officials from the necessity of responding to the needs and demands of the minority community.[208] While the Constitution may not, as the Court has observed, guarantee proportional representation for racial minorities, it does guarantee an equality of opportunity to participate in the political

---

[208] See Note, *Affirmative Action and Electoral Reform*, 90 YALE L. J. 1811, 1812-1817 & nn.7-10, 13-15, 19 (1981).

life of the community.[209] State responsibility is present where an electoral system has the effect of precluding the possibility of proportionate electoral power and political saliency for a minority community.[210]

The notion of state responsibility is not limitless. Before subjecting states to a test of serious scrutiny, the courts must consider whether the challenged ramifications of a public policy stem directly from the policy itself or more accurately from private behavior. Difficult questions may need resolution, but they are empirical questions on which courts can consider evidence.

3. *Can the courts measure disproportionate impacts?* Judgment is no doubt involved in determining whether an impact is disproportionate "enough" to raise constitutional questions. But this concern is no more problematic for judges to handle than are a vast array of constitutional questions with which they regularly deal and is indeed easier than determining intent. Objections may be raised to the imprecision involved in knowing how disproportionate an impact needs to be to be subjected to serious scrutiny. The courts may well take a "know it when they see it" approach and scrutinize those impacts too large to escape their notice and ignore those small enough to be attributable to chance.[211] This is not an area in which the courts have no precedent to follow. In the reapportionment cases, the courts have applied an "as nearly as practicable" standard which has allowed for both strictness and reasonable flexibility. The Supreme Court has also had to determine how small a jury is constitutionally too small, how divided a jury is too divided to preserve a "reasonable doubt" standard for convictions in criminal cases. In reapportionment and jury cases, the court's determination about the "numbers" was very critical as it determined the constitutionality of the challenged actions. In the disproportionate impact cases, the determination about the "numbers" only triggers serious scrutiny and does not necessarily invalidate the

---

[209] "The plaintiffs' burden is to produce evidence . . . that its members had less opportunity than did other residents in the district to participate in the political processes and to elect legislators of their choice." White v. Regester, 412 U.S. 755, 766 (1973).

[210] Justice Stevens's assertion in Rogers v. Lodge, 102 S. Ct. at 3286-89, that it is the minority status numerically that explains the limitations on black electoral strength is not entirely accurate. Systemic features are important. See note 208 *supra*.

[211] There is, of course, a statistical test for "chance" relationships. While high correlations such as in *Washington, Feeney,* or *NEA* are not proof of causation, neither are they "flukes." Our legal principles are unduly infected with the need to identify single causes. In equal protection cases it ought to be apparent to the courts that strong racial or gender-based correlations, which are not "chance" outcomes, suggest that race or gender is an important element in the outcome.

challenged policy. The constitutional implications are thus distinctly less onerous.

A serious conceptual question in disproportionate impact cases involves the relevant universe of persons from which to determine the disadvantage to minorities or women. Should one, for example, consider all of the applicants for particular jobs as the universe within which to compare success rates among various racial or gender groups? Alternatively, ought the statistics on disadvantage be considered with respect to the total population of the country? Or, should only the population of the surrounding area—from among whom employees would be hired—be considered in determining the degree of disproportionate disadvantageous impact of an employment practice? While there is no one correct scientific answer to this question, courts ought to take great care to prevent manipulation of the relevant universe to refute evidence of disadvantage or to create the impression of disparate impact where none reasonably exists.[212] There is, nevertheless, room for flexibility and judgment in determining how to measure the relevant effects of public policies on protected groups. It is a matter of determining who is really affected by the challenged policy.

Some hypotheticals may be in order. If a challenged employment policy disqualifies a significantly greater percentage of minority applicants than other applicants, this ought to create a *prima facie* case of discrimination. The public employer might, however, rebut this presumption by demonstrating that its policy would not have disproportionately disqualified a more representative sample of local minority workers. What the state would be demonstrating in this situation is that the applicant pool was skewed and did not reflect the expected pool in which minorities would have fared as well as nonminority applicants. Conversely, in cases in which actual applicants have fared equally well under the employment criteria used, plaintiffs should nevertheless have the opportunity to demonstrate that an absence of disproportionate disqualification is a function of the

---

[212] In a provocative argument on employment discrimination, Lerner has accused the courts of manipulating the relevant universe from which to measure disproportionate impacts. But her alternative for identifying the universe in "new hire" cases simply defines away the problem by pinpointing the relevant universe as the "qualified labor pool." This effectively preempts any attempt to analyze what "qualified" actually means and rejects the normative principle that impact theory seeks to protect, that is, that qualifications be defined to minimize, as far as is possible, racial and gender-based disadvantages. Lerner, note 42 *supra*, at 30-31, 39.

deterrent effect of the employment criteria. If a police department requires officers to be at least five feet eight inches tall, women of lesser height—a group which includes the vast majority of all American women—will be unlikely to seek employment as police officers. It would, therefore, be inappropriate to treat actual applicants as the relevant universe against which to measure relative male/female disqualification rates.

In disproportionate impact cases—be they employment, school segregation, housing, jury selection, or voting rights—courts must decide how to circumscribe the relevant universe for purposes of measuring impacts for their disproportionality. Judgment is clearly called for, but it requires conceptual thinking which is no different in kind from that in which judges routinely engage. The necessity of making such determinations hardly seems a basis on which to reject impact analysis.

4. *Scrutiny of disproportionate impacts will lead to race-conscious policymaking.* This is a considerable objection to an interpretation of equal protection that includes effects analysis and a concern about disproportionately harmful impacts on disadvantaged groups. But it differs significantly from the criticism that it requires judging people on the basis of their race, the criticism most often leveled against affirmative action plans that use different methods of selection or classification for different racial groups. The criticism of fostering race awareness is, nevertheless, very valid. But is it necessarily antithetical to our conception of equality to be sensitive to race or gender? While the long-run goals of color-blindness and gender nearsightedness are laudable, they are not a current reality. Anyone who begins from the premise of racial or sexual equality will find nothing attractive in a state responsibility model or in the application of serious scrutiny. But those who see the pristine principle of equal treatment as reflecting a simple judicial declaration of equality in law, and not a statement of empirical reality, will be more inclined to ask of the government that it consider the racial, ethnic, and gender-based consequences of its policies. To use a very simple analogy, we care enough about our environment to demand environmental impact statements. We should care enough about group-disadvantaging public policy to demand a similar concern.

It will be little comfort to those opposed to any official accounting of race or gender to be reminded that we already have legitimated group-conscious decisionmaking. In *Regents of the University of*

California v. Bakke,[213] *Fullilove v. Klutznick*,[214] *Steelworkers v. Weber*,[215] *Hills v. Gautreaux*,[216] *U.J.O. v. Carey*,[217] and *Morton v. Mancari*,[218] the Supreme Court has acknowledged the legitimacy of race-conscious policies of a nonstigmatizing type. The Court itself has often utilized race-conscious remedies, especially in the area of school desegregation. The *Emporia* decision, it will be recalled, was quite explicit about the equitable powers of the courts to scrutinize the actions of school districts in terms of their impact on the process of school desegregation. Racial effects were therefore made a primary policy consideration. It is similarly unclear whether a concern about race, ethnicity, or gender-conscious policymaking is a concern about its being mandated under the Constitution or its being permissible. It would appear to be the latter or else there would be no constitutionally based objection to such "sensitivities" in policymaking. But if the policymaking process must be completely oblivious to race, is the government prohibited from structuring its policies to promote integration? Is the government similarly forbidden to pass such laws as § 1985[219] which are designed to control racially motivated crime? These are examples of the most benign, yet the most race-conscious, of public policy options. Must they also be prohibited? This question may seem rhetorical to some, but it is, nevertheless, important. If the Constitution allows for racial sensitivity of a benign sort, when adopted through policy channels, then it must similarly allow for such remedies to be mandated by the judiciary, especially when such sensitivity as the judiciary orders is one founded in equality of treatment under less biased criteria of selection.

V. CONCLUSION

The decisions of the Burger Court on equal protection have been significantly influenced by the application of the intent rule. The rule has proved attractive to the Justices and to its scholarly exponents in large part because of their concern about the perceived alternatives and their apprehension about the possibility of far-reaching judicial remedies. But the arguments against intent analysis are many and

---

[213] 438 U.S. 265 (1978).
[214] 448 U.S. 448 (1980).
[215] 443 U.S. 193 (1979).
[216] 425 U.S. 284 (1976).
[217] 430 U.S. 144 (1977).
[218] 417 U.S. 535 (1974).
[219] 42 U.S.C. §1985.

varied. It inappropriately defines as the only locus of the injury the process by which the challenged policy decisions were made. As precedents from many different equal protection cases fully demonstrate, injuries can occur in the results of the decisions made. Precedents interpreting other constitutional rights argue against the validity of the proposition that only those effects that were intended by the policymakers are subject to scrutiny.

Attention to the Court's formulation and application of the intent rule has raised serious conceptual questions about what constitutes illicit intent. The analysis has also demonstrated that it is not likely that the intent rule is even capable of protecting that which it purports to protect—a policymaking process free of racism and sexism. The Court has been reluctant in nearly every case to acknowledge either the existence or importance of illicit intent, unless it has been unable to imagine any other explanation for the challenged policy. As long as any other explanation is fathomable, the Court will assume that the legitimate considerations brought about the policy in question. By following a "same decision" rule, the Court satisfied one of the most voiced, although not most critical, objections to intent analysis, that of futility.

Beyond issues of contrary authority in precedents, beyond the conceptual and pragmatic difficulties of defining and applying the intent rule, lies the most serious criticism of this aspect of equal protection law. The rule fails to hold states responsible for the substance and consequences of their decisions and their policies. Equal protection should instead be based on the state's accountability for its choices; for all of its classifications, overt and implicit, that affect members of the political community; and for the consequences of the policies it pursues. A test of serious scrutiny, reflecting a principled rather than an ad hoc balance, acknowledges that other goals besides racial, ethnic, and gender-based equity in the impact of policy are legitimate state interests. The test of serious scrutiny demands only that the state use the least discriminatory options in effecting its significant, legitimate interests.

DIANE WOOD HUTCHINSON

CLASS ACTIONS: JOINDER OR REPRESENTATIONAL DEVICE?

Each Term, the Supreme Court faces a wide variety of issues that should require a choice between two models of the modern class action: a joinder model and a representational model. Yet the Court has shown no awareness of the choices it has been making. To the contrary, when one looks at its accumulated wisdom on class actions, it is apparent that the Court has never seen the two broad patterns that emerge. It is not that this is a new problem attributable to the 1966 revision of Rule 23 of the Federal Rules of Civil Procedure. It has existed as long as class actions have been entertained by the federal courts. Nor is this an antiquated problem, in the sense that the Court has by now resolved all issues that can possibly arise so that only pedants and historians should have any remaining interest in it. The lower courts and the Supreme Court itself continue to face class action problems whose resolution ought to depend upon the conception of the class action that the Court chooses.

The joinder model, in brief, treats the class action as a device that brings together similarly situated persons for adjudication of common claims, and nothing more. Every member of a class, under this model, must independently satisfy all procedural requirements for appearing before the court in question. The only reasons to use the class device instead of simple joinder are the added convenience, for unnamed members, of having someone else take the principal responsibility for conducting the suit and the added procedural protections, such as court

Diane Wood Hutchinson is Assistant Professor of Law, The University of Chicago.

AUTHOR'S NOTE: My thanks go to David P. Currie, Frank H. Easterbrook, David B. Roe, and Cass R. Sunstein for their thoughtful comments on an earlier draft.

approval of settlements, offered by the class action rule. The representational model, in contrast, places much greater importance on the named class representative. Once this person has established his right to come before the court, he may act as legal representative for others similarly situated, whether or not they could have sued independently. Recognition of these two models, even at this late date, identifies which of them is the better reasoned and more consistent with the concept of group litigation.

I. CLASS ACTIONS FROM EQUITY PRACTICE THROUGH AMENDED RULE 23

A. PRE-1938 PRACTICE

The seeds of every important aspect of the modern class action—its representational character, the degree of shared interests required, the binding effect on absentee members—can be found in the pre-1938 equity cases. Class actions were a consistent, if somewhat difficult to explain, feature of equity practice for centuries.[1] For present purposes, there is no need to examine the English Chancery examples of group litigation, in which one person was permitted to represent the interests of the group to which he belonged. Suffice it to note that even before the Supreme Court had promulgated its first rule concerning class actions, in 1842,[2] the Court had encountered this type of suit.[3] In 1820, sitting on circuit, Justice Story explained in *West v. Randall* when the general equity rule requiring joinder of all materially interested parties was relaxed:[4]

> [F]or where the parties are very numerous, and the court perceives, that it will be almost impossible to bring them all before the court;

---

[1] See, *e.g.*, Yeazell, *Group Litigation and Social Context: Toward a History of the Class Action*, 77 COLUM. L. REV. 866 (1977); Yeazell, *From Group Litigation to Class Action, Part I: The Industrialization of Group Litigation*, 27 U.C.L.A. L. REV. 514 (1980); and *Part II: Interest, Class, and Representation*, *id.* at 1067; see also STORY, COMMENTARIES ON EQUITY PLEADINGS §120 (4th ed. 1848); 1 POMEROY, EQUITY JURISPRUDENCE §IV (5th ed. 1941); 3B MOORE, FEDERAL PRACTICE ¶23.02[1] (1982).

[2] 1 How. lvi. Only the first edition of 1 Howard contains the equity rules. Subsequent printings and editions omitted all preliminary material, including the Rules, apparently due to an internal dispute within the Court over its new Reporter and his practices. See SWISHER, THE TANEY PERIOD: 1836-1864 (5 HOLMES DEVISE HISTORY OF THE SUPREME COURT OF THE UNITED STATES) 308-09 (1974). The text of the 1842 version of Rule 48 is also in HOPKINS, THE NEW FEDERAL EQUITY RULES 52 (8th ed. 1933).

[3] See Beatty v. Kurtz, 2 Pet. 566 (1829); City of Georgetown v. Alexander Canal Co., 12 Pet. 91 (1838); see also West v. Randall, 2 Mason 181, 29 Fed. Cas. 718 (Fed. Cas. no. 17,424) (Cir. Ct. R.I. 1820) (Story, J., on circuit).

[4] West v. Randall, 2 Mason at 193, 29 Fed. Cas. at 722.

or where the question is of general interest, and a few may sue for the benefit of the whole; or where the parties form a part of a voluntary association for public or private purposes, and may be fairly supposed to represent the rights and interests of the whole; in these and analogous cases, if the bill purports to be not merely in behalf of the plaintiffs, but of all others interested, the plea of the want of parties will be repelled, and the court will proceed to a decree.

Story identified five settings in which the rule he described had been applied: (1) suits by a part of the crew of a privateer against prize agents for an account and their portion of prize money; (2) suits by a few creditors suing on behalf of the rest; (3) suits by legatees seeking relief and an account against executors; (4) suits by a few members of a voluntary society or an unincorporated body of proprietors; and (5) suits in which the lord of a manor sued representative tenants, or representative tenants sued the lord.[5]

Story understood the class device as the result both of practical difficulties and of the adequacy of representation furnished by the plaintiff. Even in attempting to give a general description of a class action, he found the device difficult to define other than in an illustrative manner. The remainder of the discussion in *West* indicates that Story at least was prepared to give conclusive effect to the decree when it was favorable to absentees, although he seemed to think that the absentees were entitled to their own day in court if the decree were adverse.[6] This question of the *res judicata* effect of class decrees on absentee rights has remained vexing to the present time. It is therefore worth noting where, for practical purposes, the Court started out.

In 1842, the Court promulgated equity rules, including Rule 48 on class practice, which purported to codify Story's analysis in *West:*[7]

Where the parties on either side are very numerous and can not, without manifest inconvenience and oppressive delays in the suit, be all brought before it, the Court in its discretion may dispense with making all of them parties, and may proceed in the suit, having sufficient parties before it to represent all the adverse interest of the

---

[5] 2 Mason at 194-95; 29 Fed. Cas. at 722-23.
[6] 2 Mason at 193, 195; 29 Fed. Cas. at 722-23. When Story later wrote his treatise on equity pleadings, he seemed more willing to accord the decree conclusive effect no matter what. In the fourth edition, he stated that "in most, if not in all, cases of this sort [*i.e.* numerous parties, impracticable to join all], the decree obtained upon such a Bill will ordinarily be held binding upon all other persons standing in the same predicament, the Court taking care, that sufficient persons are before it, honestly, fairly, and fully to ascertain and try the general right in contest." STORY, note 1 *supra*, at §120.
[7] 1 How. lvi. See note 2 *supra*.

plaintiffs and the defendants in the suit properly before it. But, in such cases, the decree shall be without prejudice to the rights and claims of all the absent parties.

Again there is the mix of concern about the practical difficulty of conducting litigation with numerous plaintiffs or defendants and the adequacy of representation on the part of those actually before the court. There is here an overt attempt to deal with the *res judicata* effect of the class decree—an attempt that stands in marked contrast to later efforts to draft procedural rules, which consistently refused to specify something as "substantive" as *res judicata* effect.[8] A noteworthy point about the last sentence of Rule 48 is that the Court promptly refused to follow it.[9]

Equity Rule 48 remained formally unchanged until 1912, when the Court issued new rules for equity cases. Rule 38 of the 1912 rules, entitled "Representatives of Class," stated with brevity: "When the question is one of common or general interest to many persons constituting a class so numerous as to make it impracticable to bring them all before the court, one or more may sue or defend for the whole."[10] Those who had reviewed the earlier Rule 48 recommended the deletion of its last sentence, for the interesting reason that "in every true 'class suit' the decree is necessarily binding upon all parties included in the decree."[11] Rule 38 thus seemed to carry within it the assumption that some lawsuits are "really" class suits, while others are not, and perhaps may not be. Rule 38 also emphasized the practical advantages of class suits: common questions, numerous persons, practicalities of joinder. This did not mean that the Court was uninterested in adequacy of representation during this period.[12] A more likely explanation for the form of Rule 38 lies in the general ossification of class procedures during that period. Certain types of cases or patterns of representation were recognized to be legitimate

---

[8] See Equity Rule 38 of 1912; original Fed. R. Civ. P. 23 (1938); amended Fed. R. Civ. P. 23 (1966). See generally MOORE, note 1 *supra*, at ¶23.11[1], explaining why the drafters of the 1938 rule did not recommend a section specifying the effect of judgment; see also Advisory Committee Note on amended Rule 23, 39 F.R.D. 105–06 (1966).

[9] See the discussion of Smith v. Swormstedt, 16 How. 288 (1853), text *infra* at note 34.

[10] Rules of Practice for the Courts of Equity of the United States, 226 U.S. 627, 659 (1912).

[11] HOPKINS, note 2 *supra*, at 240.

[12] See, *e.g.*, *In re* Engelhard, 231 U.S. 646 (1914), in which the Court refused to permit petitioner to sue on behalf of all telephone subscribers, for the apparent reason that the unnamed subscribers had not authorized the representation; see also International News Serv. v. Associated Press, 248 U.S. 215 (1918), in which the Court discussed at some length the right of the organizations to represent their members' interests.

class actions, and the Court was hesitant to extend the form to other, newer patterns.

The forms of class actions were therefore well established by 1912, and the Court saw no need to spell them out in its new Rule. Creditors' bills, which had been included in Justice Story's 1820 list, were the most obvious instance of a true and a necessary class action. Before bankruptcy laws were fully developed, one creditor could sue an insolvent debtor (or a debtor whose ability to pay was seriously questionable) and force a distribution of assets under the supervision of the court of equity. *Richmond v. Irons*[13] affords a good example of a creditors' bill class action. James Irons, a judgment creditor of a bank, sued the bank and its president, claiming fraud on the creditors in a series of transactions designed to hide assets from them. Initially, the bill was on Irons' behalf alone, but eventually, after several amendments, it was alleged expressly that it was filed on behalf of all the creditors and sought a *pro rata* distribution among them.

Justice Matthews, writing for the Court, held that the amendments were irrelevant, since a creditors' bill was necessarily on behalf of all:[14]

> In the case of an insolvent incorporation thus brought into liquidation, and wound up by judicial process at the suit of a creditor, whether he sues in his own right, or on behalf of himself and other creditors, the rule of distribution is the same, and is founded upon the principle of equality in which equity delights.

The Court also found that the statute of limitations ceased to run against all creditors of the bank no later than the 1876 amendment of the bill. Although each creditor became a party only when he appeared to prove his claim, once he made this required appearance he was treated as "virtually a party complainant from the beginning."[15]

After the litigating creditor established the claim, the normal procedure was to refer the case to a master, who would state an account of the assets, give notice (often by publication) to all other creditors of

---

[13] 121 U.S. 27 (1887). See also Ransom v. Davis's Adm'rs, 18 How. 295 (1855); Myers v. Fenn, 5 Wall. 205 (1866); Kerrison v. Stewart, 93 U.S. 155 (1876); Hatch v. Dana, 101 U.S. 205 (1879); Terry v. Little, 101 U.S. 216 (1879); Johnson v. Waters, 111 U.S. 640 (1884); Stewart v. Dunham, 115 U.S. 61 (1885); Hassall v. Wilcox, 115 U.S. 598 (1885); Gibson v. Shufeldt, 122 U.S. 27 (1887); Handley v. Stutz, 137 U.S. 366 (1890); Hale v. Allinson, 188 U.S. 56 (1903). *Cf.* Kelley v. Gill, 245 U.S. 116 (1917).

[14] 121 U.S. at 44.

[15] *Id.* at 52, 54.

the defendant that they must appear, and inform those creditors that they must establish their individual claims. Nonappearing creditors eventually lost their rights to payment.[16]

Creditors' bills were easy to recognize as "true" class actions, or necessarily class actions, because recovery for one required recovery for all. Putting intraclass distribution questions to one side, the litigating creditor clearly shared all important interests with the rest of the class. Equity found the alternative to class treatment unacceptable: giving a court-sanctioned preference to the creditor that won the race to the courthouse. The unnamed creditors were under no obligation to participate in the lawsuit until liability was established and the master had taken charge; only then were they required to "opt in" (to use an anachronistic term) to secure their right to recovery. Intervention was available, but not indispensable, for the protection of unnamed creditor rights.

For different reasons, the fraternal benefit association cases (Story's fourth category above) were seen as necessarily classwide litigation. Two kinds of cases arose within this category: those in which the voluntary association was opposed to outsiders, exemplified by the early case of *Beatty v. Kurtz*,[17] and those in which there was an internal dispute between the organization and some of its members, exemplified by *Supreme Tribe of Ben-Hur v. Cauble*.[18] In *Beatty v. Kurtz*, the governing committee of the German Lutheran Church sued the heir-at-law of a church benefactor who, the plaintiffs claimed, had given certain land to the church to be used for its meeting place and a small cemetery. Defendants challenged the right of the committee to represent the interests of the other members of the church. The Court (again per Justice Story) refused to rely only on the reasonable presumption of actual authorization from the congregation that arose from the record.[19] Instead, it went on to state, without any explanation, that this was "one of those cases, in which certain persons, belonging to a voluntary society, and having a common interest, may sue in behalf of themselves and others having the like interest, as part of the same society, for purposes common to all, and beneficial to all."[20]

In other words, the Court believed that a consent theory of group litigation was unnecessary here, because the plaintiffs before it shared

---

[16] *E.g.,* Johnson v. Waters, 111 U.S. at 673–74; Richmond v. Irons, 121 U.S. at 66.

[17] 2 Pet. 566 (1829).

[18] 255 U.S. 356 (1921).

[19] 2 Pet. at 584.

[20] *Ibid.*

interests so completely with the absent persons that adequate representation was assured.[21] Insofar as this suit concerned the intimate affairs of the church, this assumption was probably correct. It is clear, however, that the interests of absent members of the association might not always coincide so neatly or inevitably with those of the named parties, even in dealings with third parties.[22]

While the assumption of coincidence of interest among all members of an association furnished the justification for class treatment in the *Beatty*-type case, a broader assumption that all interests would be represented was necessary in the *Supreme Tribe of Ben-Hur* type. Briefly, *Ben-Hur* involved a dispute between two factions of the Tribe's members arising from a 1908 decision by the association to reorganize itself to provide a sounder financial base. As reorganized, benefit certificates that had been issued by the society up to July 1, 1908, were newly designated Class A, and certificates issued thereafter were designated Class B. Members of the association who held Class A certificates sued the Tribe (an Indiana fraternal benefit society) and its officers (also Indiana citizens), attacking the reorganization. It was obvious that the plaintiffs, some 523 out of a total of 70,000 Class A members and all citizens of states other than Indiana, were not representing the interests of the Class B members. The Court, however, stretched the concept introduced in *Beatty* to find that the named plaintiffs of Class A had indeed functioned as adequate representatives for everyone in Class A (including persons of Indiana citizenship).

The Court never discussed the interests of the Class B members, even though the final result, which upheld the reorganization, was clearly intended to be binding upon them as well. It had to have assumed that their interests in the validity of the reorganization were fully represented by the Tribe itself. In theory, the Court might have recognized a right in Class B members to mount their own challenge, but its position in several similar cases indicates that its view was otherwise.[23] Even in cases involving internal disputes, then, the Court

---

[21] Yeazell, note 1 *supra*, 27 U.C.L.A. L. REV. at 522. See discussion in Sec. II-A *infra*.

[22] Compare the problems of assuring congruence of interest in present-day Rule 23(b) (2) actions that have been noted by a number of commentators. *E.g.*, Bell, *Serving Two Masters: Integration Ideals and Client Interests in School Desegregation Litigation*, 85 YALE L. J. 470 (1976); Yeazell, note 1 *supra*, 27 U.C.L.A. L. REV. at 1107-20; Note, *Due Process Rights of Absentees in Title VII Class Actions—The Myth of Homogeneity of Interest*, 59 B.U. L. REV. 661 (1979).

[23] See Hartford Life Ins. Co. v. Ibs, 237 U.S. 662 (1915); Hartford Life Ins. Co v. Barber, 245 U.S. 146 (1917).

treated the association as a single entity, or as a representative for its members, even though the original justification for such treatment did not exist in this type of case. As long as all interests were before the court, the perceived need to come to one result for the association as a whole provided the justification for the group approach.

A similar, perhaps more compelling, rationale underlay the acceptance of class treatment in the cases involving a common fund or common property. As later became apparent under the 1938 Rule 23(a) (2), ingenuity rather than logic provided the real outer limits for this kind of case. Some of the more common fact patterns included bondholders, estates, and a true preexisting common fund.[24] The bondholder cases were almost identical to the creditors' bills; if the trustees were unable or unwilling to protect railroad bondholders, some could sue on behalf of all, and equity would take care that no one received more than his deserts.

The estate cases illustrated the need for more than just a common fund or common property to justify a class action. *McArthur v. Scott*,[25] a suit brought by after-born grandchildren to set aside a will that had been recognized in prior litigation brought by the children and then-existing grandchildren, established that the lack of the proper relationship or link between the parties to the first suit and the persons necessarily absent from it prevented the latter from being bound.

Smith v. Swormstedt[26] involved both plaintiff and defendant classes. It arose out of the split between the Northern and Southern factions of the Methodist Episcopal Church just before the Civil War. The Church's activities in selling books and other pamphlets had generated a fund, the Book Concern, out of which payments for traveling preachers and their families, for supernumerary and worn-out preachers, and for their widows and orphans would be made. When the Church split, the Northern group attempted to keep all the proceeds of the Book Concern for its own preachers. Six Southern preachers sued, successfully, on their own behalf and on behalf of approximately fifteen hundred other Southerners, for their part of the fund. The defendants were the agents of the Book Concern and a class

---

[24] Bondholders: see, *e.g.*, Galveston R.R. v. Cowdrey, 11 Wall. 459 (1870); Beals v. Illinois, M. & T. R.R., 133 U.S. 290 (1890); estates: see, *e.g.*, Shields v. Thomas, 17 How. 3 (1854); McArthur v. Scott, 113 U.S. 340 (1885); common fund: see Smith v. Swormstedt, 16 How. 288 (1853). As the description of the facts of *Smith* reveals, see text *infra* at note 26, this case could also be considered an example of a voluntary association with an internal dispute.

[25] 113 U.S. 340 (1885).

[26] 16 How. 288 (1853).

of all the Northern preachers. The Court rejected an objection to the bill for want of proper parties, citing *Story on Equity Pleadings*, and implicitly recognized (as in the later case of *Ben-Hur*) that all possible interests were before the Court: "care must be taken that persons are brought on the record fairly representing the interest or right involved, so that it may be fully and honestly tried."[27]

Finally, in blatant disregard of the language of the then-applicable Equity Rule 48, the Court in *Swormstedt* flatly stated that the decree would bind absent persons who had been represented:[28]

> For convenience, therefore, and to prevent a failure of justice, a court of equity permits a portion of the parties in interest to represent the entire body, and the decree binds all of them the same as if all were before the court. The legal and equitable rights and liabilities of all being before the court by representation, and especially where the subject-matter of the suit is common to all, there can be very little danger but that the interest of all will be properly protected and maintained.

This rationale was a good deal broader than the facts demanded.

The Court was slow to follow the implications of *Smith v. Swormstedt*'s language in the last group of cases[29]—those involving only a common question or a more general commonality of interest. It is impossible to avoid the conclusion that the Court was hostile to common question class actions, when the cases from this period are considered.[30] In these cases, where the comfort of the relationship among creditors, members of an association, or those interested in common property was absent, the Court went to much greater pains to satisfy itself that the party before it actually had the right to represent absent persons. Thus, for example, in *City of Georgetown v. Alexander Canal Co.*[31] it refused to allow the city to sue to abate a nuisance on behalf of its citizens, because the city itself had no property

---

[27] *Id.* at 303.

[28] *Ibid.* But see Wabash R.R. v. Adelbert College, 208 U.S. 609 (1908), in which the Court chose to follow Rule 48's command with respect to binding effect of judgments.

[29] See generally Yeazell, note 1 *supra*, 27 U.C.L.A. L. REV. at 1092-96.

[30] See, *e.g.*, Scott v. Donald, 165 U.S. 107 (1897); McCabe v. Atchinson, T. & S.F. Ry., 235 U.S. 151 (1914); St. Louis, I. Mt. & So. Ry. v. McKnight, 244 U.S. 368 (1917); Matthews v. Rodgers, 284 U.S. 521 (1932).

[31] 12 Pet. 91 (1838). Compare the modern case of Hawaii v. Standard Oil of California, 405 U.S. 251 (1972), in which the Court found that §4 of the Clayton Act, 15 U.S.C. §15, did not authorize a state to sue for injury to its general economy, but it noted that in a proper case a state might be a Rule 23 class representative. *Id.* at 266.

that was being affected by the nuisance. In contrast, in *United States v. Old Settlers*, where commissioners had been appointed by the Western Cherokee Indians to represent their interests in a suit before the Court of Claims, the Court readily cited *Smith v. Swormstedt* and held that the few could represent the many.[32] Similarly, the Court was hospitable to cases in which corporations came forth to represent the interests of their shareholders.[33]

In re Engelhard nicely illustrates the intersection between the Court's concern with legitimacy of representation and the common question type of suit.[34] The underlying dispute in the case concerned the validity of the rates established by the City of Louisville for the Cumberland Telephone and Telegraph Company. The Company sued the city, complaining that the rates were confiscatorily low. The rates were enjoined for the pendency of the suit, thereby forcing subscribers in the city to pay the higher amounts. Petitioner Engelhard & Sons Company sought to intervene in the suit for the purpose of suing individually and as a representative of all subscribers, to recover the excess amounts paid. The Court, after rejecting Engelhard's petition on two independent grounds, complained that it had not demonstrated actual authority to sue for the other subscribers.[35] Express authority would have been unnecessary if the case had been a proper one for class treatment. No one complained about the lack of express authority in *Smith v. Swormstedt*. As far back as *Beatty v. Kurtz*, the Court had felt free to pass over this question and to rely solely on the availability of group procedures.

The real problem was that Engelhard, like others who tried the class device during this period, failed to convince the Court that the time-honored precedents supported its case as well. In several other cases, the Court refused to allow plaintiffs to represent classes in suits challenging matters such as prohibitions on liquor imports, rate orders, and license taxes.[36] Unless there was some special relationship between the party before the court (the class representative) and the absent

---

[32] 148 U.S. 427, 480 (1893).

[33] *E.g.*, Hawkins v. Glenn, 131 U.S. 319, 329 (1889); Christopher v. Brusselback, 302 U.S. 500 (1938) (discusses when a corporation could represent its shareholders).

[34] 231 U.S. 646 (1914).

[35] *Id.* at 652.

[36] Scott v. Donald, 165 U.S. 107 (1897) (South Carolina dispensary law); St. Louis, I. Mt. & So. Ry. v. McKnight, 244 U.S. 368 (1917) (shippers injured by high rates not a class); Matthews v. Rodgers, 284 U.S. 521 (1932) (cotton dealers not permitted to challenge cotton license tax as class).

persons, or a very close similarity to the kinds of class cases described
by Story in *West v. Randall* nearly a century before, the Court in the
period immediately preceding the 1938 Federal Rules was not ready to
accept a common-question class action. It either rejected class
treatment altogether, or in the familiar cases it often went all the way
and bound absentees by the results obtained by the parties before the
court. This changed to some extent with the enactment of the 1938
version of Rule 23, but only at the cost of the confusion that
surrounded the so-called "spurious" class action for the full
twenty-eight years of its existence.

B. ORIGINAL RULE 23 (1938-66)

When the Federal Rules of Civil Procedure were adopted in 1938,
they contained a new and significantly broader rule governing class
actions, which will be referred to as "original Rule 23."[37] To begin
with, original Rule 23 was broader than any of its predecessors as a
result of Rules 1 and 2, which broadened the application of the new
procedure rules to suits at law.[38] Harry Kalven and Maurice
Rosenfield, writing in 1941, commented (not without irony) that Rule

---

[37] The text of original Rule 23 was as follows:

> (a) REPRESENTATION. If persons constituting a class are so numerous as to make it
> impracticable to bring them all before the court, such of them, one or more, as will fairly
> insure the adequate representation of all may, on behalf of all, sue or be sued, when the
> character of the right sought to be enforced for or against the class is
>
> > (1) joint, or common, or secondary in the sense that the owner of a primary right refuses
> > to enforce that right and a member of the class thereby becomes entitled to enforce
> > it;
> > (2) several, and the object of the action is the adjudication of claims which do or may
> > affect specific property involved in the action; or
> > (3) several, and there is a common question of law or fact affecting the several rights and
> > a common relief is sought.
>
> (b) SECONDARY ACTION BY SHAREHOLDERS. [Omitted.]
> (c) DISMISSAL OR COMPROMISE. A class action shall not be dismissed or
> compromised without the approval of the court. If the right sought to be enforced is one
> defined in paragraph (1) of subdivision (a) of this rule notice of the proposed dismissal
> or compromise shall be given to all members of the class in such manner as the court
> directs. If the right is one defined in paragraph (2) or (3) of subdivision (a) notice shall
> be given only if the court requires it.

Fed. R. Civ. P. 23 (1938).

[38] Rule 1 originally provided that "[t]hese rules govern the procedure in the district courts of
the United States in all suits of a civil nature whether cognizable as cases at law or in equity, with
the exceptions stated in Rule 81. They shall be construed to secure the just, speedy, and
inexpensive determination of every action." Rule 2, which has never been changed, read "[t]here
shall be one form of action to be known as 'civil action.' " Fed. R. Civ. P. 1, 2 (1938); 28 U.S.C.
§723 (c) (1940 ed.); 308 U.S. 645, 663 (1939). See also the original language of the Rules Enabling
Act, 28 U.S.C. §2072, which gave the Court the power, through rules, to abolish the distinction
between law and equity. Rules Enabling Act, ch. 651, 48 Stat. 1064 (1934).

23 "presumably represent[ed] the summary and culmination of years of experience with the class suit," and that it had been "widely regarded as a major achievement of the federal rules."[39] The new rule attempted to define more precisely when class actions had been authorized, using categories that transcended the specific factual settings that had seemed so unavoidable before.[40] In so doing, the rule adopted the now infamous classification by jural relationships among members of the class: "true" class actions, governed by original Rule 23(a) (1), were those in which the class shared a "joint, or common, or secondary" right; "hybrid" actions under original 23(a) (2) involved rights which were "several, and the object of the action is the adjudication of claims which do or may affect specific property involved in the action"; and "spurious" actions, under original 23(a) (3), involved rights which were "several, and there is a common question of law or fact affecting the several rights and a common relief is sought." Moore, who was the author of the first draft of original Rule 23, had included a section (later deleted) specifying the effect of judgment in each of the three cases. In a true class action, the judgment was to be "conclusive upon the class"; in a hybrid action, it was to be conclusive upon all parties and privies to the proceeding and upon all claims affecting specific property involved in the proceeding; and in a spurious action, it was to be conclusive "upon only the parties and privies to the proceeding."[41]

In keeping with the implications of his views on the *res judicata* effect of a judgment in a spurious class action, Moore flatly described it as a "permissive joinder device."[42] His text took (and takes) the position that "[w]hen a suit was brought by or against such a class, it was merely an invitation to joinder—an invitation to become a fellow traveler in the litigation, which might or might not be accepted. It was an invitation and not a command performance."[43] The trouble with this position, as Moore himself recognized, was that it made Rule 23(a) (3) completely superfluous, because Rule 20 already allowed the most liberal joinder. Moore tried to give some independent force to the class device by adhering to the rule established in *Supreme Tribe of Ben-Hur*

---

[39] Kalven and Rosenfield, *The Contemporary Function of the Class Suit*, 8 U. CHI. L. REV. 684, 695 (1941).

[40] See generally Original Committee Note of 1937 to Rule 23, reprinted in MOORE, note 1 *supra*, at ¶23.01[2]; Sunderland, *The New Federal Rules*, 45 W. VA. L. Q. 5 (1938).

[41] Moore, *Federal Rules of Civil Procedure: Some Problems Raised By the Preliminary Draft*, 25 GEO. L. J. 551, 557 (1937); see also MOORE, note 1 *supra*, at ¶23.11.

[42] MOORE, note 1 *supra*, at ¶23.10[1].

[43] *Ibid.*

that in a diversity case only the citizenship of the named parties would be material.[44] Each member of a spurious class had to satisfy any applicable amount in controversy requirement, but one could avoid that hurdle by the simple expedient of intervening instead of joining. For intervention, Moore believed that "members of the [spurious] class could intervene without regard to jurisdictional limitations applicable to original parties."[45]

Kalven and Rosenfield pointed out the difficulties with Moore's position in their classic article, *The Contemporary Function of the Class Suit:* "This saving function for the type (3) suit is at once irrelevant to the purpose of the class suit, trivial and probably unsound," and elaborated in a footnote:[46]

> So considered the type (3) suit functions exclusively as a trick for obtaining federal jurisdiction. . . . The rule would be absurd as stated since an original party of record who lacked the jurisdictional prerequisites can go out and come in a moment later as an intervenor. . . . The more desirable result would be to relieve the class suit of federal jurisdictional requirements designed for individual suits.

Their answer was to permit the representative party to litigate alone until liability was established, and then to hold the decree open for a time while absentee class members came in and established their right to share in the recovery before a master.[47] Since the absentee members under this procedure were in no sense parties of record before or during the trial, there was no need to be concerned with whether or not they satisfied jurisdictional prerequisites. Kalven and Rosenfield would have measured the amount in controversy by the recovery sought by the class as a whole, although they admitted that the federal rule was to the contrary.[48]

Moore captured the essense of this dispute when he recognized the two extremes that he and Kalven and Rosenfield represented:[49]

> [The Kalven/Rosenfield] article criticized the position of the 1938 edition of this Treatise which took the minimum view that the class

---

[44] *Id.* at ¶23.13, at 23-2961.

[45] *Id.* at ¶23.12, at 23-2913.

[46] Note 39 *supra*, at 704 & n.66.

[47] This is not unlike the procedure described above (see text *supra* at notes 15, 16) that was used in creditors' bill cases.

[48] Note 39 *supra*, at 704 n.66.

[49] MOORE, note 1 *supra*, at ¶23.03[1], at 23-42.

action is a procedural device to avoid multiple joinder in cases of multitudinous litigation. Instead, the authors urged a maximum goal for the class action: to allow representation of certain types of claims that would not otherwise be brought because of litigation economics and other realities. The basic controversy remains whether the proper goal for the class action should be limited to the minimum one of providing a shortcut to otherwise multitudinous litigation, or on the other hand, should be extended to the maximum one of opening court access to otherwise nonlitigable claims.

Moore asserted that this question "tended to be" more substantive than procedural, but it is not so easy to place either label on the goal. The assumption that the problem existed only in the case of the spurious action also begged the most fundamental question: When is a class action a device for group litigation that permits one person—the representative—to stand in for a number of absent other persons who are unable for some compelling reason to join the suit, and when is it a specialized form of joinder that enjoys a few extra procedural conveniences? Spurious actions raised this issue most vividly, since Moore's description of them as "permissive joinder devices" and his views on *res judicata* were quite persuasive. Yet hybrid and even true actions necessarily raised questions about the appropriateness of federal court jurisdiction in cases where some critical trait, such as diverse citizenship or amount in controversy, was improper in the unnamed members.

Because other difficulties with original Rule 23 were so striking,[50] the choice between Moore's minimum goal and maximum goal did not attract any attention when the work of revising Rule 23 was going on. Instead, the Advisory Committee identified three principal objects that it sought to attain by the amended rule: it wanted to "describe[ ] in more practical terms the occasions for maintaining class actions; provide[ ] that all class actions maintained to the end as such [would] result in judgments including those whom the court finds to be members of the class, whether or not the judgment is favorable to the class; and refer[ ] to the measures which [could] be taken to assure the fair conduct of these actions."[51] Great attention has been paid to these aspects of contemporary class actions, at the expense of attention to the issue identified by Moore.

---

[50] *I.e.* difficulties such as how to distinguish among the different jural relationships in the first place, contradictory classifications by the lower courts on indistinguishable facts, and differing views on the availability of intervention after a judgment on liability. See generally the Advisory Committee Note to the 1966 rule, 39 F.R.D. 98 (1966).

[51] 39 F.R.D. at 99; see also Kaplan, *Continuing Work of the Civil Committee: 1966 Amendments*

C. AMENDED RULE 23 (1966 TO THE PRESENT)

The 1966 revisors of Rule 23 continued and improved upon the efforts of the original drafters of the rule to clarify and generalize the criteria that ought to govern when a class suit is available. The amended rule abandoned the opaque categorizations according to jural relationships and substituted a new, two-part functional inquiry. Subdivision (a) of the amended rule, as the Advisory Committee noted, "states the prerequisites for maintaining any class action in terms of the numerousness of the class making joinder of the members impracticable, the existence of questions common to the class, and the desired qualifications of the representative parties. . . . These are necessary but not sufficient conditions for a class action."[52] Specifically, it provides, quite consistently with former rules on class actions going all the way back to Equity Rule 48 of 1842, that "[o]ne or more members of a class may sue or be sued as representative parties on behalf of all only if (1) the class is so numerous that joinder of all members is impracticable, (2) there are questions of law or fact common to the class, (3) the claims or defenses of the representative parties are typical of the claims or defenses of the class, and (4) the representative parties will fairly and adequately protect the interests of the class."[53]

Although this is, more or less, all that Equity Rules 48 and 38 required, the cases decided under those rules clearly revealed that the Court was looking for something more. In particular, common questions of law or fact, standing alone, were simply not enough to support a class action. The original Rule 23 sought to describe the "something more" that was needed with its jural relationships. In basic agreement with the necessity of additional justification for a class, the drafters of amended Rule 23 tried to describe, in the rule's subsection (b) categories, the types of situations in which the normal rules requiring joinder and permitting each individual his own day in court would be superseded in the interest of the greater fairness and efficiency of the class device. Thus, the little-used (b) (1) category focuses on the undesirability of incompatible standards of conduct for the party opposing the class and the practical possibility that litigation by one class member may substantially impair the ability of other members to protect their rights.[54] The drafters of the rule indicated

---

of the Federal Rules of Civil Procedure (I), 81 HARV. L. REV. 356 (1967).

[52] 39 F.R.D. at 100.

[53] Fed. R. Civ. P. 23(a) (1966).

[54] Specifically, Rule 23(b) (1) imposes these requirements in addition to those of 23(a):

their belief that the (b) (1) category encompassed, among other things, the old fraternal-benefit-association cases.[55]

The (b) (2) category, in a sense, further defines one kind of common question that will suffice to justify the class action: the party opposing the class must have acted or refused to act on grounds generally applicable to the class. This is enough, however, only when the type of relief sought is injunctive or declaratory.[56] The latter requirement of (b) (2) echoes the "common relief" language of original Rule 23(a) (3). It seems to have been inserted on the somewhat dubious theory that the class representative, under these circumstances, is likely to seek the same injunction for himself as the absent members of the class would want.[57]

The (b) (3) category also relies on a refinement of the common question requirement, but in its case the question may relate to anything, so long as it predominates over individual questions. Again, one extra hurdle is attached, in this case that the class action be "superior to other available methods for the fair and efficient adjudication of the controversy."[58] The (b) (3) category also carries

---

(1) the prosecution of separate actions by or against individual members of the class would create a risk of

   (A) inconsistent or varying adjudications with respect to individual members of the class which would establish incompatible standards of conduct for the party opposing the class, or

   (B) adjudications with respect to individual members of the class which would as a practical matter be dispositive of the interests of the other members not parties to the adjudications or substantially impair or impede their ability to protect their interests. . . .

[55] The Advisory Committee note on subsection (b) (1) (B) comments that "[i]n an action by policy holders against a fraternal benefit association attacking a financial reorganization of the society, it would hardly have been practical, if indeed it would have been possible, to confine the effects of a validation of the reorganization to the individual plaintiffs. . . . See *Supreme Tribe of Ben-Hur v. Cauble*, 255 U.S. 356 (1921); . . . ." 39 F.R.D. at 101. The Committee's two illustrations of a (b) (1) (A) action were an action against a municipality to declare a bond issue invalid or to condition or limit it, and litigation of the rights and duties of riparian owners or landowner rights and duties respecting a claimed nuisance. *Id.* at 100.

[56] Rule 23(b) (2) states, in its entirety: "the party opposing the class has acted or refused to act on grounds generally applicable to the class, thereby making appropriate final injunctive relief or corresponding declaratory relief with respect to the class as a whole; . . . ." As construed at present, injunctive or declaratory relief need not be the sole relief demanded; actions have been permitted under (b) (2) in which damages or back pay were sought incidently. See generally 7A WRIGHT & MILLER, FEDERAL PRACTICE AND PROCEDURE §1775 (1972); MOORE, note 1 *supra*, at ¶23.40[4].

[57] See note 22 *supra*.

[58] The full text of (b) (3) provides further guidance on these special requirements: "(3) the court [must find] that the questions of law or fact common to the members of the class predominate over any questions affecting only individual members, and that a class action is superior to other available methods for the fair and efficient adjudication of the controversy. The matters pertinent to the findings include: (A) the interest of members of the class in individually controlling the

with it a number of special procedural requirements, notably that of notice to identifiable class members and the opportunity of those members to "opt out" of the class. These special requirements, like the (b) (2) limit on available relief, are directed more to the question of the legitimacy and adequacy of representation than to any other aspect of the class device.

Finally, the revisors of Rule 23 were greatly concerned to make the decree rendered in a class action binding upon all class members. The Advisory Committee's comments on amended Rule 23(c) (3) describes these efforts and why they were made:[59]

> The judgment in a class action maintained as such to the end will embrace the class, that is, in a class action under subdivision (b) (1) or (b) (2), those found by the court to be class members; in a class action under subdivision (b) (3), those to whom the notice prescribed by subdivision (c) (2) was directed, excepting those who requested exclusion or who are ultimately found by the court not to be members of the class. The judgment has this scope whether it is favorable or unfavorable to the class.
>
> . . . Under proposed subdivision (c) (3), one-way intervention [as it had been practiced occasionally under original Rule 23(a) (3)] is excluded. . . .
>
> Although thus declaring that the judgment in a class action includes the class, as defined, subdivision (c) (3) does not disturb the recognized principle that the court conducting the action cannot predetermine the *res judicata* effect of the judgment; this can be tested only in a subsequent action. . . . The court, however, in framing the judgment in any suit brought as a class action, must decide what its extent or coverage shall be, and if the matter is carefully considered, questions of *res judicata* are less likely to be raised at a later time and if raised will be more satisfactorily answered.

The amended rule therefore took the position that any proper class action under it was entitled to the same kind of binding effect that the Supreme Court described over a century before in *Smith v. Swormstedt*.[60] The most important ground upon which courts today refuse to give binding effect to a prior class adjudication when an unnamed member of the class challenges the judgment is the lack of

---

prosecution or defense of separate actions; (B) the extent and nature of any litigation concerning the controversy already commenced by or against members of the class; (C) the desirability or undesirability of concentrating the litigation of the claims in the particular forum; (D) the difficulties likely to be encountered in the management of a class action."

[59] 39 F.R.D. at 105-06.

[60] 16 How. at 303; see text *supra*, at note 28.

adequate representation.[61] This, however, is only one aspect of the due process to which the unnamed class members are entitled. If the court considering the prior class decree finds that, in a particular case, some other due process right was violated, such as a right to notice, it will similarly refuse to give effect to the class decree. The net effect of these rules is to introduce some flexibility into the otherwise firm statement found in amended Rule 23(c) (3) on the binding effect of the decree.

II. PROCEDURAL AND POLICY CONTEXT OF THE TWO MODELS

A. PROCEDURAL CONTEXT

Although the nature of the justification for treating each of amended Rule 23's subsection (b) categories as a suitable candidate for binding group litigation varies, these differences do not have any necessary relationship to the primary questions at hand: When can the class action make possible litigation on the part of absentee class members that would otherwise be unavailable in federal court? And when is the class action only a convenience device that goes slightly beyond Rule 20 joinder? These questions differ from the problems of group litigation that were the subject of Professor Yeazell's inquiry in his article *From Group Litigation to Class Action.*[62] Yeazell wrote about two related problems in group litigation—the link that justifies treating certain persons as a single group, and the theory of representation that underlies the selection of a representative for the group: "The theoretical question . . . can be posed more specifically: what cohesion, transactions, or likenesses will justify one person's representing another in litigation—will qualify a group as a litigative entity?"[63]

On the former point, he noted that "[h]istorically group litigation has moved from the first to the last of the bases suggested by the question, requiring first the actual cohesion of a social group as its basis, then a looser series of transactions among the members of the group, and finally only the sharing of some abstractly defined common interest among the members of the class."[64] On the second point, he established that there are two distinct theories that might support the

---

[61] See, *e.g.*, Gonzales v. Cassidy, 474 F.2d 67 (5th Cir. 1973). See generally 7A WRIGHT & MILLER, note 56 *supra* at §1789; MOORE, note 1 *supra*, at ¶23.60.

[62] Note 1 *supra*.

[63] *Id.* at 515.

[64] *Ibid.*

selection of a particular representative: consent on the part of the members of the litigative group, and congruence of pertinent interests between the representative, on the one hand, and the rest of the group members, on the other.[65]

Both these theories of representation were adopted, in part, in amended Rule 23. They account for the most important differences among the three subsection (b) actions. The (b) (1) actions present the strongest instance of congruence of interest among class members, since they are premised on the practical or legal difficulty of adjudicating the claims of the members individually. Consent, therefore, is unnecessary as a legitimizing factor for either kind of (b) (1) class. A (b) (2) action also assumes that the congruence of interests among class members is sufficient to make consent unnecessary. As Yeazell and others have noted, however, the interests in modern (b) (2) classes often vary considerably.[66] Nevertheless, perhaps because of the strong substantive interest in the policies underlying the laws usually enforced in (b) (2) class actions, it has not been thought necessary to legitimize the selection of a representative through the mechanism of consent. Only in the (b) (3) actions, and there only through the veto power provided by the option to opt out, are the members of the group given a way to voice their opinions with respect to the selection of their representative.[67]

The factors that lead one to define a group, or to select a representative from the group, all derive in the end from the substantive interests shared by the group members. All have certain interests that the law, at least allegedly, recognizes. If the party

---

[65] *Id.* at 1068. Some have rejected this view of class actions in favor of a so-called "substantive" theory. *Developments in the Law—Class Actions*, 89 HARV. L. REV. 1318, 1353 (1976). This substantive view, or fairness theory, does not help particularly to answer the question how the representative is selected.

[66] See, *e.g.*, *id.* at 1114-17; see also note 22 *supra.* For example, in a (b) (2) class action challenging racial discrimination in the schools, some members of the class might favor increased expenditures for one-race schools, while others might believe strongly in integration as a remedy.

[67] Some courts of appeals have been moving toward a discretionary opt-out right for (b) (2) classes that involve monetary relief, such as back pay. See Penson v. Terminal Transport Co., 634 F.2d 989 (5th Cir. 1981) (district court has power under Rule 23(d) (2) to require an opt-out right with notice thereof in appropriate (b) (2) actions); Holmes v. Continental Can Co., 706 F.2d 1144 (11th Cir. 1983) (district court abused discretion in (b) (2) action in refusing to give opt-out rights from negotiated settlement); but see Kincade v. General Tire & Rubber Co., 635 F.2d 501 (5th Cir. 1981) (neither due process clause nor Rule 23 mandates a right to opt out from a settlement in a (b) (2) action). The need for a right to opt out (*i.e.* to consent to representation) should arise only if the named representative's interests are not sufficiently congruent with those of the class to assure adequate representation. Careful application of Rule 23(a) and 23(e) should obviate the need for (b) (2) opt-out procedures.

opposing the group wishes to challenge the existence of those interests, it may do so through the vehicles of Rule 12(b) (6) or Rule 56. The characteristics that would lead a court to treat a class action as a glorified joinder device or as a true representational action are different. Those characteristics are "procedural" in this sense: They establish one's right to sue in a federal court on the substantive claim, rather than in a state court. They include procedural traits such as citizenship of the representative and the absent members (something having nothing to do with the law providing the basis for the claim), jurisdictional amount, and personal jurisdiction. It is easy to see, for example, on the facts of *Supreme Tribe of Ben-Hur* that one could hypothetically have selected the class A certificate holder representative either by an election among all class A holders (*i.e.* consent) or by the legal presumption of identity of interest among all class A holders. The question remains in either case whether the lack of diversity between unnamed members and the opposing party violates the rule of *Strawbridge v. Curtiss*[68] and requires the federal court to dismiss for lack of jurisdiction, or at the very least to say that the class defined by the lawsuit did not include nondiverse members. One's resolution of the latter question will depend, in the final analysis, on one's acceptance of a joinder model (Moore's minimum goal) or a representation model (Moore's maximum goal).

B. THE POLICY BASIS FOR CLASS ACTIONS

The joinder model, simply stated, imposes the same procedural requirements on every class member, whether representative or absent. The representation model, as the name suggests, focuses as exclusively as possible on the procedural qualifications of the named, or representative, parties, ignoring those of the absent persons. There are a number of constraints that any acceptable model must observe, including some imposed by the Constitution (Article III and the Due Process Clauses), some imposed by statute (both the Rules Enabling Act and substantive statutes) and some imposed by Rule 82 of the Federal Rules of Civil Procedure.[69] Thus, the first inquiry must be

---

[68] 3 Cranch 267 (1806). *Strawbridge*, of course, has been construed as an interpretation of the diversity statute and not the language of Article III. See State Farm Fire & Casualty Co. v. Tashire, 386 U.S. 523 (1967). To treat absolute diversity as an Article III mandate would put a number of federal statutes in jeopardy.

[69] Rule 82 states that the Federal Rules of Civil Procedure "shall not be construed to extend or limit the jurisdiction of the United States district courts or the venue of actions therein."

whether each of the two models offers an acceptable alternative in light of constraints external to Rule 23. To the extent that both models do so, the choice between them must be governed in the end by the policies underlying the class action device, with appropriate attention to historical antecedents where they remain relevant.

The original policy supporting class actions arose out of the ordinary rigidity of the rules governing parties. Even in equity, the usual rule was that all persons materially interested in the subject of a suit had to be made parties.[70] The class action was thought of as an exception to that rule for cases in which all the parties were too numerous to be brought before the court or where there was some other substantial impediment to perfect joinder. When an opposing party wished to challenge the propriety of permitting a class to litigate, it would file an objection to the bill charging a want of proper parties to maintain the suit.[71]

This rationale was recognized by the Supreme Court in what is still one of the leading twentieth-century decisions on class actions, *Hansberry v. Lee:*[72]

> The class suit was an invention of equity to enable it to proceed to a decree in suits where the number of those interested in the subject of the litigation is so great that their joinder as parties in conformity to the usual rules of procedure is impracticable. Courts are not infrequently called upon to proceed with causes in which the number of those interested in the litigation is so great as to make difficult or impossible the joinder of all because some are not within the jurisdiction or because their whereabouts is unknown or where if all were made parties to the suit its continued abatement by the death of some would prevent or unduly delay a decree.

A bit later in the same discussion, the Court referred to the problem of a "technical defect of parties."[73] More recently, the Court stated that "[t]he class-action device was designed as 'an exception to the usual rule that litigation is conducted by and on behalf of the individual named parties only.' *Califano* v. *Yamasaki,* 442 U.S. 682, 700-701 [1979]."[74]

---

[70] See, *e.g.,* West v. Randall, 2 Mason 181, note 3 *supra.* See also STORY, note 1 *supra,* at §§95-97, 541-43.

[71] *E.g.,* Smith v. Swormstedt, 16 How. 288, 301, text at note 27 *supra.*

[72] 311 U.S. 32, 41 (1940).

[73] *Id.* at 42.

[74] General Telephone Co. of Southwest v. Falcon, 457 U.S. 147, 155 (1982).

Thus, even today something approaching the original justification for class actions is recognized as a purpose of the rule.

Further refinement of the class action rule and vastly increased experience with it have revealed that more fundamental policies support the decision to relax the rules concerning parties. Two such policies stand out in the Court's more recent opinions: one favoring efficiency and economy of litigation, and one emphasizing the role of the class action as a supplement to public law enforcement efforts.[75] To some extent, these policies have been seen as contradictory, since a class action may in fact create a lawsuit where none of the individual members would have sued alone.[76] The Court has, as convenience served, referred to both policies without attempting to reconcile them.

A typical description of the efficiency rationale appears in *American Pipe & Construction Co. v. Utah*,[77] in which the Court criticized a rule that would have permitted absent class members to intervene after a denial of class certification only if they had previously filed motions to intervene within the period of limitations. The Court stated that such a rule "would deprive Rule 23 class actions of the efficiency and economy of litigation which is a principal purpose of the procedure."[78] A few pages earlier, it had commented that "[a] federal class action is no longer 'an invitation to joinder' but a truly representative suit designed to avoid, rather than encourage, unnecessary filing of repetitious papers and motions."[79] In the 1982 Term, in two decisions that resolved some of *American Pipe*'s open questions, the Court reiterated its commitment to these purposes.[80]

On the other hand, in *Deposit Guaranty National Bank v. Roper*,[81] a consumer class action involving credit card interest rates, the Court seemed to rely almost exclusively on the private attorney-general role of the class action:[82]

---

[75] Kalven and Rosenfield emphasized the latter policy in their article. See note 39 *supra*.

[76] See Dam, *Class Actions: Efficiency, Compensation, Deterrence, and Conflict of Interest*, 4 J. LEG. STUD. 47 (1975); but see Bernstein, *Judicial Economy and Class Actions*, 7 J. LEG. STUD. 349 (1978).

[77] 414 U.S. 538 (1974).

[78] *Id.* at 553.

[79] *Id.* at 550. See also *id.* at 551.

[80] Chardon v. Soto, 103 S. Ct. 2611, 2618 (1983); Crown, Cork & Seal Co. v. Parker, 103 S. Ct. 2392, 2395 (1983).

[81] 445 U.S. 326 (1980).

[82] *Id.* at 338-39 (footnotes omitted).

The use of the class-action procedure for litigation of individual claims may offer substantial advantages for named plaintiffs; it may motivate them to bring cases that for economic reasons might not be brought otherwise.... For better or worse, the financial incentive that class actions offer to the legal profession is a natural outgrowth of the increasing reliance on the "private attorney general" for the vindication of legal rights; obviously this development has been facilitated by Rule 23.

The aggregation of individual claims in the context of a classwide suit is an evolutionary response to the existence of injuries unremedied by the regulatory action of government.

Almost in passing, the Court had taken a similar line a year earlier in *Reiter v. Sonotone Corp.*,[83] in which it held that consumers who paid a higher price for goods purchased for personal use were entitled to sue under the antitrust laws for treble damages. In a footnote, it said, "[o]f course, the treble-damages remedy of §4 [of the Clayton Act, 15 U.S.C. §15] took on new practical significance for consumers with the advent of Fed. Rule Civ. Proc. 23."[84] In concluding the *Reiter* opinion, the Court conceded that this kind of consumer class action might well "add a significant burden to the already crowded dockets of the federal courts," but it noted that "[t]hese private suits provide a significant supplement to the limited resources available to the Department of Justice for enforcing the antitrust laws and deterring violations."[85]

As long as efficiency is not seen as a simple decrease in the caseload of the federal courts, resulting from the substitution of one lawsuit for many, the two rationales underlying the modern class action can be reconciled satisfactorily. Everything depends, in the end, on the proper treatment of the concept of efficiency itself. A persuasive view of the efficiency rationale was advanced in Bernstein's article, *Judicial Economy and Class Actions.*[86]

---

[83] 442 U.S. 330 (1979).

[84] *Id.* at 343 n.6.

[85] *Id.* at 344. See also Gulf Oil Co. v. Bernard, 452 U.S. 89 (1981), in which the Court described the "customary role" of named plaintiffs as that of vindicating the "rights of individuals who otherwise might not consider it worth the candle to embark on litigation in which the optimum result might be more than consumed by the cost," citing *Roper, supra. Id.* at 99-100 n.11.

[86] Note 76 *supra*, at 349, 352-53 (footnote omitted). It may not be entirely clear from Bernstein's evidence whether it is true only that the average cost of class litigation is less than average benefits or if the marginal case is also beneficial. This is important to the extent that a generous class action rule brings more marginal cases into the court system. The general point remains, however, that a mere increase in number of class cases alone is insufficient evidence from which to infer that class actions are "inefficient."

[A]n assessment of the size of benefits flowing from class litigation is necessary to lend meaning to the concept of "economies of time, effort and expense" as a goal of class-based adjudication. Although "individually non-recoverable" claims may indeed increase not only caseloads, but also particular cases' time consumption, these additional burdens do not decrease judicial efficiency unless corresponding benefits are not conferred by the additional litigation. Otherwise, namely under a definition of judicial economy that excludes litigation benefits, *any* increase in caseloads and case-time consumption would constitute an impairment of judicial efficiency, and courts would be most efficient with no cases at all!

If it is assumed that the activities of private attorneys-general confer net benefits in the area of law enforcement, then the two rationales for the class action coexist happily. It is true, of course, that the ease of filing a complaint in federal court that satisfies Rule 8 and the ease of designating oneself a class representative/private attorney-general means that every class action may not confer a net benefit on society. Overenforcement of some laws may take place.[87] This is not the place to explore the myriad abuses, real or perceived, that exist under the present version of Rule 23. It is enough to pose the question which procedural conception of the class action—joinder or representational— better serves the two policies that the Court has recognized. It will appear that from both the historical and the policy-oriented standpoints the representational model is preferable. To the extent that the Court's decisions have followed this model, they have been sound. Those that have not followed it have given unsatisfactory answers to the problems raised on their facts and offer bad solutions to the new issues before the courts.

III. Joinder Model

A. DESCRIPTION AND ANALYSIS

The key attribute of the joinder model is its focus on each individual member of the class, whether representative or absent. Under this model, the class action is a group litigation device that brings together

---

[87] See, for example, the problems that arose in connection with Truth-in-Lending Act class actions prior to the amendment of that statute to deal specifically with group litigation. 15 U.S.C. §1640. See generally 4 NEWBERG ON CLASS ACTIONS §§7760.04–7760.05L (1977); Comment, *Class Actions Under the Truth in Lending Act*, 26 LOY. L. REV. 333 (1980); Fischer, *From Ratner to Qui Tam: Truth-in-Lending Class Action Developments*, 24 HASTINGS L. J. 813, 832–46 (1973); Note, *Class Actions Under the Truth in Lending Act*, 83 YALE L. J. 1410 (1974).

persons who are similarly situated not only with respect to their substantive claims but also with respect to their access to the forum court. The class action of Rule 23 differs from the simple joinder of Rule 20 only insofar as it offers added procedural protections for the litigants through increased judicial supervision and it does not require the unnamed members physically to come forward and conduct their own lawsuits. Thus, a class action offers a convenience to the unnamed member, but it does not improve his access to the court. The representative may not litigate the claim of any person who would not himself have the right to litigate the claim directly.

A few illustrations of what the joinder model would require in various situations may help to clarify it. Two principal problems arise in connection with a federal court's subject matter jurisdiction. First, in any suit brought under 28 U.S.C. §1332, the diversity statute, the normal rule is that there must be complete diversity between the plaintiffs and the defendants.[88] Second, in any suit brought under a federal jurisdictional statute that contains an amount in controversy requirement (usually §1332, since the repeal of the amount in controversy requirement of §1331), the normal rule is that each plaintiff must satisfy the requirement on his own.[89] The only exception to this rule occurs when the "several parties have a common undivided interest and a single title or right is involved."[90] In this instance, aggregation is permitted even under Rule 20 joinder. The joinder model for class actions would predict exactly the same results for assessing the jurisdiction of the court over the class. Every member of the class would be required to be of diverse citizenship from every opposing party, and every member of the class would be required to satisfy the amount in controversy requirement (except in instances where Rule 20 itself imposes no such requirement).

Personal jurisdiction and venue are two additional requirements that must normally be satisfied before a suit can proceed in a federal court. Personal jurisdiction over plaintiffs is not generally discussed, because

---

[88] See Strawbridge v. Curtiss, note 68 *supra*.

[89] See generally WRIGHT, FEDERAL COURTS §36 (4th ed. 1983); 14 WRIGHT, MILLER, & COOPER, FEDERAL PRACTICE AND PROCEDURE §§3704-05 (1976); 1 MOORE, FEDERAL PRACTICE ¶0.97[3] (1982). See Oliver v. Alexander, 6 Pet. 143 (1830); see also Snyder v. Harris, 394 U.S. 332 (1969). This rule has its absurd aspects. If a single plaintiff joins several claims under Rule 18, as he is permitted to do, he may aggregate the amounts in controversy for each one to reach the minimum required for federal court jurisdiction. If, however, two plaintiffs attempt to sue together pursuant to Rule 20, each one must satisfy the amount himself, despite the fact that joinder under Rule 20 is permissible only if the claims arise out of the same transactions or occurrences, while Rule 18 permits joinder of the most completely unrelated claims.

[90] WRIGHT, note 89 *supra*, at §36.

the plaintiff's act of invoking the court's jurisdiction serves as consent to the court's power over him.[91] If a plaintiff chooses to join several defendants pursuant to Rule 20(a), the court must acquire personal jurisdiction over each one, through appropriate service of process under Rule 4.[92] The general federal venue statute, 28 U.S.C. §1391, specifies three permissible venues for cases in which jurisdiction is founded solely on diversity: the district where all plaintiffs reside, the district where all defendants reside, or the district in which the claim arose. The latter two venues are the only ones available in suits not founded solely on diversity. Neither plaintiffs nor defendants need be considered if the suit is brought where the claim arose; if that district is not convenient or is difficult to ascertain, litigants sometimes choose one of the other options. Where multiple plaintiffs or multiple defendants exist as a result of Rule 20 joinder, every single one of them must reside in the same district before §1391's residence options can be used. Using the joinder model for class actions for these two procedural requirements, then, one would predict that the court must have personal jurisdiction at least over all defendants in a defendant class (and perhaps over all members of a plaintiff class as well, if the consent theory of personal jurisdiction supports the court's power over every party plaintiff), and that venue in a case based solely on diversity would lie only in the district in which *(a)* every member of the plaintiff class resided, or *(b)* every defendant resided, or *(c)* where the claim arose. Needless to say, in most cases only the third option would be realistic.

If a class action is essentially a joinder mechanism, it becomes difficult to argue that the discovery devices available only against parties should not be permitted against unnamed members of the class.[93] Similarly, there is no real reason why counterclaims should not

---

[91] Thus, for example, a plaintiff cannot complain about personal jurisdiction if the defendant chooses to file a counterclaim against him. WRIGHT, MILLER, & COOPER, note 89 *supra*, at §§1416, 1424.

[92] With regard to defendants, Rule 20 states that "[a]ll persons . . . may be joined in one action as defendants if there is asserted against them jointly, severally, or in the alternative, any right to relief in respect of or arising out of the same transaction, occurrence, or series of transactions or occurrences and if any question of law or fact common to all defendants will arise in the action."

[93] *E.g.*, interrogatories under Rule 33, production of documents and things under Rule 34, and admissions under Rule 36. Most of the discovery sanctions, for obvious reasons, operate only against parties. See Rule 37(b) (2). Note, *Obtaining Discovery From Absent Class Members In Federal Rule of Civil Procedure 23(b) (3) Class Actions*, 30 DRAKE L. REV. 247 (1980-81); Developments, note 65 *supra*, at 1439-48.

be permitted against unnamed class members.[94] There are several other problems that have plagued the Court in the context of class actions, however, that cannot be answered so readily. First, what does the joinder model predict when the claim of the representative of an uncertified class becomes moot: Can the representative continue to represent the class in the trial court? Is the representative entitled to appeal the denial of certification or anything else? Second, what answer does the joinder model give to the other "headless class" problem: the problem that arises when the named representative loses on the merits but class certification was erroneously denied?

Under the joinder model, each member of the putative class could function as the class representative, because each member is procedurally entitled to litigate on his own. That may suggest that the court should continue to allow the actual representative (and his attorney) to litigate and to appeal a denial of class certification, since it is clear that others exist who will have a right to relief.[95]

Finally, the Court has grappled with two problems in connection with class actions that may be outside the scope of either procedural model: statute-of-limitations-tolling rules, and administrative remedy exhaustion rules. Both these issues are "substantive" for most purposes. For example, the statute of limitations is clearly treated as a "substantive" matter to be governed by state law under the *Erie* doctrine, and the Court's treatment of administrative exhaustion in cases arising under federal law also uses a substantive analysis.[96] Certainly for purposes of the joinder model, the class would have to be defined and limited by the relevant statute of limitations. No one with a claim older than the outside limit under the governing law could be a class member. The joinder model would also require administrative exhaustion in all cases, ignoring for the moment what the Court has actually done in this area.

---

[94] But see Steinman, *The Party Status of Absent Plaintiff Class Members: Vulnerability to Counterclaims*, 69 GEO. L. J. 1171 (1981). Steinman's argument proceeded from the premise that absent class members are not true "parties" for many purposes, looking at the purposes behind the various rules she examined. Under the joinder model, there is no reason to exempt the unnamed members from party status just because they do not actively conduct the litigation.

[95] The problems with this approach will be discussed below in connection with the criticism of the joinder model. For now, it is important only to establish exactly what the model would call for in any given instance. See text *infra* at notes 124–28.

[96] Erie R.R. v. Tompkins, 304 U.S. 64 (1938). See Walker v. Armco Steel Corp., 446 U.S. 740 (1980) (state statute of limitations used in diversity case even where apparently inconsistent with Rule 3; the two can be reconciled in the final analysis). With regard to exhaustion, compare Califano v. Yamasaki, 442 U.S. 682 (1979), and Mathews v. Diaz, 426 U.S. 67 (1976), with

Accepting this as a workable definition of the joinder model, the first important question is whether it is consistent with all relevant constitutional and statutory constraints upon Rule 23. Article III of the Constitution imposes the first such restraint upon any action entertained in federal court. It requires that the lawsuit present a "case or controversy" that is suitable for a judicial decision: the dispute may not be moot, the parties before the court must have a stake in its resolution, and the case must be ripe for a decision.[97] For the class action, it is necessary to analyze this and the other requirements from two standpoints: first, that of the named representative of the class, and second, that of the unnamed, absent members of the class. For the latter group, the question whether class certification has been granted is also of great importance.

As long as the named member of the class satisfies the various aspects of the Article III "case or controversy" requirement, he may continue both to litigate on his own and to serve as class representative. What should happen under the joinder approach, though, if the named member's suit becomes moot, as happened, for example, in *Sosna v. Iowa*[98] in the case of a certified class and in *United States Parole Commission v. Geraghty*[99] in the case of an uncertified class? In both instances, the joinder model presupposes that every other member of the class would be entitled to continue the litigation as long as the facts giving rise to the mootness of the named member's claim did not also necessarily moot the unnamed members' claims as well. To take the case of the certified class first, the real question is whether Article III considerations prohibit the named party whose claim has become moot from continuing to stand as class representative.[100] On the strictest reading of Article III, the answer should be yes, even for the joinder model. If, however, one is willing (as the Court seemed to be in *Geraghty*) to take a "more flexible" view of Article III, one could argue that in the case of the joinder model substitution of a new class representative in the place of the one whose claim has become moot is a mere technicality.

Albemarle Paper Co. v. Moody, 422 U.S. 405 (1975) (different results reached on administrative exhaustion questions through interpretation of different statutory claims).

[97] U.S. Const. Art. III, §2. See generally WRIGHT, note 89 *supra* at §12; BATOR, MISHKIN, SHAPIRO, & WECHSLER, HART AND WECHSLER'S THE FEDERAL COURTS AND THE FEDERAL SYSTEM ch. 2 (2d ed. 1973).

[98] 419 U.S. 393 (1975).

[99] 445 U.S. 388 (1980).

[100] A related question is whether such a named party continues to satisfy the criteria of Rule 23(a). Kremens v. Bartley, 431 U.S. 119 (1977). Rule 23(c) (1) gives the court authority to alter

The underlying concern that the courts entertain only actual controversies between opposing parties is satisfied in the case of a certified class action, even if one member's claim no longer exists (the named representative). Certification is important, in this context, because it offers substantial assurance that a class, as defined by Rule 23(a) and (b), in fact exists. The other aspect of the Article III requirement—that the parties before the court pursue their respective positions vigorously[101]—is more difficult to find in the case of a named representative with a moot claim, unless one is willing to look beyond the person who is technically a party of record to his attorney. Many have commented that the class attorney is the "real party" in most class litigation, in the sense that his stake in the result is far greater than that of any individual class member.[102] If the attorney's interest can legitimately stand in for the named party's interest, or if the Court may somehow look beyond the named party directly to the absent class members, then both the central Article III concerns would be satisfied even if the named representative of a certified class had a claim that became moot after the beginning of the suit.

It is more difficult, but not impossible, to find a rationale (however tenuous) to support the continuation of a named representative with a moot claim in the case of an uncertified class. The first concern—that of an actual controversy—is satisfied for the certified class because the court's certification order assures that a class exists and the joinder model assures that every other member of the class stands in the same position as the named representative insofar as right to litigate is concerned. Without the certification order, there is no assurance that a litigative group actually exists.[103] Nevertheless, it is possible that the district court erred when it refused to certify the class. This possibility, in a sense, narrows the question of continuing right to represent the class to the question of right to appeal from the order denying certification.[104]

---

or amend a certification order "before the decision on the merits," suggesting that a failure to comply with 23(a) that arose after certification but before decision on the merits might be cause for decertification.

[101] See, e.g., Flast v. Cohen, 392 U.S. 83 (1968).

[102] See, e.g., Berry, *Ending Substance's Indenture to Procedure: The Imperative for Comprehensive Revision of the Class Damage Action*, 80 COLUM. L. REV. 299 (1980).

[103] In Pasadena City Bd. of Education v. Spangler, 427 U.S. 424 (1976), the district court did not certify a class, and the claims of the individually named plaintiffs became moot. Under those circumstances, the Court stated that the case "would clearly be moot," but for the fact that in the interim the United States had intervened. *Id.* at 430. It explicitly refused to find that counsel could represent directly the claims of the unnamed members of the purported class.

[104] Indeed, there is nothing left in the suit if the named party's claim has become moot and class

Lack of success on the motion to certify the class presents one remaining issue on which the two opposing parties have differing interests. Thus, on his own the representative party should have the right to appeal this question.[105] If he loses, the case naturally is conclusively over. If he wins, however, the appellate court would reverse the denial of certification and remand to the district court, either to reconsider the factors governing certification in the light of the correct legal standards or actually to certify. Assuming that certification results, the named representative with a moot claim in this second situation now stands in the same position as the named representative with a moot claim in the certified class situation. It is still possible that reasons extraneous to Article III might remove the mooted named representative from the case. The Court has recognized that Rule 23 itself may add to Article III's requirements.[106] For present purposes, however, it appears that an Article III justification can be found for permitting the named representative with a moot claim to continue to represent a class (under the joinder model) whether or not the class was certified.[107]

Thus, depending on how strictly Article III must be construed, it is possible to construct a theory under which a class action, viewed as a joinder device, may continue (with or without certification) when the named party's claim is moot or lost.[108] It is important to note, however, that the joinder model is more susceptible to this result than is the alternative model.

The Due Process Clauses of the Constitution present a second important constitutional limitation upon any application of Rule 23.

---

certification was denied. The question becomes somewhat more complicated if the named party loses on class certification and simply loses on the merits of his own claim.

[105] The Court has recognized an interest sufficient to support appellate jurisdiction in a disappointed class representative. See Deposit Guaranty Nat'l Bank v. Roper, note 81 *supra*; U.S. Parole Comm'n v. Geraghty, note 99 *supra*.

[106] Kremens v. Bartley, note 100 *supra*; see also East Texas Motor Freight System, Inc. v. Rodriguez, 431 U.S. 395 (1977); U.S. Parole Comm'n v. Geraghty, note 99 *supra*.

[107] The problem of the "headless" class is similar enough to that of the mooted named representative that it does not require separate analysis. See, *e.g.*, U.S. Parole Comm'n v. Geraghty, note 99 *supra*, at 390 & n.2. If a class is certified and then loses on the merits, there is clearly an interest in the named party's pursuing the interests of the class on appeal. If a class is not certified, and the named party loses on the merits of his individual claim, his interest in appealing both points clearly exists. Only if he then loses on his individual appeal but wins on the appeal of the denial of certification does the problem analogous to that of the mooted party arise. At that point, it is reasonable to treat the named party with a lost claim in the same manner as a named party with a moot claim. See Comment, *Goodman v. Schlesinger and the Headless Class Action*, 60 B.U. L. REV. 348 (1980); Note, *Satterwhite v. City of Greenville and Breathing New Life into the Headless Title VII Class Action*, 32 STAN. L. REV. 743 (1980).

[108] The implications of this result are discussed in part B of this section, *infra*.

Normally, of course, one must have notice and an opportunity to be heard before one's rights can be decided by any tribunal. In a court proceeding, if one is to be a party, one must receive appropriate service of process. Class actions have been recognized as an exception to these rules, but the extent to which the exception relieves the actual parties of various obligations remains unclear.[109] When parties have done nothing but join a lawsuit through Rule 20, each one remains fully entitled to notice of everything that happens, by means of Rule 4 or 5 as appropriate. Even under a joinder model, the class action must operate somewhat differently, or none of the policies of efficiency that the Court has identified would be served. Thus, even under the joinder model the ultimate question must be whether the procedures of Rule 23 (for example, class certification, the type of notice provided for (b) (3) classes under (c) (2), or the discretionary notice of (d) (2), court approval of settlements or dismissals) are the due process equivalents of the normal notice and opportunity to be heard that the unnamed members would otherwise enjoy.

The real problem is whether the joinder model demands more in the way of notice and an opportunity to participate than a representational model. The rationale by which most commentators agree that the courts can dispense with actual notice and actual participation for every class member is representational. Just as, for example, a trustee may often sue to bind beneficiaries, or a guardian may bind a ward, a class representative may sue and bind the class members, as long as the representation is adequate. The joinder model should not necessarily force one to adopt only the consent theory of representation and not the interest theory, because in either case the absentee members are not controlling the litigation in the final analysis. Any view of the joinder model that demanded an opt-in approach to the class action (the ultimate in consent under the modern context) would still leave the class members at the mercy of their representative after opting in. Thus, in order to answer the question whether there is any due process problem with the joinder model, it is best to ask the same question with regard to the Rule 23 procedures in general.

---

[109] See Hansberry v. Lee, 311 U.S. 32 (1940); Eisen v. Carlisle & Jacquelin, 417 U.S. 156 (1974). See also, *e.g.*, Rhode, *Class Conflicts in Class Actions*, 34 STAN. L. REV. 1183 (1982); Note, *Personal Jurisdiction and Rule 23 Defendant Class Actions*, 53 INDIANA L. J. 841 (1978); Note, *Defendant Class Actions*, 91 HARV. L. REV. 630 (1978); Note, *Due Process Rights of Absentees in Title VII Class Actions—The Myth of Homogeneity of Interest*, 59 B.U. L. REV. 661 (1979); Dam, *Class Action Notice: Who Needs It?* 1974 SUPREME COURT REVIEW 97; *Developments*, note 65 *supra*, at 1402-16.

Until the Court decided *Eisen v. Carlisle & Jacquelin,* it seemed
relatively clear that constitutional (as opposed to rule) concerns
centered upon adequacy of representation. Notice to class members
was only one aspect of the adequacy question. This was highlighted by
the fact that the class action rule, presumably the product of the best
thought on the subject that could be mustered at the time, dispensed
entirely with any notice requirement for unnamed members in 1966,
at the last revision, for two out of the three subsection (b) kinds of
classes. Historically, notice to unnamed members was never even
mentioned before the 1966 amended rule, although the courts did send
notice as a matter of discretion when they deemed it appropriate. *Eisen,*
however, contains some ambiguous language in which the Court seems
to say that adequacy of representation is not the final measure of due
process.[110] This is not the question that the Court itself purported to
address. To the contrary, the Court tried to make clear that it was
deciding only that Rule 23(c) (2) imposed an iron-clad notice
requirement for (b) (3) classes when their members were capable of
identification. Later cases, such as *Quern v. Jordan,*[111] contain language
suggesting that *Eisen* was indeed limited to the Rule 23(c) (2) problem
and did not reach the constitutional question.

The better view seems quite clearly to be that *Eisen* was so limited.
On the other hand, since *Eisen* certainly required the district courts to
follow Rule 23(c) (2), it simply shifted the inquiry in one sense. The
drafters of that rule believed that notice was constitutionally required
to bind absentee class members in that more loosely knit type of class
action. The two principal commentators on the federal rules seem to
be in agreement on that point.[112] No one originally took the position
that notice was required in (b) (1) or (b) (2) action, and commentators
seemed untroubled with the view that adequacy of representation is the
only requirement of due process there.[113] Since even for a (b) (3) class,
the rule (and the Court in *Eisen*) are willing to tolerate less than perfect
actual notice, it seems that in fact, even in (b) (3) actions, the operating

---

[110] "Petitioner further contends that adequate representation, rather than notice, is the
touchstone of due process in a class action and therefore satisfies Rule 23. We think this view has
little to commend it. . . . [Q]uite apart from what due process may require, the command of Rule
23 is clearly to the contrary." 417 U.S. at 176–77.

[111] 440 U.S. 332, 335 n.3 (1979).

[112] WRIGHT & MILLER, note 56 *supra,* at §1786; MOORE, note 1 *supra,* at ¶23.55.

[113] WRIGHT & MILLER, note 56 *supra,* at §1793; MOORE, note 1 *supra,* at ¶23.72. The Second
Circuit's position to the contrary in *Eisen II* (Eisen v. Carlisle & Jacquelin, 391 F.2d 555 (2nd Cir.
1968)) has not been widely followed.

rule is that adequacy of representation in the end will satisfy due process.

With the joinder model, then, due process constraints could be viewed in one of two ways. The extreme view would be to accord exactly the same due process treatment to absentee class members as they would have received if they had joined under Rule 20. This would, in practical effect, kill the class action, because the expense of sending papers to every member of a class would be prohibitive. The more reasonable view would be to permit the class action to serve as a convenience and money-saving device, and to assess the due process rights of the absentee members by the usual adequacy-of-representation grounds. In the case of a (b) (3) class, this would include a requirement of compliance with Rule 23(c) (2), exactly as the Court has informed us it must be read. Therefore, the joinder model either falls completely on the due process requirements, or it is essentially the same as the representational model on this count.

The last important external constraints on class actions are the Rules Enabling Act and Rule 82 of the Federal Rules of Civil Procedure. The Rules Enabling Act[114] stipulates that the Federal Rules of Civil Procedure "shall not abridge, enlarge or modify any substantive right. . . ." Since the joinder model for class actions presumes that each member of the class is equally entitled from a procedural point to pursue the litigation, and Rule 23 itself ensures (or attempts to ensure) that the substantive claims litigated through class procedures will be common, the joinder model almost by definition cannot run afoul of the Enabling Act. The mere fact that class actions will be filed at times when the individuals might not have sued on their own, because of the advantages offered by the sharing of litigation expenses, is not enough to amount to an enlargement or other modification of the underlying substantive right. The joinder model is similarly safe under Rule 82, which provides that the federal rules may not be construed to "extend or limit the jurisdiction of the United States district courts." Particularly with respect to jurisdiction, the description of the model above makes clear that a joinder approach to class actions has no such effect.

B. APPLICATION AND CRITICISM

The Supreme Court has followed the joinder model implicitly on a number of occasions. Each time it has done so, the decision has come

---

[114] 28 U.S.C. §2072.

under heavy criticism, although not precisely in these terms. The two most notable examples of the Court's joinder approach have occurred in the areas of jurisdictional amount and the continuing right of a class representative to litigate after his claim has become moot.[115] In the more substantive area of exhaustion of administrative remedies, the Court has permitted the underlying statute to govern whether or not it finds such a requirement for the unnamed members.

In *Zahn v. International Paper Co.*,[116] the Court faced the question whether the jurisdictional amount requirement of 28 U.S.C. §1332 was met in a class action brought under Rule 23 (b) (3) when the named plaintiffs presented claims exceeding $10,000 in value but at least some unnamed members of the class had claims for lesser amounts. It concluded that diversity jurisdiction would not lie unless every member of the class satisfied the $10,000 amount in controversy requirement. The Court rather blindly thought that *Zahn* presented the same issue, in another guise, that it had resolved several years earlier in *Snyder v. Harris*,[117] where it had refused to entertain a class action in which neither the named plaintiffs nor the unnamed members individually met the jurisdictional amount requirement. It held that aggregation of claims was unavailable in a class action under the 1966 rule unless it would have been available prior to that time—that is, unless the claim being litigated was one concerning a "common and undivided interest." Since the Court saw *Zahn* as another kind of aggregation case, the majority never considered the other possible approach to the case. Because the district court's jurisdiction was properly being invoked by class representatives who met that particular jurisdictional requirement, the claims of other class members could be adjudicated under a sort of ancillary concept. Although the dissenters in *Zahn* did raise the point about ancillary jurisdiction, neither side saw all implications of the question presented.

The focus on *Zahn* as another aggregation case, like *Snyder*, revived the 1938 distinction between "true" and "spurious" class actions. Since it had been clear under a great number of precedents that aggregating was impermissible in "spurious" actions,[118] the Court could have concluded that aggregation was never permissible in a class action that

---

[115] The Court has taken a significantly stricter line when the named member simply loses on the merits. East Texas Motor Freight System, Inc. v. Rodriguez, 431 U.S. 395 (1977).

[116] 414 U.S. 291 (1973).

[117] 394 U.S. 332 (1969).

[118] See, *e.g.*, Clark v. Paul Gray, Inc., 306 U.S. 583 (1939).

would formerly have been classified as "spurious." There are at least two ways of looking at the "matter in controversy" in *Zahn*, however, only one of which raises the aggregation problem. If one is concerned about the right of every member of the class to litigate, then aggregation remains relevant even in *Zahn*, since the unnamed members did not meet the required jurisdictional amount on their own. If, instead, the concern is only with the characteristics of the representatives, then the fact that the unnamed members did not meet the required amount becomes beside the point. On this narrower approach to *Zahn*, it is possible to grant for the sake of argument that *Snyder* was correctly decided. No representative appeared in *Snyder* who satisfied this jurisdictional requirement. If *Snyder* misconstrued the matter in controversy for a Rule 23 class action, then *Zahn* did so *a fortiori*.[119]

Historically, the Court had permitted "true" class actions to proceed when only the named members of the class met a jurisdictional amount requirement and not all of the absentees. In *Handley v. Stutz*,[120] a creditors' bill class action, some of the creditors had claims against the corporation exceeding $2,000 (the jurisdictional amount that then applied to the Circuit Courts) and others had claims for less. The circuit court found in favor of the creditors upon a suit by those with sufficiently large claims, and left the decree open in the usual way for the other creditors to come in. With respect to the claims for less than $2,000, the defendants filed exceptions to the master's report and moved the circuit court to dismiss for lack of jurisdiction. The court overruled that motion, and the Supreme Court affirmed its decision on appeal:[121]

> The sums alleged to be due from the corporation to the original plaintiffs amounting to more than $2,000, the Circuit Court had jurisdiction of the case, and authority to administer and distribute the amounts, due from the individual defendants to the corporation for unpaid subscriptions to stock, as a trust fund for the benefit of all the creditors of the corporation, and for that purpose to permit creditors, who had not originally joined in the bill, to come in and prove their claims before a master.

---

[119] See generally Currie, *Pendent Parties*, 45 U. CHI. L. REV. 753 (1978).
[120] 137 U.S. 366 (1890).
[121] *Id.* at 369.

Unless there is something that fundamentally distinguishes the old creditors' bill kind of case from the (b) (3) action presented in *Zahn*, it is difficult to see why the majority, the dissenters, and the lawyers for the parties did not even refer to *Handley* in the *Zahn* opinions.

The Court in *Handley* made one reference to the difference between joining together in a creditors' bill, which had to be a class action, and joining together for convenience, in which case it implied that the objection might have been good. If all (b) (3) actions are convenience class actions, the two cases are distinguishable, and the Court had no need to worry about *Handley* when it decided *Zahn*. But that proves too much in the context in which the *Handley* Court made the remark. If the creditors had simply joined together for convenience, they would probably not have been entitled to proceed together as a class at all in 1890. The case would have presented only a common question, and each would have had to join independently or to have brought his own suit. Aggregation of amounts would clearly have been out of the question. There was no talk about aggregation in *Handley* itself.

In the light of the reasons that creditors' bills were given class treatment—the certainty of identity of interest vis-à-vis the debtor, and the strong policy against court-sanctioned preferences—no reason appears why a modern class action that fully satisfies Rule 23 should be treated differently. The *Handley* facts did not require federal court jurisdiction. If the Court had been concerned about universal satisfaction of the amount-in-controversy requirement, it could have remitted the creditors to their state court remedies, just as it did with the property owners in *Zahn*. Between *Snyder* and *Handley*, *Handley* offered by far the more pertinent precedent for the Court to consider as it decided *Zahn*.

The result in *Zahn* illustrates a perfect application of the joinder model: every member of the class, present or absent, must satisfy one particular jurisdictional requirement, namely the amount in controversy rule. The Court was confusing rules about aggregation of claims, which would apply even to simple joinder cases, with the more subtle question about the extent to which a class representative is entitled to pursue litigation on behalf of others. It is interesting in this context that the Court has always permitted intervenors who qualify for intervention of right under Rule 24 or its predecessors to take advantage of the district court's ancillary jurisdiction.[122] The question

---

[122] See generally WRIGHT & MILLER, note 56 *supra*, at §§1799, 1917. See also Stewart v. Dunham, 115 U.S. 61 (1885).

then arises whether the other putative class members in *Zahn* would have qualified under Rule 24 for intervention of right and been able simply to intervene in a properly filed action by the named representatives. Others have also raised important criticisms about the Court's approach in *Zahn*,[123] but the case's unthinking adoption of the joinder model for the class action deserves critical attention on its own.

The question of the continuing right of a class representative to litigate the claims of the class after the representative's own claim has become moot is tied up inextricably with the rules on appealability of orders granting or denying class certification. Naturally, if the class representative does not have a live claim at the time the suit is filed, the court will immediately dismiss. The more difficult question arises when the class representative's claim becomes moot at some time after commencement of the action and after the court has ruled on the motion to certify the class, but before a decision on the merits. The Court has decided that an order denying class certification is not entitled to interlocutory review unless the district court and the court of appeals invoke the procedures of 28 U.S.C. §1292(b).[124] In the normal case, therefore, it is necessary to wait until final judgment to appeal the decision on the class certification motion. The Court has recognized the interest of the absentee members of the putative class in a correct decision on class certification, by permitting intervention within the time allowed for an appeal, so that the new class representative might appeal the certification decision,[125] and even by permitting an appeal on the class certification point by a representative party whose claim became moot some time during the trial phase.[126] Even when the named member pursues issues relevant to the class in the case of a certified class, as in *Sosna v. Iowa*,[127] it requires an almost complete perversion of Article III to permit the named member with a moot claim to appeal the denial of class certification. Only the strained justification in connection with the description of the joinder model suffices to support this result, and its treatment of Article III as a "mere technicality" does not withstand critical scrutiny.

---

[123] See Currie, note 119 *supra*.

[124] Coopers & Lybrand v. Livesay, 437 U.S. 463 (1978); Gardner v. Westinghouse Broadcasting Co., 437 U.S. 478 (1978); *cf.* Carson v. American Brands, Inc., 450 U.S. 79 (1981) (district court refusal to enter a consent decree in a class action is appealable).

[125] United Airlines, Inc. v. McDonald, 432 U.S. 385 (1977).

[126] Deposit Guaranty Nat'l Bank v. Roper, 445 U.S. 326 (1980); U.S. Parole Comm'n v. Geraghty, 445 U.S. 388 (1980).

[127] 419 U.S. 393 (1975); see also Franks v. Bowman Transp. Co., 424 U.S. 747 (1976).

The concept underlying the Court's decisions on this point seems to be that each member of the putative class has an interest in a correct decision on the question of certification, and that the person already before the court is in the best position as a practical matter to vindicate that interest. Even the Court has admitted, however, that the mooted representative may not be an appropriate class representative on remand.[128] If that is so, then it is hard to see what conceivable interest this person has in the question of class certification. The Court may be assuming that the lawyer who was representing the former named representative is still representing the absent members of the class, and they are the ones who have become the true opposing parties and who now furnish the "case or controversy" that Article III requires. That assumption, however, turns the class action on its head. The joinder concept, insofar as it permits the Court to look through the named representative directly to the absentee members of the class, to the extreme extent of using them for an Article III criterion, is simply unacceptable.

The consequences of the joinder approach to class actions thus range from the undesirable, in *Zahn*, to the unacceptable, in *Geraghty* and *Roper*. *Geraghty* and *Roper* are unacceptable for their perversion of Article III. The *Zahn* result is undesirable because it violates both of the policies underlying class actions identified above and because it is inconsistent with the history of the class action in this country. It leads to inefficiencies, since many actions that will be adjudicated by the federal courts anyway, due to the presence of named members with the proper jurisdictional amount, will have to be decided in state courts as well, either by means of state court class actions or individually. It also frustrates the private attorney-general function of the class action, since it is fair to assume that many of those unnamed class members who are foreclosed from federal court by *Zahn* will actually do nothing. *Zahn* is inconsistent with *Handley* and with the body of case law supporting intervention of right. Only the Court's misconceived analogy to *Snyder v. Harris* and its belief that every class member had to satisfy this particular requirement led to the result.

---

[128] U.S. Parole Comm'n v. Geraghty, 445 U.S. at 405–07; see also East Texas Motor Freight System, Inc. v. Rodriguez, 431 U.S. 395 (1977); Kremens v. Bartley, 431 U.S. 119 (1977); *cf.* General Telephone Co. of Southwest v. Falcon, 457 U.S. 147 (1982).

IV. REPRESENTATION MODEL

A. DESCRIPTION AND ANALYSIS

This model carries forward the tradition whereby one person may represent the interests of others who are not before the court and who may have no independent procedural right to appear before the court. The procedural focus is upon the named representative(s); only he (they) must satisfy the pertinent jurisdictional and other preliminary requirements for bringing suit. The model has nothing to do with the substantive similarities between representative and absent class members. It assumes that the requirements of Rule 23(a) concerning the appropriateness of the suit for class treatment and the adequacy of the representation must be satisfied, and that the suit must fit within one of the Rule 23(b) categories. It may be helpful again to see what the model would predict (apart from what the Court has done) for the usual procedural requirements.

For subject matter jurisdiction, only the named representative would be required to meet any applicable rules. Thus, only the named representative would need to be of diverse citizenship from the opposing parties (or all named representatives), and only the named representative(s) would need to satisfy the jurisdictional amount requirement. Personal jurisdiction and venue would follow similar rules. In the case of a defendant class, formal service would be necessary only on the named representative. For a plaintiff class, the consent of the named representative to a particular forum would bind the remaining members of the class. Venue rules that are defined in terms of plaintiffs' or defendants' residences would need to be satisfied only by the named representatives.

The representative model gives greater protection to the unnamed members of the class in areas such as discovery and counterclaims, as it follows from this model that absentee members should not be treated as parties for either of these purposes. On the other hand, under this model the importance of the selection of the representative and the legitimacy of the selection process is, if possible, even greater than it is under the joinder model. The right of an absentee class member to challenge the result of class litigation on the ground that he was not in fact adequately represented is also of central importance.

The question of continuing the suit after the named representative's claim becomes moot again depends in part on whether or not the class was certified, but the method of continuing it even in the case of a certified class probably differs. If the district court certifies a class and the named member's claim then becomes moot,[129] one need not consider the entire case dead, because there has been judicial recognition that a class exists and its interests are implicated. The proper procedure under the representation model, however, would be to require the intervention of a new named representative who satisfied all the procedural requirements. Otherwise, there would be no assurance that such a proper representative really existed. After timely intervention, the case would proceed with the new named representative.

The case of the uncertified class is again more difficult. If anything is clear, however, it is clear that the representation model would not permit the named representative of the putative class to continue litigating on the class's behalf after his own claim disappeared. There is no assurance even that there is a class that should have been certified; one surely cannot assume that district courts always err in denying certification.[130] Again, permitting intervention of a new representative for the class within a certain period of time after the order finding the named representative's claim moot, for purposes of appealing the certification order, seems to be the only possible solution.[131] If no class member comes forward to intervene, in either the uncertified or the certified class situation, the district court should have no choice but to dismiss the entire action in the former instance, or to decertify the class and dismiss in the latter.

The real reason why the Court may be instinctively reluctant to adopt the representation model probably stems from Article III, due process, or Enabling Act concerns. In the end, however, the representation model does a better job of meeting those concerns than does the joinder model. As the discussion above of the representative

---

[129] In this context, only the kind of mootness that would ordinarily prevent one from continuing one's own suit is important. If the named representative would be individually entitled to continue the suit on the theory that the claim is "capable of repetition but evading review," then there is no reason why he should not also be permitted to continue the claim of the class. At times, however, the Court has permitted named members to continue representing classes even when that exception to mootness does not apply. See Franks v. Bowman Transp. Co., 424 U.S. 747 (1976).

[130] Indeed, on appellate review of orders on class certification, the district court's ruling is presumed to be correct. The appellate court may reverse only if it finds that the district court abused its discretion or applied the incorrect legal standards. See generally MOORE, note 1 *supra*, at ¶23.50, at 23-436 to 23-437. The decision in Pasadena City Bd. of Education v. Spangler, note 103 *supra*, is consistent with the suggestion here that the named representative could not pursue such a suit.

[131] This is similar to the procedure permitted in United Airlines v. McDonald, 432 U.S. 385 (1977).

with a moot claim illustrates, under the representation model it is impossible to end up with a "headless class" or the anomalous situation where a person with a moot claim has the right to appeal but no right to continue as class representative. The ironclad requirement of intervention of a new class member assures that there is always an adequate class representative with a live interest in the case to pursue the interests of the class. If, at the time for distribution of a recovery, it appeared that some members of the class did not have or never had a live controversy against the opposing party, the court would simply deny them the right to share in the recovery by ensuring that the description of the class required by Rule 23(c) (3) did not include such persons.

The representation model also poses no insurmountable problems with respect to due process. It is important to reiterate some points here and to expand somewhat on the analysis. First, there is nothing in the Due Process Clauses that prohibits the fact of representation. Unions sometimes represent their members in a binding fashion; executors or administrators represent the various interests in estates such that all are bound; parents or "next friends" represent the interests of children. The question is always whether the right sort of tie exists between the representative and those who are being represented.[112] For the modern class action, Rule 23(a) attempts to answer this question. Rule 23(a), in a sense, is just the culmination of experience with the general concept of representative lawsuits dating back to the early nineteenth century in this country. To say that representation is invalid particularly in class actions would require overruling cases going back as far as *Beatty v. Kurtz, Smith v. Swormstedt,* and *Supreme Tribe of Ben-Hur.* There is no need to take such a radical position. Existing doctrine under Rule 23, supplemented by the limitation on *res judicata* when hindsight proves that representation was not adequate, is ample to legitimize representation for the modern class action. Even for the problems of divergence of interest in (b) (2) classes that have received attention, devices such as multiple representatives and subclasses are available and can be used to meet the underlying concern.

Although the Court has never expressed discomfort with the representation afforded in Rule 23 class actions in terms of notice, it is possible to wonder whether a purely representational action would fully satisfy that aspect of due process. The persons under the present

---

[112] See Yeazell, note 1 *supra,* 27 U.C.L.A. L. REV.

Rule 23 scheme with whom one would be concerned are the members of any class certified under (b) (1) or (b) (2), and any members of a (b) (3) class who prove not to be identifiable and who therefore do not receive individual notice pursuant to 23(c) (2). The Court's opinion in *Eisen*[133] switches confusingly between due process justifications for the individual notice requirement and justifications derived solely from Rule 23.[134] If representation can be validated only by means of effective notice to all class members and some form of consent, then the representation model would be administratively impracticable. The costs of such large-scale notice will often be prohibitive.[135] The resolution of this particular due process issue does not depend upon which class action model is adopted, as long as one is willing to agree with Yeazell that two alternative means of legitimizing representation exist: interest congruence and consent. The Court has always taken this position. It permits one to leave the notice problem, for purposes of the representation model, where one finds it: notice is required for identifiable (b) (3) class members, and the court may in its discretion order some form of notice for (b) (1) and (b) (2) class members.

The question under the Rules Enabling Act is whether the substantive rights of unnamed class members are "abridged, enlarged, or modified" if Rule 23 is read to permit a representational class action. More specifically, are their substantive rights so affected if those rights are adjudicated in a federal court action that the unnamed members would not have had an individual right to bring because of lack of diversity, lack of requisite jurisdictional amount, or the like? The answer to this question must be no, for several compelling reasons. Every time a federal court exercises pendent jurisdiction over a state claim, it adjudicates something that the person bringing the claim could not have submitted to the federal court absent the related federal claim. Yet no one argues that pendent jurisdiction "affects" substantive rights. It simply is one way in which a forum for the adjudication of those rights is furnished.[136] The Court's recognition of ancillary jurisdiction in a variety of contexts also rests on the fundamental assumption that provision of a federal forum does not result in the changing of substantive rights. Often ancillary jurisdiction arises in connection

---

[133] Eisen v. Carlisle & Jacquelin, 417 U.S. 156 (1974).

[134] This point is elaborated in Dam, note 109 *supra*.

[135] *Cf.* Oppenheimer Fund, Inc. v. Sanders, 437 U.S. 340 (1978).

[136] The Court has gone as far as possible in the *Erie* line of cases to ensure that the federal forum has no effect on the underlying substantive rights being adjudicated. The Rules of Decision Act, 28 U.S.C. §1652, contains the congressional command on the subject.

with the operation of the Federal Rules of Civil Procedure. For example, compulsory counterclaims under Rule 13(a) are supported by ancillary jurisdiction, even though the compulsory nature of the counterclaim is a result only of the rules.[137] When a defendant takes advantage of Rule 14(a) impleader to bring in a third-party defendant, ancillary jurisdiction again supports the claim, although the Rules created the device. Finally, intervention of right under Rule 24 needs no independent basis of federal jurisdiction, even though the intervening party had no original right to be in federal court.[138]

These examples illustrate that the fact that Rule 23 may permit some people to have their rights settled in federal court, when they may have had no such right without the rule, does not mean that the rule has changed their substantive rights. It simply provides a forum in which those substantive rights may be adjudicated. Neither does Rule 23 "extend or limit" the jurisdiction of the United States district courts or the venue of actions therein" within the meaning of Rule 82. In the first place, if Rule 23 had such an effect, then so would the other rules mentioned above: Rules 13, 14, 24. In the case of Rule 23, the problem can also be addressed from another point of view. Long before the Federal Rules of Civil Procedure existed, the Court recognized a kind of ancillary jurisdiction for class actions. Thus, in *Handley v. Stutz* it permitted representative creditors to litigate the rights of all creditors, including those who did not meet the jurisdictional amount. In *Supreme Tribe of Ben-Hur v. Cauble* it permitted representatives of diverse citizenship to litigate the rights of class members whose citizenship was nondiverse from the organization's. The advent of the 1938 rules of procedure did not change these concepts of ancillary jurisdiction, and indeed the command of Rule 82 was that they could not. Rule 82 thus has the effect of supporting jurisdiction over the claims of the absent class members rather than destroying it.[139]

Questions concerning the statute of limitations and exhaustion of administrative remedies fall far closer to the "substantive" half of the

---

[137] 3 MOORE, note 1 *supra* at ¶13.15. Some states do not recognize any counterclaims as compulsory; if the federal rules had made that choice, then ancillary jurisdiction would probably not support any counterclaim. Permissive counterclaims under Rule 13(b) require an independent basis of jurisdiction now unless a setoff is involved. *Ibid.*

[138] MOORE, note 1 *supra*, at ¶24.18[1]; WRIGHT & MILLER, note 56 *supra*, at §1917.

[139] Although the Court has taken a more hostile view with regard to ancillary jurisdiction and so-called pendent parties in recent years, it has never said anything to cast doubt on the operation of these concepts in the class action area. See Moor v. County of Alameda, 411 U.S. 693 (1973); Owen Equipment & Erection Co. v. Kroger, 437 U.S. 365 (1978).

procedure/substance distinction. In both instances, the way in which the Court has approached the problems in recent years—through analysis of the underlying statutes—implies that neither of these requirements is subject to modification by procedural rules, including Rule 23. In the 1982 Term, in *Chardon v. Soto*,[140] a majority of the Court concluded that the Puerto Rican "revival" rule for its one-year statute of limitations in cases brought under 42 U.S.C. §1983 applied by force of 42 U.S.C. §1988. Over Justice Rehnquist's dissent, the majority rejected the argument that *American Pipe & Construction Co. v. Utah*[141] had established a general rule for Rule 23 class actions. It took the position instead that each statute of limitations must be analyzed in accordance with the policies applicable to it. Similarly, the Court's treatment of the need to exhaust administrative remedies has depended upon the underlying statute. In *Albemarle Paper Co. v. Moody*[142] the Court found that preliminary filing of charges with the Equal Employment Opportunity Commission was not necessary for unnamed class members in a Title VII class action. On the other hand, in *Califano v. Yamasaki*[143] it appeared to reject the possibility of membership in a class for persons who had not personally filed for a reconsideration or waiver with the Secretary of Health, Education, and Welfare in a Social Security Act case, again relying on the language of the statute for its result. Both the statute of limitations and administrative exhaustion rules are intimately tied up with the entire scheme of recovery, and hence are suitable candidates for treatment as "substantive" and beyond the scope of any procedural rule.

It thus appears that the representation model can be followed without doing any violence to either constitutional or statutory constraints on class actions. More than that, it provides a more satisfactory solution to the intractable problem of the named representative with a moot claim than the alternative—more attractive both because it ensures that a flesh and blood representative will always exist, and because it implicitly rejects the reality of the class lawyer as real party in interest. It does this without in the least distorting the core concepts of Article III.

---

[140] 103 S. Ct. 2611 (1983).
[141] 414 U.S. 538 (1974).
[142] 422 U.S. 405, 414 n.8 (1975).
[143] 422 U.S. 682 (1979).

B. APPLICATION AND CRITICISM

Not only has the Court followed the representational model at least as often as it has the joinder model, but its descriptions of the class action make one think that it has tried to adopt this representational model. In *American Pipe* it stated that "[a] federal class action is no longer 'an invitation to joinder' but a truly representative suit designed to avoid, rather than encourage, unnecessary filing of repetitious papers and motions."[144] *Supreme Tribe of Ben-Hur* is one of the best examples of a representational suit, but it is not the only one. The Court takes a representational approach with respect to the statute of limitations in one sense: Filing on the part of the class representative tolls the statute for all class members until the ruling on certification.[145] The length of time the statute is tolled after a negative ruling on certification is subject to the substantive law at issue, but it is clear that the absent members do not need to file on their own to preserve their rights. This has been the rule with class actions at least since *Richmond v. Irons*.[146] In one case (which admittedly was never followed again), *Indianapolis School Commissioners v. Jacobs*,[147] in which a class was alleged but somehow certified improperly, the Court found that the mootness of the named representatives' claims washed out the entire case. Finally, the general language if not the holding of *Hansberry v. Lee* strongly supports the representational theory.[148]

Both policies underlying class actions support a representational approach. The history of class actions in this country does so as well. The types of efficiencies and economies of which the Court has spoken can result only if the litigation can be conducted by a certain number of representative parties. As long as those parties satisfy the procedural prerequisites for suit, there is no reason not to permit the litigation to conclude the rights of others as well, once the court is satisfied with the legitimacy and quality of representation. In this sense, the modern class action can still function as a device to avoid multitudinous litigation. The private attorney-general function is also enhanced by this hospitable view of class actions. It is important to note, however, that the representational model does not always result in a broadening of the availability of class actions. In the area of the

---

[144] 414 U.S. at 550.

[145] See *American Pipe*, note 77 *supra;* Chardon v. Soto, note 80 *supra;* Crown, Cork & Seal Co. v. Parker, *ibid.*

[146] 121 U.S. 27 (1887); see discussion text at note 16 *supra.*

[147] 420 U.S. 128 (1975). See also Pasadena City Bd. of Education v. Spangler, note 103 *supra.*

[148] 311 U.S. 32, 41 (1940); see discussion *supra*, text at note 72.

representative with a moot claim, this approach would actually be narrower both for certified classes and for uncertified classes than that which the Court has taken. It would also be more consistent with traditional concepts of the attorney-client relationship and Article III than the Court's approach has been.

The history of the class action, in the end, provides significantly greater support for the representation model than the alternative, even though the nature of the action has changed dramatically over time. Only if one looks all the way back to the English Chancery practice (in which, for example, a few tenants could sue their lord to establish manorial custom) is it unambiguous that each member of the class was equally entitled to come before the court and that the joinder model was being used.[149] In this country, *Smith v. Swormstedt* demonstrates that by 1853 the U.S. Supreme Court was taking a representational approach. It is certain that all members of the defendant class in *Swormstedt* were not served with process, and there was certainly no proof of complete diversity of citizenship between the members of the plaintiff class and the members of the defendant class. Certainly the Court took a representational approach in *Ben-Hur* and asserted this approach as the law in *Hansbury v. Lee*. Thus, the verdict of history in the United States also favors the representational model.

The final argument in favor of the representational model is its superior answer to the problem that the Court thought it was going to resolve last Term in *Gillette Co. v. Miner*.[150] *Gillette* presented the question whether minimum contacts needed to exist between unnamed members of a plaintiff class and the state in which the case was filed.[151] Defendants raised the question, even before a motion for class certification was filed in the Illinois state court hearing the case, whether the due process rights of the absent plaintiff class members would be violated if those persons had no "minimum contacts" with the State of Illinois. In briefs before the Supreme Court, defendants argued vigorously that the personal jurisdiction standards established by *International Shoe*[152] and subsequent cases should protect absent

---

[149] See Yeazell, note 1 *supra*, 77 COLUMBIA L. REV. 866.

[150] *Cert. granted*, 102 S. Ct. 1767 (1982), case dismissed for want of jurisdiction, 103 S. Ct. 484 (1982).

[151] The case also presented an issue dealing with the interest of the forum state, Illinois, in the litigation as a whole. It concerned alleged violations by the Gillette Company of certain consumer protection laws, in connection with a promotional scheme. This issue, while important, is of no moment here.

[152] International Shoe Co. v. Washington, 326 U.S. 310 (1945).

plaintiff class members as well as any defendant (including, presumably, defendant class members). The scheme of Rule 23, after all, contemplates that the plaintiff class members will be bound by the result of the litigation, and it is just as bad to lose a claim one might have had as it is to be found liable to another person. Plaintiffs responded with the basic argument that *International Shoe*'s minimum contacts were for defendants, and therefore should not apply to plaintiffs.

There is a superficial appeal to the defendants' position that quickly disappears. Defendants noted, with perfect accuracy, that the absent plaintiff class members did not ask for the action to be filed, yet they are participants in it unless they opt out (which was a possibility under the pertinent Illinois procedural rule). Thus, like defendants, they are involved in litigation at someone else's instance, even to the point of being bound by its results. On the other hand, defendants overlooked at least equally undesirable consequences of the rule they advocated. No one doubts that plaintiffs may submit themselves to the jurisdiction of a court by consent. If unnamed members of classes were not bound unless they affirmatively "opted in," the old problem of one-way intervention that was condemned in original Rule 23 would reappear in this guise. The logistical problems of proving to the court's satisfaction that each and every absent member of a plaintiff class had minimum contacts with the forum would make the problems of notice and cost discussed in *Eisen* and *Oppenheimer* pale by comparison. Finally, the focus of attention should be on the basic due process rights of those absentee class members. As the discussion above has demonstrated, their due process rights receive full protection through strict attention to the adequacy of the representation they receive.

Without realizing it, the *Gillette* defendants were asking the Court to adopt a joinder approach to class actions. They were asking the Court to treat every individual member of the class just as it would have if the class device were not being used. There is nothing wrong in principle with representation with respect to the issue of personal jurisdiction. Once the premise is accepted that adequacy of representation is a way of satisfying the due process rights of absentee class members, as *Hansberry* suggested, it should not matter whether the absentees are members of a plaintiff class or a defendant class. The court has an initial responsibility for assuring adequacy of representation, as it must be convinced that the requirements of Rule 23 (a) are met throughout the litigation. After decision on the merits, absentees are free to test adequacy in a collateral lawsuit; if representation was inadequate, they receive their day in court. If, as some have suggested,[153] there is a greater danger in defendant classes that representation will be inadequate, because a plaintiff is tempted to select a less-than-vigorous defendant representative, these two safeguards will simply come into play more frequently in defendant actions.

If the rights of the absentees are in fact adequately represented, then those persons should be bound. If representation is inadequate, existing rules of *res judicata* ensure that the absentees will be entitled to make a collateral attack on the judgment and conduct their own litigation. This issue is bound to return to the Court. When it does, the Court should take care to take full account of the implications of the class action device. Both for the reasons mentioned above and in the interest of a consistent approach to class actions, it should permit the representatives to satisfy all personal jurisdiction requirements.

V. CONCLUSION

To postulate a joinder model and a representational model is to impose a certain order on the class action cases of the Supreme Court that the Court itself has not seen fit to acknowledge. Nevertheless, the cases that have explored the relationship between class representative and absentee members, particularly with respect to procedural requirements, reveal that these two approaches have in fact been taken. Nothing has justified or explained the Court's decision in one case to view a requirement as one which every class member must satisfy and in the next case as one which the representative alone may satisfy.

There is a framework within which those decisions can be made. Some problems indeed derive from the substantive law underlying the action. Where the substantive law dictates recourse to all class members, or recourse only to the representative, it should be easy enough for the Court to follow it. Where the issue is truly procedural, the representational approach offers the better way of handling the device of class litigation. A serious adoption of the joinder approach would take the Court back even further than the original Rule 23, which for all its ambivalence about the spurious class action nevertheless permitted it to function as a representative device in some instances.

---

[153] Note, 53 INDIANA L. J. 841, note 109 *supra;* Note, 91 HARV. L. REV. 630, note 109 *supra.*

As long as adequacy of representation is assured, through whatever means seems best suited to the task, there should be no concern beyond the representative's procedural characteristics. This would give appropriate heed to the history of class actions in the United States and best serve the policies behind class actions. The chaos generated by class actions is great enough in other areas. There is room for more certainty in this one.

HOWARD B. ABRAMS

COPYRIGHT, MISAPPROPRIATION, AND PREEMPTION: CONSTITUTIONAL AND STATUTORY LIMITS OF STATE LAW PROTECTION

I. INTRODUCTION

Constitutional and statutory preemption of state laws under the Copyright-Patent Clause of the Constitution[1] and the federal copyright laws[2] has emerged as the decisive issue in a steadily growing number and variety of cases. While the copyright preemption issue has primarily revolved around the hazily defined tort of misappropriation, it has also been raised to challenge the validity of state "anti-blind bidding" statutes,[3] state trade secret laws,[4] and other forms of state actions.[5]

Howard B. Abrams is Associate Professor of Law, University of Detroit School of Law.

[1] U.S. Const. Art I, sec. 8, cl. 8.

[2] 17 U.S.C. §§101-810 (Supp. V 1981). The current Copyright Act was enacted as the General Revision of Copyright Law. Pub. L. No. 94-553, 90 Stat. 2541-602 (1976). The prior Copyright Act, 17 U.S.C. §§1-216 (1976) (repealed 1976; repeal effective Jan. 1, 1978) was the Act of March 4, 1909, ch. 320, 35 Stat. 1075. For all purposes relevant to this article, the 1976 Copyright Act became effective on Jan. 1, 1978. Pub. L. No. 94-553, TRANSITIONAL AND SUPPLEMENTARY PROVISIONS, sec. 102, 90 Stat. 2598-99 (1976). Causes of action arising prior to Jan. 1, 1978, are governed by the 1909 Act even if they are filed or tried after Jan. 1, 1978. The preemption challenge to the tort of misappropriation arises in cases under both the 1976 and the 1909 Acts.

[3] Associated Film Distribution Corp. v. Thornburgh, 683 F.2d 808 (3d Cir. 1982), rev'g, 520 F. Supp. 971 (E.D. Pa. 1981); Allied Artists Pictures Corp. v. Rhodes, 679 F.2d 656 (6th Cir. 1982), aff'g in part, remanding in part, 496 F. Supp. 408 (S.D. Ohio 1980); Warner Bros. v. Wilkinson, 533 F. Supp. 105 (D. Utah 1981).

[4] Warrington Associates, Inc. v. Real-Time Engineering Systems, Inc., 522 F. Supp. 367 (N.D. Ill. 1981); Avco Corp. v. Precision Air Parts, Inc., 1978-1981 Copyright L. Dec. (CCH) ¶ 25,207 (M.D. Ala. 1980), aff'd on other grounds, 672 F.2d 494 (11th Cir. 1982), cert. denied, 103 S. Ct. 450; M. Bryce & Associates, Inc. v. Gladstone, 107 Wis. 2d 241, 319 N.W.2d 907 (Wis. App. 1982), cert. denied, 103 S. Ct. 258.

[5] Association of American Medical Colleges v. Carey, 482 F. Supp. 1358 (N.D.N.Y. 1980)

Copyright in the United States is rooted in the Copyright-Patent Clause of the Constitution[6] which provides:

> The Congress shall have Power ... To promote the Progress of Science and useful Arts, by securing for limited Times to Authors and Inventors the exclusive Right to their respective Writings and Discoveries.

The American copyright doctrine based on this Clause is that the public interest in the creation and dissemination of intellectual works justifies the toleration of the copyright monopoly. The interests of the public are paramount and the rights of the public and the public domain are accorded primacy over the secondary concerns of the authors.[7] Theories of common-law copyright or copyright as a natural right of an author were definitively rejected in *Wheaton v. Peters*,[8] which established American copyright as being a statutory grant whose limits and prerequisites were determined by Congress.

By contrast, the tort of misappropriation first arose as a matter of federal decisional law[9] based on a perceived need to insulate business investments from destructive competition by requiring competing businesses to make independent expenditures to develop competing or identical products and services rather than copying from their rivals. The doctrine found a gradual but generally sympathetic reception in

---

(preliminary injunction issued against the enforcement of the New York Standardized Testing Act, N.Y. Educ. Law §§340-48 (McKinney Supp. 1983)); Morseburg v. Balyon, 621 F.2d 972 (9th Cir.), *cert. denied*, 449 U.S. 983 (1980) (validity of California Resale Royalties Act upheld, Cal. Civ. Code §986 (West 1982)).

[6] U.S. Const. Art. I, sec. 8, cl. 8.

[7] This philosophy is thoroughly engrained in the body of American copyright legislation and decisions. See the Committee Report accompanying the 1909 Copyright Act. H.R. Rep. No. 2222, 60th Cong., 2d Sess. 7 (1909). The 1961 Report of the Register of Copyrights, which began the legislative effort leading to the 1976 Copyright Act, in its opening section on "The Purposes of Copyright" states: "As reflected in the Constitution, the ultimate purpose of copyright legislation is to foster the growth of learning and culture for the public welfare, and the grant of exclusive rights to authors for a limited time is a means to that end." House Comm. on the Judiciary, 87th Cong., 1st Sess., Report of the Register of Copyrights on the General Revision of the U.S. Copyright Law 5 (Comm. Print 1961) (hereinafter cited as Register's Report). The Register's Report also quoted the preceding passage from the House Committee Report on the 1909 Copyright Act. *Ibid.* For a study of the historic evolution and basis of this philosophy, see Abrams, *The Historic Foundation of American Copyright Law: Exploding the Myth of Common Law Copyright*, 29 WAYNE L. REV. 1119 (1983) (hereinafter cited as Abrams, *American Copyright*).

[8] 33 U.S. (8 Pet.) 591 (1834). See Abrams, *American Copyright*, note 7 *supra*, at 1178-87; PATTERSON, COPYRIGHT IN HISTORICAL PERSPECTIVE 203-12 (1968); KAPLAN, AN UNHURRIED VIEW OF COPYRIGHT 26-27 (1967).

[9] The Supreme Court recognized the misappropriation doctrine in International News Service v. Associated Press, 248 U.S. 215 (1918).

the state courts. After *Erie R.R. v. Tompkins*,[10] copyright preemption issues inevitably arose as state law became the source of protection for the commercial exploitation of recorded performances and other forms of intellectual creations.[11] After some judicial uncertainty,[12] the Supreme Court in *Sears, Roebuck & Co. v. Stiffel Co.*[13] and *Compco Corp. v. Day-Brite Lighting, Inc.*[14] adopted a standard of sweeping federal preemption in the copyright and patent areas allegedly derived from the Constitution.[15] In *Goldstein v. California*[16] and *Kewanee Co. v.*

---

[10] 304 U.S. 64 (1938).

[11] Cases concerning the unauthorized duplication of phonograph records include A & M Records, Inc. v. M.V.C. Distributing Corp., 574 F.2d 312 (6th Cir. 1978) (applying Michigan law); Capitol Records, Inc. v. Mercury Records Corp., 221 F.2d 657 (2d Cir. 1955) (2-1, L. Hand, J., dissenting at 664-68) (applying New York law); Capitol Records, Inc. v. Erickson, 2 Cal. App. 3d 526, 82 Cal. Rptr. 798 (1969), *cert. denied*, 398 U.S. 960 (1970); Capitol Records, Inc. v. Spies, 130 Ill. App. 2d 429, 264 N.E.2d 874 (1970); Gai Audio of New York, Inc. v. Columbia Broadcasting System, Inc., 27 Md. App. 172, 340 A.2d 736 (1975); Columbia Broadcasting System, Inc. v. Melody Recordings, Inc., 134 N.J. Super. 368, 341 A.2d 348 (1975); Capitol Records, Inc. v. Greatest Records, Inc., 43 Misc. 2d 878, 252 N.Y.S.2d 553 (1964); Metropolitan Opera Association v. Wagner-Nichols Recorder Corp., 199 Misc. 786, 101 N.Y.S.2d 483 (1950); United Artists Records, Inc. v. Eastern Tape Corp., 19 N.C. App. 207, 198 S.E.2d 452 (1973); Liberty/UA, Inc. v. Eastern Tape Corp., 11 N.C. App. 20, 180 S.E.2d 414 (1971); Columbia Broadcasting System, Inc. v. Custom Recording Co., 258 S.C. 465, 189 S.E.2d 305, *cert. denied*, 409 U.S. 1007 (1972); Mercury Record Productions, Inc. v. Economic Consultants, Inc., 64 Wis. 2d 163, 218 N.W.2d 705 (1974), *appeal dismissed*, 420 U.S. 914 (1975). See also Flexitized, Inc. v. National Flexitized Corp., 335 F.2d 774 (2d Cir. 1964); Waring v. Dunlea, 26 F. Supp. 338 (E.D.N.C. 1939); Compumarketing Services Corp. v. Business Envelope Manufacturers, Inc., 342 F. Supp. 776 (N.D. Ill. 1972); Pittsburgh Athletic Club v. KQV Broadcasting Co., 24 F. Supp. 490 (W.D. Pa. 1938); Mutual Broadcasting System, Inc. v. Muzak Corp., 177 Misc. 489, 30 N.Y.S. 2d 419 (1941); Waring v. WDAS Broadcasting Station, Inc., 327 Pa. 433, 194 A. 631 (1937). But see G. Ricordi & Co. v. Haendler, 194 F.2d 914 (2d Cir. 1952); National Comics Publications, Inc. v. Fawcett Publications, Inc., 191 F.2d 594 (2d Cir. 1951); Fashion Originators Guild v. FTC, 114 F.2d 80 (2d Cir. 1940), *aff'd on other grounds*, 312 U.S. 457 (1941); RCA Manufacturing Co. v. Whiteman, 114 F.2d 86 (2d Cir.), *cert. denied*, 311 U.S. 712 (1940); Cheney Bros. v. Doris Silk Corp., 35 F.2d 279 (2d Cir. 1929), *cert. denied*, 281 U.S. 728 (1930). Federal copyright protection for sound recordings was first provided by the 1971 Sound Recording Amendment which protected all sound recordings made subsequent to its effective date of Feb. 15, 1972. 17 U.S.C. §§1(f), 5(n), 19, 20, 26, 101(e) (1976) (repealed 1976; repeal effective Jan. 1, 1978). Equivalent provisions are incorporated in the 1976 Copyright Revision Act. 17 U.S.C. §§102(a) (7), 106, 114 (Supp. V. 1981). In Goldstein v. California, 412 U.S. 546 (1972), the Supreme Court held that state law protection of phonograph records made prior to February 15, 1972, from unauthorized duplication was not preempted by the Copyright Clause of the Constitution or the copyright laws. See Abrams & Abrams, *Goldstein v. California: Sound, Fury and Significance*, 1975 SUPREME COURT REVIEW 147; Brown, *Publication and Preemption in Copyright Law: Elegiac Reflections on Goldstein v. California*, 22 U.C.L.A. L. REV. 1022 (1975); Goldstein, *Kewanee Oil Co. v. Bicron Corp.: Notes on a Closing Circle*, 1974 SUPREME COURT REVIEW 81; Kurlantzick, *The Constitutionality of State Law Protection of Sound Recordings*, 5 CONN. L. REV. 204 (1972).

[12] See notes 46-68 *infra*.

[13] 376 U.S. 225 (1964).

[14] 376 U.S. 234 (1964).

[15] See text *supra* at note 6.

[16] 412 U.S. 546 (1973).

Bicron Oil Corp.,[17] however, the Court did an abrupt about-face and granted the states broad leeway to provide copyright protection in all areas which Congress had not chosen to regulate directly.

In the wake of *Goldstein* and *Kewanee*, Congress adopted the 1976 Copyright Revision Act[18] whose §301 was intended to provide a statutory resolution of the copyright preemption issues. Section 301 preempts all state laws that provide copyright protection for subject matter eligible for copyright under the federal Act.[19] By this method Congress intended to provide "a single Federal system" of statutory copyright that "would greatly improve the operation of the copyright law and would be much more effective in carrying out the basic constitutional aims of uniformity and the promotion of writing and scholarship."[20] To achieve this desired end, "[t]he declaration of this principle in §301 is intended to be stated in the clearest and most unequivocal language possible, so as to foreclose any conceivable misinterpretation of its unqualified intention that Congress shall act preemptively, and to avoid the development of any vague borderline areas between State and Federal protection."[21]

Contradictory of this expressed hope, copyright preemption litigation has raised a series of nagging and related questions for which the language of §301 fails to provide adequate answers: Is the entire preemptive force of the 1976 Copyright Revision Act and the Copyright-Patent Clause of the Constitution exhausted by §301? If not, what criteria or tests determine if a state statute or case law doctrine is preempted? Where the statute limits the works eligible for copyright to less than what the Constitution allows,[22] should the states be able to provide copyright-like protection for omitted works even where Congress clearly rejected the idea of granting copyright protection to such works?[23] And if §301 is indeed inconclusive, what are the alternatives?

---

[17] 416 U.S. 470 (1974).

[18] 17 U.S.C. §§101-810 (Supp. V 1981).

[19] 17 U.S.C. §301 (Supp. V 1981). For the text of §301, see note 176 *infra.*

[20] H. R. Rep. No. 1476, 94th Cong., 2d Sess. 129 (1976); S. Rep. No. 473, 94th Cong., 1st Sess. 113 (1975) (identical quotation).

[21] H.R. Rep. No. 1476, 94th Cong., 2d Sess. 130 (1976); S. Rep. No. 473, 94th Cong., 1st Sess. 114 (1975) (identical quotation).

[22] 17 U.S.C. §102(a) (Supp. V 1981). Congress deliberately chose the word "works" in §102 rather than the constitutional term "Writings" to make it clear that the categories listed in §102 did not exhaust the limits of what Congress might constitutionally protect under the Copyright-Patent Clause of the Constitution. H.R. Rep. No. 1476, 94th Cong., 2d Sess. 51-52 (1976); see also S. Rep. No. 473, 94th Cong., 1st Sess. 50-51 (1975) (substantially identical).

[23] Areas specifically excluded from the coverage of the 1976 Act include dress designs and

II. THE MISAPPROPRIATION DOCTRINE

The term "misappropriation" or "wrongful appropriation" has come to signify a somewhat hazily defined business tort.[24] It is more easily defined by example than by formula. A rough working definition might be: Misappropriation is a business tort whose elements include the unauthorized taking of the results of another's efforts, typically the startup or developmental costs, in creating a valuable property and using them to provide a competitive product or service in such a way as to obtain an unfair cost saving in the relevant market without any infringement of the injured party's trade identity.[25]

The Supreme Court's decision in *International News Service v. Associated Press*[26] is usually regarded as firmly establishing the misappropriation doctrine.[27] During World War I, International News Service (INS) was barred from using the cable facilities at the battlefront to send dispatches to the agency. Unable to report promptly its own news of the most important events of the day, INS took the war news from early editions of East Coast newspapers on the Associated Press (AP) wire or from the public bulletin boards of AP

---

typeface designs. H.R. Rep. No. 1476, 94th Cong., 2d Sess. 54-55 (1976). The area of the aesthetic design of useful articles was implicitly rejected by the failure to include Title II (Protection of Ornamental Designs of Useful Articles) in the final bill. This had originally been passed by the Senate but was rejected by the House. Compare S. Rep. No. 473, 94th Cong., 1st Sess. 39-47, 161-67 (1975), with H.R. Rep. No. 1476, 94th Cong., 2d Sess. 49-50 (1976). The issue of large-scale integrated circuit designs for computer chips was not considered under the 1976 Act, but is now the subject of pending legislation. S. 1201, 98th Cong., 1st Sess. (1983).

[24] Part of the difficulty of defining the tort of "misappropriation" is that the term is used in cases involving other discrete causes of action as a synonym for "taking." In trademark infringement cases, where the tort consists of a trademark or other identification being confusingly similar to that of a competitor, the courts sometimes use the terms "misappropriation" or "wrongful appropriation" to refer to the infringer's benefit from its competitor's public recognition or good will. A number of trade secret cases also speak in terms of "misappropriating" confidential information. These usages have contributed to the confusion surrounding the misappropriation doctrine and the copyright preemption issue. Such cases are not germane to this article and are only mentioned to warn the reader of this semantic confusion of separate business torts.

[25] *Cf.* Dannay, *The Sears-Compco Doctrine Today: Trademarks and Unfair Competition*, 67 TRADE-MARK REP. 132, 134 (1977).

[26] 248 U.S. 215 (1918).

[27] Earlier cases exist. National Telegraph News Co. v. Western Union Telegraph Co., 119 F. 294 (7th Cir. 1902); Illinois Commission Co. v. Cleveland Telegraph Co., 119 F. 301 (7th Cir. 1902); Fonotipia, Ltd. v. Bradley, 171 F. 951 (C.C.E.D.N.Y. 1909); Bamforth v. Douglass Post Card & Machine Co., 158 F. 355 (C.C.E.D. Pa. 1908); Victor Talking Machine Co. v. Armstrong, 132 F. 711 (C.C.S.D.N.Y. 1904). Of these, the first two are "pure" misappropriation cases on facts remarkably similar to those of *INS*, while the others interleave the doctrine with other grounds of decision.

offices and newspapers and transmitted it over its own wire. Sometimes INS rewrote the dispatches, at other times it sent the AP news reports over its wires verbatim. INS always identified itself rather than AP as the source of the news reports INS distributed. INS also bribed some employees of AP newspapers to relay the stories being carried over the AP wires to INS. The trial court enjoined INS from bribing AP employees or subscribers to violate their duties to AP, but refused to enjoin INS from taking news from AP newspapers and bulletin boards.[28] On appeal, the Second Circuit enjoined INS from this practice as well.[29] The Second Circuit held that "news" as distinct from "facts" was property and thus protected from conversion.[30] INS was also held guilty of unfair competition on the grounds of unfairly claiming credit for AP's work product rather than as misappropriation or "passing off."[31]

The Supreme Court sustained the Second Circuit's ruling but changed the grounds of decision. In disorganized opinion, the majority defined INS's behavior as tortious without granting AP a property right in the news as against the public. The opinion vacillated between tort and property as the basis of liability. First it said:[32]

> But the news element—the information respecting current events contained in the literary production—is not the creation of the writer, but is a report of matters that ordinarily are *publici juris;* it is the history of the day. It is not to be supposed that the framers of the Constitution ... intended to confer upon one who might happen to be the first to report a historic event the exclusive right for any period to spread the knowledge of it.
>
> We need spend no time, however, upon the general question of property in news matter at common law, or the application of the copyright act, since it seems to us the case must turn upon the question of unfair competition in business.... That business consists in maintaining a prompt, sure, steady, and reliable service designed to place the daily events of the world at the breakfast table of the millions at a price that, while of trifling moment to each reader, is sufficient in the aggregate to afford compensation for the cost of gathering and distributing it, with the added profit so

---

[28] Associated Press v. International News Service, 240 F. 983 (S.D.N.Y. 1917) (Hand, J.).

[29] Associated Press v. International News Service, 245 F. 244 (2d Cir. 1917) (2-1).

[30] *Id.* at 248-49. In so ruling the court was consistent with established copyright doctrine both past and present that facts per se are not capable of being copyrighted and that copyright could only be had in the authorship of the particular "expression" of such facts. See also 248 U.S. at 234.

[31] 245 F. at 253.

[32] 248 U.S. at 234-35.

necessary as an incentive to effective action in the commercial world. . . . The parties are competitors in this field; and, on fundamental principles, applicable here as elsewhere, when the rights or privileges of the one are liable to conflict with those of the other, each party is under a duty so to conduct its own business as not unnecessarily or unfairly to injure that of the other.

The Court then argued that news could equitably be regarded as property since it had a certain more or less transient commercial value. As both parties were in the business of selling news to newspapers and ultimately to the public, the Court analogized news to the "stock in trade" of merchants and concluded that news could be regarded as "quasi property" between the parties but not as to the public.[33] Little was done in the opinion to define the elements or other criteria of the form of action thus sanctioned by the Supreme Court.[34]

With the decision of *Erie R.R. v. Tompkins*[35] in 1938, further evolution of the misappropriation doctrine became solely a matter for state law. The states embraced the doctrine, slowly at first but with a steadily growing enthusiasm. The fuzziness of definition that pervades the *INS* opinion made it a flexible tool for subsequent courts to control a fairly wide variety of competitive practices. As the misappropriation doctrine revolves around prohibiting the copying or taking other advantage of a competitor's products or services, it often appears to be a state law substitute for copyright or patent protection. With the development and application of the doctrine placed in the hands of the state courts by *Erie*, it was inevitable that the issue of preemption under the federal copyright and patent laws arose.

III. COPYRIGHT AND PREEMPTION: THE CONSTITUTIONAL CHALLENGE

A. THE COPYRIGHT CLAUSE

Copyright in the United States derives from the Copyright Clause of the Constitution. Little is known of the purpose of the Copyright-Patent Clause beyond what is contained in its language.[36] At

---

[33] *Id.* at 236.

[34] Justice Holmes, joined by Justice McKenna, concurred in the holding of unfair competition insofar as INS had claimed AP's work product as its own. 248 U.S. at 246-48 (Holmes, J., concurring). Justice Brandeis dissented. 248 U.S. at 248-67 (Brandeis, J., dissenting).

[35] 304 U.S. 64 (1938).

[36] See generally Fenning, *The Origin of the Patent and Copyright Clause of the Constitution*, 17 GEO. L. J. 109 (1929); PATTERSON, note 8 *supra*, at 192-96.

the Constitutional Convention, James Madison and Charles Pinckney presented proposals giving Congress copyright and patent powers. The proposals were referred to the Committee of Detail, and on September 5, 1787 the Clause in its final form was adopted without debate.[37] The secondary writings of the constitutional era shed little additional light on the subject.[38]

On its face, the Copyright Clause provides some limits but leaves a number of questions, including preemption, open. The Clause expresses as its purpose "[t]o promote the Progress of Science and useful Arts." It assumes that production of "Writings" by "Authors" and "Discoveries" by "Inventors" will serve this purpose and thus benefit the public. The medium of this promotion is to be Congress and the sanctioned congressional method is the grant of an exclusive right, a monopoly, that must be limited at least in terms of time. The recipient of this monopoly must be an "Author," thus confirming the act of authorship as the threshold requirement for obtaining copyright protection.[39] Finally, the item protected must be a "Writing" in at least

---

[37] MADISON, NOTES OF DEBATES IN THE FEDERAL CONVENTION OF 1787 477-78, 579-81 (Koch ed. 1966); 5 DEBATES ON THE ADOPTION OF THE FEDERAL CONSTITUTION 439-40, 510-12 (J. Elliot ed., 2d ed. 1836); 2 THE RECORDS OF THE FEDERAL CONVENTION OF 1787 324-25, 505-06 (Farrand ed., rev. ed. 1937).

[38] The commentary on the Copyright-Patent Clause found in the Federalist Papers, usually attributed to James Madison, states: "The utility of this power will scarcely be questioned. The copyright of authors has been solemnly adjudged, in Great Britain, to be a right of the common law. The right to useful inventions seems with equal reason to belong to the inventors. The public good fully coincides in both cases with the claims of individuals. The States cannot separately make effectual provision for either of the cases, and most of them have anticipated the decision of this point, by laws passed at the instance of Congress" (Federalist No. 43). This passage is not only brief but somewhat ambiguous. This probably reflects nothing more than that in the public debate over ratification of the proposed constitution, the issue of copyright was comparatively insignificant. This passage does give some indication of the philosophy embodied in the constitutional clause. The "utility" of the power and the "public good" are stressed in the argument, again reinforcing the notion of the public interest as the justification of the copyright system. Also, the right is clearly one of the author, deriving the act of authorship. The ineffectiveness of state law protection is noted, but the reasons for that inadequacy are not given. This passage tells us nothing about the balance, if any, to be struck should these interests be in conflict. See also Abrams, *American Copyright*, note 7 *supra*, at 1175-78. Dean Patterson argues that the first Copyright Act, Act of May 31, 1790, 1 Stat. 124 (Peters ed. 1845), clearly shows that the first Congress conceived of copyright as a statutory incentive designed to promote social goals rather than as a natural or property right of an author. PATTERSON, note 8 *supra*, at 197-202.

[39] The constitutional limitation of copyright to works of "Authors" has been construed to require that any works must be "original" as a necessary precondition of attaining copyright protection. 17 U.S.C. §102 (Supp. V 1981). The term "original" in copyright law means independent origination with little or no concern for aesthetic merit or creative genius. Bleistein v. Donaldson Lithographing Co., 188 U.S. 239 (1903) (Holmes, J.), is usually considered the classic case on this issue. See also L. Batlin & Son, Inc. v. Snyder, 536 F.2d 486 (2d Cir. 1976) (en banc), *rev'g* 187 U.S.P.Q. (BNA) 721 (2d Cir. 1975), *cert. denied*, 429 U.S. 857 (1976). This low threshold is really little more than a prohibition on copying, however, it does serve to prevent copyrighting of public domain sources and thus lessen the scope of the copyright monopoly.

some accepted sense of the word.[40] On the preemption issue, the constitutional language neither specifically endorses nor prohibits state law copyright protection.

The copyright preemption issue is inescapably tied to the unfair competition tort of misappropriation. Like copyright infringement, the gist of the tort of misappropriation is wrongful copying, and the remedy sought invariably includes a prohibition or restriction on the copying of the plaintiff's product. The misappropriation doctrine often seems to provide copyright or patent protection under another name.[41]

B. SOUND RECORDINGS: THE BATTLEGROUND FOR PREEMPTION

To compound the problem, copyright law has not always responded intelligently to advances in technology. New technologies made possible new products and new media for the commercial exploitation of creative works. These increasingly diverse types of subject matter and methods of communication and exploitation often fit clumsily into the existing copyright laws. These problems were exacerbated by the expansion and improvement of reproductive technologies which allowed the copiers to take advantage of the original manufacturer's developmental and startup expenditures rather than making their own. This gave the copiers a larger competitive price advantage over the originators and permitted a widespread dispersion of the copying process. Whether by accident or design, lack of congressional foresight or judicial obtuseness, the copyright laws did not always adequately define what types of works were protected or the extent of the protection. Where copyright protection was unavailable resort was made to the misappropriation doctrine as an alternate source of protection.

---

[40] The Supreme Court has defined the constitutional term "Writings" to "include any physical rendering of the fruits of creative intellectual or aesthetic labor." Goldstein v. California, 412 U.S. 546, 561 (1973). The subject-matter coverage of the 1976 Copyright Act is deliberately less than all that might be included within the constitutional term "Writings." Notes 22, 23 supra. See also Staff Comment, The Meaning of "Writings" in the Copyright Clause of the Constitution, 31 N.Y.U. L. REV. 1253 (1956).

[41] The patent laws provide a closely related basis for a preemption challenge to some forms of state law unfair competition and such cases as Sears, Roebuck & Co. v. Stiffel Co., 376 U.S. 225 (1964), Compco Corp. v. Day-Brite Lighting, Inc., 376 U.S. 234 (1964), and Kewanee Oil Co. v. Bicron Corp., 416 U.S. 470 (1974), are an essential part of the copyright preemption analysis. See text infra accompanying notes 69-75, 104-09.

Although the tort of misappropriation has been extended to cover many different situations, its major development subsequent to *INS* was in the series of cases revolving around sound recordings.[42] In §1(e) of the 1909 Copyright Act,[43] Congress had left a perceived gap in the copyright protection of recorded music by limiting the rights of songwriters and ignoring those of performers in recorded musical compositions.[44] As copyright protection was unavailable to prevent unauthorized duplication of phonograph records, resort was made to the misappropriation doctrine as an alternate source of protection.[45] It was on this issue that the preemption challenge to the misappropriation doctrine emerged most clearly.

C. CONSTITUTIONAL COPYRIGHT PREEMPTION: THE JUDICIAL VACILLATION

1. *The Learned Hand Decisions.* Following hard on the heels of *Erie R.R. v. Tompkins,*[46] the Second Circuit became the principal battleground for the issues of copyright preemption of the burgeoning doctrine of misappropriation, with Judge Learned Hand cast in the role of principal protagonist of an expansive view of federal constitutional preemption. Judge Hand eloquently articulated his philosophy in a

---

[42] See note 11 *supra.*

[43] 17 U.S.C. §1(e) (1976) (repealed 1976; repeal effective Jan. 1, 1978).

[44] The 1909 Copyright Act set the stage for much of the subsequent litigation of the misappropriation doctrine and the copyright preemption issue by the clumsy and confusing language it employed to resolve the problem of infringing player piano rolls, 1909's equivalent to phonograph records and prerecorded tapes. *Id.* The problem arose when the Supreme Court held in White-Smith Music Publishing Co. v. Apollo Co., 209 U.S. 1 (1908), that perforated player piano rolls were not copies within the meaning of the then current copyright act since they were not understandable by the unaided human eye. Congress was persuaded to amend the pending copyright revision bills to make the unauthorized duplication of player piano rolls, phonograph records, and cylinders an infringement of copyright. However, Congress was afraid of the "establishment of a mechanical-music trust." H.R. Rep. No. 2222, 60th Cong., 2d Sess. 7 (1909). See generally *id.* 4-9. To extend copyright protection to mechanical devices for reproducing music while preventing the formation of "a great music trust," *id.* at 8, Congress hit on the scheme of a compulsory license which it embodied in §1(e) of the 1909 Act. 17 U.S.C. §1(e) (1976) (repealed 1976; repeal effective Jan. 1, 1978). The copyright owner of the underlying musical composition had the exclusive right to make the first reproduction, but thereafter had to permit anyone else to make a competing reproduction conditioned on the payment of a royalty of 2 cents for each copy manufactured. *Cf.* 17 U.S.C. §114, 115 (Supp. V 1981). Congress did not address the issue of whether the performer, as distinct from the composer, had any rights in the performance of music rendered by one of these "mechanical" devices. The 1909 Copyright Act was silent on the subject of performers' rights, and there is absolutely nothing in the legislative history to show that Congress ever considered this issue. H.R. Rep. No. 2222, 60th Cong., 2d Sess. 4-9 (1909).

[45] See cases cited at note 11 *supra.*

[46] 304 U.S. 64 (1938).

series of decisions involving efforts to prevent copying of subject matter which was unprotected by the copyright laws.[47] The core issue is not one of moral rights or wrongs, but of the primacy of federal law. To Judge Hand, the copyright scheme embodied in the Constitution did not permit the recognition of "common-law property" in intellectual works once published, regardless of whether such works are within the ambit of statutory protection. It is for Congress both to prescribe the extent of copyright protection and to determine what is eligible subject matter. Subject matter left unprotected and rights left unrecognized by Congress belonged to the public domain once they were published. State law protection, whether based on "common-law property" or unfair competition, is an intolerable invasion of the rights of the public under the federal copyright scheme. State law may not prohibit the copying of that which the federal law permits to be copied. Whatever rights the claimant might have are to be subordinated to rights of the public absent a congressional grant of monopoly to the contrary.[48]

2. *The Pendulum Swings:* Metropolitan Opera *and* Capitol Records. Notwithstanding Judge Hand's strictures on the necessity for constitutional preemption of state protection of intellectual property under the guise of unfair competition, the state courts simply ignored the issue. In *Metropolitan Opera Ass'n v. Wagner-Nichols Recorder Corp.,*[49] the fountainhead for subsequent state court decisions protecting phonograph records from unauthorized copying, the defendant was enjoined from recording the radio broadcasts of performances by New York's Metropolitan Opera and then making and selling phonograph records derived from these recordings.

The court characterized the defendant's behavior as having "[a]ppropriated and exploited for their own benefit the result of the

---

[47] Capitol Records, Inc. v. Mercury Records Corp., 221 F.2d 657, 664-68 (2d Cir. 1955) (Hand, J., dissenting); G. Ricordi & Co. v. Haendler, 194 F.2d 914 (2d Cir. 1952); National Comics Publications, Inc. v. Fawcett Publications, Inc., 191 F.2d 594 (2d Cir. 1951); Fashion Originators Guild v. FTC, 114 F.2d 80 (2d Cir. 1940), *aff'd on other grounds*, 312 U.S. 457 (1941); RCA Manufacturing Co. v. Whiteman, 114 F.2d 86 (2d Cir.), *cert. denied*, 311 U.S. 712 (1940); Cheney Bros. v. Doris Silk Corp., 35 F.2d 279 (2d Cir. 1929), *cert. denied*, 281 U.S. 728 (1930).

[48] The concentration of the copyright industries in New York during Judge Hand's tenure on the bench afforded him the unique opportunity to be dominant judicial expositor of the law of copyright in the United States. Rarely, if ever, has a similar opportunity presented itself to a single lower court judge to so greatly control the evolution of doctrine in a given field. Judge Hand was the first to deal with the issue of constitutional copyright preemption and to consciously seek to resolve that issue. To this day his opinions on this issue are the most thoroughly reasoned judicial articulation of the principles he espoused. For an extended appreciation of Judge Hand's copyright jurisprudence, see KAPLAN, note 8 *supra*, at 41-74 (1966).

[49] 199 Misc. 786, 101 N.Y.S.2d 483 (1950), *aff'd*, 279 A.D. 632, 107 N.Y.S.2d 795 (1951).

expenditures, labor and skill of the Metropolitan Opera and American Broadcasting,"[50] wrongfully interfered with and impaired the value of the various contracts, impaired the earnings from the sale of authorized records, "traded on and appropriated the value of the name and reputation"[51] of the Met, and endangered the Met's reputation by selling records of inferior quality. The court noted that New York had extended the doctrine of unfair competition beyond the cases of "palming off" and had granted "relief in cases where there was no fraud on the public, but only a misappropriation for the commercial advantage of one person of a benefit or 'property right' belonging to another."[52] The court invoked the misappropriation doctrine on the strength of *INS*[53] and *Fonotipia, Ltd. v. Bradley*,[54] and ultimately justified its expansive view of unfair competition "on the broader principle that property rights of commercial value are to be and will be protected from any form of commercial immorality."[55]

Several points are worth noting. First is the court's complete failure to discuss the preemption issue. No thought is given to the allocation of authority over copyrights and patents by the Constitution or the interplay between the state law of misappropriation and the federal copyright statute. Second, the court did not consider the consequences of its decision. The court was effectively creating a perpetual copyright in the performances of the Metropolitan Opera. Not only could they not be copied now—they could never be copied in the future. The court's prohibition of copying on the grounds of misappropriation is equivalent to a perpetual common-law copyright in the performances. Yet the court's opinion shows no concern with any of the limitations that surround conventional statutory copyright to insure that the monopoly serves the public purpose of encouraging creation and dissemination of intellectual works without unduly restricting the public's interest in easy availability and ready access.[56]

---

[50] *Id.* at 791, 101 N.Y.S.2d at 487.

[51] *Id.*

[52] *Id.* at 793, 101 N.Y.S.2d at 489.

[53] International News Service v. Associated Press, 248 U.S. 215 (1918).

[54] 171 F. 951 (C.C.E.D.N.Y. 1909).

[55] 199 Misc. at 796, 101 N.Y.S.2d at 492.

[56] Copyrights are of limited duration; only "authors" can obtain protection; the subject matter must be both constitutionally and statutorily eligible; only the particularized expression of the idea—not the idea itself—is protected; and the protection is circumscribed by the "fair use" and other doctrines. On the final point, see generally SELTZER, EXEMPTIONS AND FAIR USE IN COPYRIGHT (1977).

Third, the court enthusiastically embraced *INS* and the misappropriation doctrine as the basis for a sweeping regulation of competitive behavior. The court, by accident or design, gave the greatest scope for judicial sanction of monopoly. The court proclaimed an unlimited doctrine potentially applicable to all forms of competitive endeavors. This stands in marked contrast with Judge Hand's repeated attempts to limit *INS* to its facts.[57]

It is easy to accept *Metropolitan Opera:* the defendant's behavior was a blatant and distasteful example of capitalizing on another's expenditure of time, effort, and money to that other's disadvantage. In many ways it is a classic case of trademark infringement, as the defendant represented his product as that of the Metropolitan Opera without the Met's consent.[58] But it is not the noxiousness of the defendant's behavior that is at stake in the preemption analysis, but rather where the authority rests between the federal and state governments to make the judgments as to what is acceptable and unacceptable copying.

Metropolitan Opera is clearly antithetical to the position of Judge Hand. To Judge Hand, the ultimate purpose of the copyright monopoly is to benefit the public. This mandate is embodied in the constitutional Clause by its stated purpose of promoting "the Progress of Science and Useful Arts" which requires that Congress define and limit the monopoly given as the incentive for creation. To grant a perpetual monopoly without any justification that it is in the long-range interest of the public is bad enough, that it is done by a state court where the Constitution has empowered Congress to undertake that task is a violation of the constitutional allocation of powers between state and federal authority.[59]

In *Capitol Records, Inc. v. Mercury Records Corp.,*[60] Judge Hand's position was rejected by the Second Circuit. Prior to World War II, Telefunken, a German company, granted Capitol Records an exclusive license to manufacture phonograph records from masters owned by Telefunken. After the war, the Czechoslovakian tribunal forfeited Telefunken's rights in the master recordings in Czechoslovakia. Mercury then obtained a license to distribute records made from the

---

[57] Note 47 *supra.*
[58] *Cf.* note 31 *supra.*
[59] See note 47 *supra.*
[60] 221 F.2d 657 (2d Cir. 1955).

Czechoslovakian masters in the United States. Capitol sued Mercury on grounds of unfair competition and the case came into the federal courts as a diversity matter.

The majority opinion first ruled that an interpretative performance of another's composition was a "Writing" within the Copyright Clause of the Constitution and thus Congress could provide copyright protection for recordings of such performances. But no such provision had been made. Stating that the case was controlled by the law of New York, the majority cited *Metropolitan Opera* and concluded "that the inescapable result of that case is that where the originator, or the assignee of the originator, of records of performances by musical artists puts those records on public sale, his act does not constitute a dedication of the right to copy and sell the records."[61] On this basis the injunction against Mercury was sustained. No further inquiry into the preemption issues was made.

In dissent,[62] Judge Hand agreed with the majority that (1) the performance of a work would qualify as a "Writing" under the Copyright Clause of the Constitution, (2) such performances were not included in the subject-matter coverage of the 1909 Copyright Act,[63] and (3) if the case were to be decided solely as an issue of New York law, then *Metropolitan Opera* dictated a finding in favor of the plaintiff. He then noted that if the copyright statute provided protection for such recordings, then clearly the sale of the records would have published the performance and dedicated whatever common-law rights existed to the public domain.[64] He continued:[65]

> I therefore recognize the plausibility of the possible argument that
> ... the courts of New York should be deemed free, sub nomine
> "unfair competition," to determine what conduct shall constitute a
> "publication" of a "work" not covered by the Copyright Act. It
> would then follow that they could grant to an author a perpetual
> monopoly, although he exploited the "work" with all the freedom
> he would have enjoyed, had it been copyrighted. I cannot believe
> that the failure of Congress to include within the Act all that the
> Clause covers should give the states so wide a power. To do so
> would pro tanto defeat the overriding purpose of the Clause, which
> was to grant only for "limited Times" the untrammeled exploitation

---

[61] *Id.* at 663.

[62] *Id.* at 664–68.

[63] See text accompanying notes 42–45 *supra.*

[64] 221 F.2d at 666.

[65] *Id.* at 666–67.

of an author's "Writings." Either he must be content with such circumscribed exploitation as does not constitute "publication," or he must eventually dedicate his "work" to the public. . . . I would hold the clause has that much effect *ex proprio vigore;* and that the states are not free to follow their own notions as to when an author's right shall be unlimited in both user and duration. . . . I submit that, once it is settled that a "work" is in that class, [constitutional "Writings"] the Clause enforces upon the author the choice I have just mentioned; and, if so, it must follow that it is a federal question whether he has published the "work."

Judge Hand argues that the ultimate dedication of any work to the public domain is necessary to fulfill the constitutional mandate "[t]o promote the Progress of Science and useful Arts." The copyright power is entrusted to Congress, and only Congress can determine the works to be given copyright protection and the extent of such protection. Gaps in the statutory scheme can only be changed by Congress. The states may not act even where Congress has not done so, as this would defeat the purpose of the constitutional clause. Unlimited monopoly protection based on a state's law of unfair competition is too great a distortion of the constitutional purpose of copyright to be tolerated.

Judge Hand also urged that the nature of the subject matter required the uniformity of being governed by federal law rather than risk the balkanization of conflicting state court decisions.[66] Since the decision would only be effective in New York, if other states permitted Mercury to manufacture the records New York could not exclude them. Acknowledging that "[u]nhappily we cannot deal with the situation as we should like, because the copyrightability of such works is *casus omissus* from the Act," nonetheless he was "not satisfied that the result is unjust, when the alternative is a monopoy unlimited both in time and in user."[67]

Following *Metropolitan Opera* and *Capitol Records,* the position of the law apparently was that the misappropriation doctrine stemming from *INS* was not preempted by either the Copyright Clause of the Constitution or the federal copyright statutes. It is quite striking that the preemption challenge had been articulated strongly and eloquently by perhaps the leading jurist of the day only to fail, while the opposite view had prevailed without even addressing the issue. This lack of

---

[66] *Id.* at 667.
[67] *Id.*

coherent response to the preemption challenge is more startling when it is recognized that the actual and articulated limits of the misappropriation doctrine had been broadened into a far stronger monopoly than first indicated by the *INS* decision.[68]

3. *And Swings Again:* Sears *and* Compco. These issues reached the Supreme Court in the companion cases of *Sears, Roebuck & Co. v. Stiffel Co.*[69] and *Compco Co. v. Day-Brite Lighting Inc.*[70] These cases arose as suits for the infringement of a design patent and for unfair competition in a pole lamp and a lighting fixture, respectively. Both trial courts invalidated the design patents but granted relief on the grounds of unfair competition.[71] The Seventh Circuit affirmed, basing its rulings on the Illinois law of unfair competition.[72] The Supreme Court reversed. In sweeping terms, Justice Black articulated a broad standard of federal preemption in the patent and copyright areas. He stated that "because of the federal patent laws a state may not, when the article is unpatented and uncopyrighted, prohibit the copying of the article itself or award damages for such copying."[73] Justice Black then held:[74]

> [W]hen an article is unprotected by a patent or a copyright, state law may not forbid others to copy that article. To forbid copying would interfere with the federal policy, found in Art. I, §8, cl.8, of the Constitution and in the implementing federal statutes, of allowing free access to copy whatever the federal patent and copyright laws leave in the public domain.

Sears and *Compco* announce a far-reaching standard of federal constitutional preemption. Justice Black adopts the Hand position and shares much of Hand's values, if not his meticulousness of analysis. Justice Black perceives a pervasive federal scheme that encourages free competition and imitation, with copyrights and patents being the only two carefully permitted and constitutionally authorized exceptions. Broad preemption is required by the "federal policy" that is derived from the Copyright-Patent Clause. Competitors are free to copy whatever is not exempted from the public domain by the federal

---

[68] *Cf.* cases cited at note 19 *supra*.

[69] 376 U.S. 225 (1964).

[70] 376 U.S. 234 (1964).

[71] *Id.* at 226 (*Sears*); *id.* at 234–36 (*Compco*).

[72] Stiffel Co. v Sears, Roebuck & Co., 313 F.2d 115 (7th Cir. 1963); Day-Brite Lighting, Inc. v. Compco Corp., 311 F.2d 26 (7th Cir. 1962).

[73] 376 U.S. at 232–33.

[74] *Id.* at 237.

statutes, thus providing the public with the benefit of greater market competition. The states may not restrict the right of the public to copy any items unprotected by the statutes. Only Congress, under the specific authority of the Constitution, may remove such items from the public domain. The balancing of monopoly incentive and public interest is constitutionally delegated to Congress for determination, and the states may not impinge on this congressional power.

The most serious problem with the opinions in *Sears* and *Compco* is that the underlying constitutional rationale for their position is neither seriously analyzed nor fully articulated. The basic assumptions remain inchoate, and, as a result, the opinions lose much of their cogency.[75]

Sears and *Compco* were perceived as overruling *INS* as a matter of federal law and as preempting the states from adopting its doctrine. Possibly the most notable and dramatic case to have arisen is *DeCosta v. Columbia Broadcasting System, Inc.*,[76] where the plaintiff had originated the character of Paladin, which CBS stole for the central character in its highly successful television series, *Have Gun Will Travel*. Plaintiff recovered a verdict in the trial court on the grounds of misappropriation.[77] The First Circuit reversed, stating:[78]

> Moreover, the leading case affording a remedy for mere copying, *International News Service v. Associated Press*, is no longer authoritative for at least two reasons: it was decided as a matter of general federal law before the decision in *Erie R.R. v. Tompkins;* and, as it prohibited the copying of published written matter that had not been copyrighted (indeed, as news it could not be copyrighted), it has clearly been overruled by the Supreme Court's recent decisions in *Sears, Roebuck & Co. v. Stiffel Co.*, and *Compco Corp. v. Day-Brite Lighting, Inc.* While this normally would not prevent the state court from adopting the reasoning of *INS* in fashioning a rule of state law, we think it important to consider the scope of state power in this area in view of *Sears* and *Compco. . . .*

---

[75] Justice Black's views share much of Judge Hand's values and constitutional concern, if not his meticulousness of analysis and clarity of argument. See text accompanying notes 46-48, 62-67 *supra.*

[76] 377 F.2d 315 (1st Cir.) *cert. denied*, 389 U.S. 1007 (1967). But cf. DeCosta v. Columbia Broadcasting System, 520 F.2d 499 (1st Cir. 1975), *cert. denied*, 423 U.S. 1073 (1976), discussed *infra* note 111.

[77] Without using the word "misappropriation," the court characterized DeCosta's claim by stating his "judgment can only be supported on a rule of law which would allow recovery upon proof of creation by the plaintiff and copying by the defendant and nothing else." *Id.* at 318.

[78] *Id.* at 318-19. But cf. Columbia Broadcasting System v. DeCosta, 520 F.2d 499 (1st Cir. 1975), *cert. denied*, 423 U.S. 1073 (1976), discussed *infra* note 111.

Congress has established a procedural scheme of protection by notice and registration. The necessary implication of this approach, we conclude, is that absent compliance with the scheme, the federal policy favoring free dissemination of intellectual creations prevails. Thus, if a "writing" is within the scope of the constitutional clause, and Congress has not protected it, whether deliberately or by unexplained omission, it can be freely copied.

In a series of cases involving unauthorized duplication and sale of phonograph records, however, the state courts consistently invoked the authority of *INS* to grant relief on the grounds of misappropriation,[79] notwithstanding *Sears* and *Compco*. Typical is *Capitol Records, Inc. v. Spies*.[80] The defendant bought single copies of plaintiff's records at retail from which he made and sold tape recordings. The plaintiff had spent between $50,000 and $75,000 to make the master recording of each record from which it duplicated its copies for sale. Plaintiff sought an injunction and included in the complaint a count for wrongful appropriation of its work, skill, and expenditures. The trial court denied plaintiff's motion for a temporary injunction, stating that it was compelled to do so by *Sears* and *Compco*,[81] but the Illinois Appellate Court brushed aside this argument:[82]

> We believe that the facts of the instant case are clearly distinguishable from the *Sears* and *Compco* decisions. . . . Whereas in those cases the court was concerned with the copying of products which were not patented, in the instant case Spies was actually appropriating another's property. Rather than the *Sears* and *Compco* decisions, we find that the case of *International News Service v. Associated Press* is controlling.

The court states there is a difference between "misappropriating another's property" and copying an unpatented article, but this only begs the question. No real explanation of the perceived difference is ever given. As what Spies did was to copy an uncopyrighted article, it is hard to understand what difference between the two activities the court was trying to articulate. Whatever the reason, *INS* rather than *Sears* and *Compco* was consistently deemed the controlling precedent in the record piracy cases.

---

[79] Note 11 *supra*.
[80] 130 Ill. App. 2d 429, 264 N.E.2d 874 (1970).
[81] *Id.* at 431, 264 N.E.2d at 875.
[82] *Id.* at 432, 264 N.E.2d at 876.

4. *And Yet Again:* Goldstein *and* Kewanee. *Goldstein v. California*[83] marked a fundamental shift on the issue of constitutional copyright preemption of state laws. Goldstein was convicted under a California statute[84] which made it a misdemeanor to make unauthorized duplications of sound recordings. In a five-to-four decision, the Court upheld the validity of the California statute. Writing for the majority, Chief Justice Burger treated the California Act as if it were a state copyright statute rather than an unfair competition law.[85] Chief Justice Burger stated the test for preemption was that of *Cooley v. Board of Wardens*[86] and *Southern Pacific R.R. v. Arizona.*[87] Was the subject matter of the regulation national or local in its character? This was a massive shift in constitutional doctrine. The standards the Chief Justice was employing for determining preemption issues under the Copyright Clause[88] were those developed for the Commerce Clause.[89] No consideration whatsoever was given to whether the two Clauses could or should be so interchanged.

There is no rational basis for this change. The two Clauses address separate problems in the federal system and embody different approaches to different subject matter. The Commerce Clause is a naked allocation of power over commercial activity to the federal government. Its underlying rationale is to assure federal authority adequate power to regulate interstate transactions so the national government can protect national interests. Nothing is said in the Commerce Clause about what values or purposes shall be served by any authorized legislation.

By contrast, the Copyright Clause not only allocates power to Congress, it stipulates values that shape and constrain the exercise of that power.[90] The fundamental premise of the Copyright Clause is that it is in the public interest to have a plentiful and accessible supply of intellectual works to "promote the Progress of Science and useful Arts." To achieve this goal, Congress may grant limited monopoly protection to "Authors and Inventors" as an incentive to produce "Writings and Discoveries." The public interest had consistently been

---

[83] 412 U.S. 546 (1973).
[84] Cal. Penal Code §653h (West 1970).
[85] 412 U.S. at 552.
[86] 12 How. 299 (1851).
[87] 325 U.S. 761 (1945).
[88] U.S. Const. Art. I, sec. 8, cl. 8.
[89] U.S. Const. Art. I, sec. 8, cl. 3: "The Congress shall have Power . . . To regulate Commerce with foreign Nations, and among the several States, and with the Indian Tribes."
[90] See notes 6-8 *supra* and accompanying text.

accorded primacy among the copyright values. The various limitations on the scope of copyright protection are reflections of this primacy of the public interest and serve to mitigate the inherent dangers of the copyright monopoly. The Commerce Clause has no such values or concerns and, on a constitutional level, no concerns about the limitation of monopoly or strictures limiting legislative or judicial actions by concepts of public interest.

This is not uncharted territory. The whole stream of copyright and patent litigation and legislation has pointed to the Copyright-Patent Clause as the constitutional fountainhead for analyzing these problems. From *Wheaton v. Peters*[91] to *Sears-Compco* and beyond,[92] availability and access to intellectual works and an insurance of the public domain was the primary factor in the American copyright equation.[93] Prior to *Goldstein*, it had never been remotely suggested that the Commerce Clause was an appropriate constitutional standard for the analysis of copyright or patent cases.

By shifting the preemption analysis to the Commerce Clause, Chief Justice Burger was able to avoid considering the lengthy history and jurisprudence of American copyright law. Any issues of the public interest, the public domain, or problems of a perpetual monopoly were ignored. There is no justification given for this shift to the Commerce Clause. Having established the distinction between national and local subject matter as the litmus paper test for preemption, Chief Justice Burger proceeded to analyze whether constitutional "Writings" were to be considered national or local subject matter. In an all but bizarre passage, he wrote:[94]

> Although the copyright clause recognizes the potential benefits of a national system, it does not indicate that all writings are of national interest or that state legislation is, in all cases, unnecessary or precluded. . . . In view of that enormous diversity, it is unlikely that all citizens in all parts of the country place the same importance on works relating to all subjects. Since the subject matter to which the copyright clause is addressed may thus be of purely local importance and not worthy of national attention or protection, we cannot discern such an unyielding national interest as to require an inference that state power to grant copyrights has been relinquished to *exclusive* federal control.

[91] 33 U.S. (8 Pet.) 591 (1834).

[92] Sears, Roebuck & Co. v. Stiffel Co., 376 U.S. 225 (1964); Compco Co. v. Day-Brite Lighting, Inc., 376 U.S. 234 (1964); discussed *supra* at text accompanying notes 69-75.

[93] See generally Abrams, *American Copyright*, note 7 *supra*.

[94] 412 U.S. at 556-57.

The Chief Justice's analysis of the national or local nature of the subject matter of copyright in general and of sound recordings in particular is even more dismal than the choice of the Commerce Clause as the appropriate starting point for the preemption analysis of a state copyright law. His seemingly obvious statement that "it is unlikely that all citizens in all parts of the country place the same importance on works relating to all subjects" does not at all support his conclusion that "the subject matter to which the copyright clause is addressed may be of purely local importance." In effect, he is generalizing from a singular example of a given "writing" to a statement about a generic class of "writings." It is a verbal shell game. To say that some particular book, print, song, record, or other writing may have only geographically limited appeal, or that tastes may vary locally, is unarguable but irrelevant. Copyright is concerned with "writings" generically. To conclude that the generic categories of books, prints, songs, records or other writings, or indeed all writings are of local interest, as Chief Justice Burger does, is a logical fallacy. The proposition that the constitutional category of "Writings" is not of national interest is ludicrous. Even generic categories of writings such as phonograph records are not inherently of "purely local interest." The reasoning of *Goldstein* affords no sensible explanation or justification for the assertions.[95]

When the Chief Justice turned to the question whether the federal statute required preemption of the California law his standard was *Hines v. Davidowitz:* whether the challenged state law "stands as an obstacle to the accomplishment and execution of the full purposes and objectives of Congress."[96] The Court reasoned Congress had left the area of recorded performances "unattended" in the 1909 Copyright Act,[97] leaving the states free to legislate until such time as Congress might occupy the field.[98] The issue of a conflict between state law and the federal copyright act was avoided by interpreting the federal law so that it did not cover the type of activity the state law sought to regulate. *Goldstein* thus suggests that every subject-matter issue arising

---

[95] The *Goldstein* opinion does cite six patents that were granted by the states. 412 U.S. at 557, n.13. However, these patents were all granted prior to the adoption of the Constitution so they are logically irrelevant.

[96] 312 U.S. 52, 67 (1941), cited at 412 U.S. 561.

[97] For a brief discussion of the lack of protection for performances of music embodied in sound recordings as distinct from the music performed under the 1909 Copyright Act, see note 44 *supra.*

[98] 412 U.S. at 569-70.

in copyright preemption requires an examination of the relevant congressional history.

Chief Justice Burger explicitly stated that the court was reaffirming *Sears* and *Compco*.[99] He accomplished this by reading *Sears* and *Compco* to hold that where an article is a member of a class of articles (books, machines, etc.) which are eligible for copyright or patent protection, but the particular article fails to meet the threshold standards for such protection,[100] then state law may not provide the protection that the federal law denied. If the object cannot obtain federal patent or copyright protection because it is generically ineligible, however, then the states may protect it because federal law left the area "unattended." The issue of eligibility is to be measured by the coverage of the statute rather than the purpose of the constitutional Clause, a questionable reading at best.[101]

Goldstein's conclusion is not untenable and can be justified under the Copyright Clause.[102] The danger is that *Goldstein* essentially justifies state law protection of any item of skill or manufacture regardless of the subject matter and without any concern for public interest or equivalent limiting factors imposed on the copyright and patent monopolies. Again, the fundamental criticism of the *Goldstein* opinion is that it ignores the Copyright Clause limitation on monopoly to "limited Times." To treat this merely as a limit on federal power without inquiry into its underlying policy is too naive and superficial to be acceptable.[103]

In *Kewanee*,[104] the Supreme Court considered the standards for determining whether a state trade secret law conflicted with the federal

---

[99] *Id.* at 571.

[100] For patents, the standards are novelty, utility, and nonobviousness. Graham v. John Deere Co., 383 U.S. 1 (1966), is usually considered the classic in this field. Its companion case, United States v. Adams, 383 U.S. 39 (1966), also merits study in this regard. For copyright the standard is originality. See note 39 *supra*.

[101] This reading of *Sears-Compco* seeks to explain those decisions on the basis that the design patents on the objects sought to be protected were invalid. Thus the items were members of a class which was generically eligible for design patent protection but failed to meet the standards for a valid patent, whereas phonograph records were generically ineligible for copyright. *Goldstein*'s rereading of *Sears* and *Compco* would render them compatible with *Goldstein*. However, this effort to resolve the contradictions between the opinions is really not convincing. It ignores the thrust of Justice Black's opinions, whose sweeping language suggests the preemption of all state intellectual property protection is necessary to give the federal scheme its rational scope. See Abrams & Abrams, *Goldstein v. California: Sound, Fury & Significance*, 1975 SUPREME COURT REVIEW 147, 175-77.

[102] See notes 36-38 *supra*.

[103] See notes 83-101 *supra*.

[104] 416 U.S. 470 (1974). *Kewanee* is often regarded as the companion or counterpart to *Goldstein*. Where *Goldstein* was the vehicle for the Burger Court to establish its analysis on the issue of

patent statute and was therefore invalid under the Supremacy Clause.[105] The plaintiff had developed a technique for growing larger radiation-detecting crystals than their competitors. Rather than seek a patent on this technique, the plaintiff relied on trade secret protection. The defendant company, formed by former employees of the plaintiff, produced competitive crystals employing the plaintiff's secret techniques. The District Court granted injunctive relief under Ohio's trade secret law.[106] The Sixth Circuit reversed, holding that the state law was preempted by the federal patent law.[107]

For the majority, Chief Justice Burger first summarily resolved the issue of constitutional preemption on the authority of *Goldstein*. Then, relying on *Hines v. Davidowitz*,[108] he embarked on an extended consideration of the underlying policies embodied in the patent laws (balancing the incentive for invention with the public dissemination of knowledge) and state trade secret laws (maintaining standards of commercial ethics and encouraging invention), the extent to which the availability of state trade secret protection might provide an incentive for inventors to avoid the patent system and thus frustrate the patent policy of disclosure, and other aspects of the overlapping spheres of patent and trade secret protection. He concluded that "the extension of trade secret protection to clearly patentable [but unpatented] inventions does not conflict with the patent policy of disclosure."[109]

Kewanee emphasized standards used where there was a potential conflict between state law and federal statutes. The analysis turns on identifying the underlying goals and policies of the federal statute to see if the operation of the state statute will seriously hinder them. The analytic method used in *Kewanee* suggests that even if the *Goldstein* inquiry shows that a subject matter has not been left unattended by Congress, a further inquiry must be made. The factors which *Kewanee* considered included the underlying purposes of the statutes and the overall impact of validating the state statute on the goals of the federal

---

constitutional copyright preemption, *Kewanee* provided the equivalent vehicle for statutory preemption. See Goldstein, *Kewanee Oil Co. v. Bicron Corp.: Notes on a Closing Circle*, 1974 SUPREME COURT REVIEW 81; Abrams & Abrams, *Goldstein v. California: Sound, Fury & Significance*, 1975 SUPREME COURT REVIEW 147, 178-82.

[105] Ohio had adopted the definition of trade secrets from the Restatement of Torts §757 (1939). See W. R. Grace & Co. v. Hargadine, 392 F.2d 9, 14 (6th Cir. 1968); B. F. Goodrich Co. v. Wohlgemuth, 117 Ohio App. 493, 498, 192 N.E.2d 99, 104 (1963).

[106] 416 U.S. at 473-74.

[107] 478 F.2d 1074 (6th Cir. 1973).

[108] 312 U.S. 52 (1941).

[109] 416 U.S. at 491.

legislation. *Kewanee* is willing to tolerate reliance on the secrecy of trade secret protection at the expense of the disclosure that the patent laws seek to promote.

D. THE IMPACT OF GOLDSTEIN

Between *Goldstein* and *Kewanee* and the effective date of the 1976 Copyright Act,[110] a scattering of cases arose exploring the limits of the revised copyright preemption doctrines. These cases show that *Goldstein* and *Kewanee* were generally perceived as giving approval to a broad expansion of the misappropriation doctrine and seriously limiting, if not overruling, *Sears* and *Compco*,[111] with the courts hesitant over the extent of application of the doctrine.

1. Storch v. Mergenthaler. The protection of typeface designs from copying under the misappropriation doctrine was at issue in *Leonard Storch Enterprises, Inc. v. Mergenthaler Linotype Co.*[112] Plaintiff filed an antitrust suit charging defendant with unlawful attempts to monopolize the market for film fonts for the relevant typesetting machines. The defendant counterclaimed for misappropriation of its Orion typeface design by the plaintiff. Plaintiff had been reproducing

---

[110] The 1976 Copyright Act became effective on Jan. 1, 1978. Note 2 *supra*.

[111] Perhaps the most dramatic illustration of the essential incompatibility of the positions of Chief Justice Burger in *Goldstein* and Justice Black in *Sears-Compco* came in DeCosta v. Columbia Broadcasting System, 520 F.2d 499 (1st Cir. 1975), *cert. denied*, 423 U.S. 1073 (1976). In the first *DeCosta* case, the First Circuit had reversed plaintiff's verdict against CBS for pirating his character "Paladin" for a television series on the grounds that *Sears-Compco* had overruled *INS*, and required that state law misappropriation protection be preempted. Columbia Broadcasting System v. DeCosta, 377 F.2d 315 (1st Cir.), *cert. denied*, 389 U.S. 1007 (1967). In the second *DeCosta* case, the First Circuit stated that in light of *Goldstein* it was obvious that their prior decision was in error in dismissing the misappropriation action. 520 F.2d at 510. However, the First Circuit still refused to let DeCosta recover on grounds that were essentially a law of the case rationale. *Id.* After having his creation blatantly pirated by CBS, which grossed over $14 million from its program, 377 F.2d at 317, and having his jury award of $150,000 stripped from him by the First Circuit twice, with the second opinion stating the first was wrong but that it was now too late to do justice, certainly Victor DeCosta is entitled to take his place at the head of the line of plaintiffs who are justifiably outraged at the workings of the legal system.

[112] 1978-81 Copyright L. Dec. (CCH) ¶25,092 (E.D.N.Y. 1979) (*Storch I*); and 1978-81 Copyright L. Dec. (CCH) ¶25,214 (E.D.N.Y. 1980) (*Storch II*). The first case involved a motion to dismiss on the grounds that the defendant's counterclaim for misappropriation was preempted. The second case was a disposition on the merits. *Storch I* is also reported at 202 U.S.P.Q. (BNA) 623. However, this report included only the very short opinion of the judge but not the magistrate's decision. By itself, the judicial opinion seems to suggest that since typeface designs are ineligible for statutory copyright protection under the authority of Eltra Corp. v. Ringer, 579 F.2d 294 (4th Cir. 1978), upholding the refusal of the Copyright Office to register such claims, this is sufficient to determine that state law is not preempted. Without the magistrate's opinion this would appear to be the rationale for the decision. As the judicial order approved the magistrate's opinion, it is apparent that the preemption analysis was not that one dimensional. There simply was no need for the court to recover the same ground.

the defendant's film fonts and was distributing them in competition with the defendant. By duplicating the film fonts by a photographic process, the plaintiff saved a significant amount of money over the costs it would otherwise have incurred to duplicate the film fonts.[113]

The plaintiff moved to dismiss the counterclaim on the ground that it was preempted by the federal copyright and patent laws.[114] The magistrate's opinion, approved by the court, provides an excellent illustration of why the copyright-misappropriation interface is so troubling.[115]

The opinion characterized *INS* as "[t]he early leading case involving the interrelation between state misappropriation law and federal copyright law."[116] Adopting the analysis suggested by *Goldstein*, it determined that typeface designs were generically ineligible for copyright protection rather than being eligible and failing for lack of originality.[117] *Sears* and *Compco* were thus inapplicable under the *Goldstein* rationale. *Goldstein* required an analysis of whether Congress had left the area "unattended" or intended to place typeface designs beyond the ambit of state law protection. The opinion could find no specific preemptive intent in the records of congressional activity on the topic of protecting typeface designs.[118] Since the case arose under diversity jurisdiction, the court turned to New York law and, relying primarily on *Metropolitan Opera*,[119] held that under New York law "business could not take a 'free ride' on what a competitor had done"[120] and that New York "recognized a cause of action for the misappropriation of a property right created by labor, skill and expenditure."[121] This notwithstanding the opinion's conclusion that "the form of unfair competition, commonly referred to as misappropriation, is nothing more than copyright under another name."[122]

---

[113] The gravamen of Mergenthaler's counterclaim was that "Storch photographically reproduces the essential portions of Mergenthaler film fonts, and thereby bypasses much of the cost in creating the original fonts." 1978-81 Copyright L. Dec. (CCH) ¶25,092 at 15,121.

[114] The trial court stated the motion was one to dismiss under Fed. R. Civ. P. 12(b) (6), 1978-81 Copyright L. Dec. (CCH) ¶25,092 at 15,520, but the magistrate stated the motion was one for summary judgment under Fed. R. Civ. P. 56. 1978-81 Copyright L. Dec. ¶25,092 at 15,521.

[115] 1978-81 Copyright L. Dec. (CCH) ¶25,092 at 15,521.

[116] *Id.*

[117] *Id.* at 15,523-24.

[118] *Id.* at 15,524.

[119] 199 Misc. 786, 101 N.Y.S.2d 483 (1950), *aff'd*, 279 A.D. 632, 107 N.Y.S.2d 795 (1951).

[120] 1978-81 Copyright L. Dec. (CCH) ¶25,092 at 15,525.

[121] *Id.* at 15,526.

[122] *Id.* at 15,521.

When *Storch* went to trial, the court dismissed both the complaint and the counterclaim.[123] The court saw it as a question of two competing values. Greater protection would arguably lead to a greater number and variety of new typeface designs but at a higher cost to the public. Greater freedom for copying would lead to lower prices to the public at the risk of chilling the creation of new products. The court then decided that there had not been an adequate showing that Storch's copying was unduly harmful to Mergenthaler. *Storch* added another element to the misappropriation calculus. After copying is proved, a remedy will be available only if it is necessary for the originator of the product to remain in competition with the plagiarist.

The *INS* case had articulated a similar concern. Protection was accorded to the Associated Press, not only because of the labor and money it had expended, but also because permitting the International News Service to take the news off the Associated Press wires would result in the demise or decline of the Associated Press services.[124] The opinion did not, however, make much of an issue of how much Associated Press would be hindered by the competition and how much business would actually be diverted from it. Instead, the Court then surmised there was some potential harm the Associated Press might suffer and that was sufficient. By contrast, the *Storch* court apparently had before it extensive evidence of the relative costs of the two competitors for the production of the film fonts in question and of their impact on the competitiveness of the parties.[125]

2. Synercom Technology v. University Computing. A similar set of concerns surface in the case of *Synercom Technology, Inc. v. University Computing Co.*[126] Plaintiff and defendant marketed competing stress analysis computer programs. The defendant, the second competitor to enter the market, copied the plaintiff's input formats so that plaintiff's customers could use their existing punch cards and switch to defendant's program without having to reenter their data on new punch cards. Plaintiff sued alleging, among other things, counts for copyright infringement and misappropriation of its computer formats.

---

[123] 1978-81 Copyright L. Dec. (CCH) ¶35,214 (E.D.N.Y. 1980).

[124] 248 U.S. 215, 239-40 (1918).

[125] 1978-81 Copyright L. Dec. (CCH) ¶35,214 at 16,226; 16,239-45.

[126] 462 F. Supp. 1003 (N.D.Tex. 1978) (*Synercom I*); 474 F. Supp. 37 (N.D.Tex. 1979) (*Synercom II*).

In the first opinion[127] the court took up the issue of statutory copyright protection and held that the computer input formats in question were not infringed because what was copied involved the "ideas" contained in the formats rather than their "expressions."[128] The second opinion dealt with the misappropriation issue. The court noted that the misappropriation doctrine of the *INS* case had been accepted by Texas.[129] The court began its preemption analysis by stating that under the broad language of *Sears* and *Compco* the misappropriation action would be preempted. Judge Higginbotham then candidly stated the difficulty he faced:[130]

> But since those cases the Supreme Court has issued several decisions that have cut back on at least the language of *Sears* and *Compco* and have attempted to fashion some sort of workable interplay between state and federal law in the field of intellectual property. The result of these more recent decisions is that the precise dimensions of the preemptive sweep of federal law, and, consequently, the permissible reach of state law in this area has become a matter of difficulty and confusion that requires careful analysis of each case in the light of the relevant case law. The line between the permissible and the impermissible exercise of state power has become difficult to discern.

The court wove together several strands of argument. *Goldstein* was distinguished on the ground that it was regulating conduct that was "culpable" whereas that in *Sears* and *Compco* was not.[131] As such, the statute in *Goldstein* was viewed as an extension of California's police power. The behavior in the case at bar was deemed not to be "culpable," thus avoiding the reach of *Goldstein* and *Kewanee*. The opinion next papered over the differences between *Sears-Compco* and *Goldstein-Kewanee* on the ground that they were all concerned with "whether the state law conflicted unacceptably with the goals of federal legislation."[132] Having thus rephrased the issue, the court concluded that "application of the misappropriation doctrine here would conflict with the federal policy of disclosure of and free access

---

[127] 462 F. Supp. 1003 (N.D.Tex. 1978).

[128] *Id.* at 1012.

[129] 474 F. Supp. at 39, citing Southwestern Broadcasting Co. v. Oil Center Broadcasting Co., 210 S.W.2d 230 (Tex. Civ. App. 1947); Gilmore v. Sammons, 269 S.W. 861 (Tex. Civ. App. 1925).

[130] *Id.* at 40–41.

[131] *Id.* at 41.

[132] *Id.* at 42–43.

to discoveries. The result would be that no one could copy Synercom's input formats, and so Synercom would have a favored access to customers using its program. . . ."[133] The court also noted that a lack of uniformity in this area would create serious business problems for computer services operating on an interstate basis.[134] Finally, although the input formats were deemed "writings" within the scope of the 1909 Copyright Act, copyright protection for them was barred on the basis of the idea-expression distinction and thus could not be said to have been left "unattended" by Congress.[135]

Thus, while *Storch* found no preemption of the misappropriation doctrine, *Synercom* found the doctrine preempted where a second competitor capitalized on the developmental costs of the originator. On a fundamental level, however, the cases are similar. Both courts refused to apply the doctrine to a situation which would normally seem to involve the doctrine: *Synercom* on the basis of preemption, *Storch* on a procompetition policy thesis. To say that the federal statutes embody a goal or policy to leave some things free to be imitated is the equivalent of saying that there are limits to the monopoly. Both courts are concerned with this issue, though one finds it to be the basis for preemption while the other finds no preemption but uses the monopolistic result as the basis for refusing to apply the doctrine. The major problem remains the inability to identify any hierarchy of values by which the preemption issue is to be decided. In large measure this is the result of *Goldstein*'s abandonment of the Copyright Clause analysis for that of the Commerce Clause. Neither *Goldstein* nor *Kewanee* gives any guidelines which value structures are to govern these determinations.

To some courts at least, the public interest is a factor in the misappropriation determination. *Storch* is the more explicit of the two opinions, stating that the public benefit of lower prices requires the plaintiff to show the copying has rendered it uncompetitive before relief can be obtained. In *Synercom* this theme is muted but nonetheless detectable in the court's attempts to differentiate the "culpable" copying in *Goldstein* from that in *Sears* and *Compco*.[136] This evidences a desire for a limit to the more egregious forms of monopoly protection under the misappropriation doctrine.

---

[133] *Id.* at 43.
[134] *Id.*
[135] *Id.* at 43–44.
[136] *Id.* at 41.

3. Sears-Compco *Revisited*. In *Jacobs v. Robitaille*[137] the court held that the misappropriation doctrine was preempted from preventing the copying of advertisements of one advertising guide by another with the advertiser's consent. The court's reasoning was that advertisements were eligible for protection under federal copyright law and thus were preempted even under *Goldstein*. This is perfectly consistent with the *Goldstein* gloss on *Sears* and *Compco*. In *Triangle Publications, Inc. v. Sports Eye, Inc.*,[138] the publisher of the *Daily Racing Form* sought a temporary injunction against a competing publication which used raw data obtained from the *Daily Racing Form* to prepare its listings of the various horses entered in a given race in different categories. The final information conveyed, format, and physical appearance of the two publications were quite different. The court first refused a preliminary injunction on the copyright count on the ground of lack of sufficient similarity between the works. On the misappropriation count, the court refused relief on the same ground as *Jacobs v. Robitaille*. Since the plaintiff's newspaper was copyrightable, it could not be said that it had been left "unattended" by Congress. Thus the lack of copyright protection for the raw data that the plaintiff's paper contained was deemed to be the result of deliberate congressional action and the application of the state law misappropriation doctrine was preempted.

IV. PREEMPTION: THE LEGISLATIVE HISTORY OF 17 U.S.C. §301

During the decade from *Sears* and *Compco* to *Goldstein* and *Kewanee*, Congress wrestled with the problem of copyright revision.[139] Dissatisfaction with the concept of publication as the demarcation line between federal and state authority[140] led the Register of Copyrights to

---

[137] 406 F. Supp. 1145 (D.N.H. 1976).

[138] 415 F. Supp. 682 (E.D. Pa. 1976).

[139] An overview of the lengthy legislative process is summarized at H.R. Rep. No. 1476, 94th Cong., 2d Sess. 47-50 (1976). An extensive multivolume analytical index of the legislative history is now being prepared by Professor Alan Latman and James Lightstone, of which the first four volumes have been published at this date. LATMAN & LIGHTSTONE, THE KAMINSTEIN LEGISLATIVE HISTORY PROJECT: A COMPENDIUM AND ANALYTICAL INDEX OF MATERIALS LEADING TO THE COPYRIGHT ACT OF 1976 (v. 1 1981, v. 2 1982, v. 3 1983, v. 4 1983). (The project is dedicated to the late Abraham L. Kaminstein, Register of Copyrights from 1960 to 1971 and one of the key figures in the Revision of the Copyright Laws.)

[140] Under prior law, a work obtained federal statutory copyright protection upon publication with proper copyright notice. 17 U.S.C. §10 (1976) (repealed 1976; repeal effective Jan. 1, 1978). Certain unpublished works which lent themselves to performance could also obtain federal statutory copyright by registration. *Id.* at §12. While a manuscript was unpublished, it was

suggest that the concept of publication be replaced by the concept of "public dissemination."[141] The copyright bar and commentators reacted negatively and favored a completely nationalized system in which unpublished works would be fully eligible for statutory protection.[142] This change was incorporated into the 1963 Preliminary Draft of a proposed copyright act.[143] To change to a fully federal system was felt to require preemption of state law protecting unpublished manuscripts. To accomplish this, a preemption provision was included in the 1963 Preliminary Draft.[144] After assessing the reactions to the 1963 Preliminary Draft, the Copyright Office

---

protected from unauthorized copying by "common law copyright" which protected rights in unpublished manuscripts. *Id.* at §2. The 1909 Act did not define publication but it did define the "date of publication" to be "the earliest date when copies of the first authorized edition were placed on sale, sold, or publicly distributed by the proprietor of the copyright." *Id.* at §26. The concept of publication proved slippery and difficult to work with. See generally Kaplan, *Publication in Copyright Law*, 103 U. PA. L. REV. 469 (1955); Strauss, *Protection of Unpublished Works* (1957), Copyright Law Revision—Studies Prepared for the Subcomm. on Patents, Trademarks, and Copyrights of the Comm. on the Judiciary, United States Senate, Eighty-sixth Congress, Second Session, Pursuant to S. Res. 240, Study No. 29 (Sen. Comm. Print 1960); compare Shapiro, Bernstein & Co. v. Miracle Record Co., 91 F. Supp. 473 (1950), with Rosette v. Rainbo Record Mfg. Co., 354 F. Supp. 1183 (S.D.N.Y. 1973), *aff'd per curiam*, 546 F.2d 461 (2d Cir. 1976); compare De Mille Co. v. Casey, 121 Misc. 78, 201 N.Y.S. 20 (Sup. Ct. 1923) with Blanc v. Lantz, 83 U.S.P.Q. (BNA) 137 (Cal. Super. Ct. 1949).

[141] REGISTER'S REPORT, note 7 *supra* at 39-43.

[142] Copyright Law Revision Part 2—Discussion and Comments Report of the Register of Copyrights on the General Revision of the U.S. Copyright Law, 88th Cong. 1st Sess. 184-86, 228-29, 239-40, 242-43, 245, 252-54, 263, 278-79, 292-93, 304, 351-52, 373, 382-83, 390-92 (House Comm. Print 1963).

[143] Preliminary Draft for Revised U.S. Copyright Law §§19-23, Copyright Law Revision Part 3—Preliminary Draft for Revised U.S. Copyright Law and Discussions and Comments on the Draft, 88th Cong., 2d Sess. 18-22 (House Comm. Print 1964).

[144] The 1963 Preliminary Draft provided:

§19. Pre-emption With Respect to Other Laws
(a) ... all rights in the nature of copyright in works for which copyright protection is available under sections 1 and 2, ... whether published or unpublished, shall be governed exclusively by this title. Thereafter, no person shall be entitled to copyright, to literary or intellectual property rights, or to any equivalent legal or equitable right in any such work under the common law or statute of any State.
(b) Nothing in this title shall annul or limit any rights or remedies under the law of any State:
   (1) With respect to material for which copyright protection is not available under sections 1 and 2;
   (2) ...
   (3) With respect to activities constituting breaches of trust, invasion of privacy, or deceptive trade practices including passing off and false representation.

Preliminary Draft for Revised U.S. Copyright Law §19, Copyright Law Revision Part 3—Preliminary Draft for Revised U.S. Copyright Law and Discussions and Comments on the Draft, 88th Cong., 2d Sess. 18 (House Comm. Print 1964).

submitted the draft of the 1964 Copyright Revision Bill[145] to Congress with a revised preemption section which read as follows:[146]

§19. Pre-emption With Respect to Other Laws

(a) On and after January 1, 1967, all rights in the nature of copyright in works that come within the subject matter of copyright as specified by sections 1 and 2, whether created before or after that date and whether published or unpublished, are governed exclusively by this title. Thereafter, no person is entitled to copyright, literary property rights, or any equivalent legal or equitable right in any such work under the common law or statutes of any State.

(b) Nothing in this title annuls or limits any rights or remedies under the law of any State with respect to:

> (1) unpublished material that does not come within the subject matter of copyright as specified by sections 1 and 2;
>
> (2) any cause of action arising from undertaking commenced before January 1, 1967;
>
> (3) activities violating rights that are not equivalent to any of the exclusive rights within the general scope of copyright as specified by section 5, including breaches of contract, breaches of trust, invasion of privacy, defamation, and deceptive trade practices such as passing off and false representation.

The use of the word "unpublished" in §19(b) (1) was to prevent §301(a) from being interpreted as permitting the States to provide copyright-like protection for published works that were generically ineligible for copyright protection. This was stated quite explicitly by the Register of Copyrights in his *Supplementary Report* accompanying the 1965 Revision Bill:[147]

> The word "unpublished" in clause (1) of section 301(b) deserves special note. In the United States, under the doctrine established by

---

[145] S. 3008, 88th Cong., 1st Sess. (1964); H.R. 11947, 88th Cong., 1st Sess. (1964); H.R. 12354, 88th Cong., 1st Sess. (1964) (identical bills).

[146] *Id.* §19.

[147] Copyright Law Revision Part 6—Supplementary Report of the Register of Copyrights on the General Revision of the U.S. Copyright Law: 1965 Revision Bill, 89th Cong., 1st Sess. 85 (House Comm. Print 1965).

The 1965 Copyright Revision Bill renumbered the sections of the proposed act so that the preemption section was changed from §19 to §301. Except for the changes in the numbers of the sections, there were no differences in the preemption provisions of the 1964 and 1965 Acts. No further renumbering of the preemption section took place and it was finally enacted as §301. 17 U.S.C. §301 (Supp. V 1981).

the Supreme Court in *Wheaton v. Peters*, 33 U.S. (8 Pet.) 591 (1834), common law copyright protection has consistently been held to terminate upon the publication of the work. The word "unpublished" was therefore added to this clause to avoid any implication that common law protection equivalent to copyright, for material not coming within the subject matter of the statute, might continue after its publication. What constitutes "publication" for this purpose, which is now a matter of uncertainty, would be governed by the definition of that term in the statute.

In explaining the rather pointed exclusion of misappropriation and the forms of unfair competition that did not involve some sort of deception or misleading of the public, the *Supplementary Report* continued:[148]

[W]e have resisted use of the ambiguous term "unfair competition," which in recent years has gone through some wide shifts in meaning. In some States it was greatly broadened to become, under the name "misappropriation," the virtual equivalent of a copyright; .... There is no intention to pre-empt causes of action for unfair competition involving false labeling and fraudulent representation but, to the extent that a right against "Unfair competition" is merely copyright by another name, section 301 is intended to abolish it as a common law cause of action.

This preemption scheme of these initial bills is clearly designed to give great precedence to the federal system. In §301(a), the states are explicitly preempted from giving copyright or equivalent protection to any subject matter eligible for statutory protection. Under §301(b) (1), anything that falls outside of such bounds can be protected by state law only while it remains unpublished. Once published, it enters the public domain and cannot remain private property save by qualifying for the circumscribed monopolies of copyright or patent.

In the 1967 bill, §301(b) (1) was changed to add "works of authorship not fixed in any tangible medium of expression" to the definition of unpublished works, but otherwise no change of any significance was made.[149] With this, the wording of that portion of the proposed revision bill was apparently settled and there was no further controversy or concern about of the issue until 1975.

---

[148] Copyright Law Revision Part 6—Supplementary Report of the Register of Copyrights on the General Revision of the U.S. Copyright Law: 1965 Revision Bill, 89th Cong., 1st Sess. 85 (House Comm. Print 1965).

[149] H. R. 2512, 90th Cong., 1st Sess. §301 (1967); S. 597, 90th Cong., 1st Sess. §301 (1967); H.R. 5650, 90th Cong., 1st Sess. §301 (1967); (identical bills).

The 1975 copyright revision bills introduced into Congress contained the same preemption provision as the 1967 bill.[150] In committee, both the House and Senate amended §301(b) to read:[151]

> (b) Nothing in this title annuls or limits any rights or remedies under the common law or statutes of any State with respect to:
>
>   (1) subject matter that does not come within the subject matter of copyright as specified by sections 102 and 103, including works of authorship not fixed in any tangible medium of expression; or
>
>   (2) ...
>
>   (3) activities violating legal or equitable rights that are not equivalent to any of the exclusive rights within the general scope of copyright as specified by section 106, including rights against misappropriation not equivalent to any of such exclusive rights, breaches of contract, breaches of trust, trespass, conversion, invasion of privacy, defamation, and deceptive trade practices such as passing off and false representation; . . . .

Two drastic changes were made here. First, the area removed from state regulation was drastically reduced. Prior drafts clearly forbade the states to provide copyright or equivalent protection both to works in categories eligible for protection and to published works outside those categories. The new provision provides different calculus. First, all noneligible categories of works could now be protected by the states regardless of publication. Second, by phrasing §301(b) (1) to exempt from preemption all that is not covered in §§102 and 103, the legislation creates a potential trap of staggering dimensions. Section 102(b) proclaims that copyright protection does not extend to "any idea, procedure, process, system, method of operation, concept, principle, or discovery, regardless of the form in which it is described, explained, illustrated, or embodied in such work."[152] Thus under a literal reading of the revised §301(b) (1) the states are fully empowered to provide protection for "any idea, procedure, process, system, method of

---

[150] S. 22, 94th Cong., 1st Sess. §301 (1975), introduced on January 15, 1975, by Senator McClellan; H.R. 2223, 94th Cong., 1st Sess. §301 (1975), introduced on Jan. 28, 1975, by Representative Kastenmeier. Section 301, the preemption provision of these bills, was identical to those which had been in all of the bills since 1967.

[151] S. 22, 94th Cong., 1st Sess. §301 (1975) (as amended in committee), reported in S. Rep. No. 473, 94th Cong., 1st Sess. 20 (1975), and in H.R. Rep. No. 1476, 95th Cong., 2d Sess. 24 (1976).

[152] 17 U.S.C. §102(b) (Supp. V 1981).

operation, concept, principle, or discovery" whether or not it is embodied in a copyrighted work.[153]

The explanation for this change is that some works eligible for statutory protection might never be fixed in a tangible medium of expression as required by §102(a).[154] The examples given included such examples as choreography, extemporaneous speeches, and live broadcasts. Under the prior Act,[155] state law protection was available for such works. The intent of the amendment was to permit state law protection of an author's rights in "unfixed" works. Upon being "fixed," they would be protected by the copyright act or not at all.[156] There is not one word in the explanation of this change that evinces any intent to permit the states to protect any works once they had been "fixed" and published, regardless of whether they were eligible for copyright protection. Yet the language of the change seems to do just that, accomplishing a result that does not seem to have been intended. Paradoxically, an intent to increase the scope of federal coverage dramatically and dangerously decreased it. It is hard to avoid the conclusion that Congress and the Copyright Office were oblivious to the implications of this change.

The second change, including misappropriation in the list of state actions not preempted, is an equally drastic about face. The committee reports explain this in the following terms:[157]

> "Misappropriation" is not necessarily synonymous with copyright infringement, and thus a cause of action labeled as "misappropriation" is not preempted if it is in fact based neither on a right within the general scope of copyright as specified by section 106 nor on a right equivalent thereto. For example, state law should have the flexibility to afford a remedy (under traditional principles of equity) against a consistent pattern of unauthorized appropriation by a competitor of the facts (i.e., not the literary expression) constituting "hot" news, whether in the mold of *International News Service v. Associated Press*, 248 U.S. 215 (1918), or in the newer form of data

---

[153] While this seems far-fetched, the fact is that at least one court has taken that position. Bromhall v. Rorvik, 478 F. Supp. 361 (E.D. Pa. 1979), discussed at text accompanying note 237 *infra*.

[154] 17 U.S.C. 102(a) (Supp. IV 1980). Congress felt the constitutional requirement of a writing mandated that whatever copyright could protect had to be at least tangible and perceivable even if a machine or device had to be employed. See H.R. Rep. No. 1476, 94th Cong., 2d Sess. 52-53 (1976); S. Rep. No. 473, 94th Cong., 1st Sess. 51-52 (1975).

[155] 17 U.S.C. §2 (1976) (repealed 1976; repeal effective Jan. 1, 1978).

[156] H.R. Rep. No. 1476, 94th Cong., 2d Sess. 131 (1976); S. Rep. No. 473, 94th Cong., 1st Sess. 114-15 (1975).

[157] S. Rep. No. 1476, 94th Cong., 2d Sess. 132 (1976).

updates from scientific, business or financial data bases. Likewise, a person having no trust or other relationship with the proprietor of a computerized data base should not be immunized from sanctions against electronically or cryptographically breaching the proprietor's security arrangements and accessing the proprietor's data. The unauthorized data access which should be remediable might also be achieved by the intentional interception of data transmissions by wire, microwave or laser transmissions, or by common unintentional means of "crossed" telephone lines occasioned by errors in switching.

The misappropriation doctrine, long the primary target of preemption as "copyright under another name,"[158] is given statutory sanction and is to be preempted only when it is deemed to be equivalent to copyright but not otherwise. Obviously, the statute and the committee reports indicate that some but not all applications of the misappropriation doctrine are viewed as the equivalent of copyright protection. This tribute to the amorphous nature of misappropriation cites some examples but provides no guidance to the distinct characteristics of these different types of misappropriation. The Congress seems as unable clearly to define misappropriation as the courts. *INS* is approved but no analysis is given of what elements in the *INS* facts or decision distinguish it from copyright protection other than whether the news is "hot."

How did such a drastic shift occur after nearly a decade of seeming totally uncontroversial consensus? When the House Subcommittee held its hearings in 1975, there was extensive testimony from Barbara Ringer, then Register of Copyrights. In addition to a substantial opening statement,[159] Ringer was the sole witness appearing before the House Subcommittee for the last five days of the total eighteen days of hearings. On the last day of her testimony, the subject of preemption came up. Ringer began by saying that "at one time, this [preemption] was unquestionably the most controversial and debated issue in copyright revision"[160] and then noted that "[t]his has not, however,

---

[158] See text accompanying note 148 *supra*.

[159] Statement of Barbara Ringer, Register of Copyrights, on May 7, 1975, 1 Copyright Law Revision: Hearings before the Subcommittee on Courts, Civil Liberties, and the Administration of Justice of the Committee on the Judiciary House of Representatives, Ninety-fourth Congress, First Session on H.R. 2223 Copyright Law Revision, Serial No. 36, 94th Cong., 1st Sess. 92-118 (1975) (hereinafter cited as Hearings).

[160] Statement of Barbara Ringer, Register of Copyrights, on Dec. 4, 1975, 3 Hearings, note 159 *supra*, at 1,910 (1975). The references in her testimony to chapters refer to the Copyright Office, Second Supplementary Report of the Register of Copyright on the General Revision of the U.S.

been true for at least 10 years and probably quite a bit longer than that."[161] The extent of her entire discussion of the changes in §301(b) was the following:[162]

> The Federal preemption provision in the bill has stayed pretty much the same since the early 1960's. That has happened as the result of a series of decisions by the courts, including the Supreme Court, which have had sort of a roller coaster effect with respect to Federal preemption, but which under the present law, as I think most people interpret it, requires some technical changes in section 301. These were drafted by various members of the copyright bar, and were endorsed in the Senate version. The Copyright Office endorses them.

This passage raises serious questions about just what Congress intended. There does appear to be some desire to conform the preemption provisions of the bill to the *Goldstein* and *Kewanee* decisions. There is no recognition that this would be a radical shift in the preemption issue, allowing the states broad authority over works which they were not previously allowed. Nor is acknowledgment made that this contradicts the long-stated goal of providing an expanded and fully national system of copyright protection.

If there was a desire to harmonize the pending legislation with *Goldstein*, there is no interpretation of *Goldstein* and *Kewanee* supplied. *Goldstein* never said there was any constitutional reason that Congress could not preempt the field, only that it had not done so. *Goldstein* certainly holds that Congress in its discretion could adjust the allocation of power to protect intellectual property.[163] The Supreme Court was adjudicating an issue of allocation of power between the states and the federal government, not passing on the wisdom of the misappropriation doctrine. The curiously passive attitude that

---

Copyright Law: 1975 Revision Bill October–December 1975 (Draft ed. 1975). The report noted the Senate Committee had made the changes which the House Committee subsequently adopted. *Id.* at ch. 12, 6-7. The report stated the justification for the preemption provision was establishment of a single federal system of copyright protection in place of the previously existing dual system. *Id.* at ch. 12, 2, 4-7. There was no discussion whatsoever of the changes the amendments would make from the prior provisions, the shift in attitude toward misappropriation, or the impact the amendments would have. *Id.*

[161] Statement of Barbara Ringer, Register of Copyrights, on Dec. 4, 1975, 3 Hearings, note 159 *supra*, at 1,910 (1975).

[162] *Id.*

[163] *Goldstein* clearly takes the position that once Congress has acted, that is the determinative factor in the preemption analysis. Thus, if anything, *Goldstein* suggests there is reason for Congress to take some step toward arriving at its own position on preemption rather than trying to follow the Court.

Goldstein was to be followed shows a lack of understanding of that case. If anything, *Goldstein* invited congressional study and analysis of the misappropriation doctrine; it didn't discourage it. But the Register may have regarded *Goldstein* as constitutionally forbidding the preemption of misappropriation.

If the changes are considered as an attempt to provide a reasoned decision of the proper limits of state power to protect intellectual property, the problems are even more serious. Neither Congress nor the Copyright Office seems to have had any conception of what they were doing.[164] There is no analysis of the misappropriation doctrine even as it is recast from the role of disfavored usurper of federal copyright into a recognized common-law right. No definition is given of the elements of this common-law tort which has been described as "nothing more than copyright under another name."[165] There is a nod in the direction of the early concerns, primarily with establishing federal protection that would begin at fixation rather than at publication, but nothing in the way of any inquiry into how or why §301(b) assumed its present shape. There is no consideration of the public interest of the role of public domain or of the monopolies that would be created. At best §301(b) reflects a compulsion to follow, however ineptly, the *Goldstein* decision, while ignoring the opinion's explicit statements that it was clearly the prerogative of Congress to determine the lines for preemption.

This rewriting of the preemption provision without serious discussion or analysis, as a "technical" change, was made at the last possible moment, too late for opposing views to be heard by the Subcommittee. At best it is an inept and slothful legislative performance. At worst, it is a scam on a gullible Congress by anonymous "members of the copyright bar"[166] to slip the misappropriation doctrine back into the legislation from which it had been carefully excluded.

The Justice Department apparently was also asleep at the switch when the changes in §301 were embodied in the Senate bill. In 1976, however, the Justice Department reacted to the sanctioning of misappropriation in two letters of substantially identical content.[167]

---

[164] See text accompanying notes 150–63 *supra.*

[165] See text accompanying note 148 *supra.*

[166] See text accompanying note 162 *supra.*

[167] Letter from Thomas E. Kauper, Assistant Attorney General, Antitrust Division, to Senator Hugh Scott (Feb. 13, 1976) (published in COMMERCE CLEARING HOUSE COPYRIGHT REVISION ACT OF 1976 269–272 (1976)); and letter from Michael M. Uhlmann, Assistant Attorney General,

The letters first attacked the "misappropriation" doctrine on the ground that it was anticompetitive and monopolistic.[168] Relying primarily on the opinions of Learned Hand, the letters suggested the doctrine was a minority view which was generally discredited,[169] and that the doctrine was vague and uncertain and could frustrate copyright and antitrust policies by maintaining perpetual monopolies. The core of the Justice Department's reasoning was that:[170]

> [I]mitation is the life-blood of competition. Mere commercial copying is neither unlawful, nor immoral; instead it is often a commercial and economic necessity. Copying very often supports and promotes competition—it spurs further invention and innovation, permits newcomers to enter markets, and generally, by bringing forward functionally equivalent products and services, is a necessary condition for the competitive forces of the marketplace acting to lower prices, satisfy consumer demand and allocate product optimally.

In effect, the monopolies the misappropriation doctrine would justify were an aberration from the basic competitive scheme of our internal commercial policies to which copyrights and patents were carefully limited, constitutionally created exceptions. The Justice Department noted that actions such as breach of contract presented no problem as "[t]hese are causes of action different in nature from that of copyright infringement."[171] For the Justice Department's analysis, misappropriation was copyright infringement by another name. On this topic, the letter to Congressman Kastenmeier concluded by recommending that the references to misappropriation in §301(b) (3) be deleted.

When the bill came to the floor of the House, Congressman Seiberling moved to strike the list of examples of state-protected rights which were not preempted from §301(b) (3).[172] Basing his position on

---

Legislative Affairs of July 27, 1976, to Congressman Robert Kastenmeier, Chairman, Subcomm. on Courts, Civil Liberties, and the Administration of Justice, Comm. on the Judiciary (July 27, 1976) (hereinafter cited as Uhlmann letter) (published in LAW JOURNAL PRESS, THE COPYRIGHT ACT OF 1976: DEALING WITH THE NEW REALITIES, 177-92 (1976)). A copy of the portion of the text of the Uhlmann letter dealing with preemption is attached as an appendix to Fetter, *Copyright Revision and the Preemption of State "Misappropriation" Law: A Study in Judicial and Congressional Interaction,* 27 COPYRIGHT L. SYMPOSIUM (ASCAP) 1, App. 4 at 63-69 (1982) (hereinafter cited as Fetter).

[168] Uhlmann letter, Fetter, note 167 *supra,* at 66-68.

[169] *Id.* at 66-67.

[170] *Id.* at 68.

[171] *Id.*

[172] *Id.* 122 CONG. REC. 31,977, 32,015 (1976).

the Justice Department letter, he argued that misappropriation made the preemption section meaningless, that misappropriation was based on the *INS* case which "has generally been ignored by the Supreme Court itself and by the lower courts ever since."[173] Congressman Railsback, a member of the House Judiciary Committee which had presented the bill to the House, then asked Congressman Seiberling to confirm that it was not the intent of his amendment to change the law in those states which had adopted the misappropriation doctrine. Seiberling then stated: "That is correct . . . I am trying to have this bill leave the state law alone and make it clear we are merely dealing with copyright laws."[174] Congressman Railsback then indicated he did not oppose the amendment and it passed. The subsequent Conference Committee Report did no more than note the different wordings of the House and Senate bills and state that the House version had been adopted without any explanation of the reasons for such decision.[175] Thus §301 assumed its final form.[176]

---

[173] *Id.*
[174] *Id.*
[175] H.R. Rep. No. 1733, 94th Cong., 2d Sess. 78-79 (1976).
[176] As finally enacted, 17 U.S.C. §301 (Supp. V 1981), provides:

§301:. Preemption with respect to other laws
    (a) On and after January 1, 1978, all legal or equitable rights that are equivalent to any of the exclusive rights within the general scope of copyright as specified by section 106 in works of authorship that are fixed in a tangible medium of expression and come within the subject matter of copyright as specified by sections 102 and 103, whether created before or after that date and whether published or unpublished, are governed exclusively by this title. Thereafter, no person is entitled to any such right or equivalent right in any such work under the common law or statutes of any State.
    (b) Nothing in this title annuls or limits any rights or remedies under the common law of statutes of any State with respect to—
        (1) subject matter that does not come within the subject matter of copyright as specified by sections 102 and 103, including works of authorship not fixed in any tangible medium of expression; or
        (2) any cause of action arising from undertakings commenced before January 1, 1978; or
        (3) activities violating legal or equitable rights that are not equivalent to any of the exclusive rights within the general scope of copyright as specified by section 106.
    (c) With respect to sound recordings fixed before February 15, 1972, any rights or remedies under the common law or statutes of any State shall not be annulled or limited by this title until February 15, 2047. The preemptive provisions of subsection (a) shall apply to any such rights and remedies pertaining to any cause of action arising from undertakings commenced on and after February 15, 2047. Notwithstanding the provisions of section 303, no sound recording fixed before February 15, 1972, shall be subject to copyright under this title before, on, or after February 15, 2047.
    (d) Nothing in this title annuls or limits any rights or remedies under any other Federal statute.

To say that this leaves the legislative history of preemption of the misappropriation doctrine in a state of confusion is an understatement. From this sequence of events almost any position for or against preemption of the misappropriation doctrine can be plausibly argued. Congressman Seiberling's opening remarks and reliance on the Justice Department letter clearly indicate that he intended to have the statute totally preempt the misappropriation doctrine. On the other hand, it is also plausible to view the colloquy between Railsback and Seiberling on the floor of the House as supporting the position that the amendment really made no change in the content of §301(b) (3). But Congressman Railsback's remarks can be viewed as merely being concerned with indicating that such state law actions as trademark infringement and trade secret violations, sometimes loosely referred to as misappropriation, were not preempted.[177] What weight ought to be assigned to the fact that, though the Justice Department letters did not object to state law causes of action such as breaches of contract or breaches of trust, examples were stricken along with misappropriation? The one-sided and selective arguments of the Justice Department may also weigh against the credibility of reading their antimisappropriation stance into the legislative history of the section. Yet there is no mistaking that the letters were violently opposed to any recognition of the misappropriation doctrine and strenuously urged that it be preempted. It is clear that Congressman Seiberling's amendment was inspired by these letters and sought to implement their purpose.

The lack of a satisfactory legislative history to solve problems of statutory interpretation does not relieve the need to come to grips with §301.[178] It does place an even greater emphasis on dealing with the statutory language as enacted.

On its face, §301 creates a two-pronged test to determine preemption: (1) Is the subject matter under consideration generically eligible for copyright protection under §§102 and 103? (2) Are the rights involved equivalent to the rights provided under §106? If both questions are answered affirmatively, §301 provides for absolute preemption. If either question is answered in the negative, §301 imposes no obstacle to the exercise of state power. The scheme of §301 may be represented by the diagram shown below.

---

[177] 122 CONG. REC. 32,015 (1976).

[178] Two articles which have explored this legislative history are Fetter, note 167 *supra*, and Diamond, *Preemption of State Law*, 25 Bull. Copyright Soc'y 204 (1978).

	Rights Equivalent to Rights under §106	Rights Not Equivalent to Rights under §106
§§102, 103 subject matter	States totally preempted	States not preempted
Subject matter outside of §§102, 103	States not preempted	States not preempted

Issues of preemption under §301 require courts to determine if the challenged state action involves subject matter included in the copyright statute and if the rights claimed are equivalent to those granted by §106. This seemingly simple two-step process does not end the matter. There is also the question whether the entire preemptive force of the statute is exhausted by §301. In effect, are the regulatory thrust of the statute and its underlying goals and purposes concerned solely with issues of subject-matter coverage and description of rights? If more is involved—as the courts have indicated in several cases—the §301 inquiry will not resolve all preemption issues. The courts will have the task of identifying the values and policies embodied in the statutory provisions and determining whether a given form of state law protection interferes sufficiently to be constitutionally obnoxious. This is no easy task. Identifying the values and the policies of the copyright statutes has been a subject of no little controversy and judicial vacillation. Measuring the amount of interference between state laws and federal laws is also a difficult task for it is a question of degree as well as of kind. A more fundamental question persists. Is the present preemption scheme—constitutional, legislative, and judicial—satisfactory? If not, what alternatives are preferable?

The preemption test set forth in §301 is quite mechanical. On its face all that is required is the comparison of the subject matter sought to be protected and the rights asserted under the state law with the federal law. Only if both are congruent is the state law preempted. Whether Congress left the area "unattended" or determined that a particular type of subject matter should not be protected is not an inquiry required by §301. That it should be a relevant inquiry seems obvious, but the language of §301 invites the courts to ignore this inquiry.

Even if it is assumed that the two measures of equivalent subject matter and equivalent rights adequately provide sufficient preemption to insure the proper and unimpeded functioning of the federal copyright system, the question remains whether the boundaries have been accurately defined to provide the needed preemption. In short, does the act provide adequate and useful definitions of the subject matter and rights for purposes of the preemption inquiry? The major concern is that of subject matter. By limiting the scope of preemption to subject matter eligible for copyright protection, there is the distinct possibility that state protection may be afforded to subject matter Congress would have placed in the public domain.

VI. JUDICIAL DEVELOPMENTS

A. THE §106 MEASURE

A fair portion of the litigation that has arisen under §301 is concerned with whether rights asserted under various common-law claims are equivalent to the rights granted by §106. The courts have not employed any one consistent method of making that determination. There have been too few cases to establish any "leading case" or "clear trends" indicating a preferred test or mode of analysis for determining when rights are equivalent. The courts have looked at several different factors in making the equivalency determination. Some cases use or combine more than one analytic method. More than one analytic approach may, indeed, shed useful light on the question whether state law unacceptably interferes with the goals and purposes of the federal copyright and patent laws. Nor has it been long since §301 became effective and the various state causes of action often may have little in common other than the amorphous labels of misappropriation and unfair competition.

A reasonable starting point is those cases where the courts have considered the deletion of the listed examples from §301(b) (3) on the House floor. In *Mitchell v. Penton/Industrial Publishing Co.,*[179] plaintiff wrote a book entitled *Records Retention* which allegedly provided businesses with a systematic guideline for the retention and destruction of business records in compliance with some 1,300 governmental statutes and regulations. Plaintiff claimed his book was the result of a great deal of painstaking effort and research. Plaintiff sued the defendant alleging the defendant's magazine article had been copied from his book. The first count of the complaint was for statutory copyright infringement and the second for misappropriation of the value of defendant's labor and expense in compiling the

---

[179] 486 F. Supp. 22 (N.D. Ohio 1979).

information. After noting that the language of §301(b) (3) had been amended on the floor of the House, the court went on:[180]

> By deleting the examples ... Congress must have decided it was better to permit the states in the first instance through statutory or decisional law to specify or fashion "rights or remedies" that fall within clause (3), subject, of course, to court application of the copyright law limitations of clause (3). While deleted from clause (3), those causes of action remain illustrative of "certain types of misappropriation, not preempted under section 301." However, these exemplified causes of action could only be brought as a pendent state claim in conjunction with a copyright infringement action if indeed the pendent claim was recognized as a legally sufficient state action and provided the claim did not involve a legal or equitable right that is "equivalent to any of the exclusive rights within the general scope of copyright as specified by section 106."

The court then found the right asserted to be a "broad 'misappropriation' claim"[181] which it held preempted by §301(a). In determining the misappropriation count was equivalent to a claim for copyright infringement, the court noted that the plaintiff was not alleging any showing of "passing off" and observed that if the plaintiff prevailed on its statutory claim the misappropriation count would be totally redundant.

The court's interpretation of the purpose of the Seiberling amendment is open to question. The court saw the amendment as expressing a design to permit the states to define for themselves the elements and remedies of state causes of action rather than having the listed remedies of the committee draft of the bill operate as a limitation on what a state might choose. That the amendment might have been trying to preempt the misappropriation doctrine under the 1976 Copyright Act is not considered. The discrepancies between the interpretation of the court and the thrust of the Justice Department letters on which Congressman Seiberling based his amendment are more understandable if the judge was unaware of them. As the Justice Department letters are not incorporated into either the Congressional Record or the Committee Reports, it is very easy to see how they could escape judicial attention.

The practical impact of this interpretation of the amendment is to treat the examples given in the committee reports as a partial list of

---

[180] *Id.* at 25.
[181] *Id.*

state law causes of action which may or may not be preempted depending on the application of the tests in §§301(a) and (b) on a case-by-case basis. The committee reports are taken as neither a denial nor an affirmance of any given state cause of action as being preempted. Considering the potential for confusion in the Seiberling amendment,[182] this is an eminently practical resolution of the question of the weight a court should accord to the committee reports in determining §301 issues. To the extent the court may have misunderstood the intent of Congressman Seiberling and the Justice Department, it is fair to say that they provided little rational guidance that would have helped to avoid the result.

In *M. Bryce & Associates, Inc. v. Gladstone*,[183] a trade secrets case that arose prior to January 1, 1978, the plaintiff demonstrated a management information system to the defendants after the defendants had signed a nondisclosure agreement. The plaintiff had placed copyright notice on his manuals but apparently limited their circulation to customers and others who signed confidentiality agreements. One of the issues was whether the trade secret action was preempted by the 1909 Copyright Act which was in effect at the time the action arose. The court discussed §301 of the 1976 Act and its amendment, setting forth in a footnote the text of the debate on Congressman Seiberling's amendment. The court expressed perplexity over what the amendment had accomplished, noting that the three congressmen who spoke "agreed that the examples should be deleted but seemed to differ on whether this action was to limit or expand preemption."[184] The court concluded that the 1976 Copyright Act did not displace state trade secret law.

In *Harper & Row Publishers, Inc. v. Nation Enterprises*,[185] plaintiff sued the defendant for the unauthorized publication of ex-President Ford's memoirs. The three counts of the complaint were for copyright infringement, conversion, and tortious interference with Harper and Row's licensing arrangements with Time, Inc. In deciding whether the latter two counts were preempted, the court stated that the state rights sought to be vindicated must be *"qualitatively"*[186] different from §106 rights to avoid preemption. The court observed that the

---

[182] See text accompanying notes 172–77 *supra*.

[183] 107 Wis. 2d 241, 319 N.W.2d 907 (Wis. App. 1982), *cert. denied*, 103 S. Ct. 258 (1982).

[184] *Id.* at 17,411.

[185] 501 F. Supp. 848 (S.D.N.Y. 1980).

[186] *Id.* at 852.

conversion count was not concerned with the actual possession of a physical manuscript but only with the control of its reproduction and dissemination, and thus equivalent to the §106 rights. As to the interference with contract count, the court found that the contract right allegedly injured was that of preparing derivative works, another §106 right. In response to the argument that suit for interference with contract involved additional elements of proof such as the knowledge of the existence of the contract, the court held that this did not preclude the application of §301 to preempt such a claim where the contract right involved was the right to adapt and print copies of a copyrighted work. In doing so, the court quoted from the portion of the House Committee Report that "to the extent that the unfair competition concept known as 'interference with contract relations' is merely the equivalent of copyright protection, it would be preempted."[187] This decision can be viewed as at least one judicial expression that the amendment did not alter the substantive nature of §301 or the underlying intent of the Congress as expressed in the committee reports. This conclusion is weakened by the fact that the court never discussed the amendment and its impact on the authority of the statements in the committee reports.

Thus, it is still unclear how much weight the judiciary will give to the statements in the House report, the House floor amendment, or the Justice Department letter. In *Harper & Row*, the court quoted the House Committee Report without even considering the amendment, treating it as if it had full validity. In *Bryce*, the court candidly admits its perplexity. *Bryce*, however, was governed by the 1909 Act. The court's only real concern was whether the 1976 Act had evidenced unmistakable congressional intent to preempt state trade secret laws. Concluding that the 1976 Act was not clearly opposed to state trade secret protection ended the inquiry. *Mitchell's* treatment of the weight to be accorded to the House Committee Report is perhaps the most reasonable middle ground. The list of actions simply indicates areas where Congress felt the issue of preemption might be raised and thus an indication that analysis under §§301 and 106 is called for. No opinion has yet taken into account the Justice Department letter which might lead a court to take a stronger preemption stance, particularly where the state law claim goes under the title of misappropriation.[188]

---

[187] *Id.* at 853.

[188] The cases have mentioned Congressman Seiberling's referral to the Justice Department's letter, but no case has yet considered the text of the letter itself. Given the Justice Department's

There are additional cases concerned with the issue of equivalent rights. In the criminal case of *Commonwealth v. Rizzuto*,[189] the court held that §301 required the preemption of a state law prosecution for receiving stolen property which consisted of the programs embodied on unauthorized videotape recordings of copyrighted movies. Since the act that was outlawed was the duplicating of works for sale and nothing else was being taken from the copyright owners, the court held that only the provisions of the Copyright Act were applicable to restrain the behavior in question. The court noted that the case would have been different if the actual physical copies themselves had been stolen as such a theft could be prosecuted under state law.[190] The court centered its opinion on the fact that the prohibited behavior in the case was the unauthorized duplication of a clearly copyrightable work and thus reasoned that a restraint on that activity would amount to a copyright-like restraint. In *Suid v. Newsweek Magazine*,[191] the author of a 357-page book on American war movies sued *Newsweek* for both copyright infringement and unfair competition where a *Newsweek* article had copied from some unpublished letters set forth in his book. The court gave the allegation of the common-law right short shrift with the accurate observation that "[o]ne of those exclusive rights is the right to reproduce the original work."[192]

In *John H. Harland Co. v. Clarke Checks, Inc.*,[193] the court inquired whether there were different elements of proof involved as the basis for determining if the rights were equivalent. The court held that causes of action stated under Georgia's Deceptive Trade Practices Act and the Georgia law of unfair competition were not preempted under §301(b) (3) because these causes of action required proof of confusion

---

virulent opposition to the misappropriation doctrine, if Congressman Seiberling's amendment is regarded as implementing the Justice Department position then the misappropriation doctrine was clearly intended to be preempted.

[189] 1978-81 Copyright L. Dec. (CCH) ¶25,233 (Mass. Super. Ct. 1980), *aff'd sub. nom.*, Commonwealth v. Yourawski, 425 N.E.2d 298 (1981).

[190] The court also ruled that the intangible "literary property" in the motion pictures was incapable of being property under the Massachusetts stolen property act. *Id.* at 16,382. See also Mass. Ann. Laws ch. 266, §60 (Michie/Law. Co-op. 1980).

[191] 503 F. Supp. 146 (D.D.C. 1980).

[192] *Id.* at 149.

[193] 1978-91 Copyright L. Dec. (CCH) ¶25,265 (N.D. Ga. 1980). Similarly, in George P. Ballas Buick-GMC, Inc. v. Taylor Buick, Inc., 5 Ohio Misc. 2d 16, 449 N.E.2d 805 (C. P. Lucas County 1981), *aff'd*, 5 Ohio App. 3d 71, 449 N.E.2d 503 (1982), the court held that §301 did not preempt an action labeled as misappropriation of an advertising design under Ohio's Deceptive Trade Practices Act, Ohio Rev. Code Ann. §§4165.01-.04 (Page 1980), because the plaintiff would have to prove confusion or deception of the public, elements of proof not found in a copyright infringement action.

or deception of the public, elements of proof not found in a copyright infringement action. In *Fox v. Wiener Laces, Inc.*,[194] the court ruled that plaintiff could maintain an action in contract or quasi contract in state court and the remedies could include injunctive relief barring the defendant from copying her designs. The court did not state the basis of its conclusion, perhaps assuming it to be obvious in this type of case. In *Dealer Advertising Development, Inc. v. Barbara Allan Financial Advertising, Inc.*,[195] some of the various unfair competition claims were held to allege the same acts and seek the same relief as would a statutory copyright claim. Although this would have easily justified a finding of preemption, the court instead rested its decision on the collateral claims rule which bars duplicative relief. Had the court rested its decision on preemption, the result would be unchanged.

The issue of copyright preemption arises when a plaintiff asserts a state law cause of action based on some right which the defendant has violated by duplicating some creation, work product, or other property of the plaintiff. The determination of rights equivalency can be approached in several ways. One approach is to compare the elements of proof of the respective causes of action. If the state cause of action requires the proof of some element such as confusion of the public or "passing off," this will indicate that the cause of action is not preempted. If there is no such extra element, then the state action is preempted. The *Mitchell*[196] and *John H. Harland Co.*[197] cases employ this approach.

Comparing the elements of proof of a state action with those of copyright infringement simply is not an accurate guide to whether the rights being claimed are equivalent. The preemption issue is whether the rights are equivalent, not whether they have similar or different elements of proof. If the right being claimed under the state cause of action is one of the exclusive rights listed in §106, preemption is indicated regardless of how similar or different the elements of proof may be. That the courts have not yet reached any unreasonable results is probably due to the fact that the comparison of elements has only been used in those cases where it is consistent with comparing the rights being asserted.

---

[194] 74 App. Div. 2d 549, 425 N.Y.S.2d 114 (1980).
[195] 1978-81 Copyright L. Dec. (CCH) ¶25,219 (W.D. Mich. 1979).
[196] See text accompanying notes 179-82 *supra*.
[197] See text accompanying note 193 *supra*.

A functional approach is to examine the impact and effect of the right asserted at state law and its remedy. If the effect is to place the defendant under the same kind of restrictions from copying and use as would the copyright laws, then the right is preempted. This is among the reasons articulated by the courts in *Harper & Row*,[198] *Commonwealth v. Rizzuto*,[199] and *Suid*.[200]

This approach examines the nature of the right claimed under the state cause of action rather than the elements of proof. If these rights are essentially to prohibit all others from copying,[201] then the state action is preempted.

A few cases have arisen involving preemption challenges to state trade secret laws. At first blush the preemption challenge would seem to be trivial in light of the Supreme Court's decision in *Kewanee Oil Co. v. Bicron Corp.*[202] The issue persists, however, and the reasoning in the opinions raises some analytic issues of importance.

In *Warrington Associates, Inc. v. Real-Time Engineering Systems, Inc.*,[203] the defendant was charged with having "misappropriated Warrington's secret computer software programs (Count I), unlawfully interfered with and conspired to breach contractual assurances of confidentiality owed to Warrington (Counts II and III), infringed Warrington's copyrights (Count IV), and engaged in unfair competition (Count V)."[204] The defendant's motion to dismiss all counts except the statutory copyright claim was treated as a motion for summary judgment and denied. The court quoted from the House Committee Report that "[t]he evolving common law rights of 'privacy,' 'publicity,' and trade secrets, . . . would remain unaffected so long as the causes of action contain elements such as an invasion of personal rights or a breach of trust or confidentiality."[205] The court took no notice of the deletion of the examples from §301 (b) (3) on the House floor by the Seiberling amendment.[206] After noting the Supreme Court decision in *Kewanee Oil Co. v. Bicron Corp.*,[207] the court

---

[198] See text accompanying notes 185-87 *supra*.

[199] See text accompanying notes 189-90 *supra*.

[200] See text accompanying notes 191-92 *supra*.

[101] The word "copying" is used in the broad sense of any right among those listed in §106 of the 1976 Copyright Act, 17 U.S.C. §106 (Supp. V 1981).

[202] 416 U.S. 470 (1974).

[203] 522 F. Supp. 367 (N.D. Ill. 1981).

[204] *Id.* at 368.

[205] *Id.* at 369.

[206] *Id.*

[207] 416 U.S. 470 (1974).

concluded that the trade secret claims were not preempted since "the state trade secret tort is premised on concepts of breach of trust and confidentiality, and not copying."[208]

A contrary result was reached in *Avco Corp. v. Precision Air Parts, Inc.*,[209] in which the defendant manufactured replacement parts for aircraft engines of which the plaintiff was the original manufacturer. One method for the second source manufacturer to obtain the necessary approval from the FAA for replacement parts is to show that its parts designs are identical with those of the original manufacturer. Plaintiff filed a complaint for misappropriation of trade secrets and unfair competition (Count I) and common-law copyright infringement (Count II). Plaintiff claimed that defendant had "without proper authority obtained and improperly utilized copies of Lycoming proprietary drawings and specifications to obtain PMAs for replacement parts for Lycoming engines."[210] Plaintiff further alleged that the defendant "copied or duplicated, or caused additional copies or duplications to be made from, such original Lycoming drawings and specifications"[211] of the plaintiff's designs which the defendant used to obtain its approval as a manufacturer of replacement parts.

The court dismissed the complaint for failure to state a cause of action for which relief could be granted, holding that the alleged state law causes of action were preempted under §301.[212] The court stated that state trade secret laws would be preempted if they did not require "the elements of an invasion of privacy, a trespass, a breach of trust or a breach of confidentiality."[213] The court then noted that the right plaintiff claimed to have been violated was the exclusive right to copy drawings and designs and that plaintiff had "not even alleged, much less shown that Defendant has committed any of the elements that allow the common law rights of 'trade secrets' to avoid preemption."[214]

What these cases have in common is a focus on the elements of proof needed to establish the state law tort as the basis for testing equivalency of rights under §301 (b) (3).[215] The preemption issue turns

---

[208] 522 F. Supp. at 369.

[209] 1978-81 Copyright L. Rep. (CCH) ¶25,207 (M.D. Ala. 1980), *aff'd on other grounds*, 676 F.2d 494 (11th Cir.) (statute of limitations), *cert. denied*, 103 S. Ct. 450 (1982).

[210] *Id.* at 16,156.

[211] *Id.*

[212] *Id.* at 16,160.

[213] *Id.* at 16,159.

[214] *Id.*

[215] 17 U.S.C. §301(b) (3) (Supp. V 1981).

on whether the elements of proof of the state action are different from those for copyright infringement rather than on whether the remedy for the prevailing plaintiff will enforce an exclusive right to copy equivalent to that provided by §106.[216] The cases are quite compatible with each other.[217] In *Warrington*[218] there is a finding of a breach of contract and confidential relationship as the justification for the court's restraint on copying, while in *Avco* it is the absence of these elements that sustains the preemption challenge.[219] Simply to establish that one cause of action will require proof of different elements need not change the fact that the rights being sustained may well be equivalent to those provided under §106. As applied to misappropriation cases, the argument would run that since the misappropriation doctrine involves the proof of different elements than copyright infringement,[220] it is not preempted. This overlooks the fact that the right being claimed is the exclusive right to copy a work or an article, which is precisely the essence of the rights in §106.[221] As applied to trade secret cases, this preemption argument also seems logically plausible if the analysis is

---

[216] 17 U.S.C. §106 (Supp. V 1981) provides:

§106. Exclusive rights in copyrighted works
[T]he owner of copyright under this title has the exclusive rights to do and to authorize any of the following:
(1) to reproduce the copyrighted work in copies or phonorecords;
(2) to prepare derivative works based upon the copyrighted work;
(3) to distribute copies or phonorecords of the copyrighted work to the public by sale or other transfer of ownership, or by rental, lease or lending;
(4) . . . to perform the copyrighted work publicly; and
(5) . . . to display the copyrighted work publicly.

[217] The seeming difference is that *Avco* found a state trade secret claim to be preempted while *Warrington* did not.

[218] See text accompanying notes 203-8 *supra*. See also M. Bryce & Associates v. Gladstone, 107 Wis. 2d 241, 319 N.W. 2d 907 (Wis. App.), *cert. denied*, 103 S. Ct. 258 (1982).

[219] The trade secret cases are easily reconciled. The crucial point is that the rights being asserted in trade secrets cases are not "exclusive" rights within the meaning of §106 of the Copyright Act, 17 U.S.C. §106 (Supp. V 1981), or of the Copyright Clause of the Constitution. They are only asserted against an individual who has stolen, committed a breach of a trust, or otherwise had a relationship with the claimant which members of the general public do not occupy. Provided the trade secret is independently recreated, or made public by its owner, trade secret law will not prevent the public from taking any of the acts listed in §106. The reason the elements test has worked in the trade secret cases is that the elements tested for—theft, breach of trust, etc.—are precisely those acts by which the defendant is differentiated from the general public.

[220] Typically, misappropriation is said to include such elements of proof as the severe damage done to the originator by the competitor's copying; the time, skill, and money invested by the originator; or the immorality of the competitor obtaining a "free ride" on the originator's efforts. Only the second *Storch* case has made a serious effort to explore these issues as matters of proof.

[221] See text accompanying notes 196-200 *supra* and note 300 *infra*.

limited to a narrow reading of the alleged right. However, an examination of the results of allowing the state law right will illustrate the difference between trade secret law and misappropriation. Granting trade secret protection does nothing to interfere with the right of the public to make free use of that which has entered public circulation or awareness. There is no restraint on copying by any competitor for any purpose, only a restraint on how the copied article or information is initially obtained. Misappropriation, by contrast, would forbid copying by any competitor regardless of how widespread the public distribution of the work in question.

B. THE §102 MEASURE

The other measure of the §301 test, subject-matter coverage, seems to be easier to determine. There is useful legislative history to help determine a number of questions concerning what is within the ambit of § 102(a).[222] The definitions of §101 seem adequate for most problems[223] and much of the extensive decisional law under the prior Act remains relevant so there is ample guidance for both bench and bar.

The touchy area of the "design of a useful article" was specifically excluded from the definition of "Pictorial, graphic and sculptural works" in the 1976 Act except "to the extent that, such design incorporates pictorial, graphic, or sculptural features that can be identified separately from, and are capable of existing independently of, the utilitarian aspects of the article."[224] Thus earlier cases like *Esquire, Inc. v. Ringer*[225] and *Eltra Corp. v. Ringer*[226] were clearly enough

---

[222] *See* H.R. Rep. No. 1476, 94th Cong., 2d Sess. 51-57 (1976); S. Rep. No. 473, 94th Cong., 1st Sess. 50-54 (1975).

[223] See, e.g., 17 U.S.C. §101 (Supp. V 1980) (definitions of "audiovisual works," "collective works," "compilation," "derivative work," "literary works," "motion pictures," "phonorecords," "pictorial, graphic and sculptural works," "sound recordings," and "useful article"). In Harper & Row Publishers, Inc. v. Nation Enterprises, 501 F. Supp. 848 (S.D.N.Y. 1980), in answer to a count for copyright infringement, the defense argued ex-President Ford's memoirs were not a work of authorship under §102 but merely a narrative of facts which were not eligible to copyright protection. The court had no trouble in rejecting this argument and apparently the defendant did not press it seriously.

[224] 17 U.S.C. §101 (Supp. V 1980) (definition of "Pictorial, graphic, and sculptural works").

[225] 591 F.2d 796 (D.C.Cir. 1978) (outdoor lamp pole configuration held ineligible for copyright).

[226] 580 F.2d 294 (4th Cir. 1978) (typeface designs held ineligible for copyright); but see Kieselstein-Cord v. Accessories by Pearl, Inc., 632 F.2d 989 (1980), *rev'g and remanding*, 480 F. Supp. 732 (S.D.N.Y. 1980) (belt buckle designs held valid).

reaffirmed in the 1976 Act to discourage relitigation of their issues.[227] Whatever the reason, serious litigation of the coverage of §§102 and 103 is relatively rare.[228]

This scarcity of cases, however, should not obscure the potential trap in the subject-matter test of § 301. The definition of eligible subject matter in §102(a) sought to accomplish several purposes. These included providing federal protection for unpublished works. To accomplish this goal fixation was established as the starting point of federal protection.[229] The drafters explicitly desired to have the statute protect less than the full possible range of constitutionally eligible subject matter. They were not desirous of giving copyright protection to every constitutionally eligible "Writings."[230] And, as previously noted, Congress deliberately and explicitly excluded a number of categories of constitutionally eligible subject matter.[231]

Section 301 states that there will be no preemption of state law regarding "subject matter that does not come within the subject matter of copyright as specified by sections 102 and 103." This language apparently was intended to make the preemption scheme of §301 conform to the preemption standards set forth in *Goldstein*.[232] If the

---

[227] The House Report makes it clear that the definitions of "pictorial, graphic, and sculptural works" and "useful article" in §101 of the 1976 Act embody an explicit congressional intent to exclude useful articles and their designs from copyright protection except for those elements which can be separated from the article and have an independent existence apart from the utilitarian aspects of the article. H.R. Rep. No. 1476, 94th Cong., 2d Sess. 51-52 (1976); S. Rep. No. 473, 94th Cong., 1st Sess. 50-51 (1975). The House Report also contained a list of examples of uncopyrightable articles including "the shape of an automobile, airplane, ladies' dress, food processor, television set, or any other industrial product" unless the design element in question met the test of independence and separability. The same rule was to apply to architectural works, the Committee distinguishing between" [p]urely nonfunctional or monumental structures" and "the utilitarian aspects of the structure." *Id.* at 55. The Committee chose to defer consideration of protecting typeface designs for copyright protection and made it explicit that they were outside the ambit of the Act. *Id.*

[228] Other issues the 1976 Act laid to rest were the copyrightability of computer programs and whether the subject matter coverage of statutory protection was coextensive with the maximum permitted by the Copyright Clause. Under the 1976 Act, "Copyright protection subsists . . . in original works of authorship fixed in any tangible medium of expression, now known or later developed, from which they can be perceived, reproduced, or otherwise communicated, either directly or with the aid of a machine or device." 17 U.S.C. §102(a) (Supp. V 1981). This explicitly overruled White-Smith Music Publishing Co. v. Apollo Co., 209 U.S. 1 (1908), which had denied copyright protection to player piano rolls because their perforations could not be intelligibly read by the unaided human eye. Under the 1976 Act, computer programs are deemed literary works and they are copyrightable "to the extent that they incorporate authorship in the programmer's expression of original ideas, as distinguished from the ideas themselves." H.R. Rep. No. 1476, 94th Cong., 2d Sess. 54 (1976).

[229] 17 U.S.C. §102(a) (Supp. V 1981).

[230] See note 228 *supra.*

[231] See text accompanying notes 224-27 *supra.*

[232] 412 U.S. 546 (1973).

subject matter was eligible for statutory copyright protection, the *Goldstein* interpretation of *Sears-Compco* prevents the states from providing copyright protection. If statutory protection for the subject matter was not available, then *Goldstein* requires an inquiry to determine whether the area was left unattended by Congress or the denial of protection represented a congressional decision which would preempt the states.

Congress may have gone the Supreme Court one better. On its face, §301 requires only the first of the two inquiries formulated in *Goldstein*. Even if Congress considered protecting certain subject matter and consciously and explicitly determined that such subject matter should best be left unprotected, the language of §301 by itself would not require preemption. The courts would have to take it on themselves to examine this issue without any statutory directive to do so. There is no basis in the statutory language to require such an inquiry. On this basis the states can use the misappropriation doctrine to provide what is essentially copyright protection for such things as typeface designs or dress designs and other items Congress has deliberately excluded from copyright protection.

The first opinion in *Leonard Storch Enterprises, Inc. v. Mergenthaler Linotype Co.*[233] illustrates the problem. In that case, decided under the 1909 Act, the denial of the motion to dismiss was predicated on the dual inquiry suggested by *Goldstein* (1) that typeface designs were generically ineligible for copyright protection and (2) that Congress had left the area unattended.[234] Under the 1976 Act only the first of these inquiries would be relevant. The Committee Report concerning typeface designs states:[235]

> The Committee has considered, but chosen to defer, the possibility of protecting the design of typefaces.... The Committee does not regard the design of typeface ... to be a copyrightable "pictorial, graphic, or sculptural work" within the meaning of this bill and the application of the dividing line in section 101.

If the court makes an inquiry into whether or not the area is unattended, then state protection of typeface designs is very likely to be preempted. If no such inquiry is made, then it seems almost certain

---

[233] 1978–81 Copyright L. Dec. (CCH) ¶25,092 (E.D.N.Y. 1979).

[234] *Id.* at 15,523. While there is no controversy that typeface designs were generically ineligible for copyright protection, there is a good deal of room for debate over whether Congress did this by design or by inadvertence.

[235] H.R. Rep. No. 1476, 94th Cong., 2d Sess. 55 (1976).

that there will be no preemption. It may be that other considerations will dictate a consistent resolution to each specific subject matter area;[236] the possibility for inconsistency is built into the statute.

An extreme example of the kind of problem this could create is dramatically indicated by the rationale adopted by the court in *Bromhall v. Rorvik*.[237] The plaintiff, a respected genetic research scientist, sent the defendant a copy of an unpublished nine-page summary of his doctoral thesis. The defendant asked for the information under the pretense of writing a serious article or book on the topic, but in fact used the material to lend credibility to a work of fiction which dealt with the topic in a sensational manner. Plaintiff filed suit and included in his complaint counts for infringement of his common-law copyright in the unpublished work and for equitable relief. Defendant's motion to dismiss the count for infringement of the common-law copyright was granted on the ground that the 1976 Copyright Act had abolished the common-law copyright in fixed but unpublished works, a category which clearly applied to the plaintiff's summary. The claim of common-law copyright was held to be preempted.[238]

Turning to the claim for equitable relief, the court then characterized the plaintiff's claim as one for the fraudulent appropriation of an idea,[239] and declared that Pennsylvania recognized such rights in ideas.[240] The court then stated:[241]

Finally, I am of the view that the claims asserted in count V are not governed by the Copyright Act. Copyright protection extends only

---

[236] The practical difficulties of protecting matter within one state where it is not guaranteed protection in others would prove a sufficient difficulty to cause state courts to hesitate before providing protection. For example, the courts of one state might attempt to provide protection for industrial designs arguing that since they are not within the subject matter of copyright under §§102 and 103, the state protection is not preempted under §301(b) (1). If a court accepted this argument—which is based on a literal reading of the statute—the state protection would not deter manufacturers from copying industrial designs in other states which did not recognize the right. Could the first state constitutionally bar products manufactured in the second state from being sold within its borders? The practical problem of enforcement might prove insuperable, and this could chill the desire of a court to grant such protection in the first place.

[237] 478 F. Supp. 361 (E.D. Pa. 1979).

[238] *Id.* at 366.

[239] *Ibid.*

[240] *Id.* at 367. The two cases the court cited as authority for its position that ideas could be "property" were Schott v. Westinghouse Electric Corp., 436 Pa. 279, 259 A.2d 443 (1969), and Thomas v. R. J. Reynolds Tobacco Co., 350 Pa. 262, 38 A.2d 61 (1944), cited at 478 F. Supp. at 367. These cases involved the submission of ideas for promotional campaigns to manufacturers and sought compensation on a contractual or quasi-contractual basis.

[241] 478 F. Supp. at 367.

to the *expression* of an idea, not the idea itself. Section 102 (b) of the Act reads:

> (b) In no case does copyright protection for an original work of authorship extend to any idea, procedure, process, system, method of operation, concept, principle, or discovery, regardless of the form in which it is described, explained, illustrated or embodied. . . .

Since the claims now being considered are not entitled to protection under the Act, they are not preempted by the Act. §301(b) (1) and (b) (3).

The court's position is based on a misreading of the statute but is invited by the statutory language. Section 102(b) is an embodiment of the idea-expression distinction in copyright law. The distinction between idea and expression, or the "idea-expression dichotomy" as it is often called, is the term of art used in copyright law to indicate the elements in a copyrighted work which the grant of the copyright monopoly does not take from the public.[242] It differentiates those elements in a copyrighted work which are protected from those which may be freely copied and plagiarized by the public.[243] It is the limit of the protection extended by the statutory monopoly of copyright to subject matter included under §102(a), not a definition of excluded subject matter. Section 301(b) (1) addresses the issue of preemption in terms of whether the category of work involved is generically eligible for copyright protection under §§102(a) and 103. Section 102(b) is concerned with the limits of protection available to categories of works that fall within §§102(a) and 103.

The result in the *Bromhall* case seems wrong. It is hard to see any justification for taking §301(b) (1) as a charter of authority for state protection of ideas. The notion that ideas could be protected either by copyright or the common law has always been rejected, and even the most ardent advocates of common-law copyright have consistently disclaimed any capacity of the common law to protect ideas. There is certainly not the slightest reason in the legislative history to believe

---

[242] "In no case does copyright protection for an original work of authorship extend to any idea, procedure, process, system, method of operation, concept, principle, or discovery, regardless of the form in which it is described, explained, illustrated, or embodied in such work." 17 U.S.C. §102(b) (Supp. V 1981).

[243] This doctrine has been extensively litigated in cases involving the more subtle forms of plagiarism rather than literal copying. The classic exposition of the doctrine and its application in the context of infringement is Judge Learned Hand's opinions in Sheldon v. Metro-Goldwyn Pictures Corp., 81 F.2d 49 (2d Cir.), *cert. denied*, 298 U.S. 669 (1936), and Nichols v. Universal Pictures Corp., 45 F.2d 119 (2d Cir. 1930), *cert. denied*, 282 U.S. 902 (1931).

that Congress intended §102(b) to function as a grant of authority to the states to protect facts and information. The House and Senate Reports could hardly be more explicit:[244]

> Section 102(b) in no way enlarges or contracts the scope of copyright protection under the present law. Its purpose is to restate, in the context of the new single Federal system of copyright, that the basic dichotomy between expression and idea remains unchanged.

This is the entire discussion of §102(b) in the committee reports that accompanied the 1976 Copyright Act. There is certainly nothing in this comment that can conceivably be taken as endorsing such a drastic change as to allow the states to redefine the public domain to restrict access to facts.

Similar arguments have faced the courts in a number of cases arising under the 1909 Act.[245] These cases have consistently treated facts, research, and the like as being unprotectible either by copyright or common law. *Hoehling v. Universal City Studios, Inc.,*[246] arose under the 1909 Act and after the Supreme Court's decisions in *Goldstein* and *Kewanee*. The plaintiff alleged that parts of his book on the explosion of the Hindenburg, including facts he had obtained by extensive personal research, had been copied by the defendant's movie and filed a complaint charging statutory copyright infringement and common-law unfair competition.[247] On appeal from a grant of summary judgment for the defendants, the Second Circuit first rejected the argument that there could be a copyright in facts. Identifying the policy considerations underlying this rule, the court stated:[248]

> To avoid a chilling effect on authors who contemplate tackling an historical issue or event, broad latitude must be granted to subsequent authors who make use of historical subject matters, including theories or plots. Learned Hand counseled in *Meyers v. Mail & Express Co.,* 36 C.O. Bull. 478, 479 (S.D.N.Y. 1919), "[t]here

---

[244] H.R. Rep. No. 1476, 94th Cong., 2d Sess. 56-57 (1976); S. Rep. No. 473, 94th Cong., 1st Sess. 54 (1975).

[245] Hoehling v. Universal City Studios, Inc., 618 F.2d 972 (2d Cir.), *cert denied,* 449 U.S. 841 (1980); Miller v. Universal City Studios, Inc., 650 F.2d 1365 (5th Cir. 1981), *rev'g* 460 F. Supp. 984 (S.D. Fla. 1978); Rosemont Enterprises, Inc. v. Random House, Inc., 366 F.2d 303 (2d Cir. 1966), *cert. denied,* 385 U.S. 1009 (1967); but see Toksvig v. Bruce Publishing Co., 181 F.2d 664 (7th cir. 1950).

[246] 618 F.2d 972 (2d Cir.), *cert. denied,* 449 U.S. 841 (1980).

[247] *Id.* at 977.

[248] *Id.* at 978.

cannot be any such thing as copyright in the order of presentation of the facts, nor, indeed, in their selection."

The court concluded by applying this rationale to the plaintiff's common-law claim:[249]

Where, as here, historical facts, themes, and research have been deliberately exempted from the scope of copyright protection to vindicate the overriding goal of encouraging contributions to recorded knowledge, the states are pre-empted from removing such material from the public domain. "To forbid copying" in this case "would interfere with the federal policy . . . of allowing free access to copy whatever the federal patent and copyright laws leave in the public domain."

In *Suid v. Newsweek Magazine*,[250] arising under the 1976 Act, the court was faced with the same arguments for common-law protection of research as arose in *Bromhall*.[251] In *Suid*, the complaint contained a statutory copyright count, an unfair competition count, and a count for a *prima facie* tort. The court had no trouble stating that the book was a work within the scope of §102 of the 1976 Copyright Act and, in reference to any notion that the defendant did not have a right to copy the results of research, concluded with the following quote from the Second Circuit's opinion in *Hoehling v. Universal City Studios, Inc.*: "Where, as here, historical facts, themes, and research have been deliberately exempted from the scope of copyright protection to vindicate the overriding goal of encouraging contributions to recorded knowledge, the states are pre-empted from removing such materials from the public domain."[252]

It is hard to accept *Bromhall*'s conclusion that ideas may be protected from use under state law misappropriation doctrine, yet barring any problem of preemption based on the patent laws[253] this is the conclusion that was reached by a literal reading of §301. It may be argued that there are special circumstances in *Bromhall* which would reduce the applicability of its holding (i.e., an unpublished work of serious research which is obtained by fraud and then used for a commercially oriented sensational novel), yet the fact remains that the

[249] *Id.* at 980.
[250] 503 F. Supp. 146 (D.D.C. 1980).
[251] 478 F. Supp. 361 (E.D. Pa. 1979).
[252] 503 F. Supp. at 149.
[253] See notes 41, 242-43 *supra*.

court arrived at this result by a literal if perverse reading of the Copyright Act. The simple-minded language of §301 invites just such an unthinking reaction. By reducing the preemption analysis to a simple question whether a given work is covered by the copyright statute, §301 suggests that no further consideration need be given to the issue. Thus the Copyright Act's preemption provisions are taken as an express authority for state law protection of ideas. This results from the fact that §301 states the preemption test in terms of §§102 and 106. These sections of the statute, particularly §102(b), were designed to serve totally different purposes from defining the appropriate limits on the state sphere of competence under the federal copyright scheme. Section 102(b) was meant to insure the Copyright Act did not hinder the public's access to all intellectual elements that it listed.

Even if the language of §301 is not misread in the fashion of *Bromhall*, it is clear that it invites an unthinking mechanical response to any evaluation of the goals and philosophy of the copyright system.[254] The scheme of §301 is merely concerned with line drawing without any sensitivity to any issues of the public interest or the public domain. It suggests that the problems of balancing public interest and monopoly incentives are irrelevant. Thus it invites mechanical decisionmaking to provide state law copyright protection without any sensitivity to the concern for the public interest. *Goldstein* suggested the inquiry into public interest was to be conducted and delineated by congressional action rather than by a constitutional standard. In its efforts to incorporate *Goldstein* into the preemption provisions,[255] Congress made no attempt to define the preemption standards in a rational or principled fashion.[256] Given this failure, results such as *Bromhall* must almost be regarded as disappointing but not surprising.

C. PREEMPTION OUTSIDE OF §301

There are other preemptive factors in the Copyright Act going beyond the issues of equivalency in §301. The anti-blind bidding

---

[254] Under the language of §301 the test for preemption is an inquiry of whether the subject matter is eligible for copyright protection or not. It ignores the issue of why the subject matter is ineligible and thus invites the courts to do likewise. Thus a literal application of §301 would lead to the absurd result that a congressional desire that something be free to be copied would authorize state court creation of monopoly protection.

[255] See text accompanying notes 159-63 *supra*.

[256] See text accompanying notes 150-78 *supra*.

statutes[257] present a case in point. It has become more and more the practice of the motion picture industry to engage in the practice of "blind bidding" for the distribution of its feature films. When a picture is partially finished, the distributors send various film clips, publicity, and information on the film to the various theater owners and ask them to bid on the pictures. For whatever reason, it is enough of a seller's market for the distributors to insist on both cash and percentage guarantees, minimum length of runs, and advance payment of the cash guarantees from the theater owners before the latter have even seen a finished version of the film. As one might expect, not all of the films thus secured by the theaters are box office hits, and the theater owners have felt they are being coerced into a very unfavorable situation by the practices of the movie industry.

State anti-blind bidding statutes have been the response. Essentially these statutes provide that theater owners must be given an opportunity to see the finished films before they are required to make advance payments or to give irrevocable guarantees of cash or minimum theater playing time. These statutes have resulted in at least three cases to date which have challenged the constitutionality of the statutes on various constitutional theories, including copyright preemption.[258]

The first case to arise was *Allied Artists Pictures Corp. v. Rhodes,*[259] where the validity of Ohio's anti-blind bidding statute[260] was attacked by several motion picture distributors and producers. The Ohio statute outlawed blind bidding and required that there be open bidding on the

---

[257] Alabama: Ala. Code §§8-18-1 to -6 (Supp. 1982); Georgia: Ga. Code Ann. §§106-1301 to -1305 (Supp. 1982); Idaho: Idaho Code §§18-7701 to -7708 (Supp. 1983); Louisiana: La. Rev. Stat. Ann. §§2901-05 (West Supp. 1983); Maine: Me. Rev. Stat. Ann. tit. 10, §§1901-05 (1980); Massachusetts: Mass. Ann. Laws ch. 93F, §§1-4 (Michie/Law. Co-op. Supp. 1983); Missouri: Mo. Ann. Stat. §§407.350-.357 (Vernon Supp. 1983); New Mexico: N.M. Stat. Ann. §§57-5A-1 to -5 (Supp. 1983); North Carolina: N.C. Gen. Stat. §§75c-1 to -5 (1981); Ohio: Ohio Rev. Code Ann. §§1333.05-07 (Page 1979); Pennsylvania: Pa. Stat. Ann. tit. 74, §§203-1 to -11 (Purdon Supp. 1983); South Carolina: S.C. Code Ann. §§39-5-510 to -560 (Law. Co-op. Supp. 1982); Tennessee: Tenn. Code Ann. §§47-25-701 to -704 (Supp. 1983); Utah: Utah Code Ann. §§13-13-1 to -4 (Supp. 1981); Virginia: Va. Code §§59.1-255 to -261 (1982); Washington: Wash. Rev. Code §§19.58.010-.905 (Supp. 1983); West Virginia: W. Va. Code §§47-110-1 to -4 (1980).

[258] This paper is concerned with the copyright preemption issue and will not touch upon the other constitutional issues raised in these cases. The various constitutional challenges in these cases have included lengthy arguments that the statutes violate the Commerce Clause, the First Amendment, the Due Process Clause of the Fourteenth Amendment, and are preempted under the Supremacy Clause by virtue of the federal antitrust laws.

[259] 496 F. Supp. 408 (S.D. Ohio 1980), *aff'd in part, rev'd and remanded in part,* 679 F.2d 656 (6th Cir. 1982).

[260] Ohio Rev. Code Ann. §§1333.05-.07 (Page 1979).

distribution of films. The Act also prohibited the conditioning of a license upon payment of a guarantee where the rental for the movie was based on attendance or box office receipts and the requiring of payment of guarantees or deposits more than fourteen days in advance.

On the copyright preemption challenge, the plaintiffs made their strongest argument on the theory that the state law unduly restricted the exercise of their federal rights.[261] The argument essentially had two prongs. First, the burdens of mandatory trade screenings, semipublic bidding, disclosure, inability to require guarantees as a condition of a film rental, and other restrictions were sufficiently onerous to amount to a serious deprivation of the plantiffs' rights to reproduce, perform, and lease that were given to them exclusively under §106 of the 1976 Copyright Act. Second, the requirement of a mandatory trade screening amounted to a forced performance and thus a serious curtailment and denigration of their §106 rights.

The court denied the proposition that the Copyright Act guaranteed the owner an unlimited right to market the work without state control. The court stated:[262]

> The first three contentions [of the plaintiffs] proceed from the erroneous premises that the copyright confers on its owner the right to dispose of its subject matter on the optimum terms and that the fundamental purpose of the copyright laws is to reward the owner. . . .
>
> The fundamental purpose of the constitutional grant of copyright is enunciated in Article I, §8 as "to promoted the progress of Sciences [*sic*] and useful Arts." The rationale was explained by the Supreme Court as based on "the conviction that encouragement of individuals by personal gain is the best way to advance public welfare through the talents of authors. . . ." *Mazer v. Stein*, 347 U.S. 201, 219 (1954). "The copyright law, like the patent statutes, make reward to the owner a secondary consideration." *United States v. Paramount Pictures, Inc.*, 334 U.S. 131, 158 (1948). Accordingly, the primary purpose of copyright is *not* to reward the author, but is rather to secure "the general benefits derived by the public from the labors of authors." *Fox Films v. Doyal*, 286 U.S. 123, 128 (1932); *Twentieth Century Music Corp. v. Aiken*, 422 U.S. 151, 156 (1975).

---

[261] 496 F. Supp. at 445-46.
[262] *Id.* at 446.

With the premise established that the public interest was paramount rather than the author's monopoly, the court differentiated between rights granted by the copyright statutes and the property produced and marketed under such rights. The court concluded that a statute regulating the marketing of a product was not preempted simply because it happened to be a copy of a copyrighted work. As a policy matter under both the Constitution and the statutes, the public interest did not require the preemption of a statute aimed at controlling the distribution practices of a copyright owner.

The plaintiffs' remaining copyright preemption argument was that the requirement of a screening before distribution in Ohio compelled a performance in Ohio within the meaning of the 1976 Copyright Act.[263] The court noted that the Ohio statute compelled a performance only after the plaintiffs had made their decision to distribute their motion pictures in Ohio and did not deprive the plaintiffs of their right to perform their film publicly. In an analysis reminiscent of *Kewanee*, the court found the impact of the Ohio statute was compatible with the underlying public interests in the Copyright Act. Trade screening permitted the theater owners to make more informed judgments about the films they were licensing while blind bidding denied this opportunity. Thus blind bidding tended to erase any differences in product while trade screenings would place more of a premium on creating better films. Thus a prohibition on blind bidding not only rectified a market situation the state perceived as inequitable, it reinforced the basic purpose of the copyright laws by rewarding better films. The court stated:[264]

> All of the provisions of the statute complained of tend to differentiate the reward for individual copyrights by enabling exhibitors to distinguish between proffered motion pictures. This effect and the anticipated increased opportunity the Act affords to independents for the showing of their films, far from frustrating the objectives of Congress in enacting the Copyright Act, further the wide dissemination of copyrighted works and thereby its primary object "to advance the public welfare through the talents of authors. . . ." *Mazer v. Stein*, 347 U.S. 201, 249 (1954).

---

[263] *See* 17 U.S.C. §101 (Supp. V 1981) (definition of "perform"). The court classified this as the fourth of the plaintiffs' copyright preemption arguments, however, the first three were essentially identical for purposes of analysis.

[264] 496 F. Supp. at 447.

On appeal,[265] the Sixth Circuit upheld the requirement of a trade screening and the guidelines for open bidding and remanded the pricing restrictions to the district court for further consideration under the Commerce Clause. The copyright preemption argument was quickly dismissed and the trial court's decision and reasoning fully endorsed.[266]

The second anti-blind bidding statute to be tested was that of Pennsylvania[267] in *Associated Film Distribution Corp. v. Thornburgh*.[268] On a motion for summary judgment, the trial court first distinguished the Ohio Act as far less burdensome than the Pennsylvania statute. The court then held that the Pennsylvania statute was invalid primarily on the grounds of the First Amendment. The court's argument was that motion pictures were a form of speech and that the statute unduly interfered with their distribution.

The court then turned to the copyright preemption issue, noting that even though the First Amendment issue was "dispositive," it would discuss the issue "because of the importance of this constitutional challenge to a significant state legislative enactment, in which it is claimed that the state enactment interferes with federal law."[269] The court concluded that Congress had "unmistakably ordained" that the federal laws were to govern in the area of copyright. The court read the changes made to §301(a) in 1975[270] and the deletion of the examples from §301(b) (3) as broadening the reach of these preemption provisions. Noting the Pennsylvania Act did not seek to create an alternate or conflicting copyright scheme which §301 would cover, the court redirected its inquiry into the channels of *Hines v. Davidowitz*,[271] asking whether the state act "stands as an obstacle to the accomplishment and execution of the full purposes and objectives of Congress."[272] The court turned to §§106(3) and 106(4) and to the legislative history to conclude that these rights were the statutory embodiment of the purpose stated in the Committee Reports to insure "the copyright owner would have the right to control the first public

[265] 679 F.2d 656 (6th Cir. 1982).

[266] *Id.* at 662–63.

[267] Pa. Stat. Ann. tit. 74, §§203–1 to –11 (Purdon Supp. 1983).

[268] 520 F. Supp. 971 (E.D.Pa. 1981), *rev'd and remanded for trial*, 683 F.2d 808 (3d Cir. 1982).

[269] *Id.* at 991.

[270] *Id.* at 992.

[271] 312 U.S. 52 (1941).

[272] 520 F. Supp. at 993.

distribution of an authorized copy of his work *whether by sale, gift, loan, or some rental or lease agreement.*[273] The court concluded:[274]

> [I]ts provisions [the Pennsylvania Act's] substantially restrict the conditions under which a copyright holder may distribute or license its work. Its regulation of the conditions under which "rental, lease, or lending" may take place interferes with the federally created rights granted by §106 and with copyright holder's "control over the sale or the commercial use . . ." of its work, *Goldstein, supra,* 412 U.S. at 555, in ways that the Ohio statute upheld in *Allied Artists* does not.

The court further held that the advance screening requirement forced the copyright owner to delay its release of the copyrighted motion picture thus again unduly interfering with the rights granted under §106.[275]

On appeal,[276] the Third Circuit first ruled that the issues of both freedom of speech and copyright preemption required factual determinations of the extent to which the state law interfered with the federal constitutional and statutory rights. In dealing with the copyright preemption issue, the Third Circuit noted that the issue had been decided on a grant of summary judgment and limited its inquiry to whether the Pennsylvania statute on its face was an obstacle to the accomplishment of the purposes of the federal Act. The court took a narrow and literal reading of §301, inquiring only if the Pennsylvania statute granted rights equivalent to those in §106. Relying extensively on the copyright analysis contained in the district court opinion in *Allied Artists Pictures Corp. v. Rhodes,*[277] the Third Circuit reversed the grant of summary judgment and remanded the case for trial.

A more limited issue was involved in *Warner Bros., Inc. v. Wilkinson.*[278] The plaintiff sought a declaratory judgment and injunctive relief against one provision of the Utah Motion Picture Fair Bidding Act[279] that provided that it was illegal for the distributor to require either the guarantee of a minimum payment or the setting of minimum ticket prices by the theater where the film was licensed for

---

[273] *Id.*

[274] *Id.* at 994.

[275] *Supra* note 216.

[276] 683 F.2d 808 (3d Cir. 1982).

[277] 496 F. Supp. 408 (S.D. Ohio 1980), discussed at 683 F.2d at 812-15. The Third Circuit gave most of its consideration to the other constitutional issues in the case.

[278] 533 F. Supp. 105 (D.Utah 1981).

[279] Utah Code Ann. §§13-13-1 to -4 (Supp. 1981).

a percentage of the box office receipts. The *Wilkinson* court took a different approach to the copyright preemption issue. The court's position was that this simply was not a copyright case and thus no copyright issue was involved since "[n]o one has appropriated a product protected by the copyright law for commercial exploitation against the copyright owner's wishes"[280] and the state's prohibition on certain contract terms in the licensing agreement did not amount to an involuntary transfer of copyright under §201(e). The court then stated that simply because the rights to transfer or license the work under §§106 and 201 were exclusive did not exempt them from all regulation and that it was within the power of a state to restrict the forms of enforceable agreements that private parties could enter into.

Although it did not involve an anti-blind bidding statute, the case of *Association of American Medical Colleges v. Carey*,[281] raised similar issues. At stake was the constitutional validity of New York's "Truth in Testing" law[282] which required that almost all standardized tests given for admission to college, graduate, or professional schools be made available to the takers after the examination together with copies of their examinations and the answer keys. It also required that a copy of the examination and the answer key and any validating or other data be placed on public record. Alleging that this law would destroy the validity of the Medical College Admission Test (MCAT), the plaintiff sought to enjoin its enforcement claiming, among other things, that it was preempted by the copyright laws. The gist of the plaintiff's argument was that the New York law impinged upon its exclusive right to distribute its test which it was guaranteed under §106, particularly its rights to control the distribution and reproduction of the work.[283] In reply, the defendant argued that such usage was permitted under the fair use doctrine embodied in §107 of the Copyright Act.[284] The court did not rule on this issue. Rather it stated that this was a serious question going to the merits and then examined the balance of hardships to determine if a preliminary injunction should issue. Finding that requiring the disclosure of the test questions would indeed be a serious hardship on the defendant, the court issued the preliminary injunction. Although this is not a final adjudication, it

---

[280] 533 F. Supp. at 108.
[281] 482 F. Supp. 1358 (N.D.N.Y. 1980).
[282] N.Y. Educ. Law §§340-48 (McKinney Supp. 1982).
[283] 482 F. Supp. at 1365.
[284] *Ibid.*

does demonstrate that a preemption argument outside of the ambit of §301 can be effective.

These cases involve preemption challenges to state laws that are in some way perceived to inhibit or impede the full exercise of the rights granted by the Copyright Act. Section 301 is unable to resolve these issues. It is designed to determine those conflicts where a state law would seek to inhibit the use of uncopyrighted materials. These cases, however, do not involve state law restraints on the use of uncopyrighted matter but the related issue of state law restraints on copyrighted materials.[285] As such, the issue shifts from the rights of the public to copy to the extent to which a state can regulate the use of copyrighted material without unconstitutionally impinging on the exercise of the rights granted by §106.

The reasoning of the district courts in *Rhodes*[286] and *Thornburgh*[287] exhibit a fundamental agreement on the nature of the issue and the proper analytic approach to resolving the problem. Both premise their arguments on an underlying view of the Copyright Clause as granting Congress the copyright power so that the public benefit from the production and dissemination of works can be encouraged by the incentives provided for authors. The copyright laws are viewed as the concrete congressional determination of the precise form in which this purpose shall be carried out. The inquiry then is whether a state's anti-blind bidding statute unacceptably interferes with the exercise of the congressionally granted rights. Both opinions evaluate the state statutes in terms of the extent to which they impede the exercise of the rights granted to a copyright owner under §106. *Rhodes* more explicitly phrases the issues as the extent to which the state statute interferes with the underlying goal of encouraging the production and dissemination of the motion pictures. *Thornburgh* concentrates on the precise language of §106 without explicitly relating this to the goals of the copyright system. The two courts also differ in their evaluation of the extent to which the respective statutes do interfere with rights granted

---

[285] Where the states act to nullify or unduly restrict the rights granted by the statute, §301 is irrelevant. The thrust of §301 is preventing the states from creating equivalent rights for designated types of subject matter. Obviously there can be no copyright preemption issue here if the entire preemptive force of the 1976 Copyright Act ends with §301. Thus the courts have been very consistent in recognizing copyright preemption issues beyond the scope of §301.

[286] Allied Artists Pictures Corp. v. Rhodes, 496 F. Supp. 408 (S.D. Ohio 1980), *aff'd in part, rev'd and remanded in part,* 679 F.2d 656 (6th Cir. 1982).

[287] Associated Film Distribution Corp., 520 F. Supp. 971 (E.D.Pa. 1981), *rev'd and remanded for trial,* 683 F.2d 808 (3d Cir. 1982).

to the owners under §106 and, possibly, in their evaluation of the extent of interference that is constitutionally tolerable. In *Rhodes*, the Sixth Circuit explicitly endorsed the district court's analysis and conclusions on the issue of copyright preemption.[288] In *Thornburgh*[289] the Third Circuit, relying heavily on the district court's opinion in *Rhodes*, felt the determination of the copyright preemption issue involved questions of fact and remanded the case for trial.[290] In *Wilkinson*[291] the analysis followed a different approach. The court took the position that since there was no issue of any unauthorized copy being made there was no copyright issue in the case. Thus to the *Wilkinson* court, it was simply a question of trade regulation and restrictions on permissible contract clauses under the state police power. Finally, in *Carey*[292] the preemption issue was essentially deferred for further consideration as a factual issue.

The analysis advanced in *Rhodes* and *Thornburgh* seems sound. The *Rhodes* opinion is more sensitive to the nexus between the statutory provisions and the underlying goals of the copyright system than is *Thornburgh*, but more as a difference of degree than of kind.[293] The abbreviated analysis in *Wilkinson* is hard to evaluate. The court essentially said there were no copyright issues unless there was a question of unauthorized copying of the plaintiff's copyrighted works. If the court meant that no copyright preemption issues could arise except in the context of an infringement claim, it is wrong.[294] If the court's statement is merely an abrupt way of saying that it regarded the Utah statute as an acceptable trade regulation that did not unduly impinge upon the rights granted under §106, then it is acceptable if badly phrased. The opinion presents no analysis of the limits of constitutionally acceptable interference, the extent of the interference that actually occurred, nor of the goals, purposes, or provisions of the statute with which the state law allegedly interfered. Given that this decision arose after *Rhodes* and *Thornburgh*, it may well be the court simply did not feel like remapping territory already charted. But

[288] See text accompanying note 266 *supra*.

[289] 683 F.2d 808 (3d Cir. 1982).

[290] See text accompanying notes 276-77 *supra*.

[291] Warner Bros., Inc. v. Wilkinson, 533 F. Supp. 105 (D. Utah 1981).

[292] Association of American Medical Colleges v. Carey, 482 F. Supp. 1358 (N.D.N.Y. 1980).

[293] See text accompanying notes 286-90 *supra*.

[294] The claim in all of the anti-blind bidding cases is that the state regulation unconstitutionally interferes with rights granted by the Copyright Clause. Obviously, this type of preemption challenge involves no question of infringement.

Wilkinson cites *Rhodes* only with reference to antitrust preemption and not copyright preemption. *Thornburgh* is not cited.[295] *Carey*[296] does not reach the merits of the preemption issue but acknowledges that it is a serious enough claim to support a preliminary injunction.

Rhodes, Thornburgh, and *Carey* do little directly to resolve the issue of copyright preemption of the misappropriation doctrine or of the problems of interpreting §301. The cases do illustrate that the courts are willing to recognize copyright preemption questions beyond the confines covered by §301. Further, *Rhodes* and *Thornburgh* demonstrate that the courts have no real difficulty in identifying values in the Copyright Clause of the Constitution and the copyright statutes or in translating these into workable standards for day-to-day decisionmaking. This is in sharp contrast to the *Goldstein*[297] opinion's inability to do so.

VIII. CONCLUSIONS

Certainly nothing definitive can be said about the current status of the misappropriation doctrine in light of §301 of the 1976 Copyright Act. It seems that some revision of §301 is necessary if only to provide some clarity to a chaotic situation. The concern should probably be more with the subject matter exempted from coverage than the question of equivalent rights. Both the legislative history and the adopted language of the statute specify that state rights equivalent to copyright are preempted. The issue remains whether Congress has made a determination that misappropriation indeed is or is not equivalent to copyright or whether Congress has left this to the courts.

The issue is not whether there shall be preemption but how much preemption. To some extent any conclusion will reflect the values that are perceived to be embodied in the American copyright system and the relative weight assigned to these values. At one extreme, there is the *Sears-Compco* approach.[298] The starting point for this position is the high value that is attached to the public domain and the public's right of free and unhindered access to all material therein. Thus competition and imitation are perceived as accepted and indeed desirable forms of economic behavior and any monopolistic restraints on such behavior

---

[295] Warner Bros., Inc. v. Wilkinson, 533 F. Supp. 105, 107-08 (D. Utah 1981).

[296] Association of American Medical Colleges v. Carey, 482 F. Supp. 1358 (N.D.N.Y. 1980).

[297] See text accompanying notes 83-93 *supra*.

[298] See text accompanying notes 69-82 *supra*.

are not only contrary to the public interest but can only be justified by the exercise of congressional power under the Copyright-Patent Clause. As such, state law protection of any intellectual property on the basis of misappropriation is necessarily preempted as it would conflict with the constitutional scheme. Barring an overruling of *Goldstein*, this is not likely to take place on a judicial level. On a congressional level it would require revision of §301 to provide that state law copyright protection of any published material is preempted.[299] This would provide a far simpler and more workable test than the present statute. Any issue whether the States were intended by Congress to be able to act should require a congressional declaration to that effect.

A middle-of-the-road position would accept the *Goldstein* stance, but not its reasoning, that the Constitution did not necessarily require that the States be preempted from providing copyright protection in all cases. Congress, however, could clearly provide such preemption if it felt this was the more desirable way to implement a copyright system. Thus a sufficient distaste for monopoly outside of the federal patent and copyright systems would lead to the same type of result but would base it on an exercise of congressional discretion in terms of promoting a desirable policy of the competition and utilization of public works.

The two stated positions share the object to limit monopoly control over intellectual property to a minimum outside of the carefully defined contours and limits of federal copyrights and patents. The first position derives its concept of total federal preemption from the Constitution. The second position argues that such preemption is a matter of policy to be determined by congressional decision, and that the choice as a matter of practical policy should be full-scale preemption.

A view that is more tolerant to the creation of state monopoly protection for intellectual property would still require several changes from the present structure. The two inquiries suggested in *Goldstein* would be required to determine if the subject matter were covered by the federal statute, and, if not, whether it had been left unattended or deliberately excluded by Congress. In addition, certain limitations would have to be imposed on state copyright protection to prevent its becoming too great a detriment to the public interest and the public

---

[299] This would essentially be restoring §301 to its formulation prior to the 1975 committee amendments.

domain. Three parallels to the copyright system come immediately to mind. Probably the most useful would be some form of the idea-expression distinction. This might well serve the purpose of reducing the inequality of startup and development costs that makes commercial copying potentially damaging and allows for a good deal of competition. A durational limit is another possibility. Finally, there would have to be some variation of the copyright doctrine known as fair use to permit significant public use of the works even at some cost to the originator. Obviously variations on any one or more of these themes are possible.

An approach that would be very tolerant of state law copyright protection would emulate the analysis of the *Goldstein* case. An inquiry would be made into whether the subject matter was eligible for statutory copyright. If so, the *Sears-Compco* doctrine as interpreted by *Goldstein* would indicate the state law protection was preempted. Any question of the public interest or the public domain would be ignored except as it may have been articulated by Congress.

At the opposite end of the scale is the present statute. Here the only inquiry is whether the subject matter is included in §§102 or 103 of the Act. If not, there is no preemption. *Goldstein* suggests that the public interest in the copyright system may be ignored in preemption questions unless Congress explicitly provides for it. The congressional response to *Goldstein* indicates that Congress has chosen to ignore the issue.

At this time, a fuller consideration of the misappropriation doctrine is appropriate. First, is misappropriation equivalent to copyright protection for purposes of §301? The typical argument for recognizing the misappropriation doctrine is that it entails different elements of proof than copyright does.[300] As we have seen, this argument is based on a logical fallacy. The appropriate way to determine if rights are equivalent is to examine what the right being asserted is rather than to catalog or compare its elements of proof. Whether the antecedent conditions for asserting a right under state law are identical to copyright infringement or diametrically opposed to it is simply irrelevant. The question to ask is whether the right being asserted is one of the exclusive rights listed in §106. Thus proving that the claimant has invested great time, money, and skill, or that the claimant will suffer harm, is no more germane than proving that the claimant has blue eyes.

[300] See note 220 *supra*.

A variation of this argument presents a slightly different set of questions. It could be argued that misappropriation does not claim an exclusive universal right to copy and does not universally prohibit copying. This argument usually takes one or both of two prongs: (1) misappropriation only prohibits market competitors from copying, not the public; and (2) misappropriation does not prohibit all copying, only those methods which are sufficiently efficient to permit the competitor to gain an unfair advantage or "free ride" from the originator's efforts and expenditures. The fallacies here are quite obvious. First, being able to prohibit competitors from copying is functionally the same as being able to assert a monopoly on the §106 rights in a work. Nor do competitors stand in any special relationship of trust or confidence to each other just because they are competitors, as is shown by the fact that total strangers can and do become. competitors without the slightest prior or subsequent contact or relationship. The second argument is essentially that copying is permitted only as long as it is commercially ineffective. Granted the copyright monopoly may be broader in that all modes of copying are proscribed, but the mere fact that economically undesirable modes of copying are permitted does not make misappropriation any less a copyright statute. In fact, once copying is permitted, denying the cost savings of efficient copying would simply place a greater cost burden on the public to obtain that which is already in the public domain.

The one other argument for recognizing misappropriation is essentially an emotional one. It is argued the depredations of "unscrupulous" competitors will discourage businesses from investing resources into projects that can be copied at a great cost advantage. Examples cited to demonstrate this point are legion, but among the most common are record piracy, *INS*, typeface designs, and computer chips. There is no question that, all other things being equal, any enterprise granted monopoly protection will be a more attractive investment than one that does not have such protection. However, that is not the same proposition as saying that such protection is necessarily desirable from any point of view except the monopolist's. Thus some agency has to decide that a monopoly is indeed in the public interest. Given the Copyright Clause, it is hard to resist the answer that for copyright protection that agency is Congress and only Congress. In fact, if the Seiberling amendment based on the Justice Department letter has any rational significance, it is that Congress has legislatively determined that misappropriation is equivalent to the rights under §106 and is thus preempted.

It is worth noting that the claims of chilling purposeful economic activity by such competition deserve some skepticism. In *Storch II*, the only case to actually consider this element, the court found that while the originator was required to lower prices on its typefonts, they remained profitable and its business was not jeopardized. Similarly, in *INS* there was no showing that the Associated Press had lost so much as a single subscriber or that its enterprise was in any jeopardy from the copying of its news by INS. Computer chips present perhaps the most extreme case for such protection, and it is noteworthy that the bill pending in Congress to provide such protection is expected to receive passage.[301] The Sound Recording Amendment of 1971 likewise demonstrates that Congress can and will act to provide copyright protection for such rights where it is persuaded that it should do so.[302]

In all of the preemption analysis the perspective of the public interest and the role of the public domain has been largely either relegated to the background or ignored. Yet taking this factor into consideration in the preemption equation may provide helpful guidance to solve some of the preemption issues. In essence, the preemption inquiry should include the question whether the state law cause of action would prevent the copying, plagiarizing, utilization, or other public access to something that would otherwise be available to the public. If the state law cause of action effectively removes the right of the public, competitors and noncompetitors alike, from plagiarizing, copying, using, or receiving something which is known or distributed to the public or that it otherwise would have received, it should be regarded as a *prima facie* case for preemption. If the state law right asserted does not remove anything from the public domain, then there may be no reason for the preemption question to arise.

Some examples may clarify the prior statements. This approach easily resolves any question of the preemption of state trade secret laws. It is a tautology that a trade secret must be a secret. The consequence is that granting state law protection from unauthorized disclosure does not diminish the public domain and thus does not raise any issues of

---

[301] S. 1201, 98th Cong., 1st Sess. (1983).

[302] 17 U.S.C. §§1(f), 5(n), 19, 20, 26, 101(e) (1976) (repealed 1976; repeal effective Jan. 1, 1978). See also 17 U.S.C. §§102(a) (7), 106, 114 (Supp. V 1981). See also note 11 *supra*.

copyright preemption regardless of whether the trade secret action is based on contract, tort, a right of privacy, or a breach of trust. In this view, the issue of preemption of the misappropriation doctrine will now include an inquiry as to whether the application of the doctrine will inhibit the public from obtaining access to that which otherwise would have been available to it. Thus application of the misappropriation doctrine to prevent copying of works that have been made public is at least highly suspect if not *prima facie* preempted. This viewpoint will not resolve every problem in copyright preemption but will provide some useful guides for analysis.

Assuming the statutory provisions do not change, what avenues are open to the judiciary? It is unrealistic to expect *Goldstein* to be overruled.[303] It may still be possible to shift *Goldstein's* conclusion that the states are not constitutionally preempted from any form of copyright protection from the Commerce Clause to the Copyright Clause. This would clearly restore the issues of public interest and the role of the public domain. This analysis is already taking place in a number of decisions. *Synercom,*[304] *Rhodes,*[305] and *Thornburgh*[306] show that copyright preemption analysis can use the traditional value hierarchy of the American copyright system as the starting point to arrive at rational and principled decisions. Cases such as *Bromhall*[307] indicate the danger of excluding these factors from analysis.

There is no guarantee that the judiciary will not simply take §301 literally. Indeed, there is no reason in the statute why they should not. The test of §301 is entirely mechanical and ignores any questions of underlying values, goals, or purposes of the copyright statute or of the Copyright Clause. Contrary to the expectations expressed by the congressional reports,[308] the naive and simplistic preemption scheme embodied in §301 has acted in a fashion that is anything but preemptive. While the copyright preemption issues arising under §301

---

[303] A direct overruling of *Goldstein* is not altogether impossible given the five-to-four majority by which it was decided. The majority opinion was written by Chief Justice Burger, joined by Justices Powell, Rehnquist, Stewart, and White. Justice Douglas dissented, joined by Justices Blackmun and Brennan. Justice Marshall dissented and was joined by Justices Blackmun and Brennan. However, it is most realistic to expect any shift to be more gradual.

[304] Synercom Technology, Inc. v. University Computing Co., 462 F. Supp. 1003 (N.D. Tex. 1978); 474 F. Supp. 37 (N.D. Tex. 1979).

[305] Allied Artists Pictures Corp. v. Rhodes, 496 F. Supp. 408 (S.D. Ohio 1980), *aff'd in part, rev'd and remanded in part*, 679 F.2d 656 (6th Cir. 1982).

[306] Associated Film Distribution Corp. v. Thornburgh, 520 F. Supp. 971 (E.D. Pa. 1981), *rev'd and remanded for trial*, 683 F.2d 808 (3d Cir. 1982).

[307] Bromhall v. Rorvik, 478 F. Supp. 361 (E.D. Pa. 1979).

[308] See text accompanying notes 20-21 *supra*.

are far from definitively litigated, an examination of the decided cases shows that §301 has not provided an adequate basis for judicial decisionmaking on many of the preemption questions which have arisen under the 1976 Copyright Revision Act. Section 301 leaves the judiciary with a frustrating choice between an absurdly simple literalness and a confusing search for alternative values and methods. If anything, §301 has frustrated congressional intent to create a "single Federal system" and proliferated the "vague borderline areas between State and Federal protection" which Congress so sincerely yet so artlessly sought to avoid.[309] The difficulties created by §301 have been augmented by the vagueness of the definition of the tort of misappropriation. For these reasons a reformulation of the standards for copyright preemption is essential if a rational, coherent, and useful doctrine is to develop. This is not something to be accomplished by a few "technical changes" written by anonymous "members of the copyright bar," but should be done through an intelligent and rational consideration of which allocation of authority over intellectual property will best serve to "promote the Progress of Science and useful Arts."

---

[309] H.R. Rep. No. 1476, 94th Cong., 2d Sess. 130 (1976); S. Rep. No. 473, 94th Cong., 1st Sess. 114 (1975) (identical quotation). To some extent §301 accomplished its goal. Under prior law, the states could provide protection for unpublished works, note 140 *supra*, while under the 1976 Copyright Act only federal protection is available for fixed but unpublished works which are eligible for statutory copyright protection. *Id.*; see also note 154 *supra*. However, in the area of protection of published works, §301 allows the states to act wherever the subject matter is outisde of §§102 and 103. In effect, a literal reading of §301 gives the states carte blanche to provide copyright protection for anything that Congress does not. As §301 does not even require any inquiry into the basis for the congressional exclusion, the sphere of competency of state action to regulate copying of published works is undeniably enhanced. If anything, §301 thus invites greater state activity and a greater duality in the copyright system than previously.

GEOFFREY R. STONE
WILLIAM P. MARSHALL

BROWN v. SOCIALIST
WORKERS: INEQUALITY AS A
COMMAND OF THE FIRST
AMENDMENT

In *Brown v. Socialist Workers '74 Campaign Committee*,[1] decided in
the 1982 Term, the Court held that the disclosure provisions of the
Ohio campaign reporting law,[2] which require every political party to
report the names and addresses of campaign contributors and recipients
of campaign disbursements, could not constitutionally be applied to
the Socialist Workers Party, "a minor political party which
historically has been the object of harassment by government officials
and private parties."[3] At first glance, *Brown* does not appear
controversial. It was explicitly foreshadowed by a prior decision,[4] it
was unanimous in part,[5] and it was handed down without fanfare early
in the Term. But *Brown* poses an intriguing question: In what
circumstances, if any, does the First Amendment compel the
government to exempt particular speakers from an otherwise
constitutional law of general application?

The problem of constitutionally compelled exemptions has

Geoffrey R. Stone is Professor of Law, The University of Chicago.
William P. Marshall is Assistant Professor of Law, DePaul University College of Law.

AUTHORS' NOTE: We would like to thank Erwin Chemerinsky, Geoffrey Miller, and Cass
Sunstein for their helpful comments on an earlier draft of this paper, and Kenneth Quinn for his
research assistance.

[1] 103 S. Ct. 416 (1982).
[2] Ohio Rev. Code Ann. §3517.01 *et seq.*
[3] 103 S. Ct. at 418.
[4] Buckley v. Valeo, 424 U.S. 1, 68-74 (1976).
[5] Justice Blackmun concurred in part and in the judgment. Justice O'Connor, joined by Justices
Rehnquist and Stevens, concurred in part and dissented in part.

perplexed the Court at various points throughout its constitutional jurisprudence. In the equal protection context, for example, the Court has steadfastly rejected the notion that laws, neutral on their face, are unconstitutional as applied to particular racial or ethnic groups because they have a disproportionate impact on such groups.[6] In the free exercise context, however, the Court has occasionally held that laws, neutral on their face, are unconstitutional as applied to particular religious groups.[7] In the free speech context, the Court, until Brown, had only rarely encountered the issue.

I. ANTECEDENTS

The history of constitutionally compelled exemptions under the First Amendment is brief. Prior to Brown, the Court had recognized such exemptions only twice. In *NAACP v. Alabama*,[8] the Court invalidated a court order requiring a local chapter of the NAACP to disclose its membership list to the State. The controversy began when the State charged that the NAACP had violated a state statute requiring all foreign corporations, except as exempt, to register before doing business in the State. The NAACP maintained that it was within the statutory exemption. The state court ordered the organization to turn over its membership list, along with other items of information, to enable it to determine whether the NAACP had conducted business within the State within the meaning of the statute. The NAACP refused.

In invalidating the order, the Court observed that "freedom to engage in association for the advancement of beliefs and ideas is an inseparable aspect of . . . freedom of speech.'"[9] The Court emphasized

---

[6] See, *e.g.*, Personnel Administrator of Mass. v. Feeney, 442 U.S. 256 (1979); Arlington Heights v. Metropolitan Housing Corp., 429 U.S. 252 (1977); Washington v. Davis, 426 U.S. 229 (1976); Jefferson v. Hackney, 406 U.S. 535 (1972).

[7] See, *e.g.*, United States v. Lee, 455 U.S. 252 (1982); Thomas v. Review Bd. of Indiana Employment Security Div., 450 U.S. 707 (1981); Wisconsin v. Yoder, 406 U.S. 205 (1972); Sherbert v. Verner, 374 U.S. 398 (1963). For critical analysis of exemption theory in this context, see Marshall, *Solving the Free Exercise Dilemma: Free Exercise as Expression*, 67 MINN. L. REV. 545 (1983); Garvey, *Freedom and Equality in the Religion Clauses*, 1981 SUPREME COURT REVIEW 193; Note, *Religious Exemptions under the Free Exercise Clause*, 90 YALE L. J. 350 (1980).

[8] 357 U.S. 449 (1958).

[9] *Id.* at 460. The Court first noted the "close nexus between the freedoms of speech and assembly" in NAACP v. Alabama, 357 U.S. at 460. See also Buckley v. Valeo, 424 U.S. 1 (1976); DeGregory v. Attorney General of New Hampshire, 383 U.S. 825 (1966); Gibson v. Florida Legislative Investigation Comm., 372 U.S. 539 (1963); NAACP v. Button, 371 U.S. 415 (1963); Louisiana *ex rel.* Gremillion v. NAACP, 366 U.S. 415 (1961); Talley v. California, 362 U.S. 60

that the NAACP had made "an uncontroverted showing" that on prior occasions revelation of the identity of its rank-and-file members had exposed them to economic reprisal, physical coercion, and other manifestations of public hostility.[10] The Court maintained that, in such circumstances, compelled disclosure of the NAACP's membership list was likely adversely to affect the ability of the organization and its members "to pursue their collective effort."[11] The Court thus held that to justify this "deterrent effect" the disclosure must serve a "compelling" governmental interest.[12] Applying this standard, the Court concluded that, in the light of the other evidence available, the State did not have sufficient need of the membership list to determine whether the NAACP had violated the statute to justify the indirect impairment of First Amendment rights.

Two years later, in *Bates v. City of Little Rock*,[13] the Court, relying upon *NAACP v. Alabama*, held unconstitutional as applied to a local branch of the NAACP a municipal ordinance requiring every organization operating within the municipality to report the names and addresses of its contributors. The municipality maintained that such disclosure was necessary for effective enforcement of its tax laws. As in *NAACP v. Alabama*, there was "uncontroverted evidence" that public disclosure of NAACP membership had led to "harassment and threats of bodily harm."[14] The Court observed that, in such circumstances, compulsory disclosure might work a "significant interference" with freedom of association.[15] The Court thus held that the ordinance could not constitutionally be applied to the NAACP unless the disclosure was reasonably related to a "compelling" governmental interest.[16] Although conceding that the power to tax was "fundamental," the Court found "no correlation" between the municipality's taxing scheme and the disclosure requirement.[17]

(1960); Bates v. Little Rock, 361 U.S. 516 (1960); Shelton v. Tucker, 364 U.S. 479 (1960); Sweezy v. New Hampshire, 354 U.S. 234 (1957); Watkins v. United States, 354 U.S. 178 (1957); United States v. Rumley, 345 U.S. 41 (1953). See generally Emerson, *Freedom of Association and Freedom of Expression*, 74 YALE L. J. 1, 1964; Robinson, *Protection from Compulsory Disclosure of Membership*, 58 COLUM. L. REV. 614 (1958); Douglas, *The Right of Association*, 63 COLUM. L. REV. 1361 (1963).

[10] *Id.*

[11] *Id.* at 463.

[12] *Id.*

[13] 361 U.S. 516 (1960).

[14] *Id.* at 524. The plight of blacks in this era and the struggle of the NAACP in the South are examined in KALVEN, THE NEGRO AND THE FIRST AMENDMENT 90-120 (Phoenix ed. 1965).

[15] 361 U.S. at 523.

[16] *Id.* at 524.

[17] *Id.* at 524, 525. In addition to NAACP v. Alabama and *Bates*, two other decisions involving

The Court did not have occasion to address the exemption issue again for some sixteen years.[18] Then, in *Buckley v. Valeo*,[19] the Court rejected a claim that "minor" parties were constitutionally entitled to exemption from the reporting and disclosure requirements of the Federal Election Campaign Act of 1971. The Court distinguished *NAACP v. Alabama* and *Bates* on two grounds. First, the Court observed that the disclosure requirements in *Buckley* directly informed voters about a candidate's allegiances, deterred corruption by exposing contributions, and facilitated detection of violations of the Act's contribution limitations. The Court therefore reasoned that the disclosure requirements in *Buckley*, unlike those in *NAACP v. Alabama* and *Bates*, "directly" served "substantial governmental interests."[20] Second, although conceding that "public disclosure of contributions to candidates and political parties will deter some individuals who otherwise might contribute,"[21] the Court maintained that no organization had made a specific factual showing of injury in *Buckley* similar to that made by the NAACP in *NAACP v. Alabama* and *Bates*. Thus, on the record before it, the Court concluded that the "substantial public interest in disclosure ... outweighs the harm generally alleged."[22]

The Court in *Buckley* suggested in dictum, however, that in some circumstances the balance of interests might require the government to

state requests for NAACP membership list might arguably be considered "exemption" decisions. In Louisiana *ex rel.* Gremillion v. NAACP, 366 U.S. 293 (1961), the Court, reaffirming NAACP v. Alabama and *Bates*, affirmed a temporary injunction against enforcement of a disclosure law pending factual findings of threats and harassments. In Gibson v. Florida Legislative Investigation Comm., 372 U.S. 539 (1963), the Court invalidated a contempt conviction for failure to respond to disclosure requests during a legislative committee investigation of Communist infiltration because the state had not established the requisite nexus between its interests and the information sought.

[18] The uniqueness of the remedy in NAACP v. Alabama and *Bates* is evident when those decisions are compared with other decisions of the same era in which the Court, finding a similar infringement on First Amendment rights, invalidated disclosure laws in their entirety. In Shelton v. Tucker, 364 U.S. 479 (1960), for example, the Court invalidated an Arkansas law requiring all public school teachers to file a yearly affidavit that listed all organizations to which they belonged or contributed within the past five years. Again, one of the targets of disclosure was the NAACP. In *Shelton*, however, the disclosure requirement was struck down as applied to all teachers and not simply to those teachers claiming specific harm caused by their particular associations. Similarly, in Talley v. California, 362 U.S. 60 (1960), the Court invalidated a city ordinance prohibiting the distribution of handbills unless they contained the names and addresses of the individuals who prepared, distributed, or sponsored them. Again, the Court invalidated the law in its entirety rather than only as applied to particular organizations.

[19] 424 U.S. 1 (1976).

[20] *Id.* at 68.

[21] *Id.*

[22] *Id.* at 72.

exempt particular minor parties from disclosure. The Court explained that "the governmental interest in disclosure is diminished when the contribution . . . is made to a minor party," for minor party candidates "usually represent definite and publicized viewpoints" well known to the public, and the improbability of their winning reduces the dangers of corruption and vote-buying.[23] Moreover, the potential for compelled disclosure to impair First Amendment rights may be substantially greater where minor parties are concerned, for such parties "are less likely to have a sound financial base" and "fears of reprisals may deter contributions to the point where the movement cannot survive."[24] The Court thus concluded that "[t]here could well be a case, similar to that before the Court in *NAACP v. Alabama* and *Bates*, where the threat to exercise of First Amendment rights is so serious and the state interest furthered by disclosure so insubstantial that the Act's requirements cannot be constitutionally applied."[25]

In *Brown v. Socialist Workers '74 Campaign Committee* the Court found such a case.

II. THE DECISION

The Socialist Workers Party (SWP) is a small political party with approximately sixty members in Ohio. The party states in its constitution that its aim is "the abolition of capitalism and the establishment of a workers' government to achieve socialism." The party's members regularly run for political office, but with little success. In 1980, for example, the Ohio SWP's candidate for the United States Senate received less than 2 percent of the total vote. Campaign contributions and expenditures have averaged about $15,000 annually since 1974.

In 1974, the SWP instituted a class action[26] challenging the constitutionality of the disclosure provisions of the Ohio Campaign

---

[23] *Id.* at 70. On the Court's conclusion that the views of minor parties are usually sufficiently clear that disclosure would add little insight to prospective voters, see BICKEL, REFORM AND CONTINUITY 70-71 (1971); BONE, AMERICAN POLITICS AND THE PARTY SYSTEM 300-04 (1955); EWING, PRESIDENTIAL ELECTIONS 108-09 (1940). It has also been argued that disclosure, as applied to minor parties, is of little value because (1) the press is unlikely to pay attention, Buckley v. Valeo, 519 F.2d 821, 911 (D.C. Cir. 1975) (Bazelon, C.J., concurring in part and dissenting in part); and (2) even if publicized, the information would generate little interest, see Note, *Minor Political Parties and Campaign Disclosure Laws*, 13 HARV. C.R.-C.L. L. REV. 475, 492 (1978).

[24] 424 U.S. at 71. See also Redish, *Campaign Spending Laws and the First Amendment*, 46 N.Y.U. L. REV. 900, 932 (1971).

[25] 424 U.S. at 71.

[26] The plaintiff class included all SWP candidates for political office in Ohio, their campaign

Expense Reporting Law. The Ohio statute requires every candidate for political office to file a statement identifying each contributor and each recipient of a disbursement of campaign funds and provides further that "such statements shall be open to public inspection [and] carefully preserved for a period of at least six years."[27] After extensive discovery, a three-judge district court held in 1981 that the Ohio disclosure requirements were unconstitutional as applied to the SWP.[28] The Supreme Court affirmed.

Justice Marshall delivered the opinion. Echoing *NAACP v. Alabama* and *Bates*, Marshall affirmed that " '[i]nviolability of privacy in group association may in many circumstances be indispensable to preservation of freedom of association, particularly where a group espouses dissident beliefs.' "[29]Accordingly, "[t]he right to privacy in one's political associations and beliefs will yield only . . . if there is a 'substantial relation between the information sought and [an] overriding and compelling state interest.' "[30] Marshall did not, however, hold the disclosure provisions unconstitutional on their face. Rather, relying upon the *Buckley* dictum, he held them invalid only as applied to the SWP. There was, of course, no doubt that the SWP was a "minor" party. Moreover, as in *NAACP v. Alabama* and *Bates*, there was "substantial evidence of both governmental and private hostility toward and harassment of SWP members and supporters,"[31] including threatening phone calls and hate mail, the burning of SWP literature, the destruction of SWP members' property, police harassment of a party candidate, the firing of shots at an SWP office, the discharge of several SWP members by private employers, and at least until 1976 an extensive FBI program designed to disrupt and neutralize the SWP. In the light of such evidence, Justice Marshall approved the District Court's finding that, "in Ohio, public disclosure that a person is a member of or has made a contribution to the SWP would create a reasonable probability that he or she would be subjected to threats, harassment, or reprisals."[32] In such circumstances, and in accord with

---

committees and treasurers, and people who contribute to or receive disbursements from SWP campaign committees. The defendants were the Ohio Secretary of State and other state and local officials who administer the disclosure law.

[27] Ohio Rev. Code Ann. §3517.10(B).

[28] The opinion of the District Court is unreported.

[29] 103 S. Ct. at 420, quoting NAACP v. Alabama, 357 U.S. at 462.

[30] 103 S. Ct. at 420, quoting NAACP v. Alabama, 357 U.S. at 463, quoting Sweezy v. New Hampshire, 354 U.S. 234, 265 (1957) (concurring opinion).

[31] 103 S. Ct. at 423.

[32] *Id.* at 424 n.19.

NAACP v. Alabama, Bates, and the *Buckley* dictum, Marshall held that "Ohio's campaign disclosure requirements cannot be constitutionally applied to the Ohio SWP."[33]

III. THE CONSTITUTIONALLY COMPELLED EXEMPTION

To understand why the constitutionally compelled exemption poses a unique problem, it may be helpful first to ask what differentiates *Brown* from the usual decision invalidating a restriction on expression. At one level, *Brown* seems straightforward. The Ohio statute attempts to reach too far. It is constitutional in some, but not all, of its applications. This happens all the time. Faced with this problem, the Court usually follows one of several courses. First, if a saving construction is possible, the Court may interpret the restriction narrowly to preclude unconstitutional applications.[34] Second, if the restriction is "substantially" overbroad, the Court may invalidate it on its face.[35] Third, if the restriction is not "substantially" overbroad, but the challenger's own expression cannot constitutionally be restricted, the Court may hold the restriction unconstitutional as applied.[36] And fourth, if the restriction is not "substantially" overbroad, and the challenger's own expression can constitutionally be restricted, the Court may not invalidate the restriction at all.[37]

Brown, of course, falls within the third category, for the Court invalidated the Ohio statute, not on its face, but as applied. That is neither uncommon nor unique to the constitutionally compelled exemption. In *Brown v. Louisiana,*[38] for example, the Court held a state breach of the peace statute unconstitutional as applied to a peaceful

---

[33] *Id.* at 425. The Court was unanimous in invalidating the contribution disclosure provisions. Justice O'Connor, joined by Justices Rehnquist and Stevens, dissented on the expenditure disclosure issue. See Part VI-A, *infra.* Justice Blackmun maintained that the Court should have decided the expenditure disclosure issue.

[34] *E.g.,* Arnett v. Kennedy, 416 U.S. 134 (1974); Watts v. United States, 394 U.S. 705 (1969); Scales v. United States, 367 U.S. 203 (1961). See also TRIBE, AMERICAN CONSTITUTIONAL LAW 714-18 (1978); Monaghan, *Overbreadth,* 1981 SUPREME COURT REVIEW 1; Bogen, *First Amendment Ancillary Doctrines,* 37 MD. L. REV. 679, 696-703 (1978).

[35] *E.g.,* Erznoznik v. City of Jacksonville, 422 U.S. 205 (1975); Brandenburg v. Ohio, 395 U.S. 444 (1968); Gooding v. Wilson, 405 U.S. 518 (1972); Kunz v. New York, 340 U.S. 290 (1951). See also Shaman, *The First Amendment Rule Against Overbreadth,* 52 TEMPLE L. Q. 259 (1979).

[36] *E.g.,* Spence v. Washington, 418 U.S. 405 (1974); Cox v. Louisiana, 379 U.S. 536 (1965); Edwards v. South Carolina, 372 U.S. 229 (1963).

[37] *E.g.,* New York v. Ferber, 102 S. Ct. 3348 (1982); Broadrick v. Oklahoma, 413 U.S. 601 (1973). The Court's choice among these alternatives is not always consistent. See Gunther, *Reflections on Robel,* 30 STAN. L. REV. 1140 (1968).

[38] 383 U.S. 131 (1966).

"sit-in" in a public library, even though the statute could constitutionally be applied to more disruptive activity and was not unconstitutional
on its face. Similarly, in *In re Primus*,[39] the Court held a rule prohibiting
attorneys to solicit clients unconstitutional as applied to an attorney
who was seeking to further political goals through litigation, even
though the rule could constitutionally be applied to "commercial"
solicitation and was not unconstitutional on its face.[40]

The distinctive feature of *Brown*, then, is not that the Court has
drawn a line delineating what a statute may and may not regulate. It is,
rather, the nature of the line drawn by the Court. Ordinarily, when the
Court adopts a saving construction or invalidates a law as applied or on
its face because the law reaches too far, the Court draws one of two
types of lines. First, as in the *Brown v. Louisiana* illustration, the Court
may narrow or invalidate an overbroad content-neutral restriction in
such a way as to preserve its content-neutral character. In *Martin v.
City of Struthers*,[41] for example, the Court invalidated a city ordinance
prohibiting any person from knocking on the door or ringing the bell
of any residence in order to distribute handbills, because the city could
achieve its objectives through a less restrictive alternative—it could
"punish those who call at a home in defiance of the previously
expressed will of the occupant."[42] In *United States v. Grace*,[43] the Court
invalidated a federal statute prohibiting any person from displaying
signs or banners on the sidewalks surrounding the Supreme Court
building, but noted that such sidewalks might be subject to "reasonable
time, place and manner restrictions."[44] And in *Spence v. Washington*,[45]
the Court invalidated a state statute prohibiting any person from
attaching extraneous materials to a United States flag, as applied to
"symbolic" expression that did not physically damage the flag.

Second, as in the *Primus* illustration, the Court may narrow an
overbroad content-based restriction in such a way as to make it
conform to established categories of "unprotected" or "high value"
expression.[46] In *Gooding v. Wilson*, for example, the Court held

---

[39] 436 U.S. 412 (1978).
[40] Ohralik v. Ohio State Bar, 436 U.S. 447, 456 (1978).
[41] 319 U.S. 141 (1943).
[42] *Id.* at 148.
[43] 103 S. Ct. 1702 (1982).
[44] *Id.* at 1710.
[45] 418 U.S. 405 (1975). See also Broadrick v. Oklahoma, 413 U.S. 601 (1973).
[46] The concept of "unprotected" speech, and of a hierarchy of values in First Amendment
analysis, was first enunciated in Chaplinsky v. New Hampshire, 315 U.S. 568, 571–72 (1942).
Thereafter, the Court held various categories of speech to be wholly unprotected under the First

unconstitutional a state statute that did not conform to the specific constitutional limitations of the "fighting words" doctrine.[47] In *Watts v. United States*,[48] the Court narrowly construed a federal statute prohibiting threats against the President so as not to reach mere "political hyperbole."[49] And in *Brandenburg v. Ohio*,[50] the Court invalidated a state criminal syndicalism statute because it was not limited to advocacy "directed to inciting or producing imminent lawless action and . . . likely to incite or produce such action."[51]

For all practical purposes, however, these two situations exhaust the field.[52] It is noteworthy that in neither of these situations does the Court itself draw a line, not already in the restriction, between different ideas or viewpoints within the realm of "protected" or "high" value expression. This is hardly surprising. The Court's commitment to "content neutrality" is a cornerstone of contemporary First Amendment jurisprudence.[53] Under this doctrine, it is commonplace

---

Amendment. See Valentine v. Christensen, 316 U.S. 52 (1942) (commercial speech); Beauharnais v. Illinois, 343 U.S. 250 (1952) (group libel); Chaplinsky, *supra* (fighting words); Roth v. United States, 354 U.S. 476 (1957) (obscenity). More recently, the Court has tended to treat "low"-value speech in a more speech-protective manner. See *e.g.*, Virginia State Bd. of Pharmacy v. Virginia Citizens Consumer Council, Inc., 425 U.S. 748 (1976) (holding commercial speech protected under the First Amendment); New York Times v. Sullivan, 376 U.S. 254 (1964) (libelous speech protected unless accompanied by actual malice); Cohen v. California, 403 U.S. 15 (1971) (protecting the use of offensive speech). Although the factors the Court considers in deciding whether a particular class of speech occupies only a "subordinate position in the scale of First Amendment values," Ohralik v. Ohio State Bar, 436 U.S. 447, 456 (1978), are rather elusive, it appears to focus on the extent to which the speech furthers the historical, political, and philosophical purposes that underlie the First Amendment. See Stone, *Content Regulation and the First Amendment*, 25 WM. & MARY L. REV. 189 (1983) (hereinafter cited as *Content Regulation*).

[47] 405 U.S. 518 (1972).
[48] 394 U.S. 705 (1969).
[49] *Id.* at 708.
[50] 395 U.S. 444 (1969).
[51] *Id.* at 447. See also New York v. Ferber, 102 S. Ct. 3348 (1982).
[52] This does not, of course, exhaust all of the situations in which the Court may invalidate a law under the First Amendment. Rather, it exhausts only those situations in which the Court may invalidate a law because it does not reach far enough. *E.g.*, Police Dep't v. Mosley, 408 U.S. 92 (1972); Erznoznik v. City of Jacksonville, 422 U.S. 205 (1975); Widmar v. Vincent, 454 U.S. 263 (1982).
[53] "[A]bove all else, the First Amendment means that government has no power to restrict expression because of its message, its subject matter, or its content." Police Dep't v. Mosley, 408 U.S. 92, 95 (1972). See, *e.g.*, Widmar v. Vincent, 454 U.S. 263 (1982); Consolidated Edison Co. v. Public Service Comm'n, 447 U.S. 530 (1980); Erznoznik v. City of Jacksonville, 422 U.S. 205 (1975). The Court's content-based/content-neutral distinction has sparked lively academic discussion. See, *e.g.*, ELY, DEMOCRACY AND DISTRUST 105-16 (1980); TRIBE, note 34 *supra*, at 580-94; Stone, *Content Regulation*, note 46 *supra*; Stephan, *The First Amendment and Content Discrimination*, 68 VA. L. REV. 203 (1982); Redish, *The Content Distinction in First Amendment Analysis*, 34 STAN. L. REV. 113 (1981); Farber, *Content Regulation and the First Amendment: A Revisionist View*, 68 GEO. L. J. 727 (1980); Stone, *Restrictions of Speech Because of its Content: The Peculiar Case of Subject Matter Restrictions*, 46 U. CHI. L. REV. 81 (1978) (hereinafter cited as

for the Court to invalidate content-based restrictions while at the same time suggesting that the state may achieve its objectives through less problematic content-neutral restrictions.[54] It is not at all commonplace, however, for the Court to invalidate a content-neutral restriction while at the same time suggesting that the state may achieve its objectives through a context-based restriction. Indeed, given the Court's commitment to "content neutrality," one could hardly expect the Court to hold that a content-based restriction is constitutionally compelled. But that is what happened in *Brown*. For in *Brown* the Court expressly exempted particular political parties from an otherwise content-neutral regulation for reasons directly related to the content of their expression. This, then, is the salient feature of the constitutionally compelled exemption, and the critical characteristic that distinguishes *Brown*, *NAACP v. Alabama*, and *Bates* from the mass of decisions invalidating regulations that reach too far. The constitutionally compelled exemption substitutes a content-based law for one that is content neutral. It stands the presumption in favor of "content neutrality" on its head.[55]

IV. THE COURT'S RATIONALE

In *Brown*, the Court, building upon *NAACP v. Alabama*, *Bates*, and the *Buckley* dictum, offered two explanations for its decision to exempt the SWP from the disclosure requirements of the Ohio Act. First, the Court observed that the state's interests in promoting an informed electorate and deterring corruption are "diminished" when it compels disclosure of contributions to "minor" as compared to "major" political parties, for minor parties " 'usually represent definite and publicized viewpoints' well known to the public, and the improbability of their winning reduces the dangers of corruption."[56] Second, the Court observed that "the potential for impairing First

---

Subject Matter Restrictions); Karst, *Equality as a Central Principle in the First Amendment*, 43 U. CHI. L. REV. 20 (1975).

[54] *E.g.*, Carey v. Brown, 447 U.S. 455, 470-71 (1980); Erznoznik v. City of Jacksonville, 422 U.S. 205, 212 n.9 (1975).

[55] In *Brown* itself, the disclosure law might fairly be characterized as a "subject matter" restriction, for it governs only contributions to "political" organizations. See Stone, *Subject Matter Restrictions*, note 53 *supra*. The Court, however, tends to view this sort of subject matter restriction as essentially content neutral. See *id.* at 94-95. Thus, although *Brown* technically converts a subject matter restriction into one based on viewpoint, this paper, for the sake of clarity, treats it as converting a content neutral restriction into one based on content. The analysis is unaffected by the choice of labels.

[56] 103 S. Ct. at 420, quoting Buckley v. Valeo, 424 U.S. at 70.

Amendment interests is substantially greater" when a state compels disclosure of contributions to "minor" as compared to "major" parties, for minor parties " 'are less likely to have a sound financial base and thus are more vulnerable to falloffs in contributions' " because of " 'fears of reprisals.' "[57] As a factual matter, these observations may be accurate. But neither singly nor in combination do they satisfactorily explain *Brown*.

A. "DIMINISHED" INTEREST

In some circumstances, the Court routinely considers the government's "diminished" interest in deciding whether a particular restriction reaches too far. In *Broadrick v. Oklahoma*,[58] for example, the Court held that the state could constitutionally restrict the political activities of public employees, but noted that the restriction might be unconstitutional as applied to some activities, such as wearing campaign buttons, that did not sufficiently threaten the state's interests to warrant restriction. Similarly, in *Bradenburg v. Ohio*,[59] the Court indicated that the state could constitutionally restrict express incitement, but noted that the restriction would be unconstitutional as applied to speech that is not likely to incite imminent lawless action, for in such circumstances, the speech would not sufficiently threaten the state's interests to warrant restriction.

Ordinarily, however, the Court considers this factor only when it narrows a content-neutral law or narrows a law to conform to an established category of "unprotected" or "low" value expression. Indeed, in no decision outside the *NAACP v. Alabama-Bates-Buckley-Brown* line has the Court ever cited "diminished" government interest as a justification for converting a content-neutral law into one that distinguishes on the basis of content. Rather, in considering the constitutionality of content-neutral laws, the Court ordinarily asks only whether the state interest is sufficient to justify the restriction on speakers generally, without inquiring further whether the state's interest is "diminished" as applied to specific speakers for reasons related to the content of their expression.[60]

---

[57] Id. at 420, quoting Buckley v. Valeo, 424 U.S. at 71.

[58] 413 U.S. 601 (1973).

[59] 395 U.S. 444 (1969).

[60] In *Brown*, it is clear that "diminished" interest is not itself sufficient to justify a constitutionally compelled exemption, for the Court held in *Buckley* that minor parties that could not show a record of harassment and reprisals were not entitled to exemption even though the state's interest in disclosure is "diminished" to the same degree that it is "diminished" in *Brown*.

Moreover, the Court routinely invalidates laws that are content-based on their face even when the state's interest in restricting the unregulated expression, as compared to its interest in restricting the regulated expression, is "diminished" to the same degree that it is "diminished" in *Brown*. In *Police Department v. Mosley*,[61] for example, the Court invalidated a city ordinance prohibiting all picketing near a school, except peaceful labor picketing, despite the city's contention that, as a class, labor picketing is less "prone to produce violence than nonlabor picketing."[62] Similarly, in *Erznoznik v. City of Jacksonville*,[63] the Court invalidated a city ordinance prohibiting any drive-in movie theater from exhibiting films containing nudity when the screen is visible from a public street or place, despite the city's obviously sensible conclusion that scenes without nudity are less likely to offend passersby and distract motorists than scenes containing nudity. And in *Widmar v. Vincent*,[64] the court invalidated a university policy making its facilities generally available for the activities of student groups, except for "purposes of religious worship or religious teaching," despite the university's contention that its interest in avoiding the reality or appearance of "establishing" religion was wholly inapplicable to the unrestricted expression. In these and similar decisions invalidating content-based restrictions, the differential between the strength of the state's interests as applied to the restricted and unrestricted speech does not seem markedly different from the differential in *Brown* between the strength of the state's interests as applied to "major" and "minor" political parties. In cases like *Mosley*, *Erznoznik*, and *Widmar*, however, the Court held that the differential was not sufficient to permit the state to employ a content-based restriction, whereas in *Brown* the Court held that the differential was sufficient, not merely to permit a content-based restriction, but to compel one as a matter of constitutional command.

Finally, the Court's reliance on "diminished" state interest in *Brown* cannot be explained on the ground that the state's interest in

---

See 424 U.S. at 68-72. Indeed, in virtually any case a state could assert a greater interest in upholding a restriction against some speakers than against others. The state's interest in preventing fraud in charitable solicitations, for example, would probably not be severely undercut if the Girl Scout cookie drive was exempt from regulation. If the state's interest in preventing fraud is sufficient to justify solicitation regulations, however, it is ordinarily of no constitutional import that the state's interest may be stronger as applied to some speakers than to others.

[61] 408 U.S. 92 (1972).
[62] *Id.* at 100.
[63] 422 U.S. 205 (1975).
[64] 454 U.S. 263 (1981).

compelling disclosure from the SWP is so insubstantial that it is per se insufficient to support a restriction on expression. Even as applied to the SWP, the state's interests in informing the electorate and deterring corruption are hardly frivolous,[65] and in many instances the Court has sustained restrictions on expression for reasons less substantial than those at issue in *Brown*.[66] Moreover, there is a further interest, overlooked by the Court, that would seem to provide substantial justification for the state's decision to compel disclosure even from the SWP. For the state obviously has an interest, grounded in the First Amendment, in avoiding content-based restrictions. The state, in other words, may want to avoid the reality and appearance of favoritism and improper motivation inherent in the creation of such an exemption, the possible distortions of public debate that might result from such an exemption, and the extraordinary difficulties of implementing and administering such an exemption. Indeed, for all the reasons that the Court itself ordinarily insists on "content-neutrality,"[67] the state may legitimately seek content-neutrality in *Brown*.

B. "DISPARATE" IMPACT

The second explanation offered in *Brown*—that "the potential for impairing First Amendment interests is substantially greater" when compulsory disclosure requirements are applied to the SWP than when they are applied to other political parties—is equally unsatisfactory. For in considering the constitutionality of content-neutral restrictions, the Court has generally disregarded the fact that such restrictions often have unequal de facto effects. In *Greer v. Spock*,[68] for example, the Court upheld a regulation prohibiting all political speeches and demonstrations on a military base, despite the fact that "the potential" of the regulation to impair "First Amendment interests is substantially greater" as applied to some speakers than others, for the regulation prevents exposure to "those minor candidates whose campaigns [are] neither prominent enough nor sufficiently well-financed to attract media coverage" and are thus compelled to "make do with the more old fashioned face-to-face style of campaigning."[69]

---

[65] See Buckley v. Valeo, 424 U.S. 1 (1976) (upholding disclosure requirements as applied to minor parties).

[66] *E.g.*, United States Postal Service v. Council of Greenburgh Civic Associations, 453 U.S. 114 (1981); Heffron v. International Society for Krishna Consciousness, 452 U.S. 640 (1981); United States v. O'Brien, 391 U.S. 367 (1968).

[67] The concerns underlying the Court's content-based/content-neutral distinction are examined at length in Stone, *Content Regulation*, note 46 *supra*.

[68] 424 U.S. 828 (1976).

[69] Spock v. David, 469 F.2d 1047, 1056 (3d Cir. 1972).

Similarly, in *Heffron v. International Society for Krishna Consciousness*,[70] the Court upheld a Minnesota State Fair rule restricting the opportunity to distribute written material in a peripatetic manner, despite the fact that "the potential" of the rule to impair "First Amendment interests is substantially greater" as applied to those speakers who traditionally use this means of communication. And in *United States v. O'Brien*,[71] the Court upheld a federal statute prohibiting any person from knowingly destroying a draft card, as applied to an individual who publicly burned his draft card as a symbolic expression of protest against the War and the draft, despite the fact that "the potential" of the statute to impair "First Amendment interests is substantially greater" as applied to those who oppose government policy. Who, after all, would destroy a draft card as an expression of support of government policy?[72]

In some cases, however, the Court has considered the unequal de facto effects of content-neutral restrictions. In the public forum context, for example, the Court has recognized that restrictions on leaflets and similar means of communication may have a disproportionate impact upon those who, for reasons of finances or ideology, do not have ready access to more conventional means of communication.[73] In such circumstances, the Court has held that restrictions on such traditional but unconventional means of communication must be tested by a more stringent standard of justification than other content-neutral

---

[70] 452 U.S. 640 (1981).

[71] 391 U.S. 367 (1968).

[72] Compelled disclosure may have a significant disparate impact on some major parties as compared to others. As Professor Fleischman has noted: "What is true of organizations seeking to change policy, such as the NAACP, is equally true for organizations seeking to change governmental policymakers and officeholders. In politics, there are always 'ins' and 'outs' in a natural state of opposition so that if all contributors are known to the public, the risk of reprisal is clearly present. That risk is particularly high the more heated the contest or the greater the disproportion of strength among the contestants. . . . The result is that the greater the need for opposition, the greater is the risk of associating for political purposes with challengers. The greater the risk, the more deterrence there is to giving, and the greater is the need for privacy." Fleischman, *Freedom of Speech and Equality of Political Opportunity: The Constitutionality of the Federal Election Campaign Act of 1971*, 51 N. CAR. L. REV. 389, 424-25 (1973). Nonetheless, the Court made clear in *Buckley* that an exemption would not be compelled for a major party even if it could show that its contributors had been subjected to a disproportionate degree of harassment. See 424 U.S. at 68. In the Court's view, the Government interest, if strong enough to outweigh countervailing First Amendment rights in general, is strong enough to outweigh the rights of those more seriously affected.

[73] *E.g.*, Martin v. City of Struthers, 319 U.S. 141, 146 (1943); Kovacs v. Cooper, 336 U.S. 77, 102 (1949) (Black, J., dissenting); see Metromedia, Inc. v. San Diego, 453 U.S. 490, 552 (1981) (Stevens, J., dissenting); *id.* at 563 (Burger, C.J., dissenting). See also Kalven, *The Concept of the Public Forum: Cox v. Louisiana*, 1965 SUPREME COURT REVIEW 1, 30; Stone, *Subject Matter Restrictions*, note 53 *supra*, at 102; Karst, note 53 *supra*, at 36; TRIBE note 34 *supra*, at 683.

restrictions. Similarly, in the ballot access context, the Court has held that a filing deadline or other restriction on political participation "that falls unequally on new or small political parties or on independent candidates" must be tested by a heightened standard of scrutiny.[74] In such cases, however, the Court does not create a special exemption and thus convert a content-neutral restriction into one based on content. Rather, the Court elevates the standard of review for the restriction as a whole. If the law cannot withstand the heightened level of scrutiny, it is invalidated in its entirety. If it satisfies the higher standard, it is upheld despite the fact that "the potential" of the law to impair "First Amendment interests is substantially greater" as applied to some speakers than others. In either case, a content-neutral restriction remains. A similar approach was available to the Court in *Brown*.[75] It chose instead to create an exemption.

Finally, it should be noted that, in reviewing the constitutionality of laws that are content-based on their face, the Court has not looked with special favor on restrictions that exempt particular speakers because they would be disproportionately disadvantaged by a content-neutral restriction.[76] To the contrary, the Court has never upheld a content-based restriction for this reason. In Brown, however, the Court relied on this factor to hold that a content-based restriction was constitutionally compelled.

C. "DIMINISHED" INTEREST AND "DISPARATE" IMPACT IN COMBINATION

If neither of these factors is sufficient in itself to explain *Brown*, are they sufficient in combination? No. At the outset, it is worth noting that, although both factors were present in *Brown*, neither *NAACP v. Alabama* nor *Bates* involved "diminished" interest. That is, in neither of those cases was the state's interest in compelling disclosure from the NAACP markedly less than its interest in compelling disclosure from other organizations.

Moreover, the plain and simple fact is that the Court routinely invalidates content-based laws even when both factors are present. In *Police Department v. Mosley*,[77] for example, perhaps the seminal

---

[74] Anderson v. Celebrezze, 103 S. Ct. 1564, 1572 (1983).

[75] Indeed, in other decisions the Court has invalidated disclosure laws in their entirety. *E.g.*, Shelton v. Tucker, 364 U.S. 479 (1960); Talley v. California, 362 U.S. 60 (1960).

[76] *E.g.*, Carey v. Brown, 447 U.S. 455, 468 n.13 (1980). See Cass, *First Amendment Access to Government Facilities*, 65 VA. L. REV. 1287, 1323-24 (1979).

[77] 408 U.S. 92 (1972).

decision on content-neutrality, the Court invalidated a city ordinance prohibiting all picketing near a school except labor picketing, even though the city maintained that, "as a class, nonlabor picketing is more prone to produce violence than labor picketing,"[78] and even though a content-neutral restriction prohibiting all picketing would more seriously disadvantage labor picketers, who would be unable to protest near their place of employment, than other picketers, whose messages might not be as specifically tied to the school building.[79] The point, of course, is not that the factors identified in *Brown* are irrelevant to the analysis of content-based restrictions. They are unquestionably relevant. But, prior to *Buckley* and *Brown*, the Court had never identified these factors as "special" or as sufficient in themselves to justify content-based restrictions, and there is no obvious reason to accord them such status. Other factors are also relevant and, as always, the question is one of degree.

The Court's explanation of *Brown* is inconsistent, not only with precedent, but also with the trend and tenor of First Amendment jurisprudence generally. The Court's analysis of First Amendment issues has shifted in recent decades away from ad hoc balancing and toward the formulation of precise, categorical rules. This is a salutary development.[80] *Brown*, however, if understood in terms of the Court's explanation, represents a dramatic step in the opposite direction. Ordinarily, when the Court engages in balancing, it weighs the government interests in regulating the restricted expression against the First Amendment interests of the class of speakers whose expression is restricted.[81] In *Brown*, however, the Court apparently weighed the government interests in regulating the expression of particular speakers within the restricted class against the First Amendment interests of those particular speakers. By employing such ad hoc, speaker-specific balancing, the Court has injected a new element of uncertainty and unpredictability into the First Amendment analysis.[82]

---

[78] *Id.* at 100.

[79] See also Heffron v. International Society for Krishna Consciousness, 452 U.S. 640 (1981).

[80] See ELY note 53 *supra*, at 105-16; TRIBE note 34 *supra*, at 582-84; Schauer, *Categories and the First Amendment: A Play in Three Acts*, 34 VAND. L. REV. 265 (1981).

[81] For a recent example of "general" balancing, see Anderson v. Celebrezze, 103 S. Ct. 1564 (1983) (invalidating an early filing deadline for ballot access because of its impact on independent candidates and their supporters).

[82] For example, in a typical disparate impact case, a speaker may claim that he is more seriously affected by a forum regulation than other speakers who have no special relationship to the forum. The question of relative harm in such circumstances is likely to be quite complex, however, for several groups may be disproportionately harmed by the restriction. For discussion of this issue, see Stephan, note 53 *supra;* Cass, note 76 *supra.*

Moreover, if *Brown* is understood in terms of the Court's explanation, it cuts to the very core of First Amendment doctrine, for by relying on ad hoc balancing to hold that a content-based restriction is constitutionally compelled, the Court seems significantly to have undermined its commitment to "content-neutrality." Indeed, if understood in terms of the Court's explanation, *Brown* would seem to invite legislated content-based restrictions on the plea that they are constitutionally compelled, and it would seem to invite numerous "as applied" challenges seeking to engraft content-based exemptions onto content-neutral restrictions that, up to now, have never been questioned.

Despite all this, neither *NAACP v. Alabama* nor *Bates* nor *Brown* really seems "wrong." But if they are "right," it must be for some reason other than, or in addition to, the explanation offered by the Court. What is needed is some clear limiting principle that is consistent with First Amendment analysis generally and that serves both to justify and to limit these decisions.

V. ALTERNATIVE RATIONALES

A. SPEAKER-BASED RESTRICTIONS

The exemptions recognized in *NAACP v. Alabama*, *Bates*, and *Brown* might be viewed as speaker-based rather than content-based. That is, the exemptions distinguish not between ideas or viewpoints but between speakers. The exemption in *Brown*, for example, distinguishes, not between those who espouse Socialism and those who espouse Republicanism, but between the Socialist and Republican Parties. Accordingly, the exemption may not implicate the concerns that underlie the Court's commitment to "content-neutrality."

Speaker-based restrictions—that is, restrictions that treat some speakers differently from others, but define the distinction in terms other than content—are not uncommon. In *First Nat'l Bank of Boston v. Bellotti*,[83] for example, a state statute prohibited business corporations, but not other speakers, from expending funds to affect the vote in certain types of referenda. In *Consolidated Edison Co. v. Public Service Comm'n*,[84] a Commission order prohibited public utility companies, but not other speakers, from including certain types of

---

[83] 435 U.S. 765 (1978).
[84] 447 U.S. 530 (1980).

communications in their bills. And in *Village of Schaumburg v. Citizens for a Better Environment,*[85] a municipal ordinance prohibited charitable organizations that did not use at least 75 percent of their receipts for "charitable purposes," but not other speakers, from soliciting contributions from the public by certain means. In each of these decisions, however, the Court invalidated the challenged restriction without addressing the speaker-based inequality. In two cases decided in the 1982 Term, however, the Court began for the first time to address the problem of speaker-based restrictions.

In *Regan v. Taxation with Representation,*[86] the Court, in a unanimous decision, sustained the constitutionality of a federal statute providing that contributions to an otherwise tax-exempt organization, other than a tax-exempt veterans' organization, may not be deducted on the contributor's income tax return if a substantial part of the organization's activities consist of attempts to influence legislation. In reaching this result, the Court emphasized that "a legislature's decision not to subsidize" First Amendment activity is "not subject to strict scrutiny."[87] The Court noted, however, that "[t]he case would be different if Congress were to discriminate invidiously in its subsidies in such a way as to " ' "aim[ ] at the suppression of dangerous ideas," ' "[88] but concluded that, under the challenged provisions, veterans' organizations were "entitled to receive tax-deductible contributions regardless of the content"[89] of their speech.

In *Perry Education Ass'n v. Perry Local Educators' Ass'n,*[90] the Court sustained the constitutionality of a collective bargaining agreement between a local board of education and the duly elected exclusive bargaining representative for the teachers, where the agreement provided that the exclusive bargaining representative, but no other union, would have access to the interschool mail system. Noting that the policy applied "to all unions other than the recognized bargaining representative," and that there was "no indication in the record that the policy was motivated by a desire to suppress" the views of rival unions, the Court concluded that the policy did not constitute "viewpoint discrimination barred by the First Amendment."[91] Moreover, after

---

[85] 444 U.S. 620 (1980).

[86] 103 S. Ct. 1997 (1983).

[87] *Id.* at 2001.

[88] *Id.* at 2002, quoting Cammarano v. United States, 358 U.S. 498, 513 (1959), quoting Speiser v. Randall, 357 U.S. 513, 519 (1958).

[89] *Id.* at 2002.

[90] 103 S. Ct. 948 (1983).

[91] *Id.* at 957 n.9.

explaining that the interschool mail system was not a public forum, the Court analogized speaker-based restrictions to subject-matter restrictions and declared that although such restrictions "may be impermissible in a public forum,"[92] they are permissible in a nonpublic forum if "they are reasonable in light of the purpose which the forum at issue serves."[93]

In these cases, then, the Court distinguished speaker-based from viewpoint-based restrictions, the most extreme form of content-based restriction,[94] and indicated that, at least in the subsidy and nonpublic forum contexts, speaker-based restrictions constitute an intermediate category, falling between content-neutral and viewpoint-based restrictions.

Whatever the merits of this view in *Regan* and *Perry*, it seems strained as applied to *Brown*. For the exemption established in *Brown* distinguishes, not between veterans and nonveterans, or between an exclusive bargaining representative and other unions, but between political parties. In such circumstances, the correlation between speaker identity and viewpoint is almost perfect.[95] Moreover, the justification for the exemption is not unrelated to viewpoint. To the contrary, the exemption turns explicitly on the "communicative impact"[96] of expression, for the exemption is available only if disclosure of an individual's involvement with a particular political party is likely to trigger "threats, harassment, and reprisals"[97] from those who oppose the party's views. To take a more familiar example, suppose a state law prohibits any person from making a speech that might trigger a hostile audience response. Although such a law is formally speaker-based, and does not expressly identify specific ideas for suppression, it would clearly be treated as content-based because it turns directly on "communicative impact."[98] Similarly, the exemption created in *Brown* is speaker-based in only the most formal sense. And even if the

---

[92] *Id.* at 957.

[93] *Id.*

[94] See *Content Regulation*, note 46 *supra*.

[95] See Williams v. Rhodes, 393 U.S. 23 (1968).

[96] The significance of "communicative impact" is examined in *Content Regulation*, note 46 *supra*, Part IV-B; ELY, note 53 *supra*, at 111; TRIBE, note 34 *supra*, at 580, 679, 683; Brudney, *Business Corporations and Stockholders' Rights Under the First Amendment*, 91 YALE L. J. 235, 250-51 (1981); Redish, note 53 *supra*, at 116-17; Farber, note 53 *supra*, at 743-46; Ely, *Flag Desecration: A Case Study in the Roles of Categorization and Balancing in First Amendment Analysis*, 88 HARV. L. REV. 1482, 1497 (1975).

[97] 103. S. Ct. at 424.

[98] *E.g.*, Cox v. Louisiana, 379 U.S. 536 (1965); Edwards v. South Carolina, 372 U.S. 229 (1962). See *Content Regulation*, note 46 *supra*, Parts IV-B & V-A.

speaker-based quality of the exemption is sufficient to distinguish it from more conventional content-based restrictions, the difference seems insufficient in itself to explain or to limit the doctrine.[99]

B. COURT-"CREATED" CONTENT-BASED RESTRICTIONS

A second possible explanation of *NAACP v. Alabama, Bates,* and *Brown* is that a lower standard of justification is appropriate when a content-based restriction is adopted, not by legislative or executive officials, but by the Justices of the Supreme Court. This explanation derives from the notion, clearly embraced by the Court, that "when regulation is based on the content of speech, government action must be scrutinized more carefully to ensure that communication has not been prohibited 'merely because public officials disapprove the speaker's view.' "[100] A primary concern underlying the Court's presumption against content-based restrictions, in other words, is that public officials are especially likely to adopt such restrictions at least in part because they personally agree or disagree with particular ideas or viewpoints. To ferret out such "improper" motivations, and to ensure that content-based restrictions would have been adopted even in the absence of such motivations, the Court ordinarily tests content-based restrictions with especially stringent standards of justification.[101]

In *Brown,* however, it was the Justices of the Supreme Court, and not legislative or executive officials, who adopted the content-based restriction. Arguably, the Justices are in a very different position from other public officials in terms of "improper" motivation. The Justices, after all, are acting not as discretionary policymakers but as interpreters of a written Constitution. Their discretion is limited by the constraints of interpretation, and there is thus less opportunity for "improper" motivation to affect their decisions. Moreover, the independence, insulation, objectivity, and distance of the Justices from the tumult and turmoil of the political process serve further to reduce the possibility that their decisions are motivated by "improper" considerations. Thus,

---

[99] For a more general discussion of speaker-based restrictions, see *Content Regulation,* note 46 *supra,* Part V-D.

[100] Consolidated Edison v. Public Service Comm'n, 447 U.S. 530, 536 (1980), quoting Niemotko v. Maryland, 340 U.S. 268, 282 (1951) (Frankfurter, J., concurring). *Accord* United States Postal Service v. Council of Greenburgh Civic Associations, 453 U.S. 114, 132 (1981).

[101] For a full discussion of the relevance of "improper" motivation, see *Content Regulation,* note 46 *supra,* Part IV-D; see also Symposium, *Legislative Motivation,* 15 SAN DIEGO L. REV. 925 (1978); Ely, *Legislative and Administrative Motivation in Constitutional Law,* 79 YALE L. J. 1205 (1970).

when the Justices decide that the Constitution compels a content-based restriction, the safeguards ordinarily employed to guard against "improper" motivations are arguably unnecessary, and content-based restrictions adopted in such circumstances need not be tested by the ordinary standards of content-based review.

This explanation of *Brown* would no doubt sound immodest, at best, if offered by the Court. It is, however, consistent with the most common, and perhaps the most persuasive, theory of judicial review.[102] Moreover, it is consistent with an important branch of First Amendment jurisprudence. The Court has long held that certain types of expression, such as obscenity, fighting words, commercial advertising, and false statements of fact, have only a "subordinate position in the scale of First Amendment values,"[103] and are thus entitled only to limited First Amendment protection.[104] Commentators have criticized this doctrine as necessarily injecting the Court "into value judgments concerned with the content of expression, a role foreclosed to it by the basic theory of the First Amendment,"[105] but the Court has consistently adhered to its "low" value theory. Thus, despite the Court's general commitment to "content neutrality," and despite its frequent invalidation of similar "value" judgments of other public officials, the Court routinely makes its own judgments about the "value" of expression. What is forbidden to others is allowed to the Court.

Whatever the merits of this theory generally, it does not satisfactorily explain *Brown*. First, although this theory may explain the Court's departure from the ordinary standards of content-based review when it concludes that the Constitution compels a content-based restriction, it tells us nothing of the circumstances in which the Constitution has this effect. When, in other words, are content-based exemptions constitutionally required? Second, a concern with "improper" motivation is not the only rationale for the Court's presumption against content-based restrictions. To the contrary, the presumption derives as well from a concern that such restrictions may

---

[102] See BICKEL, THE LEAST DANGEROUS BRANCH (1962).

[103] Ohralik v. Ohio State Bar, 436 U.S. 447, 456 (1978).

[104] *E.g.*, Chaplinsky v. New Hampshire, 315 U.S. 568 (1942) (fighting words); Virginia State Bd. of Pharmacy v. Virginia Citizens Consumer Council, Inc., 425 U.S. 748 (1976) (commercial speech); Miller v. California, 413 U.S. 15 (1973) (obscenity); Gertz v. Robert Welch, Inc., 418 U.S. 323 (1974) (false statements of fact); New York v. Ferber, 102 S. Ct. 3348 (1982) (child pornography).

[105] EMERSON, THE SYSTEM OF FREE EXPRESSION 326 (1970).

distort public debate[106] and from the disfavored status of the justifications usually offered in defense of such restrictions.[107] Even if constitutionally compelled exemptions avoid the motivational concern, the others remain.[108] Third, there is a back-door problem in *Brown*. That is, the exemption created by the Court is not really constitutionally compelled. *Brown* leaves the Ohio legislature with two alternatives. It may retain the disclosure requirements and exempt the SWP or it may abolish the disclosure requirements entirely. The decision whether to adopt the content-based restriction thus rests ultimately with the legislature, and that decision may of course be affected by "improper" motivation.[109] Finally, there is an internal contradiction in this theory as applied to *Brown*. Under this theory, the Court employs a less demanding test to decide whether a content-based restriction is constitutionally compelled than it employs to decide whether a content-based restriction is constitutionally permissible. In theory, this is defensible because of the reduced concern with "improper" motivation. But it is also illogical. Can a content-based restriction be constitutionally compelled if it is not adopted by the legislature, but be unconstitutional if the legislature adopts it? Under this theory, that would be the message of *Brown*.

C. "AFFIRMATIVE" ACTION

A third explanation of *NAACP v. Alabama, Bates,* and *Brown* derives from the fact that the content-based restrictions created in those decisions have three quite distinct characteristics: (1) they provide a special benefit (2) to "minor" political parties or organizations (3) whose members have historically been subjected to "threats, harassment, and reprisals." Viewed in this light, the decisions

---

[106] See *Content Regulation*, note 46 *supra*, Part IV-C.

[107] *Id.* at Part IV-B.

[108] It is at least arguable, of course, that the Justices will not adopt any content-based restriction that involves a disfavored justification or a possible distortion of public debate because they are especially sensitive to these dangers.

[109] The risk of "improper" motivation in this situation is probably less than the risk in the usual content-based context, but greater than the risk in the usual content-neutral context. Unlike the usual situation in which a legislature drafts a content-based restriction, the legislature here does not select the specific ideas or viewpoints to be restricted. Rather, the legislature here is limited to a choice between a content-neutral rule (requiring no disclosure) and a predetermined content-based rule (disclosure with a constitutionally compelled exemption). Unlike the usual situation, in which a legislature drafts a content-neutral restriction, however, the legislature here can select a restriction that has a built-in content-based exemption with full knowledge of the types of speech and speakers likely to be exempted. The attitude of the legislators towards the groups likely to qualify for exemption may thus affect their decision whether to adopt disclosure with an exemption or to abandon disclosure entirely.

take on an air of "affirmative action." Like laws that provide special benefits to blacks in the equal protection context,[110] the exemptions created in these decisions provide special benefits to groups that, in the First Amendment context, may be especially in need of extraordinary protection. Indeed, the NAACP in the Deep South in the 1950s and 1960s and the SWP in the Midwest in the 1970s and 1980s are in some ways analogous to "suspect" classes in equal protection jurisprudence, for they are discrete "minority" groups, who have traditionally been "outcasts" from the relevant political process, and whose members have historically been subjected to both private and governmental discrimination.[111]

Although the analogy may be pushed too far, an "affirmative action" understanding of *NAACP v. Alabama, Bates*, and *Brown* may help to explain the Court's willingness to depart from its ordinarily strict presumption in favor of "content neutrality." Indeed, an "affirmative action" justification tends at least to mitigate the primary concerns underlying the Court's general disapproval of content-based restrictions—"improper" motivation, distortion of public debate, and reliance on constitutionally disfavored justifications.[112] "Improper" motivation is unlikely in this context, for "major" political parties remain subject to the disclosure requirements and only "outcast" minor parties are exempt. It is thus unlikely that such an exemption would be designed to promote the exempt organizations or to suppress those that are not exempt.[113] Moreover, unlike most content-based restrictions, the exemptions adopted in *Brown* and its antecedents are unlikely to distort public debate. To the contrary, their purpose is to preserve the status quo and to prevent the distortion that would otherwise occur if the disclosure requirements were imposed on the "outcast" organizations.[114] Finally, although the Court is ordinarily especially skeptical of efforts to justify content-based restrictions on the ground that

---

[110] *E.g.*, Regents of Univ. of California v. Bakke, 438 U.S. 265 (1978); Fullilove v. Klutznick, 448 U.S. 448 (1980).

[111] *Cf.* Massachusetts Bd. of Retirement v. Murgia, 427 U.S. 307, 313 (1976) (describing a "suspect" class as one that has experienced a "history of purposeful unequal treatment").

[112] For analysis of the relationship of these concerns to the content-based/content-neutral distinction, see *Content Regulation*, note 46 *supra*, Parts IV-B-D.

[113] *Cf.* Ely, *The Constitutionality of Reverse Racial Discrimination*, 41 U. CHI. L. REV. 7 (1974); Regents of University of California v. Bakke, 438 U.S. 265, 357 (1980) (Brennan, J., concurring).

[114] Although an exemption for "outcast" parties may reduce the distortion of public debate created by disclosure, it may produce distortion of its own. That is, compelled disclosure with an exemption for "outcast" parties puts "outcast" parties in a better competitive position than they would have been in had there been no disclosure law at all.

particular ideas might provoke a hostile audience response,[115] here that consideration is used not to restrict the unpopular speech but to protect it.

An "affirmative action" understanding may also help to limit the potential scope of the doctrine of constitutionally compelled exemptions, for under this view, the doctrine extends only to those organizations which are in need of extraordinary protection because of their traditionally "outcast" status.

For several reasons, however, an "affirmative action" explanation may prove too much. First, in *NAACP v. Alabama, Bates*, and *Brown*, the Court held that the exemptions were constitutionally compelled. The Court has never held in the equal protection context, however, that "affirmative action" is constitutionally required. The most it has ever held is that "affirmative action" is constitutionally permitted. Second, in the First Amendment context, the Court has never explicitly suggested that an "affirmative action" justification is sufficient to support a content-based restriction, let alone to require one as a matter of constitutional command. Third, at the time of *NAACP v. Alabama* and *Bates*, the Court had never considered "affirmative action" even in the racial context, and it is thus unlikely that it had an "affirmative action" analysis in mind when it decided those cases. Fourth, several of the Justices who voted in *Brown* to invalidate the contribution disclosure provisions as applied to the SWP have never accepted the constitutionality of "affirmative action" in the equal protection context,[116] and it is unlikely that they would rely upon "affirmative action" considerations to hold a law unconstitutional in the First Amendment context without at least some explanation. Finally, an "affirmative action" explanation may raise more questions than it answers. After *Brown*, in what circumstances is "affirmative action" constitutionally permissible? May the Ohio legislature provide special tax benefits to the SWP?[117] May it exempt the SWP from ordinary content-neutral restrictions on expression? More to the point of Brown, when are "affirmative action" exemptions constitutionally required? Are otherwise constitutional content-neutral restrictions unconstitutional as applied to "outcast" political organizations whenever they have a disparate impact on such organizations?[118] Must

---

[115] See Content Regulation, note 46 *supra*, Part IV-B.

[116] *E.g.*, Fullilove v. Klutznik, 448 U.S. 448, 522 (1980) (Stewart, J., joined by Rehnquist J., dissenting); *id.* at 532 (Stevens, J., dissenting).

[117] *Cf.* Regan v. Taxation with Representation, 103 S. Ct. 1997 (1983).

[118] One might distinguish, for example, between a grant of affirmative "benefits," such as tax

the disparate impact be "substantial"? Must the disparate impact, as in *Brown*, be a product of the group's unpopularity? Must the government interests furthered by the restriction be "diminished," as in *Brown*, as applied to such groups?

In the end, then, although an "affirmative action" rationale might effectively limit the *NAACP v. Alabama-Bates-Buckley-Brown* doctrine, and might explain the Court's willingness to tolerate (indeed, compel) a content-based restriction, there is too little support in the opinions and in the surrounding jurisprudence to accept an "affirmative action" rationale as the full answer.

D. THE SEVERITY OF INFRINGEMENT ON FIRST AMENDMENT RIGHTS

A fourth possible explanation of these decisions concerns the nature and extent of the harm to First Amendment rights caused by disclosure. The Court has offered three quite distinct characterizations of the harm.

First, as the Court observed in *Buckley*, public disclosure will inevitably deter some individuals who might otherwise join or contribute to a political party or organization. This harm may affect individuals across the entire political spectrum. Indeed, it may affect those who wish to join or contribute to "major" as well as "minor" parties and organizations. An individual whose employer is a member of the SWP, for example, may be more reluctant to join or contribute to the Republican Party than to the SWP.

This is, of course, a significant infringement on the First Amendment rights of the "deterred" individuals, and the Court has thus employed a relatively demanding standard to test the constitutionality of even content-neutral laws that compel public disclosure of an individual's associations. In *Shelton v. Tucker*[119] and *Talley v. California*,[120] for example, the Court invalidated such laws because they did not further sufficiently weighty interests to justify the infringement on First Amendment rights. And in Buckley, the Court explained that "significant encroachments on First Amendment rights

---

subsidies, to "outcast" organizations and a grant of exemptions, such as the exemption at issue in *Brown*. Under an exemption theory, "affirmative action" would be permissible only to protect such organizations against laws that would otherwise have a disparately adverse effect on them and thus heap additional burdens on an already disadvantaged group.

[119] 364 U.S. 479 (1960).
[120] 362 U.S. 60 (1960).

of the sort that compelled disclosure imposes cannot be justified by a mere showing of some legitimate interest."[121] Rather, "the subordinating interests of the State must survive exacting scrutiny," and there must "be a 'relevant correlation' or 'substantial relation' between the governmental interest and the information required to be disclosed."[122] Unlike *Shelton* and *Talley*, however, the Court upheld the disclosure requirements in *Buckley* because in the context of campaign contributions the "disclosure requirements . . . directly serve substantial government interests"[123] even as applied to "minor" parties. And although the Court indicated in *Brown* that the government had only a "diminished interest" in compelling disclosure from the SWP, mere "diminished interest" is not in itself sufficient to justify,[124] let alone compel, a content-based exemption from an otherwise constitutional content-neutral restriction. Thus, a concern with this type of harm does not explain *Brown*.

Second, as the Court observed in *Brown*, "the potential for" disclosure to impair "First Amendment interests is substantially greater"[125] as applied to unpopular "minor" parties than other parties or organizations, for the members of such parties are more likely to be subjected to "threats, harassment, and reprisals." The concern, in other words, is with "relative" harm. There are two aspects to this issue. At the individual level, disclosure may have a disparate impact on individuals who support the SWP, as compared, for example, to individuals who support the Republican Party, for supporters of the SWP are more likely to be subjected to "threats, harassment, and reprisals" because of the "outcast" status of the organization. In absolute numbers, however, disclosure may have a disparate impact on supporters of the Republican Party, for there are many more supporters of that Party to be harmed. Insofar as the interests of individuals are concerned, in other words, it may be worse if disclosure harms one hundred out of a million Republicans than if it harms twenty out of sixty socialists. Thus, at the individual level, a concern with relative impact cannot explain *Brown*.

Disclosure may also have a disparate impact at the organizational level, *i.e.*, disclosure may more adversely affect the SWP if it harms twenty of its sixty members than the Republican Party if it harms one

[121] 424 U.S. at 64.
[122] *Id.*
[123] *Id.* at 68.
[124] See Part IV-A, *supra*.
[125] 103 S. Ct. at 423.

hundred of its one million members. But disclosure may also have a disparate impact on some "major" parties as compared to other "major" parties. In urban areas, for example, those in power may impose reprisals against city workers, contractors, and others who support the "major" party challenger. Although disclosure may have a significantly disparate impact on major "out" parties in such circumstances, the Court made clear in *Buckley* that such "major" parties are nonetheless ineligible for exemption. Indeed, the mere disparate impact of an otherwise constitutional content-neutral restriction is not in itself sufficient to require a constitutionally compelled content-based exemption.[126]

Third, as the Court observed in *Brown*, compelled disclosure can "cripple a minor party's ability to operate effectively,"[127] and, in some circumstances, even " 'deter contributions to the point where the movement cannot survive,' " thereby reducing " 'the free circulation of ideas.' "[128] Here we deal, not with a mere difference in the degree of harm, but with a fundamental difference in the kind of harm. It is this consideration that may best explain these decisions.

Content-neutral restrictions often have de facto content-differential effects. In most instances, however, these content-differential effects have only a modest impact on public debate. For example, a federal statute prohibiting any person from knowingly destroying a draft card undoubtedly has a disparate impact, as applied to expression, on those who oppose the draft. But the actual restrictive effect, although disparate, is not severe, for there remain available many alternative means of expressing the same point of view.[129] Similarly, a policy excluding all political speakers from a military base undoubtedly has a disparate impact on those who seek to address military personnel on military issues. But the actual restrictive effect, although disparate, is not severe, for such speakers may shift to alternative means of expression.[130] The point, of course, is not that these de facto content-differential effects are unimportant.[131] It is, rather, that they are not ordinarily sufficiently severe to warrant the creation of a content-based exemption.

---

[126] See Part IV-B, *supra*.

[127] 103. S. Ct. at 423.

[128] *Id.* at 420, quoting Buckley v. Valeo, 424 U.S. at 71.

[129] *Cf.* United States v. O'Brien, 391 U.S. 367 (1968).

[130] *Cf.* Greer v. Spock, 424 U.S. 828 (1976).

[131] To the contrary, in some circumstances they are sufficient to require invalidation of a content-neutral restriction in its entirety. See authorities cited in note 73, *supra*.

Disclosure requirements, however, are special. Although content-neutral on their face, such requirements can have dramatically disparate effects on different organizations, depending upon the size and relative "unpopularity" of the organization. Moreover, and more important, the actual restrictive effect of disclosure may be not only disparate but extraordinarily severe. If the organization is small, and if it is vulnerable to falloffs in membership and contributions, disclosure can deprive it, not merely of a particular means of expression, but of the resources necessary to participate effectively in public debate by any means of expression. As the Court observed in *Brown*, disclosure can "cripple" an organization's "ability to operate effectively"[132] and can deter membership and contributions to such an extent that " 'the movement cannot survive.' "[133] Thus, the harm to the First Amendment is more than simply the harm to the organization and its supporters. For the "crippling" of a political party directly affects the public's "choice on the issues"[134] and results in a " 'reduction in the free circulation of ideas both within and without the political arena.' "[135] It is this unique combination of dramatic disparate impact and potentially severe effect that makes disclosure special.[136] Indeed, it is this unique combination that explains why all of the Court's decisions involving constitutionally compelled exemptions have involved disclosure. For the Court is prepared to sacrifice the goal of "content-neutrality," as a matter of constitutional compulsion, only where, as in the disclosure context, there is a risk that particular ideas or viewpoints may be driven completely from the "marketplace of ideas."[137]

---

[132] 103 S. Ct. at 423.

[133] *Id.* at 420, quoting Buckley v. Valeo, 424 U.S. at 71. As one commentator has noted, "[w]hile the primary impact of disclosure statutes on the major parties may be to reduce the volume of their speech, the impact on minor parties could be to eliminate them entirely." *Developments in the Law—Elections*, 88 HARV. L. REV. 1111, 1247 (1975). See Buckley v. Valeo, 519 F.2d 821, 908 (D.C. Cir. 1975) (Bazelon, C.J., concurring in part and dissenting in part).

[134] Williams v. Rhodes, 393 U.S. 23, 33 (1968).

[135] Brown v. Socialist Workers '74 Campaign Committee, 103 S. Ct. at 430, quoting Buckley v. Valeo, 424 U.S. at 71. See also Anderson v. Celebrezze, 103 S. Ct. 1564, 1572 (1983). The role of "minor" parties as a source of ideas is well documented. See Sweezy v. New Hampshire, 354 U.S. 234, 250-51 (1957) (opinion of Warren, C.J.); Nicholson, *Buckley v. Valeo: The Constitutionality of the Federal Election Campaign Act Amendments of 1974*, 1977 WISC. L. REV. 323, 356.

[136] Disparate impact is essential for the doctrine to come into play, for if the effect is uniform on all speakers the restriction will pose a straightforward instance of content-neutral balancing. The exemption issue thus arises only when the restriction limits some speakers more than others.

[137] See Brown v. Socialist Workers '74 Campaign Committee, 103 S. Ct. at 420, quoting Buckley v. Valeo, 424 U.S. at 71.

This concern with the extraordinarily severe effects that content-neutral disclosure requirements may have on particular political parties and organizations seems a sensible explanation of the constitutionally compelled exemption. Because this explanation compels the creation of content-based exemptions only when the threat to First Amendment rights is truly compelling, it is consistent with the Court's general commitment to "content-neutrality." And because this explanation focuses on a specific, narrowly defined inquiry, it avoids the difficulties inherent in a more open-ended, ad hoc form of balancing. Defined in terms of this explanation, the doctrine of constitutionally compelled exemptions offers an extraordinary remedy for an extraordinary problem.

There are, however, several objections that one might lodge against this understanding of the doctrine. First, the opinions do not expressly embrace this explanation. They do, however, contain language suggesting that this concern is, in fact, at the heart of the doctrine. In *Buckley* and *Brown*, for example, the Court noted that " '[i]n some circumstances fears of reprisals may deter contributions to the point where the movement cannot survive,' "[138] and in *NAACP v. Alabama* and *Bates* the Court observed that " '[i]nviolability of privacy in group association may in many circumstances be indispensable to preservation of freedom of association, particularly where a group espouses dissident beliefs.' "[139] Moreover, it is significant that the Court has never even considered the doctrine of constitutionally compelled exemptions outside the disclosure context, and that no alternative explanation is as consistent with First Amendment doctrine generally.

Second, one might object that there was no actual finding or showing in these cases that the ability of the NAACP and the SWP to participate in public debate was in fact imminently threatened by the disclosure requirements. The standard, however, need not be that strict. Indeed, such a strict standard would create the risk that particular parties or organizations might be driven out of the "market" or effectively crippled before an order exempting them from disclosure could be obtained. And an after-the-fact holding that compelled disclosure was unconstitutional would, of course, be scant consolation to an already defunct organization. Thus, a more appropriate standard would focus, not on whether destruction is imminent, but on whether

---

[138] 103 S. Ct. at 420, quoting Buckley v. Valeo, 424 U.S. at 71.
[139] Bates v. Little Rock, 361 U.S. at 523, quoting NAACP v. Alabama, 357 U.S. at 462.

there is a realistic possibility that disclosure could eventually cripple the organization or drive it out of existence. That standard is consistent with the Court's analysis in *NAACP v. Alabama, Bates,* and *Brown.*[140]

Third, one might object that this explanation reflects too narrow a conception of the constitutionally compelled exemption. There is a vast expanse between mere disparate impact, on the one hand, and disparate impact that might drive an organization out of existence, on the other. Arguably, the line should be drawn less strictly. That is, one might hold that a constitutionally compelled exemption is warranted whenever the disparate impact of an otherwise constitutional content-neutral restriction might significantly reduce an organization's overall effectiveness in the political process. Under this formulation, the doctrine might be available to "major" as well as "minor" parties and organizations. For example, if a political party that relies heavily on large individual contributions can demonstrate that a law limiting the permissible amount of individual contributions has in fact substantially reduced its ability to participate in the political process, and has not had a similar effect on competing parties, it might, under this formulation, claim a constitutionally compelled exemption. In defense of this formulation, one might argue that the ultimate harm to First Amendment interests is "greater" if a "major" party is put at an appreciable competitive disadvantage than if a "minor" party is put out of business. There are, however, difficulties with this formulation—it adopts a debatable measure of "harm;"[141] its implementation might prove difficult, for it shifts the standard towards a more open-ended form of balancing; and the Court's repeated emphasis in *Brown* on the "minor" party status of the SWP suggests that the Court itself intended to exclude this formulation of the doctrine.

Finally, one might argue that this explanation of the doctrine does not satisfactorily explain Brown. For even if compelled disclosure of campaign contributions might effectively cripple the SWP, the SWP could readily avoid this result by no longer running candidates for political office. Given that the SWP has that option, the disclosure requirement really eliminates only a particular means of expression, for

---

[140] See Part VI-A, *infra.*

[141] It has been argued that the purposes of the First Amendment are especially furthered by the activities of "minor" parties, for their campaigns tend to bring fresh ideas and programs to the attention of the electorate. See Nicholson, note 135 *supra,* at 356; *cf.* MAZMANIAN, THIRD PARTIES IN PRESIDENTIAL ELECTIONS 67 (1974).

the SWP could still express its views by alternative means, such as leafleting, marching, and advertising. Indeed, this should not especially trouble the SWP, for as the Court noted, its candidates always lose. The notion of "alternative means of expression," however, cannot be interpreted this broadly. The ability to run candidates for office is the very essence of political activity.[142] Leafleting is simply not an alternative.[143]

Thus, although the Court's explicit explanation of *Brown*—"diminished interest" combined with "disparate impact"—is insufficient to explain the doctrine of constitutionally compelled exemptions, the doctrine is in fact both warranted and, properly understood, consistent with First Amendment jurisprudence. As the doctrine emerges from *NAACP v. Alabama, Bates, Buckley*, and *Brown*, it can be explained, in part, on the grounds that *(a)* the exemptions are speaker-based rather than content-based, and *(b)* the exemptions are created by the Court as a matter of constitutional interpretation, rather than by legislative or executive officials in the exercise of their policymaking authority, and *(c)* the usual concerns underlying the Court's presumption against content-based restrictions —possible improper motivation, distortion of public debate, and reliance on constitutionally "disfavored" justifications—are largely eliminated by the "affirmative action" quality of the exemption. The potential of disclosure to drive an unpopular "minor" party out of existence is so severe that extraordinary measures are warranted to avoid that result.

VI. ADDITIONAL QUESTIONS

A. PROOF OF HARM

How does one prove that there is a "reasonable possibility" that disclosure might cripple a political organization and perhaps drive it out of existence? The Court did not formulate the issue in precisely this

---

[142] See Anderson v. Celebrezze, 103 S. Ct. 1564, 1575 n.26 (1983); Lubin v. Panish, 415 U.S. 709, 719 n.5 (1974); see also Redish, note 24 *supra*, at 931-32.

[143] One might also object that whereas the Court relied in Brown on both disparate impact and "diminished" government interest to justify the constitutionally compelled exemption, this explanation of the doctrine places primary, if not exclusive, emphasis on the severity of the disparate impact. Nothing in *Brown*, however, suggests that "diminished" interest is an essential, rather than merely a relevant, factor. Indeed, "diminished" interest was neither mentioned nor actually present in NAACP v. Alabama or *Bates*. Moreover, there is no logical reason to require "diminished" interest, so long as the restrictive effect of the law is sufficient to outweigh the government's interest in the restriction. And, of course, even under this explanation of the

manner in *Brown*, for it did not expressly delimit the doctrine in these terms. Rather, the Court held that an organization is constitutionally entitled to exemption from an otherwise constitutional disclosure requirement if *(a)* it is a "minor" organization and *(b)* there is a " 'reasonable probability' " that compelled disclosure of its members or contributors " 'will subject them to threats, harassment, or reprisals from either Government officials or private parties.' "[144] Because "minor" political organizations are " 'less likely to have a sound financial base,' " and are thus especially " 'vulnerable to falloffs in contributions,' "[145] this two-step inquiry seems a sensible way to get at the ultimate issue—the potential impact of disclosure on the future effectiveness of the organization. There was no question in *Brown* that the SWP qualified as a "minor" party. The Ohio SWP has less than sixty members, its annual contributions have averaged only $15,000 per year, and its candidate for United States Senator in 1980 received less than 2 percent of the vote.

The more serious question was whether there was a "reasonable probability" that disclosure of the SWP's contributors would "subject them to threats, harassment, or reprisals." The SWP presented the following evidence: (1) From 1961 to 1971, the FBI engaged in "massive" surveillance of the SWP and conducted a "counterintelligence" program designed to impair the ability of the SWP to function. This program included "disclosing to the press the criminal records of SWP candidates, and sending anonymous letters to SWP members, supporters, spouses, and employers."[146] (2) In 1980, four members of the SWP were discharged by two different private employers in Ohio for reasons apparently related to their political beliefs. (3) In 1980-81, eighteen members of the SWP were discharged by two different employers in Georgia because of their political beliefs. (4) In 1979, a private individual in Pennsylvania threatened a member of the SWP. A year later, the SWP member's car was destroyed by fire. (5) In 1978, an SWP office in Illinois was vandalized. (6) In 1981, a shot was fired at an SWP office in Pennsylvania. (7) In 1980, an Ohio office of the SWP received threatening telephone calls

---

doctrine, "diminished" interest is relevant, for a disclosure requirement is more likely to be unconstitutional as applied to a particular organization if that factor is present. In the end, however, severity of impact is the key to this understanding of the doctrine, for if the restrictive effect is sufficiently severe to create the possibility of driving a political party out of existence, only an extraordinary justification, if even that, could allow the restriction to stand.

[144] 103 S. Ct. at 420-21, quoting Buckley v. Valeo, 424 U.S. at 74.
[145] 103 S. Ct. at 420, quoting Buckley v. Valeo, 424 U.S. at 74.
[146] 103 S. Ct. at 424.

and hate mail from members of the American Nazi Party. Based on this evidence, the Court held that the District Court had "properly concluded" that there was "a reasonable probability that disclosing the names of contributors . . . will subject them to threats, harassment, and reprisals."[147]

In the State's view, however, "the evidence . . . involved only isolated instances of alleged harassment, and was insufficient to establish any ongoing pattern of harassment by either government officials or private parties during recent years."[148] The State offered several specific objections to the District Court's conclusion. First, the State objected to the lack of any direct evidence that the disclosure requirements had actually deterred any specific individuals from contributing to the SWP or had actually led to the harassment of any specific SWP contributors. Echoing *Buckley*, the Court rejected "such 'unduly strict requirements of proof,' " opting for greater " 'flexibility in the proof of injury.' "[149] It is unnecessary, the Court held, to "prove that 'chill and harassment [are] directly attributable to the specific disclosures from which the exemption is sought.' "[150]

Second, the State maintained that the evidence of governmental monitoring, infiltration, and disruption of the SWP was irrelevant. The SWP's difficulties with the government antedated the Ohio statute, and there was thus no reason to believe that the failure to exempt the SWP from the disclosure requirements would in any appreciable way further the government's identification and harassment of SWP members. Moreover, the government had voluntarily abandoned its programs against the SWP several years earlier. The Court dismissed these objections in a perfunctory manner, noting only that "hostility toward the SWP is ingrained and likely to continue."[151]

Third, the State maintained that almost all the evidence of harassment and reprisals against the SWP involved incidents in states other than Ohio. Once again, the Court emphasized the circumstantial value of the evidence, explaining only that "the Ohio SWP may offer evidence of the experiences of other chapters espousing the same political philosophy."[152]

---

[147] *Id.*
[148] Brief for Appellants at 21.
[149] 103 S. Ct. at 425 n.20, quoting Buckley v. Valeo, 424 U.S. at 74.
[150] 103 S. Ct. at 425 n.20, quoting Buckley v. Valeo, 424 U.S. at 74.
[151] 103 S. Ct. at 425.
[152] *Id.* at 424 n.20.

Finally, the State argued that almost all the evidence concerning private harassment of SWP members "involved highly vocal and publicly active party members" who voluntarily maintained "a degree of public visibility concerning their controversial political views," and that such evidence therefore was "virtually" irrelevant to "the question of whether persons who merely contribute private financial support to the organization would be subjected to threats or harassment."[153] The Court did not address this objection at all.

Although largely conclusory, the Court's analysis of the evidentiary issue in *Brown* is consistent with its recognition in *Buckley* that "unduly strict requirements of proof could impose a heavy burden" on dissident "minor" parties.[154] Such parties, the Court observed, "must be allowed sufficient flexibility in the proof of injury to assure a fair consideration of their claim."[155] Thus, in *Brown*, the Court did not require direct evidence of actual harm. Rather, once the evidence established the SWP as an "outcast" organization, the Court inferred that "chilling effect" was likely. This reasoning seems sensible. As the Court recognized, even out-of-state incidents of harassment may provide important circumstantial evidence of private hostility in Ohio,[156] and recent governmental programs of surveillance and disruption, even if terminated, tend to prove not only that such programs might be renewed but also that there exists a climate for private harassment, for official reprisals often reflect the attitudes of the majority and may make private harassment seem "acceptable."

---

[153] Brief for Appellants at 21.

[154] 424 U.S. at 74. The Court explained that such parties "may never be able to prove a substantial threat of harassment, however real that threat may be, because [they] would be required to come forward with witnesses who are too fearful to contribute but not too fearful to testify about their fear." *Id.*

[155] *Id.* Various lower courts have struggled to apply the Buckley standard. In Wisconsin Socialist Workers 1976 Campaign Comm. v. McCann, 433 F. Supp. 540 (E.D. Wis. 1977), the District Court applied a liberal standard of harassment and granted an injunction against enforcement of Wisconsin's disclosure requirements. The court stated that "[t]o require evidence of specific acts of harassment of contributors would impose an unduly strict burden on the plaintiffs." *Id.* at 548. See also 1980 Illinois Socialist Workers Campaign v. State of Illinois Board of Education, 531 F. Supp. 915 (N.D. Ill. 1981). But on Oregon Socialist Workers 1974 Campaign Comm. v. Paulus, 432 F. Supp. 1255 (D. Oregon 1977), the court rejected the SWP's request for exemption, despite an evidentiary showing of specific acts of harassment. See also Socialist Workers Party v. Brown, 53 Cal.3d 879 (1975).

[156] There may be limits to this, however. Proof of harassment of the NAACP in the Deep South may not have much bearing on whether the NAACP is an "outcast" organization in New York, for example. In accepting evidence of harassment on a national scale, the Court followed the clear trend of the lower courts. See 1980 Illinois Socialist Workers Campaign v. State of Illinois Board of Elections, 531 F. Supp. 915 (N.D. Ill. 1981); Doe v. Martin, 404 F. Supp. 753 (D.D.C. 1975); In the Matter of Minnesota Socialist Workers Campaign Comm. Request for Exemption, No. H-001 (Minn. State Ethics Comm., Oct. 1974).

Thus, there could be little doubt about the SWP's status as an "outcast" organization, and in the light of the difficulties faced by dissident organizations in attempting to prove actual chilling effect, the Court appropriately concluded in *Brown* that the SWP had presented a sufficient factual case for exemption.

Brown posed a further question, however, as to how far the Court would stretch the inference from "outcast" status to adverse effect. Although the Court was unanimous in holding the contribution disclosure requirements unconstitutional, Justice O'Connor, joined by Justices Rehnquist and Stevens, dissented from the holding that the expenditure disclosure requirements were similarly invalid.

Justice O'Connor argued that "disclosure of recipients of expenditures will have a lesser impact on a minority party's First Amendment interests than will disclosure of contributors."[157] This is so, she explained, because many expenditures may "be for quite mundane purposes,"[158] such as office supplies, telephone service, bank charges, and printing and photography costs. Persons who provide such services, O'Connor reasoned, "are not generally perceived by the public as supporting the party's ideology, and thus are unlikely to be harassed if their names are disclosed."[159] Although O'Connor conceded that other recipients of expenditures, such as campaign workers who receive per diem, travel, or room expenses, "may have closer ideological ties to the party" and thus "may be harassed or threatened for their conduct,"[160] she maintained that laws requiring disclosure of such expenditures "are not likely to contribute to this harassment," for "[o]nce an individual has openly shown his close ties to the organization by campaigning for it, disclosure of the receipt of expenditures is unlikely to increase the degree of harassment so significantly as to deter the individual from campaigning for the party."[161] Thus, O'Connor concluded, a "party's associational interests are unlikely to be affected by disclosure of recipients of [its] expenditures."[162]

In such circumstances, O'Connor reasoned, "a separately focused inquiry" is necessary to determine "whether there exists a reasonable probability that disclosure will subject recipients or the party itself to

---

[157] 103 S. Ct. at 430 (O'Connor, J., dissenting).
[158] *Id.*
[159] *Id.*
[160] *Id.*
[161] *Id.*
[162] *Id.*

threats, harassment, or reprisals."[163] O'Connor was unwilling, in other words, to infer adverse effect from the SWP's "outcast" status. And, after examining the record, O'Connor concluded that, in contrast to the evidence relating to contributions, the record did not support the conclusion "that disclosure of recipients of expenditures would lead to harassment of recipients or reprisals to the party or its members."[164]

Justice Marshall, speaking for the Court, rejected what he termed the dissent's "unduly narrow view of the minor party exemption."[165] Marshall rejected "the dissent's assertion that disclosure of disbursements paid to campaign workers and supporters will not increase the probability that they will be subjected to harassment," because the "preservation of unorthodox political affiliations in public records substantially increases the potential for harassment above and beyond the risk that an individual faces simply as a result of having worked for an unpopular party at one time."[166] Moreover, Marshall noted, "individuals who receive disbursements for 'merely' commercial transactions may be deterred by the public enmity attending publicity, and those seeking to harass may disrupt commercial activities on the basis of expenditure information."[167] Indeed, Marshall added, compelled disclosure of the names of such recipients could "cripple a minor party's ability to operate effectively."[168] Thus, Marshall concluded, the expenditure disclosure requirements should be tested by the same standard as the contribution disclosure requirements. Applying that standard, Marshall held that the District Court had "properly concluded" that the "evidence of private and government hostility toward the SWP and its members establishes a reasonable

---

[163] *Id.*

[164] *Id.* at 431. A second disagreement between the majority and the dissent concerned the need for a separate and distinct "balancing" of interests to determine the validity of the expenditure disclosure requirement. Justice O'Connor maintained that "there are important differences between disclosure of contributors and disclosure of recipients of campaign expenditures" that suggest "that the balance should not necessarily be calibrated identically." *Id.* at 429. The balance, she argued, should reflect not only the arguably lesser impact of disclosure of expenditures on the SWP but also the arguably increased governmental interest in compelling the disclosure of expenditures. On the latter, O'Connor argued that the "purpose of requiring parties to disclose expenditures is to deter improper influencing of voters," and "a minor party, whose short-term goal is merely recognition, may be as tempted to resort to impermissible methods as are major parties." *Id.* In response, Justice Marshall conceded that "minor" parties might attempt to buy votes but argued that this concern is diminished as applied to minor parties because "minor party candidates are unlikely to win elections," and, in any event, "their limited financial resources serve as a built-in ceiling." *Id.* at 422.

[165] 103 S. Ct. at 421.

[166] *Id.* at 423 n.14.

[167] *Id.* at 423.

[168] *Id.*

probability that disclosing the names of . . . recipients will subject them to threats, harassment, and reprisals."[169]

The disagreement within the Court over the expenditure issue is narrow, but not without interest. Both sides accept the *Buckley* doctrine and the importance of "flexible" evidentiary standards. The dissenters, however, are skeptical of the claim that disclosure may deter political recipients from dealing with the SWP, and demand specific proof of such incidents, whereas the majority rely upon the "outcast" status of the SWP as a sufficient predicate to infer that disclosure might deter potential recipients. There is some force to the dissenters' position. The very sensitivity of First Amendment rights, which underlies the concept of "chilling effect," suggests that disclosure is more likely to deter contributors than contractors. Moreover, the difficulties of proof may be reduced in the expenditure context, for it should not be too difficult for the SWP to prove that nonideological contractors refused to deal with it because of fears of exposure and harassment. In the end, however, the majority's approach may have more to commend it, for it simplifies the evidentiary inquiry in an area that is already too complex.[170]

B. EXEMPTION OR INVALIDATION?

In *Buckley*, the Court, applying ordinary content-neutral balancing, held that campaign disclosure requirements are constitutional because they "directly serve substantial governmental interests."[171] In *Brown*, the Court held that such disclosure requirements cannot constitution-ally be applied to organizations which, like the SWP, can demonstrate that they are "minor" political parties, and that there exists "a reasonable probability that disclosing the names of contributors and recipients will subject them to threats, harassment, and reprisals."[172] What, though, is the appropriate remedy in *Brown?* Is it to leave the disclosure requirements intact for all organizations that do not qualify

---

[169] *Id.* at 424.

[170] There are limits, however, to relying on evidence of "outcast" status alone. Suppose, for example, an ordinance requires all restaurants to disclose their ownership. Is a restaurant owned by the SWP exempt from this requirement? Although disclosure may threaten the SWP's ability to operate the restaurant, it would not seriously undermine the SWP's ability to participate in public debate. It should be noted that the State did not argue that there was a difference between contributors and recipients until its reply brief before the Supreme Court. Thus, the District Court's findings, which were affirmed by the majority, did not differentiate between contributors and recipients. This procedural quirk may have affected the Court's perception of the issues.

[171] 424 U.S. at 68.

[172] 103 S. Ct. at 424.

for the constitutionally compelled exemption or is it to invalidate the requirements in their entirety? In *Buckley* and *Brown*, the Court, without explanation, endorsed the former approach. But suppose that, after *Brown*, the Republican Party challenges the disclosure requirements, modified by the constitutionally compelled exemption, as an unconstitutional content-based restriction. Are the requirements, as modified, constitutional?

It might be argued, of course, that the Court in *Buckley* had already upheld the disclosure requirements as applied to the Republican Party, and that the creation of an exemption for the SWP in *Brown* in no way undermined the *Buckley* conclusion that the governmental interests in disclosure are sufficient to override the First Amendment interests of the Republicans. There is an essential weakness in this argument, however, for it runs head-on into the Court's distinction between content-based and content-neutral restrictions on expression. This doctrine is premised on the notion that content-based restrictions are ordinarily more threatening to fundamental First Amendment concerns than content-neutral restrictions, and that content-based restrictions must therefore be tested by more stringent standards of justification.[173] Under this doctrine, it is not at all uncommon for the Court to sustain a content-neutral restriction even though it would invalidate a seemingly narrower content-based restriction. For example, although government might constitutionally prohibit all picketing near a school while school is in session, it cannot constitutionally exempt labor picketers from the restriction.[174] Similarly, although government might constitutionally restrict the political activities of public employees,[175] it cannot constitutionally exempt Republican or Socialist employees from the restriction.[176] Thus, in the disclosure context, the conclusion in *Buckley* that content-neutral disclosure requirements are constitutional does not necessarily mean that content-based requirements, exempting the SWP, are also constitutional, for in upholding the content-neutral requirements in *Buckley*, the Court employed a markedly less stringent standard than that ordinarily employed to test the constitutionality of content-based restrictions. In *Buckley*, the Court employed content-neutral balancing and held that, in the light of the degree of

[173] See generally *Content Regulation*, note 46 *supra*.
[174] Police Department v. Mosley, 408 U.S. 92 (1972).
[175] Broadrick v. Oklahoma, 413 U.S. 601 (1973).
[176] But *cf.* United States v. Robel, 389 U.S. 258 (1967); Keyishian v. Board of Regents, 385 U.S. 589 (1967).

infringement of First Amendment rights, the disclosure requirements were constitutional because they "directly" furthered "substantial" governmental interests. Under content-based review, however, the challenged law ordinarily must be "necessary" to further "compelling" governmental interests."[177]

There are at least three possible explanations for the Court's decision to exempt the SWP rather than to invalidate the disclosure requirements in their entirety. The first is that the content-based restriction created in *Brown* may in fact withstand ordinary content-based review. This depends, in part, on precisely what element of the challenged law must satisfy such scrutiny. The content-based disclosure law created in *Brown* has two elements: the underlying disclosure requirements and the exemption. Although, as the Court held in *Buckley*, the underlying disclosure requirements withstand content-neutral balancing, they probably are not "necessary" to further "compelling" governmental interests. The exemption, however, may satisfy this more stringent standard, for it is "necessary" to prevent compelled disclosure from "crippling" an already "outcast" political party.[178] Thus, whether the content-based disclosure requirements created in *Brown* can withstand ordinary content-based review depends on which element(s) of the law must be "necessary" to further a "compelling" governmental interest—the underlying disclosure requirements, the exemption, or both.

The first alternative—that only the underlying disclosure requirements must satisfy content-based review—makes no sense, for content-based review must ultimately focus on the constitutionality of the content-based distinction between exempt and nonexempt organizations. The second alternative—that only the exemption must satisfy this standard—is more plausible. If, as the Court held in *Buckley*, the underlying disclosure requirements are themselves constitutional, the only remaining concern is the constitutionality of the exemption. And if, as the Court indicated in *Brown*, the exemption is "necessary" to further a "compelling" governmental interest, the inquiry should arguably be at an end. After all, if the underlying disclosure requirements are constitutional, the "free speech" interests of the

---

[177] *E.g.*, Widmar v. Vincent, 454 U.S. 263, 270 (1981); Carey v. Brown, 447 U.S. 455, 461, 464-66 (1980). See TRIBE, note 34 *supra*, at 602.

[178] An exemption designed to prevent a violation of constitutional rights is presumably "necessary" to further a "compelling" governmental interest. See Widmar v. Vincent, 454 U.S. 263, 271 (1981).

nonexempt organizations are not violated, and if the exemption is "necessary" to further a "compelling" governmental interest, the "equality" interests of the nonexempt organizations are not violated. Thus, under this view, the exemption, even though content-based, is arguably constitutional.[179] The third alternative—that both the underlying disclosure requirements and the exemption must satisfy the content-based standard—is also plausible. Content-based restrictions ordinarily threaten several fundamental First Amendment concerns— they may distort public debate, they may be the product of "improper" motivation, and they may be defended on the basis of constitutionally disfavored justifications. A strict standard of review is employed to assure that these concerns are not threatened unless the content-based restriction is absolutely essential. Thus, both the exemption and the underlying disclosure requirements must be "necessary" to further "compelling" governmental interests. For if only the exemption satisfies this test, the content-based restriction as a whole is not necessary to further a "compelling" governmental interest. Under this view, the content-based restriction created in Brown does not satisfy the ordinary standards of content-based review, and the appropriate remedy would be to invalidate the disclosure requirements in their entirety. Although this third possibility seems the most sensible in the light of the underlying purposes of content-based review, the Court itself has never expressly addressed the question.[180]

The second possible explanation of the Court's decision to exempt the SWP rather than to invalidate the disclosure requirements in their entirety turns on the notion that the content-based restriction created in *Brown* is not an ordinary content-based restriction, and thus should not be tested by the ordinary standards of content-based review, because the content-based exemption that created the problem was itself constitutionally compelled. But that reasoning is circular, for it assumes that exemption rather than invalidation is the appropriate remedy. The essential holding of *Brown* is not that an exemption is constitutionally compelled, but that the statute cannot constitutionally be applied to the SWP. Whether exemption or invalidation is the appropriate remedy in such circumstances remains in question.

---

[179] See Farber, note 53 *supra*.

[180] The issue is often posed, but not resolved, because the Court ordinarily invalidates content-based restrictions without having to address the question. *E.g.*, Metromedia, Inc. v. City of San Diego, 453 U.S. 490 (1981); Widmar v. Vincent, 454 U.S. 263 (1981); Carey v. Brown, 447 U.S. 455 (1980).

The third possible explanation is that exemption rather than invalidation is appropriate, not because the statute cannot constitutionally be applied to the SWP, but because the creation of an exemption in such circumstances does not threaten the concerns underlying the Court's usual presumption against content-based restrictions. Several factors may support this conclusion. First, there is arguably less risk of "improper" motivation in this context than in the context of most content-based restrictions.[181] This is so for several reasons: the exemption, on its face, is speaker rather than content-based;[182] the exemption derives from constitutional interpretation rather than from the usual process of legislative formulation;[183] unlike most content-based restrictions, the exemption does not expressly specify particular groups or ideas for special treatment, but establishes criteria that are neutrally applied to all speakers;[184] there is a clear "affirmative action" quality to the exemption in the light of the nature of the groups benefited;[185] and there is clearly a compelling reason not to impose the disclosure requirements on the exempted organizations.[186] Second, there is arguably less risk of distortion of public debate in this context than in the context of most content-based restrictions,[187] for the exemption is designed to prevent the dramatic distortion that would occur if the disclosure requirements were imposed equally on all organizations.[188] And third, the exemption created in *Brown*, unlike most content-based restrictions, is not based on a constitutionally disfavored justification. That is, the exemption is based neither on a "paternalistic" desire to prevent individuals from hearing "erroneous" ideas nor on a desire to suppress expression because it may offend others or trigger a hostile audience response.[189] To the contrary, the exemption is based on a perfectly legitimate desire to protect unpopular speakers against such a hostile reaction.

---

[181] The relevance of "improper" motivation is examined in *Content Regulation*, note 46 *supra*, Part IV-D. See also the authorities cited in note 101 *supra*.

[182] See Part V-A, *supra*.

[183] See Part V-B, *supra*.

[184] See *Content Regulation*, note 43 *supra*, Part V-A.

[185] See Part V-C, *supra*.

[186] See Part V-D, *supra*.

[187] The relevance of "distortion" of public debate is examined in *Content Regulation*, note 46 *supra*, Part IV-C.

[188] The exemption itself creates "distortion," however, for exempt "minor" parties are competitively better off than they would be if the disclosure requirements were invalidated in their entirety.

[189] The relevance of "disfavored" justifications is examined in *Content Regulation*, note 46 *supra*, Part IV-B.

For these reasons, then, the constitutionally compelled exemption recognized in *Brown* may not seriously threaten the concerns underlying the Court's usual presumption against content-based restrictions. It may thus be sensible to uphold such an exemption even though it could not pass muster under the most stringent standards of content-based review.[190]

C. EXEMPTIONS FOR INDIVIDUALS?

Does exemption theory protect individuals as well as organizations? Assume that Employee is afraid to contribute to the Republican Party because Employer, an ardent Democrat, might "punish" him for his "disloyalty." Assume further that, on several occasions, Employer, after examining official campaign contribution lists recorded pursuant to a disclosure law, has either fired or demoted employees who had previously contributed to the Republican Party. In such circumstances, is Employee constitutionally entitled to exemption?

This hypothetical parallels *Brown* in two respects. First, like the SWP and its contributors, Employee will suffer a more severe harm than contributors who are not faced with the risk of reprisal. Second, like the SWP and its contributors, Employee may effectively be driven out of the "marketplace of ideas." Employee, however, unlike the SWP and its contributors, is not entitled to exemption. That, indeed, is the explicit holding of *Buckley*.[191]

That Employee's claim to exemption is denied, whereas the SWP's claim to exemption is granted, may shed light on the Court's evaluation of the relative importance of the "purposes" often said to underlie the First Amendment—individual self-fulfillment,[192] the search for truth,[193] and self-governance.[194] The Court has never embraced any one of these

[190] For examples of other content-based restrictions that may not require full content-based review, see *Content Regulation*, note 46 *supra*, Part V.

[191] 424 U.S. at 68.

[192] See Cohen v. California, 403 U.S. 15, 24 (1971) (the First Amendment protects freedom of expression, in part, "in the belief that no other approach would comport with the premise of individual dignity and choice upon which our political system rests"); Whitney v. California, 274 U.S. 357, 375 (1927) (Brandeis, J., concurring) ("Those who won our independence believed that the final end of the State was to make men free to develop their faculties . . ."). See generally, MILL, CONSIDERATIONS ON REPRESENTATIVE GOVERNMENT 203; EMERSON, note 105 supra, at 6; TRIBE, note 34 *supra*, at 578; Scanlon, *A Theory of Free Expression*, 1 PHIL. & PUB. AFF 204 (1972).

[193] See Abrams v. United States, 250 U.S. 616, 630 (1919) (Holmes, J., dissenting) ("the best test of truth is the power of the thought to get itself accepted in the competition of the market"); Virginia State Bd. of Pharmacy v. Virginia Consumers Council, 425 U.S. 748 (1976); Gertz v. Robert Welch, Inc., 418 U.S. 323, 339-40 (1974).

[194] See Buckley v. Valeo, 424 U.S. 1, 14 (1976) ("Discussion of public issues and debate on the qualifications of candidates are integral to the operation of the system of government established

theories as the "true" purpose of the First Amendment, and the Court's opinions have at times reflected all three theories.[195] In the exemption context, however, the emphasis seems clear. Both Employee and the SWP contributor have self-fulfillment interests at stake. But the fragile existence of the SWP adds an additional element to the analysis, for a loss of contributions may prevent the SWP's message from effectively entering public debate. By emphasizing this factor, the Court has tied the constitutionally compelled exemption to the search for truth and self-governance rationales.[196]

Although the Court's emphasis on the search for truth and self-governance rationales in this context may signal a subordination or even rejection of the self-fulfillment theory, alternative explanations are available. First, the distinction may be explained, not in terms of the relative importance of the rationales for free expression, but in terms of the "additive" factor. The decision to accord "greater" protection to the SWP and its contributors than to Employee may simply be the result of the fact that in the Employee situation, self-fulfillment is the primary value that is threatened, whereas in the SWP situation, all three values are threatened.

Second, the explanation may lie in the nature of disclosure laws generally. Disclosure laws are designed to add information to public debate and to promote an informed electorate. They are designed to advance the search for truth and self-governance theories of free expression. When disclosure threatens to drive a party out of existence,

by our Constitution"); Monitor Patriot Co. v. Roy, 401 U.S. 265, 272 (1971) ("[I]t can hardly be doubted that the [First Amendment's] constitutional guarantee has its fullest and most urgent application precisely to the conduct of campaigns for political office"); Williams v. Rhodes, 393 U.S. 23, 32 (1968) ("Competition in ideas and government is at the core of our electoral process and of the First Amendment freedoms"); Garrison v. Louisiana, 379 U.S. 64, 74–75 (1964) (Political speech "is more than self-expression; it is the essence of self-government"); New York Times v. Sullivan, 364 U.S. 254, 270 (1964) (There is a "profound national commitment to the principle that debate on public issues should be uninhibited, robust, and wide-open"). See also MIEKLEJOHN, POLITICAL FREEDOM (1960); Bork, *Neutral Principles and Some First Amendment Problems*, 47 IND. L. J. 1 (1971); Kalven, *The New York Times Case: A Note on the "Central Meaning of the First Amendment*," 1964 SUPREME COURT REVIEW 191.

[195] *Compare* Wooley v. Maynard, 430 U.S. 705 (1977) and Cohen v. California, 403 U.S. 15 (1971) (self-fulfillment) with Virginia State Bd. of Pharmacy v. Virginia Consumers Council, 425 U.S. 748 (1976) (search for truth) *with* Mills v. Alabama, 384 U.S. 214, 218–19 (1966) (self-government). Search for truth and self-government are often merged into one concept. *E.g.*, Anderson v. Celebrezze, 103 U.S. 1565, 1572 (1983).

[196] A concern with distortion of public debate is more closely tied to the search for truth and self-governance rationales than to self-fulfillment. Search for truth and self-governance both assume that ideas compete for acceptance. Self-fulfillment, on the other hand, is not a competitive concept. It is concerned with the effect of the restriction on the individual's expression without regard to its effect on others. That a restriction may distort public debate is irrelevant to the self-fulfillment rationale.

it may defeat its underlying purpose. In such circumstances, it may be appropriate for the Court to require consistency with the search for truth and self-governance rationales, since they are themselves the justifications for the restriction.[197]

VII. CONCLUSION

Against the backdrop of a constitutional jurisprudence committed to content neutrality, it is surprising to find a decision that holds that a content-based distinction is constitutionally compelled. Although the Court in *Brown* failed adequately to explain this seeming anomoly, the decision is in fact consistent with the fundamental principles that have shaped First Amendment jurisprudence. The simple lesson of *Brown* is that when the commitment to neutrality conflicts with the commitment to preservation of ideas in the political marketplace, the latter will prevail.

---

[197] The Court itself has often spoken in language reflecting search for truth and self-governance values when reviewing laws that affect the political arena, thus indicating that it may review laws in accord with the First Amendment purposes that the laws are designed to serve. *E.g.*, Anderson v. Celebrezze, 103 S. Ct. 1564, 1572-73 (1983); Williams v. Rhodes, 393 U.S. 23 (1968). Two other possible explanations of the distinction between "minor" parties and individuals who may be deterred from contributing to "major" parties merit note. First, the distinction might arguably be explained in terms of the special administrative problems that might arise if individuals could claim such exemptions. This seems rather weak, however, for the administrative problems in this context are neither insurmountable nor unique, and, in any event, the Court rarely accepts administrative convenience as a justification for restrictions on expression. Second, the distinction might be explained on the ground that the interests underlying disclosure are not "diminished" as applied to "major" party contributors. As applied to particular individuals, however, the governmental interests are not very weighty. Exemptions for individuals are thus not likely significantly to undermine the underlying interests.

Abington School District v Schempp......................................104, 119
298
Aguilar v Texas...305
Barclay v Florida...343
Barefoot v Estelle..585
Bates v City of Little Rock.......................................464, 499
Beatty v Kurtz..340
Billington v Missouri...288
Bivens v Six Unknown Federal Narcotics Agents.....................1, 33, 120
Bob Jones University v United States..............................414, 422
Brown v Board of Education..583
Brown v Socialist Workers' Party..586
Buckley v Valeo...479
Califano v Yamasaki...343
California v Ramos..346
Chapman v California...397, 432
City of Memphis v Greene..402, 411, 427
City of Mobile v Bolden...37
Clarke v Haberle Crystal Springs Brewing Company........................412
Dandridge v Williams..86
Davis v Beason...215, 258, 280
EEOC v Wyoming..490
Eisen v Carlisle & Jacquelin..290
Elkins v United States...334, 359
Enmund v Florida...511, 518
Erie Railroad v Tompkins..238
Fry v United States..306, 314, 419
Furman v Georgia..339
Gardner v Florida...7
General Electric Company v Gilbert......................................275
Gibbons v Ogden..93, 113
Gillette v United States...333, 359
Godfrey v Georgia..511, 527
Goldstein v Californai..291
Gouled v United States...318, 338
Gregg v Georgia...132
Hampton & Company v United States.......................................493
Handley v Stutz..479, 504
Hansbury v Lee..249
Hodel v Virginia Surface Mining & Reclamation Association...............
Illinois v Gates...299, 301
Immigration & Naturalization Service v Chadha...........................125
International News Service v Associated Press.......................513, 525
Jefferson v Hackney..397, 425
Kewanee Company v Bicron Oil Corporation...........................512, 530
Lilly v Commissioner..41
Lockett v Ohio...322, 374
McArthur v Scott..466
McCollum v Board of Education...................................88, 95, 101
McCulloch v Maryland..125, 143, 246. 275
McGautha v California..308, 393
McGowan v Maryland..397
McNabb v United States..290
Mapp v Ohio..287, 293
Maryland v Wirtz..217
Milliken v Bradley..406, 430
Motor Vehicle Manufacturers Association v State Farm Mutual Insurance Company....178
NAACP v Alabama...584
National League of Cities v Usery..................................215, 240
Norwood v Harrison..15
Quern v Jordan..490
Richmond v Irons..463
Runyon v McCrary...19, 79
San Antonio Independent School District v Rodriguez.....................430
Sears Roebuck & Company v Stiffel Company...............................528
Sherbert v Verner..21, 85, 418
Smith v Swormstedt..466, 499, 504
Stone v Powell...288, 295
Street v New York...348
Stromberg v California..347
Supreme Tribe of Ben Hur v Cauble.................................464, 499
Textile Mills Securities Corporation v Commissioner.....................38
Thomas v Collins..348
United States v California...217. 252
United States v Lee...24
Universal Camera v NLRB...199
Washington v Davis...14, 404
Wheaton v Peters..510
Wisconsin v Yoder...83, 90, 100, 108, 114
Woodson v North Carolina...323, 374
Zahn v International Paper Company......................................492
Zant v Stephens..305, 343, 347

1983

Illinois v. Gates 299
Immigration and Naturalization Service v. Chadha 125
International News Service v. Associated Press 513
Jefferson v. Hackney 397
John H. Harland Company v. Clarke Checks, Inc. 554
Kewanee Company v. Bicron Oil Corporation 512
Lemon v. Kurtzman 119
Lilly v. Commissioner 41
Lockett v. Ohio 322
M. Bryce & Associates, Inc. v. Gladstone 552
Mapp v. Ohio 287
Maryland v. Wirtz 217
McArthur v. Scott 466
McCollum v. Board of Education 88
McCulloch v. Maryland 125
McGautha v. California 308
McGowan v. Maryland 397
McNabb v. United States 290
Menora v. Illinois High School Association 23
Milliken v. Bradley 406
Mitchell v. Penton/Industrial Publishing Company 550
Motor Vehicle Manufacturers Ass'n. v. State Farm Mutual Ins. 178
NAACP v. Alabama 584
National League of Cities v. Usery 215
Norwood v. Harrison 15
Price v. Massachusetts 94
Quern v. Jordan 490
Richmond v. Irons 463
Runyon v. McCrary 19
San Antonio Independent School District v. Rodriguez 430
Sear Roebuck and Company v. Stiffel Company 528
Sherbert v. Verner 21
Smith v. Swormstedt 466
Southern Pacific Railroad v. Arizona 527
Stone v. Powell 288
Street v. New York 348
Stromberg v. California 347
Suid v. Newsweek Magazine 553
Supreme Tribe of Ben Hur v. Cauble 464
Tank Truck Rentals, Inc. v. Commissioner 43
Textile Mills Securities Corporation v. Commissioner 38
Thomas v. Collins 348
Tilton v. Richardson 119
United States v. California 217
United States v. James 45
United States v. Lee 24
Universal Camera v. NLRB 199
Walz v. Tax Commissioner 85
Washington v. Davis 14
West Virginia v. Barnette 28
Wheaton v. Peters 510
Wisconsin v. Yoder 83
Wolman v. Walter 121
Woodson v. North Carolina 323

Wooley v. Maynard 28
Zahn v. International Paper Company 492
Zant v. Stephens 305
Zorach v. Clauson 104